The Best of The Nation

THE BEST OF

Selections from the Independent Magazine of
Politics and Culture

EDITED BY
VICTOR NAVASKY
& KATRINA VANDEN HEUVEL

•

FOREWORD BY
GORE VIDAL

THUNDER'S MOUTH PRESS / NATION BOOKS
NEW YORK

Published by Thunder's Mouth Press/Nation Books

841 Broadway, Fourth Floor

New York, NY 10003

Nation Books is a co-publishing venture of the Nation Institute
and Avalon Publishing Group, Incorporated.

ISBN 1-56025-267-7

Library of Congress Cataloging-in-Publication Data

The Best of the Nation : selections from the independent magazine of politics
and culture / edited by Victor Navasky & Katrina vanden Heuvel.

p.   cm.

ISBN 1-56025-267-7

1. United States—Politics and government—1989–1993.   2. United States—Politics and
government—1993–   3. United States—Social conditions—1980–   I. Navasky, Victor S.   II.
Vanden Heuvel, Katrina.   III. Nation (New York, N.Y.)

E881 .B47 2000

973.928—dc21   00–21769

Distributed by Publishers Group West

Manufactured in the United States of America

Contents

Contents

1992

Contents

1993

Contents

CONTENTS

Contents

1996

1998

Contents

CONTRIBUTORS
• 594

THE SOUTHWEST COAST of Italy is lined with what local residents call "Norman towers." Although most of these conical stone structures were built or rebuilt by the Bourbons, the whole lot were supposedly put in place centuries earlier by the Roman emperors as a warning system. From Sicily to Rome, Morse-code-like messages could be sent by bonfires from one tower to the next so rapidly that a May-day warning might arrive on Caesar's desk rather more quickly than anything sent today by Italian Fedex. One might say that for the last one hundred thirty-five years, *The Nation* has acted as our Norman towers, a journalistic alert-system, warning of dangers too often invisible to even the most alert coastal dweller.

The Nation's Anglo-Irish founder, E. L. Godkin, wrote out of New York for the London *Daily News* until 1865 when he was offered a partnership in the New York *Times*. No doubt dreaming on things to come (Godkin was to raise, if only briefly, the standards of American book-reviewing to heights that others would swiftly—even urgently—lower), he turned down the offer from the *Times* and started a weekly review that was soon affiliated with New York's noblest and most "radical" newspaper, the Evening *Post*, whose editor for fifty-one years was William Cullen Bryant, an abolitionist and ornithologist (c.f. his "Ode to a Waterfowl"); after the ruckus at Harper's Ferry, it was Bryant who declared the revolutionary John Brown a holy martyr. Bryant was succeeded by Carl Schurz, a German school teacher who had settled in Wisconsin, supported Lincoln for president, fought as a general at Bull Run, became senator from Missouri; later Schurz worked with Godkin as editor of the Evening *Post* and *The Nation* from 1881 to 1883.

What exactly were the politics of Godkin, Bryant, Schurz? Basically, not too unlike that of a later *Nation* associate editor, Norman Thomas, five times Socialist candidate for president of the United States but then, again, not too like. Certainly, the three editors were hardly ideologues in thrall to some political system; rather, they shared a mindset that distinguished them from, say, the carefully reactionary New York *Times*; and they saw their work as the enlightenment of a citizenry usually most comfortable when lolling in absolute darkness. They prematurely favored abolition of slavery; they were permanent opponents of corruption in politics of the sort that took deep root during Grant's Gilded Age and now, like fast-growing burdock, overwhelms our amber fields of grain. Finally, they were anti-imperialists.

Schurz was also chief editorial writer of *Harper's Weekly* until, at the end of the last century but one, our rulers decided it was empiretime. Schurz quit *Harper*'s rather than support the war with Spain and the annexation of the Philippines. Finally, what did this trio actually *do* other than to warn? Well, in 1884 Godkin and Schurz—Bryant had finally soared off to join the great waterfowl in the sky—pretty much led the splinter party of Independent Republicans which was opposed to the regular Republicans' corrupt presidential candidate, James G. Blaine. For this foray into politics they were dubbed "mugwumps"— 1830s native American slang for "big-shots" (in the sense, here, of "egg-heads"). They were also thought to be having it both ways, their faces—or mugs—on one side of the Republican fence and their rumps—wumps—on the other.

For the last few decades history has made mugwumpery pretty much impossible since the fences that most matter are either set far too high to straddle or don't exist. Essentially, *The Nation* has usually inclined to a "freedom from narrow prejudice, an open mindedness" (the OED definition of liberalism, cited as of 1781), "as well as an openness to the acceptance of new ideas or proposals of reform and, finally, of political opinions favorable to changes and reforms tending in the direction of democracy." The dictionary then adds, demurely, that as of 1801, liberal was "opposite to conservative." Yes.

With this definition in mind, one can see how necessary it is for corporate America, through its media, educational and political systems, to demonize not only the word "liberal" but everything for which it stands. The process began with a famous victory. In 1868, the Fourteenth Amendment to the Constitution extended the Bill of Rights (enjoyed by each American as citizen of the republic) to each American as citizen of any one of the states as well. Senator Roscoe G. Conkling (coiner of the plangent phrase, "Let the chips fall where they may") promptly got out his axe. In a cunning bit of carpentry, he so arranged the chips as to make it possible for the Supreme Court to rule, with a presumably straight collective face, that under the Fourteenth a corporation could be regarded as a "person" with all those commensurate rights the human American citizen enjoys, including the right to act politically; hence, the endless lobbying of legislators by corporations, not to mention those floods of hard and soft corporate money that have permanently undone our political system. This great ongoing perversion of the Fourteenth would have had Godkin, Bryant, and Schurz off their fence by now. Certainly our Norman towers must now start setting ever-brighter, ever-more-frequent fires.

Meanwhile, some messages that *The Nation*'s watchtowers have sent up the line during the last decade. In 1990 the Soviet was crumbling. Steve Cohen, *The Nation*'s watchtower in Moscow, and E. P. Thompson reported on what was actually happening in Russia and Eastern Europe while the CIA was still in thrall to the notion of the Soviet's inexorable and rapid dominance of the whole world's economy. 1991: Solotaroff reports on the conglomeratizing (and dumbing down) of book publishing, while Hobsbawm notes that in the place of discarded ideologies only nationalism (aka ethnicity) seems to thrive. Molly Ivins' Norman tower blazes, as always, with burning boll weevils. Rushdie and Alexander Cockburn take Lucifer's measure. 1993: the flames are passing along mixed messages. Robert Sherrill illuminates Murdoch and the world's media monopolies. Finally, it has even been suggested that an end to the increasingly pointless NATO might steady our wobbly "global" empire.

To read these pieces over the last decade is to get a . . . well, I started with the image of the transmission of fiery messages of warning so let the decade, century, millennium (a word I've learned at last to spell) end with fireworks of the sort those now alive, "we happy billions," will always associate with Peter Jennings on ABC television as he followed, on 31 December 1999, the setting sun of the old millennium for a full twenty-four hours until we observers were as worn out by time detailed as he was energized by prime time.

Finally, on a lighter note, there is aloft in the current e-mail heaven, one "Retlaw" (Walter spelled backwards—gibbering ghost of our own gossip-king Winchell?) reveals that before Congress's last summer break: 9 members have been accused of spousal abuse; 7 have been arrested for fraud; 19 accused of writing bad checks; 117 have bankrupted at least two businesses; 3 have been arrested for assault; 71 have credit records so bad that they can't qualify for a credit card; 14 have been arrested for shoplifting; 21 are current defendants in lawsuits and, in 1998 alone, 84 were stopped for drunk driving but released after they claimed Congressional immunity. All this, of course, is merely the tip of the iceberg that "Retlaw," in his deckchair aboard the sky *Titanic*, has duly noted. I am assuming that under Prosecutor Starr's new legal ground rules, shored up by those Draconian laws that underpin our never-intended-to-be-won wars against drugs and terrorism, all of these Congress-persons are to be considered absolutely guilty until they are able to prove themselves, at great expense, innocent.

"Where," as William Bennett used to moan on Larry King's hour of charm, "is the outrage?" I suspect Godkin would find all this pretty funny—not to mention representative. Meanwhile, let us keep our watch fires burning. Great mischief this way comes.

EDITORS' NOTE

WHEN WE SAT down to select the pieces to appear in this anthology, we gave ourselves four guidelines.

First, they should indeed be the best of *The Nation*.

Second, they should reflect the spirit of *The Nation*, which is, to quote the words of its founding prospectus, "the critical spirit."

Third, there should be no more than one article from any single writer.

And finally, they should en masse give the reader a sense of the diverse political, cultural, literary, and ideological perspectives that have found a home in our pages.

What we ended up with, however, was something unplanned:

An alternative history of the last decade of the twentieth century, a unique archive of the issues, values, institutions, and personalities which preoccupied, united and divided, and ultimately defined the independent, democratic left.

Which is not to say that there is or was one left any more than there is or was a party-line from which contributors to this somewhat fractious, elegant, quirky, searching journal have never deviated or have even measured themselves against.

Thus Katha Pollitt on the arguments over the literary canon and Gore Vidal on the patriarchal state are light years apart in sensibility, style, and priorities, yet they share originality of conception, independence of thought, and a standard of literary excellence which should be model to any student of the culture.

Although the articles and reviews and poetry pieces assembled here cover the last ten years, contributors to the anthology roam far and wide—to the distant past and the unknown future. Marshall Berman's meditation on the Communist Manifesto is an illustration of the former, and Mark Crispin Miller's chart depicting the New Entertainment State of the latter.

We go to press in the midst of an unprecedented and overwhelming cascade of mergers, takeovers, consolidations in the communications biz. How sweet it is to be an island of independence in the midst of this ocean of absentee conglomerated ownership.

We would be the last to insist that editorial (and/or business) independence guarantee either literary quality or political integrity. But we suspect that the creative context made possible by *The Nation*'s 135-year history of independent publishing, so felicitously captured by Gore Vidal in his introduction, helps account for whatever originality of conception, innocence of assumption, lyricism of spirit, skepticism of the official line, and clarity of thought the reader might find in the pages ahead. Read on!

Victor Navasky and Katrina vanden Heuvel

PREZ V. UPTIGHT RE: BOLDNESS GAP

Douglas McGrath

•

WASHINGTON

OCT. 6: PREZ still taking a beating on Noriega noncoup. At p.-conf. today, Helen Thos. asked, "Didn't we miss our chance? Are you too slow to deal with unfolding events? Shouldn't we strike while the iron's hot?"

Prez said, "Keep your pants on, Helen. We've got an experienced team in place to check out all coup opportunities as they come down that creek. But I'm sorry: If the next coup we have a shot at is a loser like this one, *no sale. Return to sender. We pasadena.* But let the word of this President go out: The United States is not out of the coup business. You get a winner coup in here, one that will succeed with no risks to the Americans involved, and wham! It's ours!"

Privately, all of us v. relieved coup flopped. As Prez said re: N., "The big brown one knows everything we've done down there in that region. If we bring Nory to trial, he'll talk—and then I am history! Out of here! Mr. Impeachment-Article-Approved!"

Malta summit w/Gorb still secret. Will hold meeting at sea. This perfect as it keeps G. from getting out of limos and being popular. Sunu and Fitzy both get seasick but Prez says water at Malta is "glass-city."

Oct. 9: Began day as usual w/polling people re: Prez's numbers. Up 2% thanks to Atwa's ABC strat. on Nory flap: Always Blame Congress. At photo-op w/Jessica McClure, the Texas well girl, Prez beautifully

ABC'd the Nory story. Said: "And I think you've got to look at this Congress. Those oversight committees. These marvelous liberal laws that box us in without any way to respond: Kidnapping—can't do it. The liberals say no. Killing—can't do that either. Ixnay says Ongresscay!"

Then Nat. Sec. meeting. Scow wants a White Paper to see if the exodus of over a million people from East Germany is just P.R. CIA wants budget upped. Needs to double staff at threat-magnification desk.

Oct. 12: Supreme Court and spouses here tonight for gala dinner to kick off NRA's "Buy a Second Handgun" campaign. Had to pull Prez for call from Gorb. Gorb said he wanted Prez to know he was planning a big, bold initiative. What is it? Prez asked. Gorb just chuckled. Then he *hung up*! Prez shocked: "For heaven's sake—he ripcorded me!"

Returning to Blue Room, Prez knew everyone would be watching for signs of anxiety, so was v. Mr. Smooth. I could tell, however, he was distracted. During dessert he ate his sherbet with a knife.

Oct. 13: No change in Prez's numbers since yesterday. Q.'s numbers, though, v. odd: over 40 %—*up* from 25—said they didn't know enough about Q. to make a judgment. Thus longer people see Q., less they know about him. Baker said this could be Q.'s one asset. Atwa thinks answer is to sched. focus groups to see what people would like in Q. and then run ads telling them he has it.

Prez ordered daily intelligence briefings doubled on Gorb. V. concerned re: that phone call. Fears G. planning something big for Malta. Rode w/Prez on way to Skull & Bones fall barbecue. Prez usually so excited re: S&B. Today, though, v. quiet; mostly played w/the electric door lock. Finally he said, "You'd think he'd get tired of being bold."

Post lunch, RR called from Bel Air. Has signed a $2 million contract with Sears to endorse a line of lawnmowers. Called the Lawn Chief. Wants to use Presidential Seal on the grassbags. Will we OK?

Oct. 17: Told Fitzy to announce impending veto for funding of abortions for victims of rape or incest. Prez hedged all aft. Tried to think of a million outs, but knew Righters would kill. Finally, "I don't see any way around it: I've got to stick to my position!"

At poll meeting, slight prob. developing for Prez. Growing percentage of public (17%) can't remember if Prez is P. or V.P. Atwa fears this due to 17% not knowing who the V.P. is. Must do something w/Q. Trick is how to sneak Q. into public's thoughts w/o getting Q.'s thoughts into public's thoughts. Sig Rogich, new image man, put to work on Sublim.-Op. Will report back.

(12:30 AM) Prez called. Said he had been woken by phone call from Gorb. Gorb wanted to know if he'd told Prez that he was planning a

"big, bold initiative." Prez said he had, but not what it was. "Good," Gorb said, "just checking." And hung up! Prez frantic.

Oct. 18: Prez's numbers softening due to abortion stand. Then great news: A big quake hit San Francisco! That should take people's minds off the veto. Atwa wants to send Q. out for pics. "His numbers will kick ass when people see how much he cares about dead people and real estate." Baker all for this. Said privately to me, "This may be our best shot at getting him off the '92 ticket—with any luck, there'll be an aftershock!"

At NSC Scow ordered White Paper on likelihood that Honecker will make real and not just cosmetic changes in East G. Canceled a little after 4 when Honecker resigned. Agreed Cheney to announce $180 billion in Def. cuts. Thanks to RR's Buffer-Op., that leaves us $320 billion before we actually have to cut anything.

Oct. 21: Prez vetoed Medicaid bill on abortion for rape and incest. Sunu, w/an eye on polls and upcoming elections, told all to put out the line of the day. Prez said he feared that "someone who wasn't raped might take the money for an abortion." A "high-level White House official" was quoted in *Post* as saying, "If there's a free abortion in it, where's the incentive for a woman not to get raped?" Must review line of the day more closely with Q.

Oct. 23: Terrible day. Shevy announced that USSR apologized for its invasion of Afgh. and said it was "a moral mistake." Everyone agreed this is G.'s big, bold move. (He'd have to tear down the Berlin wall to top this.) But then a wire came. It was from G. It said, "That wasn't it."

Oct. 31: Prez. v. testy w/press portrayal of him as too prudent. The "W" thing makes him ballistic. Matters not helped by Gorb, who has started calling him "Prudy." (Prez swears that next time he goes to Moscow, "I'm going to boot in his bedroom!")

So Prez calls p.-conf. to announce Malta summit. Stahl asked, "Sir, did you arrange this summit to correct the impression that you are too timid?" Prez snapped, "Certainly not! Sit down! Is that the kind of question they teach in those marvelous 'journalism' schools?"

Lowering expectations vital for success. So Prez initiated Op. Low.-Ex. 56. He told Bob Schieffer, "We plan to bring no proposals to the meeting whatsoever. Not going to bring them. Not a proposal kind of meeting. Won't even bring the briefcase." After p.-conf., Prez immediately ordered NSC and State to draw up proposals for summit. Networks focusing on "feet-up" aspect. Press buys Op. Low.-Ex. every time. Unbelievable.

Nov. 3: Scow ordered White Paper on whether Krenz represents any real change in East G. or if it's just cosmetic. Canceled a little after 6 when half of East G. Cabinet resigned. Ordered White Paper on whether possible to get a White Paper written before it has to be canceled.

Prez completely unready for these changes. *Post* wondered today in ed. if Prez could be the "bold visionary the dramatic situation requires." Prez: "If I'd wanted to be a visionary, I would have gone into advertising!"

Is becoming obsessed w/what G. might be planning. During a meeting with Atwa re: next week's election, took extensive notes, but afterward I saw they were all doodles: "Vision thing . . . Bold gets old . . . Old Boldie . . . Old bald Boldie . . ." Went outside to throw horseshoes but was so distracted he threw one through the window and hit Q.

Q., who thinks everything is a loyalty test, said, "Good shot, sir!"

Nov. 9: Elections v. bad for us. Atwa says Prez must soften abortion stance somehow. So Prez read this statement: "Some say it's a human life, sacred and inviolate. Others say it's just a ball of cells and saliva. Some say abortion is no different an operation than plastic surgery. Others call it coldblooded murder. Obviously, this is an issue where there is room for a breadth of opinion."

Wall coming down! At last, Gorb's big, bold initiative, and it wasn't an embarrassing proposal at Malta in front of the world. Elated Prez said to summon W.H. press to Oval Office. But as I rounded them up. Gorb called. All he said was, "It isn't the wall." Then hung up. Press came in. Prez couldn't contain anger at G. during pictures. Must get Prez to not look bitter about spread of democracy.

At Prez's urging, Baker convened Vision-Boosting Study Group to coordinate bold proposals for Malta. No ideas yet. Broke up early.

Nov. 12: Q. on *Meet the Press*. Said that Soviets haven't changed. Q: "I still don't think, for instance, that you can charge things in the Soviet Union. The Communists are afraid that people will charge a lot of stuff and then defect without paying. And what about right on red? They're not even *talking* about that. If they're not ready for right on red, you think they're ever going to tear down the Berlin wall? Allow any kind of free travel to the West? Think about it."

Nov. 20: RR called. To help us make up our minds about the Lawn Chief, he wanted us to know Cabinet members will get mowers at 20% off.

Prez in Chicago today. During speech was heckled by nuns who are against the murder of priests in El Salvador. Prez barked at the nuns, "Now you be quiet!" When they continued to heckle him, he got off the dais, went down to one of them and tied her habit into a knot. On flight back, said to me, "I am pumped! Bring on the G-man!"

U.S.S. Belknap

Dec. 2: Fitzy went off diet, but it didn't matter. He's thrown it all up back here. To keep from being sick, Sunu lies on floor, legs elevated, and converts fractions.

This is the big day: Prez met Gorb. All of us frantic Gorb would spring his trap in front of the press, so right after sitting down, Prez unleashed all the proposals we said we weren't bringing: the accelerated arms control timetable, normalization of economic relations, endorsement of Gorb's reforms at home. The only proposal Gorb made was to accept everything we offered them. Nothing big or bold.

Then they met privately.

Gorb said, "You may remember I told you about a big, bold initiative I have in mind." Prez said he remembered. G. was silent for a moment, then faced the Prez. "Just kidding!" he said.

Prez looked seasick. "You mean I've been bold for nothing?" he asked. "I can't believe you're not going to be bold!"

Air Force I

On way to Brussels. Prez v. peeved. Issued new guidelines for future: no unilateral boldness. If boldness required, use covert boldness. Any public boldness should be coordinated with Soviet Union.

MICHAEL HARRINGTON, SOCIALIST

A REVIEW OF *SOCIALISM: PAST AND FUTURE.*
BY MICHAEL HARRINGTON.

Cornel West

•

THE DEATH OF Michael Harrington is the end of an era in the history of American socialism. He was the socialist evangelist of our time—the bearer of the mantles of Eugene Debs and Norman Thomas. Unlike Debs and Thomas, however, Harrington was a serious intellectual. His first book, *The Other America* (1962)—with a boost from Dwight Macdonald's famous review in *The New Yorker*—thrust him into the limelight and prompted the Kennedy Administration's campaign against poverty. His fifteen other books ranged from solid history of Western socialist movements (*Socialism*, 1972) to analysis of advanced capitalist societies (*Twilight of Capitalism*, 1976), to autobiographical reflections (*The Long Distance Runner*, 1988) to broad pronouncements about the prevailing crisis of Western civilization (*The Politics at God's Funeral*, 1984). Though far from original works, these books guided and inspired many progressives in their struggles for freedom, solidarity and justice.

Like the late Raymond Williams in Britain and the late C. B. Macpherson in Canada, Harrington carved out a vital democratic socialist space between the Scylla of Stalinism and the Charybdis of liberalism. With his early roots in Irish Catholicism he was a Pascalian Marxist who wagered boldly on the capacity of ordinary men and

women to create and sustain a socialist future. Harrington was also a
socialist in the American grain: experimental in method, moral in
motivation and optimistic in outlook. Like Walt Whitman, John Dewey
and C. Wright Mills, he believed in the possibility of social betterment
by means of creative intelligence, moral suasion and political struggle.
Yet he was the first great democratic socialist in the United States to be
well read in the Marxist classics (his translation of Georg Lukács's
"What Is Orthodox Marxism?" thirty years ago was the first in this
country) *and* to have mastered the details of progressive public policy.
Endowed with great ambition, talent, discipline and curiosity—but no
Ph.D.—he became the shining knight and activist intellectual of the
democratic left for nearly three decades.

Harrington was the product of two distinct intellectual subcultures: those of the artistic bohemian radicals (centered at the White
Horse tavern in Greenwich Village) and the anti-Stalinist socialists of
the late 1950s and early 1960s. The former changed him from a fol-
lower of Dorothy Day's Catholic social gospel (after college at Holy
Cross, a year at Yale Law School and an M.A. in English at the University of Chicago) into a secular proponent of sexual freedom and
racial equality; the latter turned him into a self-styled Marxist with
deep democratic sentiments. Both left subcultures were thoroughly
New Yorkish and disproportionately Jewish, and thus permeated by
intense conversation, bookish knowledge, oppositional outlooks and
identification with the oppressed and exploited. Harrington's superb
oratorical skills, voracious reading and links with the progressive
wing of the labor movement were fundamentally shaped by these
subcultures—which are no longer available to young intellectuals.
His charisma as a progressive leader and his heritage as a public
intellectual bore this particular historical stamp, and reflected as
well his good nature and his ability to reconcile opposing people
and ideas.

In his last book, *Socialism: Past and Future,* Harrington grapples
with the most fundamental questions facing democratic socialists: Is
socialism more than "the hollow memory of a passionate youth" or
"humankind's most noble and useful political illusion"? Can the socialist ideal once again become credible and desirable, given its heavy
"baggage of historic failure" in the form of command economies,
bureaucratic authoritarian elites and repressive regimentation of ordinary people in the "actually existing" Communist countries? What are
the analytical contents, practical socioeconomic arrangements and
moral values that define the term "socialism"? Does the term obstruct

and obscure the very ideals it purports to promote? What does it mean to be a democratic socialist today?

Harrington's attempt to reply to these pressing questions constitutes not only a re-evaluation of the socialist life he led but also a projection of his legacy. The book was begun the day he was told that he had inoperable cancer and a limited time to live. And the text is vintage Harrington—lucid, candid, tempered yet upbeat. His basic argument is that the hope for human freedom and justice in the future rests upon the capacity of people to choose and implement democratic forms of socialization in the face of "irresponsible," "unthinking" and "unsocial" versions of corporate socialization. Harrington defines corporate socialization as a fusion of Weber's notion of rationalization, or the expansion of bureaucratic hierarchies that impose impersonal rules and regulations in order to increase efficiency, and Marx's idea of commodification, or the globalization of capital. (This takes the form of centralizing corporations that concentrate power and wealth and render people increasingly dependent on market forces to satisfy their needs and desires.) For Harrington, the fundamental choice is not between rigid command economies and "free markets," or between bureaucratic collectivist regimes and capitalist democracies. Rather, the basic choice in the future will be between a democratic, or "bottom-up" socialization and corporate, or "top-down" socialization. This choice is much more complex than it appears on the surface and is a far cry from the classic Marxist choice between socialism and barbarism posed by Rosa Luxemburg.

First, Harrington's notion of democratic socialization has nothing to do with nationalization or state control of economic enterprises. Nor is it associated with a socialist "negation" of capitalism. Instead, it is a process in which social forces—especially those brought to bear by progressive groups, associations and organizations—try to broaden the participation of citizens in the economic, cultural and political spheres of society and thus control the conditions of their existence. At present these forces are weak compared with those of corporate socialization. Orthodox Marxist-Leninists have made the fatal mistake of reducing democratic socialization to elitist nationalization, creating monstrosities that are neither socialist nor capitalist, neither free nor efficient.

Second, Harrington shows that the reality of corporate socialization can be separated from rhetoric about "free markets" or the absence of state intervention in the economy. As Reagan and Thatcher illustrated, corporate socialization, despite conservative pieties about "laissez-faire" capitalism, is deeply statist, with its military buildups, socially authoritarian regimentation of the labor force, moral strictures on individual (especially women's) choices and a debt-financed public sphere.

Third, democratic socialization, in Harrington's view, entails more than workers' participation in investment decisions (including access to relevant knowledge and information) and the use of markets for nonmarket purposes. It also requires a new culture, a new civilization. Harrington's attempt to define this "new socialism" harks back to the best of the nineteenth-century utopian socialists, such as Charles Fourier, Robert Owen and the Saint-Simonians. While Harrington shuns their naïveté, moralism and messianism, he accents their feminist, communitarian and cultural radicalism. He then adds a strong antiracist and ecological consciousness that calls for a new global civilization in which wealth is distributed more equally and life is lived more meaningfully.

Harrington's project is indeed visionary. Yet he struggles to make it appear to be more than mere fantasy. So he accepts the sacred cow of the present capitalist structure of accumulation—namely, economic growth—and attempts to show how it can be channeled toward qualitative living, not merely quantitative consuming. He proposes replacing the gross national product with a new set of statistics, the qualitative national (and international) product, which would subtract from the G.N.P. environmental degradation, premature death, wasteful packaging and uninformative advertising in order to keep track of the quality of life. Further, Harrington suggests a restructuring of the United Nations and its related economic institutions—such as the World Bank and the International Monetary Fund—in order to transfer resources from North to South and promote cultural differences. He emphatically points out that Third World debt not only forces cutbacks in crucial social services for the countries' poor people but also prevents the South from consuming First World goods—consumption that could fuel economic growth in both North and South. And his trenchant critique of the calculated dependence of the export-led economies of the Four Tigers (Taiwan, South Korea, Hong Kong and Singapore)—the showcase countries for conservative economists—reveals the fragility of the present international economic order. His discussion is extremely relevant to Eastern Europeans clamoring for the "free market"—that is, full integration into the corporate-dominated economic order of the West.

How will democratic socialization come about? How do we radically reform a system while working within it? How can democratic socialist practices be more than a social democracy in which corporate priorities operate within a public sector organized by liberals and managed by bureaucratic elites? And given the fragmentation and casualization of the labor force—the de-skilling and re-skilling of workers due to the automation, computerization and robotization in the workplace—who will be the major agents of social change?

Harrington approaches these questions with candor and caution. First, he assumes that any socialist conception of social change must be epochal, not apocalyptic. He finds it impossible to conceive the triumph of democratic socialization in the next fifty years. Second, he presents Sweden's social democratic order as the major inspiration—not the utopian model or flawless example—for figuring out how to overcome the most inegalitarian effects of corporate socialization. Sweden's policy of "collective capital formation," which links growth to efficiency and democratic management, and solidaristic wage demands that first reward those at the bottom of the labor force fall far short of his vision. Yet they show what can be done when pressure is brought to bear on capital in the interests of social justice and democratic participation. Harrington acknowledges the precious gains achieved by reformers as well as the structural constraints on reform. His notion of "visionary gradualism" is an attempt to walk this tightrope of short-term strategies and tactics and long-term aims.

But is he successful? Does he remain blind to possible new social forces or silent about new strategies for change? It is extremely difficult to know how to measure "success" here. Certainly social movements he did not foresee may emerge. New cleavages in the fragile conservative camp could weaken the right offensive, and structural transformations could threaten the present forms of corporate socialization. Yet it would be unfair to blame Harrington for failure to predict such events.

The major problem I have with Harrington's impressive projects is that it remains too far removed from lived experience in advanced capitalist societies. Despite his call for a new culture, he does not discuss the civic terrorism that haunts our city streets; the central role of TV, video, radio and film in shaping the perceptions of citizens; the escalating violence against women, gays and lesbians; the racial and ethnic polarization or the slow decomposition of civil society (families, schools, neighborhoods and associations). There are no reflections in the book about the impact of the plagues of drugs and AIDS on a terrified populace or the entrenchment of jingoistic patriotism and nationalism. Although he invokes Gramsci, Harrington is more interested in the notion of "historic blocs"—coalition politics—than in the actual operations of hegemony that mobilize people's "consent" (in the forms of indifference or passivity) to the "fate" of corporate socialization. Subtle investigations into such cultural, experiential and existential realities—as intimated in the works of Georg Simmel, Lukács, Walter Benjamin, Siegfried Kracauer and other cultural critics—are needed before democratic socialization can become more than a noble ideal.

Harrington combined many of the best qualities of the old left and a genuine openness to some of the insights of the New Left. In his life and work, the fist and rose begin to come together. With the historic merger of his organization, the Democratic Socialist Organizing Committee, with the New American Movement in 1982, this unity-in-process, though full of tension, was manifest. His mere presence gave the new group, Democratic Socialists of America, a visibility and legitimacy in progressive circles far beyond its numbers (roughly 7,000).

Because the left is organizationally weak and intellectually timid relative to its conservative counterparts (it is armed more with journals and gestures than with programs and politicians), it has tended to rely on charismatic spokespersons and insurgent movements. Harrington's death makes this situation more apparent. The splitting of the old and New lefts from the black, brown, yellow and red lefts—dating back to the mid-1960s—exacerbates the predicament of progressives. This is why Jesse Jackson's Rainbow politics is so refreshing. It is a new multiracial attempt to channel the inchoate left-liberal sentiments of ordinary people into an electoral campaign of national scope. Yet the legacy of Harrington, as well as those of Martin Luther King Jr., Fanny Lou Hamer and Malcolm X, as well as the efforts of feminists, greens, the Gray Panthers and gays and lesbians, deserves a movement with deeper roots. Jackson's courageous attempt to gain power at the national level is a symptom of the weakness of the left—a sign that its capacity to generate extraparliamentary social motion or movements has waned. The best way to keep the legacy of Harrington alive is to go beyond it by building from grass-roots citizens' participation in credible progressive projects in which activists see that their efforts can make a difference. In this way, the crucial difference that Michael Harrington made in many of our lives can become contagious.

TIME FOR *OUR* SINATRA DOCTRINE

Carlos Fuentes

•

IN DECEMBER 1968—more than twenty-one years ago—Gabriel García Márquez, Julio Cortázar and I traveled to Prague. Our purpose was to show our solidarity with the Czechoslovak reform movement, which has come to be called the Prague Spring. That August, the troops of the Warsaw Pact had invaded Czechoslovakia to terminate Alexander Dubcek's experiment in democratic socialism. At the time of our arrival, Dubcek was still formally in office, and even though Prague was surrounded by Soviet tanks, the only visible signs of the invasion there were a few bullet-riddled walls and a shattered glass partition in Wenceslas Square. A soldier from one of the Soviet Union's Asian republics had smashed into it; he had never seen a glass wall before. The Czechoslovaks, who are descendants, after all, of Franz Kafka and the good soldier Schweik, instantly put up a sign: "Nothing Can Stop the Soviet Soldier."

As it turned out, the glass-breaking soldier was not an anomaly. Many of the Soviet soldiers were Asians who spoke neither Czech nor Russian. They were told they were being sent to put down a revolt in one of the Soviet republics and, thinking they were welcome liberators, they were all smiles as they drove their tanks into the city. Czechoslovak girls would offer them flowers and then spit in their faces when they bent down to take them. It was then that other wounds appeared, the internal wounds caused by this assault on socialism, on law and, above all, on hope.

What Dubcek and his advisers—Foreign Minister Jiri Hajek, President Ludvik Svoboda, the economist Ota Sik and the journalist Jiri Pelikan—were seeking was, in light of the changes now taking place in Central Europe, remarkably modest. "Socialism with a human face," simply put, consisted in carrying out Marx's dictum about the withering away of the state and its gradual replacement by the energies of civil society. Czechoslovakia, which had a tradition of political democracy and a well-developed industrial base, not only could take that step but actually did take it. The Prague Spring saw the proliferation of activities carried out by social groups within and tangential to the state. Farmers, students, industrial workers, intellectuals, people in the information sector, even bureaucrats began to take initiatives, to organize, to demand effective representation and to develop their own press. As a counterbalance, they demanded a democratization of the Communist Party and a constructive response from the state to this social dynamism.

But the petrified Communist state could make no political response to these demands being made by the very society that, ironically, the state had been involved in creating for two decades. Dubcek's reform group emerged as a response to the voices of society. That is, *glasnost* and *perestroika* were born twenty-two years ago in Czechoslovakia. It is only natural that they now return to their native land and replace the doctrine used to justify the aggression of 1968. The Brezhnev Doctrine announced that the Soviet Union had the right to intervene militarily to insure that any nation already within the Soviet sphere of influence (or even one that might someday be within it) did not drift away. In so doing, Brezhnev supplied powerful arguments to U.S. hard-liners: Those who fall into the hands of the Soviet Union never escape.

When García Márquez, Cortázar and I reached Prague in the cold winter of 1968, the operative fiction—Kafka-cum-Schweik—was that the Russians were not there at all, that the "spring" could continue right into winter. While we couldn't refer directly to the Brezhnev Doctrine, we could talk about the Monroe Doctrine, so that when we mentioned U.S. intervention in Latin America, everyone understood that we were talking about Soviet intervention in Eastern Europe.

Today the Brezhnev Doctrine is dead, and the Soviet government's witty Foreign Ministry spokesman, Gennadi Gerasimov, whose sense of humor derives from Gogol and Bulgakov, says that now it's the Sinatra

Doctrine that's operative in Eastern Europe: "I'll do it my way" is the order of the day. Or as we say in Mexico, *Cada chango a su mecate*— "Every monkey up his own tree." But the demise of the Brezhnev Doctrine in Europe, from the Elbe to the Vistula and from the Danube to the Baltic, is not being echoed by the demise of the Monroe Doctrine in the other theater of the cold war, the U.S. sphere of influence in Central America and the Caribbean.

The Monroe Doctrine is the most illustrious cadaver in all the Americas. It was born with more holes than a Swiss cheese. How could President Monroe, in 1823, proscribe any European presence in the New World without weakening the legitimacy of the United States, whose independence would never have been achieved without the military intervention of Bourbon France? It was not only the active participation of freelancers like Lafayette but also de Grasse's fleet and Rochambeau's troops that clinched the English surrender at Yorktown.

The application of the Monroe Doctrine as a weapon of intervention by the United States in Latin America reached the highest pitch of fantasy during the Falklands/Malvinas war. United Nations ambassador Jeane Kirkpatrick urged the Argentine military to embark on its disastrous adventure. In exchange for that support, the Argentines would train the Nicaraguan *contras*. But both the Argentine government and President Ronald Reagan had to realize that, when the chips were down, Washington would naturally support its old NATO ally, Britain, and not its remote South Atlantic lackey, President Leopoldo Galtieri.

Once again it was clear that the United States did not intend to use the Monroe Doctrine against Europe but against Latin America. It was simply a weapon to be deployed against any Latin American government that might be in conflict with Washington, any government that Washington might claim was working for "extra-continental" interest. It was the same argument the United States used against Mexico and the Germany of the Kaiser, against Argentina and the Axis powers, against Guatemala, Cuba, Brazil, Chile and Nicaragua with regard to "international communism." It is, therefore, hardly surprising that Latin American nations have from time to time preferred to align themselves with the distant empire, Moscow, rather than the all-too-nearby one, Washington. If only Latin Americans had been allowed to follow, unobstructed, their own national destinies without pressures from either side, how much confusion, how many perversions, how many reversals and, of course, how many human tragedies might have been avoided.

It is one of the paradoxes of this *fin de siècle* that in the era of economic interdependence and instant communication political nationalism should be enjoying such a powerful resurgence. From Armenia and Turkestan to the Ukraine and Lithuania, from Northern Ireland to Brittany and the Basque country, regional nationalism is sending tremors through the seemingly solid foundations of European unity. The "single European home" is going to require an original and flexible federalism if it is going to respond successfully to these challenges.

In Latin America, nationalism is not limited to more or less isolated regions but is an important factor in the identity of extant nations. Mexican, Nicaraguan or Venezuelan nationalism is not spilling over frontiers and endangering neighboring countries and is certainly not destabilizing states. These nations define themselves by means of nationalism. We must, therefore, recognize nationalism as a dynamic factor essential for the solution of internal problems, which should remain free of outside meddling. We Latin Americans will be able to face the challenges of our times only if we first overcome this problem of external intervention.

Mexico and Brazil have the advantage of having consolidated their national sovereignty. Now they can test that sovereignty against the problems of political and economic modernization. Countries like Nicaragua, on the other hand, must defend their nascent national institutions against constant external aggression. In fact, the Sandinista government has defeated that foreign-supported aggression—just as Benito Juárez defeated the Mexican *contras*—and now demands that its last vestiges be expunged. The end of the *contras* should also be the end of the long history of U.S. intervention in Nicaragua.

The legitimacy of the current Nicaraguan government derives in part from its being the first to act without being under Washington's tutelage. The February elections will continue the process of national recovery, the consolidation of national institutions and the growth of energy in civil society because of the active participation of twenty opposition parties. There is no way to compare what is happening in Nicaragua with the situation in El Salvador. The Farabundo Marti National Liberation Front was not invented abroad; it arose in El Salvador and will either survive or die there. The *contras* never won a battle in Nicaragua; the F.M.L.N. controls much of El Salvador and is capable of launching an offensive in the capital itself to prove to President Alfredo Cristiani that he should negotiate seriously or face the prospect of an interminable bloodletting in a no-win situation. To accuse Nicaragua of sending arms to the F.M.L.N. is to apply yet another doctrine, one invented by the Mexican conservative ideologue Lucas Alamán: blaming internal problems on foreign governments.

The Bush Administration is being criticized for its lack of initiatives with regard to the changes in Eastern Europe. I think it is more to be criticized for its abysmal behavior—threats or inaction—in Central America and the Caribbean. To go on arming the Salvadoran government while demanding that the Soviet Union stop arming the Nicaraguan government is not only a refusal to recognize that Moscow has in fact suspended all arms shipments to Central America but also a refusal to negotiate the compromise that Soviet President Gorbachev and Latin American diplomats have so often suggested, namely, that no one ship arms to central America.

Even if that were to happen, Bush—the last, albeit the most timid, of ideologues—would still be blind to the obvious facts about Central American nationalism. To call Violeta Chamorro "Washington's candidate" is to give her the kiss of death. It turns the Nicaraguan election into a struggle between Ortega and Bush, just as the 1946 Argentine election forced voters to choose between Juan Domingo Perón and his principal enemy, U.S. Ambassador Spruille Braden. Naturally, the national candidate won.

Bush cannot limit his response to Gorbachev in Central America to a denunciation of Soviet arms—which, of course, are his justification for sending U.S. arms. He must support the principle that neither great power send arms and thereby proclaim the Sinatra Doctrine for all of Central America. Every country should go its own way, with no outside intervention whatsoever. Then we would see just how quickly negotiations would take place in El Salvador and with what vigor national institutions would develop in Nicaragua.

Bush's hypocrisy in Central America is an insult. He takes a paternalistic attitude that does not recognize the ability of Salvadorans or Nicaraguans to resolve their own conflicts or determine their own destinies. Is there anyone who really believes that the victory of the F.M.L.N. in El Salvador or of Daniel Ortega in Nicaragua would endanger the United States or constitute a Soviet beachhead in Central America? In the Gorbachev era, with Solidarity governing Poland, with the Czechoslovak Politburo in total collapse, with a multiparty Hungary requesting admission to the Council of Europe, with the removal of the Berlin wall, how can anyone think that Gorbachev has either the intention or the ability to set up Stalinist dictatorships whose advantage to the Soviet Union would be doubtful, and logistically impossible, in countries so geographically remote? No one would want to be a spoke in the wheel of such a troika—assuming troikas had wheels.

The real problem, of course, is Cuba. Fidel Castro is increasingly isolated from his old allies in the Communist world. A stormy session of the Cuban Cabinet in 1968 debated the question of whether Cuba should denounce the invasion of Czechoslovakia. The Brezhnev Doctrine reinforced the perpetuation of the Monroe Doctrine in the Americas. The Cubans hoped the Czechoslovaks would resist, but there was no Sierra Maestra anywhere near the Danube. Castro, once again, was obliged to follow the policy he could enact instead of the policy he wanted to enact.

Is it possible for Fidel Castro to lead today the revolution he always wanted: Latin American and far-reaching, but a revolution that would not sacrifice democratic freedoms or social transformation? Will age, the tentacles of the system or perhaps a love of the personal exercise of power keep him from it?

The human drama in this dilemma cannot be overlooked. Castro can claim that for Cuba the cold war is not over. And everything suggests that George Bush, like his predecessors, does not want a reformed Cuba but a defeated Cuba. Given such a reality, there can be no movement on either side, just paralysis. If only Bush and Castro would simultaneously and dramatically declare an end to the cold war in the Caribbean, the mutual opening of frontiers and the demolition of their two walls. That's right, the Havana wall, so that Cubans could have free access to information and so that political prisons could be emptied. But the Miami wall must also come down: The blockade must be lifted and U.S. citizens allowed to travel to Cuba, trade with Cuba and recognize Cuba. And let's hear no more of Radio Marti's stridency.

But if the New World we either cannot or choose not to act with the clearsighted dramatism of the Europeans, it is certainly necessary that the first steps be taken for the eventual removal of the Miami and Havana walls. This must be done delicately, over a reasonable period of time and with good faith on both sides. Relations between Cuba and the United States, as lopsided as they are, and as insolent and aggressive as the White House has been and continues to be toward its former protectorate under the Platt Amendment, reveal a mutual insecurity. Castro is afraid that any relaxation of tension will be used against him by the gringos. Bush is afraid that, deprived of an enemy in Europe, the United States will have nowhere to show off its Manichean machismo. Where else can he demonstrate, with quasi-religious piety, that the Good Empire is facing up to the Evil Empire but in Cuba and

Central America? The rest of the world, however, sees in Bush's regime the profound insecurity of an empire in decline, and its belief in and respect for the United States continue to diminish.

An initiative by George Bush that would bring the agenda of the United States in the Caribbean and Cuba up to date would restore his country's diplomatic prestige, which Mikhail Gorbachev and his brilliant policies have stolen.

Are we going to be witnesses to the paradox that it will be the Soviet Union that dispenses with its useless ideological baggage while the United States persists in dealing with the world only in ideological terms? If the Soviet Union can give up the Brezhnev Doctrine for the Sinatra Doctrine, the United States can give up the James Monroe Doctrine for the Marilyn Monroe Doctrine: Let's all go to bed wearing the perfume we like best.

OUT OF THE MOUTHS OF BABES
CHILD ABUSE AND THE ABUSE OF ADULTS

Alexander Cockburn

•

IN THE SUMMER of 1983 Judy Johnson, the mother of a 2-year-old, complained to the police of Manhattan Beach, a rich seaside city in greater Los Angeles, that her son had been sodomized by "Mr. Ray." This turned out to be Ray Buckey, a teacher at the McMartin infant school founded by his grandfather. The boy was examined and pronounced to be telling the truth. Buckey was arrested, released, rearrested and then spent four years in prison awaiting trail.

In the months following his first arrest panic convulsed parents in Manhattan Beach. The police had sent them letters asking for information about abuse. By the spring of 1984 Buckey, his mother, grandmother, sister and three fellow teachers had been arrested; later they would be charged on 208 counts involving forty-one children. The police announced they had thirty-six suspects as yet uncharged and no fewer than 1,200 alleged victims of abuse. Amid the hysteria seven other infant schools in Manhattan Beach had to close.

The charges made by the children were gothic in their detail. The children said they had witnessed devil worship in a church; had been photographed naked; had had sticks, silverware and screwdrivers stuck up their bottoms; had been marched to mortuaries and cemeteries where they dug up corpses with shovels and pickaxes; had been flown in airplanes; had been given red or pink liquid that made them sleepy; had been buried alive; had seen naked priests, cavorting in a secret cellar below the school; had seen one teacher fly; had observed three abusers "dressed up as witches"; had seen Ray Buckey kill a horse with a baseball bat.

At almost exactly the same time that Judy Johnson was making the charges that provoked the longest trial in U.S. legal history (at a cost of $15million) Christine Brown of Jordan, Minnesota, was making similar accusations of abuse of her daughter by James Rud, a trash collector living in a trailer park. Among those subsequently implicated by children in the trailer park was this same Christine Brown, a twice-married mother of five, hit with eighteen counts of criminal sex conduct and of participating with other adults in oral sex with youngsters.

Christine turned for help to her older sister Helen and brother-in-law Tom Brown (they all shared the same surname), who mortgaged their house to post bail. Two months later the prosecutor, an unstable woman named Kathleen Morris, who once spat on an interlocutor in her office, had Tom and Helen arrested for child abuse. They were jailed for five days, and shortly thereafter about forty people met in City Hall to speak out against the arrests. These included an automobile painter named Bob Bentz and his wife, Lois, and an eight-year police veteran, Greg Myers. In the next few weeks Bob and Lois Bentz, Greg Myers and his wife, Jane, and Dwayne and Dee Rank, who had picked up the Browns from jail, were all arrested for child abuse. Sheriff's Deputy Don Buchan and his wife, Cindy, for whom Jane Myers had baby-sat, feared that their children might have been abused. But the more they looked into the charges, the more baseless they found them to be. The Buchans were duly arrested for child abuse.

In the end everyone except James Rud, the original accused, was released, and the prosecutor investigated by Minnesota's State Board of Professional Responsibility. Tom Brown lost his twelve-year trucking job. Police Officer Myers became a part-time construction worker. Dwayne Rank, a lathe operator, ran up $50,000 in legal costs and he and Dee had to give up their house. Buchan held his job in the sheriff's department but faces a $200,000 legal bill. The strain destroyed Bob and Lois Bentz's marriage. Christine Brown left the area. Helen Brown got her two children back after they had spent fourteen months in foster care.

The Jordan children told stories almost as lurid as those from Manhattan Beach, and the charges that destroyed lives in those two towns spread rapidly across the country in the months and years that followed. Children in more than a hundred cities, from Fort Bragg, California, to Grenade, Mississippi, came forward. In June 1984 children in

Sacramento told of witnessing orgies, cannibalism and snuff films. Two months later in Miami children reported being made to drink urine and eat feces. In Wilkes-Barre, Pennsylvania, in March 1985 two children said adults had forced them into having oral sex with a goat and eating a dismembered deer's raw heart. In November 1985 in Maplewood, New Jersey, a 24-year-old woman was indicated on 235 counts of "repulsively bizarre acts" alleged by infants, such as assaulting children with tampons, playing the piano naked and licking peanut butter and jelly off their bodies. In April 1986 children in a preschool in Sequim, Washington, charged they had been taken to graveyards and forced to witness animal sacrifice. In Chicago children said they had been made to eat a boiled baby. A boy in a Memphis preschool said his teacher, Frances Ballard, had, among innumerable perversions, put a bomb in a hamster and blown it up after children counted to 11. She was acquitted of fifteen charges but, in what seems to be an appalling miscarriage of justice, went to prison supposedly for kissing a 4-year-old boy on his genitals.

SATAN'S HOOFPRINTS

These details come from two reporters with the Memphis *Commercial Appeal*, Tom Charlier and Shirley Downing. In a magnificent series in late 1987 they surveyed nearly two score investigations of "ritual abuse" against children and compared the cases and the children's charges. Many of them have a venerable antecedent, going back at least as far as Roman accusations against Christians in the second century. Others belong to what these days is called urban legend—lurid tales endlessly recycled, like the one about the phantom hitchhiker or the prosthetic hook hanging from the car door.

Of the thirty-six investigations reviewed by Charlier and Downing, all launched after the summer of 1983 and most of them concluded by 1987, ninety-one people were arrested and charged, and of the seventy-nine defendants whose cases have been heard, twenty-three were convicted, mostly of lesser charges, some of which have been reversed.

On January 18 of this year came the denouement to the most sensational case of all. A jury acquitted Ray Buckey and his mother, Peggy McMartin Buckey, on fifty-two counts of molestation after deliberating for nine weeks over evidence presented to it over two years. On thirteen remaining counts against Ray the court was deadlocked and a mistrial declared. He could be retried on those.

Buckey's life has been effectively ruined. His mother is suing for wrongful prosecution. The woman who started it all, Judy Johnson, is quit of the case. She died in 1986 of an alcohol-related illness. She had also claimed that her son had been sodomized by an AWOL marine who she said had inflicted similar treatment (oral or anal, it is impossible to say, since the word can refer to assaults through either orifice) on the family dog. Johnson, who had a history of mental illness, also said her son—age 2, remember—had described sex rituals in churches and animal sacrifice.

THE GREAT FEAR

Why did this hysteria commence? An immediate response, by no means improper, is that "hysteria" is an unkind word for a long over-due concern with child abuse. More than 100,000 cases are reported each year, most involving incest. By the early 1980s American society had evolved sufficiently for it to confront with some measure of determination the sexual persecution of children. In 1984 the F.B.I. circulated nationally an advisory on child sex abuse which, in retrospect, may have fueled the paranoia.

It's clear from reading accounts of the various cases that many of the adults bringing the charges felt they were deeply involved in a national cause. An important issue in the Buckey trial was whether some major players in the case had themselves been abused as children. But it's also clear that some terrible injustices were done. The press was greatly to blame and so were ambitious prosecutors eager to make a name for themselves.

In a January 19–22 series on press coverage of the Buckey case, reporter David Shaw of the *Los Angeles Times* wrote a deadly account of the media frenzy that took place after the accusations first surfaced, making it clear that the essential function of most of the press had been to act as a conduit for the prosecution. The reporter responsible for breaking the story of the McMartin investigation was Wayne Satz of KABC in Los Angeles. He had an intimate relationship with Kee Mac-Farlane, who worked as a "therapist" for Children's Institute International and who interviewed the McMartin infants and promulgated their charges. Her only credential was a certificate as "welder-sculptor" from an Ohio welding school.

In the hysterical atmosphere the prosecutors felt they could get away with anything, and journalists eagerly lapped up their charges. Preposterous "experts" were dutifully quoted. One California doctor of the mind claimed to have identified symptoms in children abused by satanic cults—said symptoms including "fear of monsters," making farting noises, and laughing when other children farted. In general most expertise was rickety, often absurdly so. Examiners would tell a child to bend over, and if their scrutiny was greeted by an "anal wink"—i.e., contraction of the sphincter—they would pronounce the child abused.

But if there was a general social awakening to the reality and pervasiveness of child abuse, in which some children's testimony was taken too seriously precisely because in the past it had not been taken seriously enough, there was also the receptive atmosphere of the early Reagan years. The attempt to recreate the McCarthy hearings directly—Senator Jeremiah Denton's investigation into "terrorism"—was a comic flop. But society was ripe for a witch hunt nonetheless, and the accumulated energies poised to this end displaced themselves onto the cause of hunting for body-snatchers of the nation's children.

Indeed, commie hunters and Satan hunters share the same paranoid mind frame. The Memphis Police Department's supposed expert on satanic crimes, Sgt. Jerry Davis, known to his colleagues as Mr. Conspirator, was in the late 1960s head of a criminal intelligence unit infiltrating Memphis student groups in search of subversives. In the total war against child abusers Iowa officials sought but failed to obtain sanction to strip and probe children without parental permission in search of evidence of abuse.

The laws of this chase would have been the envy of the seventeenth-century prosecutors at Salem. The accusers were infants as young as 2 and 3, permitted in fifty states to testify without corroboration from adults or physical evidence; without cross-examination in many states; to have their charges merely reported by adults as hearsay in many states. These infants had themselves been interrogated as many as thirty times by social workers or other investigators, told they would remain separated from their parents if they retracted their charges, held in sterile environments during questioning, to a degree that one critic described as kindred to "brainwashing" in the Korean War.

So the nation went on the hunt for Satan, and the search rapidly took on the usual populist impedimenta: priests conducting perverted masses in cellars, gulping down children's blood and performing other tricks of the heterodox trade. Rocking chairs disappeared from infant schools so teachers would not be compelled to hold children in their laps. Teachers took care never to be left alone with infants. Video monitors scanned playrooms, for teachers' protection. In this purgative frenzy many lives were destroyed. Perhaps we may console ourselves that children have been fortified in confidence that at last they can tell somebody about what had happened behind the woodshed. But even here the hysteria has diminished the credibility of this infant witness.

BAD DAYS IN PLEASANTVILLE

Benjamin H. Cheever

•

WHEN I WORKED at the headquarters of *Reader's* Digest in Chappaqua, New York, every employee was given a turkey on Thanksgiving. One year the Wallaces, the couple who owned the company, found that a turkey was not sufficient expression of their holiday spirit, and we were also given a ham for Christmas. Another time we got the turkey on Thanksgiving and on Christmas we got a check for $250.

There was no turkey last year. And there was no ham. Employees were given a gift certificate worth $10 when redeemed at one of a number of local merchants. This is part of a new hardheadedness that has also resulted in substantial increases in the cost of lunch at the company cafeteria, the ending of a subsidized bus service and the lengthening of the workday by thirty minutes.

We live in the age of the bottom line, and I suppose it would be wrong to expect a continuation of nineteenth-century paternalism in the late twentieth century. But what makes the loss of the turkeys so interesting is that it comes at a time when the top executives of this same company are being treated with the sort of generosity that might have made Andrew Carnegie blush. And Carnegie sold steel. A big part of what these people market is an idea of right and wrong.

Last December, when The Reader's Digest Association filed with the Securities and Exchange Commission for approval to sell 25 million shares of its Class A nonvoting common stock, even *The Wall Street*

Journal was impressed by the financial rewards earmarked for the company's top executive. Patrick Reilly of the *Journal* commented, "[George] Grune, the chief executive, stands to benefit handsomely in the offering. The executive will receive payments totaling about $5.5 million under the terms of an equivalent stock unit plan."

The S.E.C. filling shows that Grune also owns 240,000 shares of nonvoting common stock, currently worth about $5.75 million. The company went public on February 15 with the stock at $21 a share. It is now worth about $24. Grune was paid $1,010,707 in salary and bonuses in fiscal year 1989. He got another $450,000 in bonuses earned in fiscal year 1988 and paid in 1989, according to the filing. Grune also received "performance shares" valued at $860,910 during the 1989 fiscal year. So the total nest egg—stock, salary and various bonuses—comes to well over $13 million.

I was pondering this during a recent trip to the Red Apple supermarket. I know that prices vary from market to market, so I should say that I went to the Red Apple at the corner of 82nd Street and Broadway in New York City. A turkey weighing 11.22 pounds was selling for $15.60. That didn't seem right, so I telephoned *Reader's Digest*. I worked there for eleven years, and I know these people. I asked for Grune, but he was traveling. So I asked for public relations and got Bruce Trachtenberg.

"Why did the company decide not to give away turkeys this Thanksgiving?" I asked Trachtenberg. (I suppose I should call him Bruce. He called me Ben.)

"That, ah, that was just a decision that, ah well, actually it was an opportunity. What we did is we gave, the company gave away gift certificates valued at I believe ten dollars."

"But isn't ten dollars less than what a turkey would have cost?"

"No," said Bruce.

When I asked about new working conditions, he said he didn't think they had been altered. True, the workday had been lengthened, and the bus service from the surrounding suburbs to the *Digest's* Chappaqua office had been stopped in 1986. But there had been only 350 riders at the time. *Only* 350 riders? Lunch was still heavily subsidized, Bruce said. But lunch used to cost 25 cents. Now it can cost a couple of dollars. And what about the approximately 300 employees offered early retirement in 1986? What about the scores of others who have since left under circumstances unfriendly enough to spark a number of lawsuits?

When I went to work for *Reader's Digest* in 1976 I was fully aware of the public's perception of my chosen employer. But consider my problem: I needed somebody to grow up to be like. I didn't think it was smart for me to try to grow up to be a novelist like my father. He didn't think it was smart either. I knew a number of admirable men who worked there, including a brilliant neighbor of ours. Maybe I could try and grow up to be like him.

It's widely supposed that money is the only reason anybody ever went to work for the *Digest*. Certainly money had something to do with my desire to work for *R.D.*, but it wasn't the only reason. I started out at the copy desk and was never particularly well paid. In fact, I recall a difficult afternoon when I got the printout of salaries of the people who reported to me and found that one of them was earning almost twice as much as I was.

You see, the *Digest* wasn't just a place to work, it was something to believe in. I can hear you falling away in droves, but let me try to explain. Sure the magazine is conservative. *Reader's Digest* had been a booster for the war in Vietnam. Sure, they once sent out American flag stickers to every subscriber and employee. Employees were encouraged to display the flags on their car windows.

The magazine's founder, DeWitt Wallace, believed in the American Dream. But he was also tolerant. A lot of those stickers went into the trash. Besides, while it was easy to find fault with his dogma, it was hard not to respect him for the purity and consistency of his vision. It was difficult not to admire "The Founder." His full name was William Roy DeWitt Wallace, but he asked people to call him Wally. Most everyone I knew called him Mr. Wallace, but I thought it touching that this great man, editor of the world's largest magazine, wanted to be called Wally.

He made an art of civility. After I'd been at the *Digest* only a week, my phone rang. It was the high, reedy voice I'd been told to expect. Mr. Wallace wanted to know if I had a minute. Because if I had a minute, he would like it if I could come down to his office. When I got there the world's most commercially successful editor leaped right up and shook my hand. I talked. He listened. When people listen to me, I often think it has to do with my father, but Wallace was in his late 80s when I first met him, and he didn't seem to make the connection. In fact, he asked what my father did for a living. I said that he was a writer.

"Oh," said Wallace. "It must have been a hard life."

After I'd been at *Reader's Digest* for a year or so, I was invited to lunch with Mr. Wallace, an older editor named John Allen and the representative of a charity that sought Wallace funds.

Allen introduced me to The Founder as "one of our brilliant young editors." This sort of generous overstatement was typical of John. Wallace shook my hand, studied my face and then said, "I don't believe we've met."

"I think we have, sir," I said. Wallace turned violently to the table, clearly dismayed by his failure to remember my name. He was muttering angrily, and I thought I heard him say, "Oh shit."

When I told John about this later, he wasn't surprised that Wallace had been upset about not remembering my name. But he couldn't believe that The Founder would use such foul language. Maybe it was "shucks" he said. It sure sounded like "shit" to me.

After the lunch John told me that I should write Wallace a note telling what I thought about the charity that I'd seen presented. "He'll answer you," said John. "But don't you write back again. Because he'll feel that he has to answer your second note, and it could go on forever."

So I spent most of the next day phrasing a careful, thoughtful note about the lunch. I was still on the copy desk then, but I had my own personal memo paper with my name on it and a picture of Pegasus, the company symbol. Wallace wrote back on a piece of loose-leaf notebook paper. Most of his notes were written on notebook paper, or on the backs of old envelopes.

Yes, some of Wallace's positions were reactionary. But he had ears; he listened to other points of view (he admired *The Nation*, incidentally). Certainly Wallace was a high-church optimist, and sometimes the facts in *Digest* articles were distorted to support his faith. After the magazine moved into its spanking new $1.5 million Chappaqua headquarters in 1939, the Wallaces decided to keep Pleasantville, the original Westchester County location, as a mailing address. They thought it sounded better.

DeWitt and Lila Acheson Wallace had started the magazine in a basement in Greenwich Village in 1922. They had to borrow $600 to pay for their first mailing. Their idea—which Wallace had tried unsuccessfully to shop around to a number of established publishers—turned out to be practically a license to print money.

Salaries and benefits were legendary, and the profits that couldn't be spent on employees or expansion were plowed back into the community. By 1986 the Wallaces had given away almost $200 million. Ultimately they gave *Reader's Digest* away. They had no children, so they willed the company to a series of philanthropic trusts. The Metropolitan Museum of Art, Lincoln Center, Sloan-Kettering Cancer Center and the New York Zoological Society all receive funds. So does the Lila Acheson Wallace Bird House at the Bronx Zoo.

The organizations that have received Wallace bequests are too numerous to list: The Boys Club, the Boy Scouts, local hospitals and a hospital in Beirut are a few of them. When the Wallaces were alive there was a wonderful unpredictability to their generosity. When Wallace made out his first check to the fledgling Outward Bound it was for $1 million. And he gave Hubert Humphrey a lot of money. The Wallaces were conservative, of course, but they liked Hubert.

Wallace was always generous to his employees. In 1976 he got up at the company's old-timers' party and said, "Lila and I hate to act impulsively and unilaterally without waiting for the next board of directors meeting. But . . ." He then gave all 3,300 employees a raise. Those making less than $40,000 a year got 11 percent. Those making more than $40,000 got 8 percent. Perhaps this is what George Grune was referring to when he told *The New York Times* in 1986 that he meant to continue in the Wallace tradition, but that he was not as willing as they had been to leave things to chance. "I have a penchant for planning," he said. "Doing things well means doing things according to goals and objectives."

I wonder what objectives the Wallaces achieved with a surprise raise? And why they rewarded more liberally the people at the bottom of the heap?

When the new administration took over in 1984, Grune became chair and chief executive officer, Richard McLoughlin became vice chair and William Cross, since retired, became president and chief operating officer. Kenneth Gilmore became editor in chief. Over the short term their tenure has been extremely profitable for the organization and for themselves.

The S.E.C. filing shows that McLoughlin, now president and chief operating officer, got $466,067 in salary for the fiscal year ending June 30, 1989. His bonus was $258,000. Editor in chief Gilmore got $349,267 in salary and $168,000 in bonuses. Both men were also given stock deals on a smaller scale but similar to that enjoyed by Grune. Besides this, the S.E.C. filing outlines a complicated schedule of compensation that insures that whatever the future brings, it will not bring poverty to the top men at *R.D.*

The company itself is much more profitable. But much of the profit represents savings, not earnings. In 1986 the circulation base of the domestic edition was reduced from 17 million plus to just over 16 million to save on fulfillment costs. When I was there, the *Digest* was also reducing its editorial staff. (No, I wasn't fired. Nor am I involved in any way in any legal dispute with my former employer.) I remember going to the company bookstore with another editor and having him point out that there were more employees selling greeting cards to other employees than editing any particular issue of the magazine. And revenues from the magazine itself have fallen. Last year its operating income was $61.6 million. In fiscal year 1988 it was $65.9 million.

I'm aware that what's going on at *Reader's Digest* seems harmless when compared with big corporate shuffles like the one at RJR Nabisco. But the *Digest* is a publishing company. People read the magazine. These people vote. They raise families. It matters what they think. And I believe it also matters what is being thought by the people who put out the magazine. The men at the top were editors in the old days. They thought that the words in their magazine mattered. Now the men at the top are businessmen, who see the magazine as just another product.

But people still read this product. The S.E.C. report boasts, "Today, 39 editions of *Reader's Digest* in 15 languages are read in every country in the world by an estimated 100,000,000 people each month. United States circulation is more than 16,000,000 and worldwide circulation is approximately 28,000,000."

They don't read it in Japan anymore, however, or in Spain. Both editions have been closed to save money. I don't know what these cutbacks meant to the publishing communities in their countries, but I do know what they did to the workers. Healthy Japanese companies rarely fire anybody. So when the Japanese editors of *Reader's Digest* were fired, they were in disgrace. It was widely supposed that they had done something terrible. It's bad, of course, not to make a profit, but it's not terrible. Driving to work in Chappaqua one morning, I saw a line of Japanese standing at the end of the driveway with signs protesting the treatment of workers in Tokyo. The Japanese haven't forgotten something Mr. Wallace always knew: The worker has a dignity that goes well beyond his or her immediate ability to turn a buck.

There have been other, domestic cutbacks as well. Most writers are paid much less. The educational division has been closed. It was losing money, of course, but it wasn't started to earn money. It was just another way the Wallaces had of paying back the community that had made them so rich.

And what's all this money being saved for? The charitable funds will get some of it, and will benefit from the sale of stock. But does it make sense to squeeze the employees in order to give more cash to Lincoln Center? Management has given a variety of reasons for cutting costs; one of the prime reasons was that the money was being saved in order to keep the company from having to go public—to keep it owned by the charitable trusts the Wallaces had set up. "We plan to maintain the Digest as a private company," Grune told the *Times* in 1986. Four years later he took the company public.

Now management says that the tax laws will not allow the funds to continue to own more than 50 percent of the company's voting stock after the year 2000. Besides which, if the company has to be sold, couldn't all of it be sold to the employees? Old-timers have told me that this was Wallace's original plan. And do the tax laws insist on a generous compensation for the top executives? What does the I.R.S. have to say about surprise raises—or turkeys?

The story of how the new management group won control in 1984 is a fascinating one. John O'Hara had been president and chief executive officer, sharing power with editor in chief Edward Thompson. Mr. Wallace had died. Lila Wallace was extremely ill. It was crucial to the incoming management that the old guard be out before she died, because O'Hara and Thompson were trustees of Lila's stock and executors of her will. It was a squeaker. Both were fired in time. The appointment of the new top executives was announced on the very day that Mrs. Wallace died.

Fortune ran an article titled "Intrigue Behind the Ivy at *Reader's Digest*" in June 1984. When writer Roy Rowan asked about the timing of the new appointments, he was told it was a coincidence. But Rowan wasn't convinced. So he noted that Grune himself had touched on the subject at an employee gathering. " 'You could call it a strange coincidence,' " Grune said. " 'But you could also look at it another way. Suddenly she saw the sun shining on the *Digest* and felt relieved.' "

Maybe, but when I think of what's happening in Chappaqua, I'm more inclined to remember one of the favorite sayings of William Roy DeWitt Wallace. "The dead," he liked to say, "carry with them to the grave in their clutched hands only that which they have given away."

BREAK UP THE BLOCS IN EUROPE

E. P. Thompson

•

THIS HAS BEEN a good year for peace in Europe, but not such a good year for the European peace movement. No doubt these things go together. The much-trumpeted "end of the cold war" has inevitably slackened the motivations to act urgently for peace. Exhausted activists have been picking up other themes in politics or in their personal lives. Indeed, people have told me there isn't such a thing as a peace movement anymore, a movement standing apart from and sometimes influencing profoundly other political agendas. But that is an overstatement.

Organizations and experienced offices abound in Europe (like C.N.D. and Quaker Peace and Service in Britain), and they are very much more influential than they were ten years ago. These are still at the center of significant activist lobbies. The recent Ninth Annual European Nuclear Disarmament (END) Convention in Helsinki, Finland, and Tallinn, Estonia, demonstrated how the wide spectrum of nonaligned peace forces can still meet together in an effective alliance—the Greens, Eurocommunists and Social Democrats, the feminist and Christian movements of the West, with many allies from the Third World and increasing numbers of (sometimes hesitant) allies from Eastern and Central Europe.

The European peace movement certainly still exists: as consolidated infrastructure, as known and trusted network, as wide and loose alliance, as mood and aspiration, and also as experience; that is, tens of thousands know whom they trust and whom they do not trust. All this still feeds daily and weekly into the wider political process.

Yet I look back upon the past twelve months as a time in which we in the European peace movement failed to make the most of a great moment of opportunity. There have been political reasons for this: the lack of a clear program, the failure to find the right point of intervention. As the extraordinary events of October to December 1989 unfolded, and as the giant political actors pursued their own negotiations, the peace movement was frozen into a posture of *attentisme*—a wait-and-see policy, offering commentary but abandoning the attempt to interject its own script.

Not only in Britain but in Western Europe and in the United States as well there has been a general retreat of political forces on the center and left. Some are content to stand on the sidelines and leave everything to Presidents Bush and Gorbachev. Others are in the grip of a modish defeatism. They can see nothing in the events of the past year but the triumph of Western capitalism, which is of course precisely what triumphant capitalists wish people to see.

If that premise can be sold to the people of Europe, East as well as West, then this political moment, which even now remains open, will return to closure, and a settlement can be imposed that is acceptable to unreconstructed Western militarism and diplomacy. That settlement will not end the cold war but will extend it forward for decades in a skewed form. And it could do worse than that.

The crux is the "German question," which is not a German question at all but a European question, a question of whether and how to abolish the blocs, or whether to strengthen one against the other; in short, a global question. These past months have seen an ugly attempt by NATO strategists to play a confidence trick on the people of Europe, culminating in the one-sided settlement of a reunited Germany within the structures of NATO and outside the Warsaw Pact. As a "concession" the Soviet Union has been graciously "permitted" by NATO to station some troops on former East German territory for two or three years more.

To say that such a "settlement" is a gross historical injustice is to employ a term far too abstract to engage the mind. At the risk of proving myself to be boring and senile, I must fall back on more concrete memories of World War II.

Long before that war was officially started the Nazi and Fascist (and also imperial Japanese) forces were on the offensive. Mussolini invaded Albania and Ethiopia. Hitler effected the *Anschluss* with Austria, bit off the Sudetenland, and Germany and Italy helped Franco destroy the Spanish Republic. Then came full European war: Poland was invaded (and carved up with Stalin), then Belgium, Holland, Denmark, half of France, Norway, Yugoslavia, Greece. By 1941 the only places in Western and Southern Europe free from Axis occupation were Britain, a few neutral nations, and some mountaintops in Montenegro, Bosnia and Norway, where partisans clung on.

It was a catastrophic record of defeat and retreat. Then Hitler, having failed to occupy the British skies, turned his motorized forces against the Soviet Union. For a year or more the record was the same. Vast territories were overrun—the Baltic states, the Ukraine, Byelorussia and thence deeply toward the Caucasus. Leningrad was placed under siege and the panzers were on the edge of Moscow.

Then a remarkable thing happened. For the first time the Axis forces were stopped. When it seemed impossible that the Soviet Union could still have an industry or support a war machine, the men, women and children went out and stopped the panzers with gasoline bombs and with their bare hands. In Leningrad poets and workers and scholars kept themselves alive through two bitter winters by burning their books and their floorboards and their children's toys. Moscow repeated (but with better success) the desperate people's defense of Madrid.

Meanwhile the best that the "free world" could do was to check the Axis forces before Cairo, at El Alamein. It was a serious and hard-fought battle, but not one likely to save the world. That privilege was left to the Soviet people.

No one was more aware of this than the British and Allied forces in the Near and Middle East. They knew their very survival depended on the Russians. To prompt my memory I have been looking over letters my brother wrote home in 1941–42. In November 1941 he wrote from Syria that "the sacrifices of the Russians make Coventry and London look like a couple of train accidents."

By the summer of 1942 my brother's unit was sent to Persia, partly to guard supply routes to the Soviet Union, partly as a possible backstop in case (as seemed increasingly likely) the Axis forces broke through the Caucasus and Georgia. The key to that lay in a place called Stalingrad. It has changed its name now, but I dare say there is an antique shop in North London that still has a map with the old name.

In September 1942 my brother was "knob twiddling" on his radio: "At the moment Stalingrad is the focus of all the world's broadcasting. Pick up any station—German, French, Italian, Arabic, half-a-dozen assorted Slavs . . . you won't be able to hear three sentences without the word 'Stalingrad' coming in unmistakeably." Three days later the weather began to break and he wrote in profound relief:

> All of us . . . are glad at the news of it. At the cookhouse, in the fitter's shop, in the small canteen tent where they gather for the evenings, men look with relief and gratitude to the coming rain. Rain here will mean rain at Mozdok and Tuapse. Rain here will mean rain on all the approaches to Stalingrad. Rain here will mean rain at Voronezh, Orel and Kalinin. Rain here will mean rain, and shortly snow, on the roads that lead from Viborg, Vilno, Riga, to hard-pressed Leningrad.

The rain and snow came just in time. (The second front, please remember, came twenty-one months later, although there was some serious fighting in Italy in the intervening months.) The Axis forces suffered their first shattering defeat at Stalingrad. In 1942, slowly, borne on rivers of blood, the markers on the maps began to move back.

I recall all this boring stuff, which may come strangely from a supporter of today's peace movement, because I wish to give a local habitation to that abstraction "historical injustice." The survival of the "free world" and of British democracy (if that is what we have) owes most of all to that massive transfusion of Russian blood.

That is not an apology for Stalin's policies, either before, during or after the war. It is a plea to the generations who did not live through those years to understand the justice due the Russians. The figure often cited today for Soviet losses in World War II is 20 million—that is more than the combined populations of London, Birmingham, Manchester, Norwich, Bristol and several other cities besides. These vast numbers mean that every Soviet family today lost grandparents and uncles and fathers and sisters. The custom survives for newlyweds to visit the graves on their wedding day.

The custom may die out but the historical memory will not. If suppressed it could return in unexpected and perhaps unwelcome ways. NATO's insistence on imposing an unjust and skewed "settlement," which denies due recognition to Soviet memories, a settlement which may have been accepted reluctantly by a weakened Soviet leadership in return for economic sweeteners, may well nourish a Russian nationalist or militarist comeback in 1992 or 2002.

No nation has less historical memory of Soviet suffering in World War II than the United States. The American people are constantly given the media message that they, almost alone, "won" that war. The 20 million Soviet dead are rarely mentioned, although it is more than three times the appalling figure of the Holocaust (6 million), which is mentioned constantly, as if those massacred Jews were the only victims of that war.

It follows that U.S. policy-and opinion-makers are determined to impose their unilateral settlement on Europe. They suppose themselves to be also the "victors" of the cold war. But the victors were those who brought it to an end: the forces for democracy and renewal in Eastern and Central Europe and the peace movements in the West. If either superpower can claim credit, it is the one that disengaged first from aggressive postures and started to disarm—that is, the Soviet Union.

My brother did not survive that war. Neither, dear reader, did your grandfather or uncle or mother. Neither did countless Norwegians, Dutch, Czechoslovaks, Poles, Belgians, French, Yugoslavs, Indians, New Zealanders, Canadians, Greeks and others. The settlement of the German question is not something to be imposed on all of us by the United States. It involves tender and difficult obligations—not just to future generations but to remembered friends and kin.

Countless Germans and Italians also died, and some Germans and more Italians took part in the anti-Fascist resistance. It is far from my intention to call for vindictive or unforgiving attitudes toward the German people today. On the contrary, I am convinced that German national and cultural traditions have undergone a very significant, and possibly irreversible, change.

I was fortunate enough to be present in October 1981 at the first great manifestation of the newborn West German peace movement in Bonn. All day long, unaggressive and good-humored multitudes, most in their teens or early 20s, thronged through the city like a nation reborn. In the past decade the German people have shown a far greater disposition toward constructive and peaceful diplomacies than have most European nations. They even have a Foreign Minister, Hans-Dietrich Genscher, who has from time to time been able to block Chancellor Helmut Kohl's NATO-subservient plans. The most militaristic and unconstructive policies in Europe today come not from West Germany but from France, Turkey and Margaret Thatcher's Britain.

There is no way to guarantee that a nation will not revert to its worst traditions. All that one can do is create conditions, and institutions, that foster the good. That is, of course, exactly what NATO is not doing. The peaceful traditions of the new Germany belong with the Social Democrats, the Greens, the churches, the peace movement. In every way the United States and Britain have been ignoring those voices and encouraging Kohl's nationalist *Anschluss-politik*, with its capitalist animus toward East Germany and Central Europe. Such a triumphalist West Germany will treat the workers of East Germany as a cheap labor reserve.

Nor am I asking the German people to go through the next decades with their heads perpetually bowed in guilt for the sins of the Hitler years. Guilt is an unproductive political passion, and often one that represses or disguises other passions. I am asking the German people to act now, not only for the future of Germany but also for the future of Europe and of the world.

That requires a reunited Germany in some form. But not the present one-sided settlement that privileges and strengthens NATO. I will not try to decide which alternative form of settlement would be preferable. Over the past six months Soviet, Czechoslovak and East German diplomats proposed a score of solutions. Those included a neutral and demilitarized Germany, formal membership in both NATO and the Warsaw Pact, mutual security arrangements involving both blocs or more complex arrangements involving the thirty-five nations of the Conference on Security and Cooperation in Europe. To every single proposal the reply of the United States and NATO was *nyet*—a reply coming so quickly that the proposals must have been unread. The Bush Administration does not even wish its own people to know that any alternative to Germany-in-NATO was possible. When Czechoslovak President Vaclav Havel visited the United States, he was leaned on very heavily by Secretary of State James Baker not to mention on television that the Czechoslovaks had alternative proposals. The interesting ideas of Rainer Eppelmann, a veteran of the independent peace movement and now the East German Minister of Defense and Disarmament, have gone almost unnoticed in the West.

"The underlying attitude in the Administration toward Moscow on that issue," *The New York Times* reported, "was described by one official as: 'We won, you lost. Your allies are asking you to leave, ours are asking us to stay, so we are not equals.' " Baker recently repeated that America's forces will stay in Europe for as long as they are wanted by her allies or needed. Thus the American idea of a "settlement" is for a reunited Germany—and its military forces—in NATO, and the withdrawal, or "rollback," of Soviet forces from Eastern and Central Europe and the Baltic states. Meanwhile, the Truman Doctrine remains in place, U.S. nuclear-armed navies patrol the Mediterranean and the Persian Gulf, and U.S. bases—with their Tridents and their aircraft armed with nuclear-tipped weapons—remain everywhere in the West and South, from Oxfordshire to the Turkish border with the Soviet Union.

This is no settlement at all. It is a cynical maneuver to derive advantage from the struggles for democracy on the other side. For almost a year we have been passing through a period of unusual political plasticity, when institutions and ideologies can be remolded. This moment is not anyone's triumph or anyone's defeat but everyone's opportunity. The opportunity will not wait around forever.

It is time for Europeans, East and West, to write their own script, for their own and their children's future. This means that the peace movement and its new allies in the East must show their full strength once more and impose a genuine settlement on the politicians. The object of such a settlement would be a truly symmetrical dismantling of both blocs, in which NATO at long last would make concessions that matched the concessions made in the East. The aims must be the denuclearization of Europe, an all-European security system and an all-European development program. In effect, if a reunified Germany is to be absorbed into NATO, then we must insure that NATO becomes an irrelevance.

The peace movement must shed its deference to the superpowers and its presumption that whatever Bush and Gorbachev might agree upon must be the best for us. Those two politicians may have merits (well, one of them may) but they operate within limits and within calculations of short-term political interest. The peace movement has more experience, a more disinterested stance and a longer perspective. Just because Gorbachev seems to have been tempted to give way before unrelenting NATO pressure—and economic bribes—there is no reason why the peace movement should surrender also. Our object remains to destroy the bloc system, and the German question gives us our opportunity to do so.

Both in West Germany and East Germany there are significant forces (among Social Democrats, Greens and also in the East German government) working for alternative solutions. If the German people wish to shed the guilt of the Hitler years they can do this best of all by rejecting Kohl's bullying *Anschlusspolitik* and by insisting that the German solution must and can be only a part of the European resolution of the cold war—a stage in the dissolution of both blocs, with the establishment of mutual security agreements and progressive dealignment leading to the abolition of both NATO and the Warsaw Pact.

This dealignment is a perfectly feasible project, a realistic agenda for the next two or three years. This should be the price tag set on German reunification. It would be the best insurance for the future of Europe, and in taking the leading part in securing this outcome the German people would earn Europe's gratitude.

But to secure this the European peace movement must once again move in force, as an actor and agenda maker, determined to complete the task it commenced with the END Appeal in 1980. In those early years, 1980–83, British END sometimes was accused by friends of being too sharp in its criticisms of Soviet policies. Now I believe we should say yes to the many constructive Soviet proposals. Not yes without qualification but yes to exploring them, together with the thirty-five nations. If James Baker insists that U.S. forces must remain in Europe for as long as they are wanted or needed, then we must (politely) make it plain that they are wanted and needed no more. No more than Soviet forces and bases are wanted or needed in Czechoslovakia or Hungary. What kind of a "settlement" would it be that evicted one side and left the other fully armed and holding on to all its stations?

NOTES ON OUR PATRIARCHAL STATE

Gore Vidal

•

THOMAS JEFFERSON. THIS is where it all begins. With his Declaration of Independence, he created the *idea* of the American Revolution, as opposed to the less glamorous and certainly less noble business of simply deciding who pays tax to whom. Along with the usual separated-colony boilerplate, there would be a new nation founded upon life, liberty and the pursuit of happiness. The first two foundation stones were familiar if vague. What, after all, *is* liberty? Liberty *from* what? From everyone else? From decent opinion? From accountability? That debate goes on. But the notion of freedom from tyranny is an ancient one and everyone thinks he knows what Jefferson meant, including dreamy Tom himself.

The "pursuit of happiness" is the real joker in the deck. No one is quite sure just what Jefferson meant, but I suppose he had it in mind that government would leave each citizen alone to develop as best he can in a tranquil climate to achieve whatever it is that his heart desires with minimum distress to the other pursuers of happiness. This was a revolutionary concept in 1776. It still is. With a single phrase Jefferson had upped the ante and made our Republic—in name at least—more human-scale than any other.

Eventually we freed ourselves from England, thanks to the French fleet. At the end of the struggle, there was George Washington and hardly anyone else except a group of ambitious lawyers, overexcited by the prospect of a new nation with new laws and a complex judiciary in need of powerful advocates and prosecutors and interpreters. Hence a most lawyerly Constitution that, in effect, excluded from citizenship women, slaves, Native Americans and the poor. The Constitution's famous checks and balances were designed to check the man who would be king while making certain that in the balance the people at large would have no weight at all. That is why, unlike most First World countries, the United States has elections rather than politics.

The second revolutionary note was struck in 1791. Although the Founding Fathers were, to a man, natural conservatives, there were enough Jefferson-minded pursuers of happiness among them to realize that so lawyerly a Republic would probably serve as a straitjacket for those of an energetic nature. So to insure the right of each to pursue happiness, the Bill of Rights was attached to the Constitution. In theory, henceforward no one need fear the tyranny of either the state or the majority.

Certain of our rights, such as freedom of speech, were said to be inalienable. But a significant minority has never accepted the idea of so much freedom for so many. That is why, from 1791 to the present day, the ongoing drama of our Republic has been the relentless attack of the prosperous few upon the rights of the restless many—often masked as the righteous will of the majority against the deviant few. The current Supreme Court is clearly dedicated to the removal or alienation of as many of our inalienable rights as possible, on the specious ground that what the founders did not spell out as a "right" was not a right at all but some sort of unpatriotic, un-American activity.

The result has been confusion, to put it mildly. The Fourteenth Amendment made it clear that those freedoms guaranteed to persons as citizens of the United States also applied to them as citizens of pure Utah or sex-sickened Georgia. But, so the argument goes, if the Constitution does not say that you may smoke marijuana, then any state may forbid you to smoke what a local majority thinks is bad for you. On the other hand, if the producers of death-enhancing consumer items have enough money, they can buy congresses, courts, presidents; they can also hire a consumer spokesperson like Jesse Helms to uphold the constitutional right of those who wish to pursue happiness and profits by making and selling cigarettes, which kill a half-million or so people a year, while forbidding, at huge expense, heroin, which kills in the pathetically low four figures. That neither tobacco nor heroin is good for people is agreed by all. But should either be outlawed in the sort of society that Jefferson designed for us? Finally, do we want a free society or a patriarchal one? My question is not rhetorical.

Patriarchal. From the Latin *pater*, father. As in father knows best. A patriot, then, is someone who serves the *father*land. The notion of the father as chief of chiefs is prehistoric. From this tribal conceit derives monotheism: the idea of a single god-creator who has created at least half of *us* in *his* image.

Although religion may be freely practiced in these parts, it was deliberately excluded from the political arrangements of our Republic. Unfortunately, the zealous few are always busy trying to make the many submit to their religious laws and superstitions. In the 1950s they won a great, and illegal, victory over the Constitution when they put the phrase "In God We Trust" on the currency.

Although the notion of one god may give comfort to those in need of a daddy, it reminds the rest of us that the totalitarian society is grounded upon the concept of God the father. One paternal god, one paternal leader. Authority is absolute. And error, as the Roman Catholic Church tells us, has no rights.

Each year it is discovered that when high school seniors are confronted blindly with the Bill of Rights, they neither like it nor approve of it. Our society has made them into true patriots, believers in a stern patriarchy where the police have every right to arrest you for just about anything that Dad disapproves of. The tragedy of the United States in this century is not the crackup of an empire, which we never knew what to do with in the first place, but the collapse of the idea of the citizen as someone autonomous whose private life is not subject to orders from above. Today, hundreds of thousands of Americans are only marginally free as they undergo mandatory blood tests, urine tests, lie detector tests. Speech is theoretically free but the true pulpit, electronic or print, is pretty much denied anyone who does not support the patriarchal state in all its misdeeds. It is no wonder that two-thirds of citizens under 40 have no interest in public affairs. They know they are not participants in the governance of the country. They are, simply, administrative units.

I would put the time and place of our fall as the White House in 1950. Harry Truman and his advisers decided that it would be a good idea to keep the United States on a full wartime basis even though there was no enemy on earth who could challenge us militarily or economically. Therefore an enemy had to be invented. The dictator Stalin fit the bill. So did atheistic *and* godless communism as a rival religion. But, said a Republican senator to Truman, if you really want to waste all that money on the military, you're going to have to scare the hell out of the American people. With a lot of help from Congress and from the likes of Henry Luce, Truman did just that.

Out of fairness to our inadvertent totalitarians, there was an urgent economic motive in 1950. We had made our recovery from the Depression of the 1930s *only* when the war put everyone to work. After the war, rather than run the terrible risk of a free economy in which General Motors would have to make something people wanted, like a car, we decided to take all the revenue—two-thirds anyway—of the federal government and put it into armaments.

The second reason for our garrison state is obvious: profit. There is a third reason, but I don't think most people in 1950 were aware of its consequences. A state forever at war, hot or cold, is easily controlled by the few, unlike a relatively free society, in which the governors are accountable to the people at large and to law. Today the neglected, ignored people have got the point; half the electorate refuses to vote in presidential elections. After all, was there any difference between Dukakis and Bush? Admittedly, Dukakis did not seem to mind too much if Kitty was raped by black prisoners on furlough, while Bush thought the flag was just grand, even if it was made in Taiwan. This was all good fun of the kind our rulers, who gave us prime-time television, think the idiots—us—will lap up. But then it is their job to divert public attention from the great corruption of the Pentagon and S&Ls and toxic waste. In the end there was a difference between the two: Dukakis wanted to increase the Pentagon budget by $4 billion, Bush by $11 billion. This being the extent of disagreement between the parties, it is clear that neither is an instrument by which the people might assert themselves and make known their will. As for a third party, we tried that in 1972. The People's Party. Unfortunately we hadn't realized that to have a third party you must have two other parties. We also found out that political parties, as opposed to spontaneous movements, are not possible in an oligarchy as entrenched as the one that rules us.

The small group that pays for the presidents and the congresses maintains its grip on the country through the media and the schools. After all, if people hadn't bought the idea that Noriega was the number one drug-dispenser, Panama could not have been illegally invaded so that Bush might not seem a wimp. Thousands of Panamanians died, as well as twenty-three American servicemen (nine of them killed by other Americans), for no purpose other than shoring up the image of the oligarchs' current spokesman, George Bush. Since the reading skills of the American people are the lowest in the First World, the general public is always easy prey to manipulation by television. This means that if you want to demonize drugs or the Arabs or the Japanese, you do so openly in the media. You also do it subliminally. As a result, in the past two years drugs was pushed from tenth to first place as a national worry. Now that communism has ceased to be the unholy devil, drug dealers, and users, are the enemy. Aircraft carriers are needed off the coast of Colombia to intercept drug exporters. And so two-thirds of the true budget will continue to go to the government in its latest "war"—a war that will not be won because no one has any interest in winning it, as opposed to expensively prosecuting it. The oligarchy does not care whether the citizens make themselves sick with drugs or not. What government wants is simple: total control. If this can be got by dispensing with the Bill of Rights, then that's a small price to pay. The whole tone of the Reagan-Bush management is one of open hostility to our ancient rights in particular and to the people in general. Today the poor, as Mr. Bush might put it, are in deep doo-doo. The rich are fed up with the poor. And if the poor don't shape up, the rich just aren't going to take it anymore.

The problem is money: who has it, who spends it and who gets what for what he paid. When it costs $40 million to create a presidential candidate he is not going to show much interest in the people at large. He will represent the folks who gave him the $40 million. Example: Bush. Since his election, what has he fought for? Environment? Education? No. His one crusade has been the cutting of the capital gains tax. That was the price the corporations demanded in exchange for buying him, rather than Dukakis, the presidency.

For thirty years I have made the same proposal to correct the great corruption. No candidate or party may buy time or space in the media. Give free media time and space to all candidates. Limit national election campaigns to six weeks, which is, more or less, what other First World countries do. A single act of Congress could make our elections unbuyable. However, those who have been elected by the present system are not about to change it.

The two parties, which are really one party, cannot be put to use. They are the country's ownership made carnival. Can the united action of individual citizens regain some control over the government? I think so. But it won't be easy, to riot in understatement. Attempts to cut back the war budget—whether the war be against communism or drugs or us—will be fought with great resourcefulness. When challenged with the billions of dollars wasted or stolen from the Pentagon, the establishment politician's answer is clear: Abortion is against God's law. He promptly changes the subject, the way a magician does when he catches your attention with one hand while the other picks your pocket.

Lately, though, our corporate oligarchs have become alarmed by one development in particular: the breakup of the nation-state almost everywhere. Since the nation-state, as we know it, is a nineteenth-century invention, I feel no sorrow at its demise. But those with orderly minds, eager to impose absolute order on others, are dismayed by the refusal of Latinos, say, to learn English, or Armenians to be Russian, or Québécois to be Canadian, and so on. I think this sudden worldwide desire for tribal identity is healthy, if only because our masters don't. Indeed, they have tried to make it impossible for us to use the word "race" for fear of being smeared by their media as racist—something they are but their critics are often not. Yet we are all racist to the extent that any of us feels that he belongs to a tribe, whether it be one of color or religion or some sort of shared identity.

In actuality, we are now faced with two movements. One is centrifugal: a rushing away from the confines of a nation-state, like the Soviet Union, or from any such iron order, equally unnatural, like heterosexuality, which was invented as recently as 1930.* Simultaneously, there is a centripetal force at work: a coming together of autonomous units for certain shared ends. Hence, the Common Market in Europe. Under a loose sort of confederation, the benefits of a common currency and joint environmental action can be shared by a great many tribes or races that choose, willingly, to cooperate. So we see, on the one hand, a healthy flight from the center in order to retain individuality, and, on the other, a healthy coming together to make a "more perfect life" for the residents of the common planet. Should centripetal forces defeat centrifugal longings, however, then welcome to the anthill society, and to our inglorious common death on a speck of used-up celestial matter.

Our political debate—what little there is—can never speak of the future except in terms of the past. I shall, therefore, present a formula to restore the Republic by moving boldly forward into the past. I wish to invoke the spirit of Henry Clay. Thanks to our educational system, no one knows who he is, but for political purposes he can be first explained, then trotted out as a true America Firster who felt that it was

---

* According to Jonathan Ned Katz in *Socialist Review* for February 1990, the word "heterosexual," still not acceptable to the O.E.D., first appeared in *The New York Times* (where else?) in 1930. Plainly a new category, outside the known sciences.

the task of government to make internal improvements, to spend money on education and on the enlargement of the nation's economic plant. Clay, translated in a modern context, would have us abandon all military pretensions on the ground that we are too small and too poor a country to act as a global policeman. He would also suggest that we police ourselves first, and leave—terrible thought—Nicaragua to the Nicaraguans. Yes, Clay *could* be called an isolationist, but what's wrong with that? Our economic failure is making us more and more isolated from the rest of the industrialized world anyway. We could use this quiet time to restore our economic health, to take a few hundred billion dollars from military procurement and put it into education, into finding new ways of training and utilizing the work force, new ways of preserving or restoring earth and air and water. This does not seem to me to be too ambitious a program. Also, ideologically, it is absolutely— even sublimely—reactionary, and therefore salable.

But the highly progressive military-industrial-political complex will not easily let go. Ominously, our garrison state is now turning inward to create a police state. More than a million Americans are in prison or under constraint, the largest number, per capita, in the industrialized world. At least we are first at something. Currently there is a plan to reactivate old army camps to house drug users as well as pushers. Of course we could legalize drugs and get rid of the problem but where's the money in that? Where's the fun? Where's the control over all the people all the time?

Any optimistic signs? Yes. More and more of the people who never vote are beginning to worry about their personal finances. They are looking for explanations. And now that the Reagan magic act is over, the majority that does not vote can be reached. Not through the media but through videocassettes. One can make a videocassette very cheaply, with a movie star who will work for nothing,† in order to explain, let us say, the ongoing S&L scandal. These cassettes can be given out free all over the country, which is the only way that the people can be directly addressed as they once were, in the eighteenth century, through pamphlets by the likes of Thomas Paine. I got the cassette idea from that lovable old curmudgeon Ayatollah Khomeini, who flooded Iran with radio tapes from his place of exile in Paris. With those tapes he brought revolution to Iran and overthrew the Shah. I think we can do as

---

† I know that it is elitist to use a star when a real expert, who is really boring just like everybody else, is available. But on the nuclear freeze, say, Paul Newman was worth a dozen senators.

well from our exile here at home. We will also have helped create that educated citizenry without which Jefferson felt life, liberty and the pursuit of happiness not possible.

I began this discourse with Jefferson, as did the country, and I end with his great injunction that, should all else fail, the tree of liberty must still be nourished with the blood, if necessary, of tyrants and of patriots. Have a nice millennium.

LET 'EM VOTE FOR "NONE OF THE ABOVE"

Micah L. Sifry

•

EVERY DAY EVIDENCE mounts that the public is getting sick of politics as usual. Only 50.2 percent of eligible voters cast ballots in the 1988 presidential election and only one-third of the electorate is likely to vote in Congressional and statewide races this fall. Among those who doggedly fulfill their civic duty, there is growing distaste for the two major parties and their negative campaigns, entrenched incumbents and fealty to big funders. Indeed, the voters were so disgusted by the 1988 presidential campaign that the day after the election, according to a little-noted Gallup poll, fully 30 percent said they would have been likely to vote "no confidence" in both George Bush and Michael Dukakis had there been a place on the ballot to do so.

Well, maybe institutionalizing such a choice wouldn't be a bad idea. Consider, for example, last fall's gubernatorial race in New Jersey, a nasty mud-wrestle between Jim Florio, Democrat, and Jim Courter, Republican. So disenchanted were Jerseyans with this choice that a few weeks before the election only a minority of those polled had a positive view of *either* man. Florio won the election, but in all likelihood neither candidate would have emerged victorious had voters been able to pull a lever for "none of the above" (NOTA).

A serious NOTA ballot option covering all elective offices would function as a public veto. To make it work, state election laws would have to require a special election (held according to the existing rules for when an office becomes vacant) any time NOTA got more votes than any of the candidates. Political parties would then nominate candidates by whatever method they desire—provided that those who had lost to NOTA could not be renominated for that term. NOTA would of course be on the special-election ballot as well. By threatening incumbents and contenders alike, NOTA might well introduce a real choice into elections and eventually force candidates to address the issues seriously.

The proposal is not as alien as it may seem. In its essence, it should appeal to the American belief in freedom of choice. Why should we only be able to vote "yes" for someone or abstain? Many states already require an up-down referendum on sitting judges and, interestingly, more and more of them are being defeated. A nonbinding version of NOTA has been on the ballot in Nevada since 1976. In Vermont, State Senator John McClaughry, a Republican from Caledonia County, has introduced legislation that would give voters the option of choosing "none of the above" for all elective offices, save President and Vice President. By leaving out the presidency, McClaughry is trying to avoid entanglement in the byzantine procedures of the Electoral College. My reading of the Constitution, however, suggests that each state's electors could be directed to vote for "none"; if neither of the candidates achieved a majority, the election would be thrown into Congress. In any event, the Constitution leaves to the states the power to regulate elections to Congress and to state and local offices. Under McClaughry's proposal, statewide executive offices left vacant because voters chose "none of the above" would be filled by special vote of the legislature, though there's no reason why direct elections could not be held to fill these offices as well.

At a minimum, NOTA on the ballot for offices like mayor, governor, senator and representative might discourage a good deal of negative advertising. Contenders often promise not to "go negative," but, given the fact that smear attacks do work, that pledge is frequently abandoned as races heat up. If the people could vote their revulsion at such tactics, much gutter politics would be deterred by the prospect of mutually assured destruction.

Likewise, NOTA would reduce the advantages of incumbency and the dominance of money. One out of ten House incumbents ran unopposed in 1988, and the 402 incumbents who were returned to office averaged 74 percent of the vote. Incumbents are bolstered by their relatively high name recognition, by institutional perks like franking privileges and by a whopping disparity in campaign finances. According to the Federal Election Commission, as of June 30, senators bidding for re-election this year had $83.1 million in their campaign treasuries; challengers had $25.9 million. The gap was even wider in the House, where incumbents had $112.8 million and challengers only $20.2 million. A big NOTA vote against an entrenched incumbent would at least increase the chances of recruiting serious challengers—from within the incumbent's party as well as without—the next time around. And moneyed interests might not invest so heavily in incumbents if their longevity was no longer guaranteed.

A NOTA choice might even draw some nonvoters back to the voting booth, though on this point experts like Frances Fox Piven, co-author of *Why Americans Don't Vote*, and Curtis Gans, of the Committee for the Study of the American Electorate, are skeptical. Piven doubts that people are sufficiently tuned in to the record of their local representatives to vote "no" in significant numbers but admits that in the intensity of a presidential election year, more might come out and upset the local status quo. Gans, who favors the NOTA idea, suggests that the purely advisory "none of these candidates" option extant in Nevada is a good test of whether NOTA would increase turnout. In 1976, when it was first tried, "none" received 47 percent of the vote in a Republican primary, topping two live contenders for the House of Representatives. (The "victorious" Republican nominee was trounced in the general election.) And in 1980, "none" narrowly lost to Jimmy Carter in the Democratic presidential primary, 34 percent to 38 percent. But overall turnout has declined in Nevada, albeit at a slightly slower rate than the national average. However, "none" in Nevada is only symbolic, and thus a true throwaway vote, which may be why it has drawn only in the single digits of late.

Recent elections in the Soviet Union show the power of being able to vote "no." Soviet voters cross off the names of candidates they reject rather than check the one they favor. They can thus reject all the contenders and even vote against an unopposed incumbent. Moreover, a winning candidate needs to receive an absolute majority of the vote, and the election is not valid if less than half the electorate votes. In the spring of 1989, when Soviet voters were given their first opportunity to nominate alternative candidates and vote in secret, an astounding number of local party and state officials were thrown out of office—even when they were the sole candidate. As a result nearly 200 out of 1,500 races for the Congress of People's Deputies had to be rerun.

How can we make NOTA a reality? Obviously, both parties are too comfortable with the current situation to enact anything so dramatic to enhance the democratic process. Letters to your representative are not in order. The best way to get things started is through the initiative and referendum process, which is available in twenty-three states. In the others, citizens will have to pressure their state legislators, perhaps by mounting widespread write-in campaigns or leaving their ballots blank. If a number of states independently enacted a NOTA provision, the others might follow or join in passing a constitutional amendment, in the same manner that direct election of senators was brought about at the turn of the century. Just possibly, NOTA may surface this fall in western Massachusetts, the birthplace of the nuclear freeze, where the Pioneer Valley Pro-Democracy Campaign is planning a NOTA write-in effort to protest the corruption of democracy by big money.

Pollsters could go a long way toward confirming public interest in having a real choice in elections by including a NOTA option in the battery of questions they ask about political races. Several say they would seriously consider trying it. Larry Hugick of The Gallup Organization says, "There's been so much continuing speculation about alienation, voter disaffection, et cetera, that it would probably be interesting to ask [this] more than once, especially to plot the effect of negative campaigning." Mike Kagay and Kathy Frankovic, the directors of polling at, respectively, *The New York Times* and CBS News, both noted that in the past three presidential races they asked likely voters if they wished there were other choices or if they were satisfied with the existing nominees. In October 1988, 64 percent expressed dissatisfaction.

In recent months there has been no shortage of proposed ideas to deal with what *The New York Times* has called "the trouble with politics." Former Democratic and Republican party chairs Charles Manatt and Frank Fahrenkopf have offered to abbreviate their parties' conventions in exchange for free television time from the networks later in the fall. Similarly, a bipartisan commission of academic experts convened by the Senate leadership has called for providing free television time to major-party candidates to "strengthen" the two-party system and cut campaign costs. To reduce the use of thirty-second "attack ads," Senator John Danforth has proposed legislation that would force candidates to appear in all their commercials. The John and Mary Markle Foundation has proposed the creation of a "voters' channel" on public television that would try to focus on issues rather than personalities or the horse race. For their part, network news executives have made their ritual promises to do a better job next time.

Liberal hopes are currently riding on voter registration and campaign finance reform. A promising voter registration bill that would enlarge the rolls by mandating automatic registration when people apply for or renew driver's licenses and by prohibiting purges of non-voters from registration lists passed the House by a veto-proof margin [see "Voting Block," February 12] and is now awaiting consideration in the Senate. Unfortunately, the current lack of Republican sponsors for the measure may spell its doom there. And while Senate Democrats have now passed a campaign finance reform bill that goes a long way toward driving big money out of Senate races, President Bush has already threatened to veto any bill limiting campaign spending.

These liberal reforms are undoubtedly needed, as are steps to allow same-day registration, to ease restrictions to getting on the ballot, to make free TV time available to candidates of all parties, to fully finance primary and general races from public funds and to limit the length of campaigns. But none of these measures stand much of a chance at present because one or both of the major parties see them as threats, and their technical nature makes it extremely difficult to build a movement that would force the system to respond.

Worse yet, all of these proposals, despite their good intentions, fail to address the deeper problem afflicting American democracy: the emptiness of two-party politics. It's no accident that Manatt and Fahrenkopf favor measures that would tighten their parties' hold on the political process, or that the Senate's academic advisers want free television time only for the two major parties. For all their partisan posturing on pseudo-issues like flag burning, nearly all members of the two parties actually share a variety of common assumptions on critical issues ranging from the S&L debacle to national health care. As Nelson Mandela joked at his meeting this summer with the members of the Congressional Black Caucus, "You would hardly know there was any difference between the Democratic and Republican parties. . . . In fact, we hope very soon to hear that they have merged."

Third-party campaigns are one way to break this logjam. But the state barriers to getting a third party on the ballot are high and the national ones are even higher. Ongoing efforts to transform the Democratic Party by electing progressive local officials may yet bear fruit, and the inside-outside strategy of Jesse Jackson is still worth watching.

But if we want to put real pressure on our white-bread politicians, NOTA seems to me the way to go. Who knows—a write-in/referendum campaign to put NOTA on the ballot could even galvanize a pro-democracy movement that would effectively push for the systemic reforms discussed above. One similar idea that has already got some attention is a proposal to limit Congressional and state terms to twelve years. Indeed, versions of this proposal will be on the ballot in California, Oklahoma and Colorado in November. Writing in *The New Republic* in support of a twelve-year limit, Hendrik Hertzberg marshals good arguments for breaking down the Congressional seniority system and shaking up the two parties' presidential-Congressional condominium. But he fails to explain how democracy is going to be enhanced if outgoing representatives can still use all the perks and powers at their disposal to anoint successors, or how the people's will is to be served if a genuinely popular and effective legislator is forced to step down. Hertzberg writes that "the term limit would mean that at least once every 12 years (and probably more frequently), every citizen would get a fighting chance to vote in a genuinely *political* congressional election."

Why not every two years? *The New York Times* has editorialized against a twelve-year term limit, arguing, "If voters think a member should be shown the gate, let them say so on Election Day." I agree. Let them vote NOTA.

EMBARGOED LITERATURE

Edward W. Said

•

EIGHT YEARS BEFORE Naguib Mahfouz won the Nobel Prize in Literature, a major New York commercial publisher known for his liberal and unprovincial views asked me to suggest some Third World novels for translation and inclusion in a series he was planning. The list I gave him was headed by two or three of Mahfouz's works, none of which was then in circulation in the United States. True, there were a few novels by the Egyptian master available in England, but these had never gained entry into the United States, and even in Europe were principally known only by a few students of Arabic. Several weeks after I submitted my list I inquired which novels had been chosen, only to be informed that the Mahfouz translations would not be undertaken. When I asked why, I was given an answer that has haunted me ever since. "The problem," I was told, "is that Arabic is a controversial language."

What, exactly, the publisher meant is still a little vague to me—but that Arabs and their language were somehow not respectable, and consequently dangerous, *louche*, unapproachable, was perfectly evident to me then and, alas, now. For of all the major world literatures, Arabic remains relatively unknown and unread in the West, for reasons that are unique, even remarkable, at a time when tastes here for the non-European are more developed than ever before and, even more compelling, contemporary Arabic literature is at a particularly interesting juncture.

An amusing sign of the disparity between the interest taken in Arabic literature and that in other literatures outside the Atlantic world can be seen in the treatment afforded Mahfouz and his work in English after he won the Nobel in 1988. Doubleday acquired the rights to much of his work and a few months ago began to introduce a handful of his stories and novels, including the first volume of his major work, the *Cairo Trilogy*, in what appeared to be new editions. In fact, with one exception, the translations were exactly the ones that had been available all along in England, some quite good but most either indifferent or poor. Clearly the idea was to capitalize on and market his new fame, but not at the cost of a retranslation.

Second, and more comically symptomatic, half a dozen profiles of Mahfouz appeared in American magazines, including *Vanity Fair, The New Yorker* and *The New York Times Magazine*. In effect, they were the same article rewritten over and over. Each talked about his favorite cafe, his modesty, his position on Israel (in the second sentence of its story on his Nobel Prize, *The New York Times* thoughtfully expressed the opinion of the Israeli consul in New York), his orderly and extremely uninteresting life. All of the authors, some of them reasonably accomplished essayists, were innocent of both Arabic and Arabic literature. (In *The New Yorker*, Milton Viorst delivered himself of the thought that "Arabic, an imprecise language, requires most writers to choose between poetry and clarity.") All regarded Mahfouz as a hybrid of cultural oddity and political symbol. Little was said about his formal achievements, for instance, or about his place in modern literature as a whole.

Third, now that the act has worn thin, Mahfouz has more or less been dropped from discussion—without having provoked even the more venturesome literate into finding out which other writers in Arabic might be worth looking into. Where, after all, did Mahfouz come from? It is impossible not to believe that one reason for this odd state of affairs is the longstanding prejudice against Arabs and Islam that remains entrenched in Western, and especially American, culture. Here the "experts" on Islam and the Arabs bear considerable blame. Their so called *doyen*, Bernard Lewis, still blathers on in places like *The Wall Street Journal, The Atlantic* and *The American Scholar* about the darkness and strangeness of Muslims, Arabs, their culture, religion, etc. Israeli or Jewish scholars are commonly asked to comment on things Islamic while the reverse—an Arab commenting on Hebrew literature or Israeli policy—is seldom risked. Princeton University, one of the leading American centers of Arab and Islamic studies, does not have on its faculty a single native speaker teaching Arabic language or literature. Critics, book reviewers and journal editors studiously avoid discussion of Arabic books even as they attempt prodigies of reading and interpretation where, for instance, Czech and Argentine literatures are concerned.

The bald fact is, the unavailability of Arabic literature in translation is no longer an excuse. Small but conscientious publishing houses like Al-Saqi (26 Westbourne Grove, Bayswater, London W2 5RH) and Quartet (27–29 Goodge Street, London W1P 1FD) in England, Sindbad (1 Rue Feutrier, 75018 Paris) in France and Three Continents Press (1901 Pennsylvania Avenue, Suite 407, Washington, D.C.) in the United States have assembled a diverse cross section of contemporary work from the Arab world that is still overlooked or deliberately ignored by editors and book reviewers. In addition, some larger publishers (Penguin, Random House and a handful of American university presses) have recently put out some truly first-rate literary work that has gone unnoticed and unreviewed, as if indifference and prejudice were a blockade designed to interdict any attention to texts that do not reiterate the usual clichés about "Islam," violence, sensuality and so forth. There almost seems to be a deliberate policy of maintaining a kind of monolithic reductionism where the Arabs and Islam are concerned; in this, the Orientalism that distances and dehumanizes another culture is upheld, and the xenophobic fantasy of a pure "Western" identity elevated and strengthened. (Some of these reflections have been partially instigated by the truly disgraceful level of reporting on the Iraqi military aggression in Kuwait. Most of what has passed for journalistic and expert commentary in the United States media has been simply a repetition of appalling clichés, most of them ignorant, unhistorical, moralistic, self-righteous and hypocritical. All of them derive unquestioningly in one way or another from U.S. government policy, which has long considered the Arabs to be either terrorists or mindless stooges to be milked for their money or abundant and inexpensive oil.) What is disappointing is how little compensating pressure there is from the culture at large, one that seems automatically to prefer the Mahfouz rewrites and the Islamic stereotypes to almost anything else.

The irony is that there is a good deal in recent literary material to complicate and make more interesting the current Arab scene. In less than a year three books of unique literary distinction have appeared in fine translations yet gone virtually unnoticed. Each, in its own way, is both a dissenting or oppositional work and also a work by an author well-known and admired within the Arab and Islamic tradition. In other words, while each of these works treats Arab culture as something to be fought over and contested, thereby opposing orthodoxy, unjust authority and uncritical dogma, none of them expresses the kind of alienation and estrangement from the culture that is at work in attacks by Western Orientalists.

The most intellectually stimulating of the three is Adonis's *An Introduction to Arab Poetics*, from Al-Saqi, translated with uncommon intelligence by Catherine Cobham. (The University of Texas Press plans to bring out an edition of this next spring.) Adonis is today's most daring and provocative Arab poet, a symbolist and surrealist who is like a combination of Montale, Breton, Yeats and the early T. S. Eliot. In this compilation of four essays originally given as lectures at the Collège de France, he reinterprets the whole massive Arab tradition, from pre-Islamic poetry through the Koran, the classical period and on into the present. Arguing that there has always been a literalist, authoritarian strain in the literature, Adonis presents the thesis that this has usually been opposed by poets and thinkers for whom modernity is renewal rather than conformism, transgression rather than nationalism, creativity rather than fundamentalism.

Far from being simply an academic statement, *Arab Poetics* is an uncompromising challenge to the status quo that is held in place by official Arab culture. In no uncertain terms Adonis identifies the latter equally with religious and with secular authority, clerics and bureaucrats whose retreat into either a reliquary past or the arms of a foreign patron has brought us to the cultural crisis that we as Arabs face today. Adonis's command of the texts is astonishingly true, as is the simple brilliance of his argument. One would have thought it as important a cultural manifesto as any written today, which is what makes the silence that has greeted the work so stupefying.

The two other recent works are Edwar al-Kharrat's *City of Saffron* and the Lebanese feminist novelist Hanan al-Shaykh's *Women of Sand and Myrrh*, both published by Quartet, the first translated admirably by Frances Liardet, the latter with her customary fluency by Cobham. Kharrat is a Coptic Egyptian writer whose early years in Alexandria form the subject of this semi-autobiographical text, which bears a formal resemblance to Joyce's *A Portrait of the Artist as a Young Man*. Readers who have swallowed the journalistic myth that Copts and Muslims hate each other will be informed otherwise by these meditative yet subversively intimate ruminations about childhood. One feels not only the *non serviam* of the budding artist but also a warmly confident exploration of life in a working-class Coptic family beset with physical dislocation, unhappy sex, political upheaval. Here too it is possible to read Kharrat's revelations as very much a part of contemporary Egyptian culture without ever forgetting that he disputes the official establishment's facile versions of what "realism" and social responsibility are all about. Hanan al-Shaykh's novel is a complex and demanding story of women in the Persian Gulf—oppressed, manipulated, sexually tormented and confused. Far from simple romance, *Women of Sand and Myrrh* is both breathtakingly frank and technically difficult, taking on such experiences as homosexuality and patriarchy with unexpected power. Would that more Western feminists attended to writers like Shaykh and not just to the overexposed (and overcited) Nawal el-Saadawi.

It is less the explicit subject matter than the formal and technical achievement of these three works that is so striking, and so accurate an index of how excitingly far Arabic literature has come since Mahfouz was at his peak about twenty-five years ago. The best of today's writers are oppositional figures who frequently use literary virtuosity to form an oblique critique of life in the various Arab states, where tyranny and atavism are common features of daily existence but where a large number of writers are still committed to live. But, one should add, these writers are neither alone nor unaware of what surrounds and has preceded them. Other excellent translations (again, ignored by the Anglo-American literary world) have appeared of: Abdel Rahman Munif's monumental *Cities of Salt*, by Peter Theroux for Random House's Vintage Books, the only serious work of fiction that tries to show the effect on a gulf country of oil, Americans and local oligarchy; Gamal al-Ghitani's *Zayni Barakat* in the best of all translations, by Farouk Abdel Wahab, for Viking Penguin, a superbly elegant Jamesian novel about sixteenth-century Cairo, in effect an allegory of Nasser's rule with its combination of honest reformist zeal and political paranoia and repression; Elias Khoury's *The Little Mountain*, in Maia Tabet's spare translation for the University of Minnesota Press, a postmodernist fable of the Lebanese civil war; and Emile Habiby's great *Secret Life of Saeed the Ill-Fated Pessoptimist*, the surreal Palestinian masterpiece, in only a passable version by Trevor Le Gassick and Salma Jayyusi published by Readers International, which is nevertheless astonishing in its wit and dark inventiveness.

Other recent Arabic works include Hussein Haddawy's distinguished new translation for Norton of the *Arabian Nights*; the Sudanese Tayib Salih's *Season of Migration of the North*, in an edi-

tion by the leading Arabic-English translator of our time, Denys John-
son-Davies, done for Heinemann in England and republished in the
United States by Michael Kesend; Ghassan Kanafani's *Men in the Sun*,
in Hilary Kilpatrick's rendition for Three Continents, a prescient para-
ble of three Palestinian refugees trying to smuggle themselves from
Iraq to Kuwait in a tanker truck, dying of asphyxiation and heat at the
border post; the collection of poems by Mahmoud Darwish, Samih al-
Qassim (today's leading Palestinian poets) and Adonis, *Victims of a
Map*, in a bilingual Penguin edition rendered capably by Abdullah al-
Udhari. Salih's novel can bear extremely favorable comparison with V.
S. Naipaul's *A Bend in the River*; despite their common source in Con-
rad's *Heart of Darkness*, Salih's work is far less schematic and ideolog-
ically embittered, a novel of genuine postcolonial strength and passion.

There are also the enormous compilations by Salma Jayyusi being
published over several years by Columbia University Press, of which
Modern Arabic Poetry: An Anthology is the first to have appeared. It
is fortunate that this relatively high number of recently translated Arabic works coincides with their importance and literary reputation in
the Arab world. Nevertheless, it is also sadly the case that Arab writers
themselves (as well as their publishing houses, ministries of culture,
embassies in Western capitals) have done hardly anything to promote
their works, and the discourse of Arab culture, in the West; the
absence of an Arab cultural intervention in the world debate is thus
depressing and tragic. I write these lines as the horrific waste and
potential violence of today's gulf crisis focus all efforts on war and confrontation. Is it too much to connect the stark political and military
polarization with the cultural abyss that exists between Arabs and the
West? What impresses one is the will to ignore and reduce the Arabs
that still exists in many departments of Western culture, and the unac-
ceptable defeatism among some Arabs that a resurgent religion and
indiscriminate hostility are the only answers. It may seem pathetically
utopian to offer the reading and interpretation of contemporary literature as meliorative activities, but what is so attractive about the war now
going on between Baghdad, the former Abbasid capital, and the entire
West?

WILD AT HEART

Stuart Klawans

•

A FILM PROJECTIONIST nods off in his booth and starts to dream. Separating itself from his slumbering form, a twin rises, takes from the wall a twin of his hat and goes down into the movie house to stand in the aisle and watch the film the dreamer is projecting. Then the twin approaches the screen and walks into the film.

Buster Keaton's adventure in *Sherlock Junior* has served for over sixty years as a model of how people watch movies. Not that all pictures work on an audience this way; but films, perhaps more than any other artworks, tend to set up a running commentary on their own unreality. They are like dreams in which one is aware of dreaming.

Many of the best movies balance this tendency with other character-istics of film: its unsurpassed ability to document the world; its force-fulness as a medium for argument; its rhythmic play of light and shadow, sound and silence, which allows it to border on the plastic arts. I'm thinking at the moment of Renoir's *The Crime of Monsieur Lange* and Fassbinder's *The Bitter Tears of Petra von Kant*, which played recently in New York at the Public Theater and the Bleecker Street Cinema. You may supply examples of your own, but they won't be many. Fully realized, four-dimensional films are rare. What you see most often are movies in which the tendency toward self-conscious fan-tasy predominates—which brings us to David Lynch.

Like a creature that has developed a single, oversized organ at the expense of the rest of its withered body, Lynch is a misshapen talent, oddly evolved to fit an odd cultural niche. He hasn't the slightest interest in the world around him. His images invariably seem to emerge from a soundstage, even when shot on location. His actors reveal only the gestures and turns of phrase of other actors. You will never feel the shock of recognition in a Lynch film, only shock itself. Nor is there a purpose to the jolt. Though Lynch's abundant stock of absurdities, incongruities and asides sometimes teases the viewer with a hint of profundity, nothing adds up in his pictures. He is as incapable of argument as of documentation. What he *can* do—and he does it supremely well—is draw the viewer into that mood of willful oneirism, using visual effects that are both dazzling and indelible.

Wild at Heart is his latest foray into the land of waking dreams. Based on a novel by Barry Gifford and photographed by Lynch's longtime collaborator Frederick Elmes, it is the story of young lovers on the run, from a Carolinas town called Cape Fear to New Orleans to a hellhole known as Big Tuna, Texas. Nicolas Cage plays Sailor; Laura Dern plays Lula. But the names don't really matter, since the characters are generic. They're the guy who dreams he's Elvis and the girl who's haunted by her past.

The proceedings get started with a bang. Immediately after the credits, there's an uncommonly bloody killing, which lands Sailor in jail. On his release—effected with a simple title card, announcing that time has passed—Lula picks him up in a black Thunderbird convertible. Cool cars, sunglasses and plenty of rock music are essential to a filmmaker of Lynch's aspirations. So, too, is dialogue that sounds like *Cliffs Notes* for the movie. Such is Sailor's comment when Lula hands him his beloved snake-skin jacket: "For me, it is a symbol of individuality and my belief in personal freedom." Then it's off for some hot sex, more rock and roll, more hot sex, a few flashbacks of violence. What can the lovers possibly do for a follow-up, except leave the state and break Sailor's parole?

What follows is mannered, arch, empty, labored, expertly made and intermittently thrilling. Though scene flows effortlessly into scene—no one is better than Lynch at transitions—I remember the events in pieces. A man on fire runs through a suburban living room. A young woman, injured in a car wreck, pokes uncomprehendingly at the bloody hole in her scalp. Lula, undergoing an abortion, lies under a doctor's magnifying lamp, her face appearing outsized while her tiny arms thrash helplessly. Many of the shots are enthralling, even when they're without incident—for example, the view of the roadside at night, seen as a horizontal band of shadowy green, rushing past beneath impenetrable blackness. There are also a few sequences, full of incident, that pull you all the way into the dream. The best of them, the great set piece of *Wild at Heart*, is a confrontation in a motel room between Lula and Bobby Peru (Willem Dafoe), Big Tuna's incarnation of evil. It's so intense an encounter that I could all but feel the breath coming through Bobby's rotten teeth.

Then Bobby left. He had shown his power over Lula; and Lynch had demonstrated much the same thing to me. Once more, he had proved he could push my buttons, and once more he'd turned out to have no good reason for pushing them. I felt used. I also felt that this scene, like certain episodes of *Blue Velvet*, exposed the vacuum in Lynch. In its own sick way, *Wild at Heart* is as much a brainless, heartless spectacle as *Indiana Jones and the Temple of Doom*. The difference is that Spielberg engineered his movie-as-rollercoaster for a general audience. Lynch constructs his for an audience that wants to feel wised-up, decadent, better than the Speilbergian middle class.

At this point, Lynch's fans, most of my friends among them, might object that his dreams are so troubled that one's complicit enjoyment of them is itself an act of culpability. By taking to a personal extreme the oneiric and plastic qualities of film, he draws the audience into a more conscious engagement with its desires. It sounds plausible; and if movies are indeed commentaries on a dream rather than mirrors of reality, what more can they honestly offer? So let me suggest a counterexample: Brian DePalma's *Blow Out*, a film so self-enclosed that *The Village Voice's* J. Hoberman has likened it to a Möbius strip.

Blow Out is, in fact, a circular story with a twist, and it's all surface. Based explicitly on Antonioni's *Blow-Up*, with an added debt to Coppola's *The Conversation*, the picture is at every level a film about film. The protagonist lives within movies. His setting, too, is made up: a mythical city named Philadelphia, central to the history of an imaginary nation called the United States. In this never-never land, the women all have to sell their bodies in one way or another to survive, while the men make a living selling each other pictures of the women. You realize, of course, that this is a fantasy; and DePalma tells you as much in every way he knows how. Still, you leave the theater devastated for these phony characters in their invented country, and for yourself and your own nation as well. For all its artifice, *Blow Out* has weight, purpose, moral power. It's not a balanced film, but it's a great one.

Wild at Heart, on the other hand, is not only lopsided and brilliant but utterly cynical as well. That's a striking conjunction, given the way

Lynch's work has been received. His best-known production, *Twin Peaks*, made its mark by providing just what we all want from television—sex, violence and easy laughs—delivering them more amply than the competition and with greater style. So why don't people just say that *Twin Peaks*— and *Wild at Heart* and *Blue Velvet*—are cheap thrills in expensive wrappers? (To take one example out of many: *The New York Times* puffed *Wild at Heart* just before its release by lauding the "unsettling vision" of David Lynch, "the reigning master of locating the bizarre, the surreal and the disturbing in American life.") You'd think, for all the hype, that Lynch's pictures were works of pioneering artistry, suitable to be stuck on a museum wall right next to *Un Chien Andalou*. More likely, though, they're empty artifacts of that cultural niche I mentioned at the beginning of this piece, the milieu of the institutional avant-garde.

Whenever you hear the words *disturbing, transgressive* and *subversive* tossed around, whenever rules are supposedly being broken and authorities challenged, you may assume you're in avant-garde territory. You're among the institutional avant-garde when the transgressors have M.F.A. degrees from good schools and are on a first-name basis with at least three arts administrators. This is the setting in which the avant-garde becomes avant-gardism, one more item in a repertory of styles—an approved, accredited part of the curriculum, to be studied in academies and practiced for the approbation of one's fellow professionals. If Lynch is a pioneer, it's because he has converted this outrage-by-the-numbers avant-gardism into mainstream, commercial success. Think of him as the boy voted Most Likely to Succeed, in a school where the other class notables include Robert Mapplethorpe and Karen Finley.

We might as well forgive the average tourist from Mars for assuming that the names I've just brought together represent America's greatest contemporary artists. Is that entirely a function of notoriety—sought-after and profitable in one case, unwanted in the others, who had their fame thrust upon them by a cabal of sleazoid politicians and Bible-thumpers? Or is there a real resemblance among these classmates?

Before answering, let me assure the reader that I am far from wanting to blame anyone for falling victim to Jesse Helms. More than that: I endorse the right of all artists to as much government money as they can grab, no strings attached. By all means, let the institutional avant-garde join with the Metropolitan Museum and the Metropolitan Opera to rejoice in the National Endowment for the Arts' $171 million a year. Better still, why not give the institutional avant-garde its own savings and loan? If James Fail could acquire the Bluebonnet Savings Bank along with $1.85 billion in federal subsidies after putting up just $1,000 of his own money, then surely we can do as much for Karen Finley and her friends.

Nevertheless, if we can bear for a moment to forget public policy and think about art, we might notice a powerful odor of bad faith arising from the vicinity of the institutional avant-garde. It's the smell of subversion that wants to be risk-free. First comes the self-validating gesture of declaring that all works of art should aspire to the condition of avant-gardism, if they're to be taken seriously; then comes the refusal to play out the consequences. For example: It's shabby to complain that performance artists, those descendants of the Dadaists, will soon have nowhere to perform, given that all the major venues receive government funds. Think of the *real* Dadaists in Berlin, who staged their events not in art galleries or at the local equivalent of Lincoln Center but in churches and bars and cafes, especially the ones where they weren't welcome. Think of the Berlin Dadaist Franz Jung, who in 1923 chose to express himself by hijacking a German freighter in the Baltic and taking it to Petrograd, where he turned the ship over to the Soviet authorities. There's an avant-gardist I can respect.

What I can't respect is work that denies all of the traditional, non-transgressive functions of art while simultaneously turning away from the risks of engagement with the world. Sometimes, on the excuse of favoring strong content over mere style, the artists and their flacks turn against the notion of formal skill. Sometimes, as with David Lynch, formal skill is all the artist provides. In either case, the presumed assault on bourgeois order is safely contained—in an art gallery, at a performing arts center, on the screen. The danger of the image is assumed; the image of danger is all that's demanded.

I came out of *Wild at Heart* feeling sick of images, sick of irony, sick of a copycat avant-garde that's addicted to money and applause. The poor get locked out of their jobs, get tossed out of their homes, get shot by stray bullets at the rate of one a day: and the college-educated play at wanting to be disturbed.

Tourists from Mars, wherever you travel next, try to speak kindly of us. The truth is too great a shame.

HIGH AND LOW AT MOMA

Arthur C. Danto

•

W HEN I LEARNED that the Museum of Modern Art in New York was to mount an exhibition of high and low art, I hoped for something as tonic and brilliant as the great second act of *Ariadne auf Naxos*, in which the tragic heroine is thrust into the same dramatic space as a band of scruffy buffoons, who seek to distract her from her drawn-out sorrows by snapping their fingers and singing rowdy songs. The first act of Strauss and Hofmansthal's masterpiece was given over to a debate between representatives of *opera seria* and *opera buffa* as to which should take precedence in an evening's entertainment, when Monsieur Jourdain, rich and vulgar, ordains that both operas be put on at the same time, so that the singing will end early enough for a fireworks display afterward. The second act is the result: The classical heroine sings her heavy heart out on the barren island on which her lover, Theseus, has abandoned her, also inhabited, through an impossible artistic collage, by a company of *commedia dell'arte* figures, who undertake to amuse her out of her *Schmerz* and give her some useful pointers on how to handle men. My hope was that the low art in the projected show would do something along those lines—be antic and wry, say not to take matters of art too seriously, that there has to be some basis in fun for the existence of art, that it can't be all sopranic lamentation and tragical sighs and prayers for divine intercession.

In the early years of Pop Art's ascendancy in the New York art world, the situation of Ariadne's improbable island was often enough repeated, with artists of high calling and shamanistic pretensions encountering the new irreverent stars who had challenged the premises of their painting: It was like watching misdialogues between Prince Hamlet and Mickey Mouse. In Victor Bockris's superb life of Andy Warhol, there is an eloquent anecdote about a party given by Larry Rivers in the Hamptons, at which Warhol approached an admittedly drunk Willem De Kooning with an affable "Hi, Bill!" He was rebuffed with the following aria: "You're a killer of art, you're a killer of beauty, and you're even a killer of laughter. I can't bear your work." (As someone who took the scenario of the comic strip seriously, Warhol *had* to have said "Ulp!!!") It was an operatic, or at least a dramatic moment. The Abstract Expressionists perceived themselves as in touch with chthonic forces and the dark metaphysical tides of Being. They believed in magic, mystery and art's high spiritual vocation. And suddenly the art world was invaded by twerps, who painted soup cans and fashioned hamburgers out of plaster-soaked muslin, and who monumentalized Chef Boyardee spaghetti (the pasta revolution had not as yet overtaken the land) or actually made paintings of Donald Duck and Goofy, or the teary faces of vapid girls, those vehicles of teenage love dreams expressing moony sentiments in thought-balloons.

"A painting by Lichtenstein," Max Kozloff wrote in the art pages of *The Nation*(!), "is at once ingenuous and vicious, repulsive and modish—the latest sensation." In another journal he ascribed to these artists "the pin-headed and contemptible style of gum-chewers, bobby-soxers, and, worse, delinquents." This attitude lives on in those whose artistic ethos was formed in Abstract Expressionist times, though it differs greatly from my own. When *The Nation* denounced Pop, *The Journal of Philosophy* declared it philosophically profound; and when, in a review of Warhol's posthumous retrospective at MoMA, I proposed that he was the nearest thing to a philosophical genius the art world had produced, even good friends turned on me. It was essential to their estimate of art and of themselves that Warhol be dumb and *buffa*, while the art that his succeeded was smart and *seria*. And the fact that Pop's images were intinctured with the logos and slogans of commercial semiography contributed to the general suspiciousness with which it was received by high culture, whose priests looked down the very noses that had been popped out of joint.

One of the marvelous expressions of Pop ideology, which affirmed as it subverted the stigma of commercialism, and at the same time sought to paint out the boundary between high and low art, was Claes

Oldenburg's *Store*, which operated on East 2nd Street in Manhattan from December 1961 to January 1962. The very idea that art might be purveyed in a store rather than displayed in a gallery, that it might exchange hands across a counter and consist of objects that engaged ordinary men and women in the ordinary moments of life—little monuments of the commonplace, as it were—was in its own way as intoxicating as the aesthetic collisions in *Ariadne*. Here were cheeseburgers with lettuce, slabs of pie, girls' dresses and gym shoes, fashioned out of plaster-stiffened cloth and painted to resemble items in the *Lebenswelt* that no one who lived the everyday culture, to which they belonged, could fail to recognize. They might, to be sure, have some difficulty in recognizing the objects as *art*. But, as if to forestall that problem, Oldenburg dripped paint over their raw surfaces in such a way as to give them a kind of gaiety and an artistic authenticity at once, inasmuch as it was the reigning dogma of that moment that painting was painting; that paint itself, fluid, shiny, puckered, dribbled, dropped and dripping, was the soul and substance of art. It was through the handling of paint that Oldenburg claimed oneness with the heroes of Abstract Expressionism who disdained the subject matter he celebrated joyously. Paint may, indeed must, have given these works their artistic authenticity in the terms of that era; but what Oldenburg was interested in was the language of everydayness. "I am for an art," he wrote, in a manifesto that has since become famous, ". . . that does something other than sit on its ass in the museum. I am for an art that grows up not knowing it is art at all, an art given the chance of having a starting point of zero. I am for an art that embroils itself with the everyday crap & still comes out on top."

It is, of course, among the ironies of artistic success that coming out on top, for an artwork, means just "sitting on its ass" in some museum or other. It somewhat symbolizes the spirit of the exhibition, "High & Low: Modern Art and Popular Culture," that its authors, Kirk Varnedoe and Adam Gopnik, should have made an ingenious and metaphoric salute to Oldenburg's *Store* by appropriating a window, rarely used before in the architecture of MoMA, and treating it *as* a store window in which several of Oldenburg's confections of that era are displayed: "39 Cents (Fragment of a Sign)," "Auto Tire With Price," "White Gym Shoes" and so on. It is a delicate, elegant gesture of fraternity across the decades, but it is easily subject to the gross critical discourse of our own sour era, which sneers at what it sees as the commodification of art and is already disposed to regard the museum as a kind of store for the elite, in which cultural bric-a-brac carry implicit price tags (to be sure in $$$$$$ rather than in ¢¢¢¢¢¢). And inevitably, inasmuch as the identification of high art with spirituality often coexists in the same critical breast with that attitude, Varnedoe himself has been attacked as a latter-day Monsieur Jourdain, whose philistine disregard of class differences among artworks has forced the tragedians of high art to consort with the ragamuffins and low-lifers of pop culture. "The museum, having abdicated its role as cultural referee by putting what used to be out on the streets inside its sanctuary," ironizes the editorialist of *The Journal of Art*, "sheds the dreary temple/tower image that threatens the triumph of populist tolerance." And Varnedoe— who "claims the sacred mantle of Alfred Barr Jr."—is accused of playing to the galleries in both senses of the term, attempting to please both the pinheaded gum-chewers and the merchants who traffic in art (but clearly not the high-minded editorialist herself).

In truth, the wonderful window, which opens the museum to the street in a complex metaphorical transfer in which the light of art spreads outward as the light of day spreads inward, is a precise expression of what the exhibition is really undertaking to do. Its intention is to relocate, in the historical conditions that gave them nourishment, works of art that have been "sitting on their asses" as eternal aesthetic presences for too long. "We hope to take objects that have too often been isolated as 'timeless' or 'transcendent' and resituate them within the changing, dynamic contradictions of real life," says the catalogue. It is the genius of modern art that it has drawn heavily on vital fragments of popular culture, just as it was the genius of Wittgenstein to find philosophical inspiration in Street and Smith's *Detective Story Magazine*, or the genius of phenomenology, which Sartre was thrilled to learn from Raymond Aron one boozy night in Montparnasse, to make philosophy even out of cocktail glasses. It is in part a *causal* and an *explanatory* thesis that the exhibition advances and sustains, a partial art-historical narrative in which, instead of the influence of genius A and genius B, the story is told of how genius C and genius D found inspiration in scraps of newsprint, theatrical posters and commercial labels, in the sullen scrawls of prisoners and delinquents, or in the lurid imagery of the funnies. "It is quite a feat to subsume Dubuffet and Cy Twombly under the category of graffiti inspired artists," *The Journal of Art* sneers. It is no feat at all if the thesis is one of historical explanation. Nor is it in any sense a reduction of these artists if the explanation in fact is true, for it does not in the least imply that no artistic criterion distinguishes Dubuffet and Twombly from the chalk scribbles and scratchings each may have drawn upon. "High & Low" is in fact a heroic and difficult *exposition à thèse*, but one almost impossible to mount and completely impossible to indemnify against critics unprepared to rethink the categories of modernist works, when construed as cultural artifacts with complex genealogies.

Wittgenstein said, powerfully and beautifully, that "an expression has meaning only in the stream of life." Much the same may be said of art, with suitable qualification of expressions, even if art historians and critics tend to treat works as though they draw their meaning only from the stream of art. Standard historical and critical practice sees works evolving out of other works by formal modification alone, so that the history of art is a string of begats, and works are scions of other works. That is by no means an absolutely wrong way to think of art history, and it is certainly a way of thinking congenial to Varnedoe. But in this show he has undertaken something grandly different, by inserting some of the icons of modernism into the lifestreams that nourished them and to which they owe dimensions of their meaning. The recreated store window—literally a window of opportunity—is one of several built into the 53rd Street facade of MoMA in the renovations of 1984, but it normally is blocked up by sheetrock to increase the sense of blank enclosure and intensify the sensory focus to which the museum's galleries have mainly aspired—chaste cubicles of visual delight. In uncovering the window, Varnedoe is symbolically opening the museum itself up to the stream of life, to the world of commonplace objects from which his displayed objects derived their sustenance and vitality.

There is more than a simple causal thesis of lifestream-to-artwork implied in this show; the artwork-to-lifestream influence, though somewhat understressed in the exhibits, was prominent in its intention. The catalogue cities a 1954 text from an in-house publication of Young & Rubicam: "If we were to eliminate, in any one issue of *Life*, all advertisements that bear the influence of Miró, Mondrian, and the Bauhaus, we would cut out a sizable proportion of that issue's linage." And the "modern" look has itself been aspired to by designers for whom MoMA (when it was still referred to as "The Modern") was an immense quarry for forms that became adopted as emblems of modernity: the boomerang-shaped coffee table, the black-and-orange butterfly chair, the kidney-shaped silver brooch, the mobile over the crib. In the ideal life-art-life cycle, "stylistic inventions often propelled the movements of specific manners and strategies from high to low to high to low again: billboards affect avant-garde painters whose work later affects billboard designers . . . or techniques of sales display get picked up in structures of art that in turn change the look of commerce."

The structure of such a cycle is more apparent in some of the five categories of "low" genres with high-art resonances than in others. "Comics" and "Words," for example, work somewhat better than "Caricature" and "Graffiti," and all those rather better than "Advertising," which is in many ways a seriously flawed installation, despite its inspired moments.

Consider, to begin with, "Words." By this the curators have in mind words *as printed*, where the mode of lettering carries meanings beyond those carried by the words themselves. Thus, the characteristic sans-serif style of the newspaper headline conveys a kind of annunciatory or proclamational significance. There are, one might say, "print acts" in definite analogy with what philosophers have termed "speech acts," where the fact that the speaker uses certain words or intonations augments or modifies the meanings of the words themselves were they to be taken merely lexically. The Cubists, for particular example, tore out fragments of banner headlines for insertion into early collages. These allowed the possibility of mischievous puns. Picasso incorporated only "UN COUP DE THE" from a headline which had to have read "UN COUP DE THEATRE." The latter doubtless referred to a political happening of some drama, but the fragment to a shot of tea or even a cup of tea—just the thing for a still life. But it also allows an interpretation in which the dramatic event is a tempest in a teacup. In *Landscape With Posters*, Picasso took the word "KUB"—the brand name of a bouillon cube widely advertised but singularly apt in a (K)ubist composition, since it denotes but fails to exemplify cubicity. The sans-serif style of lettering gets taken up by the Constructivists, who used it brilliantly in posters and for book designs, conveying the urgency of headlines. One such book cover, by Aleksandr Rodchenko, gives graphic excitement to a volume of Mayakovsky's poetry. This 1923 design is appropriated by the curators of this very show for the cover of their catalogue, and its handsome red exclamation point—a high wedge over a low dot—serves as the show's emblem. So lettering migrates from newspaper to painting to design. And the catalogue cover is ambiguous as to whether it is merely graphic art or a high-art statement in the postmodern genre, referring to a style it also appropriates and endorses, to make a sophisticated statement of the theme of the exhibition.

The placement of Picasso and Braque near the threshold of the show has exposed the latter to some severe but, in my view, misguided criticism. The critic of *The New York Times*, uncharacteristically intemperate, writes, "Mr. Varnedoe and Mr. Gopnik review the inception of Cubist collage as if last year's 'Picasso and Braque: Pioneering

Cubism' had never happened." To begin with, paintings have different meanings in different streams of life and art, and it is instructive to situate Cubist works in the stream of graphic design and convention. But secondly, not every visitor to the show will view it as a professional critic does, comparing show with show the way sportswriters compare games with games. *Landscape With Posters* has an altogether different weight and reference in Varnedoe's inaugural show than it could have had in William Rubin's valedictory show. The difference that exhibitional context can make when viewing identical works—which carry differing meanings and references in various exhibitions—is one of the things a show like the present one makes clear. And yet, it exacts a heavy price from the viewer, who must identify from the work alone the stream in which it is to have the meaning that Varnedoe and Gopnik mean to evoke (if the show is to be experienced as they intended). But sometimes there is no obvious reason why a work is included, and unless one has recourse to the extremely detailed and ambitious catalogue, one will be in the dark. In fact, the catalogue stands to the show in a very different relation from that in which catalogues normally do. These days, catalogues are vast scholarly achievements, even the lifework of historians and specialists. They are indispensable to other specialists (and, in candor, to critics required to review the shows) but generally optional to the average museum visitor, depending upon his or her interest. "High & Low" is a catalogue-driven exhibition, however, to the point that a great many of the exhibits make no sense unless one has read the text (and may still make little sense afterward). In a way, the individual exhibits serve as illustrations for a text. And the text cannot be easily deduced from the illustrations alone.

Take, for egregious example, Duchamp's notorious *Fountain* of 1917, which we all know is a urinal signed "R. Mutt" and dated. Why is it in the "Advertising" section of the show? And why alongside it is Meret Oppenheim's hardly less notorious fur-lined "*coup de the*"? The *Times* critic has every reason to complain that "the visitor might as well be upstairs in the museum's permanent collection galleries." But even when one reads the text that is to justify inclusion of these Dada works, the connections are tenuous: "[Duchamp's] statement also has a curious parallelism with the way the merchandisers of plumbing promoted their wares." And the catalogue shows us as well some vintage photographs of plumbing supply houses with windows full of sinks and tubs and toilets. But who, even if long immersed in the discussions surrounding *Fountain*—philosophical, critical, historical—could conceivably appreciate *this* connection between Duchamp and advertising?

And which ordinary visitor could infer that this was the sort of point being made in locating the work in a vitrine in the "Advertising" portion of the show? The principle for including in the same section works by Joseph Cornell is hardly more compelling. The blissful rednecks that *The Journal of Art* fears MoMA's curators are pandering to will hardly be up to the erudition in ephemera that an appreciation of the show exacts as a condition.

The show—and of course the catalogue—concludes with "Contemporary Reflections." This may be read as an effort by Varnedoe as a new director of MoMA to come to terms with the difficult and perhaps intractable art history of the present moment, in connection with which this particular museum has a particular problem of identity. "Modern" must originally have been in part a kind of indexical term, indicating *now* in contrast with *then*. But "modern" also turns out to have been a pretty identifiable style—exactly that style the Young & Rubicam writer must have had in mind in referring to the derived stylistics of the 1950s magazines. If MoMA identifies with that style, its contents and its missions are historically circumscribed. If it adheres to the temporal sense of "modern," these limits are modified, but the work it must deal with is now no longer *modern* in the stylistic sense. It remains open to question whether location in low-high-low cycles is the best way into the art of the present moment. It may be the best entry into the work of Jeff Koons, but hardly, one must feel, with the works actually shown. There ought, instead of stainless steel decanters and displayed vacuum cleaners, to have been his megakitsch frights on which Gopnik has written so instructively elsewhere. Possibly there is a low-high connection for Jenny Holzer, with whom the show closes, inasmuch as she has found inspiration in LED banner billboards for putting her thought up in lights. And, with the help of the catalogue, one can find out why Elizabeth Murray, clearly a favorite of Varnedoe and Gopnik, belongs here. Her work has a kind of cartoon derivation.

One of Murray's works can be seen as a gigantesque pair of shoes with holes in them. These, she claims, derive from the comic strip *Blondie*; and the catalogue concludes with an almost lyrical celebration of big shoes, as a sort of leitmotif of the show. It integrates the big shoes of Mickey, or the trucking character of R. Crumb, perhaps the white gym shoes of Oldenburg, and other works as well. The shoes are emblems of a kind of aesthetic pilgrimage the curators themselves have made, and the walker through the show will have made as well, into the present, so far as it lies across the final threshold of the show. "The deal is that you have to go without a map, and you can only get

there on foot." You cannot, however, get through the show itself without a map, and even with one in hand you will at times be lost. Still, it is
a remarkable and valuable exhibition, the implications of which for the
temple of modern art itself we shall all now watch for with the greatest
interest.

THE PRIEST AND HIS PEOPLE

Amy Wilentz

•

IN FRONT OF A burned-out church in downtown Port-au-Prince, Haiti, a crowd of several hundred gathered a few weeks ago to greet a priest. They were blocking the capital's main street, and it was hot out, but they didn't care. They had come to see the man they call "The Prophet." They snatched him up when he arrived, a small man in a guayabera with a bulletproof vest underneath it, and they hoisted him onto their shoulders. During the entire rally, his feet did not once touch the ground.

The priest, Jean-Bertrand Aristide, was no longer permitted to say mass at the church across the street, where he had once preached (or at any other Catholic church). That seemed to matter less now than it had two years ago, when he was expelled from his religious order for preaching politics, just three months after his church had been sacked and burned during his Sunday mass by forces loyal to the military dictatorship. It mattered less because now Aristide had become a politician. And the crowd greeted him not as a priest but as a presidential candidate.

On October 18, two days before candidate registration closed for Haiti's third attempt at elections in the five years since the dictator Jean-Claude Duvalier was ousted from power, Aristide declared his long-rumored candidacy. The announcement met with wild enthusiasm among the priest's youthful supporters, although some of his closest advisers did not approve and have chosen to remain aloof from the campaign. Like Aristide, these dissenters have always argued against elections, saying that until criminals from the old regimes have been brought to trial, no election in Haiti can be considered free and fair.

But many Haitians clearly feel—as Aristide seems to—that any election in which Aristide is a candidate is an election worth voting in. After he declared, voter registration for the December 16 election surged, especially in the department that includes Port-au-Prince, where more than a third of Haiti's registered voters live. Indeed, Aristide has always been a favorite with Haiti's outcast urban populations. In 1985 he began giving fiery good-versus-evil sermons that eventually helped bring the urban masses out onto the streets to protest Duvalier's regime. And as the Duvalierist forces regrouped and grew strong again after Duvalier's fall, Aristide did not cease to speak out against them and their presence in the post-Duvalier regimes, at a time when most opposition leaders were holding their peace, either out of fear or because they had begun to compromise. Aristide has been perceived for years as the unshakable, unswerving and unsuppressible spokesperson for Haiti's poor—which in Haiti means almost everyone.

The months preceding this year's presidential and legislative vote have been full of fits and starts. The stage was set for a reasonably democratic vote this past March, when Ertha Pascal Trouillot, one of the Supreme Court's least offensive members, was named President in the wake of the fall of Gen. Prosper Avril. More important for the success of elections than Trouillot's weak government, however, will be the cooperation of the Haitian military—if it agrees to cooperate—and the presence of international election observers. In October the United Nations and the Organization of American States formally announced that they would send huge observer teams to the elections.

The military is still a powerful retrogressive force in Haiti, as are the rich and corrupt Duvalierists. This year's electoral process is tainted by the memory of Haiti's 1987 elections, which also seemed to be going forward properly, only to end—on Election Day, November 29—in bullets, machetes, massacre and the declaration of a military dictatorship. The 1990 electoral calendar was tarnished last summer by the return to Haitian soil of Dr. Roger Lafontant, a former interior minister and leader of Duvalier's pampered paramilitary thugs, the Tonton Macoutes. Although a warrant was issued months ago for his arrest, the military has thus far been unable or disinclined to bring the doctor in. Lafontant declared his candidacy only to have it rejected by the electoral council in November. In 1987 a number of Duvalierist candidates were similarly denied a place on the ballot, and they are the ones, along with some military officers, who masterminded the attacks on voters that Election Day.

Already, this year's electoral violence has begun. On December 5, a group of armed men attacked an evening rally in Pétionville, a wealthy suburb of Port-au-Prince where a crowd of some 10,000 had gathered to hear Aristide speak. At least five people were killed and more than fifty wounded. Presumably, the assault was the work of the Duvalierists. The military remained aloof: "It's a political matter," the Pétionville commander was reported to have commented. Political or otherwise, it was obviously an attempt to scare Aristide's supporters away from the polling places. Few were able to forget the words of the Duvalierist youths who had participated in the attack on Aristide's church in 1988: "Wherever he preaches, there will be a mountain of corpses."

Although he was the latest entry into the electoral fray, Aristide is the clear front-runner. His closest competitor, Marc Bazin, a center-right former World Bank official, is not-nearly as popular as the priest, though Bazin was a candidate in the 1987 elections and has built up a more impressive election organization than Aristide. Bazin's coalition party, the National Alliance for Democracy and Progress, is the only one putting up candidates for almost all of the 110 seats in the legislature. Aristide's group, the National Front for Change and Democracy, has managed to put up only fifty.

It is more than possible to imagine a stalemate should Aristide win the presidency and a Bazin coalition take the Parliament. In such a case, an impatient military—and the military is always impatient in Haiti—might be quick to step in. Perhaps hoping to avoid such a dangerous impasse, Aristide has reportedly been courting the socialist wing of Bazin's coalition (in Haiti, politics makes the strangest bedfellows), led by Serge Gilles, an intellectual with strong ties to the French Socialists. Aristide's people have encouraged rumors that Gilles may decide to go with Aristide's front, thereby giving the priest the parliamentary clout he would need in a future government. In such an administration Aristide would be President and Gilles Prime Minister. Bazin would be completely marginalized.

All this is, of course, to talk about Haiti as though it were accustomed to clean elections and as though its politicians, its military and other sectors of its ruling classes have a tradition of obeying constitutional norms and parliamentary protocol. Such anticipatory talk about the 1987 election, for example, proved ridiculous in retrospect, as voters lay decapitated and eviscerated at the polling places.

The United States, which has encouraged Haiti's post-Duvalier elections, has been extremely anxious to see that this one goes off better than the last two (a fraudulent presidential election in January 1988 gave rise to a civilian government soon toppled by the army that had put it in power). After Aristide (who has often been labeled a "radical firebrand" in embassy cables) announced his candidacy, Ambassador Alvin Adams continued to give assurances of U.S. neutrality in the electoral process.

But then the Ambassador, who is famous in Haiti for speaking in ambiguous Creole proverbs, cited this one: "Apre bal, tanbou lou" (When the party is over, the drums grow heavy). According to Haitians, he meant that after the fun of Aristide's campaign will come the hard task of governing, for which Aristide is ill suited.

The charges most often leveled against Aristide during his short campaign (by his adversaries but also sometimes by his friends) are that he is a charismatic religious figure singularly unfit for administrative work; that this unsuitability will lead to a crisis in which he is forced to take absolute power or cede power to the military; that he has no longstanding organization behind him; and that his popularity is based on a cult of personality like that of François (Papa Doc) Duvalier, which can lead to dictatorship.

But Aristide himself believes that he is running to bring the Haitian people to power, and that the firm connections he has made with progressive middle-class technocrats and intellectuals over the years will stand him in good stead as an executive. Aristide, no slouch himself on the proverb front, replied to Adams, "Anpil men, chay pa lou" (With many hands, the burden is never heavy).

JANUARY 28, 1991

THE RISE OF LOUIS FARRAKHAN
PART ONE

Adolph Reed, Jr.

•

LOUIS FARRAKHAN IS ALL over America. In the past year he has been the subject of widely publicized feature-length interviews in *The Washington Post* and *The Washington Times*, and in other nonblack publications as well. He tore up the campaign trail on behalf of local and Congressional candidates in the Nation of Islam's first direct foray into electoral politics. He was prominent at rallies and demonstrations in support of embattled former Washington Major Marion Barry, despite having denounced him only a few months earlier as a drug fiend and philanderer. Farrakhan has even been a featured solo guest on *Donahue*. He has kept up a torrid pace of speaking engagements and, of late, has begun to stake out a position critical of U.S. intervention in the Persian Gulf.

Recognition of Farrakhan as a public figure has been growing since his involvement in Jesse Jackson's first campaign for the Democratic presidential nomination in 1984. But understanding what his rise means in American life requires going back much further than that.

Louis Farrakhan, now 57, has been around a long time. Like Otis Redding, Aretha Franklin and hip-hop, he had considerable visibility among blacks before whites discovered him. For well over thirty years he has propagated a vision of political separatism and a program of moral rearmament, "self-help" business development and an idiosyncratic brand of Islamic religion. That vision and program, as well as his personal stature, grew from the soil of black nationalist politics in the civil rights/black power era. To make sense of Farrakhan requires situating him within the organizational and ideological contexts from which he emerged. Doing so, moreover, indicates that his anti-Semitism and whatever he might think of whites in general are ephemeral in comparison with the truly dangerous tendencies he represents.

In the early 1960s, as Louis X, Farrakhan was minister of the Nation of Islam's important Boston mosque and a kind of understudy to Malcolm X. He sided conspicuously with Elijah Muhammad, founder and "Messenger" of the Nation, against Malcolm in the bitter 1963–65 conflict that ended with the latter's murder. Farrakhan replaced Malcolm as minister of the Harlem mosque and later became Muhammad's national representative.

The Messenger's core teachings include claims that blacks were the world's "original" race, from which all others derived; that black Americans are descended from an ancient, "lost" Asian tribe; that the white race originated from a demonic laboratory experiment and that Elijah Muhammad was divinely inspired. Following nationalist convention, the Muslims advocate the subordination of women, drawing on a rhetoric of domesticity, moral purity and male responsibility; predictably, they denounce feminism and gay rights as white decadence and as strategies to undermine black unity and moral fiber.

The Nation's secular program has always focused on "nation building," which in practice has meant business development and the creation of separate schools and other institutions. Those activities have been harnessed to the ultimate goal of political separation and the formation of an independent state. Under Muhammad that goal remained inchoate, appearing mainly as a millenarian dream, but for Farrakhan it figures more directly into programmatic rhetoric. Discussion of the proposed state's citizenry characteristically elides the distinction between the membership of the Nation of Islam and black Americans in general, but Farrakhan recently has indicated that one possible model entails putting the former in charge of the latter. The nation-building agenda also reinforces the organization's natalist ideology and longstanding opposition to abortion, which both Muhammad and Farrakhan have denounced as genocidal as well as immoral.

Farrakhan rose to prominence during the late 1960s and early 1970s, when Muhammad's Nation was trying to become more visible in public life and to establish a greater presence in the black activist arena. As Muhammad's representative, he participated in national black political forums, addressed the 1970 Pan-African Congress of nationalist activists (as did first-time black Mayors Richard Hatcher of Gary, Indiana, and Kenneth Gibson of Newark; Ralph Abernathy; National Urban League director Whitney Young Jr.; Jesse Jackson and others) and frequently spoke on black college campuses. During that period the Nation also expanded its business development agenda, which until then had centered mainly on mom-and-pop restaurants, takeout sandwich and baked goods shops, cut-and-sew operations catering to the organization's members (to satisfy the Muslim dress code) and the newspaper *Muhammad Speaks*. The Nation unveiled a set of ambitious goals, including establishment of agribusiness in the South, a medical complex in Chicago and large-scale international commerce anchored by fish imports from Peru. There was even talk that Muhammad would take advantage of Richard Nixon's definition of "black power" as "black capitalism" and apply for funds from minority economic development programs in the Office of Economic Opportunity or the Small Business Administration.

Two personal encounters I had with Farrakhan in late 1970 and early 1971 neatly reflect the discordant aspects of the Nation of Islam's thrust then and his place in it. One was a speech he gave at the predominantly black Fayetteville State University in North Carolina, where he scored mainstream civil rights spokesperson for their spinelessness and lack of vision. Of Ralph Abernathy's pledge to pursue King's "dream" as his successor at the Southern Christian Leadership Conference, Farrakhan quipped, "Talking about dreaming somebody else's dream! Don't you know that when you're dreaming, you're *asleep? Wake up*, black man!" And he chastised his mainly student audience for putative moral weakness. "Just as a bootmaker molds a boot, so the teacher molds the hearts and minds of the youth of our nation," he said, playing on the institution's history as a teachers' college. "And what are you going to teach them, *drunkard*? What are you going to teach them, *dope fiend*? What are you going to teach them, *foul, frivolous woman* who will lie down with a teacher to get a passing grade?" (Note that the woman, not the teacher, is his target.) With striking theatricality and stage presence, he punctuated each charge by pointing to a different section of the auditorium, as if exposing particular culprits.

The second encounter came soon thereafter. Along with other field-staff members of the North Carolina-based Foundation for Community Development, I was called in to Durham to attend a meeting with Farrakhan. He had come to the area as Muhammad's delegate, mainly to pursue contacts with officials of a well-established black bank and the North Carolina Mutual Life Insurance Company, then one of the largest black-owned businesses in the United States. He also wanted to examine the operations of the community development corporation that our agency had helped the local poor-people's organization create. At the meeting his demeanor was reserved, almost stilted, and he seemed (or tried to seem) in thrall to an image of black Durham as a center for business enterprise. (He had attended college in Winston-Salem during the early 1950s and quite likely imbibed that image then.) Although he made perfunctory gestures of appreciation for our reputation for grass-roots activism and black-power radicalism, he expressed only polite interest in the participatory and cooperative aspects of our community development approach. He was not much moved by the idea of organizing poor people to act on their own behalf.

While the Nation seemed to be growing and consolidating itself as a corporate enterprise, many of us in movement circles who watched from the outside wondered then how it would resolve the evident tension between its flamboyant rhetorical posture, so clear that night at Fayetteville State, and its very conventional business aspirations. Central in our minds was anticipation of the succession crisis likely to occur when Muhammad, who in 1970 was already a feeble septuagenarian, died or stepped down. For not only could Muslim operatives be seen hanging out with denizens of the underworld, but sectarian zealotry often condoned a strongarm style.

The Uhuru Kitabu bookstore in Philadelphia, for example, was firebombed in 1970 when its proprietors—former Student Non-Violent Coordinating Committee workers—refused to remove a Malcolm X poster from the store's window after threats from local Muslims. In Atlanta in 1971 a dispute between Muslims and Black Panthers over turf rights for streetcorner newspaper hawking erupted into a hundred-person brawl. In 1972 strife within New York's Temple Number 7 culminated in a three-hour fight and shootout that began in the mosque and spilled outside. A purge of remaining Malcolm X loyalists followed in New York and elsewhere, and factions within the Nation were implicated in assassinations of outspoken followers of Malcolm in Boston and in Newark, where the presiding minister of the mosque was gunned down.

Most chilling, in January 1973 a simmering theological dispute with members of the Hanafi Islamic sect in Washington ignited into an attack of which only zealots or hardened killers are capable. Seven Hanafis were murdered in their 16th Street residence, owned by Kareem Abdul-Jabbar; five of the victims were children, including babies who were drowned in the bathtub. (The Hanafis held the Nation responsible and four years later occupied a government building and B'nai B'rith center and took hostages to press their demands for retribution.)

In that climate it was reasonable to worry, upon Elijah Muhammad's death in 1975, that the friction might lead to open warfare among the organization's contending factions, particularly between those identified with Farrakhan, who stood for the primacy of ideology, and the Messenger's son Wallace (Warith) Deen Muhammad, who had been linked much more with the Nation's business operations than with its ideological mission. Consequences of that sort did not materialize, and W. D. succeeded his father without apparent conflict, or at least with no immediate, publicly noticeable disruption.

The tension between the two agendas inevitably came to a head, however. Since the early 1970s the Nation had sought explicitly to recruit a middle-class membership as part of its drive for economic development. College students and professionals who joined were likely to be rewarded with responsible positions in the administrative hierarchy, but the Nation had only limited success in gaining petit-bourgeois adherents. It was, after all, a bit much to expect a college-educated constituency to accept as religious principle that the pig is a hybrid of the dog, the cat and the rat or that whites derive from an evil wizard's botched experiment on subhuman creatures.

At the same time, instability grew in the Muslim business operations. For whatever reasons—probably among them was a reluctance to open records to outside scrutiny—the organization retreated from its ambivalent interest in pursuing federal economic-development support. Yet the projects on the board required both considerable specialized expertise and capitalization surpassing the Nation's liquidity. A $3 million "loan" from the Libyan government in 1972 was a stopgap. Despite its ideological boost as a statement of Islamic solidarity, however, the Libyan deal was also a signal that the Messenger Muhammad could not finance his bold schemes internally and was unwilling to do so through regular outside sources.

The desire to broaden the Nation's class base rested on more than a need for expertise. The early newspaper and the bean pie, restaurant and fish ventures relied on the super-exploitation of members' labor. The religio-racial ideology—much like family ideology in a mom-and-pop store—could impose on members, at least in the short run, jobs offering low wages, no benefits and sometimes even no wages. But while it might help keep a newspaper solvent or finance a new restaurant, that ideologically driven accumulation strategy could not begin to support hospital construction or complex international commerce. Tithes or direct investment by a more affluent membership might better help meet capital needs.

Thus, when W. D. Muhammad inherited the Nation of Islam, it was stymied by a fundamental contradiction: The motors of its success— the religio-racial ideology, hermetic separatism and primitive strategy of capital accumulation—had become impediments to realizing the objectives that success had spawned. Negotiating the contradiction was constrained, moreover, by Farrakhan, who constituted himself on the right flank as guardian of the Messenger's orthodoxy, ready to challenge deviations.

Those contrary tendencies coexisted no more than three years. Before the split became public knowledge Muhammad had introduced sweeping changes. He repudiated his father's idiosyncratic religious doctrines—no more Yacub, the evil wizard—in favor of conventional Islamic beliefs. He changed the sect's name to the World Community of Islam in the West to reflect a move toward traditional Islam. He rejected the Messenger's insistence on abstaining from secular politics: Instead, he actively urged political participation. In 1976 Muhammad gave up on the goal of economic independence, dismantled the group's holdings and considered seeking Small Business Administration assistance for member-entrepreneurs. (Rumor has it that titles to all the Nation's assets were held not by the organization but by the Messenger himself, who died intestate. Supposedly, W. D. hastened to sell off everything and divided the proceeds equally among all his father's legitimate and illegitimate offspring.)

W. D. had been a very close ally of Malcolm X, reputedly even through the break with his own father, and within his first year as leader of the organization he renamed the Harlem mosque in Malcolm's honor. To Farrakhan's partisans, who often pointed to W. D.'s support for Malcolm as evidence of filial impiety, that gesture must have affirmed suspicions of his blasphemous inclinations. More strain must have developed from W. D.'s proclamation in 1975 that whites thenceforth would be welcome as members of the sect. In 1978 Farrakhan announced his departure and the formation of a new Nation of Islam on the basis of the Messenger's original teachings. In 1985 the World Community of Islam in the West officially disbanded, leaving Farrakhan's group as Elijah Muhammad's sole organizational legacy.

Through the early 1980s Farrakhan maintained a relatively low profile as he built his organization by replicating the old Nation's forms and cultivating a membership drawn from its main social base on the margins of black working-class life. He re-established the Fruit of Islam, the paramilitary security force, and he restored the old ideology, Yacub and all. He even concocted a version of the old bean pie-and-fish economic development formula via Power Products, a line of household and personal items. (To date, the line has not done well, and Farrakhan seems not to have given it much attention.) As if to underscore his loyalty to the elder Muhammad's vision, Farrakhan resumed his old title, national representative of the Honorable Eli ah Muhammad and the Nation of Islam. The chief public signal of the Nation of Islam's return was the appearance of young men on inner-city streets wearing the group's distinctive suit and bow tie and aggressively selling the *Final Call* newspaper, which, but for the different title, follows the format of the old *Muhammad Speaks*.

The original Nation of Islam had grown in prominence in the years after the Supreme Court's 1954 *Brown v. Board of Education* decision because the organization, primarily through Malcolm, chose to operate within the discursive realm created by the developing activist movement. Debate about politics and racial strategy—at widely varying levels of sophistication—was extensive, and the rising tide of activism lifted all ideological and organizational boats.

In the early 1980s, though, there was no hint of a popular movement, and black political discourse had withered to fit entirely within the frame of elite-centered agendas for race-relations engineering. The cutting edge of racial advocacy, for example, was what political scientist Earl Picard described astutely at the time as the "corporate intervention strategy," pioneered by Jesse Jackson at Operation PUSH and adopted with less rhetorical flair by the National Urban League and the N.A.A.C.P. This strategy consisted in using the threat of consumer boycott to induce corporations to enter into "covenants" binding them to hire black managers, contract with black vendors, deposit in black banks and recruit black chisees. (For a while, the N.A.A.C.P. concentrated on Hollywood, identifying the fate of the race with its representation in the film industry.) At the same time Ronald Reagan was pressing ahead with a rhetoric and battle plan steeped in racial revanchism, and official black opposition ranged from feeble to incoherent. In that context, the Fruit of Islam selling newspapers outside the supermarket looked for all the world like living anachronisms.

In the race for the 1984 Democratic presidential nomination, however, Farrakhan demonstrated the new Nation of Islam's political departure from the old. Unlike Elijah Muhammad, Farrakhan did not remain publicly aloof from electoral politics. He openly supported

Jackson's candidacy and even provided him with a Fruit of Islam security force. Because of Farrakhan's and the Nation's long association with anti-Semitic rhetoric, his closeness to Jackson was thrown into relief in the wake of the "Hymietown" controversy.

Milton Coleman, the *Washington Post* reporter who disclosed Jackson's remarks, was condemned widely as a race traitor, but Farrakhan raised the ante: "We're going to make an example of Milton Coleman. One day soon, we will punish you by death, because you are interfering with the future of our babies—for white people and against the good of yourself and your own people. This is a fitting punishment for such dogs." (Farrakhan has always denied he made these remarks.)

That inflamed rhetoric, along with Farrakhan's reference to Judaism as a "gutter religion," prodded a temporizing Jackson to distance himself publicly from Farrakhan, and the incident made sensationalistic copy throughout the information industry. For those with longer memories Farrakhan's attack on Coleman was a chilling reminder of the thuggish currents of the past. Indeed, his therefore most notoriously threatening pronouncement—against Malcolm X—had set a frightening precedent. In December 1964 he wrote in *Muhammad Speaks*:

> Only those who wish to be led to hell, or to their doom, will follow Malcolm. The die is set and Malcolm shall not escape, especially after such foolish talk about his benefactor in trying to rob him of the divine glory which Allah has bestowed upon him. Such a man as Malcolm is worthy of death—and would have met with death if it had not been for Muhammad's confidence in Allah for victory over the enemies.

Two months later Malcolm was assassinated.

In retrospect, the significance of the Milton Coleman incident lay in how it propelled Farrakhan into the new, mass-mediated space in Afro-American politics first carved out by Jesse Jackson. Jackson's 1984 campaign oscillated between simplistic racial appeals ("It's our turn now!") and claims to represent some larger "moral force." As I have argued in *The Jesse Jackson Phenomenon*, that oscillation was rooted in a contradiction between the campaign's public posture as the crest of a broadly based social movement and the reality that it could rely on black votes only. The pressure to increase the black vote justified a mobilization strategy that often approached pure demagogy. In an August 1984 interview with *Ebony*, Jackson described himself as the carrier of "the emotions and self-respect and inner security of the whole race." The messianism implicit in that perception of his racial role appeared more clearly in his insinuation in that same interview that a Virginia supporter's terminal cancer was cured by going to a Jackson rally. In the midst of the Reagan counterrevolution and black elites' typically uninspired and ineffectual responses, that sort of demagogic appeal found a popular audience. With no more promising agenda available, racial cheerleading at least offered a soothing catharsis. The promise of deliverance by proxy, of racial absorption into Jackson's persona, consoled some with simple explanations and apparently easy remedies ("If all black people could just get together behind Jesse . . .")

But between 1984 and 1988 Jackson moved to consolidate his position as a racial broker in mainstream national politics and to expand his domain to include putative representation of all the "locked out." That shift required soft-pedaling the race line, and instead of making sharp denunciations of the nasty grass-roots racism expressed in Howard Beach and Forsyth County, Georgia, he attempted to invoke the common interests of poor whites and poor blacks. Jackson's transition from the posture of militant insurgent to a more subdued insider's style left vacant the specific racial space that he had created and that had proved to be marketable. Louis Farrakhan's emergence as a national political figure is largely the story of his efforts to replace Jackson as central embodiment and broker of the black race-nationalist political persona. Those efforts began, at least symbolically, with Jackson's grudging acquiescence to white pressure to criticize Farrakhan after the "Hymietown" incident.

The notoriety acquired in that incident fueled Farrakhan's rise in two ways. First, it simply increased his name recognition, especially among a younger generation with no recollection of the old Nation of Islam and his role therein. Second, the heavy barrage of sensationalistic coverage and the sanctimonious white response to the affair afforded an image of Farrakhan and Jackson joined in racial martyrdom. Repudiation of Farrakhan has become a litmus test imposed by white opinion makers for black participation in mainstream politics, and many blacks perceive the test as a humiliating power play. Farrakhan's messianic pretensions, moreover, give him a style something like a counterpunching boxer, and he deftly turned the assault on him into evidence of his authenticity as a race leader. Whites and their agents, the argument goes, expend so much energy on discrediting him because he is a genuine advocate of black interests and thus a threat to white racial domination. In that view, the more he is attacked, the greater his authenticity and the more emphatically he must be defended.

Farrakhan hardly invented this style. Jackson and his black supporters have routinely dismissed criticism by accusing critics of either
racism or race treason. Marion Barry, Gus Savage and legions of less
prominent malefactors have wrapped themselves in red, black and
green rhetoric to conceal abuses of public trust or other failings. Nor is
the practice an "African survival," Jimmy Swaggart, Billy James Har-
gis, Richard Nixon and Oliver North all claim to have been beleaguered
by a comparable conspiracy of liberal-communists. Farrakhan stands
out because he has been cast in our public theater—like Qaddafi and
Noriega, both of whom he has defended—as a figure of almost car-
toonishly demonic proportions. He has become uniquely notorious
because his inflammatory nationalist persona has helped to center public discussion of Afro-American politics on the only issue (except affirmative action, of course) about which most whites ever show much
concern: What do blacks think of whites?

All for One and None for All: The Rise of Louis Farrakhan

Part two

Adolph Reed, Jr.

•

THE HYPOCRISY IN the white reaction to Louis Farrakhan's "hate mongering" is transparent. And beneath the platitudes and fatuities about Martin Luther King Jr.'s dream, black Americans are aware of the dual standard governing public outcry. David Duke's racism and anti-Semitism have been more direct and vitriolic than Farrakhan's, but Duke has not provoked comparable public anxiety and denunciation—despite the fact that the ex-Nazi/Klansman has won a seat as a Louisiana State Representative, has run as a "legitimate" candidate for the U.S. Senate and harbors gubernatorial intentions. The heavy metal group Guns n' Roses maintains a repertoire that is unremittingly and unapologetically misogynistic, homophobic, racist and xenophobic, yet the group has escaped the outrage and public censure heaped upon the no more (nor less, certainly) racist and misogynistic Public Enemy. The scurrilous Andrew Dice Clay is granted television specials and a film contract; the no more repugnant 2 Live Crew is censored for obscenity. Recognition of this hypocritical Jim Crow standard for targeting public scorn naturally breeds resentment and racial defensiveness. The retrograde racial climate fostered by Reaganism particularly stimulates that defensive tendency. It is also reinforced and cultivated by black elites of all sorts—from the national civil rights advocacy organizations, the Congressional Black Caucus and Jesse Jackson to small-town politicians, journalists and academics, who opportunistically reproduce a political discourse among black citizens that takes race as its only significant category of critical analysis.

The Marion Barry case exemplifies the dangerous limitations of that discourse. With very few honest exceptions, black spokespersons failed to take a principled stand denouncing both the Bush Administration's disingenuous, irresponsible (and yes, racist) use of public power in pursuit of Barry *and* the Mayor's culpability—not simply for his tawdry personal life but, much more seriously, for the contempt and neglect that his entire pattern of governance has directed toward his poor black constituents. One source of the reticence is the mutual protectiveness that operates within all elite networks; it is intensified no doubt by being in a beleaguered community. But it also reflects the absence of explicit norms of civic life and ideals of political economy other than those connected immediately to principles of equity among racial groups. Without such norms and ideals, race stands out as the sole unequivocal criterion of good and bad, right and wrong, truth and falsity. That context nurtures a variety of demagogues, hustlers and charlatans; in addition, it underlies an important characteristic of Farrakhan's black support.

Farrakhan has been attacked so vigorously and singularly *in part* because he is black. He is seen by whites as a symbol embodying, and therefore justifying, their fears of a black peril. Blacks have come to his defense *mainly* because he is black and perceived to be a victim of racially inspired defamation; he gets points in principle for saying things that antagonize whites. Few who rally to vindicate him know or have anything substantive to say about his program; most defend him as a strong black voice that whites want to silence. Farrakhan's wager is that he can build a personal following by asserting his apparent victimization as de facto evidence of political legitimacy.

Can he succeed? To what extent has he already succeeded? What difference does it make whether or not he ensconces himself as a major force in national Afro-American politics? The first two questions, commonly asked, express clear, immediate concerns but can be answered only contingently. The third is almost never asked, but it goes to the heart of the most disturbing qualities of the Farrakhan controversy and what it says about the state of black politics.

If mass conversion to the Nation of Islam is the measure of success, then Farrakhan does not seem to have got very far. Nor is it likely that he will. The organization's strict dietary code and other behavioral disciplines—not to mention its bizarre and non-Christian theology—

greatly limit his membership pool, as they did Elijah Muhammad's. There is, however, an intermediate zone between adhering to the Nation's doctrines and *pro forma* support, and I suspect that is the terrain on which Farrakhan has staked his aspirations.

He seems to have made some headway, at least within the college-age population, in propagating an image of himself as the quintessential representative of black assertiveness. Black student groups now almost routinely make headlines and raise hackles by paying top-shelf lecture fees (reportedly $17,000 for speaker and entourage at the University of Massachusetts, Amherst) to hear Farrakhan's message. And those in both college and noncollege networks drop his name as a signifier of being conversant with the state of chic in race militancy, just as semi-reverent, faux intimate invocations of Michael Jordan or Teddy Riley convey being *au courant* in other contexts.

Embracing Farrakhan's image—like wearing an Africa medallion— is an act of vicarious empowerment. More clearly on the campuses but probably outside student life as well, it is a totemic act of the sort distinctive to mass-consumption culture: highly salient but without clear meaning, effortlessly accessible but somehow bestowing in-group status. For college students, inviting Farrakhan forges identity with a power that counterattacks racism and isolation and soothes the anxieties around upward mobility or class maintenance. For non-students, invoking his name forges identity with a power that consoles fleetingly in the face of a marginalized life showing little hope for improvement.

Not surprisingly, the youthful Farrakhan constituency in each domain seems preponderantly male. On the one hand, Farrakhan's stridency and martial style have a distinctly macho appeal. On the other, women of any stratum are not likely to respond enthusiastically to his philosophy, which assigns them subordinate status in a patriarchal family, stresses childbearing and child raising as their main functions and ties them to the domestic realm in a state of modified purdah.

How far that kind of ephemeral constituency can go is an open question. Some slender cohort will enter the Nation of Islam from the student and nonstudent populations, and Farrakhan's decision to have the Nation operate in electoral politics will probably help campus recruitment by providing a visible public career path, though that tactic has yet to produce any substantive victories. The vast majority will either retain a mainly symbolic identification by recycling signature catch phrases, lose interest entirely or move back and forth between those two positions according to the vagaries of biography.

The impetus to invite Farrakhan to speak on campuses is driven by a combination of localized *cri de coeur* and protest, competition and solidarity with black students at other institutions, faddishness and racially mediated adolescent rebelliousness and anxiety. But what happens when he comes? What message does he deliver? What do students hear and how do they receive it? What can that tell us about the depth and meaning of his support?

For many the act of consuming the event is the principal gratification. In that sense going to a Farrakhan speech is identical to going to an M. C. Hammer concert; it is the happening place to be at the moment. Farrakhan is a masterful performer and spellbinding orator. He offers his audience a safely contained catharsis: visceral rebellion without dangerous consequences, an instant, painless inversion of power and status relations. As a talented demagogue, Farrakhan mingles banalities, half-truths, distortions and falsehoods to buttress simplistic and wacky theories. The result is a narrative in which he takes on the role of racial conscience and, in Malcolm's old phrase, "tells it like it is." He cajoles, berates, exhorts, instructs and consoles—all reassuringly, without upsetting the framework of conservative petit-bourgeois convention.

Indeed, Farrakhan has reproduced the contradiction within the old Nation of Islam, the tension between militant posture and conservative program. But that contradiction fits the ambivalent position of the student audience. Their racial militancy often rests atop basically conventional, if not conservative, aspirations: for example, the desire to penetrate—or create black-controlled alternatives to—the "glass ceiling" barring access to the upper reaches of corporate wealth and power. Radical rhetoric is attractive when it speaks to their frustrations as members of a minority, as long as it does not conflict with their hopes for corporate success and belief in their own superiority to a benighted black "underclass."

The combination of cathartic, feel-good militancy and conservative substance is the source as well of whatever comparable following Farrakhan may have generated among the older population. It is also what makes him a dangerous force in American life—quite apart from what he thinks of whites in general or Jews in particular. He weds a radical, oppositional style to a program that proposes private and individual responses to social problems; he endorses moral repressiveness; he asserts racial essentialism; he affirms male authority; and he lauds bootstrap capitalism. In defining his and the Nation's role as bringing the holy word to a homogeneous but defective population, moreover, he has little truck for cultivation of democratic debate among Afro-Americans, and he is quick to castigate black critics with the threatening language of race treason.

Reports of Farrakhan's growing presence typically note that the crowds drawn to his speaking tours include many older, apparently well-off people who indicate that they appreciate his message of race pride and self-help community development. Observers from Benjamin Hooks to Phil Donahue have anointed his antidrug and bootstrap rhetoric as level-headed and unobjectionable, the stuff of an appropriate and reasonable approach to the problems of black inner cities. But his focus on self-help and moral revitalization is profoundly reactionary and meshes perfectly with the victim-blaming orthodoxy of the Reagan/Bush era.

To Farrakhan the most pressing problems confronting the poor and working-class Afro-American population are not poverty and dispossession themselves but their putative behavioral and attitudinal byproducts: drugs, crime, social "pathology." In an August interview in *Emerge* he declared that to improve black Americans' condition it is necessary first to "recognize that we as a people are sick." In his March 13, 1990, *Donahue* appearance he maintained that blacks suffer from a dependent, welfare mentality inculcated in slavery; there and elsewhere (in a March 1, 1990, *Washington Post* interview, for example) he has implicitly trivialized and challenged the propriety of the Thirteenth Amendment, alleging that at Emancipation the infantilized blacks "didn't have the mentality of a free people to go and do for ourselves." (In this view Farrakhan echoes not only Daniel Patrick Moynihan's notorious 1965 report on the black family but also much older racist representations: the common belief in the early twentieth century that emancipated blacks would die out because of their incompetence at independent life in civilized society and the antebellum view that justified slavery as a humanitarian service for childlike savages who could not exist independently.)

Farrakhan romanticizes the segregation era as a time of black business success and laments that "throughout the South the economic advancement that we gained under Jim Crow is literally dead." He suggested in *Emerge* that civil rights legislation has done black citizens general harm because "women, gays, lesbians and Jews have taken advantage of civil rights laws, antidiscrimination laws, housing laws, and they have marched on to a better life while the people who made it happen are going farther and farther behind economically." He proposed the "real solution" in a very sympathetic July 23, 1990, interview in *The Spotlight*, organ of the ultra-reactionary Liberty Lobby:

If I am sick and I'm a member of your household and I have a com-
municable disease, what you do (so that the disease does not affect the
whole family) you remove me from the house and you put me in a place
which is separate to allow me to come back to health. Then I can return
to my family. Here, when people have been under oppression for 400
years, it produces an ill effect. ⸴ . . You have . . . millions of [Black] people who are out of it in terms of our ability to take advantage of even the
laws that are on the books right now. We are not creating jobs for ourselves. We are sitting in a dependent posture waiting for white people to
create a job for us. And if you don't create a job for us we threaten to
picket or wait on welfare to come.

Farrakhan's views of politics and government also share significant
features with the Reaganite right. The flip side of his self-help notion is
rejection of government responsibility for the welfare of the citizenry.
The highly touted Muslim "Dopebusters" drug program in Washington's Mayfair Mansions (where I lived as a child, incidentally) is, after
all, advertised as a case of successful privatization. Predictably, Farrakhan shows little regard for the state's integrity as a secular institution. In announcing the Nation's foray into running candidates for
public office (for the Washington school board and two Congressional
seats, one of them contested by Dr. Abdul Alim Muhammad of Dopebusters fame), he maintained in the Nation's organ, *The Final Call*,
that politics needs "somebody trained in divine law, then trained in the
law of the land" and announced that the Nation of Islam has been
"given by Allah the right guidance for our people and the right guidance for our nation." Like Reagan, he assumes the classic demagogic
tack of an antipolitical politics, presenting himself and his subalterns
as redeemers coming from outside the political realm and untainted by
its corruptions. Their mission is to bring moral order.

Clearly, this is a very disturbing, regressive social vision, and it is
instructive that Farrakhan has received the Liberty Lobby's enthusiastic stamp of approval. The good news is that his vision is most unlikely
to win mass Afro-American adherence; the bad news is that doing so is
not a necessary condition for Farrakhan's becoming a central race
spokesperson. Instead, he seems to be following the route that Jesse
Jackson pioneered.

With his 1983 speaking tour Jackson gained acclamation as a paramount figure in Afro-American politics by parlaying media images of
enthusiastic audiences into a claim to represent a mass constituency.
He succeeded without having articulated a program or coherent vision

for those supposed constituents to accept or reject. In claiming to embody their aspirations simply in his being, he also sought to merge collective racial fortunes into his own, a strategy that entailed defining support of Jackson as an act of race loyalty.

Jackson's strategy exploited longstanding and hegemonic presumptions in American society that black people naturally speak with a single voice as a racial group, that the "leaders" who express the collective racial interest emerge organically from the population and that the objectives and interests of those organic leaders are identical with those of the general racial constituency. Those presumptions eliminate the need to attend to potentially troublesome issues of accountability, legitimacy and democratic process among Afro-Americans, and they give whites easy, uncomplicated access to a version of black thinking by condensing the entire race into a few designated spokespersons. They also simplify the management of racial subordination by allowing white elites to pick and choose among pretenders to race leadership and, at their own discretion, to confer "authenticity." Thus Jackson generated the dynamic of personalistic legitimation that created his national status almost as self-fulfilling prophecy, without regard to the specific character of his popular support. Jackson has shown that it is possible to penetrate the innermost circles of the national race-relations management elite without coming from a clearly denominated organizational, electoral or institutional base. Farrakhan could follow that same path, though he might be constrained as well as aided by the fact that he does have an organizational base, and by that base's particular nature.

Operation PUSH under Jackson was purely an extension of his person, and it cohered around opportunism as a raison d'être. The National Rainbow Coalition Inc. today is an organizational fiction. Both have therefore been well suited to the protean style that Jackson employed to establish himself first as embodiment of insurgent mass racial aspirations and then as generic "moral force" in elite national political circles. While the Nation of Islam is an extension of Farrakhan's objectives, it also has a governing ideology and world view. He may be limited—in the same way that he hampered Wallace Muhammad—in his ability to bend that orthodoxy to suit his immediate political purposes.

Farrakhan may differ from Jackson in yet another consequential way. Where Jackson's history has been marked by self-promotion more than propagation of a durable set of beliefs, Farrakhan—though obviously opportunistic—has built his career and organization around a clear, aggressive ideology. His ambitions appear to be in a way narrower, in a way broader than Jackson's. Farrakhan is more likely to be content with a status defined in purely racial terms and has been less inclined to moderate his race line in exchange for access to privileged insider status. On his own and through the Nation he has been sharply censorious and disparaging of what he construes as Jackson's knuckling under to white criticism. In part, I suspect, that difference reflects the fact that Farrakhan has an organizational apparatus that permits him to maximize the returns of a purely racial focus by engineering symbols of legitimacy and continual mobilization (rallies, conferences, community visibility). The difference also underscores the fact that Farrakhan's ideology decrees an explicit racial mission—purification (by the Nation's standards) of Afro-American life. Unlike Jackson, who has capitalized on the image of control of the black American population, Farrakhan wants real control.

His suggestion that some 600,000 incarcerated blacks be released to his authority in Africa is more than a publicity stunt. It expresses a belief that in the best-case scenario he should be put in charge of black Americans. His request in the *Washington Post* interview to be "allowed the freedom to teach black people unhindered" sounds mild enough, but only because it leaves ambiguous what he considers improper hindrances. Opposition of any sort falls into that category, and his 1984 threat to Milton Coleman for race treason in the "Hymietown" affair reveals the place of dissent in the society he would make. Of the model of racial authority he would assert, he makes a revealing comparison in the *Emerge* interview: "I am to black people as the Pope is to white people." That enlarged self-image can approach a lunatic megalomania. He alleges in *Emerge* that the revival of interest in Malcolm X is the work of a conspiracy aimed at undermining his mission; to *The Washington Post* he traced the spread of crack in inner cities to a similar conspiracy against him, and he claimed to have been transported in 1985 into a spaceship where Elijah Muhammad gave him general instructions and prophesied Reagan's attack on Libya.

How can it be that Farrakhan's actual vision of and for black America has been so noncontroversial? Why have the civil rights establishment and other liberal black opinion leaders not publicly expressed more vocal concern about its protofascist nature and substance? Some of the reticence may derive from fear of being attacked for race disloyalty, but the black petit-bourgeois chorus of praise for the Nation's rhetoric of self-help and moral rearmament reveals a deeper reason for the absence of criticism. The same repugnant, essentially Victorian view of the inner-city black poor as incompetent and morally defective that undergirds Farrkhan's agenda suffuses the political discourse of the black petite bourgeoisie. That view informs the common sense, moreover, even of many of those identified with the left. Of course, not many would admit to the level of contempt that Farrakhan has expressed publicly:

> Not one of you [*Spotlight* editorial staff] would mind, maybe, my living next door to you, because I'm a man of a degree of intelligence, of moral character. I'm not a wild, partying fellow. I'm not a noisemaker. I keep my home very clean and my lawn very nice. . . . With some of us who have learned how to act at home and abroad, you might not have problems . . . Drive through the ghettoes, and see our people. See how we live. Tell me that you want your son or daughter to marry one of these. No, you won't.

Some, like Harvard sociologist Orlando Patterson, share Farrakhan's contention that the black poor's pathology is a product of the slavery experience. Others, like the Carter Administration's Equal Employment Opportunity Commission director and newly elected Washington Congressional delegate Eleanor Holmes Norton or Chicago sociologist William Julius Wilson, maintain that this pathology is a phenomenon of the post-World War II or even postsegregation era. Still others, like Roger Wilkins, have embraced both narratives of origin. There is, however, nearly unanimous agreement with Farrakhan's belief that defective behavior and attitudes are rampant among the poor. In a recent article in *Dissent*, Patterson points to an underclass bent on "violence and destruction." Norton, calling for "Restoring the Traditional Black Family" in *The New York Times Magazine* (June 2, 1985), sees a "self-perpetuating culture of the ghetto," a "destructive ethos" that forms a "complicated, predatory ghetto subculture." Wilson frets over the "sharp increase in social pathologies in ghetto communities" in his opus on urban poverty, *The Truly Disadvantaged* (1987). Wilkins cites in *The New York Times* the authority of Samuel Proctor—retired Rutgers professor, civil rights veteran and minister emeritus of Harlem's Abyssinian Baptist Church—who fears that the "uneducated, illiterate, impoverished, violent underclass" will "grow like a cancer," producing "losers who are destroying our schools . . . who are unparented and whose communities are morally bankrupt." Being associated with the more radical left does not imply immunity from the rhetoric of spreading pathology among the black poor. In *The Progressive* Manning Marable reproduces uncritically the mirage of "growing numbers

of juvenile pregnancies" among his litany of "intractable social problems proliferating" in black inner cities despite his observation that
such problems have structural causes and his call for good social-demo-
cratic solutions. Cornel West in *Prophetic Fragments* sounds the alarm
about the cities' "cultural decay and moral disintegration."

This often lurid imagery of pathology naturally points toward a
need for behavioral modification, moral regeneration and special tutelage by black betters, and black middle-class paternalism is as shameless and self-serving now as at the turn of the century. Patterson,
Norton, Wilson and Wilkins announce the middle class's special role in
making certain that the poor are fit into properly two-parent, male-
headed families. Proctor, presumably giving up on adults, wants to use
military discipline to insure that children have "breakfasts with others
at a table." West would send them into churches for moral rehabilitation. And the Committee on Policy for Racial Justice of the Joint Center for Political Studies (whose members include Norton, Wilkins and
Wilson) lauds self-help in its manifesto, *Black Initiative and Governmental Responsibility*, and calls on black "religious institutions, civic
and social organizations, media, entertainers, educators, athletes, public officials, and other community leaders" to "emphasize . . . values."
It was a master stroke of Reagan's second-term spin doctors to sugar-
coat the offensive on the black poor with claptrap about special black
middle-class responsibility for "their" poor and the challenge of self-
help. The black leadership elite fell right into line and quickly institutionalized a cooing patter of noblesse oblige.

From that hegemonic class standpoint there is little room and less
desire to criticize Farrakhan's contemptuous, authoritarian diagnosis
and remedy. As he instructed *The Spotlight:*

> We must be allowed the freedom first to teach our people and put
> them in a state of readiness to receive justice . . . Blacks in America have
> to be concentrated upon, to lift us up in a way that we will become self-
> respecting so that the communities of the world will not mind accepting
> us as an equal member among the community of family of nations . . .
> But when we [the Nation of Islam] get finished with these people, we
> produce dignified intelligent people. The American system can't pro-
> duce that. We can.

In sum, Louis Farrakhan has become prominent in the public eye
because he appeals symbolically both to black frustration and alienation in this retrograde era and to white racism, disingenuousness and

naïveté. He also responds to the status anxiety, paternalistic class prejudice and ideological conservatism embedded within black petit-bourgeois race militancy. His antiwhite or anti-Semitic views are neither the most important issue surrounding Farrakhan nor the greatest reason for concern about his prospects for growing influence. After all, he will never be able to impose his beliefs—no matter how obnoxious or heinous—on any group of white Americans. More significant, and more insidious, is the fact that racial units are his essential categories for defining and comprehending political life. That fact obviously establishes him on common conceptual ground with all manner of racists. (*The Spotlight* was happily curious about whether he and David Duke actually would disagree on anything in a debate rumored to be in the works.)

His racial essentialism has an appeal for many blacks in a purely demagogic way. It also gives him an outlook that seems disarmingly sensible to whites—at least those who can overlook his fiery pro-black sentiments and devil theories—because it fits into the hoary "What do your people want?" framework for discussing black Americans. That essentialist outlook also underlies his self-help rhetoric, which appeals to both whites and middle-class blacks. Whites like it because it implies that blacks should pull themselves up by their bootstraps and not make demands on government. Middle-class blacks like it because it legitimizes a "special role" for the black petite bourgeoisie over the benighted remainder of the race. In both views, "self-help" with respect to ordinary black Americans replaces a standard expectation of democratic citizenship—a direct, unmediated relation to the institutions and processes of public authority. Self-help ideology is a form of privatization and therefore implies cession of the principle that government is responsible for improving the lives of the citizenry and advancing egalitarian interests; it also rests on a premise that black Americans cannot effectively make demands on the state directly as citizens but must go through intermediaries constituted as guardians of collective racial self-interest. Ironically, "self-help" requires dissolution of the autonomous civic self of Afro-Americans.

The link between self-help rhetoric and racial custodianship is as old as Booker T. Washington, the model of organic racial leadership Farrakhan articulates. The idea that black racial interests can be embodied in a single individual has always been attractively economical for white elites. Giving Washington a railroad car for his own use to avoid Jim Crow was a lot cheaper for white elites and less disruptive than socioeconomic democratization and preservation of citizenship rights. Jesse

Jackson updated the claim to organic racial leadership and brokerage by enlisting mass media technology to legitimize it, and Farrakhan is following in Jackson's steps. Because of his organization and ideology, however, Farrakhan more than his predecessors throws into relief the dangerous, fascistic presumptions inscribed at the foundation of that model. That—underscored by the brownshirt character of the Fruit of Islam and the history of the old Nation during Farrakhan's ascent—is what makes him uniquely troubling. But demonizing him misses the point; it is the idea of organic representation of the racial collectivity that makes him possible.

It is that idea, whether expressed flamboyantly by Farrakhan or in the more conventional petit-bourgeois synecdoche that folds all black interests into a narrow class agenda, that most needs to be repudiated. Its polluting and demobilizing effects on Afro-American political life have never been more visible, thanks to promotion by the mass media's special combination of racist cynicism and gullibility. Cheap hustlers and charlatans, corrupt and irresponsible public officials and perpetrators of any sort of fraud can manipulate the generic defensiveness decreed by a politics of organic racial representation to support their scams or sidestep their guilt—all too often for offenses against black constituents. A straight line connects Washington's Tuskegee Machine, which sought to control access to philanthropic support for racial agendas, to Jackson's insinuation that "respect" for him is respect for all black Americans to Farrakhan's death threat against Milton Coleman to the pathetic specter of the rogues' gallery of Farrakhan, Illinois Representative Gus Savage, the Rev. Al Sharpton, the Rev. George Stallings and Tawana Brawley sharing the stage with Marion Barry at a rally to defend the corrupt Mayor's honor. That image captures the depth of crisis of political vision that racial organicism has wrought.

BEATING ABOUT EXECUTIVE PRIVILEGE

•

No sooner did he say—with a vibrato
    of vainglory in the saying,
    less grievance than gratification—
        "I've had it!" than he
was moved, or behooved, to equivocate
    his past possession by a less
    martial note (having had it, does one
        ever get it back?),
and he then observed, "I'm not trying to sound
    the tocsin of war." And by that phrase,
    in what we are pleased to call the Media
        (denoting the mid-
province of speech, neither phatic nor refined),
    panic was sown: "To sound the *what?*"
    asked one reporter, floored. "What do TOXINS
        sound like anyway,
and how in hell would *he* know?" Another phoned
    from Camp David to inquire if
    tocsins were like trumpets and, being so,
        could sound . . . uncertain.
CNN, ever mindful of literary
    precedent in White House matters,
    heard "dachshunds of war" and pondered if this
        could be a condign
allusion to "cry 'Havoc!' and let slip
    the dogs of war"—the kind of thing

regularly bruited about the green
    quadrangles of Yale.

It is not dogs which have been let slip, not
    dachshunds of war, nor the other
kind of toxin (though appropriate
    enough, that poison,
to our circumstance): the dread alarum
    which he was "not trying to sound"
the world has heard, and because *he* has had
    whatever it was,
we are having it. Across the country, night
    by night, our sleepless bedrooms glow
with the blue languor of opium dens.
    Who was it first said
TV is the opiate of the masses?
    If he was right, and we are hooked,
then war must be the crack of presidents . . .
    All week we watch as
the huge projectiles rise like . . . penises,
    and we wonder, before quashing
such speculation as absurd, childish,
    out of the question, if on either side—*our* constitutional
dictatorship and *their* frenzied
    following—we are mustered and mastered
    by anything more
than such erectile follies; whether all our
    bad history is but the mauled
extension of our rulers' . . . yes, just so,
    of our rulers' *rule*?

Richard Howard

CHOICE CAN *SAVE* PUBLIC EDUCATION

Deborah W. Meier

•

BEFORE DECIDING TO go down in history as a war president, George Bush called himself our "education President," announcing ambitious goals to make American schoolchildren first in the world by the year 2000. These goals were applauded by politicians, educators and corporate leaders across the political spectrum. America's future itself, they all declared, is at stake, but, unlike the gulf war, they believe this future can be bought cheaply.

The conservatives have the answer: choice. It's a solution, they note, that doesn't require throwing money at schools. And furthermore it's politically correct. The marketplace, they remind us gloatingly, will cure what a socialistic system of schooling has produced: the miseducation of our young. The most articulate and contentious proponents of marketplace choices in education are John Chubb and Terry Moe, whose articles, speeches and book, *Politics, Markets, and America's Schools*, have sparked widespread debate. But this is not merely a battle of words. A number of localities and several states have initiated systems of choice, often using Chubb and Moe's data to support their programs. While Chubb and Moe contend that they favor public education, what they mean is public funding for education. Public institutions are their enemy. They make no bones about it: Private is good, public is bad. Private equals enterprising, public equals stifling bureaucracy and destructive political influence.

The original right-wing challenge to public education, vouchers for private schools, went down to a resounding defeat. The newest star on the right, choice, is both a more powerful challenger and a more interesting one. Because progressives are on the defensive, their concern with equity leads them to attack choice reflexively as inherently elitist (naturally, it has few friends among educational bureaucrats either). This is, I believe, a grave mistake. The argument over choice, unlike the one about vouchers, offers progressives an opportunity. After all, it wasn't so long ago that progressive educators were enthusiastically supporting schools of choice, usually called "alternative schools." However, those alternatives were always on the fringe, as though the vast majority were doing just fine, thanks. We now have a chance to make such alternatives the mainstream, not just for avant-garde "misfits" and "nerds" or those most "at risk."

Americans have long supported a dual school system. Whether schools are public or private, the social class of the students was and continues to be the single most significant factor in determining a school's intellectual values and how it works. The higher the student body's socioeconomic status, the meatier the curriculum, the more open-ended the discussion, the less rote and rigid the pedagogy, the more respectful the tone, the more rigorous the expectations, the greater the staff autonomy. Numerous studies have confirmed a simple fact: The primary factor in determining the quality of schools (as well as programs within schools) is not whether they are public or private but who attends them. Changing this is what education reform is all about. What we need is strategies for giving to everyone what the rich have always valued. After all, the rich have had good public schools as well as good private schools. If we use choice to undermine public education, we will increase the duality of our educational system. If we want to use it to undermine the historic duality of our schools, the kind of plan we adopt is more important than choice advocates like Moe and Chubb acknowledge.

When I first entered teaching, and when my own children began their long trek through urban public schools, I too was an unreconstructed advocate of the strictly zoned neighborhood school. I knew all about choice, a favorite tactic of racists escaping desegregation. There were even moments when I wished we could legally outlaw any selective public or private institutions, although I could readily see the risks—

not to mention the political impossibility—of doing so. That's no longer the case. My change of heart has personal overtones: I've spent the past sixteen years in a public school district in East Harlem that has pioneered choice, and I have founded a network of small schools of choice in that community: the Central Park East schools. All of District 4's schools are small, largely self-governing and pedagogically innovative. They are schools with a focus, with staffs brought together around common ideas, free to shape a whole set of school parameters in accord with those ideas.

It would have been impossible to carry out this ambitious agenda without choice. Choice was the prerequisite. It was an enabling strategy for District Superintendent, Anthony Alvarado, who wanted to get rid of the tradition of zoned, factory-style, bureaucratically controlled schools that has long been synonymous with urban public schooling and replace it with a different image of what "public" could mean. The District 4 way was deceptively simple; it required no vast blue print, just a new mindset. Within ten years, starting in 1974, District 4 totally changed the way 15,000 mostly poor Latino and African-American youngsters got educated without ever pulling the rug out from under either parents or professionals. The words "restructuring" and "reform" were never used—this was, after all, the late 1970s and early 1980s. The Superintendent sidestepped resistance by building a parallel system of choice, until even its opponents found themselves benefiting from it.

To begin with, Alvarado initiated a few model schools open to parental choice, locating them within existing buildings where space was available. He sought schools that would look excitingly different, that would have a loyal, if small, following among families and would have strong professional leadership. Alvarado and his Alternate Schools director, Sy Fliegel, gave such schools extraordinary support in the form of greater flexibility with regard to staffing, use of resources, organization of time, forms of assessment and on-site advice and counseling. Wherever possible, they also ran interference with Central Board of Education bureaucracy. When people in the "regular" schools complained of favoritism, Alvarado and Fliegel assured them that they'd be favorites too if they had some new ideas they wanted to try. Some even accepted the challenge. Each year, more schools were added. They generally started with a few classes and the largest grew to no more than 300 students. Some stayed as small as fifty. Within half a dozen years most of the students in the middle and junior-high grades were attending alternative schools, and each district building housed several autonomous schools.

Schools were no longer equated with buildings. Where there had been twenty-two schools in twenty-two buildings, in less than ten years fifty-one schools occupied twenty buildings (along with two housed in a nearby high school). Only then did the Superintendent announce Stage Two: Henceforth no junior high would serve a specific geopraphic area. All families of incoming seventh graders would have to choose. The district provided sixth-grade parents and teachers with lots of information to assist them in their choice, although probably word-of-mouth was the decisive factor (as it is in private schools). Sixteen neighborhood elementary schools remain intact, with space reserved first for those living within the designated zone, but Alvarado promised that parents were free to shop around if space existed. In addition, the district supported the creation of twenty alternative elementary schools, eight of them bilingual. As a result, the neighborhood elementary schools became smaller and, in effect, also schools of choice. Alvarado even enticed a former independent elementary school to enter the public sector, leaving intact its parental governing board.

A majority of the new schools were fairly traditional, although more focused in terms of their themes (such as music, science or journalism) and more intimate and family-oriented due to their small size. Size also meant that regardless of the formal structure, all the participants were generally informally involved in decisions about school life. Most of the schools were designed by small groups of teachers tired of compromising what they thought were their most promising ideas. As a result there was a level of energy and esprit, a sense of co-ownership that made these schools stand out. They developed, over time, differences in pedagogy, style of leadership, forms of governance, tone and climate. A few schools (such as the three Central Park East schools) used this opening to try radically different forms of teaching and learning, testing and assessment, school/family collaboration and staff self-government. In this one small district, noted only a decade earlier as one of the worst in the city, there were by 1984 dozens of schools with considerable citywide reputations and stature, alongside dozens of others that were decidedly more humane, where kids found it hard to fall through the cracks and teachers were enthusiastic about teaching. A few were mediocre or worse; one or two had serious problems. The consensus from the streams of observers who came to see, and those who studied the data, was that the change was real and lasting. What was even more important, however, was that the stage was set for trying out more innovative educational ideas as professionals had the opportunity to be more directly involved in decision making. It was not a cost-free idea, but the added expense was small compared with many other heralded reform efforts; it was less than the cost of one additional teacher for every newly created school.

If this were the best of all possible worlds, the next ten years would have been used to launch Stage Three. The district would have studied what was not happening within these fifty-three small schools, examined more closely issues of equity, tracked their graduates over time, studied the families' reasons for making choices and looked for strategies to prod schools into taking on tougher challenges. The Central Board would have worked out ways to legitimize these "wild-cat" schools while also encouraging other districts to follow a similar path. Under the leadership of Alvarado's successor, Carlos Medina, District 4 launched Stage Three. But it was not the best of all worlds, and the district found itself on the defensive for reasons that had nothing to do with education in the fifty-three schools. As a result, Medina's efforts to move ahead were thwarted, and new leadership hostile to choice was installed. Today, in 1991, District 4 stands once again at a crossroads, with new sympathetic leadership both within the district and at the Central Board, although badly hobbled by the threat of draconian budget cuts. That the fifty-three schools have survived the past few years in a system that not only never officially acknowledged their existence but often worked to thwart them is a tribute to the loyalty and ingenuity that choice and co-ownership together engender.

While the District 4 story suggests that choice is fully compatible with public education and an efficient vehicle for setting in motion school reform, it is foolhardy not to acknowledge that in the political climate of the 1990s choice runs the risk of leading to privatization.

However, it's not enough these days to cry out in alarm at the possible demise of public education. If public schools are seen as incapable of responding to the demand for wholesale reform, why should we expect the public to resist privatization? Maybe private schools aren't much better, but if public education has proved so inept at meeting the challenge, if it has had such a poor history of serving equity or excellence, it's easy to see the lure of privatization. Given this history, why not just let the chips fall where they may?

The question is a good one. If we want to preserve public education as the norm for most citizens then we'd better have important and positive reasons for doing so, reasons that are compelling to parents, teachers and the broader voting public. To do so we must make the case that the rationale for improving education goes far beyond the problem employers face in recruiting sufficient numbers of competent and reliable workers or our chagrin at finding the United States at the bottom in test scores for math and science. At least as important is the role education plays as a tool in reviving and maintaining the fabric of our democratic institutions. While public education may be useful as an industrial policy, it is *essential* to healthy public life in a democracy. The two go together, and never has this been clearer than it is today. If we cannot make a convincing case for this, we will see our public schools dismantled in one way or another, either by a misused choice or by erosion and neglect as funds dry up for public education and private schooling becomes the norm for those who can afford to opt out. The status quo plus cosmetic changes won't save public education, at least not in our major urban areas.

The alternative to privatization is good public education, and choice is an essential tool in the effort to create such education. It is the necessary catalyst for the kind of dramatic restructuring that most agree is needed to produce a far better educated citizenry. Virtually all the major educational task forces, for example, agree that dramatic changes will require removing the stifling regulations that presently keep schools tied to outmoded practices, to doing things in lockstep. They agree that if we want change, we'll have to put up with non-conformity and some messiness. We'll have to allow those most involved (teachers, administrators, parents) to exercise greater on-site power to put their collective wisdom into practice. Once we do all this, however, school X and school Y are going to start doing things differently. How then can we ignore personal "tastes"? Besides, it's a lot easier to undertake difficult innovations successfully if teachers, parents and students are in agreement.

We can't expect the marketplace, public or private, to stimulate this kind of reform magically. Private schools as an example of the market at work aren't very inspiring when it comes to innovation. They may encourage livelier educational practice, but in general they are as convention-bound as public schools. They mostly differ in an invidious way, much like their public school sisters. There's a hierarchy among them, based mostly on how choosy the school can be about whom it accepts. The fact that the choosiest schools attract higher-status families and select only the most promising students insures their success; replication, by definition, is impossible. Their value lies in their scarcity. This kind of marketplace has led not to innovation but to imitation on a steadily watered-down basis, appealing not so much to different "tastes" but to different means and expectations. The dual system has remained alive and well in the private sector. But if the marketplace is not a magical answer, neither, experience suggests, can we expect that forced change from the top down will work. What results from such bureaucratically mandated change is anger and sabotage on the part of unwilling, unready parents and professionals as well as the manipulation of data by ambitious bureaucrats and timid administrators. The end result: a gradual return to the status quo.

To improve education for all children will require more than one simple cure-all. It requires a set of strategies. For starters, federal, state and local initiatives can stimulate districts to adopt one or another variation of the District 4 story: providing incentives to districts to break up their oversized buildings and redesign them into many small schools, easily accessible for families to choose from. Once we think small, we can even imagine locating new schools in other available public and private spaces, near workplaces as well as residences, in places where young people can interact with adults going about their daily business. While no system of rules and regulations can insure equity, public policy can assure that resources are fairly allocated. It can go further by establishing guidelines that promote appropriate social, ethnic, racial and academic diversity.

We'll also need a better quality of information if we want to promote long-range school change. We'll need a public that is not confused by misleading data or quickly discouraged by the absence of dramatically improved statistics. Who knows today what the definition of a high school dropout is or what "reading on grade level" means? We'll need to place less reliance on standardized high-stakes testing systems. Good lay information will encourage the kind of lively, even contentious, dialogue about the nature and purpose of education that is so badly needed. Choice offers no guaranteed solution to these concerns, but the existence of clear and coherent alternatives encourages such debate.

Similarly, greater school-based autonomy goes well with choice. School-based management itself does not trigger innovation, but it offers a much better audience for such innovation. Empowered faculties and families are better able to hear new ideas and less likely to sabotage them. Innovation no longer appears threatening. School-based management combined with the idea of small schools of choice allows both parents and teachers to embrace new ideas even if they cannot convince all their colleagues or all the school's parents. Furthermore, once we set loose those who are already eager to "restructure," it will be easier to encourage successive waves of innovators and risk takers. While R&D in education can't take place in labs separate from real life, as it can in most industries, no one wants to be a guinea pig. Creating a school different from what any of those who work in the system are familiar with, one that runs counter to the experiences of most families, is possible only if teachers, parents and students have time to agree on changes and a choice on whether or not they want to go along with them.

Since school officials, like parents, are naturally conservative and reluctant to change their habits, we don't need to sign them all up at once. What's needed first is a range of models, examples for teachers and the public to scrutinize and learn from. Credibility will require a critical mass of such schools; at this stage it is hard to know how many. But we can go only as fast and as far as those who bear the burden of change can tolerate. Putting more money into schools does not guarantee success but it can accelerate the pace of change. Of course, taking money out slows down the possibilities for change too.

In short, choice is necessary but not sufficient. There's something galling about the idea that you're stuck in a particular school that's not working for you unless you are rich enough to buy yourself out of it. Still, if it worked for most students, we'd put up with it, but it doesn't. What's not necessary is to buy into the rhetoric that too often surrounds choice: about the rigors of the marketplace, the virtues of private schooling and the inherent mediocrity of public places and public spaces. By using choice judiciously, we can have the virtues of the marketplace without some of its vices, and we can have the virtues of the best private schools without undermining public education.

TAKING THE DEMOCRATIC WAY

Mary Kaldor

•

DURING THE 1980S I had three wishes. I wished for the end of the cold war, for democracy in Eastern Europe and for a disarmament process to begin. I wished for them every time I stirred a Christmas pudding, caught an autumn leaf or shared a chicken wishbone. And all my wishes came true. But just as in the fairy stories, what I got was quite different from what I expected.

Instead of entering an era of peace, harmony and cooperation, we seem to be sliding into an era of chaos, violence and division. The Western military machine thundered away in the Persian Gulf. The economies and environments of Eastern Europe are devastated, and a new "golden curtain" is dropping to protect the rich West from Eastern economic refugees. New nationalist, religious and ethnic fundamentalisms—what Jacques Delors, president of the European Commission, calls "ideologies of exclusion"— are growing everywhere. Bloody civil wars in the Soviet Union seem increasingly likely. Meanwhile, the West is still doing business as usual. Arms cuts have been minor. NATO not only still exists but has expanded to include a united Germany, even though the Warsaw Pact has disintegrated. There is no commitment to solving any of the deep-rooted global problems we face. For the most part, the West has not shed its cold war conditioning. Only in Eastern Europe has the cold war ended.

There were two main Western reactions to last year's events in East-

ern Europe. Both stem from long-held assumptions about the nature of
the cold war, and both have very dangerous consequences. One is the
mood of triumphalism and self-congratulation. This was alleged to be a
victory for the West, for American as opposed to European values. The
West, said Margaret Thatcher, held out a "beacon of freedom" to the
peoples of the East. This is the "end of history," said Francis
Fukuyama, the victory for the "universal homogeneous state," which
combines political freedom and consumerism. Western triumphalism is
an expression of the orthodox view of the cold war as an epic struggle
between freedom and totalitarianism. The West was identified with freedom and the East with totalitarianism. It was Western military strength
that was supposed to have kept totalitarianism at bay. For some thinkers,
freedom is inextricably linked to free markets and a neoliberal ideology.

The problem is that the West cannot be equated with freedom. Certainly, Western countries are democratic countries and Eastern Europeans lusted after Western democracy. But the West did little to
support struggles for freedom either in the Third World or in Eastern
Europe. On the contrary, Western governments supported brutal military dictatorships in the Third World. And the creation in the late
1940s of a West German state and a Western military alliance entailed
the abandonment of the peoples of Eastern Europe.

Far from countering a Soviet military threat to Western Europe,
NATO legitimized the Soviet presence in Eastern Europe. In the 1970s,
during the détente period, there seemed to be a possibility of some
evolution toward more open societies in Eastern Europe. Then came
the emergence of Solidarity in 1980. The crackdown on Solidarity
occurred at the height of the new cold war, in 1981, and was rationalized in terms of aggressive Western postures. The renunciation of the
Brezhnev Doctrine triggered the wave of revolutions in Central Europe
in 1989. That would have been impossible without the Intermediate
Nuclear Forces (I.N.F.) treaty and the new détente mood engendered
after 1985 by the arms control process.

The Western triumphalists see little necessity for big reductions in
military spending or for increased economic cooperation with Eastern
Europe or the Third World. Conservatives argue that if Western military strength brought Communism to its knees, then the same approach
can be applied in other parts of the world—to tin-pot dictators actually
created by the West. Hence, the gung-ho attitude in the gulf. The struggle between freedom and totalitarianism is being reproduced against
fundamentalists, fanatics and dictators in the Third World, those who,
in Fukuyama's words, are still in the throes of history.

The orthodox recipe for Eastern European economies is neoliberal-ism: "Copy us and you can join the West." But of course Eastern Euro-peans are being urged to adopt policies of structural adjustment that the West would not dream of adopting. Imagine the United States reducing its deficit and external debt through austerity measures such as those imposed on Poland. Imagine if Western Europe had adopted full convertibility and free trade after World War II. Already, real wages in Poland have fallen by more than a quarter. Unemployment, poverty and inequality, as well as environmentally induced diseases, are all increasing.

The danger is that Eastern Europe will join the Third World, not the West. A new West-East division of Europe, along the Oder-Neisse Line, could well parallel the North-South rift in the Americas. A Mexi-can border could split the continent of Europe. And the Third Worldization of Eastern Europe could give rise to "ideologies of exclu-sion" and new forms of authoritarianism. It could produce some fanat-ics and fundamentalists to join the band of new enemies in the Third World.

The second Western reaction to the fall of Eastern European Communism is one of nostalgia. Realists like John Lewis Gaddis or John Mearsheimer regret the passing of the "long peace." They view the cold war as a form of great-power rivalry, and they argue that bipolar structures are much more stable than multipolar structures. But this "long peace" was largely confined to northwestern Europe. Eastern Europe was neither peaceful nor stable. There were periodic uprisings (Berlin, 1953; Hungary, 1956; Czechoslovakia, 1968; Poland, 1980–81) that were brutally suppressed. There were wars and revolutions throughout the Third World; indeed, more people have died in wars since 1945 than in the two world wars. There have even been wars in Europe—in Greece and Turkey, and in Northern Ireland.

The realists assumed that nationalism and religious fundamentalism were somehow deep-frozen during the postwar period and would emerge intact when the ice melted. The truth is that these primitive attitudes were nurtured by forty years of totalitarian rule. They were a reaction to a lifetime's experience of lies and oppression. After all, the coalition governments elected after World War II in Central Europe were center-left governments. Without the cold war, those countries might have been as stable as Austria or Finland.

The realists cannot envisage a future without superpowers. Paul Kennedy, author of *The Rise and Fall of the Great Powers*, describes a cyclical process stretching indefinitely into the future. Great powers become powerful through economic strength, but then they find it necessary to spend their wealth on military power. The Soviet Union has collapsed and the United States is declining economically, so goes the argument; now it is the turn of Western Europe and Japan. A new military structure is needed to maintain stability in Europe. In particular, the idea that Western Europe should establish a unified defense community, so that it can join the select club of global policemen, is gaining ground. The proposal for Western European defense integration has acquired considerable impetus during the gulf crisis. Essentially, this is a vision of a world of competing military blocs, in which the rich countries insulate themselves militarily from the "instability" generated by the cold war years.

Both Western reactions presuppose a fundamental conflict between East and West. Both emphasize the role of military strength in defeating totalitarianism (the triumphalists) and keeping the peace (the realists). Both are views from above, addressed to government policy-makers. But another view emerged from the dialogue between parts of the Western European peace movements and Eastern European peace, green and human rights groups during the 1980s. That is the view that there was not a fundamental conflict *between* East and West. Rather, there were fundamental conflicts *within* East and West. The idea of an East-West conflict, the invocation of the "other," was a method by which governments could manage these domestic conflicts.

I use the term "imaginary war" to describe this process. "Deterrence" did not represent preparation for some future war; rather, it was a way of acting out the East-West conflict day after day throughout the postwar period. Through military exercises, the deployment of troops and weapons, the scenarios of military planners, the games of espionage and counterespionage, and the research, development and production of military technology we behaved as though we were in a war situation, as though World War II had never really ended. This imaginary war had profound consequences for the way society was organized in both East and West. There were two distinct systems in East and West: One was democratic and capitalist and the other was socialist and totalitarian. But the two systems were not in conflict. On the contrary, they complemented each other. They shared a need for an imaginary war.

According to this interpretation, the cold war was ended by a wave of popular movements in both East and West that challenged the imaginary-war hypothesis and discredited the cold war idea. It was the Eastern European democracy movements, not Western governments, that brought about the final collapse of Communism. And it was the Western European peace movements that first challenged the status quo in Europe. Some 5 million people demonstrated in the capitals of Western Europe against the new cold war in 1981 and again in 1983.

It was the pressure of public opinion that led to the zero-option proposal on which the I.N.F. treaty was based. And it was from the Western European peace movement that Gorbachev drew a plethora of ideas and proposals unleashed after 1985. Even more important perhaps was the strategy of "détente from below," which gained importance during the second half of the 1980s. This was the strategy of building links with independent groups in Eastern Europe campaigning for democracy.

"Détente from below" was important in two respects. First, it established the integrity of large parts of the peace movement. It made it impossible to marginalize the peace movement, as had been done in the past, with the charge that peace activists were agents of the Kremlin. Second, it helped to encourage and provide support for the new peace and human rights groups that emerged during the 1980s all over Eastern Europe, groups that played a key role in the revolutions of 1989.

From the perspective of the peace movement, the end of the cold war offered a historic opportunity to reduce reliance on military force and to develop more cooperative forms of international relations, between both East and West, and North and South. What is needed now in Europe is to incorporate Eastern Europe into European institutions and to develop cooperative relationships so that Western Europe does not have to build a new wall. Many people are now talking about the role of the Conference on Security and Cooperation in Europe, better known as the Helsinki process. This new European security system would also include all of the Soviet Union and North America and would displace the bloc system and put more emphasis on nonmilitary aspects of security. There is also talk of a Marshall Plan to help clean up the environment of Eastern Europe.

Some of these ideas can be applied to the Third World. Western military strength cannot counter the new enemy—regional dictators, fanatics, terrorists and so on. In the long run, the only way to cope with the Husseins and Qaddafis of the world is through the control of military technology and through real efforts to develop cooperative relationships—to address the social, economic and political conditions that give rise to authoritarianism. But alas, the gulf conflict has put war and militarism back on the agenda. It reinforced the cold war assumption that military strength is the way to cope with totalitarian dictatorships. The Western victory in the gulf could destroy, at least for a time, the hopes held out by the end of the cold war. It will be taken as confirmation that both the triumphalists and the realists are right.

Perhaps the most important lesson of the 1980s is the role of pressure from below. If we are to keep alive a peaceful vision of the post—cold war world, then what is important is to confront the cold war culture—to work for changes in attitudes, new forms of self-organization, the development of democratic relationships. One of the key concepts of the democratic movements was the rediscovery of civil society—the notion that change comes about through the development of autonomous citizens' groups, movements or initiatives that can articulate public discontent, organize social activities and negotiate with governments.

Liberal Western commentators have interpreted the current emphasis on civil society in Eastern and Central Europe as the traditional eighteenth-century concept of civil society, as opposed to anarchic society; of democratic relationships replacing relations of violence. Writers like Ralf Dahrendorf and Timothy Garton Ash have suggested that there were no new ideas in the revolution of 1989. Yet, as articulated by Adam Michnik, George Konrad and Vaclav Havel, the concept of civil society suggests an entirely new form of politics appropriate to confront both the repression and bureaucracy of the single-party state and the electoral machinery of modern Western parties. They emphasize strengthening autonomous, self-organized civic institutions rather than capturing state power; changing the relationship between state and civil society; and, above all, generating an informed debate among those who are not seeking power, who are not watching polls or manipulating public opinion through slogans and advertising. All this has had considerable resonance in Western Europe. Havel has talked about the need to "make a real political force out of a phenomenon so ridiculed by the technicians of power—the phenomenon of the human conscience."

The Helsinki Citizens Assembly, founded in Prague in October 1990, is intended to institutionalize this idea, to provide the kernel of an all-European civil society. The assembly, which was opened by Havel, attracted some 900 people from all over Europe and North America, representing a wide range of citizens' groups and civic institutions. For the first time, Lithuanians and Azerbaijanis, Scots and Welsh, Canadians and Americans, Germans from both East and West, not to mention Scandinavians and Italians, sat down together to discuss one another's experiences and plan future projects. They agreed to set up a working group to study economic alternatives to neoliberalism, to create a Forum for Reconciliation to find ways of solving national issues in a peaceful way, to plan campaigns for disarmament and for the democratization of European institutions, and to build a range of networks on nuclear energy, arms conversion, women's issues, etc., in Europe and North America. The aim is to avoid a new cold war between a rich consumerist and armed West and the fundamentalists and fanatics of East and South—to seek a democratic alternative to both.

THE LOSS

•

Russia has lost Russia in Russia.
Russia searches for itself
   like a cut finger in snow,
     a needle in a hayloft,
like an old blind woman madly stretching her hand in fog,
searching with hopeless incantation for her lost milk cow.

We buried our icons.
   We didn't believe in our own great books.
     We fight only with alien grievances.

Is it true that we didn't survive under our own yoke,
becoming for ourselves worse than foreign enemies?
Is it true that we are doomed to live only in the silk
nightgown of idealism, eaten by moths?—
   Or in numbered prison robes?

Is it true that epilepsy is our national character?
Or convulsions of pride?
   Or convulsions of self-humiliation?
Ancient rebellions against new copper kopecks,
Against such foreign fruits as potatoes—
   now only a harmless dream.

Today's rebellion swamps the entire Kremlin
   like a mortal tide—

Is it true that we Russians have only one unhappy choice?
The ghost of Tsar Ivan the Terrible?
   Or the Ghost of Tsar Chaos?
So many impostors. Such "imposterity."

Everyone is a leader, but no one leads.
We are confused as to which banners and slogans to carry.
And such a fog in our heads
   that everyone is wrong
      and everyone is guilty in everything.

We already walked enough in such fog,
in blood up to our knees.
Lord, it's enough to punish us.
Forgive us, pity us.

Is it true that we no longer exist?
Or are we not yet born?
We are birthing now,
But it's so painful to be born again.

March 1991
Yevgeny Yevtushenko
Soviet poet
Translated by James Reagan and the author

THREE DAYS THAT SHOOK THE KREMLIN

Katrina vanden Heuvel

•

THE IGNOMINIOUS COLLAPSE of the eight-man junta that sought to overthrow Mikhail Gorbachev was an astonishing reversal of fortune and a stunning repudiation of the authoritarian past. But the crisis inside the Soviet Union is not over. The institutions that sent the tanks into the streets may be discredited but the problems that gave the reactionaries their pretext still exist. It appears that we have witnessed a victory in the battle for Soviet democracy—but not the end of the war itself.

It was never a mystery whom the coup leaders represented. All Soviet institutions are split between reformers and conservatives, but the people who orchestrated this counterreformation spoke for the reactionary wings of the military, the K.G.B., the Communist Party bureaucracy and the state industrial and agricultural ministries, which have branches in all of the fifteen republics. Centered in Moscow, with octopuslike tentacles extending to every town, these pillars of the old order have long been viewed by democratic forces as a kind of ominous "sixteenth republic."

Behind the scenes, the hard-liners had ferociously opposed Gorbachev's reforms since they were launched in 1985. But the last straw was the Nine-Plus-One accord, which Gorbachev signed with Russian President Boris Yeltsin and other republic leaders last April. It promised a new union treaty, a democratic constitution and multiparty national elections next year. The specter of even more, and institution-alized, democracy was too much. The sixteenth republic struck back.

The extraordinary images of popular resistance in Moscow's streets, led by Boris Yeltsin from the headquarters of the Russian Republic's popularly elected Parliament, should not lead us to believe that the law and order promised by the coup leaders lacked popular support. Soviet public opinion polls show that a sizable part of the population ranks the fostering of democratic values below increasing the food supply, solving consumer shortages and cutting street crime. This is not sur-prising in a country with centuries of unbroken authoritarian rule—czarist and Communist. Compared with that tradition, democratic experience, limited to the *perestroika* years, and democratic values are new. Authoritarianism and democracy have coexisted uneasily for nearly seven years and were in open conflict last week over a fissure run-ning through the political soul of the nation.

For years Western commentators and ultraradical Soviet intellectu-als have charged Gorbachev with implementing his reforms too slowly. Last week those critics saw the true nature of the forces that have blocked, menaced and threatened his *perestroika* program since 1985. After belittling what Gorbachev accomplished, they should now marvel at how much he has achieved.

Here in the United States, we must ask what the Bush Administra-tion did and did not do—and what it should now do—to truly help Gorbachev's reform process. When he first came to power calling for "fundamental reforms" of the neo-Stalinist system, he was dismissed by the majority of American commentators as little more than a tech-nocrat, "a Stalin in Gucci shoes." Many Western policy-makers charac-terized Gorbachev as an obstacle to rather than a force for democracy. And though the struggle was and remains essentially an internal Soviet matter, it is both untrue and irresponsible to deny that the United States could have played a more positive and supportive role in the struggle for democracy.

Despite Bush's noisy embrace of him (and Yeltsin) last week, Gor-bachev was wagering his personal authority and, as it turned out, his own life, when he conducted a conciliatory policy toward Washington in hopes of enticing it to meet him halfway. By any measurement, the United States has not traversed a quarter of the way. All the conces-sions have been on the Soviet side, further undermining Gorbachev's position at home among the national security elite. Moreover, the 1989 invasion of Panama and the war in Iraq dealt a severe blow to Gorbachev's "new thinking," which ruled out force to settle international differences, and thus radically undermined his argument that it was necessary and safe to demilitarize the Soviet system. The gulf war also emboldened and strengthened the zealous guardians of the old national security order, already enraged by Gorbachev and former foreign minister Eduard Shevardnadze's policies. Forced to watch in dismay as Communist parties collapsed in Eastern Europe, they resented the betrayal of their prized ally in the Middle East.

As the friends and foes of tank politics confronted each other inside the Soviet Union last week, there could be no doubt about what Gorbachev had achieved and what was at stake. For the first time in Russian and Soviet history, after centuries of authoritarian rule, the country's leader had crossed the Rubicon to democracy. That historic step alone has earned Gorbachev a remarkable place in his country's, and the world's, history. For those who continue to insist that he did too little too late, let it be said that without Gorbachev's reforms, there would have been no citadel of democracy in Yeltsin's Russian Parliament, no nationalist movements in the republics, no press struggling to stay free and, in all likelihood, few if any demonstrators in the streets.

A reformation of such historic dimensions as *perestroika* could not be expected to unfold quickly, painlessly, smoothly or without tragedies. In the coup's collapse, the world has witnessed an extraordinary case of democratic ideas defeating naked force. But the battle for democracy is not over.

CANON TO THE RIGHT OF ME . . .

Katha Pollitt

•

FOR THE PAST couple of years we've all been witness to a furious debate about the literary canon. What books should be assigned to students? What books should critics discuss? What books should the rest of us read, and who are "we" anyway? Like everyone else, I've given these questions some thought, and when an invitation came my way, I leaped to produce my own manifesto. But to my surprise, when I sat down to write—in order to discover, as E. M. Forster once said, what I really think—I found that I agreed with all sides in the debate at once.

Take the conservatives. Now, this rather dour collection of scholars and diatribists—Allan Bloom, Hilton Kramer, John Silber and so on—are not a particularly appealing group of people. They are arrogant, they are rude, they are gloomy, they do not suffer fools gladly, and everywhere they look, fools are what they see. All good reasons not to elect them to public office, as the voters of Massachusetts recently decided. But what is so terrible, really, about what they are saying? I too believe that some books are more profound, more complex, more essential to an understanding of our culture than others; I too am appalled to think of students graduating from college not having read Homer, Plato, Virgil, Milton, Tolstoy—all writers, dead white Western men though they be, whose works have meant a great deal to me. As a teacher of literature and of writing, I too have seen at first hand how ill-educated many students are, and how little aware they are of this important fact about themselves. Last year I taught a graduate seminar in the writing of poetry. None of my students had read more than a smattering of poems by anyone, male or female, published more than ten years ago. Robert Lowell was as far outside their frame of reference as Alexander Pope. When I gently suggested to one student that it might benefit her to read some poetry if she planned to spend her life writing it, she told me that yes, she knew she should read more but when she encountered a really good poem it only made her depressed. That contemporary writing has a history which it profits us to know in some depth, that we ourselves were not born yesterday, seems too obvious even to argue.

But ah, say the liberals, the canon exalted by the conservatives is itself an artifact of history. Sure, some books are more rewarding than others, but why can't we change our minds about which books those are? The canon itself was not always as we know it today: Until the 1920s, *Moby-Dick* was shelved with the boys' adventure stories. If T. S. Eliot could single-handedly dethrone the Romantic poets in favor of the neglected Metaphysicals and place John Webster alongside Shakespeare, why can't we dip into the sea of stories and fish out Edith Wharton or Virginia Woolf? And this position too makes a great deal of sense to me. After all, alongside the many good reasons for a book to end up on the required-reading shelf are some rather suspect reasons for its exclusion: because it was written by a woman and therefore presumed to be too slight; because it was written by a black person and therefore presumed to be too unsophisticated or to reflect too special a case. By all means, say the liberals, let's have great books and a shared culture. But let's make sure that all the different kinds of greatness are represented and that the culture we share reflects the true range of human experience.

If we leave the broadening of the canon up to the conservatives, this will never happen, because to them change only means defeat. Look at the recent fuss over the latest edition of the Great Books series published by Encyclopedia Britannica, headed by that old snake-oil salesman Mortimer Adler. Four women have now been added to the series: Virginia Woolf, Willa Cather, Jane Austen and George Eliot. That's nice, I suppose, but really! Jane Austen has been a certified Great Writer for a hundred years! Lionel Trilling said so! There's something truly absurd about the conservatives earnestly sitting in judgment on the illustrious dead, as though up in Writers' Heaven Jane and George and Willa and Virginia were breathlessly waiting to hear if they'd finally made it into the club, while Henry Fielding, newly dropped from

the list, howls in outer darkness and the Brontës, presumably, stamp
their feet in frustration and hope for better luck in twenty years, when
Jane Eyre and *Wuthering Heights* will suddenly turn out to have qualities of greatness never before detected in their pages. It's like Poets'
Corner at Manhattan's Cathedral of St. John the Divine, where mortal
men—and a woman or two—of letters actually vote on which immor-
tals to honor with a plaque, a process no doubt complete with electoral
campaigns, compromise candidates and all the rest of the underside of
the literary life. "No, I'm sorry, I just can't vote for Whitman. I'm a
Washington Irving man myself."

Well, a liberal is not a very exciting thing to be, as *Nation* readers
know, and so we have the radicals, who attack the concepts of "greatness," "shared," "culture" and "lists." (I'm overlooking here the ultra-
radicals, who attack the "privileging" of "texts," as they insist on
calling books, and think one might as well spend one's college years
deconstructing *Leave It to Beaver*.) Who is to say, ask the radicals,
what is a great book? What's so terrific about complexity, ambiguity,
historical centrality and high seriousness? If *The Color Purple*, say,
gets students thinking about their own experience, maybe they ought
to read it and forget about—and here you can fill in the name of whatever classic work you yourself found dry and tedious and never got
around to finishing. For the radicals the notion of a shared culture is a
lie, because it means presenting as universally meaningful and politically neutral books that reflect the interests and experiences and values
of privileged white men at the expense of those of others—women,
blacks, Latinos, Asians, the working class, whoever. Why not scrap the
one-list-for-everyone idea and let people connect with books that are
written by people like themselves about people like themselves? It will
be a more accurate reflection of a multifaceted and conflict-ridden society, and will do wonders for everyone's self-esteem, except, of course,
living white men—but they have too much self-esteem already.

Now, I have to say that I dislike the radicals' vision intensely. How
foolish to argue that Chekhov has nothing to say to a black woman—or,
for that matter, myself—merely because he is Russian, long dead, a
man. The notion that one reads to increase one's self-esteem sounds to
me like more snake oil. Literature is not an aerobics class or a session at
the therapist's. But then I think of myself as a child, leafing through
anthologies of poetry for the names of women. I never would have
admitted that I needed a role model, even if that awful term had
existed back in the prehistory of which I speak, but why was I so
excited to find a female name, even when, as was often the case, it was

attached to a poem of no interest to me whatsoever? Anna Laetitia Bar-
bauld, author of "Life! I know not what thou art/But know that thou
and I must part!"; Lady Anne Lindsay, writer of languid ballads in
incomprehensible Scots dialect; and the other minor female poets
included by chivalrous Sir Arthur Quiller-Couch in the old *Oxford
Book of English Verse*: I have to admit it, just by their presence in that
august volume they did something for me. And although it had nothing
to do with reading or writing, it was an important thing they did.

Now, what are we to make of this spluttering debate, in which
charges of imperialism are met by equally passionate accusations of
vandalism, in which each side hates the others, and yet each one seems
to have its share of reason? Perhaps what we have here is one of those
debates in which the opposing sides, unbeknownst to themselves, share
a myopia that will turn out to be the most telling feature of the whole
discussion: a debate, for instance, like that of our Founding Fathers
over the nature of the franchise. Think of all the energy and passion
spent pondering the question of property qualifications or direct versus legislative elections while all along, unmentioned and unimagined,
was the fact—to us so central—that women and slaves were never considered for any kind of vote.

Something is being overlooked: the state of reading, and books, and
literature in our country at this time. Why, ask yourself, is everyone so
hot under the collar about what to put on the required-reading shelf? It
is because while we have been arguing so fiercely about which books
make the best medicine, the patient has been slipping deeper and
deeper into a coma.

Let us imagine a country in which reading is a popular voluntary
activity. There, parents read books for their own edification and pleasure, and are seen by their children at this silent and mysterious pastime. These parents also read to their children, give them books for
presents, talk to them about books and underwrite, with their taxes, a
public library system that is open all day, every day. In school—where
an attractive library is invariably to be found—the children study certain books together but also have an active reading life of their own.
Years later it may even be hard for them to remember if they read *Jane
Eyre* at home and Judy Blume in class, or the other way around. In college young people continue to be assigned certain books, but far more
important are the books they discover for themselves—browsing in the
library, in bookstores, on the shelves of friends, one book leading to
another, back and forth in history and across languages and cultures.
After graduation they continue to read, and in the fullness of time pro-

duce a new generation of readers. Oh happy land! I wish we all lived there.

In that other country of real readers—voluntary, active, self-determined readers—a debate like the current one over the canon would not be taking place. Or if it did, it would be as a kind of parlor game: What books would *you* take to a desert island? Everyone would know that the top-ten list was merely a tiny fraction of the books one would read in a lifetime. It would not seem racist or sexist or hopelessly hidebound to put Hawthorne on the syllabus and not Toni Morrison. It would be more like putting oatmeal and not noodles on the breakfast menu—a choice part arbitrary, part a nod to the national past, part, dare one say it, a kind of reverse affirmative action: School might frankly be the place where one read the books that are a little off-putting, that have gone a little cold, that you might pass over because they do not address, in reader-friendly contemporary fashion, the issues most immediately at stake in modern life, but that, with a little study, turn out to have a great deal to say. Being on the list wouldn't mean so much. It might even add to a writer's cachet *not* to be on the list, to be in one way or another too heady, too daring, too exciting to be ground up into institutional fodder for teenagers. Generations of high school kids have been turned off to George Eliot by being forced to read *Silas Marner* at a tender age. One can imagine a whole new readership for her if grown-ups were left to approach *Middlemarch* and *Daniel Deronda* with open minds, at their leisure.

Of course, they rarely do. In America today the assumption underlying the canon debate is that the books on the list are the only books that are going to be read, and if the list is dropped no books are going to be read. Becoming a textbook is a book's only chance; all sides take that for granted. And so all agree not to mention certain things that they themselves, as highly educated people and, one assumes, devoted readers, know perfectly well. For example, that if you read only twenty-five, or fifty, or a hundred books, you can't understand them, however well chosen they are. And that if you don't have an independent reading life—and very few students do—you won't *like* reading the books on the list and will forget them the minute you finish them. And that books have, or should have, lives beyond the syllabus—thus, the totally misguided attempt to put current literature in the classroom. How strange to think that people need professorial help to read John Updike or Alice Walker, writers people actually do read for fun. But all sides agree, if it isn't taught, it doesn't count.

Let's look at the canon question from another angle. Instead of asking what books we want others to read, let's ask why we read books ourselves. I think the canon debaters are being a little disingenuous here, are suppressing, in the interest of their own agendas, their personal experience of reading. Sure, we read to understand our American culture and history, and we also read to recover neglected masterpieces, and to learn more about the accomplishments of our subgroup and thereby, as I've admitted about myself, increase our self-esteem. But what about reading for the aesthetic pleasures of language, form, image? What about reading to learn something new, to have a vicarious adventure, to follow the workings of an interesting, if possible skewed, narrow and ill-tempered mind? What about reading for the story? For an expanded sense of sheer human variety? There are a thousand reasons why a book might have a claim on our time and attention other than its canonization. I once infuriated an acquaintance by asserting that Trollope, although in many ways a lesser writer than Dickens, possessed some wonderful qualities Dickens lacked: a more realistic view of women, a more skeptical view of good intentions, a subtler sense of humor, a drier vision of life which I myself found congenial. You'd think I'd advocated throwing Dickens out and replacing him with a toaster. Because Dickens is a certified Great Writer, and Trollope is not.

Am I saying anything different from what Randall Jarrell said in his great 1953 essay "The Age of Criticism"? Not really, so I'll quote him. Speaking of the literary gatherings of the era, Jarrell wrote:

> If, at such parties, you wanted to talk about *Ulysses* or *The Castle* or *The Brothers Karamazov* or *The Great Gatsby* or Graham Greene's last novel—Important books—you were at the right place. (Though you weren't so well off if you wanted to talk about *Remembrance of Things Past*. Important, but too long.) But if you wanted to talk about Turgenev's novelettes, or *The House of the Dead*, or *Lavengro*, or *Life on the Mississippi*, or *The Old Wives' Tale*, or *The Golovlyov Family*, or Cunningham-Grahame's stories, or Saint-Simon's memoirs, or *Lost Illusions*, or *The Beggar's Opera*, or *Eugen Onegin*, or *Little Dorrit*, or the *Burnt Njal Saga*, or *Persuasion*, or *The Inspector-General*, or *Oblomov*, or *Peer Gynt*, or *Far from the Madding Crowd*, or *Out of Africa*, or the *Parallel Lives*, or *A Dreary Story*, or *Debits and Credits*, or *Arabia Deserta*, or *Elective Affinities*, or *Schweik*, or—any of a thousand good or interesting but Unimportant books, you couldn't expect a very ready knowledge or sympathy from most of the readers there. They had

looked at the big sights, the current sights, hard, with guides and glasses; and those walks in the country, over unfrequented or thrice-familiar territory, all alone—those walks from which most of the joy and good of reading come—were walks that they hadn't gone on very often.

I suspect that most canon debaters have taken those solitary rambles, if only out of boredom—how many times, after all, can you reread the *Aeneid*, or *Mrs. Dalloway*, or *Cotton Comes to Harlem* (to pick one book from each column)? But those walks don't count, because of another assumption all sides hold in common, which is that the purpose of reading is none of the many varied and delicious satisfactions I've mentioned; it's medicinal. The chief end of reading is to produce a desirable kind of person and a desirable kind of society. A respectful, high-minded citizen of a unified society for the conservatives, an up-to-date and flexible sort for the liberals, a subgroup-identified, robustly confident one for the radicals. How pragmatic, how moralistic, how American! The culture debaters turn out to share a secret suspicion of culture itself, as well as the antipornographer's belief that there is a simple, one-to-one correlation between books and behavior. Read the conservatives' list and produce a nation of sexists and racists—or a nation of philosopher kings. Read the liberals' list and produce a nation of spineless relativists—or a nation of open-minded world citizens. Read the radicals' list and produce a nation of psychobabblers and ancestor-worshipers—or a nation of stalwart proud-to-be-me pluralists.

But is there any list of a few dozen books that can have such a magical effect, for good or for ill? Of course not. It's like arguing that a perfectly nutritional breakfast cereal is enough food for the whole day. And so the canon debate is really an argument about what books to cram down the resistant throats of a resentful captive populace of students; and the trick is never to mention the fact that, in such circumstances, one book is as good, or as bad, as another. Because, as the debaters know from their own experience as readers, books are not pills that produce health when ingested in measured doses. Books do not shape character in any simple way—if, indeed, they do so at all—or the most literate would be the most virtuous instead of just the ordinary run of humanity with larger vocabularies. Books cannot mold a common national purpose when, in fact, people are honestly divided about what kind of country they want—and are divided, moreover, for very good and practical reasons, as they always have been.

For these burly and energetic purposes, books are all but useless. The way books affect us is an altogether more subtle, delicate, wayward and individual, not to say private, affair. And that reading is being made to bear such an inappropriate and simplistic burden speaks to the poverty both of culture and of frank political discussion in our time.

On his deathbed, Dr. Johnson—once canonical, now more admired than read—is supposed to have said to a friend who was energetically rearranging his bedclothes, "Thank you, this will do all that a pillow can do." One might say that the canon debaters are all asking of their handful of chosen books that they do a great deal more than any handful of books can do.

THE PAPERBACKING OF PUBLISHING

Ted Solotaroff

•

IN HIS RESPONSE to Jacob Weisberg's rip at book editors a few months back in *The New Republic*, John Baker, who runs the trade magazine *Publishers Weekly*, plaintively asks, "Is the outside world really as interested in publishing as so many newspaper and magazine editors seem to think?" Baker suggests the beginning of an explanation in noting the ambivalence of the press, which shuttles between fascination with the power and glamour of the trade book publishers and disapproval of much of their operation and product.

This ambivalence springs from several general facts. The first is that for writers, a term now covering almost anyone with a word processor, trade publishing is the place where their dream of fame and fortune could come true. Hence the wide and intense interest in how it works, rewards and frustrates. Second, publishing is our most representative cultural institution because it is the most comprehensive: the place where *People* meets *The New York Review of Books*, an encounter that causes a good deal of anxiety on both sides of the browline. Finally, trade publishing has been the flagship institution, the one that carries the cargo of our heritage along the routes of the present to the ports of the future. If it is paying only lip service to this mission and changing its course to transform itself into another busy carrier in the infotainment business, with its own big players and deals and lawsuits, that confirms the general feeling of decline in the midst of expansion, of a whole culture selling out.

Each of these general facts and the curiosity and concern they give rise to lurk in the background of Weisberg's article like major witnesses who have not yet been called to the stand. Because they have not, his indictment of publishers and editors is about 60 percent right and 60 percent wrong. He has got the crime—the decline of editorial standards—mostly right but the perpetrators and motive mostly wrong. His evidence is thin, much of it uncorroborated hearsay. He has missed virtually all of the extenuating circumstances, not to mention the distinctions, comparisons and conflicts, that form the real interest and drama of the case.

Weisberg's main presumption is that the publishing business and the editorial profession should somehow be spared the economic and social forces that everywhere create conglomerates, expand and standardize markets, and undermine product quality and professional standards. Given the profit pressures, pricing limits and distribution problems that the industry has to contend with, the remarkable fact, as Weisberg acknowledges, is not how few quality books are published but how many. (Keeping them in print is another matter.)

As for publishing's ethos, again a little perspective is in order. Even a house like Simon and Schuster, Weisberg's worst offender, is still a nun in the whorehouse alongside the major players in the music industry and the art market or, to take a comparable industry elsewhere in the economy, some of the ethical drug companies. As for professional standards, Weisberg almost stumbles on the truth when he compares his "working editors" (those who edit rather than lunch and phone around) to "college professors with a vocation for teaching" instead of, presumably, those working the academic career tracks of chasing Defense Department grants. Indeed, many institutions of higher learning today cost-account a professor's courses in much the same way that publishers evaluate an editor's list of authors. When virtually every profession is seeing its standards being eroded by the flow of big money, it is as bootless for Weisberg to view book editors in the context of forty years ago as it would be to do so with physicians or investment bankers or members of Congress.

Except for the few remaining privately held quality houses and some imprints, which probably employ less than 10 percent of the editors, there isn't much choice for a trade editor but to work in a go-go corporate environment, most of whose revenue comes from books that do well in the shopping malls. This is the basic change in publishing that Weisberg ignores, except for glancing potshots here and there: the enormous expansion of the book market as part of a service economy. That is why hardcover publishing today more and more resembles mass-market paperback publishing of twenty years ago—books for all kinds of consumers—and why the large paperback houses are now prominent in hardcover publishing. Also, it's no accident, as they used to say in Marxist circles, that now the heads of the publishing conglomerates and even of the hardcover houses within them typically come from the paperback side of the business.

This in turn has a significant effect on the way hardcover books, and their editors and authors, are handled. The traditional, editorially driven house, such as Farrar, Straus & Giroux or W. W. Norton, closely identifies itself with the content of a book and regards its package (jacket illustration, type design, cover copy, flap copy, etc.) in terms of appropriateness and good taste. The paperback mavens who are moving into hardcover publishing regard content as more or less a given— much as they regard the content of the titles they acquire to reprint. Their forte is packaging and marketing them to a broader public. Hence erotic jacket art, as on Philip Roth's *Deception*, for which Weisberg takes Simon and Schuster to task, has been standard practice in paperback publishing since it got going after World War II. (We're also seeing the telltale advent of glitzy embossed type and selling copy on hardcover jackets.) Or take Weisberg's next exhibit in his hall of shame: Bret Easton Ellis's *American Psycho*. When Sonny Mehta, president of Knopf, picked it up after it had dropped from the nervous hands of Richard Snyder, C.E.O. at S&S, and with little editorial concern or interest published it as a paperback original, he was behaving exactly like the paperback editor he has been for most of his career. Or again, Weisberg takes S&S to task for publishing conflicting accounts of the Reagan ménage by Kitty Kelley and Lou Cannon. Snyder, who came up through the ranks of paperback marketing, defends this decision with the cant of the reprinter: "To publish is to disseminate. Our aim is to present both sides." A more honest explanation would have been, "It's all product."

The influence of the paperback mentality now pervades hardcover publishing from the well, as it were, to the pump. The auction by which the paperback houses acquire reprint rights has become prevalent among hardcover houses in competition for the "big book," and even the possibly prestigious one, that hasn't been nailed down contractually or preemptively. Once the book is acquired, the emphasis, as with reprints, is on marketing. Discussions of a title and jacket can go on for hours and weeks, while the house's editorial position is usually settled in a five-minute discussion. Similarly, the number of titles that acquisitions editors and production editors are responsible for has expanded drastically in recent years, approaching the quotas of their counterparts in the paperback houses. At the marketing end the similarities become even more telling. The reprinter puts his promotion money behind the two or three leaders on his monthly new releases and leaves the rest to stand or fall on their own. This has become the mindset in hardcover publishing. In the past most houses would allocate 10 percent of the cover price times the first printing to advertise and promote the book; today hardcover books are like the biblical faithful and faithless or the Reagan/Bush public: To those that have, even more shall be given, and for those who have not, what little they do have shall be taken away. Even at the final stage of the process, hardcover publishers dispose of their unsold copies much as the mass-market reprinters have always done—abundantly and quickly.

The much deeper pockets of the reprinters derived from the fact that the cover price of their product was roughly ten times its cost, about twice the ratio for a hardcover book. Paperback printings were, as a rule of thumb, ten times larger, while the number of returned copies was only about five times larger. Also, paperbacks were much less sensitive to economic conditions: Until things began to go out of whack in the late 1970s from overspending for titles, the paperback houses weren't much affected by recessions because they provided such bargain pleasures.

In effect, then, the reprinters provided most of the operating capital for the hardcover houses to do their thing, much as the merchant fortunes subsidized the refinements of the aristocracy without much affecting its ethos. The *haut en bas* nature of the industry was reflected in the fact that the paperback houses were called reprinters by their betters on the other side of Fifth Avenue, who reserved the term "publisher" for themselves, and were kept at telephone distance during the six-and seven-figure auctions in which they weren't even told whom they were bidding against. In such ways did the profession protect itself from the demotic side of the business: The hardcover houses had the standards and the paperback houses had the élan. In 1979, when I went from Bantam to Harper and Row, it was like going from *Time to The Yale Review*.

That was also the time of sackcloth and ashes on both sides of Fifth Avenue. Amid the oil-shortage recession, publishing was having its own private downturn as a result of the spending sprees that had been set off by the first generation of conglomerate takeovers. Confusing best-selling authors with brand-name products, expanded lists and ship-ments with market share, and a shotgun wedding of a hardcover and a paperback house with a magnetic marriage, publishers poured in mil-lions in search of authors, titles and "synergy" and wreaked mostly havoc. But while publishing executives were learning to be more cau-tious and frugal, a succession of print-media giants—Bertelsmann, Pearson, Newhouse, Murdoch and Maxwell—were arriving on the scene. Although they understood book publishing better than the first-generation conglomerateers at Times Mirror, RCA and CBS had, and ran a tighter and more ruthless ship, the economies they effected by slashing overhead flowed into a second tidal wave of money for acquisi-tions of books. Like George Steinbrenner, they believed in buying heavy hitters and consistent winners, which is not surprising since that is how they built their empires. But unlike Steinbrenner's Yankees, whose vast subsidiary income from TV rights covered the multitude of his acquisition mistakes, and unlike newspapers and magazines, which stay afloat on advertising revenue, book publishers have only the direct income from their books—three out of four of which lose money—to increase profit levels and meet interest payments. Hence their extrava-gant competition for major best sellers, which, because of the expanded distribution that the giant book chains provide, can be cash cows. Also, having a Robert Ludlum, Tom Clancy or Danielle Steel pro-vides what little stability and realistic planning is possible amid the wild vicissitudes of trade publishing.

The advent of these new or rebankrolled high-stakes players was not lost on the dealers of the game, the agents, who raised the table stakes, or advances, beyond what they had been before. The sharpest ones did so not only for the rainmaking authors but also for the image-making ones: the much-vaunted older novelist or the much-publicized younger one, the classy contemporary historian, the outstanding travel writer, the philosophical gardener, and so forth. A particularly effective ploy was raising the ante for keeping an author whose reputation the house was building. The agent would slip the manuscript to a competitor or sometimes just make a few discreet phone calls, and the deed was done. As Gerald Howard, one of the few editors willing to spill the beans, has written, "The publishers are scared stiff of the powerful agents. . . . The million-dollar contracts you read about are paid over with silent screams."

That the megapublishers are susceptible to these shakedowns brings us to the gray moral complexion of the subject that Weisberg paints in stark black and white. Overpaying for an author whose book has only to show up to sell a million or more copies makes its own kind of economic sense, or at least makes understandable the terror of losing her. But why double or even triple the advance of an author whose last book hasn't earned out despite all its prominent reviews?

The publisher will say, "We can't afford to lose this author." What that means is quite complicated: first, that an author's reputation and sales have reached a point—25,000 copies or so—that his next book may launch him into orbit as a literary star and the red ink of his previous books will turn green. Second, it means that the house will lose status and, to some extent, acquisition position in the quality market if it loses him. These are the more or less objective reasons. The subjective ones are that most publishers, even the most market-minded ones, are subject to the lingering aura of cultural prestige that is associated with their house: what Weisberg shrewdly calls their "ghosts." It is these authors who enable Random House or HarperCollins or Viking to hold on to their former distinction with their left hand, as it were, while the right goes about the business of business. More subtle, but perhaps even stronger, is the surviving influence of the serious book culture within the house. Although the ownership and the market have altered conditions, the people who go into publishing do so because they like to hang around books enough to endure its abysmal salaries for the first ten years or so. They create a kind of secondary milieu of taste, irony and dedication that reinforces the better side of the publisher's pride and his desire to be respected by his staff, which in turn is most tangibly acted upon by going out on a limb for an author who matters.

So there are still two cultures in most hardcover houses: the book one and the product one. Since the latter is generally the dominating one, it has the most direct impact on the younger editors, conditioning them to be more responsive to the market, more entrepreneurial and competitive than editors of my generation were, and less guided by a sense of cultural mission. Also, the product culture is hardly a refuge from the cynicism and careerism of their generation. Does this mean they don't edit? No. They tend to get their start as editors by handling consumer books that senior editors turn over to them and develop one or another of those areas—cookbooks, sports books, pop psychology, etc.—as a career base. And since these books often require more editing than the classier ones, they are Weisberg's "working editors" from the start and are likely to remain so until they become part of management.

Some senior editors and some nominal ones who compete with one another for publicity and product have ridden the crests of the sea change in hardcover publishing. Even their troughs become crests as they go from one overpaid acquisition to the next and, often enough, from one big house or imprint to the next. As Joni Evans—whose new imprint, Turtle Bay, is likely to take trendiness to new heights—recently remarked, "When they stop writing about you, you know you're no longer hot." Since her type is so visible as well as indicative of how the major money nexus confounds and devastates the profession of editing, one wonders why Weisberg didn't write about them. Someone should, other than Roger Cohen, their flack at *The New York Times*.

Meanwhile, most acquisitions editors of serious books have all they can do to keep their heads above water. Their ability to acquire and to influence the publishing of their books has been curbed, when not crushed, by the product culture. The Pantheon debacle is their story writ large; the fate of Allen Peacock at Simon and Schuster or Jonathan Galassi at Random House or James Landis at William Morrow, to take the more glaring of many examples, is their story writ individually. The essential plot is that marketing and sales managers, subsidiary rights and publicity directors, along with those editors who have got the new religion, have become the ranking subordinates of the big-time publisher. They have the decisive input on print quotas, advertising and promotion budgets (or the lack thereof), and even the spin put on a book by its jacket, flap copy and publicity. Even more onerous, they often decide on the merits and potential of the manuscript or project that an editor has proposed to acquire and develop. Years of experience and prowess in doing so can count for nothing alongside the skepticism of people whose main contact with the life of the mind is a marketing report, and who view the editorial process in terms of overhead and the writing career in terms of advances.

During my own stint at Simon and Schuster in the early 1970s, when the twig of the present megapublisher was being bent, I was told by the editor in chief that instead of developing young or little-known authors I should be luring the ripe ones from the small houses that had established them: *That* was "exciting publishing" (he proved to be a much more successful, as well as prophetic, editor than I was). After taking a month to edit a novel I was told by the publisher, who had it from the above-mentioned colleague, who prided himself on editing a 700-page novel over a weekend, that I was, in the publisher's characteristic idiom, "slow as shit." To which I could only reply, "So are brain surgeons," as I gazed at the handwriting on the wall.

An acquisitions editor today who does quality books at a big-time house has a number of Hobbesian choices. She can try to function within the slender margin left for her, keep her overhead low, beginning with her salary, and hope that one or two of her authors turn into an Anne Tyler or a Barry Lopez and that her reputation sends a few other rising stars her way before the authorities blow the whistle. The problem with that is being out of the loop, which on Publishers Row means the major money nexus, and she may well lose such an author to an editor within it, one who will "kill to get him." The agents don't think of her when they're looking for major money from the Alfred A. Doubledays.

Much has been written about editors abandoning authors by jumping from house to house and very little about authors abandoning editors who brought them into the limelight, the very limelight that their new heavy-hitting agent is exploiting to drive up the asking price. As I've said earlier, there are quality authors the megapublisher can't afford to lose, but there are more whom it is glad to lose. In addition, the frustrations and bruises that develop between ambitious authors and relatively powerless editors become further grounds for divorce. Meanwhile, a new editor has come courting who loves every word the author has published and who has dollar signs in his eyes. Authors don't have to be told anymore that the higher the advance, the more money and attention will be given to promoting their book, though they seldom foresee what will happen in their new marriage if the book doesn't succeed.

In the mid-1980s I was told that the income from my books didn't justify my overhead and salary as a senior editor. Since I was developing a list of promising authors and didn't want to move or lose them, I worked part time until I acquired a bestselling one and regained my former position, with some added clout. This, in turn, enabled me to play a stronger hand at acquisitions and marketing meetings. Such are the conditions that drive an editor to double his standards and join the hunt for commercial books. What used to be called selling out is today simply a strategy for surviving. But the risks and consequences of doing so haven't changed just because there is more company. At best, he wastes more and more time and spirit catering to authors he would have little use for if he didn't have so much need for them. Some editors can do so without developing a dual editorial personality connected by cynicism. Instead, they become consumed by the overwork involved in fast-track management during the day and their professional work nights and weekends. Others become mainly the wheelers and dealers that Weisberg confuses with all acquisitions editors or else end up playing a losing hand of sardonic halfheartedness with both their quality and commercial authors.

The other two ways of surviving are to become part of management or find a publisher who will bankroll one's own imprint. Both positions give the editor more clout to acquire and effectively publish books and even less time to work with authors. Both positions raise profit, anxiety and distraction levels beyond the point that makes sense for a working editor.

But, then again, little in publishing does make sense these days— besides closing the door, punching the Do Not Disturb button and pulling out a manuscript or flap copy or working on some other useful, skilled task. That's why there is still a book culture, powerless or divided as many of its members may be. That's why editing standards haven't declined nearly as much as editorial ones, that is, what a house chooses to publish, which is mostly out of its editors' hands. That's why the mobility of editors today that outsiders like Weisberg attribute to opportunism is more often the desperation of someone trying to reach possibly higher ground in a flood.

THE PERILS OF THE NEW NATIONALISM

Eric Hobsbawm

•

AT A TIME when the Marshall Islands have just been admitted to the United Nations, nearly twenty of whose members have a population of less than 250,000, the argument that a territory is too small to constitute a state can no longer be convincingly maintained. Of course such states—even much larger ones—are not independent in any meaningful sense. Politically and militarily they are helpless without outside protection, as Kuwait and Croatia show. Economically they are even more dependent. Few separatist movements hope to go it alone. They want to exchange dependence on a single state economy for dependence on the European Community or some other larger unit that limits its members' economic sovereignty just as much.

Still, if a territory wishes to run up its flag outside the U.N. building in New York and acquire all the other fringe benefits of statehood—a national anthem, a national airline and a few embassies in attractive or politically important capitals—the chances today seem better than ever.

But why should anyone wish to set up such a state, mostly by breaking up existing political units in Eurasia and Africa? (There is so far no significant tendency to do so in the Americas, except in Canada.) The usual reason given by would-be state-builders is that the people of the territory concerned have constituted a "nation" from the beginning of time, a special ethnic group, usually with its own language, which cannot live under the rule of strangers. The right of self-determination, they argue, implies states that coincide with nations.

Almost everything about this argument is historically wrong, but as Ernest Renan noted more than a century ago, "Forgetting history, and even historical error, are an essential factor in the formation of a nation." However, we are concerned not with history or with rationality but with politics. Here one thing has to be stated very clearly. The nationalist belief, first expressed in the nineteenth century by Giuseppe Mazzini, that every nation should form a state, and that there should be only one state for each nation, is and always was quite unworkable in ethnic-linguistic terms.

There are, with the exception of some island ministates, probably not more than a dozen ethnically and linguistically homogeneous states among the 170 or so of the world's political entities, and probably none that include anything like the totality of the "nation" they claim to embody. The territorial distribution of the human race is older than the idea of ethnic-linguistic nation-states and therefore does not correspond to it. Development in the modern world economy, because it generates vast population movements, constantly undermines ethnic-linguistic homogeneity. Multiethnicity and plurilinguality are quite unavoidable, except temporarily by mass exclusion, forcible assimilation, mass expulsion or genocide—in short, by coercion. There is only a dark future for a world of nation-states such as the new government of Georgia, which wants to deny citizenship rights to any inhabitant who cannot prove that his or her ancestors were Georgian speakers and lived in the territory before 1801.

There are today four rather different reasons such sentiments, and their political expression in separatism, are widely supported. The first is that the collapse of the Communist system, which imposed political stability over a large part of Europe, has reopened the wounds of World War I, or, more precisely, of the misconceived and unrealistic peace settlements after it. The explosive nationalist issues in Central and Eastern Europe today are not ancient ethnic conflicts but those created during the formation of the successor states to the collapsing multiethnic Habsburg, Ottoman and Czarist Russian empires. Baltic and Caucasian separatism, and conflicts between Serbs and Croats, and Czechs and Slovaks, were not serious problems in 1917, or could not have existed before the establishment of Yugoslavia and Czechoslovakia. What has made those problems acute is not the strength of national feeling, which was no greater than in countries like Britain and Spain, but the disintegration of central power, for this forced even Soviet or Yugoslav republics that did not dream of separation, like Kazakhstan and Macedonia, to assert independence as a means of self-preservation.

The breakdown of Communist systems has given separatist agitations elsewhere enormous encouragement, but it has no direct bearing on them. Such as they are, the prospects of independence for, say, Scotland, Quebec, Euskadi (the Basque country) or Corsica remain the same as before. They do not depend on what happens in the East.

The second reason is more general, though probably more important in the West than in the East. The massive population movements of the past forty years—within and between countries and continents—have made xenophobia into a major political phenomenon, as the earlier mass migrations of 1880–1920 did to a smaller extent. Xenophobia encourages ethnic nationalism, since the essence of both is hostility to other groups (the "not-we"). United States nationalism is by origin entirely nonlinguistic. It is only because of mass Hispanic immigration that today demands are made, for the first time, that English should be the *official* language of the United States. However, mutual ethnic hatred does not necessarily produce separatism, as the United States also proves.

The third reason is that the politics of group identity are easier to understand than any others, especially for peoples who, after several decades of dictatorship, lack both political education and experience. In Central Europe, argues Miroslav Hroch, a leading Czech historian, language is once again replacing complicated concepts like constitutions and civil rights. Nationalism is among the simple, intuitively comprehensible beliefs that substitute for less understandable political programs. It is not the only one.

The fourth reason is perhaps the most fundamental. To quote the Czech historian: "Where an old regime disintegrates, where old social relations have become unstable, amid the rise of general insecurity, belonging to a common language and culture may become the only certainty in society, the only value beyond ambiguity and doubt." In the former Communist countries this insecurity and disorientation may derive from the collapse of the predictable planned economy and the social security that went with it. In the West there are other forms of disorientation and insecurity that have built up during the past decades, when the world and human life changed more rapidly and profoundly than ever before in human history.

Is it an accident that Quebec separatism as a serious political factor emerged at the end of a decade when a traditional, Catholic, pious and clerical community that had preserved the values of seventeenth-century French peasants suddenly gave way to a society in which people no longer went to church and the birthrate fell almost vertically? After two generations, when continents of peasants have become continents of city dwellers, when the relations between the generations, and increasingly between the sexes, have been transformed and past wisdom seems irrelevant to present problems, the world is full of people who long for something that still looks like an old, and unchallengeable, certainty. It is not surprising that at such times they turn to group identity, of which national identity is one form, or that the demand for a political unit exclusively for the members of the group, in the form of ethnic-linguistic nation-states, once again comes to the fore.

However, if we can understand the forces that lead to a revival of the politics of national consciousness, and even sympathize with the feelings that inspire it, let us have no illusions. Adding another few dozen to the member-states of the U.N. will not give any of them any more control over their affairs than they had before they became independent. It will not solve or diminish the problems of cultural or any other autonomy in the world, any more than it did in 1919.

Establishing nation-states on the post-World War I model is not necessarily a recipe for disaster. Among the potential new nation-states there may well be one or two future Netherlands and Switzerlands, bastions of tolerance, democracy and civilization. But who, looking at Serbia and Croatia, at Slovakia and Lithuania, at Georgia, Quebec and the rest, would today expect many of the newly separated nation-states to go that way? And who would expect a Europe of such new states to be a zone of peace?

CLINTON AND RICKEY RAY RECTOR

Christopher Hitchens

•

BERTIE WOOSTER'S AUNT Dahlia once warned him sternly against having anything at all to do with girls who spelled ordinary names in extraordinary ways: "No good can come of association with anything labelled Gwladys or Ysobel or Ethyl or Mabelle or Kathryn, but particularly Gwladys." Presuming this to extend to any Gennifers of the species, it seems that a failure to profit by Aunt Dahlia's counsel is the harshest verdict we are allowed to pass on Governor Clinton's ethical "judgment." All right, so these are lax times. That is why the name Gennifer Flowers is notorious and the name Rickey Ray Rector— surely just as euphonious—is not.

When Dostoyevsky wrote about the horrific torture of telling a man the date of his own death, and then keeping him waiting, he said that a man would endure any privation to escape that trap. This wouldn't be applicable in Rickey Ray Rector's case, since he was lobotomized as a result of a self-inflicted bullet wound. So I suppose it could be said that Governor Clinton was sparing him some of the agonies of the condemned when he refused to grant executive clemency and had him destroyed by lethal injection on January 24. This was the big *60 Minutes* weekend for the Governor, and you can well imagine that the last thing he felt he needed was idle talk about his softness on crime.

One is tempted to be pontifical about this moral contrast—a temptress on one side and an execution on the other, and the mob turning from the medicalized gibbet to the exposed love nest—but actually the Rector case tells us nothing that we do not already know only too well. The lessons are that capital punishment is cruel and unusual, that especially in the South it is applied in a racist manner, that humane and defensible alternatives to it are within easy reach, and that Bill Clinton is a calculating opportunist.

The first point is easily established. As well as degrading the medical profession in a more intimate way than the use of gassing, hanging, shooting and electrocution, "lethal injection" is just as barbarous as the sub-modern methods. As the U.S. Court of Appeals for the D.C. Circuit was constrained to observe in 1983: "There is substantial and uncontroverted evidence . . . that execution by lethal injection poses a serious risk of cruel, protracted death. . . . Even a slight error in dosage or administration can leave a prisoner conscious but paralyzed while dying, a sentient witness to his or her own asphyxiation."

Point number two is as old as America, and older than Europe. It's well put by Clinton Duffy (another good name, by the way), who as a San Quentin warden was witness to more than 150 snuffings. Capital punishment, he said, is "a privilege of the poor." Is there any thinking person who does not know what this means in a state like Arkansas? The latest and the driest phrasing of the problem comes from the General Accounting Office, reporting to the Senate and House judiciary committees this very month:

> Our synthesis of the 28 studies shows a pattern of evidence indicating racial disparities in the charging, sentencing and imposition of the death penalty. . . . In 82 percent of the studies, race of victim was found to influence the likelihood of being charged with capital murder or receiving the death penalty, i.e., those who murdered whites were found to be more likely to be sentenced to death than those who murdered blacks. This finding was remarkably consistent across data sets, states, data collection methods and analytic techniques.

As for point three, it's pretty clear that Rickey Ray Rector met all the customary pragmatic objections to clemency. He had blown half his brain away after committing murder (I take it he was guilty, though miscarriages have been known), and he wasn't going anywhere. He was, by most standards, unfit to plead. He was, in any case, condemned by definition to confinement without parole. In short, by all the usual limiting cases his sentence would have been commuted. And in no other "civilized" country, such as for example any member of the Council of

Europe, could he have been condemned to death in the first place.

In discussion with partisans of Governor Clinton's decision to license the lethal injection, I have found myself more powerfully nauseated than in past arguments with rednecks and racists who really don't know any better. The strategic and tactical thinking displayed by his supporters—I asked Clinton himself, but he refused to favor me with a reply—convicts him of a base, hungry cunning. The last two executions he authorized, of John Swindler in June 1990 and Ronald Gene Simmons later in the same month, were both of white men. Thus, it is argued, by staying the execution of Rickey Ray Rector, Clinton would have opened himself to the charge of affirmative action. I cannot offhand think of a more contemptible reasoning. The mentally devastated Rector had to die because two men of a different shade had already been put to death? In other words, never act justly now, for fear you may have to act justly later. After all, justice can set that frightful thing—a precedent.

It's also impossible to acquit Clinton of the charge of having people snuffed to suit his own political and career needs. In a candidates' debate on January 19, the Governor bragged of his firmness in dispatching Swindler and Simmons, as if to pre-empt any Hortonizing of his future ambitions. And when he briefly lost the Arkansas Statehouse to a neolithic Republican named Frank White in 1980, Clinton was considered "vulnerable" to White's demagogic charge that he was weak on law and order. The element of low calculation in the Rector decision is so evident and so naked that it makes one gasp.

So what is all this garbage about "the new paradigm" of Clinton's forthright Southern petit-bourgeois thrusting innovative fearless blah blah blah? In a test of principle where even the polls have shown that people do not demand the death penalty, he opted to maintain the foulest traditions and for the meanest purposes. As the pundits keep saying, he is a man to watch.

PEARL

•

Suppose that a warrior forgot he was wearing his pearl on his forehead, and
sought for it somewhere else . . .

—HUANG-PO

      Well, I admit
A small boy's eyes grew rounder and lips moister
To find it invisibly chained, at home in the hollow
Of his mother's throat: the real, deepwater thing.
  Far from the mind at six to plumb
X-raywise those glimmering lamplit
Asymmetries to self-immolating mite
    Or angry grain of sand
Not yet proverbial. Yet his would be the hand
    Mottled with survival—
  She having slipped (how? when?) past reach—
  That one day grasped it. Sign of what
But wisdom's trophy. Time to mediate,
Skin upon skin, so cunningly they accrete,
    The input. For its early mote
        Of grit
  Reborn as orient moon to gloat
In verdict over the shucked, outsmarted meat. . . .
One layer, so to speak, of calcium carbonate
  That formed in me is the last shot
  I took the seminar I teach

In Loss to a revival—
Of Sasha Guitry's classic "Perles de la Couronne."
   The hero has tracked down
His prize. He's holding forth, that summer night,
At the ship's rail, all suavity and wit,
   Gem swaying like a pendulum
From his fing—oops! to soft bubble-blurred harpstring
Glissandi regaining depths (man the camera, follow)
Where an unconscious world, my yawning oyster,
      Shuts on it.

James Merrill

THE GULF WAR AS TOTAL TELEVISION

Tom Engelhardt

•

HERE WE'VE JUST cruised past the first anniversary of the bombing of Iraq—Gulf-War-plus-one (plus)—and the packs of Desert Storm bubble-gum cards are long gone from newsstand counters. The war to re-establish war, American-style, seems to have vaporized even before Gen. H. Norman Schwarzkopf (retired) could get his memoirs into print. All that's left here of that twenty-four-hours-a-day, eye-burning, blood-pumping, high-tech, all-channel media event are self-satisfied military men and resentful journalists, both acting as if the initial bombing run on Baghdad had had CNN's outpost at the Al-Rashid Hotel as its target. But those who now claim that the media were the "losers" in the Gulf War, that censorship, press pools and military handlers galore represented an epic Bush Administration triumph over reportorial independence, still can't see the screen for the pixels.

What we viewed last year was less the death of independent media than the birth of "total television," a new co-production process to which normal labels of media critique and complaint largely don't apply. The Gulf War can, in fact, be seen as the ur-production of the new media conglomerate. For it, the war proved promising exactly because the boundaries between military action and media event broke down in such a way that military planning could become a new form of media reality.

Total television can be seen to have its antecedents neither in traditional war reportage nor in American war mythology. It was not even the child of Vietnam, which was not (as is so often said) our first television war but our last nontelevision one in its inability either to adhere to precise scheduling or achieve closure. Instead, total TV was born in certain mesmeric moments in the eighties when the whole nation seemed to have been mobilized at couchside to start at the same images across many channels.

Starting with the Iran hostage crisis of 1979–81 and running through the Gulf War, these glimpses of total TV generally had the theme of America or Americans held hostage—most humiliatingly in Iran; most tragically in various terrorist plane-nappings and murders; most pathetically in the Challenger disaster, in which a schoolteacher's life was hostaged to the failure of American technology; most absurdly in the little girl hostaged to the elements by her fall down a well shaft in Texas; most triumphantly in the images of students kissing American soil after their ostensible rescue from Grenada.

From the media's point of view, most of these events were, fortunately, quite limited. One kidnapped plane on an airport runway; one embassy surrounded by a crowd; a few film clips of an explosion replayed a hundred times—all of the above surrounded by talking heads; or one small war in a distant place with only the most minimal government-supplied visuals. To create more expansive total TV scenarios would have been ruinously expensive without outside help. Even Ted Turner's Cable News Network, set up for any and all twenty-four-hours-a-day media events, would have quickly felt the financial strain of total TV if left purely to its own devices. Just the attempt to re-create the Good War for the miniseries adapted from Herman Wouk's novel *The Winds of War* proved a financial catastrophe for ABC. It was not enough to mobilize an audience. New forms of sponsorship were needed.

Here we have to remember the corporate context within which the possibility for Gulf War-style total television developed. On the one hand, during the eighties media giants like Time-Warner, Murdoch's News Corporation and the Maxwell combine were being stapled together, and under their roofs distinct media forms were blurring into mix-and-match TV/movie/newspaper/magazine/book/music/theme-park entities. On the other hand, just to put such entities together (as corporations gobbled and were gobbled up, merged and purged their way through the decade) was to incur incalculable billions of dollars of debt. The burden of this debt—and a crumbling ad market by

decade's end—gave rise to new pressures to "downsize" these un-
wieldy, not especially synergistic new entities. Fewer personal and
cheaper production methods were instantly needed to make them more
financially palatable to nervous owners (or suddenly anxious potential
buyers).

General Electric, Capital Cities and the Tisch family operation,
which had come to control respectively NBC, ABC, and CBS, also
found themselves facing an assault on their audiences and their advertisers from cable television and Murdoch's new fourth network, Fox.
The swift erosion of network dominance in the late eighties led money
managers within each network to hack away at their prestigious but
often unprofitable news fiefdoms. If the Gulf War revealed the media's
ability to mount technical operations on an unprecedented scale, it also
exposed the need of the financially pressed media giants (and their
upstart competitors) for sponsorship on a scale hitherto unimaginable.
This is what the Bush Administration seemed to offer in the Gulf
War—an outside production company able to organize a well-pro-
duced, subsidized total event that could be channeled to the American
public at, relatively speaking, bargain-basement prices.

With its million or more uniformed extras, its vast sets and its six-
month preproduction schedule filled with logistical miracles (and a few
fiascos, too), the Gulf War production involved intense military/media
planning on a global scale. It had its own built-in "coming attractions"—the many variations on "Showdown in the Gulf" that teased
viewers with a possible January opening on all screens in domestic mul-
tiplexes across the nation. It had its dazzling Star Wars-style graphics,
theme music and logos, as well as stunningly primetimed first moments
(Disneyesque fireworks over Baghdad).

To succeed as a production company, the Pentagon had to offer the
networks five things: first, funding based on a relatively limited financial contribution from the networks themselves. This was accomplished
by a State Department/Pentagon financing team that sought out foreign investment much as any Hollywood production team might
have—from the Japanese, the Germans, the Saudis and so on—$50 bil-
lion, you might say, for "foreign rights," money that insured a break-
even point on the government side of the enterprise almost before the
first missile was fired; second, the ability to organize round-the-clock,
on-location support systems across a vast theater of operations; third, a
pre-edited flow of visuals available to all channels; fourth, control over
access to the set of the production, thus limiting internetwork competition and consequently network costs (those last two usually fall under

the rubric of "censorship"); and finally, the sort of precise scheduling and closure that television craves.

At the Pentagon, much thought had already gone into matters of scheduling and closure—this, out of a post-Vietnam desire to create a Third World battlefield where maximal weaponry and minimal U.S. casualties would guarantee public support. In the eighties, a new wave of "smart" (and not-so-smart) but highly destructive weaponry was brought on-line to complement an already impressive Vietnam-era arsenal. In the Persian Gulf, as a result, the preponderance and superiority of American weaponry—as well as the near nonappearance of the "enemy"—made slaughter on a vast scale, at will and with an eye to television's tight time requirements, achievable.

What President Bush then could promise the nation—and the media—was a war that could be scheduled, and this promise was structured not only into war planning but into the minds of the warmakers. As Bob Woodward reported in his book *The Commanders*, "In the White House, Bush, Quayle, Scowcroft and Sununu gathered in the small private study adjacent to the Oval Office to watch television. When the sounds of bombing could be heard behind the voices of the reporters still in their Baghdad hotel rooms, Bush, visibly relieved, said, 'Just the way it was scheduled.' "

Pressure for closure was built into the war's logo-ized form—"The War in the Gulf, Day X"—and reassurance on this score was forthcoming from the war's first moments. In fact, one striking feature of the war how often the viewing public was told that it was unfolding "on schedule." Nearly every military news conference included such a reminder, and the schedule being referred to was clearly television's. The public was constantly assured by the war's supporters that it would be clean, manageable, foreseeable, endable—in short, a program.

In the past, the reporting of war had been successfully organized and controlled by governments, and generals had polished their images with the press or even, like Douglas MacArthur, had had publicists do it for them—and, of course, images of war and generalship American-style had been re-created on-screen innumerable times by actors. But never had generals and war planners gone before the public as actors, supported by all the means a "studio" could muster on their behalf, and determined to produce a program that would fill the entire day across the dial for the full time of a "war." What we have to imagine (for we were not shown it) is that behind the dark curtains that screened off the multiple daily press conferences of the various actors, each in his distinctive fashion/camouflage outfit, each wielding his distinctive sitcom quips and put-downs, each giving his distinctive impression of the Victorious General or the In-Control Press Spokesman, lay a globe-spanning network of scriptwriters, makeup artists, fashion consultants, graphic designers, production managers, film editors (otherwise known as "censors") and even a military version of the traditional network Standards and Practices department, with its guidelines for on-air acceptability.

Only military pre-editing of virtually all aspects of the Gulf War made total television's six-week-long ratings hit a possibility. Hence, despite the uneasiness of some journalists on the scene, the TV networks understandably offered no significant protest against the censoring and controlling mechanisms of the Bush Administration—which were largely in their interest. In fact, no well-known media company was willing to join more marginal publications like *The Nations* and New York's *Village Voice* and journalists like *Newsday*'s Sydney Schanberg in their legal challenge to Pentagon censorship policies. In this way, the Gulf War experience, which offered the media giants new possibilities in the production of entertainment, also brought journalism's already tattered post-Watergate, post-Vietnam heroic self-image down to earth.

It's not surprising, then, that reporters in hotel lounges in Dhahran watching the war on TV just like everyone else would see the military's media role mainly as a censorious one, but this was to miss the point. A more useful comparison would be to those TV production companies that, in the early eighties, began creating a new-style children's television program. Usually done in conjunction with toy companies and their ad agencies, these shows in one quick leap eliminated the boundaries between ad and show by making what were essentially animated, program-length catalogues for toys.

In a similar way, the Gulf War production launched a major new form of the program-length commercial. It was as if the whole post-Vietnam era in America had built toward this forty-three-day-long ad, intent on selling both domestic and foreign markets on the renewal of American virtues. If you want to feel good, be U.S. If you want to experience technology and triumph, buy U.S. It even used the simplified visual language of the eighties ad—the upbeat, brightly colored (sales) story, whose happy ending was meant to confound the darkness of the world beyond the screen with the sprightliness of the product. No one looking at the many carefully framed visuals of the Gulf War could doubt the advertorial nature of the show, segmented as it was into sets of mini-ads for various aspects of itself.

What made this program-length ad unique, though, was the length of the program, and the fact that its newness and its commercial form unexpectedly threw into question the nature of normal television advertising. If *this* was The Ad, then what were those? Although CNN, ready-made for total TV, experienced rising ad rates and revenues during the war, for the networks it was another story. Non-CNN advertisers were unsure of how their ads would coexist with "war" in this puzzling new version of entertainment time. Of course, the war they, like so many media experts, military men and journalists, were imagining was a war of body bags. In the end, their failure to grasp the nature of this new media experience and their consequent refusal to support the production helped make total television into a financial fiasco for the big three networks. They found themselves showing a vast commercial while losing revenue from the very advertisers who felt more comfortable inside *Cheers* than inside the cheering framework of a war to destroy Iraq. (According to media critic John Mac-Arthur in his new book, *Second Front: Censorship and Propaganda in the Gulf War*, NBC, which like CBS ran behind ABC in the ratings, claimed losses of $55 million on its war coverage, including $20 million in withdrawn ad revenue. One postwar result at CBS, at least, was a further downsizing of its news department.)

This confusion over sponsorship reflected not only total television's primitive state but the likelihood that "war" might not be its ultimate venue. For one thing, the military, with its adversarial attitude toward the media, inhibited the flow of fresh images that might have fed total television's voracious appetite, and so left Monday Night War's color commentators like Anthony Cordesman (ABC) and retired Gen. Michael Dugan (CBS) trapped at halftime with no game to call.

In fact, no greater problem faced the military/media production team than its inability to establish a suitably epic story at the heart of total television. From the initial "Battle in the Gulf" (the 1981 dogfights with Libyan MIGs over the Gulf of Sidra) to the invasions of Grenada and Panama, the Reagan and Bush administrations had engaged in a decade-long experiment in the controlled presentation of American battlefield triumph. This attempt to re-establish a triumphalist American war story via the media and in the wake of Vietnam ended up, in the Persian Gulf, as little more than a passing advertorial. Missing in action in the war's coverage were not so much independent media, which had seldom existed in the history of American warfare (if anything, military censorship and misleading reportage were far more severe in World War II and Korea), but any sense of what form a lasting, empathetic war narrative could take without a military struggle in which to ground itself.

Off-screen, events in the gulf were closer to a mass electrocution than a war, and as a result, on-screen no Iraqi aggressors fell by the hundreds from their charging camels in the sort of battle our film tradition called for. Nor could armies be discovered clashing in their multi-thousands, nor tank battles—billed as potentially the largest since World War II—ranging across desert vistas. In fact, the crucial production number, D-day, renamed "G-day" (for ground war day), turned out to be no day at all. The penultimate event of the post-Vietnam era, in which the Not-Vietnamese were to be crushed in battle, had to be elided, for at the heart of this technically awesome spectacle was an embarrassingly plotless and unwatchable slaughter. The best that could be offered from an enemy who refused to put in an appearance were scenes of bedraggled Iraqis emerging from their dugouts to surrender and shots of Iraqi-commandeered cars, trucks and buses turned to charred rubble on the highway out of Kuwait City by American planes.

In fact, only when reporters were loosed to dash ahead into Kuwait City was there a hint of an on-screen story. If the liberation-of-Paris-style crowds were sparse in population-decimated Kuwait, at least the visuals flowed and journalists had an opportunity to simulate war reporters of the past, down to their safari jackets.

If the Gulf War's lack of a story line accounts, in part, for its remarkable disappearance from American politics and culture, it was not for want of the footage of death. This was, after all, a screen war at the "front" as well as at home. We know, for instance, that cameras shooting through the nightvision gunsights of Apache AH-64 attack helicopters caught graphic scenes of confused and helpless Iraqi soldiers being blown to bits by unseen attackers. But these outtakes would have been appropriate only to a very different production—one geared to a horror film, not a war story.

Given its prodigious vanishing act, perhaps the Gulf War will indeed have little lasting effect on our society. (Its effects on Iraq and the rest of the Middle East are obviously another matter.) Total television, however, could have far more staying power, hinting at possible media and advertising futures we can hardly imagine today. It points toward a world in which, increasingly, everything gets done for the media; in which the more fully meshed media systems of the twenty-first century will need to discover new, more powerful, more all-purpose sponsoring relationships, ones that, at the very least, can raise to a higher power the single-sponsor show (*The Alcoa Hour, General Electric Theater*) of a simpler corporate age. Whichever media giants dominate in the years ahead, the problem of how to pay for such global entertainment shows, what those shows can possibly be and what stories they can be made to tell must be faced. What form total television will take in the future— whether on screen we will see slaughter or some friendlier sport—and who will be its sponsors we can hardly guess.

THE KARMA RAN OVER MY DOGMA

Clancy Sigal

•

MY PAL DEREK, the Liverpool dance hall dynamiter, slugged a screw at Wakefield prison one week before he was due to release. Mollie, who used to deposit her burglary loot with me in brown paper bags and stole the Assistant Police Commissioner's white Mercedes as a fuck-you to established authority, did her best to break the law, any law, after she finished her sentence at Holloway women's prison, where she had discovered her gay identity and lots of warm friends. Here in the States my friend Claud, a permanent U.S. military AWOL, always finds ways of messing up shortly before they parole him from whatever institution he aims for like a beagle in heat.

It's called "gate fever," and I know a lot of people on the left who have it now that the prison gates are unlocked forever.

Speaking for myself, the collapse of Communism—Berlin wall crumbling, Stalin's statues melted down, all that—is a huge load off my dogma-weary shoulders. For years I've been waiting for my release papers. Dreaming of it, working for it, virtually shaping my life toward a New Dawn for Man-and Womankind represented by the discrediting of socialism, my mother's creed and mine.

Arthur Koestler once hinted that the man who gets what he's always wanted will probably plunge into a suicidal depression. Very likely that explains some of what happened to Koestler—a shrewd prophet of anticommunism—after the 1956 Hungarian uprising, which proved he was right all along, that people inevitably will rebel against an "idealistic" tyranny. Of course, being Magyars the Hungarians then unpredictably refused to self-destruct and went on to live quite well (by Eastern European standards) under their tormentors, who had learned from the Budapest bloodshed how to step back smartly from the brink. The lessons of real, paroled life are so often at variance with out prison-forced dreams.

Now the dog is dead. The thing many of us lived for. Call it socialism or communism, defense of the Soviet motherland or any of its "progressive" variations. All gone, just like Scarlett O'Hara's Tara. Well, tomorrow is another day, except it has just arrived, now, this moment.

I suspect the sequel to *G.W.T.W.* fails to mention it, but surely Scarlett's first task, after the glorious fade-out, is to earn a living for herself. That is what the left has to do now. Not "rebuild socialism" or re-create the socialist project (whatever that is). But we have to survive, as individuals, in a disintegrating economy, each of us in different ways, without the solace, or any real hope, of healing our wounds by achieving a traditional utopia in our time.

I am a born utopian. I cannot live a day of my life without also imaginatively inhabiting another planet altogether, where men and women are reduced to children, orphans really, seeking the Golden City where all fatherless and motherless kids are given open asylum without question or demur. Inside the American left, as a Communist and later left-socialist and now who-knows-what, or within the European left, where I have worked hard to eliminate Stalinism (as an editorial board member of *L'Etincelle*) and Toryism in Britain (as a "founding father" of the *Universities and Left Review*), where I am a paid-up member of the Chalk Farm ward of the Camden Labor Party, I have always been part of a broad "people's movement" to kick state-or-bourgeois capitalism in the crotch. It's been wonderful. The left draws in some of the best and worst people. We often don't treat one another well; our eyes sometimes are so fixed on a distant egalitarian prize that we do not feel our brother's or our sister's pain, or cries unvoiced because the comrades won't listen. But life without leftism would have been a bore.

After a respectable breather, no doubt we'll soon be up and at 'em again. But this time around, dear heart, no bullshit. No blather or hyphenated, postmodern, Derridean-induced, M.L.A.-approved, Leninist-fathered, neo-Hegelian prison-house of abstractions ("the people," "progressive coalition," any word starting "multi-"), soupy generalities ("forces of reaction," "gender-based") and waffle that feel like iron bars around my sense of reasonable syntax, and that always—

I repeat always—end up in an authoritarian mess. We now know, beyond a shadow of a doubt, that the impulse to use left rhetoric comes from the same primeval fear of reality, and down deep a hopelessness about the possibilities of changing our condition, as that felt by the L.A.P.D. cops as they slugged the brains out of Rodney King. Since 1917 (and even before, if you read your Marx, including "young Marx") socialism has rested one hand uneasily on its unholstered gunhip.

I too am a Marxist. Fat lot of good it does me. I cannot walk away from my past, the friends and comrades I have made, the mistakes I've committed, the hopes we shared. It is part of me the way that Freud is part of me—the way that (I fear) John Wayne's effeminate cowboy stride and Myrna Loy's laugh are part of me.

But I no longer have to spend my life in thrall to Hollywood-made images and the ideas they represent. Now is the time to stop already with the stale fantasies and Seconal rhetoric and think for ourselves, afresh, out of our own unique, unassailable (except by ourselves) personal experience, that which we know in our bones to be true about how daily life is won or lost by ourselves and our neighbors. Bad marriages, menstrual cramps, male hysteria, secrets of the heart locked so tightly inside our puritanical zeal—or the bad manners and surly-mouthedness that is its mirror image—that a real politics becomes impossible: That is what "community" is really about, not some glib label that a few able rhetoricians slap on an agenda for themselves and their fiery cousins.

Of course we mourn for the collective soul of socialism. But revolutionary grief, which is real, absurd and lastingly painful, locks us in a nostalgic dementia that can paralyze our language, tactics and abilities.

The hardest thing to do is think for ourselves. But we have models (not "role models," whatever that abomination is). Men and women who spoke, lived and wrote before the Deluge of Crap. (Incidentally, if you want to hear the latest version of Orwellian first-speak, not from the left this time, try Bill Clinton's invocation of "the Amurrican people" or Jerry Brown's litany of "take back this country"—from whom, to what? Not for nothing did Clinton study how to twist and slaughter the Mother Tongue at Oxford.)

Americans once spoke eloquently, plainly, sparely. Try the text of the Lincoln-Douglas debates. Or Sam Adams's exhortations to the Boston mob. Or Washington's Second Inaugural. Or Gene Debs's platform speeches, or Edmund Wilson's more cantankerous essays, or Randolph Bourne, or (to be unpatriotic) Virginia Woolf's *A Room of One's Own*. Today, I lean to the spiky women, Paglia and Ivins and Florence King (yes, that right-wing King). And for a real purgative to Bill C's never-inhale lying caterwauls, I do recommend a glance at how, not a word misplaced, Alexander Hamilton confessed in 1797 to screwing a fellow embezzler's wife. That's prose!

How do we regain a forgotten language? *The Nation* tries. Occasionally, it succeeds in publishing plain English written with force and point. But most of us are guilty, and there is a long way to go before we free ourselves of the whining, sentimental, self-serving, martyred, declamatory, Prussian-descended narrow rhetoric that is as much my radical reflex as yours. My mother and father, both labor organizers, were astonishingly free of this bilge—so there's no excuse for me. Maybe it was because they never went to college. Or because they had to learn to speak basic Yiddish, Russian, Croat, Polish, Italian and some Spanish before they could hope to earn the ears of their largely illiterate clients.

One part of me looks to the past for clarity, another warns that is how I got into trouble in the first place, by looking over my shoulder at the "authorities." I'm a big boy now. As they used to say on old-time news desks, it's time to go with what I've got. Meaning, each of us has an enormous, often despised, inner safety-deposit box of brilliantly lived experience, for which there simply was no room on all previous lefts. This experience—ordered, articulated, sealed at the joins by common sense and quiet decencies—is all we've really got. The door swings open with a huge and glorious clang. Let's go.

BAD BEARS NEWS—EXCHANGE

"William Seagraves" and Andrew Kopkind

•

Here Andrew Kopkind and "William Seagraves" (correspondent and author Dan Greenberg, now based in Washington D.C.) perpetrate the last in a series of animal hoaxes, stretching back to the early sixties. The first, in *The New Statesman*, also involved bears (Greenberg wrote in as an eminent British zoologist from Firmley-on-Clitt to inform Mr. Kopkind that his report about a dead bear thrown on the doorstep of a black family in the South to harass them was incorrect: The bear was not dead but hibernating). The duo have also skirmished about, among others, the eminent Mr. Preston Duck of Peking (in *The New Republic*) and in the April 2, 1988, *Nation* a Mr. "Loyal Chien" wrote in to protest Kopkind's "snide reference" to a golden retriever. Kopkind replied that "reader should know that correspondent Chien has been dogging my steps for many years on matters carnivorous. Years ago in another country, we were at each other tooth and claw over the hibernation (or estivation) habits of bears. . . ."

—THE EDITORS

BAD BEARS NEWS
Lowell, Mass.

Regarding "No Miracle in Lowell" by Andrew Kopkind [March 30]: I find it inconceivable that the author, in enumerating the many changes that Senator Tsongas produced in Lowell, likens the results to "Yellowstone or Yosemite. Without the bears."

It was only because of Senator Tsongas's intervention in an agricultural appropriations bill that funds were provided for the establishment of the Lowell Institute for Ursine Studies, now widely regarded (see *U.S. News* of Feb. 16, 1988) as the number-one center of ursine research in the United States. I can assure you that we are not confined to computer studies of bears, though we take considerable pride in having pioneered in developing that field, particularly in simulations of bear depredations against honey-producing hives, statutorily specified under the U.S.D.A. grant for this institute.

To the contrary, in our forest annex, we have in residence at the moment fourteen bears. Admittedly, they are not within the city limits of Lowell, but that point is not relevant to the present discussion, as they are no more than twenty-five minutes from downtown. On one occasion for a festival at town hall, we delivered a bear, on short notice, in little more than that time. By any reasonable measure, Lowell is not "without the bears." I hope you will publish this letter as a correction to a serious error.

WILLIAM SEAGRAVES

•

KOPKIND REPLIES
Guilford, Vt.

Readers have a right to know that Professor Seagraves is no ivory-tower scholar but the same "Smokey" Seagraves employed for many years by the U.S. Park Service and responsible for the notorious "Don't Feed the Bears" campaign, which resulted in widespread starvation, alienation and, ultimately, violence among this codependent species. Seagraves lost his job when he came under investigation by the I.R.S. for listing several bears (by name) for deductions as his "children," resulting in a net loss of income for over twenty years. It is widely believed in Lowell that Senator Tsongas managed to quash an indictment against him. Then, in a perfect example of the public-private "revolving door" pattern, replicating the whirligig movements of Tsongas from the U.S. Senate to Boston Edison to the Democratic presidential contest, Seagraves landed on his feet at UMass Lowell, where he continues his predations on the noble bear.

The more properly termed ursine-Americans (i.e., bears who reside in the United States) of Lowell are actually kept nowhere near the city, but are imprisoned in a barren and dismal pen *across the state line* in the Pheasant Lane Mall parking lot in Nashua, New Hampshire, where the enlightened laws of Massachusetts regarding the protection of our ursine cousins do not apply. This mall, of course, is one of the principal reasons for Lowell's recent decline: Residents have abandoned the expensive boutiques of the city for the cheaper shops in tax-free New Hampshire. Smokey and his bears are thus contributing to the failure of the experiment in urban renaissance undertaken by Tsongas.

And by the way, the "festival" Seagraves cites was in reality a rowdy brawl staged by Tsongas on a Greek national day, during which the poor bear was forced to drink ouzo and retsina, turned feral and vicious, mauled several small children and had to be put down. So much for ursine studies in Lowell.

ANDREW KOPKIND

IN L.A., BURNING ALL ILLUSIONS

Mike Davis

•

LOS ANGELES

THE ARMORED PERSONNEL carrier squats on the corner like *un gran sapo feo*—"a big ugly toad"—according to 9-year-old Emerio. His parents talk anxiously, almost in a whisper, about the *desaparecidos*: Raul from Tepic, big Mario, the younger Flores girl and the cousin from Ahuachapan. Like all Salvadorans, they know about those who "disappear"; they remember the headless corpses and the man whose tongue had been pulled through the hole in his throat like a necktie. That is why they came here—to ZIP code 90057, Los Angeles, California.

Now they are counting their friends and neighbors, Salvadoran and Mexican, who are suddenly gone. Some are still in the County Jail on Bauchet Street, little more than brown grains of sand lost among the 17,000 other alleged *saqueadores* (looters) and *incendarios* (arsonists) detained after the most violent American civil disturbance since the Irish poor burned Manhattan in 1863. Those without papers are probably already back in Tijuana, broke and disconsolate, cut off from their families and new lives. Violating city policy, the police fed hundreds of hapless undocumented *saqueadores* to the I.N.S. for deportation before the A.C.L.U. or immigrant rights groups even realized they had been arrested.

For many days the television talked only of the "South Central riot," "black rage" and the "Crips and Bloods." But Emerio's parents know that thousands of their neighbors from the MacArthur Park district—home to nearly one-tenth of all the Salvadorans in the world—also looted, burned, stayed out past curfew and went to jail. (An analysis of the first 5,000 arrests from all over the city revealed that 52 percent were poor Latinos, 10 percent whites and only 38 percent blacks.) They also know that the nation's first multiracial riot was as much about empty bellies and broken hearts as it was about police batons and Rodney King.

The week before the riot was unseasonably hot. At night the people lingered outside on the stoops and sidewalks of their tenements (MacArthur Park is L.A.'s Spanish Harlem), talking about their new burden of trouble. In a neighborhood far more crowded than mid-Manhattan and more dangerous than downtown Detroit, with more crack addicts and gangbangers than registered voters, *la gente* know how to laugh away every disaster except the final one. Yet there was a new melancholy in the air.

Too many people have been losing their jobs: their *pinche* $5.25-an-hour jobs as seamstresses, laborers, busboys and factory workers. In two years of recession, unemployment has tripled in L.A.'s immigrant neighborhoods. At Christmas more than 20,000 predominantly Latina women and children from throughout the central city waited all night in the cold to collect a free turkey and a blanket from charities. Other visible barometers of distress are the rapidly growing colonies of homeless *compañeros* on the desolate flanks of Crown Hill and in the concrete bed of the L.A. River, where people are forced to use sewage water for bathing and cooking.

As mothers and fathers lose their jobs, or as unemployed relatives move under the shelter of the extended family, there is increasing pressure on teenagers to supplement the family income. Belmont High School is the pride of "Little Central America," but with nearly 4,500 students it is severely overcrowded, and an additional 2,000 students must be bused to distant schools in the San Fernando Valley and elsewhere. Fully 7,000 school-age teenagers in the Belmont area, moreover, have dropped out of school. Some have entered the *vida loca* of gang culture (there are 100 different gangs in the school district that includes Belmont High), but most are struggling to find minimum-wage footholds in a declining economy.

The neighbors in MacArthur Park whom I interviewed, such as Emerio's parents, all speak of this gathering sense of unease, a perception of a future already looted. The riot arrived like a magic dispensation. People were initially shocked by the violence, then mesmerized by the televised images of biracial crowds in South Central L.A. helping themselves to mountains of desirable goods without interference from the police. The next day, Thursday, April 30, the authorities blundered twice: first by suspending school and releasing the kids into the streets; second by announcing that the National Guard was on the way to help enforce a dusk-to-dawn curfew.

Thousands immediately interpreted this as a last call to participate in the general redistribution of wealth in progress. Looting spread with explosive force throughout Hollywood and MacArthur Park, as well as parts of Echo Park, Van Nuys and Huntington Park. Although arsonists spread terrifying destruction, the looting crowds were governed by a visible moral economy. As one middle-aged lady explained to me, "Stealing is a sin, but this is like a television game show where everyone in the audience gets to win." Unlike the looters in Hollywood (some on skateboards) who stole Madonna's bustier and all the crotchless panties from Frederick's, the masses of MacArthur Park concentrated on the prosaic necessities of life like cockroach spray and Pampers.

Now, one week later, MacArthur Park is in a state of siege. A special "We Tip" hotline invites people to inform on neighbors or acquaintances suspected of looting. Elite L.A.P.D. Metro Squad units, supported by the National Guard, sweep through the tenements in search of stolen goods, while Border Patrolmen from as far away as Texas prowl the streets. Frantic parents search for missing kids, like mentally retarded 14-year-old Zuly Estrada, who is believed to have been deported to Mexico.

Meanwhile, thousands of *saqueadores*, many of them pathetic scavengers captured in the charred ruins the day after the looting, languish in County Jail, unable to meet absurdly high bails. One man, caught with a packet of sunflower seeds and two cartons of milk, is being held on $15,000; hundreds of others face felony indictments and possible two-year prison terms. Prosecutors demand thirty-day jail sentences for curfew violators, despite the fact that many of those are either homeless street people or Spanish-speakers who were unaware of the curfew. These are the "weeds" that George Bush says we must pull from the soil of our cities before it can be sown with the regenerating "seeds" of enterprise zones and tax breaks for private capital.

There is rising apprehension that the entire community will become a scapegoat. An ugly, seal-the-border nativism has been growing like crabgrass in Southern California since the start of the recession. A lynch mob of Orange County Republicans, led by Representative Dana Rohrabacher of Huntington Beach, demands the immediate deportation of all the undocumented immigrants arrested in the disturbance, while liberal Democrat Anthony Beilenson, sounding like the San Fernando Valley's Son-of-Le-Pen, proposes to strip citizenship from the U.S.-born children of illegals. According to Roberto Lovato of MacArthur Park's Central American Refugee Center, "We are becoming the guinea pigs, the Jews, in the militarized laboratory where George Bush is inventing his new urban order."

A BLACK *INTIFADA*?

"Little Gangster" Tak can't get over his amazement that he is actually standing in the same room of Brother Aziz's mosque with a bunch of Inglewood Crips. The handsome, 22-year-old Tak, a "straight up" Inglewood Blood who looks more like a black angel by Michelangelo than one of the Boyz N the Hood, still has two Crip bullets in his body, and "they still carry a few of mine." Some of the Crips and Bloods, whose blue or red gang colors have been virtual tribal flags, remember one another from school playground days, but mainly they have met over the barrels of automatics in a war that has divided Inglewood— the pleasant, black-majority city southwest of L.A. where the Lakers play—by a river of teenage blood. Now, as Tak explains, "Everybody knows what time it is. If we don't end the killing now and unite as black men, we never will."

Although Imam Aziz and the Nation of Islam have provided the formal auspices for peacemaking, the real hands that have "tied the red and blue rags together into a 'black thang' " are in Simi Valley. Within a few hours of the first attack on white motorists, which started in 8-Trey (83rd Street) Gangster Crip territory near Florence and Normandie, the insatiable war between the Crips and Bloods, fueled by a thousand neighborhood vendettas and dead homeboys, was "put on hold" throughout Los Angeles and the adjacent black suburbs of Compton and Inglewood.

Unlike the 1965 rebellion, which broke out south of Watts and remained primarily focused on the poorer east side of the ghetto, the 1992 riot reached its maximum temperature along Crenshaw Boulevard—the very heart of black Los Angeles's more affluent west side. Despite the illusion of full-immersion "actuality" provided by the minicam and the helicopter, television's coverage of the riot's angry edge was even more twisted than the melted steel of Crenshaw's devastated shopping centers. Most reporters—"image looters" as they are now being called in South Central—merely lip-synched suburban clichés as they tramped through the ruins of lives they had no desire to understand. A violent kaleidoscope of bewildering complexity was flattened into a single, categorical scenario: legitimate black anger over the King decision hijacked by hard-core street criminals and transformed into a maddened assault on their own community.

Local television thus unwittingly mimed the McCone Commission's summary judgment that the August 1965 Watts riot was primarily the act of a hoodlum fringe. In that case, a subsequent U.C.L.A. study revealed that the "riot of the riffraff" was in fact a popular uprising involving at least 50,000 working-class adults and their teenage children. When the arrest records of this latest uprising are finally analyzed, they will probably also vindicate the judgment of many residents that all segments of black youth, gang and non-gang, "buppie" as well as underclass, took part in the disorder.

Although in Los Angeles, as elsewhere, the new black middle class has socially and spatially pulled farther apart from the deindustrialized black working class, the L.A.P.D.'s Operation Hammer and other anti-gang dragnets that arrested kids at random (entering their names and addresses into an electronic gang roster that is now proving useful in house-to-house searches for riot "ringleaders") have tended to criminalize black youth without class distinction. Between 1987 and 1990, the combined sweeps of the L.A.P.D. and the County Sheriff's Office ensnared 50,000 "suspects." Even the children of doctors and lawyers from View Park and Windsor Hills have had to "kiss the pavement" and occasionally endure some of the humiliations that the homeboys in the flats face every day—experiences that reinforce the reputation of the gangs (and their poets laureate, the gangster rappers like Ice Cube and N.W.A.) as the heroes of an outlaw generation.

Yet if the riot had a broad social base, it was the participation of the gangs—or, rather, their cooperation—that gave it constant momentum and direction. If the 1965 rebellion was a hurricane, leveling one hundred blocks of Central Avenue from Vernon to Imperial Highway, the 1992 riot was a tornado, no less destructive but snaking a zigzag course through the commercial areas of the ghetto and beyond. Most of the media saw no pattern in its path, just blind, nihilistic destruction. In fact, the arson was ruthlessly systematic. By Friday morning 90 percent of the myriad Korean-owned liquor stores, markets and swapmeets in South Central L.A. had been wiped out. Deserted by the L.A.P.D., which made no attempt to defend small businesses, the Koreans suffered damage or destruction to almost 2,000 stores from Compton to the heart of Koreatown itself. One of the first to be attacked (although, ironically, it survived) was the grocery store where 15-year-old Latasha

Harlins was shot in the back of the head last year by Korean grocer Soon Ja Du in a dispute over a $1.79 bottle of orange juice. The girl died with the money for her purchase in her hand.

Latasha Harlins. A name that was scarcely mentioned on television was the key to the catastrophic collapse of relations between L.A.'s black and Korean communities. Ever since white judge Joyce Karlin let Du off with a $500 fine and some community service—a sentence which declared that the taking of a black child's life was scarcely more serious than drunk driving—some interethnic explosion has been virtually inevitable. The several near-riots at the Compton courthouse this winter were early warning signals of the black community's unassuaged grief over Harlins's murder. On the streets of South Central Wednesday and Thursday, I was repeatedly told, "This is for our baby sister. This is for Latasha."

The balance of grievances in the community is complex. Rodney King is the symbol that links unleashed police racism in Los Angeles to the crisis of black life everywhere, from Las Vegas to Toronto. Indeed, it is becoming clear that the King case may be almost as much of a watershed in American history as Dred Scott, a test of the very meaning of the citizenship for which African-Americans have struggled for 400 years.

But on the grass-roots level, especially among gang youth, Rodney King may not have quite the same profound resonance. As one of the Inglewood Bloods told me: "Rodney King? Shit, my homies be beat like dogs by the police every day. This riot is about all the homeboys murdered by the police, about the little sister killed by the Koreans, about twenty-seven years of oppression. Rodney King just the trigger."

At the same time, those who predicted that the next L.A. riot would be a literal Armageddon have been proved wrong. Despite a thousand Day-Glo exhortations on the walls of South Central to "Kill the Police," the gangs have refrained from the deadly guerrilla warfare that they are so formidably equipped to conduct. As in 1965, there has not been a single L.A.P.D. fatality, and indeed few serious police injuries of any kind.

In this round, at least, the brunt of gang power was directed toward the looting and destruction of the Korean stores. If Latasha Harlins is the impassioned pretext, there may be other agendas as well. I saw graffiti in South Central that advocated "Day one: burn them out. Day two: we rebuild." The only national leader whom most Crips and Bloods seem to take seriously is Louis Farrakhan, and his goal of black economic self-determination is broadly embraced. (Farrakhan, it should

be emphasized, has never advocated violence as a means to this end.)
At the Inglewood gang summit, which took place on May 5, there were
repeated references to a renaissance of black capitalism out of the
ashes of Korean businesses. "After all," an ex-Crip told me later, "we
didn't burn our community, just *their* stores."

In the meantime, the police and military occupiers of Los Angeles
give no credence to any peaceful, let alone entrepreneurial, transformation of L.A.'s black gang cultures. The ecumenical movement of the
Crips and Bloods is their worst imagining: gang violence no longer random but politicized into a black *intifada*. The L.A.P.D. remembers
only too well that a generation ago the Watts rebellion produced a gang
peace out of which grew the Los Angeles branch of the Black Panther
Party. As if to prove their suspicions, the police have circulated a copy
of an anonymous and possibly spurious leaflet calling for gang unity
and "an eye for an eye. . . . If L.A.P.D. hurt a black we'll kill two."

For its part, the Bush Administration has federalized the repression
in L.A. with an eye to the spectacle of the President marching in triumph, like a Roman emperor, with captured Crips and Bloods in
chains. Thus, the Justice Department has dispatched to L.A. the same
elite task force of federal marshals who captured Manuel Noriega in
Panama as reinforcements for L.A.P.D. and F.B.I. efforts to track down
the supposed gang instigators of the riots. But as a veteran of the 1965
riot said while watching SWAT teams arrest some of the hundreds of
rival gang members trying to meet peacefully at Watt's Jordan Downs
Housing Project: "That ole fool Bush think we as dumb as Saddam.
Land Marines in Compton and get hisself re-elected. But this ain't
Iraq. This is Vietnam, Jack."

THE GREAT FEAR
A core grievance fueling the Watts rebellion and the subsequent
urban insurrections of 1967–68 was rising black unemployment in the
midst of a boom economy. What contemporary journalists fearfully
described as the beginning of the "Second Civil War" was as much a
protest against black America's exclusion from the military-Keynesian
expansion of the 1960s as it was an uprising against police racism and
de facto segregation in schools and housing. The 1992 riot and its possible progenies must likewise be understood as insurrections against an
intolerable political-economic order. As even the *Los Angeles Times*,
main cheerleader for "World City L.A.," now editorially acknowledges,
the "globalization of Los Angeles" has produced "devastating poverty
for those weak in skills and resources."

Although the $1 billion worth of liquor stores and minimalls destroyed in L.A. may seem like chump change next to the $2.6 trillion recently annihilated on the Tokyo Stock Exchange, the burning of Oz probably fits into the same Hegelian niche with the bursting of the Bubble Economy: not the "end of history" at the seacoast of Malibu but the beginning of an ominous dialectic on the rim of the Pacific. It was a hallucination in the first place to imagine that the wheel of the world economy could be turned indefinitely by a Himalaya of U.S. trade deficits and a fictitious yen.

This structural crisis of the Japan-California "co-prosperity sphere," however, threatens to translate class contradictions into interethnic conflict on both the national and local level. Culturally distinct "middleman" groups—ethnic entrepreneurs and the like—risk being seen as the personal representatives of the invisible hand that has looted local communities of economic autonomy. In the case of Los Angeles, it was tragically the neighborhood Korean liquor store, not the skyscraper corporate fortress downtown, that became the symbol of a despised new world order.

On their side, the half-million Korean-Americans in L.A. have been psychologically lacerated by the failure of the state to protect them against black rage. Indeed, several young Koreans told me that they were especially bitter that the South Central shopping malls controlled by Alexander Haagen, a wealthy contributor to local politics, were quickly defended by police and National Guard, while their stores were leisurely ransacked and burned to the ground. "Maybe this is what we get," a U.C.L.A. student said, "for uncritically buying into the white middle class's attitude toward blacks and its faith in the police."

The prospects for a multicultural reconciliation in Los Angeles depend much less on white knight Peter Ueberroth's committee of corporate rebuilders than upon a general economic recovery in Southern California. As the Los Angeles *Business Journal* complained (after noting that L.A. had lost 100,000 manufacturing jobs over the past three years), "The riots are like poison administered to a sick patient."

Forecasts still under wraps at the Southern California Association of Governments paint a dark future for the Land of Sunshine, as job growth, slowed by the decline of aerospace as well as manufacturing shifts to Mexico, lags far behind population increase. Unemployment rates—not counting the estimated 40,000 jobs lost from the riot, and the uprising's impact on the business climate—are predicted to remain at 8 to 10 percent (and 40 to 50 percent for minority youth) for the next generation, while the housing crisis, already the most acute in the nation, will spill over into new waves of homelessness. Thus, the "widening divide" of income inequality in Los Angeles County, described in a landmark 1988 study by U.C.L.A. professor Paul Ong, will become an unbridgeable chasm. Southern California's endless summer is finally over.

Affluent Angelenos instinctively sensed this as they patrolled their Hancock Park estates with shotguns or bolted in their BMWs for white sanctuaries in Orange and Ventura counties. From Palm Springs pool-sides they anxiously awaited news of the burning of Beverly Hills by the Crips and Bloods, and fretted over the extra set of house keys they had foolishly entrusted to the Latina maid. Was she now an incendiarist? Although their fears were hysterically magnified, tentacles of disorder did penetrate such sanctums of white life as the Beverly Center and Westwood Village, as well as the Melrose and Fairfax neighborhoods. Most alarmingly, the L.A.P.D.'s "thin blue line," which had protected them in 1965, was now little more than a defunct metaphor, the last of Chief Gates's bad jokes.

EMERGENCY ROOM (TURNPIKE, ANYWHERE, U.S.A.)

•

The patient coffee machine urinates
endless specimens into little white cups
for tasters who find
something indeed is terribly wrong,
but never remember to send their reports to doctors
who could, perhaps, treat the condition.

The big soft drinker in the corner
is obsessed with her female operation.
She keeps saying to herself and anyone who will listen,
"They took everything out. I just feel so *empty*."
The experienced leave her alone, but the innocent
come up to her, offer warm conversational coin,
but expect something in return,
some womanly soothing for their *own* needs.
She only repeats her one statements, ". . . . so EMPTY."
until they feel like kicking her.
Some of them do.

The normally hot-blooded soup is stiff from chill,
the iceberg lettuce salad is limp from fever.
Side by side in their bins,
passing the time by chatting away,
they think they may suffer from the same disorder.
"I don't feel at all like myself."
"You do look awful."

"They let us sit here all day without any attention."
"Maybe an icepack would help you."
"You've got to keep yourself good and warm."
"It's obviously something going around."
"I hear it's a regular epidemic."

Left on a table to die, a sandwich
can hardly believe this has happened to him.
Having heard it said so often about
his friends and neighbors, he still never expected
his own epitaph to be:
"They opened him up, took one look,
and just closed him up again."

In an adjoining section sufferers can see
disjointed bits of medical training taking place.
A long, nearly unmoving queue of them
suggests that primarily women, these days,
wish to be surgeons.
Each comes out, after what must have been
a long, laborious scrub,
looking annoyed, holding her dripping hands
well away from body and shoulderbag,
shaking them violently to dry in the air,
since the snappers-on of the rubber gloves
must be practicing someplace else.

The male trainees shoot expeditiously in and out
of another door behind which must be required
only the briefest demonstration
of some minor but useful skill—
perhaps of assuming the look of dignified relief
and self-satisfaction,
the look that is still on the face of each when he exits,
that, when he's fully qualified, announces
to waiting relatives from far down the hall
"Yes, a-a-ah yes,
everything came out well."

Mona Van Duyn

A FEW KIND WORDS FOR LIBERALISM

Philip Green

•

TOWARD THE BEGINNING of the Reagan Administration James Watt, Secretary of the Interior, remarked that though he used to think there were two kinds of Americans, Republicans and Democrats, he'd now become convinced that we were divided into Americans and liberals. Just a few short years after that neofascist invocation, Mike Dukakis fled from the "L word" as though he had been accused of card-carrying Communism; and now Bill Clinton is doing the same. Liberal-baiting has replaced redbaiting as the favorite pastime of venomous conservatives.

How has it come about, this curious phenomenon of liberalism on the defensive in a cultural milieu that Louis Hartz famously described, in his *The Liberal Tradition in America*, as wholly and uniquely liberal? More curiously, why does liberalism seem to have, at least in the United States, such a self-annihilating history?

As Hartz pointed out, liberalism is an import from Britain, where it developed on the historical stage as a doctrine of individual property right (John Locke); unencumbered business enterprise (Adam Smith); utilitarian social reform to increase the general happiness (Jeremy Bentham); and equal civil liberty for all, individuals as well as collectivities, minorities as well as majorities (John Stuart Mill). In the United States it reached its modern apotheosis in the New Deal, but its direction can be seen as early as 1848, in Mill's *Principles of Political Economy*, in

which, after countless encomiums to the "free market," he concludes
with a discussion of "the grounds and limits of the laisser-faire or non-
interference principle" that virtually lays out a complete theory of the
contemporary welfare state.

Although it's sometimes said that the reformism and egalitarianism
of Bentham and Mill have displaced the private-property, free-market
orientation of Locke and Smith, what has always remained central to
liberalism is the notion of a social order in which individual liberty will
be able to flourish equally for all to the limit of their capacities, regardless of anyone's membership in a social group other than the one that
defines itself as "the majority." The great statements of this tradition
have become classics, and deservedly so:

> On any of the great open questions . . . if either of the two opinions has
> a better claim than the other, not merely to be tolerated, but to be encour-
> aged and countenanced, it is the one which happens at the particular time
> and place to be in the minority. That is the opinion which, for the time
> being, represents the neglected interests, the side of human well-being
> which is in danger of obtaining less than its share. [Mill, *On Liberty*]

> The entire history of social improvement has been a series of transi-
> tions, by which one custom or institution after another, from being a
> supposed primary necessity of social existence, has passed into the rank
> of a universally stigmatised injustice and tyranny. So it has been with
> the distinctions of slaves and freemen, nobles and serfs, patricians and
> plebeians; and so it will be, and in part already is, with the aristocracies
> of colour, race, and sex. [Mill, *Utilitarianism*]

> If there is any principle of the Constitution that more imperatively
> calls for attachment than any other it is the principle of free thought—
> not free thought for those who agree with us but freedom for the
> thought that we hate. [Justice Oliver Wendell Holmes Jr., dissenting in
> *U.S. v. Schwimmer*, 1929]

> Our Constitution is color-blind, and neither knows nor tolerates
> classes among citizens. In respect of civil rights, all citizens are equal
> before the law. The humblest is the peer of the most powerful. [Justice
> John Harlan, dissenting in *Plessy v. Ferguson*, 1896]

Why, it seems reasonable to ask, should this tradition of equal citizenship for all be so much on the defensive in a democratic culture?

Most obviously, liberalism stands in a very uneasy relationship to democracy, which enshrines majority rule. Even leaving aside the institution of judicial review, the principles of liberal tolerance and equality call for an incredible degree of self-restraint on the part of those who think of themselves as a majority—silent or vocal. Where the majority is white-skinned, liberals demand equality for people whose skins are of a different color. Where the majority believes in traditional religious values and behaviors, liberals demand equality not just for people who have different values and behaviors but even for those who loudly flaunt them. Liberals can give their overt assent to conventionally honored buzzwords such as "family" and "community," and their sympathetic attention to those who live and die by those concepts; but when push comes to shove, liberals cannot give equal respect to patriarchal families that oppress women, or to communities that practice bigotry and exclusion. Liberalism is hopelessly cosmopolitan in a world of parochialisms; tolerant of every deviation imaginable but scornful of intolerance, even when intolerance of one kind or another is the way of life of the ordinary person; respectful of religious diversity but unable to respect dogma or fanaticism.

It's sometimes claimed that liberalism has lost its cachet because it has forsaken its origins, the allegedly single-minded dedication to private accumulation of Locke or Smith. That may be true for the Bushes and Quayles among us, who suffer the indignity of having to run for offices they once would have inherited. But the attacks on liberalism by the wealthy and their spokespersons should not resonate so intensely among other classes merely because liberals appear to them to have accommodated to the wealthy! For although liberalism stands in such an uneasy relationship to democracy, that does not explain why conservatism, its most visible opponent, has been able to reap the benefit of that difficulty. For conservatism, as opposed to liberalism, is actively hostile to democracy. Since the inception of socialist and social democratic movements, conservatives have had to make peace with democratic values, but that has rarely been from conviction, only from opportunism. For their actual views one has only to look at the obscene posture of the Bush Administration toward the Motor Voter Registration Bill; or the evisceration of the right to strike or even to organize labor unions after twelve years of conservative dominance.

Similar to those attempts to thwart popular mobilization are the Reagan/Bush efforts to shut down all avenues toward open government, and to hide information from the public; to extend presidential prerogative to the point of excluding any representative voice at all in the conduct of foreign affairs, and to develop a secret, illegal, unelected government for that purpose. As Theodore Draper has pointed out, the entire purpose of the Iran/*contra* scheme was to shelter policymaking not from the nation's "enemies," who knew perfectly well what was going on, but from the American people themselves, the only ones who were in the dark.

Whatever liberals seem to stand for, then, contemporary conservatives stand for bureaucratic autocracy and corporate plutocracy as much as they do for "free markets." And yet conservatism, in the version that British sociologist Stuart Hall calls "authoritarian populism," can also pretend to stand for "the people" in a manner debarred to liberalism. For the authoritarian populist version of conservatism purports to represent a self-conceived monolithic majority that, even when angry, is resigned to its exclusion from power and wealth no matter who rules, but correctly believes that conservatives will better defend the only prerogatives it has remaining to it, e.g., to determine who is going to move in next door, or to police the sexual behavior of its children.

In addition, liberalism has an even deeper difficulty. Where democracy invokes the people and the majority, and imagines that through simple acts of honest representation their virtuous will can be made into virtuous law, liberalism substitutes an intellectual policy elite of administrators and judges. The problem is not who runs liberal institutions—whether it is the allegedly "undemocratic" Supreme Court, or even "pointyheaded bureaucrats"—but what they do and how they do it. The unpleasant truth, first elucidated by Max Weber, is that in the modern democratic age "democracy" is the facade behind which administrative experts, in one guise or another, get the real job done. To take a historically crucial example: For simple, apparently populist solutions to economic crises, like the use of greenbacks in place of specie, or free silver, liberalism substituted what has become the impenetrable system of the Federal Reserve. Or, again, for democratic class conflict, liberalism substitutes a legal *right* to strike, a right that is less a guarantor of action than a system of formal legal constraints on it. Thus it often appears that liberal government is not on the side of the working class but is instead neutral when labor clashes with what John L. Lewis called its "deadly adversary" (and even worse than neutral when conservatives take over administration and make institutions like the National Labor Relations Board into handmaidens of business power). In other words, everywhere the putative democratic majority looks, it sees what it thought was its power dissolve into the evanescent web of administrative relationships, and what it thought was its moral virtue scathingly criticized by the moral experts of liberal tolerance. Liberal reform often represents the replacement of mass uprising and mass resistance by professionally defined regulation and control; and a critique of traditional mass values by philosophical ethics.

Moreover, liberal reform has a fatal predilection for weakening its primary tool—government. Since Bentham and Mill, liberals have insisted that government is the only agency capable of reforming the conditions that make democratic equality unachievable. Under the sway of liberal reformers, however, government promises much but delivers very little, and so government in general comes to bear the onus of failure to achieve a real measure of that equality. Liberalism thus pays a price for its unfulfilled pretenses, and its lack of credibility worsens as conservatives, when they control government, deliberately corrupt and cripple it.

This weakness of liberal government, moreover, is based in large part on the conviction that the private sector is itself not "political," a conviction that stems from liberalism's own founding myth of private property and free enterprise. Liberals, committed to that belief along with a belief in the individual and minority rights rather than class struggle, thus find it difficult to make an unequivocal alliance with the only class that has an interest in challenging that myth.

For better or worse, then, Dan Quayle is not totally off the mark when he attacks the "liberal cultural elite" that allegedly dominates our public discourse. Liberalism's commitment to social reform, as opposed to conservatism's dedication to ideological revanchism, requires and has always brought to the forefront a class of intellectual (and, more recently, therapeutic) experts: policy-makers and policy exponents who speak a language of progress through science, education and an ideal of tolerance that is modern liberalism's equivalent of moral virtue. Like Senator Roman Hruska defending the nomination of G. Harrold Carswell to the Supreme Court on the ground that even mediocre people deserve representation, the buffoonish Vice President speaks for those who lack access to that language of progress. (That his speeches are written for him and his positions articulated by paid-up members of the cultural elite such as William Kristol is another matter—though of course, not really.)

Furthermore, Quayle is also correct in another important respect. "Liberal" is exactly the word to describe, for example, Diane English, creator of *Murphy Brown*, or Hillary Clinton or Bill Clinton's good friend Linda Bloodworth-Thomason of *Designing Women*—and, like Dukakis before them, Clinton and Albert Gore. By the standards of

Mill, John Dewey, John Rawls, Teddy Kennedy or Hillary Clinton, Clinton and Gore may not be very good liberals, but liberals are indubitably what they are; as Joe Louis said of one of his opponents, he can run but he can't hide. The whole bag of sleazy diversions, from slavering over executions to denouncing Sister Souljah, will not fool any of the new redbaiters, who can look at Gore's high rating on Americans for Democratic Action's roll-call vote scale, or Clinton's remarks about "denial" and "neglect" after the Los Angeles riots and his proposal for public works investment in urban areas, or his calls for a tougher income tax on the wealthy. But as the electorate eventually becomes skeptical of their self-evidently evasive tactic of chastising the name-callers for calling names, what should compromised liberal politicians do—always keeping in mind that there is no such thing as an uncompromised politician of any kind?

Most simply, they ought to understand that Louis Hartz was right about America being a liberal milieu. He may have underestimated the corrosive effects of race, gender and sexuality on the polity. Yet it is, in the end, an undeniably liberal polity, and aspects of that heritage are worth standing on no matter how divisive they may seem at present; worth standing on not merely for those who want to be morally correct but for those who want to win as well. Yes, there are many illiberal votes for censorship of avant-garde art, but anyone who runs on a ticket of that *and* "right to life" is going to lose in most parts of the nation. The right to be let alone by the government is fundamental to Americans; there are no votes to be lost, and many to be gained, by emphasizing its application to abortion policy. The same is true of the right to vote, the cornerstone of equal citizenship; a liberal who is not in a constant rage about the Republican opposition to simplified voter registration is not committed to either democracy or liberalism, and will deserve the apathy with which a large portion of the potential electorate will greet his candidacy.

As for liberal reform, it is obvious that we cannot expect ringing endorsements of affirmative action in the present political climate, despite its being a fundamental and typical instance of liberal rectification. We can expect, though, that a liberal President will (learning a lesson from his conservative counterparts) appoint judges who will preserve rather than eviscerate it. And if we can't expect even liberal democrats today to join enthusiastically in an antiracism crusade, we can expect them at least to be committed to other fundamental aspects of liberal equality. The basis of equal citizenship is that all people should have the chance to perform up to their fullest capabilities, and this is an ideal that in principle few Americans will deny. Thus liberals should be unashamed to stand on the utilitarian notion that every time a potentially productive worker is lost to drugs, crime, illiteracy, unemployment or underemployment, we are all losers. "Workfare" may be a political necessity these days, but it is an illusion; education, though, is the real thing, and proposals for universal access to education from Head Start through graduate school (and for educational rather than military solutions to the drug problem) are both liberal and "American," and genuinely productive as well. So too is compensatory aid to cities, to rectify years not just of neglect but of policies deliberately designed to reward white suburbs and strangle nonwhite inner cities. So too is effective day care, for women who want to or who must participate in the nondomestic work force; and proper health care, for all who deserve it because they are ill, not because they have one level of income instead of another. And although liberal and not-so-liberal Democratic politicians may be in thrall to the banks and insurance companies and communications empires and fractions of industrial capital that finance their campaigns, none of this need prevent them from the obvious step of guaranteeing organized labor's bottom line for attacking the imbalance between capital and the working class: a law forbidding the hiring of replacement workers during strikes, and the promise of appointments to the N.L.R.B. that will at least treat the right to strike as a right, and the right to strikebreak as an abomination.

These are only examples; my point is not to come up with one more potpourri of liberal programs but to suggest that there is still an American liberalism, combining both rights and reform, that political leaders can successfully embrace rather than shun. And if none of this will even begin to solve the profound structural problems of the American economy, the armchair radicals who never tire of pointing this out do not have the faintest realistic idea themselves what might be done.

As for the traditional attitude of the radical left toward liberals, the first thing that ought to be evident to anyone capable of coherent thought is that there is not going to be a revolutionary Marxist system or an androgynous utopia or even a social democratic commonwealth in the United States in the near future, or perhaps any future. Yes, given liberalism's origins, liberals have to be reminded that capitalism by its nature reproduces exploitation and injustice; and that the opportunity to fulfill individual capacities is considerably more available to well-born white men than to the children of the poor or people of color or women. Still, the horror with which radicals perennially discover that

liberals are really liberals—that they are committed to impartial government, class neutrality, tolerance of manifest evil, and lesser-evil
reform rather than revolution—has become a tiresome imitation of
Claude Rains in *Casablanca*: "I'm shocked, *shocked* to find that gambling is going on in here!" We ought to give it a rest. We ought to be
aware of making implicit unholy alliances with the right by attacking
liberal tolerance because it falls short of embracing racial, ethnic or
sexual "difference"; the welfare state because it perpetuates private
property and wage labor; government because it entails bureaucracy;
free speech because hurtful things get said.

Liberal tolerance and the liberal version of civic equality, though
perhaps they can be improved on, are in the end not dispensable. An
American society without liberalism would be a sinkhole of racism,
sexism, and every form of unabashed bigotry. It would be a society in
which black men got tried by juries of white men and routinely executed for crimes they may not have committed; in which people of
color couldn't go to public schools or colleges and universities of their
own choice; books like *Our Bodies, Ourselves* couldn't get distributed;
union organizers couldn't speak to potential members anywhere without fear of being beaten up or arrested; gays wouldn't dare speak their
name; blasphemy against Christian dogma would be a crime; and so on.
There isn't much civility in American society today, but most of what
there is has been nurtured by liberal policies and attitudes.

What the left should finally recognize is that conservatives are right.
Liberalism, properly considered, makes immense demands on the
social order; it indeed deserves, or at least can deserve, the epithet of
"creeping socialism." From the moment of formation of the First
International, if not before, liberals, as Mill's *Principles* testifies, have
been under constant pressure to extend their understanding of the
extensiveness of the changes necessary to make good the promises of
liberal equality; and they have constantly done so. Thus the "Reagan
Democrats" who consistently tell interviewers that the Democratic
Party has "gone too far" in representing black people have a sadly inaccurate idea of what civil rights legislation and affirmative action have
actually accomplished; but they are a lot closer to the truth than those
on the left who castigate liberals for "not really" opposing racism. The
task for radicals, then, is never to let up their pressure, always to point
out how much remains to be done after the latest bout of liberal
reform, but not to treat liberalism but rather a compromised and half-
hearted version of it that makes supine compromises with political

power brokers or corporate moneybags. What's wrong with liberals, usually, is not that they're liberal but that they're not liberal enough.

As for liberals, *their* real task is to have the guts to go on being liberal, however they may feel they have to treat the word itself; and however they may have to modify contemporary liberal rhetoric. Liberalism may not be *the* American way, but it is indeed *an* American way, and despite all its limitations still the best one realistically available to us.

NOTES FROM ANOTHER COUNTRY

Molly Ivins

•

HOUSTON

NOTHING LIKE A Republican convention to drive you screaming back into the arms of the Democrats. Especially this convention. The elders of the press corps kept muttering they hadn't seen anything like it since the Goldwater convention in '64. True, the Republicans spent much of their time peddling fear and loathing, but it was more silly than scary, like watching people dressed in bad Halloween werewolf costumes. During the buildup to the convention, the most cockeyed optimists among the Democrats were in hopes the Republicans would tear themselves apart over abortion. No need. The party was dead meat on arrival.

I am a cautious political bettor. It's silly to put money down any closer than six weeks out from Election Day, and one should never underestimate the ability of the Democrats to screw up. But the Republicans have nothing going for them and nothing they can try works. They got a three-point bounce out of their convention. The in-depth polling shows the great majority of the public didn't care for the gay-bashing, didn't care for the feminist-bashing, didn't care for the Hillary-bashing and thought the whole exercise was too negative. It was.

The most surprising aspect of the convention was George Bush, and the surprise was—no surprises, not even a mini-idea. His own advisers were pushing the line that his big speech would finally, at long last, answer all the questions—how to get out of the recession, what the domestic agenda should be and what his vision thing actually is. They even promised that after four long years we would learn who the hell he is and what he really believes. We got nothing.

On the economy, one more time, he pushed a capital gains tax cut. There is little historical evidence that a cap gains cut stimulates the economy, and recent studies by academic economists (as opposed to the political kind) show that half of realized capital gains go straight into consumption. It's the dumbest kind of tax subsidy to conspicuous consumption you can try.

You can argue, as both Paul Tsongas and Bill Clinton do, that a targeted capital gains cut would be beneficial. Bush not only wants the cut with no strings, he's even arguing for a cut on past investments, which is nothing but a windfall for richies.

The confabulation in Houston was not, however, without its charms. I loved Ronald Reagan's speech (apparently he, not Peggy Noonan, actually wrote it)—especially the line about Thomas Jefferson. Until it occurred to me to wonder what would have happened if Jefferson, surely the finest intellect this soil has ever produced, actually did meet Reagan. Imagine the conversation:

"Ignorance is preferable to error; and he is less remote from the truth who believes nothing, than he who believes what is wrong."

"Well. Make my day."

(Such ruminations may be a consequence of the brain damage caused by listening to Republicans bloviate for hours on end. In the line of journalistic duty, I attended the God and Country Rally featuring Phyllis Schlafly, Pat Robertson and Pat Boone, and am filing a worker's compensation claim against *The Nation*.)

Many people did not care for Pat Buchanan's speech; it probably sounded better in the original German.

No one could decide whether Phil Gramm or Pat Robertson made the worst speech of the convention, perhaps because no one listened to them.

In trying to determine just how far to the right the G.O.P.'s loony wing will go, it's worth noting how Pat Robertson, past and possibly future G.O.P. presidential candidate, is fighting Iowa's proposed equal rights amendment. Pat says feminism "encourages women to leave their husbands, kill their children, practice witchcraft, destroy capitalism and become lesbians."

Listening to George Bush, toward the end of his speech, read the poetry written by Ray Price with the gestures scripted by speech coach

Roger Ailes, I was struck anew by the elaborate charade of emperor's clothing in which the American press is so supinely complicit. Bush has no more sense of poetry than he does of grammar. After the speech there was much division in the pundit corps over whether Bush had just "hit it out of the park" (both sports and war metaphors were much in vogue) or whether we had just heard a load of nasty political drivel without a single redeeming idea. But all hands were solemnly pretending we had just heard George Bush, the nation's most incoherent speaker, stand up and make a fifty-eight-minute political address.

George Bush without a Teleprompter can scarcely produce an intelligible sentence. I've been listening to him since 1966 and must confess to a secret fondness for his verbal dyslexia. Hearing him has the charm and suspense of those old adventure-movie serials: Will this man ever fight his way out of this sentence alive? As he flops from one syntactical Waterloo to the next, ever in the verbless mode, in search of the long lost predicate, or even a subject, you find yourself struggling with him, rooting for him. What is this man actually trying to say? What could he possibly mean? Hold it, I think I see it!

Imagine, for a mad moment, George Bush in the British Parliament, where the members are not only fluent in English but expected to think on their feet as well. I am told that public policy is often hammered out in the exchange of thought there. How would anyone ever figure out that Bush thinks? This is not a matter of grammar: Anyone who has ever heard some canny country legislator fracture the language while making his point knows clarity is not synonymous with syntax. The fact is that unless someone else writes a speech for him, the President of the United States sounds like a border-line moron. But the media sit around pretending that he can actually talk—can convince, inspire and lead us.

We have long been accustomed to hearing Republicans exploit racial fears, usually by talking about crime. The "family values" issue is a more subtle exploitation of the doubt, confusion and guilt felt by American women. Women are receiving so many conflicting messages from this society that no matter what choices we make, or more often, what roles necessity forces on us—work, family or the difficult combination of both—we all feel guilty about what we're doing. It's quite true that full-time homemakers resent the condescension in remarks like Hillary Clinton's "What did you expect me to do, stay home and bake cookies?" But this is a society in which people's worth is judged by how much money they make, and the esteem in which our society holds wives and mothers is reflected in their salaries.

For a political party that has consistently opposed every effort to build a support network for working mothers to then condemn and guilt-trip them is despicable. Natal leave, parental leave, day care—the whole complex of programs that exist in other industrialized nations to help working mothers does not exist here, thanks to the Republican Party. Most women in this country work because they have to. Most are still stuck in the pink-collar ghettos of sales personnel, clerical personnel and waitressing. Clerical workers are in a particular bind as more and more corporations replace them with "temporary workers" in order to avoid having to pay health and retirement benefits.

The gay-bashing at the convention would have been offensive even without the AIDS epidemic. Have they no shame, at long last have they no shame? I watched delegates who are the mothers of gay sons sit there and listen without protest. I don't know what it says about their family values.

I'm not even sure why any of this was discussed at the political convention, except that the R's clearly see political gain in it. The Constitution says the purpose of our government is "to form a more perfect union, establish justice, insure domestic tranquillity, provide for the common defense, promote the general welfare, and secure the blessings of liberty to ourselves and our posterity." The President is nowhere designated in the Constitution as arbiter of our sexual morals.

Trying to figure out from whence and why came the nastiness at that convention, I found two sources.

There are lots of nice Republicans in this world, perfectly decent, quite bright people. When Peggy Noonan, Reagan's speechwriter, covered the Democratic convention for *Newsweek*, she wrote: "There was much talk of unity, but what I saw was the pretty homogenized gathering of one of the great parties of an increasingly homogenized country—a country that has been ironed out, no lumps and wrinkles and grass stains, a country in which we are becoming all alike, sophisticated, Gapped, linened and Lancômed." It occurred to me that Noonan not only did not attend the same Democratic convention I did, she does not live in the same country I do.

Turns out she lives in East Hampton, Long Island, which may account for it. Despite having lost her job at the White House a few years ago, she does not seem to have spent any time in the unemployment line. In her country, people aren't worried about their jobs, they aren't caught in hideous health insurance binds, they aren't watching their standard of living slip slowly down, their hopes for a home slip slowly away, their dreams for the future dwindle. It's another country, the country of those who are Doing Well.

The second source of the nastiness is cynical political professionals pushing divisiveness for political reasons, exploiting fear and bigotry because it works. Old dog. Still hunts.

The professionals around Bush seem, like the man himself, not to believe in much of anything except their own entitlement to power. They are not the true believers of the Reagan years, nor even like the angry lower-middle-class Nixonites feeling snubbed by the Eastern Establishment. Too many years, too many limousines. They're out of touch with the country and fighting like piranhas not for ideas or any vision of a better America—they're fighting to keep their limousines.

THE CHARACTER OF PRESIDENTS

E. L. Doctorow

•

MR. BUSH HAS said, by way of defaming Mr. Clinton's character, that the character of a presidential candidate is important. So it is. The President we get is the country we get. With each new President the nation is conformed spiritually. He is the artificer of our malleable national soul. He proposes not only the laws but the kinds of lawlessness that govern our lives and invoke our responses. The people he appoints are cast in his image. The trouble they get into, and get us into, is his characteristic trouble. Finally, the media amplify his character into our moral weather report. He becomes the face of our sky, the conditions that prevail. One four-year term may find us at reasonable peace with one another, working things out, and the next, trampling on each other for our scraps of bread.

That a President is inevitably put forward and elected by the forces of established wealth and power means usually that he will be indentured by the time he reaches office. But in fact he is the freest of men if he will have the courage to think so and, at least theoretically, could be so transported by the millions of people who have endorsed his candidacy as to want to do the best for them. He might come to solemn appreciation of the vote we cast, in all our multicolored and multigendered millions, as an act of trust, fingers crossed, a kind of prayer.

Not that it's worked out that way. In 1968 Richard Nixon rebounded from his defeat at the hands of Jack Kennedy, and there he was again, his head sunk between the hunched shoulders of his three-button suit and his arms raised in victory, the exacted revenge of the pod people. That someone so rigid, and lacking in honor or moral distinction of any kind, someone so stiff with crippling hatreds, so spiritually dysfunctional, out of touch with everything in life that is joyful and fervently beautiful and blessed, with no discernible reverence in him for human life, and certainly with never a hope of wisdom, but living only by pure politics as if it were some colorless blood substitute in his veins—that this being could lurchingly stumble up from his own wretched career and use history and the two-party system to elect himself President is, I suppose, a gloriously perverse justification of our democratic form of government.

I think of the President's men cast in Mr. Nixon's character: convicts-to-be Ehrlichman, Haldeman and Mitchell; and Henry Kissinger, who seemed to go through the ranks as if magnetized, until he stood at the President's side, his moral clone in the practice of malefic self-promotion. I think of the events sprung from Mr. Nixon's character: the four students going down in a volley of gunfire in the campus park of Kent State University. More than 7,000 antiwar marchers detained in a stadium in Washington, D.C. The secret bombing of Cambodia, the secret deaths, the secret numbers, the always secret *Realpolitik* operations. And one other lingers in the mind: the time he ordered plumed golden helmets, Bismarckian tunics and black riding boots for the White House honor guard.

The subsequent two holders of the office, Mr. Ford and Mr. Carter, showed hardly any character at all, the one a kind of stolid mangler of the language whose major contribution to American history was to pardon Richard Nixon, the other a well-meaning but terribly vacillating permanent-pressed piety who ran as a liberal and governed as a conservative. We jogged in place during their terms of office. Nobody in America can remember where they were during Mr. Carter's term, or what they were doing, or if they had any waking life at all. Mr. Carter's biblical fundamentalism gave him exceptional patience in the negotiation of a peace between Israel and Egypt, but Washington looked nothing like the Sinai and did not inspire him. The ancient Near East was his glory and, with the failed desert operation to rescue the hostages in Iran, his downfall. He did define human rights as a factor in international relations, but did not become an honorable champion of the idea until he had left office. His vapidity is remembered, like the nervous smiles flitting across his face, as an invitation to the electorate to bring in the wolves of the right who had all this time been pacing back and forth and fitfully baying in the darkness beyond the campsite.

And so in 1980 we found ourselves living the mystery of Ronald Reagan.

With not much more than his chuckles and shrugs and grins and little jokes, Mr. Reagan managed in two elections to persuade a majority of the white working/middle class to vote against their own interests. The old self-caricaturing B-movie actor had the amazing capacity to destroy people's lives without losing their loyalty. He was said to go blank without a script, and his political opponents could think of nothing worse to call him than, in the words of Clark Clifford, an "amiable dunce." But his heartfelt pieties and simplistic reductions of thought, his misquotations and exaggerations, his mawkish appeals to rugged self-reliance spearheaded a devastating assault on the remedial legislation that had been enacted from the New Deal to the Great Society, set off new brazen white racist furies across the land and culminated in the most dangerous conspiracy against American constitutional government in the twentieth century.

The old deaf actor who nodded off in staff meetings managed always to wake up in time to approve schemes at variance with his oath of office. He refused to enforce civil rights laws, subverted the antitrust statutes, withheld Social Security payments from disabled people, cut off school lunches for needy children and gave into private hands the conduct of American foreign policy in Central America. Under the persona of this fervent charmer, we were released into our great decade of deregulated thievery, and learned that the paramount issues of our age were abortion and school prayer. Meanwhile the rich got filthy rich, the middle class turned poor, the profession of begging for alms was restored to the streets and the national debt rose to about $3 trillion.

Now there was a President with character.

Since the end of the war in Vietnam, American government under Republican Presidents has been punitive. Their philosophy is called conservatism, but the result in these many years of its application has been to dissipate the wealth of the country and lower the standard of living, health and hopes of an education of all but the top economic stratum of society. That is punitive. What Mr. Clinton refers to, inadequately, as the trickle-down theory is really the oligarchical presumption that no one but an executive citizenry of C.E.O.s, money managers and the rich and well-born really matters. When Mr. Reagan talked of getting "the government off our backs" what he meant was freeing this executive from burdens of public polity. No regulatory agency must stand in the way of our cutting timber, no judge can enjoin us from acting to restrain the competition, no labor law must stop us from moving a manufacturing plant to Indonesia, where they work for a tenth of the wage. For that matter, women will have no legal rights in the conduct of their own personal lives, and the fate of all citizens, as well as the natural world they live in, or what's left of it, is to be entrusted perpetually to the beneficent rule of the white male businessman to whom God in His infinite wisdom has given the property interests of the country.

There is an electoral strategy for implementing this nineteenth-century baronialism, and we are seeing and hearing it again in this campaign because it has always been very effective. It relies on the mordant truth that the right-wing politician has less of a distance to go to find and exploit our tribal fears and hatreds than his opponent who would track down and engage our better selves. That it seeks out and fires the antediluvian circuits of our brains is the right's advantage in every election. Pat Buchanan at the Republican convention was the Cro-Magnon baring his canines and waving his club.

The right will always invoke an enemy within. They will insist on a distinction between real Americans and those who say they are but aren't. This latter is your basic nativist amalgam of people of the wrong color, recent immigration or incorrect religious persuasion. At the beginning of the cold war "fellow travelers" and "pinkos" were added to the list (Communists being historically beyond the pale). Mr. Nixon contributed "effete intellectuals"; Mr. Reagan's Secretary of the Interior, James Watt, threw "cripples" into the pot with Jews and blacks; and this President and his men have consigned to perdition single parents, gays and lesbians, and a "cultural elite," by which they mean not only the college-educated; cosmopolitan (Jewish and their fellow-traveling) residents of both coasts who write or work in publishing, films or television but really any person in any region of the country who is articulate enough to compose a sentence telling them what a disgrace they are.

Mr. Clinton's dissenting actions during the Vietnam War place him at the head of the dark and threatening coalition of faux Americans. He is, finally, the treacherous son who dares to oppose the father. As far as Mr. Bush and his backers are concerned, when the young people of this country rejected the war in Vietnam, they gave up their generational right of succession to primacy and power. They could no longer be trusted. Neither could the democracy that spawned them like an overly permissive parent ever again be trusted.

All the Presidents since Vietnam, from Nixon to Bush, have been of the same World War II generation. They will not be moved. The thrust of their government has been, punitively, to teach us the error of our ways, to put things back to the time when people stayed in their place and owed their souls to the company store.

In June 1989 Mr. Bush vetoed a bill that would have raised the minimum wage to $4.55 an hour over three years. In October 1989 he vetoed a bill that included a provision for the use of Medicaid funds to pay for abortions for poor women who were the victims of rape or incest. In October 1990 he vetoed the Civil Rights Act enacted by Congress to set aside Supreme Court rulings that make it more difficult for women and minorities to win employment discrimination suits. In October of the next year he vetoed a bill extending benefits to people who had exhausted their twenty-six weeks of unemployment insurance (reversing himself in November to sign a more modest extension). On June 23 of this year he vetoed a bill that would have allowed the use of aborted fetuses in federally funded research. In September he vetoed the family leave bill, which would have entitled workers to be allowed unpaid time off for births or medical emergencies in their families. In July he vetoed the "motor voter" bill, which would have allowed citizens to register to vote when applying for driver's licenses.

The would-be beneficiaries of these bills—people who sweep floors, kids who work at McDonald's, poor women, blacks, the critically ill, people who've lost their jobs, working mothers and fathers, and non-voters (can't have too many of those)—always heard from Mr. Bush at the time of the veto that they had his sympathy, but that somehow, or someway, the bills on their behalf would not have done what they were designed to do and in fact would have made their lives worse.

Mr. Bush is a man who lies. Senator Dole, who ran against him in 1988, was the first to tell us that. Vice President Bush lied about his opponents in the primaries, and he lied about Mr. Dukakis in the election. President Bush lies today about the bills he vetoed as he lies about his involvement in the arms for hostages trade with Iran and continues to lie, even though he has been directly contradicted by two former Secretaries in the Reagan Cabinet—Schultz and Weinberger—and a former staff member of the National Security Council. He lies about what he did in the past and about why he is doing what he is doing in the present. He speaks for civil rights, but blocks legislation that would relieve racial inequities. He speaks for the environment but opposes measures to slow its despoliation.

You and I can lie about our actions, and misrepresent the actions of others; we can piously pretend to principles we don't believe in; we can whine and blame others for the wrong that we do. We can think only of ourselves and our own and be brutally indifferent to the needs of everyone else. We can manipulate people, call them names, con them and rob them blind. Our virtuosity is inexhaustible, as would be expected of a race of Original Sinners, and without doubt, we will all have our Maker to answer to. But as to a calculus of damage done, the devastation left behind, the person who holds the most powerful political office in the world and does these things and acts in these ways is multiplied in his moral failure to a number beyond the imagining of the rest of us.

Nevertheless, there is something hopeful to be discerned in all of this. Mr. Bush is a candidate on the defensive. His term in office has been disastrous. This presidential heir to the conservative legacy of Mr. Nixon and Mr. Reagan has about him the ambience of the weak dauphin. His own right-wing constituency is disgusted with him possibly because he portends the end of an age, the decadence of a ruling idea or merely the played-out vein of the Republican gold mine. Certainly he is, in all his ways, less than resolute. Lying is a tacit admission of having done something inadmissible. A mosaic of presidential lies offers the cryptic image of a better world.

All else being equal, what sort of presidential character is most likely to take us there?

Who would not wish for someone, first of all, who realizes that once elected, he cannot be the President merely of the constituency that empowered him but, if he would fill the defining role of the office, a President on behalf of everyone? That is a simple grade-school concept, and, given the relation in America of money to politics, cannot be anything more than that. But the President who had the courage to live by it would immediately lead a reformist movement to erase the advantages big money accords to itself by its political contributions and its lobbying. This would presume a morally intelligent President as well as a courageous one.

I would wish for a developed historical sense in the President, one that could understand and honestly acknowledge that the political philosophy of what we lovingly call the free market has in the past justified slavery, child labor, the gunning down of strikers by state militias and so forth.

I would want a presidential temperament keen with a love of justice and with the capacity to recognize the honor of humble and troubled people. And the character of mind to understand that even the borders of the nation are too small for the presidential service—that willy-nilly and ipso facto we're planetary blunderers now.

The true President would have the strength to widen the range of current political discourse, and would love and revere language as the best means we have to close on reality. That implies a sensibility attuned to the immense moral consequence of every human life. Perhaps even a sense of tragedy that would not let him sleep the night through.

Also, I should think he would be someone who really likes kids, who laughs to be around them, and who is ready to die for them—but who would never resort to the political expedient of saying so.

Perhaps Mr. Bush's major contribution to this campaign is his raising of the idea of character in the public mind. He cannot have though it through: We've been living with him. We know his mettle. When a candidate is up for a second term we don't have to rely on his actions as a 23-year-old graduate student at Oxford to determine if he's got the goods. But it may be finally a great service to the electorate, and even a personal redemption of sorts, that he invites us to imagine by contrast with his own and his predecessors' what the character of a true American President should be.

NOVEMBER FIRST

•

The season with its gray clouds,
And the statue of the forgotten conqueror
On his horse
Covered with dry leaves and graffiti.

There were so many soldiers that day,
So many refugees crowding the roads.
Naturally, they all vanished
As in a conjurer's trick.
History licked the corners of its bloody mouth,
As my father used to say.

I made a great effort to feel,
But the unexpected mildness of the evening
Overtook me with gentle indifference.
I went strolling with my eyes on the clouds.
They are constantly rethinking themselves.
They glory in their ambiguities.
They'll be there even on Judgement Day.

This is my heroic serenity speaking.
Like that general on his horse
Whose absurdity only the rain and the birds appreciate,
As he threatens the clouds with his raised sword
And imagines them fleeing like the infidels they are.

Charles Simic

Women Hide Behind a Wall of Silence

Slavenka Drakulić
Zagreb, Croatia

•

THE ROOM IS tiny, with one small window letting in almost no light on a gloomy winter morning. Outside, it's bitter cold, minus 15 degrees centigrade. Stiffly frozen pieces of hand-washed clothing are hanging on lines stretched between the barracks.

This is my first visit to Resnik, a camp near Zagreb housing 9,000 refugees, mostly Muslims, from Bosnia and Herzegovina. They have lived here for months now, ten to fifteen of them in one room. They are not allowed to cook, they have to fetch their water from outside faucets and the nearest toilets are fifty meters away. In the room of the Kahrimanovic family there are six bunk beds, one tin stove, no table, no chairs, no closet. All they possess is laid out on the beds: clothes, toys, cans of food, two or three pots. Yet these people, from a village near Kozarac in Bosnia, consider themselves lucky because they have survived.

The crowded room smells of freshly brewed coffee, of dampness and unwashed bodies. Eight men, five women and four or five children are sitting in a circle, eager to talk. They have nothing to do but wait. When I ask them what they're waiting for, they are not certain. Three of the men are waiting for a foreign country to accept them as immigrants; the others do not know what they are waiting for. One woman waits for a sign that her husband is alive, another just cries.

The women prefer to talk about the war, how much land they once owned, how many cattle, how big their houses were. The men talk about how they survived Omarska and Trnopolje concentration camps. None of them will mention the subject they know I've come here to talk about. Finally, I ask them if they have heard about mass rapes. Have they seen any? At first there is a silence; even the children are quiet for a moment, as if that horrible word leaves them speechless. I sense it is the wrong way to ask this question, or the wrong time or context, but it is too late—I feel the doors are closing. Then I get an answer: "There were no women raped in our village. We were just lucky, I guess," says one of the women. We heard that it happened in other villages, cautiously adds Smail, the oldest man in the room. The conversation suddenly stops. People get up and start leaving, a sign that I should do the same. As I am walking out the door, an old woman, Hajra, says in a low voice, "Come tomorrow, my child. Then we'll tell you what we know. We can't talk about these things in front of men, you know."

I expected this kind of reaction. I was warned by colleagues who have tried to talk to rape victims. Since September, when news stories, eyewitness accounts and official reports began appearing in the press, it has been clear that mass rapes are taking place in Bosnia. Now refugee women are questioned almost every day. A reporter gets off the plane at Zagreb and, like the old American journalists' joke, barges into one of the five or six refugee camps nearby, asking, "Anyone who was raped and speaks English?"

But most of the time one runs into a wall of silence. This silence is driving everyone crazy: reporters, feminist activists, U.N. officials, European Community delegates, Human Rights Watch, Helsinki Watch and Amnesty International envoys—all of them enter small and crowded rooms in this or another camp in Croatia, hoping to get closer to the real picture, to hear eyewitness testimony. But in vain. The likelihood is that they will leave empty-handed or hear the same stories from the same few women willing to talk. If they are persistent and patient, they will eventually find a victim who will tell her story. Or they will go to Bosnia—to the towns of Tuzla or Zenica, where women and doctors are a bit more open, perhaps because they are in the war zone. Otherwise, they leave confused and disappointed that, after all the fuss that the rapes have caused in the world media, the women are reticent. Why *won't* they talk? Don't they know it is good for them?

The matter is more complicated than outsiders realize. That their cases might provide evidence against war criminals is not these women's main concern. They barely survived the terrors of the war; many have lost family members or have husbands and sons who are still fighting there—or are held in concentration camps or have disappeared and it's not known if they are alive or dead. If the women talk, they could jeopardize the men's lives. Besides, once they are safely out of Bosnia, they want to forget what happened to them as quickly as possible. The third, and perhaps the most important, reason is that they want to hide it. Even though each woman is one among the many victims of a mass rape, what happened to them is in the domain of unspeakable things, the ultimate humiliation and shame. The invisible scars are never going to heal, but it is better if they can hide their hurt and shame from others, even relatives and neighbors.

A doctor told me a story about three sisters. One of them was raped but didn't dare to tell the other two until her pregnancy became evident. After all, under normal conditions only one out of ten rape victims reports the crime. Why would women who are raped in wartime be more forthcoming? Most of the victims are Muslims from strongly patriarchal communities; they simply do not want to revive the pain they went through. I asked one if the women talk about it among themselves. No, she said, they prefer to face it all alone.

Still another problem is that it is extremely difficult to gather solid evidence under wartime conditions, with daily shelling and lack of food, water and electricity. In Bosnia, governmental commissions are investigating war crimes and are compiling affidavits. Such documentation is also collected by local clubs of exiles, the police, the Interior Ministry, hospitals, individual doctors and social workers. But these are random efforts and the results are not made available to the public. In fact, the barely functioning Bosnian government is not using rape reports as propaganda. If it were, the evidence and documentation would be more available. But all the officials have been able to do up to now is publish a few bulletins containing estimates of the number of victims and excerpts from victims' testimony; one report was submitted to the U.N. It's almost as if they prefer to hide the information rather than go public with it.

And yet, by now there is sufficient evidence to conclude that tens of thousands of women in Bosnia and Herzegovina have been raped. The European Community recently put the number of rape victims at 20,000. The Sarajevo State Commission for Investigation of War Crimes estimates that 50,000 women were raped up to October 1992.

The numbers are highly controversial, and it may be that the truth will not be known until after the war, if ever. It could well be that, because of the wall of silence and the difficulty in documenting actual cases, the number is far greater than the world is ready to believe.

When I returned to Resnik the day after my first visit, there were only five women in the room. The youngest one, 17-year-old Mersiha, who just the day before strongly denied that she'd ever seen any rape, spoke up: "Yes, I knew that five of my school colleagues were raped and killed afterward. I saw them lying in a ditch. They were there for days and each time I passed by I didn't want to look, but I did. It was in June. Their clothes were torn off them and I could see that they had been tortured. I saw knife wounds on their breasts, on their stomachs. Then, one afternoon, when we were coming back from a concentration camp where my brother was imprisoned—there were about fifty women walking back to our village through the woods—we saw that armed Serb Chetniks were waiting for us. We knew what was going to happen, but it was impossible to escape. They stopped us and chose two women. Then about ten Chetniks raped them in front of us. We were forced to stand and watch. It was dark when they released us, and I still remember how one of the women shivered when I took off my jacket and put it over her naked shoulders."

When Mersiha talked, the other women didn't comment. They stared at the floor as if they were guilty, as if they were to blame. I asked Mersiha, But what about you? She looked at her mother, sitting there and listening, as if asking her for permission to say more. "No, it did not happen to me," she said, but I doubted her. Maybe, if I came on another day, she would decide to tell me her true story. That is how it works; only patience and empathy can break the wall of self-protection.

But Mersiha did tell me about a cousin who was raped. Her story led me to a refugee camp in Karlovac, as if she had given me an Ariadne's thread leading to an underground network—a secret, silent, frightened network of women who know about one another's misery but prefer to hide it. The 30-year-old cousin had been raped by four perfectly normal-looking Serbian boys, barely over 20—not drunk, not crazy, not beasts. In fact, they were the boys next door; she knew them because they were from a nearby Serbian village. "After all these months," she said, "I cannot get rid of a feeling of carrying some kind of visible stamp, of being dirty, physically dirty and guilty." When I asked her if she would go back, she said something that I heard over and over from many Muslims—and not only from rape victims or even women: "Under no condition would I return to live in the same village with

Serbs as before. I would never let my children go to a school with their children. I would not work with them. In fact, I would not even live in the same state with them."

These words reveal the role that mass rape plays in the Serbian program of "ethnic cleansing." As Susan Brownmiller and other feminists have pointed out, women have been raped in every war: as retaliation, to damage another man's "property," to send a message to the enemy. Rape is an instrument of war, a very efficient weapon for demoralization and humiliation. In World War II, Russian and Jewish women were raped by Nazis, and Soviet soldiers raped German women by the hundreds of thousands. Chinese women were raped by the Japanese, Vietnamese by Americans. What seems to be unprecedented about the rapes of Muslim women in Bosnia (and, to a lesser extent, the Croat women too) is that there is a clear *political* purpose behind the practice. The rapes in Bosnia are not only a standard tactic of war, they are an organized and systematic attempt to cleanse (to move, resettle, exile) the Muslim population from certain territories Serbs want to conquer in order to establish a Greater Serbia. The eyewitness accounts and reports state that women are raped everywhere and at all times, and victims are of all ages, from 6 to 80. They are also deliberately impregnated in great numbers (the Bosnian government estimates that some 35,000 of them have been impregnated, unbelievably as it may sound), held captive and released only after abortion becomes impossible. This is so they will "give birth to little Chetniks," the women are told. While Muslim men are killed fighting or are exterminated in about 100 concentration camps (the Bosnian government estimates that as many as 120,000 people have been killed or have died in the Bosnian war up to now and some 60,000 are missing, while the U.S. State Department estimate for those killed is as low as 17,000), women are raped and impregnated and expelled from their country. Thus not only is their cultural and religious integrity destroyed but the reproductive potential of the whole nation is threatened. Of course, Croats and Muslims have raped Serbian women in Bosnia too, but the Serbs are the aggressors, bent on taking over two-thirds of the territory. This does not justify Croat and Muslim offenses, but they are in a defensive war and do not practice systematic and organized rape.

Women who have been raped have almost no future. Besides the psychological damage, and in spite of a *fatwa* issued by the highest Bosnian Muslim authority, the Imam, that men should marry these women and raise the progeny of the rape in a Muslim spirit, each of them knows that this is unlikely to happen. It may seem very abstract to speak of rape as a method of ethnic cleansing, but it becomes quite clear and understandable when one talks to the victims and witnesses. One woman told me that if she were raped, she would kill herself, even if her husband did not reject her. She could not stand the shame and humiliation, she could not face her children afterward. "I would prefer to be killed than raped"; "I thought about killing myself so many times"—this is what they say. One of the most disturbing and painful things to hear is their attitude toward the children born of this violence. All the women I have spoken with or heard about or whose statements I have read—whether or not they are victims or eyewitnesses—with no exception said they would kill such a child ("I'd strangle it with my own hands," as Hajra put it) or abandon it.

To hear such statements from women, many of them mothers, gives an idea of how strongly they feel about rape, what intense negative emotions mass rape has stirred in them. In their view, the rapes are only one of the things the enemy is doing to them and are directly linked to other kinds of aggression, from shelling and attack to imprisonment, torture, killing, deportation and, finally, exile from their own homes, from their own country. They are suffering not only a loss of pride but also the loss of their identity and of their country—the loss of everything they ever had. This is why the mass rapes of women in Bosnia cannot be discussed without taking into account the political context.

What the rape victims care about most is the reaction of their immediate social group—their husbands, fathers, brothers and other relatives, their neighbors, their village, their compatriots. Their lives are strongly rooted in community, and any help they might receive individually will be inadequate. As one of them who declined psychiatric care said to me: "I refused the doctors' help because I cannot see how they could help me. I need the understanding of my relatives. I need to go back home." The most important therapy is reintegration of the victims into normal life, but this is almost impossible. Reintegration is not going to happen soon; people cannot go home because of the war. And integration into the few countries that have accepted some half-million refugees is problematic. Western Europe is closing its borders because of a rising tide of xenophobia and racism and because of the recession.

About half of the nearly 2 million Muslims who lived in Bosnia are now in exile. Europe has no policy on what to do with the greatest migration of refugees since World War II, on how to stop the bloodshed in Bosnia and bring about a sensible political solution that would be acceptable to all three sides. Without a political solution, rape victims are left to themselves and to partial solutions that offer only short-term relief. It is easy to invoke the familiar feminist argument that rapes in wartime only draw wider attention when they are used as propaganda. If this is so, in Bosnia the propaganda hasn't been working. The mass media have mainly focused on the sensationalistic aspect and have treated it as a woman's problem only, without considering the wider context, in terms of arousing public pressure for a comprehensive political settlement.

But even if the rapes were used for political propaganda, this could be justified because of the Serbian policy of exiling and destroying the Muslim population. If an entire ethnic group is systematically destroyed to the point of genocide, it is legitimate to "use" accounts of rape (or anything else, for that matter) as a means of getting attention and influencing public opinion.

Strangely enough, the women themselves—the five in Resnik camp, for example—are fully aware of this, much more than are the many politicians, humanitarians, feminists, activists or journalists who are taking their side and trying to help them. They also know something else, of which Europe is not yet aware: If there is no political solution soon, the Muslims will turn to terrorism as a last resort. Bosnia's Muslims are the Palestinians of Europe, and they will not willingly give up the right to their land.

As I was about to leave the little room in Resnik, a boy entered and listened to the end of our conversation. "I will slaughter Serbs with a dull knife," he said, matter-of-factly. I asked him how old he is. Thirteen, he said. In two years he will be doing just that, if there is no other future for him. But he won't kill just Serbs. There will be a price to pay for those who prefer to close their eyes now. It was easy to see it on that boy's face.

SISTERS UNDER THE SKIN— EXCHANGE

Katha Pollitt

•

"Marooned on Gilligan's Island: Are Women Morally Superior to Men?" (Dec. 28), Katha Pollitt's look at "difference feminism," drew mail of all types from all quarters. Women and men wrote in equal numbers—on the positive side ("I agree with Pollitt that women do not have a special claim to 'virtue,' " "Pollitt is right when she bases equality on the full humanhood of women," "Especially delightful was her skewering of psychological theories that cater to upper class[es]," "Pollitt unearthed the upper-middle-class bias of those fraudulent feminist professors") and on the negative side ("uncharacteristically careless analysis," "Gilligan did not maroon women on an island, she sent them a lifeboat," "Why put down a woman who chooses to be a housewife"/ "mother?"). And the letters were wide ranging: Animal rights activists in four cities decried a phrase on the wearing of fur; a reader wrote that the real issue was a national lack of balance between the principles of yin and yang; another, that the Hebrew word *rachmonos*, which embodies the virtues mercy and sympathy, derives from the Hebrew *rechem*, or womb; another, that Pollitt was wrong—Portia was "a lying lawyer persecuting an innocent outcast . . . supporting Pollitt's thesis that a woman can be as good or as bad as a man." One reader thinks "the real 'difference' . . . is that males bear their burdens stoically . . . without forever bitching and moaning like 'feminist' prima donnas." Kenneth J. Schmidt of New York City sent this letter. "Sir. Women are morally superior to men because they are superior to men in every way."

THE EDITORS

New York City

We were disturbed that feminist Katha Pollitt would seek to degrade and misrepresent other feminist ideas, trivializing, for example, the experience of mothers by comparing them to "gardeners blamelessly tending their innocent flowers." We wish to focus on Sara Ruddick's *Maternal Thinking*, a brilliant and original explanation of a central human experience. Working from her own experience as a mother, a philosopher and a feminist theorist, Ruddick tries to uncover how mothers think, never suggesting, as Pollitt claims, that mothers are "patient, peace loving, attentive to emotional context and so on." Pollitt is setting up a paper tiger "essentialist" for the pleasure of knocking her down.

Briefly, Ruddick's thesis is that the experience of caring for children in a daily way, by men as well as women, may imply a perspective that includes ideas of nonviolent conflict resolution and an impassioned relation to the vulnerable developing human body.

Pollitt asks if women who are not mothers can or should identify with mothers. She does not believe they can do so without endorsing essentialism. If Pollitt is right that there is a problem of essentialism in the history of women and mothers in peace movements, Ruddick's thinking offers a solution. Anyone who thinks about the demands of maternal work could link women and mothers with peace, even though many mothers and women are not peaceful. It is the ideas and values that are superior if they lead to well-being and peace, certainly not women or mothers. But the importance of maternal work is widely unrecognized, and the fact that it requires thought work that is philosophically demanding, as much or more than any other philosophical problem, is Ruddick's original contribution.

Are women essentialists if they identify with mothers or theorize a certain kind of thinking as maternal thinking? No. We identify with or as mothers in order to honor the enormously difficult and crucially important questions they have wrestled with—not to claim their solutions have been correct. Women can and should identify with mothers in the sense of being friendly to or connected to, not in the sense of being defined as or reduced to.

Pollitt refuses to recognize the difference between traditional essentialist thought and the provocations of contemporary feminist thinking. She wants women to be the same as men. In her survey of views she calls "difference feminism" she does not present the extremely useful analyses and interrogations of the concept of equality that have been done by various feminists, including the subtle elaboration of equality in terms of equivalence and other challenges to the equation "equality-the same as."

Another of Pollitt's criticisms is that "Ruddick claims to be describing what mothers do, but all too often she is really prescribing what she thinks they ought to do." But Ruddick *is* talking about what mothers do. They consider the questions of the three demands of "preservation, growth and social acceptability" that she has identified as definitive of maternal work. Ruddick is contributing to the articulation of the kind of thought that it is useful and desirable to coax from within maternal work. The failure of mothers at times to meet these demands and reasons for this are central to Ruddick's understanding: (1) Mothers are not perfect, not superior; (2) the identification of women with mothers has the effect of not allowing women a separate identity; (3) there is a lack of social support, both material and symbolic; and (4) maternal work is devalued because it is done by women and because of the peaceful implications of its demands. Representation of failure is as crucial to Ruddick's analysis as the many ordinary successes of maternal care.

Ruddick, whose primary work lies in peace studies, explores historical instances, such as the Madres movement in Argentina, in which ordinary maternal experience had led to political consciousness; Ruddick does not assert that mothering guarantees these politics, only that the Madres offer a historical example of this possibility. Ruddick is always careful to acknowledge the violent role women have sometimes played as warriors, haters and supporters of war. Nevertheless, she suggests, there is an important strain in the history of mothering that speaks to a particular way of valuing and protecting human life.

JAN CLAUSEN
BARRIE KARP
YNESTRA KING
JANE LAZARRE
GRACE PALEY

•

Arlington, Mass.

While there is much to address productively in the work of the writers attacked in Katha Pollitt's article, her muddled and often irresponsible diatribe does little to illuminate the subject. If *Nation* readers are

interested in a clear discussion of what Pollitt dubs "difference feminism"—also known as the ethic of care—they should consult Mary
Jane Larabee's book *An Ethic of Care*, or Joan Tronto's essay "Women
and Caring: What Can Feminists Learn about Morality From Caring?"

Pollitt's attack seems to suggest that those concerned with an ethic
of care are not authentic feminists but rather some of its worst enemies. Her article throws together a jumble of writers—some of whom
(Chodorow and myself, for example) could not be more different—and
often concentrates on ten-or twenty-year-old texts that their authors
have moved beyond. Pollitt's core argument is remarkable for its willful
misrepresentations. She contends that we argued that women are
morally superior to men and that "difference" and "equality" feminism are fundamentally opposed.

But none of the writers in question ever argue—or would dream of
arguing—in terms of "moral superiority." Because she challenged
Lawrence Kohlberg—one of the world's leading moral theorists, whose
developmental hierarchies give an A+ in mature moral development to
men and an F to women—Carol Gilligan talks not of moral "superiority" but of moral "maturity." And I never mention or allude to "gender traitors" or suggest that women do not have to "wage tough
political struggles over the redistribution of resources and justice and
money," Indeed, my book considers how women can wage those struggles and why more of them don't.

Similarly, "difference feminists" have not pursued their work in the
interests of discovering some gimmick to help stay-at-home mothers or
women in the "caring professions" feel good about being assigned a
subordinate place in our society, as Pollitt alleges. Rather we are all
longtime participants in the arduous struggle for female independence
and equality. All of us are attacking the ideological systems—ideas
about "mature" psychological and moral development, about legitimate and worthwhile work, about success and achievement—that have
for centuries been used systematically to oppress women. Pollitt may
disagree with our work, but to charge that the work of committed feminists in any way resembles that of Victorian promoters of the cult of
traditional feminine purity is a sorry tactic.

It is one, however, that seems inevitable given Pollitt's lack of real
interest in what the writers she attacks say. She is, for example, so hostile to Gilligan that she cannot even situate that work and its importance. Like her or not, what Gilligan has done is help to propel feminist
thinking into mainstream philosophical debate. Before Gilligan,
"women's concerns" were a kind of moral and philosophical aside—a

set of issues ghettoized in applied ethics. Moreover, with only a few notable exceptions, male-dominated philosophy maintained a radical split between the private and the public, between sentiment, habit and perception and rights, universal principles and procedural approaches to justice. Gilligan's work has brought women's concerns to a level of theoretical challenge and has called attention to what philosophers had hitherto overlooked—an ethic that would speak to the care of the young, the old and the vulnerable.

Feminists are now involved in the old debate about principle-based ethics and an ethics that focuses primarily on contracts between autonomous individuals. Dozens of other feminist philosophers are expanding on, rather than jettisoning, the rights and justice framework of philosophical argument, bringing justice into the private sphere and care into the public.

Sara Ruddick on the other hand is trying to expand our understanding of valuable work. Like many others she is attempting to correct a historical system of labor valuation that has limited women's lives for centuries. As historian Jean Boydston explains in her excellent volume *Home and Work*, ever since the colonial period, women's work in the home and then later in the care-giving professions has been systematically robbed of its economic and social value. A gendered definition of labor has decreed that legitimate work is that performed by men for individual gain outside the home.

Today, more women have moved into this sphere of "legitimate labor." This critical accomplishment has not, however, managed to alter understanding of the complex and challenging work undertaken by either sex in the home and caring professions. Extending our view beyond the exploitation patriarchy has imposed on women's work so we can consider as well the power of the principles and practices embedded in that work is an essential step in encouraging women to engage in those tough political struggles that all of us "difference feminists," in fact, currently wage.

Pollitt seems determined to give care ethics and care-giving a bad name. But our work addresses some of the most critical problems of the age, indeed of the human condition. How can people who deal with the sick and young and vulnerable and dying be led to assert for themselves as well as others? How does one move from moral agency to moral action? How can an ethic of rights and justice be expanded by an ethic of care and responsibility? How can men be encouraged to bear their fair share of the care-giving in our society? How, in short, can we help people understand not only their systematic oppression but their important contributions? The latter is essential to the creation of resistance and to struggles against oppression that we will one day hopefully win.

SUZANNE GORDON

·

POLLITT REPLIES
New York City

While working on my essay I lay awake nights wondering if I was failing to understand Ruddick's *Maternal Thinking*. Could it really be as muddled and sentimental as I thought? The letter from Clausen et al. reassures me on that point. Even Ruddick's smartest defenders cannot explain in a clear and straightforward way how we are simultaneously to conflate "women" with "mothers"; to regard mothering as a single practice despite vast individual and cultural differences, and to connect child-raising with a set of social, political and philosophical values—e.g., nonviolence—few actual mothers subscribe to.

Maybe they can't do it because it can't be done. Clausen et al. respond to none of my specific arguments. Instead, they resort to wiggle-words to assert and disclaim a thesis in a single sentence. Thus, caring for children "may imply" a nonviolent perspective— or, then again, it may not. Ruddick is not saying what mothers "ought to do" but merely clarifying "the kind of thought it is useful and desirable to coax from within maternal work"—in other words, Ruddick thinks some aspects of mothering are "useful" and "desirable" objects of reflection, and others, presumably, are useless and undesirable. As I said in my essay, that's prescriptive.

Nowhere do the Furious Five address my points about the vast variation in actual maternal behavior. I'd like to hear them try to square that "impassioned relation to the vulnerable developing human body" with, for example, the 80 million girls genitally mutilated worldwide. Why are those girls' mothers the exception and the Madres of Argentina the exemplar? In what sense is having your child tortured to death by Fascists an "ordinary maternal experience," but clitoridectomizing your child not "ordinary," although practiced by whole nations of women as a matter of course? My point is not that mothers are good or bad, or that child care is not an important and serious human endeavor, but that there is no such coherent, unified thing as "maternal practice" or "maternal thinking"—certainly nothing you can hang nonviolence on without putting on a fairly spectacular set of blinders.

Suzanne Gordon says that Gilligan makes no claim for women's "moral superiority." It's true Gilligan does not use those words. But I am hardly the only person to have drawn this inference from her work, which consistently lauds "relationship" and "caring" while belittling "rights," "autonomy" and "rationality," and which firmly associates the former with women and the latter with men. Gordon herself does so throughout her letter. I'm not going to respond point by point, since it doesn't have much to do with what I wrote. I will say, however, it's absurd to accuse me of trying to give "care-giving" a "bad name." Why would I do that? I'm a mother (ahem) myself. My concern is that caring and nurturing not be linked in a false, sentimental, ahistorical and ultimately restrictive way with women. I object with the same fervor to the equally false association of logic and justice with men, ground that feminists of the Gilliganian stripe are only too glad to concede.

A final note. I was a little shocked to find myself on the receiving end of a collective letter attacking what was, after all, not a position paper or a misogynous diatribe but a discussion of rather complex intellectual and political issues about which, surely, reasonable people may differ. What is feminism coming to when five writers—including, I was sorry to see, Grace Paley, whose fiction I greatly admire—feel group action is the appropriate response to criticism of their friend and colleague Sara Ruddick's ideas? Do Clausen and Co. believe frank debate among feminists is unsisterly? Is public disagreement a movement no-no? I like a good fight, and would be happy to continue this one, but I deeply resent this little visit from the thought police.

KATHA POLLITT

A Guide to the Ghettos

Camilo José Vergara

•

IF YOU WERE among the nearly 11,000 people who lived in two-story row houses in north Camden, New Jersey, in the 1960s, you could walk to work at Esterbrook Pen, at Knox Gelatin, at RCA or at J. R. Evans Leather. You could shop on Broadway, a busy three-mile commercial thoroughfare, nicknamed the Street of Lights because of its five first-run movie theaters, with their bright neon signs.

Today, hundreds of those row houses—once counted among the best ordinary urban dwellings in America—have been scooped up by bulldozers, their debris carted to a dump in Delaware. Walking along the narrow streets, one passes entire blocks without a single structure, the empty land criss-crossed by footpaths. The scattered dwellings that remain are faced with iron bars, so that they resemble cages.

With nearly half of its overwhelmingly Latino population on some form of public assistance, this once-thriving working-class neighborhood is now the poorest urban community in New Jersey. In 1986, former Mayor Alfred Pierce called Camden a reservation for the destitute. The north section of the city has become the drug center for South Jersey; it also hosts a soup kitchen and a large state prison.

North Camden is not unique. Since the riots of the 1960s, American cities have experienced profound transformations, best revealed in the spatial restructuring of their ghettos and the emergence of new urban forms. During the past decade, however, the "underclass" and homelessness have dominated the study of urban poverty. Meanwhile, the power of the physical surroundings to shape lives, to mirror people's existence and to symbolize social relations has been ignored. When scholars from across the political spectrum discuss the factors that account for the persistence of poverty, they fail to consider its living environments. And when prescribing solutions, they overlook the very elements that define the new ghettos: the ruins and semi-ruins; the medical, warehousing and behavior-modification institutions; the various NIMBYs, fortresses and walls; and, not least, the bitterness and anger resulting from living in these places.

Dismissing the value of information received through sight, taste and smell, or through the emotional overtones of an informant's voice, or from the sensation of moving through the spaces studied, has led to the creation of constructs without character, individuality or a sense of place. And although the limitations of statistical data—particularly when dealing with very poor populations—are widely acknowledged, the dependence on numbers is fiercely defended. Other approaches are dismissed as impressionistic, anecdotal, as poetry or "windshield surveys."

Yet today's ghettos are diverse, rich in public and private responses to the environment, in expressions of cultural identity and in reminders of history. These communities are uncharted territory; to be understood, their forms must be identified, described, inventoried and mapped.

An examination of scores of ghettos across the nation reveals three types: "green ghettos," characterized by depopulation, vacant land overgrown by nature and ruins; "institutional ghettos," publicly financed places of confinement designed mainly for the native-born; and "new immigrant ghettos," deriving their character from an influx of immigrants, mainly Latino and West Indian. Some of these communities have continued to lose population; others have emerged where a quarter-century ago there were white ethnic blue-collar neighborhoods; and sections of older ghettos have remained stable, working neighborhoods or have been rebuilt.

A TAXONOMY OF THE AMERICAN GHETTO

Green ghettos, where little has been done to counter disinvestment, abandonment, depopulation and dependency, are the leftovers of a society. Best exemplified by north Camden, by Detroit's East Side, Chicago's Lawndale and East St. Louis in Illinois, they are expanding outward to include poor suburbs such as Robbins, Illinois, and are even found in small cities such as Benton Harbor, Michigan.

Residents, remembering the businesses that moved to suburban malls, the closed factories, the fires, complain of living in a threatening place bereft of jobs and stores and neglected by City Hall. In many sections of these ghettos, pheasants and rabbits have regained the space once settled by humans, yet these are not wilderness retreats in the heart of the city. "Nothing but weeds are growing there" is a frequent complaint against vacant lots, expressing no mere distaste for the vegetation but moral outrage at the attitude that produces such anomalies.

Vegetation grows wildly on and around the vestiges of the former International Harvester Component Plant in West Pullman, Chicago. Polluted fluids—mixtures of oil, rainwater, solvents and chemicals used during years of operation—can be seen through the uncapped sewer holes, their covers stolen by scavengers. Derelict industrial buildings here and in other ghettos have long ago been sacked of anything of value. Large parcels of land lie unkempt or paved over, subtracted from the life of the city. Contradicting a long-held vision of our country as a place of endless progress, ruins, once unforeseen, are now ignored.

By contrast, in New York City, Newark and Chicago one finds large and expensive habitats—institutional ghettos—publicly regulated for the weakest and most vulnerable members of society. Institution by institution, facility by facility, these environments have been assembled in the most drug-infested and devastated parts of cities. They are the complex poorhouses of the twenty-first century, places to store a growing marginal population officially certified as "not employable." Residents are selected from the entire city population for their lack of money or home, for their addictions, for their diseases and other afflictions. Nonresidents come there to pick up medications, surplus food and used clothes; to get counseling or job training; to buy drugs or sex; or to do a stint in prison.

As Greg Turner, the manager of a day shelter on the Near West Side of Chicago, puts it: "They say, 'Let's get them off the streets and put them together in groups.' It is like the zoo; we are going to put the birds over here, we are going to put the reptiles over there, we are going to put the buffalo over here, we are going to put the seals by the pool. It is doing nothing to work with the root of the problem, just like they do nothing to work with the children, to teach them things so they don't grow up and become more homeless people or substance abusers."

Although individual components—for instance, a homeless shelter or a waste incinerator—may be subject to public debate, the overall consequences of creating such "campuses" of institutions are dismissed. The most important barrier to their growth is cost.

Such sections of the city are not neighborhoods. Along the streets surrounding Lincoln Park in south Newark, an area that includes landmark houses, former public buildings and an elegant hotel was chosen by CURA and Integrity House, two drug-treatment programs, because six of its large mansions would provide inexpensive housing for treatment. On the northwest corner of the park, a shelter for battered women just opened in another mansion, and a block north in a former garage is a men's shelter and soup kitchen. The largest structures overlooking the park, a former hotel and a federal office building, house the elderly, who fear going out by themselves. No children play in the park or travel to and from school; no parents go to or come home from work. This is a no man's land devoted to the contradictory goals of selling drugs, getting high and just surviving, on the one hand, and becoming clean and employed, on the other.

In other parts of New York and Chicago a community of recent immigrants is growing up, but this type of ghetto is most visible in South Central Los Angeles and Compton, where the built environment is more intimate than in older ghettos, the physical structures are more adaptable and it is easier for newcomers to imprint their identity. Here paint goes a long way to transform the appearance of the street.

The new immigrant ghettos are characterized by tiny offices providing numerous services, such as driving instructions, insurance and immigration assistance; by stores that sell imported beer, produce and canned goods; and by restaurants offering home cooking. Notable are the businesses that reflect the busy exchange between the local population and their native country: money transfers, travel agencies, even funeral homes that arrange to have bodies shipped home.

To get by, most residents are forced to resort to exploitative jobs paying minimum wage or less and usually lacking health benefits. For housing they crowd together in small, badly maintained apartments or in cinder-block garages and trailers.

Not being eligible for public housing may in the long run prove to be a blessing for the people. Although forced to pay high rents, immigrants tend to concentrate in neighborhoods that are part of the urban economy, thus avoiding the extreme social disorganization, isolation and violence that characterize other types of ghettos. Because of the huge influx of young people with expectations that life will be better for their children and grandchildren, these ghettos are more dynamic and fluid, resembling the foreign-born communities of a century ago.

BEHIND GHETTO WALLS, A COMMON FATE

No single ghetto is completely green, institutional or immigrant in character. Although the overwhelming trend is toward greater waste, abandonment and depopulation, these three models are related, channeling people and land to one another. Fires and demolitions in the green ghettos provide large tracts of cleared land where poverty institutions and other facilities can be built. By default the most desperate people and neighborhoods become wards of the government in communities where, in the words of a Brooklyn organizer, "all the social disasters of the city are located."

If nothing is done to prevent it, within a decade more working-class communities are likely to belong to one of these types. Conversely, some institutional ghettos, such as the Near West Side of Chicago, are likely to be squeezed out by expanding sports and medical complexes. And the same forces of abandonment that can open the way for the modern poorhouses can at other times free land for townhouses built for working families.

These are the "reclaimed ghettos." With their horror stories of violence, public incompetence and waste, ghettos are used to provide moral justification for privately managed programs of redevelopment. Under the leadership of churches, community organizations, private developers and recent immigrants, such ghettos have kicked out most of the dependent poor and have refused to admit the institutions that serve them. Instead, they focus on attracting working families, keeping out drug dealers and building guarded enclaves.

These communities are on the verge of melding into mainstream society. But when examining the contribution of community development corporations, we need to ask ourselves whether their efforts are leading to the elimination of ghettos or toward the creation of minicities of exclusion within a larger wasteland.

For it is at the boundaries that the individual character of ghettos reveals itself most clearly: around embattled clusters of dwellings where ethnic groups assert themselves, in blocks where strong buildings share a wall with dilapidated crack houses, and along the perimeter of hospitals, universities and other citadels. Borders where white meets black are stark, presenting a graphic contrast between a seemingly victorious white community and what appears to be a defeated minority community. Along Mack Avenue as it crosses from Detroit's East Side into affluent Grosse Pointe, and along Chicago's East 62nd Street, the border between Woodlawn and Hyde Park (home of the University of Chicago), a history of race relations has been written into the landscape. Security measures, guards, dead-end streets, green grass on one side; vacant land, abandoned buildings, people out of work, hanging out, on the other.

Writers in the mainstream press call ghettos intractable, expressing concern with the public burden they impose. The system works for those who are motivated, many outsiders say, pointing to the presence of minorities in more affluent suburbs, to reclaimed ghettos and to the economic success of recent black, Latino and Asian immigrants.

But among many ghetto dwellers, particularly native-born African-Americans, there is growing ideological hardening and a yearning to close ranks, to re-emerge from destitution and to prosper among themselves. A journalist in Gary, Indiana, a city almost completely abandoned by whites, remarked, "I don't know why people have to have white people to succeed." A Chicago construction worker called blacks who moved to the suburbs "imitation white people." A Newark woman suggested that such people have sold out, are living a lie. "They need to take a good look in the mirror," she said.

Echoing Malcolm X, most ghetto residents I have encountered see the devastation and violence in their communities as part of a white strategy of domination. Drugs are widely perceived as part of a monstrous plot to destroy and contain poor blacks and Latinos. A Chicago minister states, "White supremacy, a system of oppression that comes out of Western society, is the real problem." A Brooklyn artist declares, "People of color have a right to be paranoid."

Within ghetto walls a new generation is growing along with new activities, ideologies, institutions and drugs. Crack sells briskly across the street from drug-treatment centers, and children walk past homeless shelters. An army of men strips cars, and hordes of scavengers push loaded shopping carts along the streets. Houses stand alone like fortresses, enclosed by fences. Dozens of cities are falling into ruin, and along their streets billboards beg people to stop killing one another.

Today, there is renewed talk of strategies to bring jobs, to improve education, to build better housing and provide adequate health care for all Americans. Such developments would certainly improve the conditions in poor communities but would not change their isolation, racial composition and fragmentation. Ghettos would continue to expand, new ones to emerge, and the anger of their residents would remain unabated.

Public policy must also address the unique characteristics of our ghettos. A crucial step is to change practices that concentrate in these communities the poor and the institutions that serve them. We need regional and national approaches to population redistribution, such as the building of low-income housing in wealthy suburbs and the elimination of the barriers that define ghettos. And as we once did in the 1960s, we need to convince ourselves that as a nation we have the power not just to improve the ghetto but to abolish it. To do this we need to go beyond the statistics and into the streets, alleys and buildings.

In reply to those to whom dreams of a more just society have lost their power, and for those who believe that ghettos are necessary to have strong communities elsewhere, stand haunting, defiant and despairing words scribbled on the stairway of an East Harlem highrise: "Help me before I die, motherfucker."

TROUBLE STILL IN FORREST CITY

Robert Scheer

•

OVER AT THE Holiday Inn on I-40, after the catfish lunch, the Mayor of Forrest City, Arkansas, once again launched into his favorite dog and pony show, telling some local insurance agents just how great the proposed federal prison would be. As he earnestly worked his flip charts, the statistics of the coming good life flowed: "One thousand federal jobs for starters and then there's your multiplier, and with a thousand prisoners one-third will have visitors every week, and I don't need to tell you those folks need to eat and stay in motels." The audience didn't need to be sold.

It's all anyone here in St. Francis County can talk about—the prison. And how it's certain to come now that Bill Clinton's been elected President. "The prison was his idea in the first place," Mayor Danny Ferguson recalled.

As Governor, Clinton was committed to solving the seemingly intractable economic problems of a region dominated by crushing poverty. He also served as chairman of the Delta Commission, a congressionally mandated project to improve life in an impoverished belt of the Mississippi River running through six states, including the part of eastern Arkansas where Forrest City is located. In his economic address to Congress, Clinton once again promised "to end welfare as we know it," and he observed, "I have worked on this issue for the better part of a decade." Forrest City is the center of that ten-year effort, and it is a dismal failure.

Clinton may have won the presidential election by telling people across the nation that he "grew the economy" with his job-training and job-creation programs, but around here the only tangible hope of economic growth is the prison. The President is given full credit for trying: he garnered big majorities upward of 70 percent in these areas (62 percent in St. Francis), while barely carrying the state as a whole with 53 percent of the vote. But with the exception of the expected prison, it's hard to point to anything in this much-touted program for fighting poverty and creating jobs that really worked.

Clinton did try quite a few programs, including education reform, industrial development and Project Success, which he still claims took thousands of people off welfare and put them into the labor force. But despite considerable effort by the Governor to lure business with the promise of tax breaks and cheap labor, the expected jobs did not materialize. For three years running St. Francis County led the state in unemployment, and the rest of eastern Arkansas followed close behind. Now about 30 percent of the population qualify for food stamps.

Cotton is still king in the Delta, but machines now do the picking. The poorer and mostly black rural population have been forced off the land and into dismal town ghettos, where if they are lucky they live in dreary shotgun HUD housing projects and get on the welfare rolls. Aid to Families with Dependent Children and food stamps are the major sources of income for most of the 50 percent of the country's population that are black, and for quite a few of the whites as well. It provides a meager existence. A single person is eligible for only $111 in food stamps a month, and a mother with one child gets $162 per month in an A.F.D.C. grant in addition to food stamps.

It was easy for Clinton to say in his address to Congress, "I want to offer the people on welfare the education, the training, the child care, the health care they need to get back on their feet, but say after two years they must get back to work, too, in private business if possible, in public service if necessary." This is the mantra of the neolibs now gearing up for yet another assault on everyone's favorite target, the imperfect fifty-eight-year-old A.F.D.C. program.

Sounds great until you realize that the vast majority of welfare recipients are children, and that the rest of this potential work force is composed of their overburdened mothers. Meager as welfare payments are—and they have been declining steadily in real dollars over the past decade—they still provide a subsistence income, along with medical coverage.

"People would come off welfare in droves if there were jobs, but there aren't any," says Mayor Ferguson, who has spent his entire forty years here. Although he is devoted to the country's future Mayor, who is white, reports that most of his relatives have left the area for better economic climes. While the white population has steadily declined—in most of the Delta region the percentage is in the low teens—blacks are far less mobile. A segregated educational system that persisted until the sixties left them largely illiterate and without non-farming job skills. Illiteracy as a whole in the county is thought to be around 35 percent, and it is much higher among blacks.

During the late fifties and into the sixties Forrest City experienced a light manufacturing boom that provided work for its unskilled but eager labor force. But while the lure of cheap labor, much advertised by lobbyists for the state, brought in some manufacturing, those companies eventually found even more exploitable work forces abroad. Playing the "cheap labor" card is now generally viewed as a dead end, but few workers here are qualified to enter the high-tech industries of the future.

Modern industries require a more educated work force and thus tend to be attracted to the mostly white northwestern section of the state, which has been favored in economic development planning and has better school systems. "We don't have a level playing field," says Perry Webb, the energetic head of Forrest City's Chamber of Commerce. Webb, the white 36-year-old son of a Baptist minister, is much respected by all races for what are perceived as his heroic efforts to attract business. In the ten years before he took the chamber job only eight companies had come to look over Forrest City for possible relocation. Thanks largely to Webb's efforts, in the last year alone eighteen considered the place. But so far none have bought the bait of cheap local labor, a tax-reducing enterprise zone and on-site job-training programs paid for by the state. "Companies look for reasons not to move into a community," Webb observed. "We have a higher minority population that is poorly educated and dislocated from agriculture—they'll give you an honest day's work, but it's not a silicon-chip work force."

Eight years ago, the local labor force proved to be not quite as docile as runaway industries from the North might prefer. At that time, a nationally covered, initially violent twenty-one-day strike hit the Sanyo plant, the town's major employer, and the town was left with an image of a recalcitrant labor force. Nothing could be further from the truth, says Sanyo general manager Joji Suwa, who claims that "labor relations here are excellent." Sanyo is still unionized, but the assembly line is now highly mechanized, so the plant's labor force is down from a high of 2,200 at the time of the strike to around 500 today. The workers, about evenly divided between black and white, assemble finished television sets from components produced in factories elsewhere. They are paid an average of $8.50 an hour, an attractive wage in these parts.

The plant was built in 1967 by Warwick, a subsidiary of Whirlpool, but by the mid-seventies declining profit margins raised the prospect of its closure. In 1977 Sanyo, which along with other Japanese companies was under intense U.S. government pressure to shift some manufacturing to this country, bought the plant in a joint-venture agreement with Sears.

For a while things went well. The output of the plant's million-set-a-year television assembly line and its microwave oven division was marketed primarily under the Sears label: Wood cabinetry was used in larger TV consoles, and this labor-intensive but semiskilled work was nicely adapted to the local labor force. Then came a decline in demand, which Chamber of Commerce and Sanyo officials attribute to Sears changing its product mix to feature name brands, the loss of the microwave market to Korean manufacturers and the end of wood cabinets.

A more jaundiced view, expressed after a few beers in Charlie's bar by a local concrete contractor and echoed by the other patrons, is that Sanyo was shocked by the strike and went to Mexico in search of a more tractable labor force. General manager Suwa denies this, pointing out that the plant still produces a million TV sets annually, though it requires fewer workers to do so. But it is also true that the Sanyo operation in Tijuana, which produces a similar product line, has been expanding.

There seems to be general agreement that the Sanyo plant would have closed had it not been for intense lobbying by Clinton, who met with Sanyo's chairman in Japan. More important, perhaps, when Sears cut back drastically on its orders Clinton brokered a deal in which the Arkansas-based Wal-Mart chain committed itself to marketing a good portion of the Sanyo plant's output.

But despite similar heroic efforts by the Governor and local leaders, the job market here has continued its decline. And without job creation none of the vocational education and welfare reform programs seem to matter.

Not that Forrest City hasn't vigorously pursued the Governor's nationally publicized social agenda for getting people off welfare and into the job market. Gwendolyn Williams, a 40-year-old black woman who was born in this town when it was still segregated, now runs the Project Success office. She remains deeply committed to Clinton's notion that through proper motivation people can be moved from welfare to jobs. And she is proud of the successes of her program. They may not seem like big achievements, but they were hard won.

Williams mentions the two welfare mothers now holding jobs at the Roadrunner Truck Stop; one who is working at the library; and yet another who is employed by the county. The problem with the Roadrunner jobs, the only ones in the private sector, is that they pay the minimum wage and do not carry medical benefits. Forrest City sold its county hospital to the private Baptist Hospital, so a poor person without medical benefits has a hard time getting care. Nor does Forrest City have a municipal transportation system that would enable poor people, most of whom do not have cars, to get to such jobs.

Project Success does help the takers of such positions with a temporary aid program that provides van transportation, baby-sitting support and the continuance of Medicare benefits. But after the supplementary aid is withdrawn, the former welfare mother and her children will be worse off. Then too, because of limited state funding the program is open to only a fraction of welfare recipients.

Any A.F.D.C. and/or food stamp recipients who refuse to participate in the project lose their benefits. So their participation is often little more than a desultory routine of going through the motions of finding a job—as a session of the local Job Club demonstrated.

The Job Club is a four-hour-a-day, one-week program run by Project Success. The morning I was there four young men and two women were in attendance. An absurdly patronizing banner hung across the front wall: "Hi Ho, Hi Ho, it's off to work we go." A representative of Mary Kay Cosmetics spoke on grooming; she said her main job was with Southern Pacific Railroads, but they were cutting back and she didn't suggest applying. She did hold out some hope of becoming a Mary Kay representative, however. The only upbeat moment came when she offered free facials to anyone who filled out a card and called for an appointment. In the meantime, she said, they should feel free to come up and examine her product line. There were no free samples.

There was additional instruction by the human resources case worker on filling out job applications, handling embarrassing questions about arrests (leave it blank, get in the door first) and bringing a pen to job interviews.

In later interviews all of the Job Club students described rather extensive efforts to find jobs. One had traveled to Detroit and another to Arizona. They seemed quite articulate and knowledgeable about the local job market, including how many applications a company had taken and the going wage rate. They seemed beyond the need for the advice given at the Job Club, and there was nothing about their grooming that would have put off a job recruiter for, say, Sanyo. But no such recruiters show up here or at the nearly deserted state employment office.

An executive at the Sanyo company confessed to me that he and his colleagues had never heard of Project Success. Indeed, the program may be better known in some of the other states where Clinton campaigned than it is in Arkansas. One social worker told me, "In Tennessee they call it Choices. It's the same thing, just a different label, but the main thing is there are no jobs."

Project Success director Williams is aware of the futility of sending people out endlessly to look for jobs that don't exist. Her answer is to funnel as many welfare recipients as possible into classes at the local vocational college or junior college to get advanced vocational education. The latter's program has produced some registered nurses, and Williams is hopeful that some students who are now taking courses there might end up as prison guards.

Perhaps the main success of Project Success is that it has spawned a new bureaucracy in which some poor people can find jobs. One of those is Quinlock Rooks, a 38-year-old mother of three who had been on welfare. She completed the training program and went to work for the program itself in a low-paying clerical capacity. At first her pay was so low that she qualified for food stamps even though she was a state employee. But, being diligent and bright, she managed to pass various qualifying tests and now earns $15,000 a year as a case worker and no longer requires food stamps.

Not everyone can work for the state, of course. Rooks readily understands the plight of those on welfare who can't find jobs: "My best friend worked for General Industries for eleven years. Then they moved and she has not been able to land a steady job since. So she's on welfare with her kids and her situation is deteriorating—five kids in a one-bedroom house. She's a smart girl, finished high school and keeps looking. But she can't find a decent job.

"The jobs that are available are at the fast-food outlets and hotels near I-40, but they mostly want the young and are part time, so they don't have to provide medical. My clients beat the doors looking for jobs and there's nothing for them. There are 150 who show up for any kind of job."

When General Industries deserted Forrest City, it moved to Searcy, just outside Little Rock. This sort of intrastate flight frustrates Webb of the Chamber of Commerce. "We have a dog-eat-dog fight between states and between counties within a state," he says, after discussing with Mayor Ferguson and me all the failed efforts to attract industry. "We are just moving the cards around without shuffling the deck." The problem, Webb contends, "is that we don't have a national jobs and relocation policy. We can't level the playing field on our own. Clinton as Governor couldn't, but maybe as President he can do something. He's familiar with the problem, I'll say that."

Ferguson sighed. "You know, a reporter from Little Rock asked me how I would feel about Forrest City coming to be known as the prison capital of Arkansas. I said, 'It sure beats being the unemployment capital.' "

Despite an enlightened local leadership, a hard-working Mayor and a Governor who cared, the jobs have not come. If Forrest City, strategically located on the interstate linking Memphis and Little Rock, is unable to enter the modern economic age, one wonders what even a decently motivated President can accomplish for this and other desperately poor areas. It certainly is a good thing that Clinton may now try to focus federal resources to create jobs and improve educational opportunities in such communities. But if the jobs don't come, why put the onus for ending poverty on the poor rather than on the failure of the economy?

THE GAY MOMENT

Andrew Kopkind

•

THE GAY MOMENT is unavoidable. It fills the media, charges politics, saturates popular and elite culture. It is the stuff of everyday conversation and public discourse. Not for thirty years has a class of Americans endured the peculiar pain and exhilaration of having their civil rights and moral worth—their very humanness—debated at every level of public life. Lesbians and gay men today wake up to headlines alternately disputing their claim to equality under the law, supporting their right to family status, denying their desire, affirming their social identity. They fall asleep to TV talk shows where generals call them perverts, liberals plead for tolerance and politicians weigh their votes. "Gay invisibility," the social enforcement of the sexual closet, is hardly the problem anymore. Overexposure is becoming hazardous.

While gays organize what may be the biggest march on Washington ever, set for April 25, Congress ponders the pros and cons of granting gays first-class citizenship, in the civilian order as well as the military. Courts consider the legality of discrimination against the last community in the country officially excluded from constitutional protection. Senator Edward Kennedy and Representative Henry Waxman hope to introduce a new national lesbian and gay civil rights bill soon. But until that passes—certainly not for many years—the ruling federal precedent is the notorious decision by retiring Supreme Court Justice Byron White in the 1986 *Bowers v. Hardwick* case, in which he invoked the entire Judeo-Christian tradition of patriarchy and homophobia to deny gay people the rights all other Americans enjoy. Newspapers censor progay comic strips, television stations ban gay programs, schools proscribe gay-positive materials, church hierarchs forbid gay people from preaching—and parading, state electorates revoke existing antidiscrimination laws and outlaw passage of new ones, and bullies on streets of every city beat and bash gays and lesbians with escalating hatred. Some 1,900 incidents of anti-gay violence were reported in 1992. Except for a small number of enlightened workplaces in college towns and the big cities of both coasts, American institutions make it dangerous or impossible for millions of gays to leave their closets and lead integrated, fulfilling lives.

But it is the contradictions rather than the cruelties of sexual struggle that define the moment. Despite the difficulties, most gays would agree that life as a homosexual is better now than ever before in American history. The Rev. Al Carmines's hopeful but unconvincing post-Stonewall song, "I'm Gay and I'm Proud" now reflects a widespread reality. Responding to the rigidity of the old order, younger gay men and "baby dykes" have created a queer culture that is rapidly reconfiguring American values, redesigning sensibilities and remodeling politics. The gay movement, broadly constructed, is *the* movement of the moment. Devastated by a plague that threatens the very existence of their community, gay men have converted horror and grief into creative energy and purpose. AIDS has given a new sense of solidarity to lesbians and gay men who for years have often pursued separate agendas. Broadway is bursting with gay plays, big book awards go to gay authors, even Hollywood is developing movies with gay themes, and gay people of every age and social stratum are shattering their closets with explosive force. "Queer theory"—also known as lesbian and gay studies—is explored by scholars and students at hundreds of colleges.

Suddenly, "out" gays inhabit high and midlevel positions in journalism and publishing, law, academia, medicine and psychiatry, the arts and creative professions. They have made it not only possible, but comfortable and natural for younger lesbians and gay men to come out at the entry level. More out gays are in public office throughout the land, at least up to the sub-Cabinet level of the federal government. A quarter of a century of gay and lesbian political action has produced, *inter alla*, the first progay White House—despite distressing backsliding. Gay couples are winning recognition as legal families by some city governments and a few corporations (*The Nation* is one), although valuable benefits have been extended to only a small number of registrants.

And a complex infrastructure of activist, educational and professional organizations give gay life a formidable institutional base and contribute to the general appreciation of "gay power." Morley Safer was not way over the top when he suggested to his *60 Minutes* audience that it "face up to the gay nineties."

Ten years ago there might have been one gay issue in the news every month or so. Now there are dozens at the same time. The tortured topic of gays in the military is far from the "nonstarter" the late Bush reelection campaign, incredibly, assumed it to be. It strikes at the authority of the defense establishment in political life and, on a deeper level, subverts traditional gender and sexual roles as no movement has done since the dawn of modern feminism.

In the aftermath of Colorado's passage last November of Amendment 2, making it illegal for the state or any locality to protect gays from assaults on their civil rights, Christian fundamentalist churches and other right-wing groups are mounting campaigns for retrograde referendums in a dozen states, many of which had already enacted antidiscrimination laws for gays after exhausting campaigns. (Target states: Idaho, Oregon, California and Florida.) Gays and, for the first time, a significant number of straight allies are pushing a boycott of the "hate state" of Colorado. William Rubenstein, the American Civil Liberties Union point man on gay issues, marvels at the broadening of anger against homophobia. "The kind of outrage that Barbara Streisand and other celebrities are registering on gay issues has simply never been seen before."

Gays start at a disadvantage in resources. The fundamentalists can mobilize literally millions of people in a few days to phone or fax Congress and send money to antigay campaigns. There are perhaps 1,200 radio and TV outlets operated by religious broadcasters that may be available for homophobic propaganda and fundraising. Now that international communism is a dead issue, and abortion is no longer leading edge, homosexuality is the Christian right's number one bogy and its chief source of money.

During the campaign around the Oregon gay-rights proposition last year, Christian militants produced a sensationalist video called *The Gay Agenda*, which is up there with the Nazi film *The Eternal Jew* as a work of pure hate and fear. The video has had saturation distribution. The Joint Chiefs of Staff showed it to one another (their response to the expanse of male flesh and repeated crotch shots is unrecorded) and passed it on to members of Congress. One general personally sent it to Representative Pat Schroeder, who blasted back an angry public reply.

A group of filmmakers in New York City, working as the Gay and Lesbian Emergency Media Campaign, is trying to rush out countervideos,
but it's hard to drive really bad politics out with good.

Gays and straights together in New York are busy devising strategies
to counter the bitter backlash of homophobia that followed the sacking
of city schools chancellor Joseph Fernandez in February. Fernandez, an
East Harlem street tough and doper who made good, was uniquely
qualified to connect with the kids in his charge. Faced with increasing
violence and even murder throughout the system, he sought to teach
tolerance with a "rainbow curriculum" of recommended books and
other materials that teachers from the first grade on were free (but not
compelled) to use according to their personal inclinations. Since young
gay pupils are routinely taunted, and worse, in schools everywhere, and
a third of all youthful suicides are gay-related (according to a government report never disseminated by the Bush Administration), it
seemed only natural to Fernandez that the curriculum should include
materials that would promote respect for sexual minorities as well as
racial and ethnic ones.

But that, and his insistence that schools distribute free condoms to
all students who request them as a way of reducing the appalling
spread of AIDS and curbing unwanted teenage pregnancies, enraged
conservative Catholics as well as many antifeminist and antigay blacks,
and Orthodox Jews. Fernandez's contract was terminated, but that
wasn't the whole of it. Led by Pat Robertson's Christian Coalition, parents and organizers are working feverishly to seize power in community
school boards in dozens of neighborhoods around the city in elections
called for May 4. Candidates such as Allan Parham, a 24-year-old black
veteran of the Gulf War, were fired up by antigay videotapes produced
by a Brooklyn Catholic activist. Parham told a reporter that if elected
to the school board he would make sure the schools would "spend no
time on topics like homosexuality." The issues are vitally important in
the effort to normalize gay life and to combat aggressive homophobia,
which does incalculable damage to children and teenagers. Heterosex-
ism—like institutionalized racism and sexism—is so pervasive that
most people may never recognize it. But again these battles have been
framed by the right. In cities from San Diego to Tampa, gay cavaliers
must prepare to joust with Christian roundheads for the right to protect their young sisters and brothers.

The Ancient Order of Hibernians' exclusion of a gay Irish group
from New York's St. Patrick's Day parade became an international
scandal, and inspired (successful) attempts by other Irish gays to

march in similar parades in Ireland and the United States. No sooner was that fuss over than members of a gay synagogue began negotiating to march under their own banner in New York's annual Salute to Israel parade. "Oy Gay" headlined the *New York Post*, which, by the way, has an openly gay journalist, Joe Nicholson, in its ranks. (Long Island's *Newsday*, along with papers in Los Angeles, San Francisco, Detroit, Philadelphia and Chapel Hill, North Carolina, print columns on gay issues by out gay writers.) Newspapers in the smallest towns are beginning to carry same-sex "marriage" notices on the weddings page. Gay coupling celebrations haven't cracked the *New York Times* society pages yet, but the breakthrough surely is only a few months or a year away. The *Times*, which allowed the word "gay" as a descriptive and synonym for "homosexual" to be used only a few years ago, had a startling change of heart (with the retirement of executive editor A. M. Rosenthal) and is now consistently progay. New York City, with the biggest out gay population in the world, is singularly bereft of credible gay newspapers, so the *Times* and *The Village Voice* have more or less filled the vacuum. A decade ago, no one was out at the *Times*—even in one big bureau where the majority of the reporters were gay, and two were lovers. Last winter, reporter and editor Jeffrey Schmalz came out in print (as gay and a person with AIDS) and has been burning up the pages with passionate pieces about gay life and death issues, as well as about gays and gay sensibility in the arts and pop culture. The *Times* has just appointed a gay man, Adam Moss, to be a top editor at its Sunday *Magazine*. And *The New Republic* has logged so much P. R. mileage from the appointment of Andrew Sullivan as the first out gay editor (and Gap fashion model) of a mainstream national magazine, it should be able to fly free for the rest of the decade.

Four years ago, when *thirtysomething* showed a gay male character in bed with another man, advertisers were so panicked that they canceled $1 million in buys and forced the otherwise liberal creators of the program to banish the character and withdraw the offending segment from reruns that summer. Now TV is entering the gay nineties. There was a lesbian kiss on L.A. Law. MTV's *Real World* put a prominent gay character in the loft where the twentysomethings lived, loved and acted out. *Melrose Place* has a minor gay male character, although unlike the straight ones, he's invariably involved in situations in which his sexuality is somehow an issue or a problem. Last year, sixty-odd PBS stations began showing *In the Life*, the first gay series on any network—a signal event even if it had not been produced by my longtime partner, John Scagliotti. CBS has signed Harvey Fierstein (*Torch Song Trilogy*) to co-star in his own sitcom pilot to be aired this summer or fall. *Roseanne*, the top-rated sitcom on television, is the first to have a recurring genuinely lesbian character—played by Sandra Bernhard, once known as Madonna's girl-toy. And Ms. Ciccone herself, the premier sex symbol of the decade, is graphic about her own Sapphic activities. More important, her videos have shown same-sex couples in intimate poses—a crucially legitimizing image for the MTV generation. Pop music stars such as k. d. lang and Elton John came out; the late Freddie Mercury (of Queen) was outed after he died of AIDS, while others, such as Pete Towshend (of The Who) and Kurt Cobain (of Nirvana), have more or less matter-of-factly talked about bisexual times of their lives. Prince exudes androgyny, and what more can be said about Michael Jackson in that department? Only Brooke Shields knows for sure. Perhaps the most consequential gay moment in music was a single line in the new Garth Brooks country hit, "We Shall Be Free," which instructs the Nashville nation to be accepting of same-sex love. Brooks, who outsells Michael Jackson and everyone else in music these days, told Barbara Walters that he wrote it in support of his lesbian sister. *Newsweek* devoted an entire page to the song and the "turmoil" it has engendered among the hee-haw set.

The New York theater is now almost exclusively about gays, Jews and blacks—with considerable overlap. *Angels in America*, the gay-themed play by Tony Kushner that just won a Pulitzer Prize, is the most ballyhooed opening of the Broadway season (it comes to New York via London and L.A.). William Finn's moving and funny *Falsettos*, a Sondheimlich *singspiel* about a gay male couple, one of the men's child and ex-wife, their friends and their psychiatrist, won a couple of Tonys and is on national tour while continuing on Broadway. Paul Rudnick's *Jeffrey* and Larry Kramer's *The Destiny of Me* are popular crossover hits. Gays now direct some of the most prestigious theater companies. And there is a thriving lesbian and gay theater and performance scene as well.

Hollywood is about to take the plunge, or at least a sitzbath, in gay issues. For sixty years the industry has indulged in cinematic gay-bashing, consigning lesbians and gays to roles as psychopaths, clowns, suicides, hustlers, alcoholics and drug fiends, spinsters and corpses. The late Vito Russo was the great archivist of Hollywood's shameful treatment of gays; now his seminal work, *The Celluloid Closet*, is being made into a documentary by the Academy Award-winning filmmaker of *The Times of Harvey Milk*, Jonathan Demme, whose *Silence of the Lambs* was criticized by some gays for featuring an *apparently* gay serial killer (Demme insisted the character—a transvestite with a dog named Precious—was meant to be merely *confused* about his sexuality), has just finished shooting *Philadelphia*, the story of a gay lawyer (played by a painfully thin Tom Hanks) who has AIDS. Barbra Streisand bowdlerized the important gay element in the *The Prince of Tides;* she made the sister of the protagonist, who seemed to be a lesbian in the Pat Conroy novel, into a presumptive heterosexual, but gave her a gay male neighbor. Now Streisand is developing Larry Kramer's AIDS play, *The Normal Heart*, for the screen. Oliver Stone was planning to direct *The Mayor of Castro Street*, a biopic based on Randy Shilts's history of Harvey Milk, the first openly gay San Francisco City Supervisor, who was assassinated in 1978. But severe criticism leveled at Stone by some gays for his gratuitous treatment of the gay demimonde in *JFK* led him to delegate the project to someone else, rumored to be Gus Van Sant, the first officially out director in Hollywood (*My Own Private Idaho*). The movie, which Stone will produce, may appear in time for the twenty-fifth anniversary of Stonewall in 1994—which looks to be a yearlong gay culture fest.

Neuroanatomist Simon LeVay's quest for the anatomical seat of homosexuality, begun in the wake of the AIDS death of his lover, has spurred a wide-ranging investigation into the biological basis of sexuality. The search is now down to specific proteins or strings of them in DNA. The City University of New York has established the Center for Lesbian and Gay Studies, the first free-standing academic institute in the field. The influence of gay and lesbian sensibilities in modern culture is at last being examined; indeed, there would hardly be modern art, literature or philosophy without gay sensibility.

Nor is a *tour d'horizon* of the gay moment complete without a mention of *The Crying Game*, the most successful mainstream movie to deal frankly with a straight/gay relationship—with full frontal nudity. Never in the history of film has a single penis shot grossed so much: $54 million at this writing.

Most heterosexuals and perhaps many homosexuals never focus on the elements of gay culture that have infiltrated everyday life: the homoerotic advertising spreads, the ironic style in journalism and literature, the fashions on the street, the new political calculus. All of it began in a few metropolitan areas, but has been transported by the media into the remote reaches of the country. The world has turned since the Stonewall rebellion in 1969, when the gay theater meant a wink and a nod in *West Side Story*, gay politicians were scandalized in

Advise and Consent, and lesbians and gay men had to be content with *The Well of Loneliness* and Judy Garland records as public expressions of their dreams and desires.

While the arrival of the gay moment is unmistakable, its provenance and history are ambiguous and debatable. There is a feeling prevalent in the lesbian and gay community that Bill Clinton's groundbreaking progay campaign and election made all the difference in the world. The *Times*'s Schmalz began an important state-of-the-gays article in the paper's *Magazine* last fall with an account of Clinton's long friendship with David Mixner, an influential, openly gay consultant and fundraiser, and how that relationship led to Clinton's stand.

The two first met, Mixner says, at a 1969 reunion for people who had worked on Eugene McCarthy's presidential campaign the year before. Mixner was still in the closet; Clinton was heading to Oxford. In time, Clinton returned to Arkansas and became a politician; Mixner went to California and became a political consultant. He came out—to the world and his old friend Bill—in the mid-1970s, and immersed himself in gay politics. In 1978 he ran the successful campaign to defeat the Briggs Initiative, which would have effectively barred gays from teaching in the state's public schools. (His most important ally in that struggle was, of all people, Ronald Reagan, who had recently retired as governor to run, again, for the presidency. Mixner got one of Reagan's top gubernatorial aides, a gay man who had become a department store executive, to sensitize his former boss to the issue. Just before Election Day, Reagan announced his opposition to the initiative.)

Mixner kept in contact with Bill and Hillary and, by his account, instructed the couple in the elements of gay oppression and liberation. Mixner was on the Clinton presidential bus from day one, served as the campaign's co-chair in California and as a senior adviser to the candidate nationally. He also helped bring huge pots of gay money to the campaign and to position Clinton to win in excess of 75 percent of the gay vote, a crucial component of the Democratic totals in big cities where gays are concentrated (compare New York Republican Senator Al D'Amato's recent support for lifting the ban on gays in the military, coincident with the right-winger's contemplation of a run for governor). The Human Rights Campaign Fund and the Victory Fund, the two leading gay money-raising groups in Washington, estimate that $3.5 million was contributed to Clinton; perhaps three to four times that was given to all political campaigns.

But it was the crisis engendered by the military's antigay policies and the many challenges by lesbians and gays in the service that set the stage for Clinton's stance on homosexuals' rights. And it was Paul Tsongas who, in a manner of speaking, brought Clinton out on the issue. Campaigning in frigid Iowa before the caucuses there, Tsongas was asked by a reporter at an airport stop whether the candidate favored letting gays into the military. "Everybody's in, nobody's out," Tsongas replied, in a phrase he would often use.

Soon, all the other Democratic candidates would second Tsongas's motion. Clinton, who was plummeting in New Hampshire after the Gennifer Flowers story broke, could not afford to give Tsongas an advantage with the liberal Democrats who work hard and vote often in the early primaries, and he added his support for lifting the ban. Senator Tom Harkin—furthest from the boomer sensibility—was the least enthusiastic of the candidates. But even he was inspired by the exigencies of the moment, personalized by his own campaign aide, Richard Socarides, an out gay lawyer who now works as one of Harkin's legislative assistants in Washington. In his speech withdrawing from the race, Harkin vowed to fight sexism, racism and homophobia.

Clinton's national strategy derived from polling done by Stanley Greenberg, a former left-wing Yale professor, who centered the campaign on the "Reagan Democrats," those middle-and lower-middle-class white suburbanites, including many Catholics and churchgoing Protestants, who would respond to progressive class issues (such as tax "fairness") but not liberal social issues (such as affirmative action for minorities and civil rights for gays). Accordingly, Clinton remained mute on the military ban and other gay issues (except AIDS, which has its built-in escape clause) until the end of May, just before the California primary, when he gave an extraordinary speech to an absolutely delirious gay audience at the Palace Theater in Los Angeles.

Flanked by Mixner and an array of gay notables, Clinton reiterated his promise to reverse the military's ban, and in the course of citing a Defense Department study that supported such a move, all but outed the high-profile Pentagon "spokesperson who himself was said to be gay" who released it to the press. He promised to put gays in government jobs, to start a "Manhattan Project" crash program to combat AIDS, to appoint an AIDS czar, and to "make a major speech on AIDS to a nontraditional group of Americans," presumably gays, who had never been so addressed by Reagan or Bush. Clinton choked with emotion as he praised the gay and lesbian community for its courageous and committed work against AIDS: "This nation owes you thanks for that, and I want to give you my thanks and respect for that struggle today." And in a moving peroration he added:

> If I could, if I could wave my arm for those of you that are HIV positive and make it go away tomorrow, I would do it, so help me God I would. If I gave up my race for the White House and everything else, I would do that. . . . There are things we can and cannot do. . . . [But] this country is being killed by people who try to break us down and tear us up.

A videotape was shot, of course, and it quickly made the rounds of gay activists as well as Republican "opposition researchers," who never quite got up the gumption to use it against Clinton in the campaign. Clinton asked Bob Hattoy, another gay friend and early campaign adviser, who has AIDS, to speak at the Democratic National Convention—but about AIDS, not gay rights. Clinton argued with Hattoy, Mixner and other gays on his staff up until the last minute before his acceptance speech about whether to include *the word* "gay" in his text. Reports filtered onto the convention floor: It's in, it's out, it's back in. At length, Clinton used the g-word, in the predictable litany of diverse groups he would include in his Administration. But that was practically the last time he initiated a discussion of gay issues in his campaign. In fact, when he talked in Oregon in October he pointedly failed even to mention the battle then in progress around a virulently antigay ballot referendum. After his speech, reporters dragged a grudging word of disapproval from him on the referendum.

As the political campaign progressed, it dawned on many gay and lesbian activists that from now on every Democratic candidate for President would be progay. The reason that Mike Dukakis was so bad on gay issues in 1988 and Bill Clinton was good enough in 1992 had less to do with their characters or their ideologies than with their personal histories. For Dukakis, as for most straights and gays of the 1950s generation, the sexual closet was a reassuring structure of social architecture. He had close gay associates—indeed, one of the top men in his 1988 campaign was out in certain corners of the gay community—but none of them were open about their identity.

Openness has enormous power in the politics of personal relationships. Straight friends and relatives of gays have to confront truths about themselves and their social environment that they have long denied. Clinton, boomer child of the sixties, when Stonewall broke open the closet, had mixed easily with gays for years. More than that, he must deal all the time with openly gay journalists, politicians, lobbyists and advisers. For the better part of a year Clinton traveled day and night with *Newsweek* reporter Mark Miller, who was preparing the Clinton story for the magazine's special issue that would detail "how the candidate won." Miller, who is gay, did not hide his interest in gay issues, and Clinton apparently responded earnestly.

It was Miller who also pressed Clinton, at his first televised press conference in March, to admit that he would consider segregation of gays in the military. Miller seemed to be barely restraining his anger at Clinton's apparent betrayal of his own promise to end discrimination in the service, and it could be that if Miller had not been there the issue would have been blurred or buried. Even the presence of gay people in an office, a classroom, a legislative hall or a city room changes the political dynamics. Within hours after the press conference, Mixner and Hattoy were denouncing their friend the President with exceptional vehemence. Meetings were hastily called at the White House and in New York, where millionaire contributors explicitly threatened Democratic National Chairman David Wilhelm with a financial boycott of the party if Clinton didn't recant on segregation.

It is doubtful that Clinton knew from the start how immensely complex lifting the ban would become. But he should have. He reiterated his campaign pledge on the morning after his election, in response to a reporter's question. A brief but intense firestorm followed, and then seemed to subside. But according to a White House source, machinations continued below sea level. The Joint Chiefs and top Pentagon brass were unhappy at the prospect of admitting homosexuals into the service, but they were equally concerned about losing power in what they feared would be an instinctively antimilitary Administration, headed by a draft dodger and antiwar protester, for Chrissake. They worried about budget cuts, cancellation of weapons systems and the organization of Congressional forces hostile to the Pentagon.

The generals apparently tried to stop Clinton before the election by pitching the gays in the military issue to Bush, but for some reason— perhaps because of the backlash to the gay-bashing that went on at the G.O.P. convention in August—the Bushies passed. But soon after Les Aspin was chosen as Secretary of Defense, the brass began working with him to undermine the expected executive order on gays, and in the process stake out a perimeter around their own turf.

Clinton did not "stack" the ban-lifting order with those on the abortion counseling "gag rule," on fetal-tissue research and on experimentation with the abortifacient RU-486, all of which he issued two days after taking the oath of office. If he had, then he might have outflanked the opposition—a tactic endorsed by some gay activists, *The New York Times* and others who wanted to see the ban lifted. Instead, he did the worst thing, which was to talk about lifting the ban, but not do it.

Over the weekend after the inauguration, a kind of quiet military coup was leveraged, with the gay ban as the lever. Morton Halperin, then an Aspin adviser (he has since been nominated Assistant Secretary of Defense for Democracy and Human Rights), prepared a memo, which he also leaked to the press, predicting dire consequences in Congress if the ban was lifted. He recommended postponing the order until summer. The week's delay also allowed the Christian right around the country to mount an impressive antigay letter-writing campaign to Representatives in Washington. Right-wing talk-show jocks were out in force on the issue. But the consequences were in a sense predetermined by the Pentagon, which, with Aspin's compliance, had been lobbying key legislators to form the promilitary bloc the Joint Chiefs wanted. Halperin (an occasional *Nation* contributor) had served on Richard Nixon's National Security Council and had suddenly turned civil libertarian after he found out Henry Kissinger tapped his telephone. In recent years he headed the Washington office of the A.C.L.U. where he worked on cases of gay people harassed and cashiered by the military. He was close to and completely trusted by lesbians and gays involved in the struggle against the military. But during what Washington gay activists call, with dismay, "the week," when the expected executive order seemed to slip away, Halperin's role was crucial but ambiguous, and estimations of his effect on the events around the executive order differ according to one's sense of political possibility. A gay lawyer who is still fighting to lift the ban is convinced of Halperin's loyalty to the cause, and believes he had to orchestrate a delay to have a chance of winning the issue. But there is the smell of sellout in the air. A gay Democratic source says, ruefully, "Mort's no friend of ours." By doing the bidding of the Joint Chiefs and Congressional conservatives, Halperin undercut the potential strength of a Clinton *coup de foudre*, and made it all the more likely the hearings and negotiations would produce a defeat for gay rights in the guise of a "compromise" that would reinforce the military closet and keep things pretty much as they were. (Halperin declined to talk about the issue; his secretary referred *The Nation* to the Pentagon press office.)

For most gay people, the military ban was not the issue of choice. As one former "gayocrat" who left gay politics in Washington rather than devote all his time to fighting the ban said, "Why should I spend my life getting queers the right to kill or be killed? The best thing about being gay was that you *didn't* have to go in the army."

But it was the issue of opportunity. For as far as gays have come, they cannot yet determine the order of their own social agenda. There is also a serious disjunction between the gayocracy and the millions of lesbians and gays around the country who have quite different needs and demands form the fundraisers and check-writers who are the active participants in gay politics. There is no real nationwide gay organization of activists similar to the great movements for civil rights, women's liberation and radical social change that blossomed in the 1960s and soon after. The National Gay and Lesbian Task Force claims a membership of 26,000, and it performs many useful services, such as its national campaign to counter the homophobic right and to win validation for lesbian and gay families. But for the most part membership means annual giving. ACT UP around the country has been able to muster several thousand shock troops for demonstrations and civil disobedience, but there is no national coordination and, besides, it is not specifically a gay organization. Queer Nation, which was formed on the ACT UP model to deal militantly with gay issues, is small and decentralized, and riven with dissension where it still exists. There are hundreds of new organizations formed by gays in professions (journalism, law, medicine, psychotherapy, teaching), and lesbian and gay groups now thrive on many college campuses. All of them contribute to the moment, but not one has assumed a leading role.

AIDS has had a painfully paradoxical effect on the movement. At the same time that it ravaged the gay male community in institutional as well as personal terms, it has unquestionably contributed to the visibility of gay people against the social background. AIDS contains many tragedies, but first and still foremost it is a catastrophe for gay men in America. What is happening is the destruction of an effectional community very much like an ethnic or national community. Half the gay men in San Francisco are said to be infected with HIV, and the numbers in New York and other big cities are staggering; there is nothing yet to keep most of them from dying. Clinton has dithered in launching his "Manhattan Project" for AIDS. Ever fearful of the right, he refused to reverse the Reagan/Bush order excluding people with HIV from immigrating. As of mid-April he had still not appointed an AIDS czar, even though he had indicated it would be a first order of business. He has included full funding for the Ryan White Act programs to help care for people with AIDS and for education to prevent its spread, but the sum of appropriations for that and AIDS research is nowhere near what the crisis demands.

But again the contradictions intrude. Clinton is failing to live up to his promises, but at least he made them. Reagan and Bush were virtually unapproachable on the subjects of AIDS and gay rights. Now homosexuality is—by presidential directive—a positive qualification for an Administration job. Gays in Washington are finding Administration jobs for themselves and other gays, but they are also trying to convince closeted gays (in the super-closeted capital) that coming out would help, not hurt, the chances of getting hired.

So far, San Francisco lawyer and former City Supervisor Roberta Achtenberg, nominated to be Assistant Secretary of Housing and Urban Development for Fair Housing and Equal Opportunity, is the highest ranking gay person in the federal government. But the Admiration had trouble handling persistent rumors broadcast by some gays and some gay-haters that two Cabinet choices are lesbians.

Donna Shalala, Secretary of Health and Human Services, had been "outed," without supporting evidence, by students at the University of Wisconsin, where she was chancellor. According to an Administration official, she was asked many times during the transition, by co-chair Warren Christopher and others, whether the rumors were true. Moreover, the Clintonites repeatedly tried to assure her that *it was O.K.* to be gay, and they would support her coming out. "It began to sound like a *Seinfeld* stick," one Washington insider told me. When the press repeated the rumor, Shalala made a statement: "Have I lived an alternative life style? The answer is no." That ended it for the White House, but lesbians and gays were upset. "Life style" is *their* word, not ours. Homosexuality is an orientation or an identity, never a life style.

Attorney General Janet Reno, another unmarried Cabinet officer, had been called a lesbian during one of her election campaigns as Dade County prosecutor. When Clinton announced her nomination, the same old enemies started faxing the allegation all over Washington, according to National Public Radio's star reporter, Nina Totenberg. It was picked up by the ultraright Accuracy in Media, which issued a coy press advisory: "As President Clinton steps to the plate in his effort to drive home his latest nominee for attorney general, the count is two strikes and no balls. Janet Reno . . ." Reno affirmed her heterosexuality, more or less: "I'm attracted to strong, brave, rational and intelligent men," she said to a reporter. Totenberg said on the air that the rumors would not affect her nomination, and that an Administration source told her "the White House satisfied itself that Reno is not gay." We don't know by what method the satisfaction came.

What has changed the climate in America is the long experience of gay struggle, the necessary means having been, first, coming out, and second, making a scene. Sometimes it is personal witness, other times political action, and overall it is the creation of a cultural community based on sexual identity.

The ascension of gay people to positions of authority in key sectors of society has made a huge difference in the weather. The prerequisite for their influence is being out—which is why the destruction of the closet is the most vital issue of gay life, beyond any act of censorship or exclusion. It is also the reason that "outing" has become such a charged political question.

Every opinion survey shows that people who say they have a gay friend or family member are twice or three times as likely to support gay rights than are those who say they know no gay people. What the surveys don't report is the opinion of people who know out gays. None of the events and activities listed above—the political victories, the cultural successes achieved by gays in the past short period of time— would have been possible if closets were shut.

The military establishment, schools, churches all understand the importance of the closet in maintaining institutional order. That is why the services never cared a damn about gays who did not proclaim their identity, by word or deed. It is why school superintendents have lived for centuries with lesbian and gay teachers, but panic when anyone comes out. It's why churches countenance lesbian nuns and gay priests and ministers as long as they lie about themselves.

Andrew Sullivan wrote recently in *The New York Times* that dropping the military ban on gays would be a deeply conservative act, in that gays who join up would be, by definition, patriotic and traditionalist. That may be true in the particular, but in general and historical terms, nothing could be more radical than upsetting the sexual apple cart. The patriarchal power of the military consists precisely in the sexual status quo, and when gays become visible they undercut that power. Randy Shilts asserts in his study of gays in the service, *Conduct Unbecoming*, "The presence of gay men [in the military] . . . calls into question everything that manhood is supposed to mean." And homophobia—like is blood relations, racism, misogyny and anti-Semitism—is an ideology that rationalizes the oppressive uses of male power. When cruel and self-hating homophobes such as J. Edgar

Hoover and Roy Cohn are outed, even posthumously, the power system is shaken.

The counterpower of coming out has given the gay movement primacy this year in the unfinished civil rights revolution. It's more than appropriate that the N.A.A.C.P. has decided to participate in the April 25 march on Washington, along with every major civil liberties and civil rights organization in the country. Labor unions, which have not been particularly supportive of the gay movement, are also sending bus loads of marchers. Modern American feminism has a natural affinity with gay liberation: The latter was, in a sense, born of the former. The two have not always been on the best of terms, but increasingly, adherents of both movements understand how closely allied are their ideologies, how similar their enemies and how important their coalition. Pat Schroeder (ironically, a Representative from the "hate state"), one of Congress's leading feminists, is also the most vocal and effective advocate for gay rights. The kind of broad "rainbow" coalition now developing was unthinkable only a few years ago.

But the gay nineties is not only about civil right, tolerance and legitimacy. What started tumbling out of the closets at the time of Stonewall is profoundly altering the way we all live, form families, think about and act toward one another, manage our health and well-being and understand the very meaning of identity. All the crosscurrents of present-day liberation struggles are subsumed in the gay struggle. The gay moment is in some ways similar to the moment that other communities have experienced in the nation's past, but it is also something more, because sexual identity is in crisis throughout the population, and gay people—at once the most conspicuous subjects and objects of the crisis—have been forced to invent a complete cosmology to grasp it. No one says the changes will come easily. But it's just possible that a small and despised sexual minority will change America forever.

THE TRUTH ABOUT THE A.B.A.

Elisabeth Sifton

•

EVERY YEAR AT the height of spring a strange tribal rite takes place at the heart of American culture, and most of us know nothing about it. A trade fair pulls together tens of thousands of booksellers and publishers—this year in Miami over the Memorial Day weekend—with their buyers, sales directors, rights managers, publicists, sales reps and big-time executives in attendance. Like every ritual that displays bizarre deformations of once meaningful human behavior, this meeting was once quite reasonable and effective, but now it has become almost unimaginably incoherent. Books are what draw the merrymakers together, but books all too often are precisely what is least on their minds.

The initial purpose was to enable buyers from bookshops all over the country to place orders for the next season's books with the publishers' salespeople. Faxes, computers and other important changes in the business have made this serious and lively commercial activity virtually obsolete, and it's been pushed to the sidelines. When the American Booksellers Association now convenes its disputatious members, and the rites center on displays and events organized and paid for by violently competitive publishers, especially poignant confusions lurk in every encounter—and this is beyond the intense, erotically charged hysteria that characterizes all big conventions. The participants affectionately acknowledge the mysteries, but they don't like to talk about them to the uninitiated; still, in 1993 they are no longer endearing, and in fact haven't been for seasons. The whole business is in a deep mess, and American readers and writers are suffering as a result.

Like other unexamined premises of the book business, the basic physical setup of the A.B.A. hasn't changed in years. Publishers still pay huge sums of money—a hefty percentage of their annual budgets, sometimes—to install a "booth" along one of the aisles of the convention floor to do their business in. University presses and smaller regional or specialty firms actually display real books, still believing in them as they do. (At the outer edges, some of the tiniest outfits are beguilingly loony, yet there are always impressive companies that you're embarrassed not to have known about before, doing fine work with very good books.) Salespeople stay "on the stand" and chat with visitors who come along by appointment or merely pass by—not only booksellers who want to go over forthcoming titles and place orders but book-review editors from newspapers and magazines, TV and radio people, other publishers scoping out the competition, real writers.

At the mainstream houses, this model has been grotesquely inflated and transformed in the past ten or fifteen years. The booth will be an elaborately designed area as big as or bigger than a spacious New York City apartment, with huge illuminated signs (revolving, sometimes) showing the jackets of next autumn's Big Books, maybe a TV screen or two with promotional videos. Dozens of sales reps and managers, publicists and executives will be on hand for the hundreds of people who throng the place—doing what? No books are on display, and it's all but impossible to have a purposeful conversation or do real business in the midst of the hullabaloo; there are never enough tables and chairs. Occasionally piles of glossily jacketed advance proofs of some hyped best-seller-to-be will appear; during weird binges of acquisitive fervor, these, along with tote bags, T-shirts, posters and other freebies, are eagerly gobbled up. I've spent plenty of time myself rushing about the floor of an A.B.A. convention looking for goodies before the supply is exhausted, which happens in minutes, and I've done this in the company of some of America's most prominent publishers; they snicker about what they consider the infantile behavior of the booksellers, suckers, they think, for this kind of commercial nonsense, but they are indulging in it themselves. We all claim we're at the A.B.A. for the Good of the Book and To Promote Business, but we're also there to schmooze and flirt and mess around.

Meanwhile, the big-shot publishers are doing another kind of business: They are creating and adjusting images of power and intention about just four or five of their biggest books in the next year, they are making deals that they hope will safeguard these precious properties. At breakfasts and lunches (organized by the booksellers) their famous authors talk up their books; later the celebrities will sign copies by the hundreds; in the evening the publishers throw giant parties for themselves or for the celebs, and more image-mongering goes on. (For the cognoscenti, the agenda-free, well situated *New York Review* party is always the toniest; the Crown bashes, often for books *about* parties, the most wizardly lavish. I can't forget a surreal moment in Las Vegas where I watched John Updike meet Donald Trump and Anne Rice at a Random House reception for the last two.)

The money spent on all this is quite out of hand, naturally. Yet the only senior member of the tribe to call it for what it is—Tom McCormack, president of St. Martin's Press, who withdrew his company from the A.B.A. convention several years ago, denouncing it as a shameful waste of money—was not followed or supported by his fraternal peers. It gets fancier and more intense every year.

And every year the publishers encourage their foreign colleagues to come by to grab a famous or potentially famous name, so that the carefully orchestrated sale of foreign rights can add to the hype about a title, possibly one they have won at auction. (They all seem to be interested in the same handful of titles, which is why their booths look alike and give off the same abstract glitzy air. But I can remember when you could instantly tell the difference between a Random House, Houghton Mifflin, Little Brown, Simon and Schuster or Viking booth, as you could between their books; they once had different styles, "house authors" and distinctive personalities.) This last development occurred over the strong opposition of the A.B.A. itself, which rightly thought it would help to obliterate the fundamental work of placing and taking orders on domestic sales. But it lost that battle, and the A.B.A. convention is now as much a rights fair (like the famous international one in Frankfurt every fall) as it is a booksellers' one.

The irresponsible giddiness of all this spending is stunning. The country is in a grave, long recession; book sales have been flat or worse for years, despite huge growth in certain sectors of the market; libraries are underfunded and underused; functional illiteracy is rising; and polls tell us that Americans spend only 5 to 6 percent of their "leisure time" reading (and 30 percent watching television). More and more books are published and go out of print; writers justifiably feel neglected, the best sellers rarely earn out and countless numbers of people in the business will tell you they hate the way it's going. Why is this?

Book people used to take comfort in the idea that like lawyers and liquor stores they could thrive during a depression, when books were appreciated as a means of inexpensive enjoyment and self-improvement. But in the 1930s the book had little competition in this regard; local, state and national funds supported all the structures of a print culture, and publishers believed in a reading public. None of this is true today.

Any sensible business person will tell you that when sales are flat it is axiomatic to "stay close to the source of supply and close to the customer." In the book trade, this would mean that publishers should stay close to writers and close to booksellers. Indeed, great publishers always have, and still do; it is the only possible way to survive, since the known truth is that income, nay profit, depends not just on the big sellers in the current season but steady sales of the older titles ("backlist" books, published more than a year ago, provide a huge proportion of most publishers' income). You must cultivate writers and readers for both.

But even the most superficial glance at the behavior of the principal trade-book companies in America will show you just the opposite: The business is dominated by people who rarely read books or hang out with writers, who spend their time with other executives and with agents, making deals and "running the numbers," who relegate the work of dealing with writers and with the marketplace to lower-echelon editors and salespeople whose expertise they frequently defy. Alfred Knopf himself observed this decades ago when he commented dryly on the purpose of editors: "When I started in this business, writers wrote books and publishers read them in order to choose which ones they wanted to publish. The rise of the editor has occurred because now publishers can't read and need editors to do it for them; writers can't write, and need them for the same reason."

The major media manipulators now rise, balloonlike, above and beyond the world where books are read and valued. Indeed, they seem almost not to value them at all, affirming a book's worth only in terms of its spinoff utility ("potential") in other media—the mini-series, the movie, the author's TV appearances, the audiotape, the electronic capabilities, etc. The only other validation of a book's worth that they recognize is not their own opinion of the text but someone else's; therefore if a book club, or another publisher, or a reader for a movie studio likes a book, they will like it too, but not before. They develop strong peripheral vision, watching everyone else's moves, yet they develop none of their own. "Let's see how it goes. . . . This one is review-driven. . . . The clubs had doubts. . . . The writer isn't telegenic." They lack the courage or good manners to be honest and acknowledge that they haven't read and don't care about the book. They want to be like Hollywood television and movie people. They aspire to deals.

These anxious publishing executives have their counterparts throughout the trade—indeed, throughout the media—and they all respond to the retail gloom at ground level with fearful and greedy hyperactivity, putting all their chips on one or two big items, masking their fundamental lack of trust in the true power of books to do well on their own (and their justifiable lack of trust in their own judgment). In short, they aren't book people, and when they go to the A.B.A., they seek out other non-book people with whom they cut the deals. In all the palaver, they are talking discount schedules like everyone else, but in very different accents.

How have the booksellers, meanwhile, responded to the recession, and what are they doing about it? There have never been so many good booksellers in our history—resourceful, socially active and committed, well-read and good at business. Many of them might in earlier times have been ministers or teachers: They have an all but evangelical fervor about increasing readership and literacy, they believe that Americans can and should read books (few publishers today hold to this once sacred dogma), they truly care about multiculturalism, they want the United States to live up to its promises, they are astonished and pleased by the huge possibilities that its culture offers to writers and readers. They look on the horrifying statistics on the decline of reading—more than half of American households in a given year may never purchase a book, and so on—merely as indicators of what huge growth potential their business has; all those unconverted nonreaders to bring into the fold! There is nowhere to go but up!

One couldn't have better colleagues than these brave, shrewd independent booksellers, who reinvented the idea of the well-stocked cavernous bookstore which encourages browsing and unexpected purchases, which presents books as the physical and mental pleasure they are. These business people, some of whom have expanded their stores into mini-chains of their own, are the people who learned from, challenged and in some respects prevailed over the chains—Walden, Dalton, Crown—that shortsighted Cassandras claimed a decade ago would kill off the independents. With equal savvy about inventory control and marketing strategy, but a subtler, more responsible and community-based sense of how to develop and expand the customer pool, the independents soon forced the big chain companies to copy them, which they are now doing with the famous superstores.

Writers have been quick to appreciate that all this has changed the shape and nature of literary life in America. They happily accept invitations (worked out jointly between publisher and bookshop) to give readings and talks at the stores, which function like community cultural centers, filling the vacuum left by the demise of town halls and local libraries and churches; they come to know the buyers, meet the retail purchasers, develop local audiences one by one across the country. These new encounters are mostly paid for by the publishers, but they were invented by the booksellers.

None of this work could be done without the computerized technologies that make it feasible to control vast and complex inventories of hardcover, paperback, old and new books. The entire trade can develop and sustain an accurate, nuanced picture of sales and stock—this was never possible before. And computers also allow it to attack with much sharper and more flexible instruments the issue of "the numbers." At the A.B.A., the talk is all about numbers, about discounts, about price, about advertising dollars.

Among booksellers, disputes rage on many fronts. The independents and chains must both develop strategies to counter the new clout of "price clubs," the wholesalelike outfits pushing deeply discounted best sellers and other popular merchandise. The chains, regrouping in the post-Reagan years, their overly confident spread into the overly implausible malls having been arrested, build their brazenly aggressive superstores; but the long-term success of their huge national purchasing policies may not be assured, since in the end the local merchants, with well-trained staff and local knowledge, are unbeatable. Still, if they go down they'll take out good small stores with them. And independents are exploring how, or whether and which of them might band together in groups to match, as single units buying for their members, the commercial power of the biggies—allowing them to sweep up quantities of remainders, say, or other offerings from the publishers that now they may be last in line to get. And in all these cases, as never before, the disputes show total confusion as to how much books are worth—literally, confusion as to what price to put on them.

Writers know they get a royalty calculated as a percentage of the retail price of their book. Few of them notice that their contracts specify that if the discount at which the publisher sells a book goes above 49 or 50 or 52 percent (significant variants, these), the royalty will be halved—i.e., the royalty is cut in half when the book is sold at essentially a wholesale discount, not a regular trade one, which hovers in the 40 to 48 percent range. This ancient boilerplate, like so much of the book-business infrastructure, was devised a half-century ago, when only a handful of accounts merited unusually steep trade discounts. Now half or more of a commercial book's initial orders may go to wholesale or quasi-retail accounts that merit discounts of 50 percent or higher. Unless a savvy agent has negotiated the author's contract with this possibility in mind, the writer will, ironically, earn only half of what should be her income for these sales betokening her widespread popularity. Brand-name bestseller writers have contracts that make sure this doesn't happen; but as in so many other dark corners of the book business, the less-known surprise writer will not only have less chance of these big sales but a smaller piece of the action if she's lucky enough to land them.

Meanwhile, other books will be sold at lower discounts, other publishers will focus on short-discounted books for the institutional market, small stores will try to consolidate their orders over a range of titles in order to get better discounts (weighing, too, the advantages of buying from wholesalers rather than from the publisher directly). An amazingly high proportion of the total dollars, though, will be paid for those few titles that the auto-intoxicated trade chooses to believe will dominate the best-seller list, titles sold in the largest quantities. Certain books will be offered at their printed retail price of, say, $20 and elsewhere at $18 or $16 or even $10, and it will be clear that no one knows, actually, what the book is worth.

The resulting chaos is so extreme that the A.B.A members cannot agree as to how it might be straightened out. Some of them argue for an abolition of the printed retail price as the base line, favoring instead a "net price agreement" such as prevails in a number of other countries. This would, they believe, level the playing field both when everyone buys from the publishers at the same net price and when everyone sells to the readers at differing retail prices, since the prices will vary according to what kind of "value added" service, custom and availability they are offering the customers in their stores. Others vehemently oppose this. The publishers warily avoid discussing the issue among themselves—such a seminar would probably violate Sherman antitrust regulations—and mostly they just look for the angles, trying to sink as many balls as they can in this zany pool game. Sharp practices abound at all levels: There is so much stock flowing around the country, in and out of warehouses, trucks and storage rooms—and there is so much money to be made!

Naturally the competition is even more murderously greedy when outlets placing the biggest orders also heavily discount the *retail* price paid by the *retail* customer for a book that the publisher wants to have land, and therefore probably will land or already has landed, on the *New York Times* best-seller list. Thus does the scorpion swallow its tail, and thus is the business deformed around a purposefully self-fulfilling prophecy. In the ensuing blizzard of competition, the retail price becomes a fiction—the least respected and most contested figure in the arithmetic. This has been called inevitable retail development, the well-known phenomenon of standardized chains (K Mart, Toys 'R' Us, Staples) driving out local custom. But the commodities sold in those other chains don't have writers or intellectual property at issue, which requires a still point somewhere, on which the *author*'s income may be calculated. And they don't involve the *culture* in anything like the same way.

In the noise of the A.B.A. convention—where sensory overload taxes the body and wearies the soul—sensible, wise men and women can be heard doing honorable work against great odds. Lively writers, vivacious booksellers and canny publishers raise glasses together and collaborate as best they can. Stupendous wastage despoils the landscape—slagheaps of dreadful books, vulgar displays, unethical deals, pretentious pseudo-publishing. The odds are, as ever, against the brave, the plucky and the kind. Readers and writers will feel temporarily abandoned there, forgotten. But if we are lucky, and if the economy improves, and if reason occasionally prevails, the chances of our intellectual and literary life continuing into the next century will not be wholly lost.

IDENTITY POLITICS IN NEW YORK CITY

Michael Tomasky

•

AS YOU PROBABLY know, David Dinkins, the 106th Mayor of New York City and the first African-American one, did not march in the St. Patrick's Day parade. The holders of the permit of New York's largest and oldest ethnic parade, the Ancient Order of Hibernians, wouldn't allow an Irish gay and lesbian group to march under a banner that so identified it, and the Mayor of all the people of New York could not sanction this bald assault on tolerance and diversity. It was quite a ruckus.

Seven weeks later, the holders of the permit for the Salute to Israel parade, the American Zionist Youth Foundation, denied a mostly gay and lesbian synagogue from Greenwich Village the right to march in *its* parade, even though the synagogue's rabbi had made an agreement with the group that would've kept Sam Nunn on a leash: She said that her congregation would march under a banner that bore simply the name of the synagogue, without the words "gay" or "lesbian" or any-thing like them. Still the answer was no. (The foundation claims that the rabbi, Sharon Kleinbaum, broke other parts of the agreement.)

Discrimination again, right? Wrong. In this parade, Dinkins marched. So did most of the city's top Democratic officials. The papers never came right out and said it, but the obvious reason for the double standard is as follows: Dinkins figures the Irish vote is lost, but the

Jews are another matter. So politically, it's smart to offend the Irish and stand up for gays and lesbians (even though, in inimitable Dinkins style, he ended up offending them too, after police arrested 218 demonstrators who held a countermarch). But to a Democrat who'll need every vote he can get this November, Jews are several positions ahead of gays on the vote charts. Straight up Fifth Avenue, your honor, and don't forget to put this on your head!

It's campaign season in New York, and if you thought electoral politics couldn't possibly get any more superficial than they were last year, consider that the comedian Jackie Mason was, until he dropped out last month, running—for an office called Public Advocate, the devalued version of the already useless post of City Council President. Andrew Stein, current holder of said useless office and a person no one takes seriously, began by running for mayor but dropped out to seek re-election as Public Advocate after realizing that no one (aside from his multimillionaire father, who bankrolls him) takes him seriously. Rudolph Giuliani, the former Reagan Administration Justice Department official and U.S. Attorney for the Southern District of New York, is running for mayor again, but until just recently his main adviser had pretty much been keeping him out of the papers because the last time he was in them in a big way, he was screaming through a megaphone to an assemblage that was the nearest thing to the Beer Hall Putsch since David Duke counterdemonstrated at the Chicago Eight trial.

New York politics is a vaudeville act, in large part because the city's marvelous, mischievous tabloids play it that way. But behind all that, there's starkly serious business at hand. People thought 1989 was a watershed election, and it was—a referendum against twelve increasingly hateful years of Ed Koch, and a chance for the city to rise above its past prejudices to elect a black Mayor. But in crucial ways, this year's election is far more momentous. Now, the black Mayor and the social movements that started in the 1960s and eventually lifted him into the city's highest office face a referendum themselves. His coalition—black and Latino activists, and what are called, in P. C. shorthand, "progressive whites"—teeters on the brink of the identity politics cliff. And a new coalition—white outer-borough ethnics, newer immigrants and people of color who weren't schooled in traditional liberalism and who increasingly distrust its postures and buzzwords—stands ready to supplant it. Though Dinkins can by no means be written off today, he's not looking like a winner. If that's how the dice land, the fault will lie partly with the Mayor himself, so dismally disappointing in so many areas, and partly with his coalition, so full of unity and tolerance in its tropes but so lacking them in its behavior.

It was hard not to be excited by Dinkins's victory in 1989. Oh, we knew very well what we were getting—an old-line clubhouse pol, a Harlem heeler whose career had been largely occupied by dreary patronage jobs. In a room, he was an ancillary presence. As a speaker, he stuck to the script comma for comma and droned his way toward completion. It was comical, in 1989, at certain campaign stops where Jesse Jackson introduced him, to watch Jackson holding back on his firepower so as not to upstage Dinkins, who looked tiny and awed next to the Reverend.

And, as a longtime Democratic fixture, Dinkins was a pal of, and received campaign contributions from, the army of real estate barons, lawyers, lobbyists, fixers and *machers* who really run the city. There is a famous Dinkins quote in which he assures austerity guru and financier Felix Rohatyn of his willingness to get tough with the municipal unions, without whose endorsements he could not have won: "don't worry, they'll take it from me."

But supporters brushed that sort of thing aside as history tapped this clerk on the shoulder and said, "Come with me." For reasons that had little to do with Dinkins, the circumstances were right in 1989, as they had never been despite repeated attempts since 1969, for a black to make it to the top. Victory, coming as it did first against the race-baiting Koch, and then in the general election against the Reaganaut Giuliani, was all the sweeter.

But more important than the candidate himself was the potential his victory represented. Because New York has always been defined by the flow of its immigrants, its politics have always been ethnic and racial in nature. That has not necessarily been a bad thing. For decades, liberal and socialist Jews had a deep impact on the Irish conservatives of Tammany who ran the city from about 1860 onward. Later, blacks and Puerto Ricans turned the machine's eyes in other directions, and by about 1960, no white Democratic politician could win city-wide office without supporting civil rights. Of course, things have gone rather downhill since then for the reasons everyone knows about, and that's precisely why Dinkins's ability to win over one-third of the Jewish vote against a white opponent was such a triumph. Jews—at least enough of them—had rejected Giuliani's unsubtle language about Dinkins being a "Jesse Jackson Democrat" and the like. Two-thirds of Latinos, historically in constant competition with blacks over the meager spoils thrown the two groups, backed Dinkins, as did almost all black voters, and gays and lesbians. The outs were finally in, and there was much rhetoric about a new era of cooperation, empowerment and progressive agendas, all produced with white-hot vigor by the Mayor's "gorgeous mosaic."

Today, that coalition faces possible collapse. On the surface, it's because of Dinkins's failures as a politician. Groups expect things in return for their support, and many feel Dinkins hasn't executed his half of the bargain: for Latinos, too few appointments, their people no better off than under Koch; for gays and lesbians, no effective domestic partnership law. And so on.

But on a level deeper than political trade-offs, the problem is that Dinkins, and progressive New York in general, speak only in the coded language of identity politics and entreaties to oppressed subgroups. It's a language that sounds noble when talking of black or Latino "empowerment," cloaking itself in the rubrics of civil rights, comity and love of fellow person, but that in the end is the same old interest-group palm-greasing, just like the Irish pols used to play it, dressed up in a multicultural tuxedo. It pretends to be something it is not. And it dismisses those who do not buy into its precepts as Neanderthals, as relics, as being somehow *in the way* (of what is not clear).

What moral code, for example, dictates that a black Mayor denounce the prejudice of an Irish parade that excludes gays and lesbians, but put that denunciation aside to march with Jews? The answer is, none does. No, check that; the answer is, the moral code of Tammany Hall does. Dinkins's stock response, in explaining the apparent contradiction, is that the Irish Lesbian and Gay Organization asked that he not march, while Congregation Beth Simchat Torah said that, however saddened it was at its exclusion, the Mayor or anyone else should go ahead and march to show support for Israel. It takes about a second and a half to slice that rationalization away. Regarding the St. Pat's parade, Dinkins did not say, "I won't march because some people don't want me to"; he said, "I won't march on principle." Apparently, in the seven weeks between the two events, that principle became conditional. The Irish, lacking the "progressive" credential, could be tossed away.

Yes, the Irish spent many years throwing blacks away, and now, blacks may say, it's our turn. So that's all it is—a revenge game? When you claim a higher moral ground, as progressives always do, you'd better stay up there.

In such a milieu, knees jerk to the left as easily as to the right. Let's take a quick look at three case studies—three highly charged racial incidents that took place during David Dinkins's term—to see just how wrong assumptions can be, and just how inadequately Dinkins and his coalition have reacted.

- Flatbush, Brooklyn, 1990. The assistant manager of a Korean deli is alleged to have beaten a Haitian woman shopping in his store. A black-led boycott ensues, seeming at first to express legitimate grievances, which involve not only racial discrimination but economic issues such as lack of access to credit. But soon enough it turns racist, with protesters screaming, "What's the fortune cookie say? No money today!" The woman's lawyer describes severe pelvic and abdominal injuries to his client. Meanwhile, a judge issues an order that protesters be kept fifty feet away from the store, but Dinkins refuses to enforce it. The papers urge Dinkins to shop in the store, symbolically killing the boycott. He dawdles. The boycott's leaders are so uncompromising that eventually Dinkins has no choice but to go into the store and buy something—eight months after the boycott starts. Finally, a jury acquits the assistant manager, agreeing that the woman suffered only a facial scratch, if that.
- Washington Heights, Manhattan, 1992. A white cop shoots and kills a young Dominican man. Later, during riots, another white cop is accused of pushing another Dominican off a roof, based on a single eyewitness account. These cases sound open and shut, right? Hang the racist cops! Murals are painted in memory of José (Kiko) Garcia, the man who was shot, and calls for justice ensue. Some Dominicans charge that the cop was a rogue, on the take. But a grand jury finds that Garcia was a drug dealer and was packing heat, and that the officer, Michael O'Keefe, acted properly. In the other case, the eyewitness confesses under oath that he lied. Dinkins supports the grand jury, but it doesn't undo the damage of a highly public press event the Mayor staged with Garcia's family, before any of the above facts were known.
- Crown Heights, Brooklyn, 1992. A jury acquits Lemrick Nelson, a young black man, of the murder of Yankel Rosenbaum, a Hasidic divinity student who had the bad fortune of trying to walk home during the Crown Heights riot of 1991. Rosenbaum, it is disputed by no one, was killed purely because of his appearance, which marked him as a Jew. Dinkins responds to the acquittal by announcing that we live in "a society requiring that we accept and abide by the jury system." Jews—not just

Hasidim and conservatives—are outraged at Dinkins's tepid response.

What's the common thread? In each case, Dinkins showed no moral leadership; he placated constituencies. The boycotters were as obstreperous as they were because they gambled, correctly, that Dinkins wouldn't move to "alienate his base." In Washington Heights, the Mayor did make one good move: He spent a great deal of time in the community after the shooting, and his presence probably did help cool tempers and keep the rioting to a minimum. But Dinkins's meeting with the family (along with John Cardinal O'Connor, who was looking after his own Dominican Catholic constituents) was a bad call. He jumped the gun, implicitly pushed by the imperatives of his coalition—though no one would ever admit this—to the assumption that the white cops must be guilty.

In Crown Heights, Dinkins's tame response to the Nelson verdict was breathtaking. Jews reacted to the verdict with the suspicion that justice would never be served for this murder, and that's precisely where a mayor needs to step in—to calm, and to demonstrate an understanding of the anger. But Dinkins said nothing to assure Jews at all. He deplored the murder but did little else. Meanwhile, no one disputed that Nelson was part of the group of teens roaming the streets looking for Jews. After the acquittal, Nelson's lawyers celebrated at a dinner with some members of the jury. Dinkins said little about either of the events. Nor was he among the politicians who called for a federal investigation of the murder. Today, not a soul has been arrested, and there's no evidence that Dinkins has any continuing interest in the matter. You can bet the Mayor's silent posture is abetted by the fact that the victim was Hasidic. One suspects that if David Dinkins has given Yankel Rosenbaum any thought, it's been only to hope that he doesn't have to hear Rosenbaum's name much between now and Election Day.

So is Rudy Giuliani any better? He's carrying some heavy baggage. As head of the Justice Department's criminal division in the early 1980s, he personally oversaw the repatriation of Haitian exiles back into the waiting arms of the Tonton Macoutes (he had traveled to Haiti and come back saying "repression simply does not exist now"). As a prosecutor, he put some baddies in stir, but he was also a grand-stander and publicity seeker of unchecked proportion, having Wall Street traders led from their offices in handcuffs.

But the image of him that sticks, and hard, is of his speech at a police rally in front of City Hall last September. Let's just say that Leni

Riefenstahl should've been there to film it. Off-duty cops, most of them white, many drinking beer (this was in the morning), some carrying their sidearms, held an anti-Dinkins "rally." There was muttering about the "nigger Mayor" and the usual crude "jokes." Giuliani, the featured speaker, denounced the Mayor's various failings through a bullhorn to a madly cheering throng. He claimed afterward that he actually helped cool things off, because he moved some officers from the City Hall steps, where things were turning ugly, further down the street. It's true that he did speak away from the steps, but that didn't matter; what mattered was the picture of Giuliani inciting a group of people who are supposed to uphold order as they expended massive energy in creating disorder.

The rally brought into focus the element of Giuliani's character that I think makes people uncomfortable. After all, for a Republican, he's kind of moderate, a professed supporter of abortion rights, social spending and, at least rhetorically, gay rights. But people see him as a peeper—a snoop, a dick, an investigator who wants to get tough on crime, and if it requires looking into people's bedroom windows or forgetting once in a while about Miranda rights to ferret the creeps out, then so be it. This is serious business in New York, where people don't hold their rights to privacy and their liberties lightly.

Problem number two is that for a "moderate," Giuliani sure has some strange pals. Cardinal O'Connor is probably the most reactionary and hypocritical "leader" in New York today: reactionary in using his pulpit to espouse various planks of the Republican Party platform (homosexuality is evil, abortion is murder, etc.), and hypocritical because somehow, his church always gets away with pretending it's not involved in politics per se (even though, in May's school board elections, his Catholic churches distributed a voter's guide prepared by a local Pat Robertson group!). Giuliani adores the Cardinal, and despite the policy differences noted above, it's unlikely that as mayor he'd buck the archdiocese when push came to shove.

Hypothetically placing Giuliani in Gracie Mansion during the three test cases examined above does little to make one feel comfortable. There is reason to suspect, since law and order is his background, that he would've had the Flatbush boycotters immediately arrested, leading to God knows what kind of tsuris. And he probably wouldn't have paid much mind to what few legitimate claims the boycotters did have concerning the racist lending practices of banks, for example. In Washington Heights and Crown Heights, we know what he did—he stood with the police in the former and the Hasidim in the latter as reflexively as

Dinkins did the opposite, and for the same reason: Go where your votes are. If Giuliani has any vision of a higher plane of racial politics, he has not displayed it. His nascent alliance with Herman Badillo, a respectable man who dropped out of the mayoral race to run for Comptroller on a ticket with Rudy, may signal that vision, or it may just be a cheap and quick way for Giuliani to win some coveted Latino votes.

I haven't even mentioned how New York's doing under Dinkins. I did a small canvass, asking people to name the administration's signal achievements. "Hmmm, gotta take another call now," said a friend.

The truth is that Dinkins has faced horrible economic times. More than 350,000 jobs have been lost to the city since he took office. More than 1 million New Yorkers are on welfare. The schools range from mediocre to disgraceful. The streets aren't safe. It's reckoned a good year when fewer than 2,000 people are murdered. Many of New York's problems, of course, aren't his fault. They reflect changes in national and global economies, and social conditions well beyond one man's control, even if he is Mayor. But his administration has been directionless, launching a handful of programs here and there, reversing itself on policies concerning the homeless, for example, and generally doing very little to give New Yorkers a sense that their city, where their daily lives get more difficult each year, is moving forward. The bureaucracies are immovable. The unions are intractable. Wall Street is imperious. The bond raters are skeptical. Nothing seems to get done.

Historically speaking, it wasn't so long ago—forty, fifty years—that New York was the *best*. The mass transit was the best, the public housing was the best, the schools, believe it or not, were the best. Back then, New York was building the most beautiful public urban spaces known to humankind. It's impossible to imagine New York building anything beautiful today. The only major skyscraper topped off in recent years, Worldwide Plaza in west Midtown, makes architectural nods to that history but is generally a humdrum affair. Unlike the lithe, elegant Chrysler Building (1931), which seems to soar to the sky with the sum of human hopes, Worldwide Plaza sits there thick as an old tree stump, with no grace at all. Why? So the developer could maximize the floor area, and hence the profits.

At the same time, New York remains the most dazzling, wonderful city on Earth, and those of us who knock it still love it ferociously. We just don't expect much of it anymore—or of its leaders. And none of it stands much chance of changing until we find a civic language that goes beyond identifying various aggrieved groups and placating them. Until the city's political leaders confront that, everything—the public schools, the workplaces, the courts, the community development programs, the city university system—will be a battleground for competing, particularist agendas.

There has to be a way out, and all concerned, whether they admit it or not, know it. Anyone who has a child in a public school or who pays attention to the schools knows, for example, that the Rainbow Curriculum, the multicultural project of outgoing Schools Chancellor Joseph Fernandez, which was whole-heartedly backed by Dinkins, is a long way from being the most important reform the schools need now. While it's true that some opponents whipped up homophobia, the curriculum failed because of Fernandez's imperious style and, more important, because working-class parents—of all colors—see "tolerance" as a bit of a luxury when they have to chip in out of their salaries to buy chalk, erasers, and mops. Dinkins's only response to the controversy was the usual pro-Fernandez spiel, and he lost. And every year spent fretting about rainbows and not about equity in school funding, or whether high school graduates can actually read and write and think, is a year that the people who send their kids to private schools and who shelter their taxes away from the public schools—and we all know who *they* are—can pass in leisurely laughter at the circus below them. There has to be a potent political strategy that recognizes this fact and fights this fight.

And above all, there must be a single standard for civil behavior, a standard based on decency and respect—a standard that doesn't have exceptions or make excuses. Prejudice is prejudice, whether perpetrated by Irish or Jews in a parade, blacks in a boycott, or Dominicans whispering smears against the good reputation of a white cop. Until David Dinkins, or someone else, governs accordingly, the city will continue down the sinkhole.

CESAR'S GHOST

Frank Bardacke

•

CESAR, WHO WAS always good at symbols, saved his best for last: a simple pine box, fashioned by his brother's hands, carried unceremoniously through the Central Valley town he made famous. With some 35,000 people looking on.

Here was meaning enough, both for those who need it blunt and for those who like it subtle. No one—especially not the newspaper and TV reporters whose liberal sympathies had been one of his main assets— could fail to hear that pine box speak: Cesar Chavez's commitment to voluntary poverty extended even unto death. And perhaps a few among the crowd would get the deeper reference. Burial insurance had been Cesar's first organizing tool in building the National Farm-workers Association back in 1962. Many farmworkers, then and now, die so badly in debt that they can't afford to be buried. By joining up with Cesar and paying dues to the association, workers earned the right to take their final rest in a pine box, built by brother Richard.

The funeral march and picnic were near perfect. The friendly crowd was primarily Chicano, people who had driven a couple of hours up and over the Grapevine from Los Angeles to honor the man who was the authentic representative of their political coming of age in postwar America. Martin Luther King is the standard comparison, but Cesar Chavez was King and Jackie Robinson, too. Chicanos and Mexicans had played well in their own leagues—they built a lot of power in the rail-road, mining and factory unions of the Southwest—but Cesar forced his way into the political big leagues, where Chicanos had always been excluded. And, like Robinson, he played on his own terms.

Not only Chicanos but all manner of farmworker supporters marched at the funeral: liberal politicians, celebrities, Catholic priests, grape and lettuce boycotters. This was fitting too, as Chavez had always insisted that his greatest contribution to the farmworker movement was the consumer boycott. The boycott, he argued, ended the debilitating isolation of farmworkers that the boycotters marched at Cesar's funeral, and it was their buttons (the word "grapes" or "uvas" with a ghostbuster line through it) that everyone wore.

What the march lacked was farmworkers, at least in mass numbers. Several buses had come down from the Salinas Valley, and farmworkers from the immediate area were well represented, but as a group, farm-workers added little weight to the funeral. I saw no banners from U.F.W. locals, nor did I see a single button or sign proclaiming the idea of farmworker power. And this, too, was symbolically perfect, for at the time of Cesar Chavez's death, the U.F.W. was not primarily a farm-worker organization. It was a fundraising operation, run out of a deserted tuberculosis sanitarium in the Tehachapi Mountains, far from the fields of famous Delano, staffed by members of Cesar's extended family and using as its political capital Cesar's legend and the warm memories of millions of aging boycotters.

It was my second funeral march for Cesar Chavez. The first had been two days earlier, back home in Watsonville, in the Pajaro Valley, four and a half hours by car from Delano. Throughout the 1970s, Wat-sonville, together with nearby Salinas, had been a center of U.F.W. strength. Back then, most of the major growers (the two valleys spe-cialize in vegetable row crops) were signed up with either the U.F.W. or the Teamsters, and pushed by the militancy of several hundred Chavis-tas, the two unions had won increasingly better contracts. In the 1980s the entry-level hourly wage moved up over $7, and working conditions on U.F.W. crews significantly improved. But by the end of the decade that had all come apart. In Watsonville, the U.F.W. now has only a cou-ple of apple contracts, covering no more than a few hundred workers. In Salinas, the Teamsters still have a contract with the giant Bud Antle/Dole, but for most workers, unions have been replaced by farm labor contractors, and average hourly wages have fallen to around $5.

So I was surprised by the farmworker presence at that first funeral march. Fewer than 200 people had shown up, but a good number of

them were field workers. I ran into my old friend Roberto Fernandez,*
the man who taught me how to pack celery in the mid-seventies and
who helped me make it one a piece-rate celery crew, where on good days
we made over $15 an hour. Roberto came to California first as a bracero
in the early 1960s and later as an illegal. We worked side by side for
three years, and I have a lot of memories of Roberto, but my fondest is
when we were on a picket line together, trying to prevent a helicopter
from spraying a struck field. We were with a group of other strikers,
half-jokingly using slings to throw rocks at the helicopter as it flew past.
Suddenly, Roberto ran into the field, directly at the oncoming helicopter, a baseball-size rock twirling in the sling above his head, screaming
a warrior's roar. The rest of us were astounded; God knows what the
pilot thought as he yanked the helicopter straight up and away from the
kamikaze attack.

Roberto, his 6-year-old daughter and I walked a short while on the
march together, and when the other folks went into Asunción Church
to pray, the three of us walked back into town. I had seen Roberto off
and on since I left our celery crew after the 1979 strike, but we had
avoided discussing farmworker politics. Roberto is a committed Chav-
ista and always could be counted on to give the official U.F.W. line. He
was currently working on one of the few union contracts in town—not
with the U.F.W. but with a rival independent union, as the U.F.W. no
longer has any celery workers under contract. I asked him what went
wrong in the fields.

"The Republicans replaced the Democrats and ruined the law, and
we no longer had any support in Sacramento."

"That's it? All the power we had, gone just because Deukmejian
replaced Brown?"

"The people were too ignorant."

"What do you mean?"

"We got swamped by people coming from small ranchos in Mexico
who didn't know anything about unions. When the companies were letting our contracts expire and bringing in the labor contractors, we
would go out to the people in the fields and try to explain to them about
the union. But they didn't get it. They just wanted to work."

"I don't believe that. We had people from ranchos in Mexico on our
U.F.W. crews. They were strong unionists; unions are not such a hard
thing to understand."

*A pseudonym.

"Well, Frank, you aren't ever going to believe that the workers were at fault, but I was there and I talked to them, and you weren't."

I never could beat Roberto in an argument, and although I like to think I would have had a better chance in English, probably not. Two days later I drove to Delano with another old friend, Cruz Gomez. Cruz's father was a farmworker—a year-round employee on a good-size farm outside Santa Barbara. The family was relatively well off compared with the braceros and the other seasonals who worked on the ranch. Nevertheless, her father worked thirty-seven years without a paid vacation, his body slowly breaking down as he passed middle age. As we were driving, I asked Cruz about Chavez.

"For me, Chavez was it, that's all, just it. He was the main man. I remember when I met him. It was 1967 or '68, I was a college student at the University of California at Santa Barbara. I was divorced and had two small children, a kind of mother figure in the MEChA student organization. We went up to Delano as a group, and sat around and talked with him. It was very informal, but he was all there. He gave us his full attention."

When Cruz returned to U.S.C.B. she, as they say, had been organized. She soon switched majors from biology to sociology, where a few influential teachers taught her that it was her obligation to "give back to the community." In 1971 she found herself working in a local community organization. She has been doing the same kind of work ever since, moving to Watsonville in 1978, spending her days listening to the problems of migrant farmworkers.

Unlike so many others with similar backgrounds, Cruz had never gone to work in Delano or even spent much time working in a boycott organization. From her contact with farmworkers she was well aware that the U.F.W. had become pretty much a nonfactor in the Pajaro and Salinas valleys, but she had no idea why. She asked me what had happened.

Roberto and the U.F.W. are not far wrong. The virtual destruction of a unionized work force in the fields of California in the 1980s was due finally to the overwhelming social, financial and political power of the biggest business in our Golden State. The weight of the internal errors of the U.F.W. is secondary to the longstanding anti-union policies of the people who own and operate the most powerful agro-export industry in the world.

Nevertheless, in the late seventies, at the height of the U.F.W.'s strength among farmworkers, some in California agribusiness had come to the conclusion that Chavez's victory was inevitable and that they would have to learn to live with the U.F.W. Why wasn't the union—with perhaps 50,000 workers under contract and hundreds of militant activists among them—able to seize this historic opportunity?

The short answer is that within the U.F.W. the boycott tail came to wag the farmworker dog. While it was not wrong of Chavez to seek as much support as possible, this support work, primarily the boycott, became the essential activity of the union. Ultimately, it interfered with organizing in the fields.

It was an easy mistake to fall into, especially as the failure of the first grape strikes was followed so stunningly by the success of the first grape boycott. The very best farmworker activists, the strongest Chavistas, were removed from the fields and direct contact with farmworkers, so that they could be sent to work in the boycott offices of major cities. From the point of view of building the boycott, it was a genius decision. But from the point of view of spreading the union among farmworkers themselves, it was a disaster.

The manipulative use of farmworkers gave the union boycott its texture and feel. In the mid-1970s a story circulated in Salinas about a union meeting in the Imperial Valley called to recruit workers to go to a press conference in Los Angeles to support one of the boycotts. For the workers it meant a ten-hour round-trip drive on one of their days off, but many of them were willing to do it. These particular farmworkers were mostly young piece-rate lettuce cutters who earned relatively high wages, and who, like a lot of working-class people able to afford it, put their money into clothes and cars which they sported on their days off. They were proud people, volunteering to spend a weekend in Los Angeles organizing support for their movement. As the meeting closed, Marshall Ganz—one of the union's top officials at the time—had a final request. At the press conference everybody should wear their *work* clothes.

The union officials didn't want farmworkers to appear as regular working people appealing for solidarity. They had to be poor and suffering, hats in hand, asking for charity. It may have made a good press conference, but the people who told the story were angered and shamed.

What the U.F.W. called publicity strikes hurt quite a bit too. Typically, the union would enter a small spontaneous walkout (a tactic California farmworkers have been using for more than a hundred years to drive up wages at harvest time), escalate local demands as a way of publicizing the overall plight of farmworkers and then leave. This played well enough in New York and Chicago, but made it more difficult for farmworkers to win these local battles.

The union's strategy after passage of California's Agricultural Relations Act in 1975 was similar. The union would aim to win as many certification elections as possible, thereby demonstrating to Governor Jerry Brown, allies in the California legislature, boycott supporters around the world and even agribusiness that it had the allegiance of a large majority of California farmworkers. The U.F.W. hoped that this would result in some sort of statewide master agreement, imposed from above, that would cover farmworkers in most of the larger agribusiness companies.

As with the publicity strikes, the U.F.W. came onto a ranch with its high-powered organizing techniques, explained how important it was for people to vote for the union, usually won the elections and then left. Less than a third of the elections resulted in union contracts, however; too many workers felt used and deserted; and opposition to the U.F.W. grew in the fields.

Just how out of touch the U.F.W. was with farmworker sentiment is perhaps best illustrated by its approach to the question of undocumented workers. Most all California farmworkers have people in their families who have trouble with their legal status, so any union trying to organize them cannot risk taking the side of the I.N.S., the hated *migra*. Yet the U.F.W. sometimes supported the use of the *migra* against scabs, sacrificing long-term respect for a possible short-term gain.

It was the lack of strength among farmworkers that made the 1983 change in the Governor's office and the weakening of boycott support so devastating. Some of the biggest ranches reorganized their operations and replaced union contracts with labor contractors. Others let their U.F.W. contracts expire and refused to renegotiate them. In both cases, the union was powerless to stop them; the years of neglecting farmworker organizing finally took their toll.

A natural question arises: How could a farmworker organization staffed by so many intelligent people of good will, and led by one of the heroes of our time, make so many mistakes? The answer is just as direct. Structurally, the U.F.W. is one of the least democratic unions in the country. Officials in the local field offices are not elected by the workers under contract in those areas, as they are in most other unions. They are appointed by the U.F.W. executive board and were under the direct control of Cesar.

This meant that local farmworker leadership had no way of advancing within the union, other than by being personally loyal to Cesar or other high-level officials. Complaints about the union and its practices, although freely discussed among workers on the job, could not influence union policy.

This criticism does not fall from some idealized heaven of union democracy. Many staff members, who either resigned or were purged from the union, have complained privately about Chavez's authoritarian style and the lack of democracy within the U.F.W. They have rarely gone public, however, because they believed that any criticism of the U.F.W. would only help the growers, and because they were intimidated into silence by Chavez himself or by others on the U.F.W. staff. Even now people are reluctant to speak for fear of reprisals.

Philip Vera Cruz, onetime vice president of the union, who worked in the grapes for twenty years before Chavez came along, is the only staff member who put his criticism into print. Vera Cruz, who could not be guilt-tripped into silence, describes in an oral history, taken by Craig Scharlin and Lilia Villanueva, a U.F.W. staff where "power was held by Cesar alone." His conclusion is straightforward:

> One thing the union would never allow was for people to criticize Cesar. If a union leader is built up as a symbol and he talks like he was God, then there is no way you can have true democracy in the union because the members are just generally deprived of their right to reason for themselves.

The most crucial U.F.W. purge was not against the union staff but against its own farmworker members—people who dared to give the union some alternative, middle-level leadership. The trouble began when the 1979 contracts provided for full-time union grievers, elected by the workers, to handle specific complaints from the work crews. Some of the people elected in Salinas, the first workers in the hierarchy to have any real power independent of Chavez, regularly criticized several internal union policies.

At the union's 1981 convention in Fresno these men and women supported three independent candidates, not previously approved by Chavez, for election to the U.F.W.'s executive board. Afterward, they were fired from their jobs back in Salinas. Although they eventually won a nearly five-year court battle against Chavez and the union, the damage was done. No secondary leadership emerging from the ranks would be tolerated in the U.F.W.

I talked to one of the men, Aristeo Zambrano, a few weeks after the funeral. Aristeo was one of eleven children born to a farmworker family in Chavinda, Michoacán. His father worked as a bracero between 1945 and 1960, and after getting his papers fixed, he brought his son, then 14, to Hayward, California, in 1969. Aristeo moved to Salinas in 1974 and got a job cutting broccoli at a U.F.W.-organized company— Associated Produce. He was elected to the ranch committee in 1976; for the next six years he was an active unionist, re-elected to the committee every year and then to the position of paid representative, until he was fired by Chavez.

I asked him the same question I had asked Roberto Fernandez. What went wrong? How did the union fall so far so fast? His answer took several hours. Here are a few minutes of it.

"The problem developed way before we were fired in 1982. In the mid-seventies, when I became an activist, Chavez was making every decision in the union. If a car in Salinas needed a new tire, we had to check with Cesar in La Paz. He controlled every detail of union business. And nobody was allowed to say Chavez made a mistake, even when he had. And when you talked to him you had to humble yourself, as if he were a King or the Pope. . . .

"I remember in particular a closed meeting during the strike, just before the Salinas convention in 1979. He called together about twenty of us—the elected picket captains and strike coordinators—and told us that he was going to call off the strike and send us on the boycott. We refused, and we told him so. We thought the strike should be extended, not called off. And we damn sure were not going on any boycott.

"Well, he couldn't call off the strike without our support, and we did continue to fight and we won. Which made us stronger. That meeting, and its aftermath, was a political challenge to Cesar. It meant that the situation in the union had changed. He was going to have to deal with us—with the direct representatives of the workers—and, in some way or other, share power with us.

"And that was what he couldn't do. He was incapable of sharing power. So after the 1982 convention—the first U.F.W. convention that was not simply a staged show, the first convention where true disagreements came to the floor—he fired us. First he tried to organize recall elections, so that farmworkers would replace us. But he couldn't do it. We had too much support in the fields.

"We went back to the fields, and tried to continue organizing, but it was impossible. The damage had been done. People were scared or gave up on the union. They could see that the union did not belong to the workers, that it was Chavez's own personal business, and that he would run his business as he pleased. Farmworkers were good for boycotting, or walking the picket lines, or paying union dues, but not for leading our union. . . .

"Chavez built the union and then he destroyed it. The U.F.W. self-destructed. When the Republicans came back in the 1980s and the growers moved against the union, there wasn't any farmworker movement left."

What happens next? There was a feeling of optimism at the funeral. So many people together again, united by their respect for Chavez, pledging themselves to renewed effort. In her own fashion, Dolores Huerta, one of the founders of the union, expressed the hope of the crowd in her eulogy. "Cesar," she said, "died in peace, in good health, with a serene look on his face. It was as if he had chosen to die at this time . . . at this Easter time . . . He died so that we would wake up. He died so that the union might live."

In the several weeks since the funeral, I have pondered Dolores's image of Chavez as the U.F.W.'s Christ, dying so that we might live. In one way, it is perfect. All the talk of Alinsky and community organizing aside, Cesar Chavez was essentially a lay Catholic leader. His deepest origins were not in Alinsky's radical community Service Organization but in the *cursillos de Cristiandad* movement, the intense encounters of Catholic lay people, first developed by the clergy in Franco's Spain and transplanted to the New World in the 1950s. The song they brought with them was "De Colores," and their ideology was a combination of anticommunism and personal commitment of ordinary lay people to the Gospel's version of social justice. Chavez, throughout his public life, remained true to that commitment. What many of the liberals and radicals on the staff of the union could never understand was that all the fasts, the long marches, the insistence on personal sacrifice and the flirting with sainthood were not only publicity gimmicks, they were the essential Chavez.

Chavez died so that the union might live? What Dolores seems to have meant was that people, inspired by Chavez's life, would now rejoin the cause and rebuild the union. That might happen, but rebuilding the union *among farmworkers* will require a complete break with the recent past by the people who now control the U.F.W.

The U.F.W. is no longer the only group trying to organize in the fields of California. Teamster Local 890 in Salinas, with more than 7,000 field workers under contract, recently has been taken over by reformers with long experience in the Chicano and Mexican cannery worker movement. They would like to begin a new organizing drive in the Salinas Valley. In Stockton, Luis Magaña and the Organización Laboral Agrícola de California have established close contacts with the newest migrant stream in California agriculture, the Mixtec and Zapotec Indians from Oaxaca. In many areas small community groups have gone beyond simply providing services to farmworkers and have helped them organize to fight for better housing, better schooling for their kids, and against violations of labor laws by farmworker contractors.

Up until now, these small beginnings have had an uneasy relationship with the U.F.W. Viewing them as competitive organizations, Chavez often tried to block their activities, even when the U.F.W. was not organizing in the same areas. Now that Chavez is gone, could the U.F.W. learn to cooperate with these other groups? Could people who were originally inspired by the heroic example of Chavez's life, and who now no longer have Cesar around to interfere with their work, make a hundred flowers bloom in the California fields?

Si se puede.

Giving the Devil His Due— Exchange

Salmon Rushdie and Alexander Cockburn
•

London

Alexander Cockburn makes grave charges ["Beat the Devil," July 26/Aug. 2], accusing me of "spiteful abuse" of Turkish secularists. I heard the news of the atrocity in Sivas, Turkey, on the evening of Friday, July 2. Within half an hour I put out a statement condemning the fundamentalist murderers, and elaborated on this in a live telephone interview with the main BBC radio news program that evening. The next day I appeared on BBC TV, ITN and Sky Television, and spoke on the telephone to journalists from several British newspapers. In every case the primary importance of denouncing the murderers formed the main thrust of my contribution.

The *Observer* piece that Cockburn takes exception to appeared on Sunday, July 4, in the wake of all these actions. In the week that followed it, I wrote a further text (July 6), published as the leading letter in the London *Independent*, in which I tried to speak up for Bosnia's Muslims and in which I also defended those who died in Sivas against the charge that "such heinous—such *inflammatory*— offences as atheism" had provoked their murderers into murdering them. I gave interviews on this subject to several European newspapers. Finally, I published a text, which some of your readers may have seen, in *The New York Times* (July 11) discussing the need to pay attention to and support the dissidents of the Muslim world—including those in Turkey—who are at present under such vicious and lethal attack.

It is a pity Cockburn did not trouble to check the facts—he made no attempt to contact me or my agents or the Rushdie Defence Campaign based at Article 19 in London—before letting fly. After almost two weeks in which hardly a day has passed without my speaking up for secularist principles and against religious fanaticism, it is really quite extraordinary to be vilified in your pages for not having done so.

The *Observer* piece itself—as Cockburn concedes—also laid the blame for the Sivas massacre firmly on the local religious fanatics, and expressed my outrage at what they had done. It is true, however, that I criticized the behavior of the journalist Aziz Nesin, in whose newspaper *Aydinlik* unauthorized extracts from *The Satanic Verses* had been published in May. Nesin, commenting on what I said, reveals a view of the truth that is as selective as Cockburn's.

Cockburn quotes Nesin thus: "I had met Rushdie in London and discussed the possibility of publishing his book in Turkish." This is simply untrue. In 1986—the only time I ever met Nesin—*The Satanic Verses* was not even finished. Nesin says of me: "He stopped defending his work." I have not done so. Nesin goes on: "The only thing he lately cares for is whether he receives his copyright fees or not." This is not so. I have no interest in receiving whatever monies may be due to me from *Aydinlik*. I am, however, vitally interested in how, and by whom, my work is published.

Nesin and *Aydinlik* published the pirated extracts from my novel in the most polemical manner possible, denigrated my work, attacked my integrity as a man and an artist, and made a lot of money by doing so— Cockburn reveals that the paper's circulation trebled during the period of publication. Certainly these were not people I would have chosen to be the first publishers of *The Satanic Verses* in a Muslim country. Yet Cockburn believes I was wrong to defend myself, even though, that weekend, British Muslim "spokesmen" and sections of the British media were attempting to make me the person responsible for the Sivas killings. It appears to be Cockburn's view that all this—the theft of my work, the assaults on my character, the lies about my public positions and the responsibility for having caused a "Rushdie riot"—is just fine, whereas my wish to set the record straight is evidence of an even deeper perfidy.

In a letter, the Turkish writer Murat Belge, one of the friends whose advice I sought, says: "It is quite legitimate to criticize Nesin for his rather childish behavior. However, the way all the politicians are now blaming him for everything is infuriating. . . . It is as if Nesin has killed these people, and the murderers who actually burned them alive are innocent citizens." This is exactly my view, which I have expressed over and over again in the past fortnight. I am sad that it has not managed to get through to Alexander Cockburn.

SALMAN RUSHDIE

COCKBURN REPLIES
Petrolia, Calif:

I can't speak to what Rushdie precisely told television and radio reporters, but it's disingenuous for him now to suggest that such statements pre-empt what he told print journalists and what he wrote himself right after the thirty-six secularists were burned alive in Sivas. Rushdie appears to be suggesting that there was a substantial time lapse between his initial reaction and the composition of the *Observer* piece. But they were all generated within the space of a few hours. Sunday's *Independent* (July 4) carried a story whose fifth paragraph reported that "Mr. Rushdie condemned the attack, but also distanced himself from Mr. Nesin. 'I have been used yet again by people who have no interest in me as a human being, or as a writer, but seek simply to force their own confrontation and to dump the blame on me.' "

Rushdie must have said this to the *Independent* reporter on Saturday, about the time he was working on the *Observer* article. Certainly, it's exactly the sentiment of Rushdie's piece for *The Observer*, about which he is now understandably demure but whose message the editors at the paper had no trouble discerning. The subhead reads thus: "After the riot and hotel fire in which at least 40 people died, the author of *The Satanic Verses* condemns militant secularists and religious bigots who exploit his work for their own ends."

So I don't think it's true that in the first instance Rushdie saw his prime task as denouncing the murderers. His stance was highly qualified. He distanced himself from the secularists. He said he was a pawn in their game. As he put it in *The Observer*, as the first order of business before he denounced the killings, "Nesin and his associates did what they did, under the cover of free-speech rhetoric, precisely to provoke the violent confrontation that has now resulted. They wanted to bring matters to a head. Now, it seems, they have got more than they bargained for."

By the start of the following week Rushdie was evidently having second thoughts about this response, and his revised reaction duly showed up on the opinion page of *The New York Times* the Sunday following: "Let us not fall into the trap of blaming . . . the Turkish writers for 'provoking' the mob that murdered them."

I don't know why Rushdie tries this silly business of my not troubling "to check the facts." If I'd heard secondhand some rumor about Rushdie being critical of the secularists and saying they'd brought it on themselves, then I would have tried to contact him to verify the story. This was no rumor but a substantial article in one of Britain's major Sunday newspapers. He should take responsibility for what he wrote instead of pretending that it doesn't reflect his views. The factual excavation that did need doing, and which I attempted, was to disinter the secularists and Nesin from Rushdie's self-centered and patronizing abuse.

It's plain that one of the main reasons for Rushdie's pique is that Nesin said he didn't care for *The Satanic Verses* as a literary work but saw its publication in Turkish as an important political act. Rushdie shouldn't conflate unpalatable literary criticism with a principled defense of free speech. Many defenders of *The Satanic Verses* haven't read it, any more than the Ayatollah did, and many who have did not care for the novel any more than did Nesin.

There have been unauthorized translations of the so-called offensive portions of the novel in Iran and throughout the Arab world by proponents of secular democracy. Would Rushdie denounce all such activity? His work is a factor, a weapon in a vast political and intellectual struggle, and it really is a bit childish to start bleating about misuse and "decontextualization," given what has happened since the Ayatollah rushed to judgment.

As for Rushdie's public positions, he shouldn't get too upset if he is reminded now and again that for a time he presented himself as a convert to Islam, denouncing secularists for having misused his work, thus leaving these, his defenders and advocates, high and dry.

ALEXANDER COCKBURN

WORDS ARE ALL I HAVE—EXCHANGE

Carlin Romano

•

We received an unusually high volume of mail responding to Carlin Romano's review of Catharine MacKinnon's Only Words, Cass Sunstein's Democracy and the Problem of Free Speech and Lynn Hunt's The Invention of Pornography ("Between the Motion and the Act," Nov. 15). Most of the mail was in spirited disagreement with Romano's method of reviewing MacKinnon's book. About 75 percent of the letters came from women, three of whom canceled their subscriptions. Two self-described men's antirape groups called for an apology. Many letters contained lines like "I'm no fan of MacKinnon, but . . ." or "I'm a feminist who never expected to be defending MacKinnon, but . . ." The opening of the review was characterized as "a backlash against feminism," "uncommonly arrogant," "morally offensive," "repulsive," "misogynous," "dangerous and sickening." It left a reader "shaking with anger" and gave another "a sinking feeling."

Romano's opening paragraphs (no one objected to the body of the review) were intentionally provocative and offensive, but he gave us (and readers in the review itself, and in his reply, which follows) a plausible rationale for that approach. The thought experiment—which is not the same as a sexual fantasy—is a familiar technique in philosophical writing. Romano made clear that he despises rape, and while the tone of his essay was fervently opposed to one woman, it did not seem to us to be antiwomen.

When our friends at Harvard University Press write that Romano's "words . . . for some will have successfully snuffed out MacKinnon's ideas," they metaphorically equate the review to the type of pornography known as snuff video, in which an actress is supposedly really murdered. This is the kind of thought and language—provocative and offensive—that Romano sought to call attention to and criticize. Restrictions on speech (in hate-speech codes, for example) and on pornography are hotly contested on the left as they have been for years among feminists. We reiterate our commitment (not shared by all our readers) to untrammeled speech; we have welcomed this outpouring of emotion and opinion from our community.

—THE EDITORS

New York City

Carlin Romano does his own cause harm when he begins his critique of *Only Words* "Suppose I decided to rape Catherine MacKinnon. . . ." Romano's point is well taken—MacKinnon's arguments blur thought and action. But his hypothetical "thought experiment" expresses precisely the attitude of privilege against which the MacKinnonites rail.

Would Romano write, and *The Nation* run, an article that started, "Suppose I decided to lynch Clarence Thomas," or "Suppose I decided to put Norman Podhoretz in a gas chamber. . . ."? No friend of MacKinnon's fetishistic fundamentalism, I'm glad the government censors aren't snipping at Romano's text. Sensitivity, not statutes, will make us free(er). Unfortunately, Romano's approach shows just how far we have to go. And he gives MacKinnon one more clipping for her file: "male, left, woman-hater, t.b.i. (to be ignored)."

LAURA FLANDERS

•

Chicago, Ill.

Carlin Romano's review gives the extremely misleading impression that my book *Democracy and the Problem of Free Speech* is basically about pornography and is mostly an argument for state regulation of sexually explicit materials. Pornography is only a very small part of the book—just one section of the seventh chapter. In fact, my approach would probably allow less regulation of sexually explicit speech than does current law. In my brief discussion, I stress that sexually explicit materials usually deserve constitutional protection and that the Supreme Court's current "obscenity" approach wrongly allows speech to be regulated merely because it is offensive.

My book is concerned mostly with promoting free speech—by insuring more vigorous public discussion; by reducing the effects of sensationalism and soundbites during campaigns; by allowing campaign finance reform; by forbidding discrimination in government subsidies to artists and others; and by reducing advertiser and other economic pressures on the system of free expression. My "two-tier" approach to the First Amendment is designed to promote and protect political speech, and it would allow little restriction of nonpolitical speech—even if it would allow government to stop false advertising, to punish criminal conspiracy and sexual harassment and to allow celebrities to recover damages under libel law for public lies about them; does Romano disagree with any of this?

CASS R. SUNSTEIN

•

Cambridge, Mass.

I believe firmly that publishers should not respond to the reviews of their books. You publish a book. You stand by it. You do not intervene in its critical reception. And we stand by Catharine MacKinnon's work. But Carlin Romano's piece is so vile that I cannot refrain from telling you how horrified I am by it.

Thanks to the work of Professor MacKinnon and many others, we have been alerted to the wrongness, to put it mildly, of the use of rape as a tool for the conduct of war as it is being waged now in Bosnia. *I* hope that all of you at *The Nation* will now become alert to the wrongness of the use of rape as a tool for the conduct of criticism. For this is exactly what Romano did in his piece. Or, to be precise, this is what he did by proxy in a cowardly way by ascribing the deed to a composite figure of Nat Hentoff and Ronald Dworkin. To have a man do this deed and in *The Nation*—of all places—was deeply disturbing. The argument, the attempted *reductio ad absurdum* that ends up an attempted rape, is philosophically wrong. The force of the review depends on the denial that words are sometimes acts. This denial is false. Romano's words perform an act. For some they will have successfully snuffed out MacKinnon's ideas. But much more upsetting than the philosophical gaffe is that Romano trivializes MacKinnon's concerns. People agree that pornography does create attitudes that are harmful to women. I am a man, and I am amazed that the male reviewers of this book seem to think MacKinnon is driven by her personal obsessions. Have none of them a mother, a sister or a daughter who has been raped? It is tasteless in the extreme to construct a rape fantasy about any woman, let alone a scholar and lawyer who has dedicated her life to fighting violence against women. If Romano thinks that the way for him to fight the fire of MacKinnon's passion for justice is with the fire of his fantasy, he has things mixed up. The inappropriateness of using such incivility, such a misogynous attitude in the name of civil rights chills the bones.

I admire *The Nation*. I have contributed essays to *The Nation*. I hope to continue admiring it. I have known Carlin Romano for years. *The Nation*, just like any of our books, is not above criticism. In fact, our books and your essays only come to life in critical debate. But there are limits. Romano has violated them.

LINDSAY WATERS, HARVARD UNIVERSITY PRESS
CO-SIGNERS: CLAIRE SILVERS
MARIA EUGENIA QUINTANA
PAUL ADAMS, CHRISTOPHER PALMA
STEPHANIE GOUSE, AIDA DONALD

ROMANO REPLIES
Cambridge Mass

Lindsay Waters and his colleagues are welcome to disagree, but I didn't write an antifeminist, prorape review of *Only Words*. I wrote an anti-exaggeration, proreality review. I *despise* real rape and didn't rape anyone by writing *about* rape in my review (an old-fashioned distinction, I'll admit, but there you are). Catharine MacKinnon's book offended me with its own vile view of men, its imprecise arguments, its lack of philosophical sophistication, its censorious spirit, its hypocrisy in regard to legal reform and its ugly Us-against-Them mentality, which fuels too many conflicts in the world today. It accomplished that despite my prior view, which I still hold, that she's an energetic and innovative legal theorist whose independence of mind, jurisprudential extremism and political commitment shake up establishment thinking in a healthy way.

At the same time, I think it's MacKinnon who trivializes real rape by equating it with everything from *Playboy* to graffiti. After reading her book, I felt her offensive rhetoric about men, and her failure to distinguish publication of pornography from physical rape of women, disinclined me to examine her more persuasive points (though I went on to do so). It also raised a traditional free-expression issue: How should we deal with material that simultaneously offends us and makes points usually protected within those "limits" of free expression whose placement Waters declares himself so sure of? How, I wondered, would MacKinnon and her supporters deal with a "hypothetical" (really a better word for my opening example than "fantasy") that took them at their word on the equivalence of rape and pornography but tested their notions of causation, the fungibility of act and word, and so on.

So I decided to begin my review with an experimental, *intentionally offensive* counterprovocation: an example of two actions ordinarily considered different (my imagined rape of MacKinnon and "Dworkin Hentoff" 's actual crime) but arguably considered the same under MacKinnon's view. I threw in a possible casual link to complicate the matter. Rather than address any of that example's implications, or the multiple arguments in my review against *Only Words*, MacKinnon's editor predictably responds with the suggestion that I *really* raped MacKinnon in my review, that I'm a Bosnian Serb who slipped into *The Nation* and that my review amounts to pornography even though its purpose was philosophical rather than prurient. I end up thinking what I thought before: MacKinnon and her supporters tropistically respond to vigorous challenges of their views with censorious instincts, and show little enthusiasm for freedom of expression or precise analysis.

To my mind, MacKinnon's general view of pornography, and my rejection of it, should be judged in light of Mill's second and third reasons in *On Liberty* for opposing legal *or* social censorship. If MacKinnon's view or mine contains mostly falsehood and only a small "portion of truth," responding to it helps us to refine some larger, sounder truth. Even if her view or mine is wholly false, it *still* shouldn't be suppressed because having to confront it keeps what we wind up valuing as truth from becoming mere "dead dogma." So I hope Waters continues to violate what he "firmly" believes by standing up in print for his books (though a little more argument and a little less solidarity might be desirable). I hope to keep saying what I think as well.

Regarding Sunstein's complaint, no sensible reader of my review could think that *Democracy and the Problem of Free Speech* is "basically about pornography." Sunstein should put more trust in his title. In a review mainly about MacKinnon, his book didn't get equal time. Lacking an equal protection remedy, he opts for resourceful self-promotion and offers an "In Short" of his book. It is, I think, a shrewd and stimulating book, though ultimately hostile to freedom of expression because it favors a stingy, academic notion of what counts as politically valuable speech. May it nonetheless receive many reviews.

Sunstein, however, is probably not the most trustworthy reviewer of his book. He, not I, wrote that "much pornographic material lies far from the center of the First Amendment." Yet he states that an approach operating from that premise "would probably allow less regulation of sexually explicit speech than does current law." Not likely. As I suggested, Sunstein will fight to the death to defend our First Amendment freedom to publish Op-Ed pieces and other forms of "political" speech that he and other upper-class professionals deem important to democracy. After that, we—and many people without access to forums dominated by the well educated and connected—are at the mercy of the jurisprudential elite. I, for one, don't want Sunstein choosing which books or movies are good for my democratic soul. I suspect his taste is too suit-and-tie for my blood.

Flanders's objection leaves me unsure what "privilege" my opening example expressed beyond freedom to question MacKinnon's modus operandi with a counterexample aimed at problems created by her overkill style. Flanders's two alternate sentences raise tricky issues because lynching and gassing lack obvious positive flip sides, while MacKinnon's open-ended concept of rape encompasses activities that others might view as vicariously enjoyed sex. But if Clarence Thomas had suggested in print that being lynched and watching a film of a convicted serial murderer being executed were equivalent experiences, or if Norman Podhoretz had suggested that being put in a gas chamber and being anesthetized for a medical operation were equivalent experiences, those sentences might be defensible critical gambits.

THE AGE OF REASON, 1794-1994

Ring Lardner, Jr.

•

THE STATEMENTS BELOW are some of the strange things Americans believe 200 years after Thomas Paine published *The Age of Reason*. None of them can meet the ordinary standards of proof required in a court of law or in an objective scholarly investigation, but each is considered true by a sizable minority, or in some cases perhaps a majority of the American population:

- The human species was divinely created a few thousand years ago in the Garden of Eden.
- The movements of constellations and planets shape human character and influence events.
- All illness is an illusion to be overcome by the mind, not by doctors or medicine.
- Captured Americans are still being held alive in secret Vietnamese prisons.
- It is possible to foretell future events by means of palm-reading, tarot cards, tea leaves or special powers bestowed on certain individuals.
- Jews organized and financed the African-American slave trade.
- Vehicles from other solar systems have visited our planet and occasionally taken Earth residents aboard as passengers.

- Certain restless dead people, refusing to accept extinction, return to their earthly premises and harass the current occupants.
- The United States has the highest standard of living in the world.
- The United States has the highest, or one of the highest, rates of literacy in the world.
- The United States has the highest taxes compared with those of other developed nations.
- American schools provide the level of education required to cope with the modern world.
- American prison sentences are lenient compared with those of other nations.
- "Deficit reduction" lowers the national debt.
- Camels store water in their humps.
- Lemmings commit mass suicide by drowning.
- Bulls are enraged by the color red.
- The music played by an Indian snake charmer exerts a benign influence on a deadly cobra.
- Eating fish is good for the brain.
- Human weather forecasters are less reliable than bears, groundhogs, squirrels, caterpillars and sea gulls.
- Lightning never strikes twice in the same place.
- January 1, 2000, will be the first day of the next century.
- People called dowsers can locate underground water with a forked stick.
- An area called "the Bermuda Triangle" has been the site of many marine disasters without any natural explanation.
- There was once an island or continent called Atlantis that disappeared.
- Certain "psychics" can communicate with one another at great distances by some form of extrasensory perception.
- The scientific term "theory" applied to evolution means that the concept is still an undecided issue among biologists.
- John F. Kennedy was the victim of a conspiracy involving the military-industrial complex, the F.B.I. and the C.I.A.
- A second coming of Jesus Christ is imminent.
- Infant baptism is an offense against the teachings of Christ.
- No one will go to Heaven who has not been baptized.
- No one will go to Heaven who doesn't recite the Islamic creed, face Mecca and pray five times a day, practice charity, fast dur-

ing Ramadan and make at least one pilgrimage to Mecca if physically and financially able.
- The Bible was written by God or writers He inspired and rendered infallible.
- The Pope is infallible on matters of faith and morals.
- All the words attributed to Jesus Christ in the Bible were actually spoken by a single individual of that name.
- Blood transfusions are an impermissible violation of divine law.
- An Israelite tribe immigrated to North America in 609 B.C. and built a great civilization of which no trace remained except a set of gold plates discovered in 1822 by Joseph Smith of Manchester, New York, with the help of an angel named Moroni.
- God selected the Jews as His "chosen people" and aided them in annihilating other nations of people who were equally the products of His creation.
- Genuine religious fervor can produce "the gift of tongues," enabling believers to speak and understand languages previously unfamiliar to them.
- Black people are genetically inferior to white people except in some areas such as basketball, sprinting, long jumping and running with a football under one arm.
- Dreams can and do foretell future events.
- Before Columbus, even educated people thought the world was flat.
- Capital punishment has a significant deterrent effect.
- There never was a Holocaust.
- Homosexuality is a deliberate perversion practiced by immoral men and women in defiance of God's express command.
- Most of the more precious properties of Western civilization, such as the alphabet, science, philosophy, the legal code and democracy, originated in Africa.
- The first, microscopic, fertilized human cell already contains an immortal soul that retains a single, intact identity through all the trillions of cell divisions yet to come.
- A white capitalist conspiracy encourages the importation of drugs in order to degrade and subjugate minority groups.
- We, or at least many of us, have had past lives on this planet, details of which some of us are able to recall.

¡ZAPATISTA! THE PHOENIX RISES

Paco Ignacio Taibo II

•

I

THEY'VE COME OUT of nowhere. From its perennially censorious perspective, the television repeatedly displays without understanding the faces of the Zapatista rebels, hooded by ski masks or covered with quintessentially Mexican *paliacates* (the red, yellow and black bandannas worn by Mexican campesinos).

What the hell is this? Paloma wakes me up in midmorning and puts me in front of the TV. The Zapatista guerrilla army has taken half a dozen cities in Chiapas, including the state's traditional capital, San Cristóbal de las Casas.

The first words delivered by the rebels to the TV cameras are enunciated in shaky Spanish with a peculiar syntax: *Vinimo de aquí porque no aguantamos, ¿qve?, el ejército que persigue a nosotros. Vinimo a la guerra.* "We came here because we couldn't take it, see?, the army persecuting us. We came to the war."

Among the guerrillas are some officers, very few, whose speech gives away their urban origins; they could be members of a far left group, students who fled chronic unemployment to burrow into the jungle in what the language of the left called *trabajo de topo*, mole's work (teaching literacy classes, barefoot doctoring, organizing cooperatives), or schoolteachers who went through twenty years of ceaseless struggle in order to win the right to earn $200 a month and, in a handful of regions, to elect union representatives. But the vast majority are indigenous. Tzeltales, Choles, Mijes, Tojolabales. From the tribal babel of Chiapas, where the lingua franca of almost 60 percent of the population is not Spanish but one of the indigenous dialects.

Their weapons are indigenous, too. The images show an AK-47 here and there, an assault rifle stolen from the Mexican Army, but the majority are carrying shotguns and .22 caliber hunting rifles, even machetes and stakes, or wooden guns with a nail in the tip of the barrel. A lot of them are women and children. They're uniformed: green baseball caps, green pants, homemade black vests, *paliacates* around their necks or covering their faces.

The country enters the year 1994 with an insurrection and no one except the rebels understands anything.

II

They call themselves Zapatistas.

History repeats itself. In Mexico it always repeats itself. Neanderthal Marxists never get tired of reiterating that it repeats itself as farce, but that has nothing to do with it. It repeats itself as vengeance. In Mexico, the past voyages, rides, walks among us. Zapata is the key image: stubbornness, the dream cut short but not sold out.

III

In the first confrontation, twenty-four policemen died. In the fight for control of the town halls, the insurgents clashed with the state police, known as *judiciales*, and with the municipal police forces. The nation sees images of their dead bodies lying in the plazas. A lot of hate is stored up there. The *judiciales* are traditionally the landowners' white guards; they go into communities and ransack, make arrests, torture. Overheard on the second day of January in the Mexico City metro: *Los judiciales no son gente; no son personas.* "The judiciales aren't decent people; they aren't people."

IV

Are they crazy? How many of them are there? Where did the Zapatista army come from? Do they really think they can face in open combat a modern army that has air power, helicopters, heavy weapons, artillery?

In the first wave of attacks they've taken control of the entrances to the Lacandón jungle, the road from Chiapas to Guatemala and the second largest city in the state. The following day, they keep their promise and attack the military zone where the 31st Army Division is head-quartered. Then they disappear, falling back into the shadows. A reserve force of Zapatistas remains in Altamirano, Las Margaritas and Ocosingo, the towns that serve as gateways to the jungle.

They have announced that they took up arms against a government founded on an electoral fraud, that they have decreed a new agrarian reform, that they will no longer endure any abuses by the police, the army and the latifundios' caciques, that the North American Free Trade Agreement is the final kick in the stomach to the indigenous communities.

V

A couple days later, the coordinator of the coffee cooperatives of the Chiapas will tell me that this rebellion was announced in advance. The air was full of forewarnings that the government didn't want to hear. No one would admit to being in the know.

An anthropologist friend who knows the region tells me that at the end of last summer the communities voted not to sow their crops. This, for groups that live from the precarious economy of corn, is death. There's no going back. He tells me that the rebel organization's work began ten years ago. Looking back over the newspapers from the past few months I find bits of news here and there of clashes between the army, the police and the indigenous communities.

At the end of March last year, the *judiciales*, in pursuit of an armed group that had killed two soldiers in an ambush, entered San Isidro Ocotal: Indigenous men—old men and one minor—were arrested. Some were tortured. In May, the same story. There were rumors of a guerrilla force. Everyone denied them. Soon afterward, the *judiciales* entered Patate Viejo, firing their guns. They assembled the residents of the small community in the basketball court, picked out eight at random, arrested them and took them to the penitentiary in Cerro Hueco.

Mexico's Secretary of Gobernación (who is in charge of internal political affairs and police) acknowledged a few days after the fighting broke out that he knew of the existence of fifteen guerrilla training centers.

VI

I haven't left the house in three days except to buy the newspaper. I talk on the phone, listen to the radio, watch the television with the fascination of a blind man seeing an image for the first time.

An agrarianist friend explains to me that 15,000 indigenous people have died of hunger and easily curable diseases in Chiapas in the past few years. Without crop rotation, the fields are not very productive. The price of coffee has dropped, so the landowners have seized more land for cattle; they create conflicts between the communities and assassinate community leaders. Although the land cannot feed any more people, the population has been growing by 6 percent annually with the arrival of indigenous refugees from Guatemala and the internal migration of Indians whose land has been taken by the owners of the large haciendas. All this in a region where there is no electricity, 70 percent of the population is illiterate, most houses have no sewage systems or hookups for potable water and the average monthly income of a family is less than $130.

VII

In *La Jornada*, I read a fascinating story. The night they took San Cristóbal, the Zapatistas burned the municipal archives, the financial records, the land titles. The director of the historical archive negotiated with them: "You aren't going to burn the historical archive. The papers there tell the history of the origin of this city. The history of the seventeenth-century campesino rebellions and the Tzeltal uprising are there." The Zapatista committee met. Not only did they not burn it, they posted someone to guard it.

VIII

In an amazing burst of lucidity, Toño García de León, one of our best anthropologists, foretold what was going to happen in a book published nine years ago, *Resistencia y Utopia*. García says, "The elements of the past are still here, as alive as phantoms and wandering souls . . . The subsoil of Chiapas is full of murdered Indians, petrified forests, abandoned cities and oceans of petroleum."

Chiapas lies at the asshole of the world, where Jesus Christ lost his serape and John Wayne lost his horse. After the nineteenth-century uprisings had ended, the governors had their pictures taken standing next to defeated midgets. The Mexican Revolution got here twenty years late, at a fraction of its original strength, leaving the large haciendas intact. The Lacandóns, a nearly extinct Indian tribe, buy electric lamps to put in rooms without electricity, towns without electricity, whole regions without electricity—in a state that has the country's largest hydroelectric dams. San Cristóbal, a gathering place for hippie tourists, has three Zen centers and hundreds of satellite dishes, and barefoot Indians walk through its streets unable to find work as bricklayers.

IX

A popular Mexican bandit of the 1920s, el Tigre de Santa Julia, died in a rather unseemly manner, trapped and pumped full of lead by the police while he was sitting on the toilet. When you're caught off guard, people say, "They got you like el Tigre de Santa Julia."

The Mexican state has been taken by surprise, like el Tigre de Santa Julia. Did they believe their own lies? Here are the results of the last few elections in Chiapas: According to official figures, the Institutional Revolutionary Party (PRI) won in 1976 with 97.7 percent of the vote, in 1982 with 90.2 percent, in 1988 with 89.9 percent. Were they so stupid that they believed the official figures? They must have been the only ones.

People say Salinas had information on what was being planned and preferred to ignore it so as not to cast a shadow over the celebration of the implementation of NAFTA.

But elections are coming up. The chief opposition again is the Democratic Revolutionary Party (P.R.D.), led by Cuauhtémoc Cárdenas. To confront it with a new electoral fraud while a civil war is brewing would throw gasoline on the flames.

X

In post-1968 Mexico, the forces of the new left opted to work for social organization among the masses. Thousands of students were mobilized by the union movement, the struggle in the slums, the slow work of assistance to campesino insurgent movements. A minority took up arms. There was never much sympathy between the two groups, who accused each other of being "ultras" and "reformists." The guerrillas, caught up in a crazed spiral of minor confrontations that led to new clashes until their final annihilation by the police, never took any interest in working with the people. They heated things up, and years of union or campesino work were often endangered by their sectarian adventures. In short, the majority of the left was never attracted to the idea of armed struggle. But the Zapatista uprising generates a wave of sympathy.

"How could I not like them?" Ernesto, a university union organizer, tells me, "since I agree with their program for a new democracy, and since they're not some tiny group, they don't want to be anybody's vanguard, they don't impose their path, they're indigenous, they're an uprising of the masses and on top of that they've been screwed over even worse than I have."

XI

The army deployed 10,000 soldiers in the first days of the conflict, and the figure slowly rose to 17,000, one-third of the Mexican Army. Jeeps with machine guns, tanks, helicopters, German G-3 rifles, Saber planes.

XII

The dead will always be dead. The horror draws nearer. In the face of horror, political explanations are not moving. Reasons are harsh in wartime. I'm disturbed by the repeated sight of the bodies of campesinos, riddled with bullets, lying in ditches along the road. I see terrible images of a baby girl killed by a grenade fragment, her body lying in a cardboard box.

XIII

An enormous demonstration is held in Mexico City against the government's policy in Chiapas and for peace, with close to 150,000 attending. One of the chants: "First World, ha ha ha." Again we see the faces of the old and new left, but also of thousands of students joining the movement for the first time. The Zapatistas are not alone. Their program and the faces and motives of the indigenous rebels are greeted with a massive outpouring of sympathy that is reflected in the press. Something new, something different, is happening.

XIV

The Department of Gobernación has decided to invent an enemy phantom. The real phantoms, the Chiapan rebels, aren't of much use in the great propaganda war that is being launched—they're too likable. One of the ski-masked *comandantes*, the one who led the occupation of San Cristóbal de las Casas and who said his name was Marcos, is chosen. He is useful because he appears to be from the city; he isn't indigenous and might even be foreign. A verbal portrait is disseminated across the country. His vital statistics: six feet tall, blond hair, green eyes, speaks three languages (where the hell did they come up with that one? and why not four languages, or five?). The newspaper-reading sector of the country laughs at the absurdity. People call you on the phone to tell you that Marcos is their cousin, that he's the milkman. The phantom is welcomed in a wave of affection. The newsmagazine *Proceso* has just sanctified him by putting a close-up of him on the cover of its first issue on Chiapas. A Venezuelan biologist doing research on the endangered jaguars of the Lacandón jungle—and whose closest contact with a jaguar to date was the sight of some excrement—is arrested and beaten. The *judiciales* want him to confess to being the guerrilla commander in chief. Marcos himself laughs at his popularity in a joking letter to the media.

But does Commander Marcos really exist? Interviewed in the municipal palace of San Cristóbal at dawn on the first day of January, after the Zapatistas had made a clean sweep of the *judiciales*, the phantasmagoric Marcos avows that he is there to carry out the policies of a committee of indigenous campesinos; he is only a *subcomandante*, and he warns that the name "Marcos" is interchangeable—anyone can put on a ski mask and say "I am Marcos." He invites people to do so.

XV

"It's like Vietnam," says a soldier talking on the phone, overheard by an alert *La Jornada* reporter standing in line behind him. "They come out of the mist."

XVI

The jungle air is full of messages. At night, 150 short-wave radio stations saturate the ether over the ravines and footpaths with cryptic messages: "Six for Uruguay, do you copy?" "Truckloads of green cement passed in Paris." Zapatista bases identifying themselves as Two, Zero and Thunder are the most important. The helicopters try to avoid the antennas that rise through the trees.

XVII

Bombs in the Distrito Federal of the capital. The war comes nearer to the monster city. The "bombers" aren't Zapatistas. A mini-sect of the extreme left, said to be fully infiltrated by the Department of Gobernación, is responsible. Even so, the feeling that the war is getting closer and could burst out of the TV screen and explode on the corner of your street sweeps the city for a week.

XVIII

The government tightens its grip. A general mobilization of the army has been ordered. Then, the armed resistance of the Zapatistas and the almost unanimous response of the intellectual community (with the lamentable exception of Octavio Paz, who weeps for a lost "modernity"), along with the demonstration in Mexico City, force the government to draw back. It changes its line, changes its personnel, dismisses the Secretary of Gobernación, the Attorney General, the governor of Chiapas. The soft line takes over. Manuel Camacho Solís, whom Salinas recently rejected as the PRI candidate for the presidency, is now Salinas's man once more and becomes a negotiator. An amnesty is proclaimed.

In a desperate quest to end the conflict, economic support plans rapidly succeed one another, institutions are created to protect the indigenous people (from whom? from themselves?) and the official discourse adopts the critiques of the left and incorporates them, chameleonlike. The jaguar is a Mexican species. The Venezuelan biologist should have known that.

A cease-fire is declared—a tense cease-fire.

XIX

On TV there are images of soldiers vaccinating children and distributing food. The women standing in line for food in Ocosingo's plaza don't get any the second day if they don't bring their husbands. The soldiers distributing food are there to identify Zapatistas.

XX

Rumors again. Phone calls from journalist friends, low-voiced conversations during a Cárdenas rally on the esplanade of the Insurgentes metro station. Provocations are expected. There will be armed clashes. Does the army want to avenge the affront? The country grows uneasy once more. In Quintana Roo, only four kilometers from the Disneyland with real sharks known as Cancún, the *judiciales* arrest campesino leaders supposedly because they were armed. A secretary photographs a *judiciale* taking AK-47 bullets out of his sock and putting them inside a roll of toilet paper in the offices of the campesino union: This will be the proof. The *judiciales* unleash an enormous operation in the state of Guerrero. During the meeting of a powerful organization of agrarian unions on the Isthmus of Tehauntepec in the state of Oaxaca, many voices are heard protesting against the pacifism of the leaders: "If we'd rebelled, people wouldn't have died from the epidemic, there would be a hospital by now and the fraud would have fallen flat on its ass." The states of Tabasco and Michoacán are worried. The Cárdenas-led opposition won the elections there and a spectacular fraud was carried out. During the past two years, campesino community leaders who were members of the P.R.D. have been assassinated.

XXI

The Zapatistas aren't in any hurry. They're waging a masterful media war, keeping up the pressure while dissidents across the country go on the alert and mobilize. The pressure must be kept up in order to establish nonfraudulent conditions for the next elections.

A space for the social movements opens. Some of the townships that were occupied in the coastal region of Chiapas throw out mayors accused of fraud; indigenous communities in Oaxaca, Michoacán and Puebla mobilize; 10,000 teachers in Chiapas march to demand a 100 percent increase in salary. During this impasse, Zapatismo acquires social legitimacy through T-shirts, posters, continuous declarations of allegiance.

The electoral campaign of the left and center left, a broad front led by Cárdenas, is growing and has adopted the Zapatistas' program as its own. A ring is forming around the PRI that will make it difficult for the party to stage more fraudulent elections in August.

Are we nearing the end of the oldest dictatorship in the world? From 1920 to 1994 they have governed this country in the name of modernity and a betrayed revolution. Has their moment passed?

XXII

For now we're walking on shadows, disturbed and filled with hope. We are waking up with the distinct feeling that we slept among phantoms.

LAND OF THE DEAD

John Pilger

•

GIANT GHOST GUM TREES rose out of tall grass; then without notice this changed into a forest of dead, petrified shapes and black needles through which skeins of fine white sand drifted like mist. Such an extraordinary landscape reminded me of parts of central Vietnam, where American aircraft dropped ladders of bombs and huge quantities of chemical defoliants, poisoning the soil and food chain and radically altering the environment. In East Timor this is known as the "dead earth."

It is an area whose former inhabitants are either dead or "relocated." You come upon these places on the plateaus and in the ravines of the Matabian Mountains, in the eastern part of the island, where the roads are perilous. It is not difficult to understand why an untried Indonesian army took years to get the better of the guerrillas of the East Timorese resistance, popularly known as Fretilin. Jakarta's troops never conquered these mountain passes; Indonesian pilots in their low-flying American aircraft did.

Following the Indonesian invasion in December 1975, American OV-10 Broncos and Skyhawks were used to devastating effect. Cannon fire, bombs and napalm saturated the valleys and hillsides where the civilian population had fled behind the guerrillas. "Ours was the last Fretilin village to fall," said a survivor, Abel. "They made the rocks turn white. The bombardment never stopped, day in, day out; I can still hear it."

On the rim of these areas, which lie like patches of scar tissue all over the body of East Timor, are the crosses.

There are great black crosses etched against the sky—crosses on peaks, crosses in tiers on the hillsides, crosses beside the roads. In East Timor they litter the earth and crowd the eye. Walk into the scrub and they are there, always it seems, on the edges of riverbanks and escarpments, commanding all before them. Look at the dates on most of them, and they reveal the extinction of whole families, wiped out in the space of a year, a month, a day. "R.I.P. Mendonca, Crissmina, 7.6.77 . . . Mendonca, Filismina, 7.6.77 . . . Mendonca, Adalino, 7.6.77 . . . Mendonca, Alisa, 7.6.77 . . . Mendonca, Rosa, 7.6.77 . . . Mendonca, Anita, 7.6.77. . . ."

When I entered East Timor secretly last September, I had with me a hand-drawn map showing the site of a mass grave where some of those murdered in the 1991 massacre of at least 271 people in Dili, the capital, had been dumped; I had no idea that much of the country was a mass grave, marked by paths that end abruptly, fields inexplicably bulldozed, earth inexplicably covered with tarmac; and by the legions of crosses that march all the way from Tata Mai Lau, the highest peak, 10,000 feet above sea level, down to Lake Tacitolu, where a calvary line of crosses looks across to where the Pope said mass in 1989 in full view of a crescent of hard salt sand beneath which, say local people, lie human remains.

What has happened in East Timor is one of the world's great secrets. Alan Clark, the former British Defense Minister who licensed a $1 billion sale of British Hawk aircraft to Jakarta, once asked, "Does anyone know where East Timor is?" When I repeated this to him recently, he said, "I don't really fill my mind much with what one set of foreigners is doing to another." His riposte allowed a glimpse of how the unthinkable has been made acceptable; how decisions taken at great remove in distance and culture and time have had unseen and devastating effect on whole nations of people. East Timor is a horrific example.

Half of an island 300 miles north of Australia, East Timor was colonized by Portugal 450 years ago. The Portuguese partly Latinized the territory and insulated it from the upheavals of the western half of Timor, which was part of the Dutch East Indies that became Indonesia in 1949. In 1974, the old Salazarist order in Lisbon was swept aside by the "Carnation Revolution" and Europe's last great empire disintegrated virtually overnight. With the Portuguese preoccupied with events at home, the Indonesian military dictatorship of General Suharto invaded East Timor the next year, and has illegally and brutally occupied it ever since. The result: some 200,000 Timorese, or a third of the population, dead.

Western governments knew in advance the details of almost every move made by Indonesia. The C.I.A. and other American agencies intercepted Indonesia's military and intelligence communications at a top-secret base run by the Australian Defense Signals Directorate near Darwin. Moreover, leaked diplomatic cables from Jakarta, notably those sent in 1975 by the Australian Ambassador Richard Woolcott, showed the extent of Western complicity in the Suharto regime's plans to take over the Portuguese colony.

Four months *before* the invasion Ambassador Woolcott cabled his government that Gen. Benny Murdani, who led the invasion, had "assured" him that when Indonesia decided to launch a full-scale invasion, Australia would be told in advance. Woolcott reported that the British ambassador to Indonesia had advised London that it was in Britain's interests that Indonesia "absorb the territory as soon as and as unobtrusively as possible"; and that the U.S. ambassador had expressed the hope that the Indonesians would be "effective, quick and not use our equipment."

On December 5, 1975, Henry Kissinger and President Gerald Ford arrived in Jakarta on a visit a State Department official described to reporters as "the big wink." Two days later, as Air Force One climbed out of Indonesian airspace, the bloodbath in East Timor began. On his return to Washington, Kissinger sought to justify continuing to supply the Indonesian dictatorship by making the victim the aggressor. At a meeting with senior State Department officials, he asked, "And we can't construe [prevention of] a communist government in the middle of Indonesia as self-defense?" Told that this would not work, Kissinger gave orders that he wanted "to stop arms shipments quietly," but that they were secretly to "start again" the following month. In fact, as the genocide unfolded, U.S. arms shipments doubled.

In 1975 C. Philip Liechty was a C.I.A. operations officer in the U.S. Embassy in Jakarta. We met in Washington last November. "Suharto was given the green light [by the U.S.] to do what he did," Liechty told me. "There was discussion in the embassy and in traffic with the State Department about the problems that would be created for us if the public and Congress became aware of the level and type of military assistance that was going to Indonesia at that time. It was covered under the justification that it was 'for training purposes'; but there was concern that this might wear thin after a while, so the decision was taken to get the stuff flowing from San Francisco as fast as possible, to get it on the high seas before someone pulled the chain. As long as the Indonesians continued to certify that they were only using the equipment 'for training,' then we could get it through the bureaucracy.

"Without continued heavy U.S. logistical military support the Indonesians might not have been able to pull it off. [Instead] they were able to stay there at no real cost to them; it didn't put any pressure on their economy and on their military forces because American taxpayers were footing the bill for the killing of all those people and for the acquisition of that territory, to which they had no right whatsoever.

"The only interest that I ever saw expressed, the only justification I ever heard for what we were doing there was concern that East Timor was on the verge of being accepted as a new member of the United Nations and that there was an excellent chance that the country was going to be either leftist or neutralist and not likely to vote [with the United States] at the United Nations. For extinguishing that one vote, maybe 200,000 people, almost all of them noncombatants, died." I asked him what would have happened if he or his colleagues had spoken out. "Your career would end," he replied.

I had entered East Timor pretending to be a businessman. Lying down in the back of a Land Rover, I crossed the border from West Timor early one Sunday morning. I found a nation of unsmiling people; no one, it seemed, had been spared. "Of fifteen in my immediate family," said Abel, "only three are left. Up until 1986, most of our people were concentrated in what they called the central control areas. We lived in concentration camps for a long, long time. Indonesians use local people to spy on the others. People usually know who the spies are and they learn to deal with it. Certain things are not to be said widely even within the family. I mean, we the people in East Timor call it the biggest prison island in the world. You must understand that. For us who live here it's hell."

Today there are probably no more than 800 guerrillas under arms, yet they insure that four Indonesian battalions do nothing but pursue them. Moreover, they are capable of multiplying themselves within a few days, for they are the locus of a clandestine resistance that reaches into every district and has actually grown in strength over the years. In this way they continue to deny the fact of "integration" with Indonesia.

Domingos is 40 and has been in the jungle since 1983. "My wife was tortured and burned with cigarettes," he said. "She was also raped many times. In September [1993] the Indonesians sent the population of her village to find us. My wife came to me and said, 'I don't want to see your face because I have been suffering too much.' At first I thought she was rejecting me, but it was the opposite; she was asking me to fight on, to stay out of the village and not to be captured and never to surrender. She said to me, 'You get yourself killed and I shall grieve for you, but I don't want to see you in their hands. I'll never accept you giving up!' I looked at her, and she was sad. I asked her if we could live together after the war, and she said softly, 'Yes, we can.' She then walked away."

Domingos and his wife came from Kraras, now known by the Timorese as the "village of the widows." During the summer of 1983, 287 people were massacred there. Their names appear on an extraordinary list compiled in Portuguese by the church. In a meticulous, handwritten script, everything is recorded: the name and age of each of the murdered, as well as the date and place of death and the Indonesian battalion responsible.

Every time I pick up this list, a testimony of genocide, I find it strangely compelling and difficult to put down, as if each death is fresh on the page. Like the ubiquitous crosses, it records the slaughter of whole families, and bears witness to genocide: Feliciano Gomes, 50; Jacob Gomes, 50; Antonio Gomes, 37; Marcelino Gomes, 29; Joao Gomes, 33; Miguel Gomes, 51; Domingos Gomes, 30; Domingos Gomes, 2—"shot."

So far I have counted forty families, including many children: Kai and Olo Bosi, 6 and 4, "shot"; Marito Soares, 1, "shot"; Cacildo Dos Anjos, 2, "shot." There are babies as young as 3 months. At the end of each page, a priest has imprinted his name with a rubber stamp, which he asks "not to be used in the interests of personal security."

I drove into the capital, Dili, in the early afternoon. It was too quiet: not the quiet of a town asleep in the sun but of a place where something cataclysmic has happened that is not immediately evident. Fine white colonial buildings face a waterfront lined with trees and a promenade with ancient stone benches. The beauty of this seems uninterrupted. From the lighthouse, past Timor's oldest church, the Motael, to the long-arched facade of the governor's offices and the four ancient cannons with the Portuguese royal seal, the sea is polished all the way to Atauro island, where the Portuguese administration fled in 1975. Then, just beyond a marble statue of the Virgin Mary, the eye collides with rusting landing craft strewn along the beach. They have been left as a reminder of the day Indonesian marines came ashore and killed the first people they saw: women and children running down the beach, offering them food and water, as frightened people tend to do.

The November 12, 1991, massacre of unarmed young people in the Santa Cruz cemetery in Dili was different because foreigners were present, and it was videotaped. But after the foreigners were arrested and deported (one was killed), a second massacre took place, and it has never been reported.

"After the killings in the cemetery," said Mario, "I escaped being hit. So I pretended to be dead. The soldiers came and searched all the bodies and me, and hit me on the head so that I bled. They threw me with the other bodies onto a pickup truck. They took us to the mortuary, locked the door and went upstairs. Some of my friends were still alive, crying. They were calling out for water. I told them the only water was dirty, so we must pray together. I saw with my very own eyes that among the bodies were children and old people. Suddenly I heard steps approaching and I lay down again, pretending to be dead. Two soldiers came in. One of them picked up a big stone, and the other got a tablet from a jar. They then said out loud that if anyone was able to walk they had to stand up. When some of my friends got up, one of them was hit on the head by the soldiers with the stone; he died later. I heard the blows, and it sounded like coconuts cracking as they fall from trees. As they got close to me I stood up so suddenly that the soldiers were taken aback. I told them I was an informer, that I really worked for them. I didn't want to lie, but this saved my life."

Abilio, a Timorese orderly at the military hospital in Dili, took up the story. "I was at the hospital receiving the dead and wounded," he said. "Most of them were dead, but some were pretending to be. The soldiers didn't unload the bodies one by one; they just pushed them down on the ground. If they spotted one that was alive they killed him by running the van over him. Some of the soldiers were afraid of killing more. So they ordered the Timorese who were there to kill them. People said no, or they ran and hid in the toilets. The Indonesians then tried to inject them with sulfuric acid. But the soldiers stopped doing this as the people screamed too loudly."

Amnesty International has said of the Jakarta regime: "If those who violate human rights can do so with impunity, they come to believe they are beyond the reach of the law."

The United States has, as usual, the power to stop this. The Clinton Administration has declared its concern about East Timor; this, together with a proposed Congressional ban on further arms sales to

Indonesia, has worried the regime—although Jakarta also understands that in the American political system such statements are often just rhetoric. The crosses should not be allowed to multiply on the hillsides. The people of East Timor should be helped to get rid of their oppressors and to exercise their right of self-determination—albeit nineteen years late. Their great suffering, resistance and courage deserve nothing less.

CONFESSIONS OF A TOBACCO FIEND

John Leonard

•

It is only in lighting this cigarette that I discover my concrete possibility or, if one prefers, my desire to smoke.

—JEAN-PAUL SARTRE, *BEING AND NOTHINGNESS*

SO, WITH A with a bill to ban smoking anywhere in the United States except my downstairs closet stalled in fuddy-duddy Congress, Labor Secretary Robert Reich and his band of merry trolls at the Occupational Safety and Health Administration propose by ukase to purge the workplace of every last filthy weed, except in New Jersey. This, on top of a House subcommittee proposal to sextuple the federal tax on a pack of coffin nails, from 24 cents to $1.49, in order to bankroll a health care system overhaul, if there is one, by socking the poor and sinful. Plus Representative Henry Waxman, the California Democrat who dreams out loud of criminalizing nicotine while listening to David Kessler, the Food and Drugs Commissioner, who can't make up his mind whether the tobacco companies are souping up their product with extra addictive syrup, which he seemed to suggest in a February 25 letter to the Coalition on Smoking OR Health, or merely that they possess the patented technology to do so if they want to, which is all he allowed himself to say on March 25 to Waxman, after news reports of the $10 billion libel suit Philip Morris slapped on ABC for having alleged in its *Day One* magazine show that the companies *do* want to and *have* done so. Not to mention the class-action suit by flight atten-

dants over secondhand smoke that recently survived a Florida appeals
court challenge. And the unseemly scramble, as if for African colonies,
of vote-grubbing city councils in half the nation's toxic dumpsites to
shut down mild-mannered restaurants, even bars, where once upon a
time our Bogeys and our Bacalls gazed at each other through a pall of
mall. And the frightwig who just sat herself down next to me in an otherwise empty *smoking* section at the local coffee shop, wearing the pelt
of a dead marsupial, smelling like the guts of a sperm whale, to complain immediately about the cigarette I'd already stubbed out because
I've been browbeaten into feeling ashamed of my pariah self in a
shameless *Republic* of moralizing busybody bullies, professional cry-
babies, post-therapeutic vegetarian hysterics and Rogaine-abusing
Health Nazi joggers.

This is not a brief for the Merchants of Death. They wouldn't read
it, anyway, so busy are they suppressing research papers on the behavior of nicotine-addicted dope-fiend rodents. This is a brief for the
dope-fiend rodents. To feel better about the world, according to
Richard Rudgley's forthcoming book *Essential Substances: A Cultural History of Intoxicants in Society* (Kodansha): Siberian shamans
from the Stone Age on partook of the fly-agaric mushroom. Nor would
the rock paintings of San bushmen of the Kalahari and Shoshonean
Coso of the California Great Basin have looked the same without some
sort of hallucinogen. We know from the bat caves of southern Spain, as
well as from the tomb art and Breton megaliths of Neolithic France,
that poppies were about, as they had been in the Late Minoan III period
of the ornamental vases. Hemp was around on the Pontic Steppes, all
over the Carpathian Basin, in "pipe cups" from the Caucasian Early
Bronze Age and in grave chambers at the Hochdord Hallstaff D in
Stuttgart. Among Scythians, an ecstatic vapor bath was as much of a
favorite back then as it is now among Arctic peoples. In the Indian *Rig
Veda* and the Iranian *Avesta* there is an awful lot of *soma* mentioned,
and no other way to account for the geometries of Persian carpet
design. The *mang* consumed to secure the visions of that third-century
classic of Zoroastrian literature, the *Book of Arda Wiraz*, probably
contained some of the same chemicals found in the Amazonian jungle
vine *Banisteriopsis* (or *yajé*), used by Amerindians for the clairvoyant
detection of criminal activities, as well as for seeing jaguars. Bird-bone
snuffing tubes! Spatulas! Cactus! To initiate themselves in the secrets of
male identity the Bimin-Kuskusmin, a Mountain Ok people in New
Guinea, first use ginger, then tobacco, and finally mushrooms. Tukano
Indians boil bark for *ayahuasca*. In Peru, Ecuador and Bolivia, they

chew coca; in Yemen, Ethiopia, Somalia and Kenya, *khat*; in West Africa, kola nuts; and to meet their minimum daily requirement of apomorphine, Mayans used to smoke water lilies.

And I continue to stick burning leaves in my food-hole. Nor am I entirely alone, not even at *The Nation*, where your executive editor is known to puff, and the "Minority Report" columnist never stops, and until a couple months ago I couldn't go to a square dance without "Reading Around" and "Subject to Debate" bumming my charcoal-filters. Kurt Vonnegut, Molly Ivins and Susan Brownmiller smoke. So do Vaclav Havel and Lech Walesa. So did Pablo Picasso, Mary McCarthy, Franklin Roosevelt and George Sand. Charles Kuralt can't go to Los Angeles from New York without flying first to London or Antwerp or Mexico City, which may be why he quit CBS instead of cigarettes. One of the many pleasures of going to Sweden for the last December's Nobel Prize was firing up late at night with Toni Morrison, Fran Lebowitz and Sonny Mehta. *In Stockholm they've got ashtrays in the elevators.* We're undercover everywhere, like moles at Langley. And from the opprobrium, you'd think we were gay or Jewish or maybe even Violence on Television. Some of us probably are. But whatever happened to Live and Let Cough? Get a life; save a seal; bomb an abortion clinic.

We've *always* known that tobacco's bad for us. For the Iroquois of New York and the Maya of Yucatan, to whom the leaf was god, maybe lung cancer and emphysema are a payback to Europe for such user-friendlies as smallpox and syphilis. Consult the social history in Richard Klein's witty and subversive new book *Cigarettes Are Sublime* (Duke University) and you will find that as early as 1604, King James I warned his British subjects that "the habit of smoking is disgusting to sight, repulsive to smell, dangerous to the brain, noxious to the lung"—though James was also out to get Sir Walter Raleigh, who is said to have puffed away in the Tower of London. An alarmed Parlement of Paris, in 1631, outlawed smoking in prisons. The equally alarmed city fathers of Colmar in 1659 prohibited the bourgeoisie from partaking. By our own 1890s, twenty-six states had banned cigarettes, till World War I overnight made puffing patriotic. Anti-tobacco hysteria rises and falls according to phases of social moons with their own ulterior agendas, the way the Inquisition tried to stamp out peyote among the Toltecs and Chichimecas when it got to Mexico in 1571.

Exceptions will always be made in the middle of moralizing. At the very moment that Joseph Califano, Jimmy Carter's Secretary of Health, Education and Welfare, launched a $50 million campaign against smoking, his President was swearing to a group of North Carolina tobacco growers, with tears in his eyes, that he'd never sanction cutting off their subsidies. On the very same day that Louis Sullivan, George Bush's Secretary of Health and Human Services, declared war on the Merchants of Death, the White House Chief of Staff was cutting a deal with the majority leader of the Senate to gut the Clean Air Act. Nor is any administration about to mess with yearly exports exceeding $4 billion worth of American tobacco abroad; we close our eyes and think of the balance of payments. You'll have noted that on the very day Labor Secretary Reich called for banning all smoke in the workplace, the United States was the only Western nation at the Geneva talks of the Organization for Economic Cooperation and Development to vote against banning the export of toxic industrial wastes to Russia, Eastern Europe and the Third World.

But Klein, a Cornell professor of French and the editor of *Diacritics*, engages us on another level. He quit cigarettes himself upon finishing a book that was rejected by twenty-five publishers before they loved it on Tobacco Road. *Cigarettes Are Sublime* is literary criticism, pop-cultural analysis, political harangue, "an ode to cigarettes," an exercise in hyperbole ("the rhetorical figure that raises its objects up, excessively, way above their actual merit . . . not to deceive by exaggeration . . . but to allow the true value, the truth of what is insufficiently valued, to appear"), and also an act of mourning. In the secret history, peculiar physiology, depth psychology and symbolic culture of smoking, he finds "a crucial integer of our modernity."

As if they were linked rings of smoke we are asked to contemplate Molière, Baudelaire, Mallarmé, Pierre Louáuys, Jules Laforgué and J.P. Sartre; Mérimée's *Carmen* and also Bizet's (she worked, of course, in a cigarette factory in Seville); Svevo's great novel about smoking and psychoanalysis, *The Confessions of Zeno*; war novels by Erich Maria Remarque, Hemingway, Mailer and Styron; movies like *Casablanca*, in which everybody smoked incessantly and symbolically *except* Ingrid Bergman; the dandy, the prostitute, the Goya, the Cassanova and Immanuel Kant on the concept of the sublime; the iconography of Gauloises (the Soldier) and of Gitanes (the Gypsy); the humble weed as a source of aesthetic satisfaction, an aid to reflective consciousness, a variety of religious and artistic expression, a tool for managing anxiety, a symbol of sexual and political freedom, minor god, lyric muse, mystic joy, consolation, sacred and erotic object, parenthesis, prayer and "principle of camaraderie."

Now listen up. Hitler, who hated smoking, especially hated seeing women do it; there were signs saying so all over the Reich. A European Community health survey indicates that women are much more likely to smoke in countries like Holland, where they were most liberated from traditional places and roles, than in countries like, say, Portugal. "A woman who smokes in public," Klein says, "offends those who think that women are supposed to be veiled." This suggests to me that *the antismoking hysteria is misogynistic.* And then there's smoking "not only as a physical act but a discursive one," "a wordless but eloquent form of expression," "a fully coded, rhetorically complex, narratively articulated discourse with a vast repertoire of well-understood conventions that are implicated, intertextually, in the whole literary, philosophical, cultural history of smoking. . . . In the present climate, the discursive performance of smoking has become a form of obscenity, just as obscenity has become an issue of public health." This suggests to me that *prohibition is censorship!* And finally there is "the popular ethic of democratic generosity associated with tobacco in general, and with cigarettes in particular." As cats can look at kings, beggars can bum from Bourbons. "If Prometheus had stolen fire from Heaven to light his cigarette," wrote Mme. de Giradin in 1844 to the Viconte de Launay, "they would have let him do it." This suggests to me that *smoking is a form of socialism.*

Never mind that they won't let me smoke anymore even at the A.A. meeting to which I have dutifully reported for the past eight years. These days when bums ask for a light, we burn them alive in our parks. Years ago, injured in my camaraderie, I left No-Smoking Berkeley on the last flight to New York before tobacco was banned on domestic flights, as if on the last American chopper out of Saigon. I'd spent three days in the Third World capital of Flower Power and my youth, unable anywhere to light up and having everywhere to listen to assistant professors of Yup and Jog complain about the homeless and the derelict on Telegraph Avenue, while eating at Chez Panisse and shopping at Andronico's, with its thirteen varieties of shrimp and twenty-seven different sauces. I thought: We no longer live in a civil society. And I also wondered: Isn't it kind of stuck-up, wanting to live forever?

"THE AMERICAN NEO-NAZI MOVEMENT TODAY"
by David Levine—July 16/23, 1990

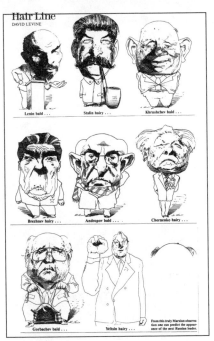

"HAIR LINE"
by David Levine—March 2, 1992

"FROM RUSSIA WITH LOVE AND SQUALOR"
by Maris Bishofs—January 18, 1993

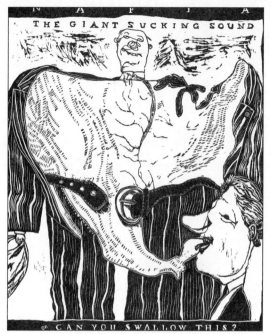

NAFTA
by Frances Jetter—January 17, 1994

"Contract on America"
by Robert Grossman—December 12, 1994

"Medicine and the Madness of the Market"
by Edward Sorel—January 9/16, 1995

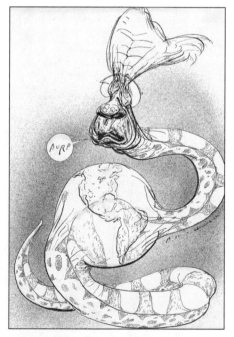

"Citizen Murdoch"
by Steve Brodner—May 29, 1995

"NATIONAL RORSCHACH"
by Art Spiegelman—October 30, 1995

"THE INFLATION OF ALAN GREENSPAN"
by Steve Brodner—March 11, 1996

"THE CIGARETTE PAPERS"
by Gary Trudeau—January 1, 1996

Tom Tomorrow cartoon—January 1, 1996

"MAD POLITICIANS DISEASE"
by Sue Coe—May 13, 1996

om Tomorrow cartoon—May 20, 1996

LET'S ALL DO THE TWISTER!"
by Robert Grossman—June 3, 1996

"THE SUPREMES"
by Robert Burke—October 14, 1996

"POLITICAL DESCENT '96"
by Edward Sorel—November 4, 199

"Preachers to Power"
by Edward Sorel—July 13, 1998

Impeachment Trail Highlights"
by Steve Brodner—January-11/18, 1999

"UNCLE SAM AT THE MILLENIUM"
 by Edward Sorel—October 17, 2000

June 20, 1994

A Deserter from Death

Daniel Singer

•

ONE OF THE first signs of old age, I'm told, is when a young woman offers you her seat on a bus (and the next stage, presumably, is when you accept it). But there is a surer proof of the passing of time: when events from your adolescence are being commemorated as ancient history—as is now the case with the fiftieth anniversary of D-day. While giving you a jolt, it also puts you in a privileged position. At a time when neo-Fascist ministers are returning to government in Europe, when creeping revisionism is gaining ground, when items from Soviet archives are cleverly selected to blur the past and convince us that Communist and Nazi, resister and collaborator, victim and executioner were all the same—it is important both to say "No, it wasn't so," and to ponder the purpose of such manipulations.

Let it be admitted from the start that this is not the neutral testimony of an objective historian but rather the committed one of a miraculous survivor of World War II who owes his life to sinus trouble. Before the war, in the Poland of my childhood, the gap between the haves and the have-nots was huge, as it was in the rest of Eastern Europe. Thus my father, a very successful journalist, hearing that the Mediterranean climate would be good for his youngest child's sinusitis, could afford to send me, my mother and my sister to the French Riviera. This happened in August 1939. After the war broke out we tried to rush back home, but—second stroke of fortune—it was too late.

Not that I was untouched by the bloody conflict. Far from it. My father was sent to the gulag in distant Siberia, my older brother was killed in the battle of Tobruk and my sister jumped from a second floor in Marseilles rather than face deportation. To escape the Nazis, I had illegally crossed the border into Switzerland and on the way I mistook in the dark the greenish uniform of the Swiss for the *Feldgrau* of the Germans. After such an experience, you grow up very fast indeed. At the time that Allied troops were landing in Normandy, I was attending Calvin's high school in Geneva and treating my classmates as kids. But in another sense, I was a youth like any other, reading Rimbaud, discovering not only the Surrealists but also the "surprise parties," as they were called, at which we jitterbugged to Mezz Mezzrow and smooched to "Blues in the Night"—instead of providing fodder for the gas chambers as did my aunts, uncles and innumerable cousins.

The reactions to D-day in Occupied Europe were, naturally enough, contrasting. At one extreme, among the resisters and the victims, the Allied invasion buoyed hopes and strengthened the conviction that, whatever cruel damage the enemy might still inflict, it was the beginning of the end. At the other extreme, those who had linked their fate with the *Herrenvolk* were either getting ready for a last stand or wondering how best to climb on a new bandwagon.

But what about the mass of the people in between? By 1944 any illusions they had held about the occupiers and their collaborators had long vanished. The bulk of the population was yearning for change. True, because of the understandable obsession with food, most people's aspirations were down-to-earth. But there was also a growing revulsion against the prewar regimes that had made such a conflict possible. Only by grasping that feeling can one understand why, say, young British soldiers would vote in Labor and throw out wartime leader Winston Churchill; or why the French Resistance proclaimed that the moneyed interests would never again be allowed to dominate the press. How romantically unreal it all sounds today! Actually, on D-day the initial reaction, as a French writer reminded us, was to exclaim, *"Les Anglais!"* because in the popular imagination Britain was the first nation to be associated with the struggle against the Nazis. The Americans' turn (whatever their actual role in the invasion) would come later. As the G.I.s spread across the liberated Continent they brought with them the myth of a distant cornucopia—the magic land of nylon stockings and Glenn Miller's "In the Mood." But it was the British who, at least to begin with, symbolized defiance of fascism. Or rather, the British and the Russians.

A personal aside: Nowadays, in these silly times, even when stating an obvious fact, one must first establish one's credentials. So let me say that I have been an anti-Stalinist almost from childhood and that my antagonism toward the Georgian tyrant, because of crimes committed in the name of socialism, has in no way diminished. Having said that, I find preposterous the current attempts to minimize either the role of Communists in the European resistance movements after 1941 or the part played by the Red Army in the Allied victory. Military experts will tell you that the landing in Western Europe would have been quite a different story if the bulk of crack German divisions had not been bogged down in the Soviet Union. Let me simply add that for someone who lived through those years of despair and contempt in France, the moments of hope were mostly connected with news from the Eastern Front. There was a joke at the time that ran, Which town is the biggest in the world? Answer: Stalingrad. Why? Because the Germans marched and marched and marched and never got to the railway station. This witticism, based on boastful Nazi communiqués claiming their troops were advancing toward the station, sounds quaint today. But at the time it was a flash of hope in a time of gloom, an optimistic message that the arrogant enemy might not be invincible.

UNIQUE AND COMPARABLE

After the landing came the liberation of the occupied territories and then the invasion of Germany itself. Accompanying the hour of glory was the horrifying discovery of the concentration camps with their ossuaries and their walking skeletons. Even we who lived close to the camps and were supposed to know were completely shattered by those pictures from hell, defying the imagination of a Hieronymus Bosch, and will probably be haunted by those images for the rest of our lives.

Whenever I am asked, or ask myself, what it means to be a Jew—as one who does not think of Jews as a race, who is a nonbeliever and was not brought up in Hebrew or Yiddish culture—I find the rudiments of an answer in my relationship to those corpses. I know and fully accept the proposition that we should share our sympathy and solidarity with the victims, the exploited, the downtrodden and humiliated without distinction of nationality, religion or skin color. Yet I could have ended up in that charnel house myself. I almost wrote "should have ended up," assuming, with utter irrationality, that I am a deserter from the army of the dead.

Words should be handled with care. Not every reactionary and repressive regime is fascist. Not every horror of our time can be equated with the Holocaust. The organized, systematic, almost scientific extermination of a people on alleged racial grounds and on such a scale seems to me to be a unique event in human history. Unique but not incomparable; quite the contrary. We are living in a crazy and increasingly dangerous world. When Jews, even if a small proportion of the whole population, can rejoice, both in public and in private, over the mad massacre of praying Palestinians; when the death of one race-car driver in the Grand Prix takes five times more space in the media than that of 200,000 blacks in Rwanda; when "ethnic cleansing," which one thought had been discredited forever, becomes bloody purification in the former Yugoslavia and looks highly contagious; when blood ties, once again, seem to negate all other forms of solidarity across national frontiers—when all this happens it is important to recall the Holocaust as a reminder of what humans are capable of performing and as a warning that it can happen here, there and everywhere if we don't tackle the deadly disease from its earliest symptoms.

For historians the past has an attraction in its own right. They wish to study events in their proper context, understand their causes and consequences. For the rest of us, the main value of history lies in the lessons it provides for our own times.

Past and Present

"We don't know yet what our past is going to be" goes the old Eastern European jest, underscoring the fact that mastery of the past is often an instrument of current struggle. Stalin was a champion at the rewriting of history, but he was not alone in this nefarious trade. Indeed, we are now witnessing in Russia (though it is probably being prompted from abroad) a vast operation involving the doctoring of documents and the manipulation of memoirs for purposes that go well beyond commercial exploitation.

Let there be no mistake: We leftists are for open diplomacy. We are in favor of the declassification of secret documents both in general and in this particular case. Although the Soviet Union should never have been a model, we can learn from its bitter experiment with socialism— and the more we know the better. Nor should we be hostile to stern judgments on that experiment, provided they are made in a historical context (taking into account, say, foreign intervention and the White as well as the Red terror). Actually, it is only in such a historical framework that a judgment can make sense. This, incidentally, is also true of studies, fashionable in recent years, of the infatuation of Western, particularly French, intellectuals with the Soviet Union. A fascinating subject, if the authors had painted in the background: the Great Depression before the war, with millions of unemployed; the anticolonial struggle in Algeria, Vietnam and elsewhere after the war. Otherwise it is, at best, merely a more sophisticated form of propaganda.

In other words, we are for truth, but the whole truth; for the systematic publication of documents (and not just in Russia) under the supervision of serious historians. Otherwise, you never know whether the text was tailored to suit a purchaser who wants to prove that the Rosenbergs were guilty, that Alger Hiss was a spy. Actually, this whole campaign seems to be aiming beyond such individual targets and probably beyond the objectives of some of the participants. If we were to accept its basic premise, namely that Hitler was merely a disciple, that the real trouble started with Stalin, nay, with the Bolshevik Revolution, we would have to reappraise our whole conception of modern history.

Revisionism itself is being revised. Its cleverest practitioners have realized they could not wipe out the Holocaust; those dead millions will not vanish into thin air. But you can make light of its importance and shift the blame for it. The revisionist historians in Germany no longer deny that Martin Heidegger was a Nazi. Instead they argue that, faced with the choice of two evils—Communism and National Socialism— he wisely chose the lesser, i.e., Nazism. In France you can't yet go as far. Nevertheless, even there a brazen attempt was made last year—with a book, a television show, a press campaign and, naturally, a "Russian document," to describe the leader of the Resistance on French soil, Jean Moulin, as a Soviet agent. The whole fraudulent construction was rapidly destroyed by prominent resisters and principled historians. The purpose, however, was obvious: If even the hero Moulin was a spy, Soviet or Nazi, what does matter, *ma chère*? Whom can we trust and whom should we blame? The next stage came in Italy, where the neo-Fascist Gianfranco Fini, the chief ally of the new Prime Minister, Silvio Berlusconi, proclaims that Fascism is no longer a relevant problem and that Benito Mussolini "was the greatest statesman of the century."

History's image is growing faint not only because of the passage of time and because many of the actors are gone. It is being distorted because the political climate has changed and conscious efforts are being made to change it still further. In the circumstances, anything that refreshes the memory—books, films, trials or celebrations, and particularly anything that transmits the true image to the younger generation—is very precious. Earlier this year the French tried 79-year-old Paul Touvier, who during the war was chief of intelligence and operations of the Vichy militia in Lyons. What is important is not that this former executioner and still unrepentant Jew-hater was sentenced to life. What matters is that many people learned about the past from his trial and that a Frenchman was for the first time condemned for his participation in "crimes against humanity"; they also learned about the role of a section of the Catholic Church in hiding and protecting the culprit. Touvier, however, was a mere thug, a flunky with blood on his hands. If, as may be hoped, Maurice Papon, a more important figure, is finally brought to trial later in the year, the complicity of the French administration will be illustrated and the impact will be greater.

But aren't D-day celebrations the best opportunity of all to teach about the past, with the beaches as the stage, the television cameras focused and the entire world as an audience? And are we not lucky to have rulers able to rise to the occasion and proclaim in our name from Normandy our revulsion from Fascist tyranny and Nazi crimes? We would be luckier still if the same honorable men were not to embrace, next month in Naples, the newcomer Berlusconi, who whitewashes Fini, who thinks that Mussolini, etc. And they do all that because our masters believe that the new regime, with its businessman boss and its Thatcherite ministers, will keep Italy safe for capitalism. The French have a good expression for their empty talk: *des paroles verbales*, verbal words. If we say much more on the subject, we could be sued for insulting our heads of state.

But we owe it to the Americans, the Canadians and the British who risked and in many cases lost their lives to free us from the Nazis; we owe it to all the victims and to those who fought on other fronts, particularly in Eastern Europe; I owe it to the 23-year-old kid whose head was blasted by a German bullet in Tobruk and who, by a quirk, will remain my big brother forever, to say what was the true nature of their struggle. Undoubtedly, they fought to break the barbarian rule of Hitler and his thugs. They also fought so that this world war would be the last. Yet in doing so, each one in his fashion and with varying degrees of consciousness, they also battled for a different world. It is this struggle that we must carry on, or rather resume. This is our heritage on D-day as dark clouds are, once again, gathering over Europe.

A SOCIALISM OF THE SKIN

Tony Kushner

•

IS THERE A relationship between homosexual liberation and socialism? That's an unfashionably utopian question, but I pose it because
it's entirely conceivable that we will one day live miserably in a thoroughly ravaged world in which lesbians and gay men can marry and
serve openly in the Army and that's it. Capitalism, after all, can absorb
a lot. Poverty, war, alienation, environmental destruction, colonialism,
unequal development, boom/bust cycles, private property, individualism, commodity fetishism, the fetishization of the body, the fetishization of violence, guns, drugs, child abuse, underfunded and bad
education (itself a form of child abuse)—these things are key to the
successful functioning of the free market. Homophobia is not; the system could certainly accommodate demands for equal rights for homosexuals without danger to itself.

But are officially sanctioned homosexual marriages and identifiably
homosexual soldiers the ultimate aims of homosexual liberation?
Clearly not, if by homosexual liberation we mean the liberation of
homosexuals, who, like most everyone else, are and will continue to be
oppressed by the depredations of capital until some better way of living together can be arrived at. So then are homosexual marriages and
soldiery the ultimate, which is to say the only achievable, aims of the
gay rights movement, a politics not of vision but of pragmatics?

Andrew Sullivan, in a provocative, carefully reasoned, moving, troubling article in *The New Republic* a year ago, arrived at that conclusion. I used to have a crush on Andrew, neocon or neoliberal (or whatever the hell they're called these days) though he be. I would never have married him, but he's cute! Then he called me a "West Village Neil Simon," *in print*, and I retired the crush. This by way of background for what follows, to prove that I am, despite my wounded affections, capable of the "reason and restraint" he calls for at the opening of his article, "The Politics of Homosexuality."

Andrew divides said politics into four, you should pardon the expression, camps—conservative, radical, moderate and liberal—each of which lacks a workable "solution to the problem of gay-straight relations." Conservatives (by which he means reactionaries, I think, but he is very polite) and radicals both profess an absolutist politics of "impossibilism," which alienates them from "the mainstream." Moderates (by which he means conservatives) practice an ostrich-politics of denial, increasingly superseded by the growing visibility of gay men and lesbians. And liberals (moderates) err mainly in trying to legislate, through antidiscrimination bills, against reactive, private-sector bigotry.

Andrew's prescription is that liberals (with whom he presumably identifies most closely) go after "pro-active" government bans on homosexual participation in the military and the institution of marriage. Period. "All public (as opposed to private) discrimination against homosexuals [should] be ended and . . . every right and responsibility that heterosexuals enjoy by virtue of the state [should] be extended to those who grow up different. And that is all." Andrew's new "liberal" gay politics "does not legislate private tolerance, it declares public equality . . . Our battle is not for political victory but for personal integrity."

The article is actually a kind of manifesto for gay conservatism, and as such it deserves scrutiny. Every manifesto also deserves acolytes, and "The Politics of Homosexuality" has earned at least one: Bruce Bawer, who appeared this year in *The New Republic* with "The Stonewall Myth: Can the Gay Rights Movement Get Beyond the Politics of Nostalgia?" Bruce, however, is no Andrew. He's cute enough; he looks rueful and contemplative on the cover of his book, *A Place at the Table*, though if you've read it you'll know Bruce doesn't like it when gay men get dishy and bitchy and talk sissy about boys. He thinks it makes us look bad for the straights. Bruce is *serious*, more serious even than Andrew, as the big open book in the cover photo proclaims: He's read more than half of it! (Lest anyone think I habitually read *The New*

Republic, the playwright David Greenspan gave me Andrew's article, and Andrew Kopkind among others drew my attention to Bruce's.)

Bruce is not only more serious than Andrew, he's more polite, no easy trick; he's so polite I almost hate to write that he's also much easier to dismiss, but he is. His article is short and sloppy, and he has this habit of creating paper tigers. Take the eponymous "Stonewall Myth," to which "many gay men and lesbians routinely" subscribe: According to Bruce, these "many" believe that gay history started with Stonewall and regard the riot as "a sacred event that lies beyond the reach of objective discourse." Huh? I don't know anyone who believes that, and I've never encountered such a ridiculous statement in any work of gay criticism or reportage or even fiction. But Bruce goes on for pages tilting at this windmill and the "politics of nostalgia" that accompanies it. He's also, and I mean this politely, a little slow. It took him five years to figure out that maybe a gay man shouldn't be writing movie reviews for the viciously homophobic *American Spectator*. In his book he is anguished: "Had I been wrong to write for so reactionary a publication? If so, then how did one figure out where to draw the line? Should I refuse to write for the *Nation* because its editors frequently appeared to be apologists for Communism," etc.

In the article Bruce decides that our real problem is a fear of acceptance, fear of failure, a "deep unarticulated fear of that metaphorical place at the table," and so we march in front of TV cameras in our underwear, confirming for all the world that we really are sick. (Clothes, worn and discarded, are always bothering Bruce; spandex and leather, business suits and bras, his writing is littered with the stuff.) I'll focus mostly on Andrew's meatier, seminal (oops!) text. (For a polite but mostly thorough reaming of *A Place at the Table*, read David Bergman in the Spring '94 issue of *The Harvard Gay and Lesbian Review*.)

In "The Politics of Homosexuality," Andrew concedes quite a lot of good will to those farthest to the right. He draws an odd distinction between the "visceral recoil" of bigots and the more cautious discomfort of homophobes—those who "sincerely believe" in "discouragement of homosexuality," who couch their sincere beliefs in "Thomist argument," in "the natural law tradition, which, for all its failings is a resilient pillar of Western thought." Bigotry, too, is a resilient pillar of Western thought, or it was the last time I checked. Andrew realizes bigotry "expresses itself in thuggery and name-calling. But there are some [conservatives] who don't support antigay violence." Like who? George Will, Bill Buckley and Cardinal O'Connor have all made token clucking noises about fag-bashing, but the incommensurability of these faint protests with the frightening extent of the violence, which has certainly been encouraged by the very vocal homophobia of "conservatives," might force one of question the sincerity of their admonitions, and further, to question the value of distinguishing "Thomist" homophobes from the "thugs" who in 1993 attacked or killed more than 1,900 lesbians and gay men (at least those are the hate crimes we know about).

Andrew takes a placid view of people on the reactionary right because he is convinced their days are numbered. But does he really believe that Pat Buchanan is now "reduced to joke-telling"? Such a conclusion is possible only if one ignores the impressive, even terrifying, political energies of the religious right. Since Andrew decides political discourse can countenance only "reason and restraint," he of course must exclude the Bible-thumpers, who are crazy and *loud*. But the spectrum is more crowded, and on the right less well-behaved, than a gentleman like Andrew cares to admit. His is an endearing reticence, but it is not wise.

Andrew is at his best describing the sorts of traumas homophobia inflicts on its victims (though to nobody's surprise he doesn't care for the word "victim"), yet despite his sensitivity, he's alarmingly quick to give up on the antidiscrimination legislation of those he calls liberals. "However effective or comprehensive anti-discrimination laws are, they cannot reach far enough." They can't give us confidence, and they only "scratch the privileged surface." "As with other civil rights legislation, those least in need of it may take fullest advantage : the most litigious and articulate homosexuals, who would likely brave the harsh winds of homophobia in any case."

It's unclear whether Andrew opposes such legislation, which, it seems to me, is worthwhile even if only moderately effective. I assume that in limiting the gay rights movement's ambitions to fighting "proactive" discrimination, he is arguing against trying to pass laws that impede "reactive" discrimination, though I can't find anything in his very specific article that states this definitively. (In any case, his distinction between "reactive" and "pro-active" discrimination falls apart as soon as one considers adoption laws or education or sexual harassment.) Perhaps he's vague because he knows he hasn't much of a case. What worries him especially is that the right will make effective propaganda out of the argument that "civil rights laws essentially dictate the behavior of heterosexuals, in curtailing their ability to discriminate." And he believes further that this argument contains "a germ of truth."

The argument is unquestionably good propaganda for homophobes, but it's identical to the N.R.A.'s argument for giving every nutbag in the country access to a semi-automatic. We have to argue such propaganda down, not run away from the legislation that inspired it. As for the "germ of truth," Andrew writes:

> Before most homosexuals have even come out of the closet they are demanding concessions from the majority, including a clear curtailment of economic and social liberties, in order to ensure protections few of them will even avail themselves of. It is no wonder there is opposition.

This is a peculiar view of the processes by which enfranchisement is extended: Civil rights, apparently, are not rights at all, not something inalienable, to which one is entitled by virtue of being human or a citizen, but concessions the majority makes to a minority if and only if the minority can promise it will use those rights. Antidiscrimination laws are seen as irrelevant to creating a safer environment in which closeted or otherwise oppressed people might feel more free to exercise their equality; laws apparently cannot encourage freedom, only punish transgressions against it.

The argument that antidiscrimination laws violate "majority" freedoms has already been used to eliminate the basis of most of the legislation from the civil rights movement. Affirmative action, housing and employment laws, and voter redistricting can all be said to curtail the freedom of bigots to discriminate, which is, of course, what such measures are supposed to do. The connection that such legislation implies between gay rights and other minority rights displeases Andrew, who resists the idea that, as forms of oppression, homophobia and racism have much in common.

With homosexuality, according to Andrew, "the option of self-concealment has always existed," something that cannot be said about race. (I could introduce him to some flaming creatures who might make him question that assessment, but never mind.) "Gay people are not uniformly discriminated against; openly gay people are." Certainly there are important differences of kind and degree and consequence between racism and homophobia, but the idea that invisibility exempts anyone from discrimination is perverse. To need to be invisible, or to feel that you need to be, is to be discriminated against. The fact that homophobia differs significantly from racism—and, loath as I am to enter the discrimination olympics, I'd argue that the consequences of racism in America today are worse than those of homophobia—does not mean that people engaged in one struggle can't learn from another, or that the tools one oppressed people have developed can't be used to try to liberate others.

Andrew is joined by Bruce in his anxiety to preserve the differences among various kinds of oppression, but they both seem less interested in according each group its own "integrity," as Andrew rightly calls it, than in keeping gay rights from being shanghaied by the radical left. "The standard post-Stonewall practice . . . indiscriminately link [s] the movement for gay equal rights with any left-wing cause to which any gay leader might happen to have a personal allegiance . . ." (this is Bruce). "Such linkages have been a disaster for the gay rights movement: not only do they falsely imply that most gay people sympathize with those so-called progressive movements, but they also serve to reinforce the idea of homosexuality itself as a 'progressive' phenomenon, as something essentially political in nature." Andrew, meanwhile, warns against the "universalist temptation," which exercises "an enervating and dissipating effect on gay radicalism's political punch."

Gay radicalism's political punch is not something either Andrew or Bruce wishes to see strengthened. Conservative gay politics is in a sense the politics of containment: Connections made with a broadly defined left are what must be contained. The pair predicts the emergence of increasing numbers of conservative homosexuals (presumably white—in both Andrew's and Bruce's prophecies they come from the suburbs), who are unsympathetic to the idea of linking their fortunes with any other political cause. The future depends not on collectivity and solidarity but on homosexual individualism—on lesbians and gay men instructing the straight world quietly, "person by person, life by life, heart by heart" (Andrew), to "do the hard, painstaking work of *getting* straight Americans used to it" (Bruce).

Like all assimilationists, Andrew and Bruce are unwilling to admit that structural or even particularly formidable barriers exist between themselves and their straight oppressors. And for all their elaborate fears that misbehaving queers alienate instead of communicate, nowhere do they express a concern that people of color or the working class or the poor are not being communed with. The audience we are ostensibly losing is identified exclusively as phobic straights, "families" (which one suspects are two-parent, middle-class) and gay teenagers.

Bruce and Andrew are very concerned about young gay people. Watching a "lean and handsome" 15-year-old leaf through *The Native* at the start of his book, Bruce worries that queer radicalism, sexual explicitness and kink frighten gay kids and the families from whence they come. Probably it is the case that teenagers are freaked by photo ads for The Dungeon. But *The Native* is not produced for teenagers. Images of adult lesbian and gay desire can't be tailored to appeal to 15-year-olds and their straight parents. Our culture is the manifest content of our lives, not a carefully constructed recruiting brochure. True, there aren't readily available, widely circulated images of homosexual domesticity or accomplishment or happiness, but I'm more inclined to blame the homophobic media than gay radicalism for that. Nor does the need for such images mandate the abandonment of public declarations of the variety of sexual desire, the public denial and repression of which is after the The Problem. Lesbian and gay kids will have less trouble accepting their homosexuality not when the Gay Pride Parade is an orderly procession of suits arranged in monogamous pairs but when people learn to be less horrified by sex and its complexities.

Out of the great stew of class, race, gender, and sexual politics that inspirits the contentious, multiplying, endlessly unfixed lesbian and gay community in America, gay conservatism manages to make a neat division between a majority that is virtually indistinguishable in behavior and aspirations and *Weltanschauung* from the straight world, and a minority of deviants and malcontents who are fucking things up for everyone, thwarting the only realizable goal, which is normalcy.

Andrew says up front that politics is supposed to relieve anxiety. I'd say that it's supposed to relieve misery and injustice. When all that can be expected from politics, in the way of immediate or even proximate social transformation, are gay weddings and gay platoons, the vast rest of it all, every other agony inflicted by homophobia, will have to be taken care of by some osmotic process of quiet individualized persuasion, which will take many, many, many years. It's the no-government, antipolitics approach to social change. You can hear it argued now against school desegregation, or any attempt to guarantee equal education; you can hear it argued against welfare or jobs programs. It's the legacy of trickledown, according to which society should change slowly, organically, spontaneously, without interference, an approach that requires not so much the "discipline, commitment, responsibility" that Bruce exhorts us to—we already practice those—but a great, appalling luxury of time (which maybe the editor of *The New Republic* and the erstwhile movie critic of *The American Spectator* can afford), after the passage of which many, many, many more miserable lives will have been spent or dispensed with. I am always suspicious of the glacier-paced patience of the right.

Such a politics of homosexuality is dispiriting. Like conservative thought in general, it offers very little in the way of hope, and very little in the way of vision. I expect both hope and vision from my politics. Andrew and Bruce offer nothing more than that gay culture will dissolve invisibly into straight culture, all important differences elided.

I think both Andrew and Bruce would call this assessment unfair, though I don't mean it to be. Andrew's politics may be roomier than Bruce's; Andrew is more worldly and generous (except, apparently, when it comes to the theater). Both men have a vision. They see before them an attainable peaceable kingdom, in which gay men and lesbians live free of fear (of homophobia, at least), in which gay kids aren't made to feel worthless, or worse, because they're gay.

But what of all the other things gay men and lesbians have to fear? What of the things gay children have to fear, in common with all children? What of the planetary despoilment that kills us? Or the financial necessity that drives some of us into unsafe, insecure, stupid, demeaning and ill-paying jobs? Or the unemployment that impoverishes some of us? Or the racism some of us face? Or the rape some of us fear? What about AIDS? Is it enough to say, Not our problem? Of course gay and lesbian politics is a progressive politics: It depends on progress for the accomplishment of any of its goals. Is there any progressive politics that recognizes no connectedness, no border-crossings, no solidarity or possibility for mutual aid?

"A map of the world that does not include Utopia is not worth even glancing at, for it leaves out the one country at which Humanity is always landing." This is neither Bruce nor Andrew, but that most glorious and silly gay writer, Oscar Wilde. Because this is the twenty-fifth anniversary of Stonewall, that mythic moment that lies beyond all objective discourse (just kidding, Bruce!), we are all thinking big. That's what anniversaries are for, to invite consideration of the past and contemplation of the future. And so, to lift my sights and spirits after the dour, pinched antipolitics of gay conservatism, I revisited Oscar, a lavish thinker, as he appears in political drag in his magnificent essay, "The Soul of Man Under Socialism."

Oscar, like our two boys, was an individualist, though rather more individual in the way he lived, and much less eager to conform. It would be stretching things to say Oscar was a radical, exactly, though if Bruce and Andrew had been his contemporaries, Lord knows how they would have tut-tutted at his scandalous carryings-on.

Oscar's socialism is an exaltation of the individual, of the individual's immense capacities for beauty and for pleasure. Behind Oscar's socialist politics, wrote John Cowper Powys, is "a grave Mirandola-like desire to reconcile the woods of Arcady with the Mount of Transfiguration." What could be swoonier? Or, with all due deference to Andrew and Bruce's sober, rational politics of homosexuality, what could be more more gay?

Powys wrote that Oscar's complaint against capitalism and industrialism is "the irritation of an extremely sensitive skin . . . combined with a pleasure-lover's annoyance at seeing other people so miserably wretched." If there is a relationship between socialism and homosexual liberation, perhaps this is it: an irritation of the skin.

"One's regret," Oscar tells us, "is that society should be constructed on such a basis that man has been forced into a groove in which he cannot freely develop what is wonderful; and fascinating, and delightful in him—in which, in fact, he misses the true pleasure and joy of living." Socialism, as an alternative to individualism politically and capitalism economically, must surely have as its ultimate objective the restitution of the joy of living we may have lost when we first picked up a tool. Toward what other objective is it worthy to strive?

Perhaps the far horizon of lesbian and gay politics is a socialism of the skin. Our task is to confront the political problematics of desire and repression. As much as Bruce and Andrew want to distance themselves from the fact, Stonewall was a sixties thing, part of the utopian project of that time (and the sixties, Joan Nestle writes, is "the favorite target of people who take delight in the failure of dreams"). Honoring the true desire of the skin, and the connection between the skin and heart and mind and soul, is what homosexual liberation is about.

Gay rights may be obtainable, on however broad or limited a basis, but liberation depends on a politics that goes beyond, not an antipolitics. Our unhappiness as scared queer children doesn't only isolate us, it also politicizes us. It inculcates in us a desire for connection that is all the stronger because we have experienced its absence. Our suffering teaches us solidarity; or it should.

BATTUES

•

Never more alien never born farther away
    never less acquiescent all that on all sides
is taken for granted never hearing with such
    fatal clarity the full intent of the voices
as when they ring the upland out of thickets
    along the edges of oak woods and beside hollows
still harboring sweet night and spring up from shadows
    in cleft rocks that gaze out over the naked
stony barrens those rough shouts suddenly struck from
    raw metals commanding the dogs whipping them on
echoing over the lit baying of the streaking
    hounds those voices that have called to each other all
their lives growing up together with this pitch always
    in them they know it this fire shaking and beating
burning as one toward the careful cellars of badgers
    boars' coverts the tunnels of foxes the bursting owls
to the end of flight and the cornered eyes they go on
    I keep hearing them I know them they are the cavalry
at Sand Creek they are Jackson's finest rooting out
    the infants of the Seminoles they are calling
names I know words we speak every day they are using
    language that we share which we say proves what we are

W. S. Merwin

BEHIND HAITI'S PARAMILITARIES

Allan Nairn

•

EMMANUEL CONSTANT, THE leader of Haiti's FRAPH hit squad, is a protegé of U.S. intelligence. Interviews with Constant and with U.S. officials who have worked directly with him confirm that Constant recently worked for the C.I.A. and that U.S. intelligence helped him launch the organization that became the FRAPH. Documentary evidence obtained from other sources and confirmed in part by Constant also indicates that a group of attachés—some of them implicated in some of Haiti's most notorious crimes—have been paid for several years by a U.S. government-funded project that maintains sensitive files on the movements of the Haitian poor.

In my October 3 *Nation* article ("The Eagle Is Landing") I quoted a U.S. intelligence official praising Constant as a "young pro-Western intellectual . . . no further right than a Young Republican" and saying that U.S. intelligence had "encouraged" Constant to form the group that emerged as the FRAPH. Reached at his home on the night of September 26, Constant confirmed the U.S. official's account. He said that his first U.S. handler was Col. Patrick Collins, the U.S. Defense Intelligence Agency attaché in Haiti, whom he described as "a very good friend of mine." (Constant spoke of dealing later with another official he called "[the United States'] best liaison," but he refused to give a name.) Constant said that Colonel Collins had first approached him while Constant was teaching a training course at the headquarters of the C.I.A.-run National Intelligence Service (SIN) and building a computer database for Haiti's notorious rural Section Chiefs at the Bureau of Information and Coordination in the General Headquarters of the Haitian coup regime.

Giving an account that dovetailed closely with that of the U.S. official, Constant said that Collins began pushing him to organize a front "that could balance the Aristide movement" and do "intelligence" work against it. He said that their discussions had begun soon after Aristide fell in September 1991. They resulted in Constant forming what later evolved into the FRAPH, a group that was known initially as the Haitian Resistance League.

Constant at first refused to go beyond his usual public statements on the FRAPH, but opened up after I told him that I understood that he knew Colonel Collins. Our initial interview took place on the first day of the bold anti-FRAPH protests on the streets of Port-au-Prince. Constant said that he wanted to offer his men as "guides" for the occupation force, saying that "I've participated in the stabilization of this country for the past three years, and the United States knows it very well, no matter what agency you talk to."

Two days after that, as a crowd marched past FRAPH headquarters, FRAPH gunmen opened fire, killing one demonstrator. Five days later, in the wake of the embarrassing media coverage of the continued mayhem by the FRAPH and of a U.S. raid on a supposed pro-Aristide terrorist camp that turned out to be a world-famous dance school, U.S. occupation forces raided the FRAPH's downtown Port-au-Prince headquarters, carting away two dozen street-level gunmen (and women) as live cameras and cheering crowds looked on. Some U.S. reporters proclaimed that this was the death of the terror system, and CNN's Richard Blystone, announcing that there was more crackdown to come, said that Constant was now "at large" (a claim also made by the next morning's New York Times).

Five minutes after Blystone's CNN broadcast, I reached Constant by telephone at his Port-au-Prince home. He said that the arrests had been only of low-level FRAPH people, and that he still intended to put his men at U.S. disposal. He said that there were no U.S. troops outside his house and worried that it might be set upon by mobs. Then he said that he had to leave for a meeting "on the street" with a U.S. Embassy staffer who was hitherto unknown to him but who he thought might be from the C.I.A.

He said that he would call back after the meeting, but he didn't, and I couldn't reach him again. But the next day Constant appeared in pub-

lic guarded—for the first time—by U.S. Marines. He stated his fealty to
the occupation and his support for the return of Aristide.

Much of the U.S. press played this as a stunning about-face, but
Constant had been saying those things in public and to me all week. He
had told me that the Carter/Powell/Nunn-Cédras pact was "the last
chance for Haiti," and had expressed no worry about the return of
Aristide, saying that the new Parliament, to be chosen in December,
would be constituted in a way that would hem him in.

Colonel Collins is now back in Haiti (his last tour ended in 1992).
The Clinton Administration has brought him back for the occupation,
and he has refused to comment on the record. But a well-informed
intelligence official (speaking before the FRAPH furor broke) confirmed that Collins had worked with Constant and had, as Constant
says, guided him and urged him on. Collins has, in recent weeks, spoken quite highly of Constant and has said that Constant's mission from
the United States was to counter the "extreme" of Aristide. Collins has
also said that, when he first approached him, Constant "was not in position to do anything . . . [but] things evolved and eventually he did come
up, [and] what had been sort of an idea and technically open for business—all of a sudden, boom, it takes on national significance."

When the relationship started, Constant was working for the C.I.A.,
teaching a course at the agency-run SIN on "The Theology of Liberation" and "Animation and mobilization." At that time, the SIN was
engaged in terrorist attacks on Aristide supporters, as were Constant's
pupils, army S-2 field intelligence officers. The targets included, among
others, popular church catechists. Constant says that the message of
the SIN course was that though communism is dead, "the extreme
left," through *ti legliz*, the grass-roots Haitian "little church," was
attempting "to convince the people that in the name of God everything
is possible" and that, therefore, it was right for the people to kill soldiers and the rich. Constant says he taught that "Aristide is not the only
on: There are tens of Aristides."

Collins has recently acknowledged that the FRAPH has indeed carried out many killings, but he has said that they have not been as
numerous as the press and human rights groups claim. He has said, in
reference to Haiti's political problems, "The only way you're going to
solve this is . . . [that] it'll all end in some big bloodbath and there'll be
somebody who emerges from it who will establish a society of sorts and
a judicial system and he's going to say: 'O.K., you own the land, you
don't—that's it,' whether it's fair or not."

Though most U.S. officials would never speak that way, it's universally acknowledged that the FRAPH is an arm of the brutal Haitian security system, which the United States has built and supervised and whose leaders it has trained, and often paid. When I asked Constant, for example, about the anti-Aristide coup, he said that as it was happening Colonel Collins and Donald Terry (the C.I.A. station chief who also ran the SIN) "were inside the [General] Headquarters." But he insisted that this was "normal": The C.I.A. and D.I.A. were always there.

A foreign diplomat who knows the system well says that it is from those very headquarters that Haiti's army, with the police and the FRAPH, has run a web of clandestine torture houses (one of them in a private home at No. 43 Fontamara), some of which are said to still be working as this article is written on the occupation's seventeenth day. According to the diplomat—who quoted internal documents as he spoke—the walkie-talkies of house personnel are routinely monitored by the U.S. Embassy, which, he said, also listened in on conversations of the U.N. Civilian Mission. Some interrogators wear shirts emblazoned "Camp d'Application" (an army base). The diplomat also detailed a command structure of seven chief attachés who have arranged killings and brought victims to the torture houses.

Four of those senior attachés (as well as other, lower-ranking ones), according to documents and interviews, appear to have worked out of the Centers for Development and Health (C.D.S.), a large multiservice clinic funded mainly by the U.S. Agency for International Development. One of them, Gros Sergo (who was killed in September 1993), listed C.D.S. on his résumé, writing that he worked in its archives and was a "Trainer of Associates" there. Another, Fritz Joseph—who, Constant says, is the key FRAPH recruiter in Cité Soleil and who, according to official records, has been a chief attaché since the coup—is acknowledged by the C.D.S. director to have worked at C.D.S. for many years. The two others, Marc Arthur and Gros Fanfan (implicated by the U.N. in the September 1993 murder of prominent pro-Aristide businessman Antoine Izmery), have been named in sworn statements as having regularly received cash payments from C.D.S. Constant confirms that FRAPH leaders and attachés are working inside C.D.S. (and specifically that Marc Arthur has worked there) and says he speaks often on the phone with the clinic's director, Dr. Reginald Boulos. Boulos denies that he speaks to Constant. He says that Sergo's résumé is wrong, that he does not knowingly employ attachés, and that he did not know until recently that Fritz Joseph was a FRAPH leader and that he fired him when critics pointed out that he was. Boulos said that C.D.S.

files track "every family in Cité Soleil" but insisted that, as far as he knows, attachés don't have access to the archives. Boulos said he hadn't seen Sergo in years, and when told of an entry from Sergo's calender that appeared to contradict that, he said it was mistaken. He also downplayed the fact that Sergo had listed him as a personal reference, along with coup leader Raoul Cédras. (Another A.I.D.-funded unit in Haiti, Planning Assistance, has also said that it employs FRAPH personnel.)

Sergo's papers indicate that he reported to the now-exiled Police Chief, Lieut. Col. Michel François (he had a pass, written on the back of François's card, authorizing him and Marc Arthur "to see the Chief of Police at all hours of the day and night"), that he and his hit squad organized anti-Aristide demonstrations, that, just before his work for C.D.S., he was in the Interior Ministry's "intelligence police," and that he had appointments to meet with the C.I.A.'s SIN chief, Col. Silvain Diderot, and with the Mevs, one of Haiti's ruling families.

Though some Haitian officials claim that François was on the C.I.A. payroll, this is denied by Lawrence Pezzullo, the former U.S. special envoy to Haiti. But Pezzullo did reveal that the C.I.A. paid François's brother, Evans, now a diplomat in the Dominican Republic. (Pezzullo joked, regarding the colonel himself, "You couldn't pay him enough to buy him.")

The FRAPH emerged as a national force in the latter months of 1993, when it staged a series of murders, public beatings and arson raids on poor neighborhoods. In one such attack, Mrs. Alerte Belance had her right hand severed by a machete.

Later, when it was convenient for him, President Clinton used photos of these macabre assaults to (accurately) brand Haiti's rulers as "armed thugs [who] have conducted a reign of terror." But, in the moment when that terror was actually at its height, Clinton used the FRAPH killings to pressure Aristide harshly to "broaden" his already broad Cabinet in a "power-sharing" deal. Pezzullo, in part echoing Collins's original vision for Constant (though he denies any knowledge of the arrangement), says that the FRAPH was "a political offset to Lavalas" and that as the "bodies were starting to appear" "we said [to Aristide]: The only people seen operating politically now are the FRAPHistas," and that he and the United States had to "fill that gap with another force with the private sector—otherwise these FRAPH people will be the only game in town."

It is often pointed out that the FRAPH embarrassed the United States by chasing off the transport ship Harlan County last year, but in that case U.S. officials could not agree about whether the ship should even be there. Constant says he got no U.S. guidance, but he had openly announced his dockside rally the day before and apparently did not get any U.S. warning to call it off.

On the fundamentals, though, U.S. officials have been united in pressing Aristide from the right. Constant said in our first interview (well before his Marine press conference) that he might now be "too high profile" for the United States. But even if he is, U.S.intelligence is a *system*, not dependent on any single individual. And—as Constant once taught about Aristide—there are others in the wings.

1953

•

Dylan Thomas and I got drunk on the same night
in the same city. He did it with style.
He stood at the bar downing shot after shot
while reciting the poems of Thomas Hardy until
that enormous voice filled the world. Meanwhile
in a hotel room off Central Park I sat alone
staring out the window as the spring night came on
wondering where she was, the dark-haired woman
who promised she would show. That was 1953,
his time was running out; mine was not, yet
it was he was who was full of fire and language and I
—not yet twenty-six—could not even cry out
against the evening falling between the trees
and the filthy window that gave me back only me,
the bedside table with its lamp, the silent TV,
and no more. I thought I was seeing who I was
when I wasn't, when I closed my eyes and saw half
of what was there. When he closed his did he see
my darkness? Your darkness? Or did he see
from the hills above Swansea the world he'd left,
the small houses crowded together like children
afraid of their parents, the church steeple, tiny
from so far off, the harbor, the sea deepening
as dusk settled down and separate lights came on?

Philip Levine

CHARACTER IN BIOGRAPHY

Carol Brightman

•

IN THE SECOND year of my maiden voyage into biography, early in 1986, when I was still writing history, and the character of my subject, Mary McCarthy, lay submerged in her tank, I came across the following piece of advice from Edmund Wilson:

> It is important in writing a biography to remember that you are telling a story, and the problems of presenting the material are in many ways just the same as those of presenting a subject in fiction. You cannot take for granted on the part of the reader any knowledge of your particular subject. You will have to introduce it to him so that he will understand it every step of the way, and you have to create your characters and backgrounds and situations just as you would those of fiction.

Characters, backgrounds and situations, in other words, along with ideas, I might add, must be made to stand on their own, even though they're drawn from events existing outside them.

This is no news to most biographers, or to the theoreticians of biography, now massed in academe, who never tire of discoursing on biography's traffic with fiction, all the more because professional questions of genre—of turf—are involved. As they are, as well, in autobiography, whose scholar/critics, haunted by Foucault, struggle to position themselves in relation to discourses on "truth" and "identity" when they are not policing gender hierarchies. "Stabilizing the canon," Leigh Gilmore calls it in *Autobiographics: A Feminist Theory of Women's Self Representation* (Cornell).

For me, Wilson's reminder was a revelation. I'm sure it encouraged me to step back from the index cards I had accumulated on the intellectual life of the 1920s, '30s and '40s, which is what I did in February that year, plunging straightaway into the thick of a story that had been ringing in my ears ever since I heard it from Mary McCarthy the summer before.

In *Writing Dangerously*, the scene opens Chapter 10, "Seduction and Betrayal":

> It started late one Saturday morning in October 1937, when Mary McCarthy arrived at *Partisan Review's* office near Union Square. She wore a slinky black dress and her Grandmother Preston's fox stole, remnants of the Vassar years. Edmund Wilson was there, "short, stout, middle-aged, breathy . . . ," wearing a two piece gray suit and a white shirt. Introductions were made, and Wilson complimented Miss McCarthy on her reviews in *The Nation*. . . . But his eyes, faintly bulging in the photographs of the period ("popping reddish-brown eyes," McCarthy describes them), made a swift appraisal. She had been noticed and she knew it.

Stripped of the quoted material about Wilson, which I added later, after McCarthy had written the story up herself shortly before her death in 1989, this is the paragraph that set me on my course.

What "started late one Saturday morning" was McCarthy's secret courtship and marriage to Wilson (only four months later), and with it, briefly, her career as a madwoman, followed by a longer-running performance as a dramatist of memory and an author of scandalous fictions. (Her critical talents were already in place.) But the "it" that had finally started was also the book itself, which, like a certain kind of fiction, found its throughline only after the primary characters were caught in the act of being themselves.

Character, in my opinion, is always the starting point, but not necessarily the end, of biography. An interesting character, one who acts outside the norms of society but whose work or deeds survive to illuminate that society (and perhaps some recesses of our own), may, in the hands of a thoughtful storyteller, offer a vision of an age all but lost to conventional wisdom. Such, in any event, was the expectation that guided me in writing about Mary McCarthy. The dissenters' dissenter, whose critical faculties remained intact long after those of many of her contemporaries had ossified, she offers a perch from which the complicated legacy of the last great age of ideas can be explored anew.

"Concerning the Age which has just passed," Lytton Strachey writes in *Eminent Victorians*, "our fathers and our grandfathers have poured forth and accumulated so vast a quantity of information . . . that the perspicacity of a Gibbon would quail before it." I have always felt the same about the 1930s and '40s (whose fathers and grandfathers had been more garrulous); another "singular age," whose secrets, I hoped, you might submit to Strachey's "subtler strategy" of "attack-[ing] his subject in unexpected places; falling upon the flank, or the rear." The military metaphor couldn't be more Edwardian, but Strachey, who pioneered the "New Biography," remains one of a handful of biographers who have done justice to what he himself called "the most delicate and humane of all the branches of the art of writing." Hence, the lasting appeal of *Eminent Victorians*, whose four portraits of English eccentrics, traditionally cast as paragons of pious rectitude—Cardinal Manning, Florence Nightingale, Dr. Thomas Arnold and General Gordon of Khartoum—remain as provocative today as they were seventy-five years ago.

Here is Strachey on the end of General C. G. Gordon, formerly known as Chinese Gordon for his defeat of the Taiping Rebellion, a man whose service to the Empire was strangely colored by the fact that "his admiration was reserved for his enemies." Thirteen years after Gordon's bloody fall at Khartoum in 1884 at the hands of the Sudanese Mahdi—and indirectly, of the Governor-General in Cairo, Sir Evelyn Baring, who refused to order relief troops until it was too late—British forces had finally smashed the Mahdi's kingdom. After that, "it was thought proper that a religious ceremony in honor of General Gordon should be held at the Palace at Khartoum," Strachey writes. Led by Catholic, Anglican, Presbyterian and Methodist chaplains, the service ended with a performance of "Abide With Me," the General's favorite hymn, by an elite company of Sudanese buglers.

> Everyone agreed that General Gordon had been avenged at last. Who could doubt it? General Gordon himself, possibly, fluttering, in some remote Nirvana, the pages of a phantasmal Bible, might have ventured on a satirical remark. But General Gordon had always been a contradictious person—even a little off his head, perhaps, though a hero; and besides he was no longer there to contradict . . . At any rate it had all ended very happily—in a glorious slaughter of twenty thousand Arabs,

a vast addition to the British Empire, and a step in the Peerage for Sir Evelyn Baring.

An exemplary passage, alongside which much contemporary biography withers, not only for lack of wit and style but also because it wants historical imagination. Strachey's finale has everything Wilson ordered, and more: background and foreground, the character's spirit flying in the face of the spirit of the age, which is also invoked, along with the biographer's appreciation of history's swift reversals, heightened by the narrator's ironic detachment from precisely those events that deeply move him.

This construction of the past couldn't be more different from the piling up of documentary fact and testimony, like overstuffed furniture on a stage that passes for history in standard biographies. Nor does it resemble the clinical dissections of personal history popular in many current biographies and memoirs, whose subjects, like patients etherized upon a table, fail to come to life—very often, I think, because they have been drained of their public lives. Of course, the comparison is not really fair. Most biographers today are innocent of any entanglement with history, past or present, as they are unencumbered by a dramatic concept of character, "formed in the world's torrent," as Goethe put it.

Biography, as a genre, has undergone a fundamental shift in recent decades, one that has taken it closer not to fiction, whose techniques it will always use, but to what the market in its infinite wisdom calls "Advice, How-To and Miscellaneous." Especially among women writing about women for women (who today account for 60 percent of biography's readers), "curiosity" has been replaced by "caring . . . as the dominant reason for continuing to read. Identification with the subject," Linda Wagner-Martin notes approvingly in her version of "The New Biography," *Telling Women's Lives* (Rutgers), "is the attraction of the form."

Wagner-Martin, a professor of English and comparative literature at the University of North Carolina and one of the Sylvia Plath biographers inspected in Janet Malcolm's *The Silent Woman* (Knopf), goes on to argue that "the biographer's positive depictions are what readers expect," on the assumption that the only "logical reason for any biographer's choice of subject . . . is admiration"—as if biography was a lonely hearts club for women seeking affirmation from other women. The same brief extends to autobiography, whose protagonists are exhorted to select "events that will make the plot both plausible and dramatic," while still gaining their readers' "admiration and their compassion."

Wagner-Martin is so serenely unaware of the retrograde nature of this position, a feminist variation of the hagiography Lytton Strachey battled, that one shrinks from taking her book seriously. And yet the idea that biography and autobiography should be good for women, "instructing us about our lives," as Jill Ker Conway asserts in *Written By Herself*, an anthology of autobiographical extracts by prominent American women, is very much around. As is the related demand, which Wagner-Martin ascribes to Carolyn Heilbrun, that the biographer should always "let the reader know where she or he stands on the topic in question."

This last was a complaint Heilbrun lodged against *Writing Dangerously* in *The Women's Review of Books* in January 1993; namely, that "it is far from clear how Brightman felt about McCarthy," whom Heilbrun clearly abhorred ("a nasty woman of vaulting ambition, capable neither of compassion nor of revealing the hidden wound that made compassion forever impossible"). What did she mean? I wondered at the time. For the notion that a biographer should stand in judgment of her subject's personal life—which is what concerned Heilbrun— together with the proviso that "the biographer must both deeply respect and simply like her subject," would seem to violate biography's Hippocratic oath. That is, that "it is not [the biographer's] business to be complimentary" (Strachey again), much less to rap knuckles when the subject offends public morals, but rather "to lay bare the facts of the case, as he understands them . . . dispassionately, impartially, and without ulterior interests."

Of course, it's no longer so simple, if it ever was. And Strachey's canon is nowhere more suspect than among feminist critics for whom "objectivity" has come to be regarded as a male construct, and adherence to it something like fellow-traveling on the wrong side of the gender war. In *Telling Women's Lives*, this line of thinking leads Wagner-Martin to assert that Edith Wharton, Ellen Glasgow and Willa Cather had to play "the male literary game" when they were writing their first fiction, because the novels they learned to write from were "European, Russian, and British, all very masculine in language and theme. The normal literary sentence was what could be called masculine," she reports blithely, quoting a toothsome passage from *The Pickwick Papers* to show that "one aim of serious nineteenth-century writing was to impress the reader with the writer's vocabulary, ease of syntactic movement, and sonority."

Biography itself, meanwhile, has entered a hall of mirrors, where the motives of biographers, their clandestine relations with sources and subjects (dead or alive), not to mention the forces behind a reviewer's hidden hand, have usurped objective considerations of the quality of the portraiture, most notably in the influential book-length essay by Janet Malcolm. Following Malcolm down the Rue Morgue of Plath biographers, one feels an excitement probably unmatched by a perusal of any of the five biographies.

The ability of this Macavity of West 43rd Street to slowly, gently divest her subjects of their professional and personal *amour-propre*, while chatting over tea and biscuits, is a kind of literary ravishment that is fascinating to watch. It reminds me of a night in Hamburg in the summer of 1960 when my father, having found a suitable cabaret for his family not far from our hotel, sat astonished, as did his wife and daughter, while the pretty blond girl at the piano was slowly, meticulously stripped of her frock and undergarments by the music-master.

One wishes Malcolm's territory extended beyond literary politics and the art world—beyond highbrow entertainment, guaranteed not to ruffle advertising feathers—to more challenging turf such as Wall Street, the foundation circuit or publishing. But it's only fair to assess her on home ground. In *The Silent Woman*, that means evaluating Malcolm's fervent defense of Plath's former husband, Britain's poet laureate Ted Hughes, first against the hollow-eyed deconstructionists, "libbers" and advocates of "dead lib" (who "want to restore to Sylvia Plath the rights she lost when she died"), and then against the charge that in destroying one, possibly two, of Plath's journals, covering the three years before her suicide in February 1963, Hughes censored his estranged wife's literary archive.

With some exceptions (A. Alvarez and Jacqueline Rose are not entirely disposed of), Malcolm succeeds in outmaneuvering the biographers and journalists who, like Wagner-Martin, rest their case with the "suicidal poetess" against the faithless husband. Malcolm's own vivid identification with the "uneasy, shifty-eyed generation" that grew up in the 1950s, which included Plath, the biographer Anne Stevenson and herself—"the three of us were almost the same age," Malcolm points out—introduces a historical context that is missing from the prevailing construct of Plath as "the abandoned and mistreated woman." It also fills in a piece of the emotional ground underlying Malcolm's odd attraction to Hughes, whose letters, with their "clotted, irregular unrepentantly messy pages brought back the letters we [Malcolm's friends] used to write one another in the nineteen-fifties and sixties on our manual Olivettis and Smith Coronas."

Ted Hughes supplies Janet Malcolm with her motive, the one "the writer, like the murderer, needs . . . Writing," she asserts in a much-quoted passage, "cannot be done in a state of desirelessness." To rid the princely Hughes of his harpies, even to bump off his ally Anne Stevenson—whose book (marred by a "pallid judiciousness") was disparaged, Malcolm suggests, because "nobody wanted to hear it was Hughes who was good and Plath bad"—is the challenge she has set herself. That she embraces it with flags waving, declaring her "tenderness toward Hughes . . . his reality, his aliveness, his stuckness," right from the start, is what gives this *essai à clef* its panache.

Malcolm's more serious argument, and the one likely to outlast the defense of Ted Hughes, is the debunking of the possibility of objectivity in biography. "The pose of fair-mindedness, the charade of even-handedness, the striking of an attitude of detachment," Malcolm contends, "can never be more than rhetorical ruses; if they were genuine, if the writer *actually* didn't care one way or the other how things came out, he would not bestir himself to represent them."

It is a strange assertion, which confuses caring with taking sides. One might argue, on the contrary, that genuine curiosity about the subject is what keeps a biographer honest. You want to gaze at him or her from unexpected angles, avoid conventional poses, question easy judgments. You would like to spare this character with whom you have to live on such intimate terms for so long the donkey work of being somebody's hero or someone's villain. If historically your subject has been both, as Mary McCarthy was and remains, well, then, you report that. You put it in the story that the story never ends.

But you don't have to take sides. If you've done your homework, honored the facts in the case, and the counter-facts—the ambiguities in the record—the sides will assert themselves. Most readers, in any event, will continue to find what they expect, no matter what you do. Carolyn Heilbrun will find her "man's woman," and wonder how the biographer let McCarthy get away with her nasty gossip about Simone de Beauvoir. McCarthy's good friend Frances FitzGerald will find her life "celebrated" in the book, "warts and all [as] she would wish."

I myself found in Mary McCarthy "the agent for my liberation," as I wrote to her happily in April 1985, from the New York Public Library's Allen Room on 42nd Street, where I had settled in after leaving *Geo* magazine and signing a contract for the book. "In a stroke," I continued, "I have been licensed to work alone, to study, to think & to write . . . a source of unspeakable satisfaction."

There was more to it than that. There was certain correspondences without which I would not have made the effort or felt the pleasure I did in making it. One went back to 1958 when I read *Memories of a Catholic Girlhood* at Vassar, and was in the throes of "losing my faith," as Mary McCarthy does in the book, in a scene, at a Sacred Heart convent retreat, that was familiar to me. She was younger, and the circumstances were different, but the mingled fear and elation that she evokes when she finally walks away from the priest who has been arguing for her salvation echoed what I felt then.

It was my first encounter with this writer, a woman and living (two strokes against her at the University of Chicago, where there was opposition to overcome from my thesis adviser Norman Maclean when I made McCarthy the subject of a master's paper in 1962, along with Simone de Beauvoir and Anaïs Nin); but already we shared a turning point. Later, I became more interested in her political and intellectual life in the 1930s, '40s and '60s, when Vietnam brought us together; and in her talent for dramatizing the moral dilemmas of her generation of radicals. But that first brush, largely subliminal, was the seed.

The biographer's relationship with the biographee—which can blossom in the course of writing into an unseemly intimacy, as the newly fashionable confessions of biographers attest—is a fascinating thing: almost theatrical in its manifestation. Nowhere is this more evident than at biography conferences, whose participants, having been closeted with their eminences for years, come out to defend their impersonations. I could hear it in my own voice at a biography seminar in Key West in January 1994, when a certain declamatory rise and fall of timbre announced the arrival of a Mary McCarthyism. And it was sheer Broadway when Blanche Wiesen Cook slipped into Eleanor Roosevelt—Franklin, too—and Off Broadway when David Levering Lewis merged with W. E. B. Du Bois.

Lewis's moment occurred during a discussion of his use of Freudian analysis to understand Du Bois's contradictory relations with women. As is often the case when biographers touch on personally relevant aspects of their subjects' lives (Cook, brightening, when she observed how "many of our most important foremothers were voluptuaries, *really!*"), Lewis's ordinarily avuncular voice quickened when he described the contrast between Du Bois's principled feminism and his poor treatment of women. "I was grateful," he said, "when a few psychologists allowed me to impersonate Du Bois and talk about his mother and the other women in my life." *My life.*

Far from muddying the waters, such projections enliven the enterprise, and rescue biography from the flatness of narrative to which it is prone. If Hannah Arendt's biographer Elisabeth Young-Bruehl is correct in contending that to empathize with your subject means not " 'putting yourself in another's place . . . [but] putting another person *in yourself*, becoming another person's habitat' " (and I think she is right), then this sort of psychic leakage is bound to occur. The danger arises when the biographer's ego, in need of reinforcement, swallows the subject whole; or reshapes the life to enhance its own fragile image, or to validate images that are thrown up by powerful agencies in the surrounding culture.

This last phenomenon is evidenced by the cluster effect one sees in biography, which has fads like everything else: sexual deviance and abuse cashing in as ingredients most likely to meet the current demand for the nitty-gritty. But the reshaping of a subject's life may also spring from what Sharon O'Brien, the author of *Willa Cather: The Emerging Voice*, calls the "critical conversations" available to biographers at the time of writing.

"Without the feminist scholarship that was exploding around me," O'Brien writes in "My Willa Cather: How Writing Her Story Shaped My Own" (*The New York Times Book Review*, February 20, 1994), "I simply could not have told the story of Cather's literary emergence in the way that I did." That was to present her "not only as a woman writer trying to find a voice within a male literary tradition but also as a lesbian writer," something Cather, who vigilantly guarded her privacy, didn't want addressed.

Whether or not this retelling of Cather's early life deepens our understanding of her life and work, I cannot say, not having read the book (which leaves the second half of Cather's complex career "unnarrated . . . because," O'Brien remarks, "it did not mesh with the tale of emergence I then found so compelling"). But it is not reassuring to be told the author "felt called or chosen to tell this story . . . [of] Cather's movement from silence into speech," not because the feminist perspective she adopted offered such tantalizing analytical tools but because "I wanted to move beyond my own silences." "Like hers," O'Brien asserts, "they were not absences of language but language shaped for the approval of others. In writing her story," she hoped, "perhaps I could shape my own."

Cather, she gambled, would help her "escape from scholarly obscurity." By standing up to a powerful figure, moreover, who disdained "literary upstarts" and meddlesome professors, O'Brien might exorcise a genie who had undermined her confidence in herself, "a certain kind of woman—powerful, self-involved, convinced of her own rightness," who intimidated her "more profoundly than the most patriarchal male." Behind Willa Cather stood "a gargantuan gym teacher . . . a humorless nun . . . and farther back, my own mother, whose interrogations always left me speechless."

With concerns such as these, we have entered the gaseous realm of psychotherapy, the kind that extends to Jill Conway's appropriation of the uses of female autobiography to help us "examine our own inner texts with these powerful models in mind . . ." The hallmark of this drama is the Dream, in which the biographer confronts the great figure, as O'Brien does when she dreams that Cather invites her to her Bank Street apartment in New York for tea. " 'I want you to know,' she said, pouring me a cup, 'that I am not gay.' 'What about the letters to Louise Pound [Cather's friend from the University of Nebraska]?' " O'Brien asks, whereupon the figure vanished.

In another dream, Cather's companion Edith Lewis telephones to ask that the word "lesbian" be left out of the book. When O'Brien tells her that isn't possible, she hangs up. In either case, O'Brien couldn't tell if she had "silenced or convinced" her interlocutor; only that "what was happening was the subtle power shift that eventually occurs in a biography: I, the once powerless daughter, was becoming a literary mother."

A biographer's archetype, the nocturnal encounter with the master, is the climax of a Henry James story, "The Real Right Thing," in which the angry ghost of a dead "man of letters" persuades his would-be scribe to abandon the project. In "Terminating Mark Rothko: Biography Is Mourning in Reverse" (*The New York Times Book Review*, July 24, 1994), James E. B. Breslin, who relates this story, presents a dream of his own. Like O'Brien's it is more reassuring.

He meets Rothko on the subway, strikes up a conversation, careful not to offend the great man, who is subject to violent outbursts, and is gratified to see that Rothko "likes" him, thinks he's "funny." Emboldened, he confesses he has written a biography (*Mark Rothko: A Biography*). Rothko doesn't "object." Breslin is "amazed to find that he didn't actually kill himself, that he's been alive all along," and quickly arranges to visit him the next day to get material for new sections of his book.

Naturally, biographers dream of winning their "awesome and powerful" subjects' approval, Breslin proposes, because they have "penetrated" their "secrets," blown their cover. They're uneasy, and need reassurance. Nevertheless, "that transgression is itself very pleasurable," Breslin adds, which is why he really "brought Rothko back to life, so his life could go on, so *I* could go on, writing his life forever."

Remedial biography, one might call it. Meanwhile, there is a not-so-subtle "power shift" in Breslin's dream, too; a masculine fantasy, in which he and Rothko "circle around each other," as in "a boxing match in which an aging heavyweight . . . has been put in the ring with a younger fighter, smaller and faster, more 'a student of the art.' " It's Hemingway straining to get into the ring with Tolstoy: another trope. Is Breslin aware of it? Does Sharon O'Brien recognize the Electra myth shimmering behind "the once powerless daughter . . . becoming a literary mother"?

Like the biographer in Henry James's story, who occupies his dead friend's study, reads his books, stirs his fire and fancies the great man becoming his "mystic assistant" because, in fact, he wants to supplant him, Breslin and O'Brien are not really interested in discovering the sources of Rothko's or Cather's achievement—at least not in these reflections. It is not their subjects' stories that enthrall them but their own.

Maybe this is the neo-New Biography. Not "the revenge of little people on big ones," as Edmund White calls "the moralizing energy" behind so much contemporary biography, but something like it. No doubt the biographers' stories, cloaked in literary journalism's psychobabble, will be supplanted in a few years by other *divertissements*. Biographies that outlast a season—Isaac Deutscher's Trotsky trilogy, Justin Kaplan's *Walt Whitman*, Elisabeth Young-Bruehl's *Hannah Arendt: For Love of the World*, Elizabeth Frank's *Louise Bogan*—will continue to be produced by writers for whom there is a real world out there, with real people in it: not a desert inhabited by people spouting "texts." *Luftmenschen*, Hannah Arendt might have called them: air people. Not tongues in trees, sermons in stone or books in running brooks either, but trees, stones, brooks are what we want—and writers for whom character is an index of history.

RACISM HAS ITS PRIVILEGES

Roger Wilkins

•

THE STORM THAT has been gathering over affirmative action for the past few years has burst. Two conservative California professors are leading a drive to place an initiative on the state ballot in 1996 that will ask Californians to vote affirmative action up or down. Since the state is beloved in political circles for its electoral votes, advance talk of the initiative has put the issue high on the national agenda. Three Republican presidential contenders—Bob Dole, Phil Gramm and Lamar Alexander—have already begun taking shots at various equal opportunity programs. Congressional review of the Clinton Administration's enforcement of these programs has begun. The President has started his own review, promising adherence to principles of nondiscrimination and full opportunity while asserting the need to prune those programs that are unfair or malfunctioning.

It is almost an article of political faith that one of the major influences in last November's election was the backlash against affirmative action among "angry white men," who are convinced it has stacked the deck against them. Their attitudes are shaped and their anger heightened by unquestioned and virtually uncheckable anecdotes about victimized whites flooding the culture. For example, *Washington Post* columnist Richard Cohen recently began what purported to be a serious analysis and attack on affirmative action by recounting that he had once missed out on a job someplace because they "needed a woman."

Well, I have an anecdote too, and it, together with Cohen's, offers some important insights about the debate that has flared recently around the issues of race, gender and justice. Some years ago, after watching me teach as a visiting professor for two semesters, members of the history department at George Mason University invited me to compete for a full professorship and endowed chair. Mason, like other institutions in Virginia's higher education system, was under a court order to desegregate. I went through the appropriate application and review process and, in due course, was appointed. A few years later, not long after I had been honored as one of the university's distinguished professors, I was shown an article by a white historian asserting that he had been a candidate for that chair but that at the last moment the job had been whisked away and handed to an unqualified black. I checked the story and discovered that this fellow had, in fact, applied but had not even passed the first threshold. But his "reverse discrimination" story is out there polluting the atmosphere in which this debate is taking place.

Affirmative action, as I understand it, was not designed to punish anyone; it was, rather—as a result of a clear-eyed look at how America actually works—an attempt to enlarge opportunity for *everybody*. As amply documented in the 1968 Kerner Commission report on racial disorders, when left to their own devices, American institutions in such areas as college admissions, hiring decisions and loan approvals had been making choices that discriminated against blacks. That discrimination, which flowed from doing what came naturally, hurt more than blacks: It hurt the entire nation, as the riots of the late 1960s demonstrated. Though the Kerner report focused on blacks, similar findings could have been made about other minorities and women.

Affirmative action required institutions to develop plans enabling them to go beyond business as usual and search for qualified people in places where they did not ordinarily conduct their searches or their business. Affirmative action programs generally require some proof that there has been a good-faith effort to follow the plan and numerical guidelines against which to judge the sincerity and the success of the effort. The idea of affirmative action *is not* to force people into positions for which they are unqualified but to encourage institutions to develop realistic criteria for the enterprise at hand and then to find a reasonably diverse mix of people qualified to be engaged in it. Without the requirements calling for plans, good-faith efforts and the setting of broad numerical goals, many institutions would do what they had always done: assert that they had looked but "couldn't find anyone qualified," and then go out and hire the white man they wanted to hire in the first place.

Affirmative action has done wonderful things for the United States by enlarging opportunity and developing and utilizing a far broader array of the skills available in the American population than in the past. It has not outlived its usefulness. It was never designed to be a program to eliminate poverty. It has not always been used wisely, and some of its permutations do have to be reconsidered, refined or, in some cases, abandoned. It is not a quota program, and those cases where rigid numbers are used (except under a court or administrative order after a specific finding of discrimination) are a bastardization of an otherwise highly beneficial set of public policies.

President Clinton is right to review what is being done under present laws and to express a willingness to eliminate activities that either don't work or are unfair. Any program that has been in place for thirty years should be reviewed.

Getting rid of what doesn't work is both good government and good politics. Gross abuses of affirmative action provide ammunition for its opponents and undercut the moral authority of the entire effort. But the President should retain—and strengthen where required—those programs necessary to enlarge social justice.

What makes the affirmative action issue so difficult is that it engages blacks and whites exactly at those points where they differ the most. There are some areas, such as rooting for the local football team, where their experiences and views are virtually identical. There are others— sometimes including work and school—where their experiences and views both overlap and diverge. And finally, there are areas such as affirmative action and inextricably related notions about the presence of racism in society where the divergences draw out almost all the points of difference between the races.

THIS LAND IS MY LAND

Blacks and whites experience America very differently. Though we often inhabit the same space, we operate in very disparate psychic spheres.

Whites have an easy sense of ownership of the country; they feel they are entitled to receive all that is best in it. Many of them believe that their country—though it may have some faults—is superior to all others and that, as Americans, they are superior as well. Many of them think of this as a white country and some of them even experience it that way. They think of it as a land of opportunity—a good place with a lot of good people in it. Some suspect (others *know*) that the presence of blacks messes everything up.

To blacks there's nothing very easy about life in America, and any sense of ownership comes hard because we encounter so much resistance in making our way through the ordinary occurrences of life. And I'm not even talking here about overt acts of discrimination but simply about the way whites intrude on and disturb our psychic space without even thinking about it.

A telling example of this was given to me by a black college student in Oklahoma. He said whites give him looks that say: "What are *you* doing here?"

"When do they give you that look?" I asked.

"Every time I walk in a door," he replied.

When he said that, every black person in the room nodded and smiled in a way that indicated recognition based on thousands of such moments in their own lives.

For most blacks, America is either a land of denied opportunity or one in which the opportunities are still grudgingly extended and extremely limited. For some—that one-third who are mired in poverty, many of them isolated in dangerous ghettos—America is a land of desperadoes and desperation. In places where whites see a lot of idealism, blacks see, at best, idealism mixed heavily with hypocrisy. Blacks accept America's greatness, but are unable to ignore ugly warts that many whites seem to need not to see. I am reminded here of James Baldwin's searing observation from *The Fire Next Time*:

> The American Negro has the great advantage of having never believed that collection of myths to which white Americans cling: that their ancestors were all freedom-loving heroes, that they were born in the greatest country the world has ever seen, or that Americans are invincible in battle and wise in peace, that Americans have always dealt honorably with Mexicans and Indians and all other neighbors or inferiors, that American men are the world's most direct and virile, that American women are pure.

It goes without saying, then, that blacks and whites remember America differently. The past is hugely important since we argue a lot about who we are on the basis of who we think we have been, and we derive much of our sense of the future from how we think we've done in the past. In a nation in which few people know much history these are perilous arguments; because in such a vacuum, people tend to weave historical fables tailored to their political or psychic needs.

Blacks are still recovering the story of their role in America, which so many white historians simply ignored or told in ways that made black people ashamed. But in a culture that batters us, learning the real history is vital in helping blacks feel fully human. It also helps us understand just how deeply American we are, how richly we have given, how much has been taken from us and how much has yet to be restored. Supporters of affirmative action believe that broad and deep damage has been done to American culture by racism and sexism over the whole course of American history and that they are still powerful forces today. We believe that minorities and women are still disadvantaged in our highly competitive society and that affirmative action is absolutely necessary to level the playing field.

Not all white Americans oppose this view and not all black Americans support it. There are a substantial number of whites in this country who have been able to escape our racist and sexist past and to enter fully into the quest for equal justice. There are other white Americans who are not racists but who more or less passively accept the powerful suggestions coming at them from all points in the culture that whites are entitled to privilege and to freedom from competition with blacks. And then there are racists who just don't like blacks or who actively despise us. There are still others who may or may not feel deep antipathy, but who know how to manipulate racism and white anxiety for their own ends. Virtually all the people in the last category oppose affirmative action and some of them make a practice of preying upon those in the second category who are not paying attention or who, like the *Post*'s Richard Cohen, are simply confused.

THE POLITICS OF DENIAL

One of these political predators is Senate majority leader Bob Dole. In his offhandedly lethal way, Dole delivered a benediction of "let me now forgive us" on *Meet the Press* recently. After crediting affirmative action for the 62 percent of the white male vote garnered by the Republicans, he remarked that slavery was "before we were born" and wondered whether future generations ought to have to continue "paying a price" for those ancient wrongs.

Such a view holds that whatever racial problems we once may have had have been solved over the course of the past thirty years and that most of our current racial friction is caused by racial and gender preferences that almost invariably work to displace some "qualified" white male. Words and phrases like "punish" or "preference" or "reverse discrimination" or "quota" are dropped into the discourse to buttress this view, as are those anecdotes about injustice to whites. Proponents of affirmative action see these arguments as disingenuous but ingenious because they reduce serious and complex social, political, economic, historical and psychological issues to bumpersticker slogans designed to elicit Pavlovian responses.

The fact is that the successful public relations assault on affirmative action flows on a river of racism that is as broad, powerful and American as the Mississippi. And, like the Mississippi, racism can be violent and deadly and is a permanent feature of American life. But while nobody who is sane denies the reality of the Mississippi, millions of Americans who are deemed sane—some of whom are powerful and some even thought wise—deny, wholly or in part, that racism exists.

It is critical to understand the workings of denial in this debate because it is used to obliterate the facts that created the need for the remedy in the first place. One of the best examples of denial was provided recently by the nation's most famous former history professor, House Speaker Newt Gingrich. According to *The Washington Post*, "Gingrich dismissed the argument that the beneficiaries of affirmative action, commonly African Americans, have been subjected to discrimination over a period of centuries. 'That is true of virtually every American,' Gingrich said, noting that the Irish were discriminated against by the English, for example."

That is breathtaking stuff coming from somebody who should know that blacks have been on this North American continent for 375 years and that for 245 the country permitted slavery. Gingrich should also know that for the next hundred years we had legalized subordination of blacks, under a suffocating blanket of condescension and frequently enforced by nightriding terrorists. We've had only thirty years of something else.

That something else is a nation trying to lift its ideals out of a thick, often impenetrable slough of racism. Racism is a hard word for what over the centuries became second nature in America—preferences across the board for white men and, following in their wake, white women. Many of these men seem to feel that it is un-American to ask them to share anything with blacks—particularly their work, their neighborhoods or "their" women. To protect these things—apparently essential to their identity—they engage in all forms of denial. For a historian to assert that "virtually every American" shares the history I have just outlined comes very close to lying.

Denial of racism is much like the denials that accompany addictions to alcohol, drugs or gambling. It is probably not stretching the analogy too much to suggest that many racist whites are so addicted to their unwarranted privileges and so threatened by the prospect of losing them that all kinds of defenses become acceptable, including insistent distortions of reality in the form of hypocrisy, lying or the most outrageous political demagogy.

THOSE PEOPLE' DON'T DESERVE HELP

The demagogues have reverted to a new version of quite an old trick. Before the 1950s, whites who were busy denying that the nation was unfair to blacks would simply assert that we didn't deserve equal treatment because we were *inferior*. These days it is not permissible in most public circles to say that blacks are inferior, but it is perfectly acceptable to target the *behavior* of blacks, specifically poor blacks. The argument then follows a fairly predictable line: The behavior of poor blacks requires a severe rethinking of national social policy, it is said. Advantaged blacks really don't need affirmative action anymore, and when they are the objects of such programs, some qualified white person (unqualified white people don't show up in these arguments) is (as Dole might put it) "punished." While it is possible that color-blind affirmative action programs benefiting all disadvantaged Americans are needed, those (i.e., blacks) whose behavior is so distressing must be punished by restricting welfare, shriveling the safety net and expanding the prison opportunity. All of that would presumably give us, in William Bennett's words, "what we want—a color-blind society," for which the white American psyche is presumably fully prepared.

There are at least three layers of unreality in these precepts. The first is that the United States is not now and probably never will be a color-blind society. It is the most color-conscious society on earth. Over the course of 375 years, whites have given blacks absolutely no reason to believe that they can behave in a color-blind manner. In many areas of our lives—particularly in employment, housing and education—affirmative action is required to counter deeply ingrained racist patterns of behavior.

Second, while I don't hold the view that all blacks who behave badly are blameless victims of a brutal system, I do believe that many poor blacks have, indeed, been brutalized by our culture, and I know of *no* blacks, rich or poor, who haven't been hurt in some measure by the racism in this country. The current mood (and, in some cases like the Speaker's, the cultivated ignorance) completely ignores the fact that some blacks never escaped the straight line of oppression that ran from slavery through the semislavery of sharecropping to the late mid-century migration from Southern farms into isolated pockets of urban poverty. Their families have always been excluded, poor and without skills, and so they were utterly defenseless when the enormous American economic dislocations that began in the mid-1970s slammed into their communities, followed closely by deadly waves of crack cocaine. One would think that the double-digit unemployment suffered consistently over the past two decades by blacks who were *looking for work* would be a permanent feature of the discussions about race, responsibility, welfare and rights.

But a discussion of the huge numbers of black workers who are becoming economically redundant would raise difficult questions about the efficiency of the economy at a time when millions of white men feel insecure. Any honest appraisal of unemployment would reveal that millions of low-skilled white men were being severely damaged by corporate and Federal Reserve decisions; it might also refocus the anger of those whites in the middle ranks whose careers have been shattered by the corporate downsizing fad.

But people's attention is kept trained on the behavior of some poor blacks by politicians and television news shows, reinforcing the stereotypes of blacks as dangerous, as threats, as unqualified. Frightened whites direct their rage at pushy blacks rather than at the corporations that export manufacturing operations to low-wage countries, or at the Federal Reserve, which imposes interest rate hikes that slow down the economy.

WHO BENEFITS? WE ALL DO

There is one final denial that blankets all the rest. It is that only society's "victims"—blacks, other minorities and women (who should, for God's sake, renounce their victimological outlooks)—have been injured by white male supremacy. Viewed in this light, affirmative action remedies are a kind of zero-sum game in which only the "victims" benefit. But racist and sexist whites who are not able to accept the full humanity of other people are themselves badly damaged— morally stunted—people. The principal product of a racist and sexist society is damaged people and institutions—victims and victimizers alike. Journalism and education, two enterprises with which I am familiar, provide two good examples.

Journalistic institutions often view the nation through a lens that bends reality to support white privilege. A recent issue of *U.S. News & World Report* introduced a package of articles on these issues with a question on its cover: "Does affirmative action mean NO WHITE MEN NEED APPLY?" The words "No white men need apply" were printed in red against a white background and were at least four times larger than the other words in the question. Inside, the lead story was illustrated by a painting that carries out the cover theme, with a wan white man separated from the opportunity ladders eagerly being scaled by women and dark men. And the story yielded up the following sentence. "Affirmative action poses a conflict between two cherished American principles: the belief that all Americans deserve equal opportunities and the idea that hard work and merit, not race or religion or gender or birthright, should determine who prospers and who does not."

Whoever wrote that sentence was in the thrall of one of the myths that Baldwin was talking about. The sentence suggests—as many people do when talking about affirmative action—that America is a meritocratic society. But what kind of meritocracy excludes women and blacks and other minorities from all meaningful competition? And even in the competition among white men, money, family and connections often count for much more than merit, test results (for whatever they're worth) and hard work.

The *U.S. News* story perpetuates and strengthens the view that many of my white students absorb from their parents: that white men now have few chances in this society. The fact is that white men still control virtually everything in America except the wealth held by widows. According to the Urban Institute, 53 percent of black men aged 25-34 are either unemployed or earn too little to lift a family of four from poverty.

Educational institutions that don't teach accurately about why America looks the way it does and why the distribution of winners and losers is as it is also injure our society. Here is another anecdote.

A warm, brilliant young white male student of mine came in just before he was to graduate and said that my course in race, law and culture, which he had just finished, had been the most valuable and the most disturbing he had ever taken. I asked how it had been disturbing.

"I learned that my two heroes are racists," he said.

"Who are your heroes and how are they racists?" I asked.

"My mom and dad," he said. "After thinking about what I was learning, I understood that they had spent all my life making me into the
same kind of racists they were."

Affirmative action had brought me together with him when he was
22. Affirmative action puts people together in ways that make that kind
of revelation possible. Nobody is a loser when that happens. The country gains.

And that, in the end, in the case for affirmative action. The arguments supporting it should be made on the basis of its broad contributions to the entire American community. It is insufficient to vilify white
males and to skewer them as the whiners that journalism of the kind
practiced by *U.S. News* invites us to do. These are people who, from the
beginning of the Republic, have been taught that skin color is destiny
and that whiteness is to be revered. Listen to Jefferson, writing in the
year the Constitution was drafted:

> The first difference that strikes us is that of colour. . . . And is the
> difference of no importance? Is it not the foundation of a greater or less
> share of beauty in the two races? Are not the fine mixtures of red and
> white . . . in the one, preferable to that eternal monotony, which reigns
> in the countenances, that immoveable veil of black which covers all the
> emotions of the other race? Add to these, flowing hair, a more elegant
> symmetry of form, their own judgment in favor of the whites, declared
> by their preference for them, as uniformly as is the preference of the
> Oran-ootan for the black women over those of his own species. The cir-
> cumstance of superior beauty, is thought worthy attention in the propa-
> gation of our horses, dogs, and other domestic animals; why not in that
> of man?

In a society so conceived and so dedicated, it is understandable that
white males would take their preferences as a matter of natural right
and consider any alteration of that a primal offense. But a nation that
operates in that way abandons its soul and its economic strength, and
will remain mired in ugliness and moral squalor because so many people are excluded from the possibility of decent lives and from forming
any sense of community with the rest of society.

Seen only as a corrective for ancient wrongs, affirmative action may
be dismissed by the likes of Gingrich, Gramm and Dole, just as
attempts to federalize decent treatment of the freed slaves were dismissed after Reconstruction more than a century ago. Then, striking
down the Civil Rights Act of 1875, Justice Joseph Bradley wrote of

blacks that "there must be some stage in the progress of his elevation when he takes the rank of a mere citizen, and ceases to be the special favorite of the laws, and when his rights, as a citizen or a man, are to be protected in the ordinary modes by which other men's rights are protected."

But white skin has made some citizens—particularly white males—*the special favorites of the culture*. It may be that we will need affirmative action until most white males are really ready for a color-blind society—that is, when they are ready to assume "the rank of a mere citizen." As a nation we took a hard look at that special favoritism thirty years ago. Though the centuries of cultural preference enjoyed by white males still overwhelmingly skew power and wealth their way, we have in fact achieved a more meritocratic society as a result of affirmative action than we have ever previously enjoyed in this country.

If we want to continue making things better in this society, we'd better figure out ways to protect and defend affirmative action against the confused, the frightened, the manipulators and, yes, the liars in politics, journalism, education and wherever else they may be found. In the name of longstanding American prejudice and myths and in the service of their own narrow interests, power-lusts or blindness, they are truly victimizing the rest of us, perverting the ideals they claim to stand for and destroying the nation they pretend to serve.

ONE VIOLENT CRIME

Bruce Shapiro

•

NEW HAVEN

ALONE IN MY home I am staring at the television screen and shouting. On the evening local news I have unexpectedly encountered video footage, several months old, of myself writhing on an ambulance gurney, bright green shirt open and drenched with blood, skin pale, knee raised, trying desperately and with utter futility to find relief from pain.

On the evening of August 7, 1994, I was among seven people stabbed and seriously wounded in a coffee bar a few blocks from my house. Any televised recollection of this incident would be upsetting. But the anger that has me shouting tonight is quite specific, and political, in origin: My picture is being shown on the news to illustrate why Connecticut's legislature plans to lock up more criminals for a longer time. A picture of my body, contorted and bleeding, has become a propaganda image in the crime war.

I had not planned to write about this assault. But for months now the politics of the nation have in large part been the politics of crime, from last year's federal crime bill through the fall elections through the Contract With America proposals currently awaiting action by the Senate. Among a welter of reactions to the attack, one feeling is clear: I am unwilling to be a silent poster child in this debate.

The physical and political truth about violence and crime lie in their specificity, so here is what happened: I had gone out for after-dinner coffee that evening with two friends and New Haven neighbors, Martin and Anna Broell Bresnick. At 9:45 we arrived at a recently opened coffeehouse on Audubon Street, a block occupied by an arts high school where Anna teaches, other community arts institutions, a few pleasant shops and upscale condos. Entering, we said hello to another friend, a former student of Anna's named Christina Koning, who the day before had started working behind the counter. We sat at a small table near the front of the cafe's; about fifteen people were scattered around the room. Just before 10, the owner announced closing time. Martin stood up and walked a few yards to the counter for a final refill.

Suddenly there was chaos—as if a mortar shell had landed. I looked up, heard Martin call Anna's name, saw his arm raised and a flash of metal and people leaping away from a thin bearded man with a ponytail. Tables and chairs toppled. Without thinking I shouted to Anna, "Get down!" and pulled her to the floor, between our table and the cafe's outer wall. She clung to my shirt, I to her shoulders, and, crouching, we pulled each other toward the door.

What actually happened I was only able to tentatively reconstruct many weeks later. Apparently, as Martin headed toward the counter the thin bearded man, whose name we later learned was Daniel Silva, asked the time from a young man named Richard Colberg, who answered and turned to leave.

Without any warning, Silva pulled out a hunting knife with a six-inch blade and stabbed in the lower back a woman leaving with Colberg, a medical technician named Kerstin Braig. Then he stabbed Colberg, severing an artery in his thigh. Silva was a slight man but he moved with demonic speed and force around the cafe's counter. He struck Martin in the thigh and in the arm he raised to protect his face. Our friend Cris Koning had in a moment's time pushed out the screen in a window and helped the wounded Kerstin Braig through it to safety. Cris was talking on the phone with the police when Silva lunged over the counter and stabbed her in the chest and abdomen. He stabbed Anna in the side as she and I pulled each other along the wall. He stabbed Emily Bernard, a graduate student who had been sitting quietly reading a book, in the abdomen as she tried to flee through the cafe's back door. All of this happened in about the time it has taken you to read this paragraph.

Meanwhile, I had made it out the cafe's front door onto the brick sidewalk with Anna, neither of us realizing yet that she was wounded. Seeing Martin through the window, I returned inside and we came out together. Somehow we separated, fleeing opposite ways down the street. I had gone no more than a few steps when I felt a hard punch in my back followed instantly by the unforgettable sensation of skin and muscle tissue parting. Silva had stabbed me about six inches above my waist, just beneath my rib cage. (That single deep stroke cut my diaphragm and sliced my spleen in half.) Without thinking, I clapped my left hand over the wound even before the knife was out and its blade caught my hand, leaving a slice across my palm and two fingers.

"Why are you doing this?" I cried out to Silva in the moment after feeling his knife punch in and yank out. As I fell to the street he leaned over my face; I vividly the knife's immense and glittering blade. He directed the point through my shirt into the flesh of my chest, beneath my left shoulder. I remember his brown beard, his clear blue-gray eyes looking directly into mine, the round globe of a street lamp like a halo above his head. Although I was just a few feet from a cafe full of people and although Martin and Anna were only yards away, the street, the city, the world felt utterly empty except for me and this thin bearded stranger with clear eyes and a bowie knife. The space around us—well-lit, familiar Audubon Street, where for six years I had taken a child to music lessons—seemed literally to have expanded into a vast and dark canyon.

"You killed my mother," he answered. My own desperate response: "Please don't." Silva pulled the knifepoint out of my chest and disappeared. A moment later I saw him flying down the street on a battered, ungainly bicycle, back straight, vest flapping and ponytail flying.

After my assailant had gone I lay on the sidewalk, hand still over the wound on my back, screaming. Pain ran over me like an express train; it felt as though every muscle in my back was locked and contorted; breathing was excruciating. A security guard appeared across the street from me; I called out to him but he stood there frozen, or so it seemed. (A few minutes later, he would help police chase Silva down.) I shouted to Anna, who was hiding behind a car down the street. Still in shock and unaware of her own injury, she ran for help, eventually collapsing on the stairs of a nearby brownstone where a prayer group that was meeting upstairs answered her desperate ringing of the doorbell. From where I was lying, I saw a second-floor light in the condo complex across the way. A woman's head appeared in the window. "Please help me," I implored. "He's gone. Please help me." She shouted back that she had called the police, but she did not come to the street. I was suddenly aware of a blond woman—Kerstin Braig, though I did not know her name then—in a white-and-gray plaid dress, sitting on the curb. I asked her for help. "I'm sorry, I've done all I can," she muttered. She raised her hand, like a medieval icon; it was covered with blood. So was her dress. She sank into a kind of stupor. Up the street I saw a police car's flashing blue lights, then another's, then I saw an officer with a concerned face and a crackling radio crouched beside me. I stayed conscious as the medics arrived and I was loaded into an ambulance—being filmed for television, as it turns out, though I have no memory of the crew's presence.

Being a victim is a hard idea to accept, even while lying in a hospital bed with tubes in veins, chest, penis and abdomen. The spirit rebels against the idea of oneself as fundamentally powerless. So I didn't think much for the first few days about the meaning of being a victim; I saw no political dimension to my experience.

As I learned in more detail what had happened I thought, in my jumbled-up, anesthetized state, about my injured friends—although everyone survived, their wounds ranged from quite serious to critical—and about my wounds and surgery. I also thought about my assailant. A few facts about him are worth repeating. Until August 7 Daniel Silva was a self-employed junk dealer and a homeowner. He was white. He lived with his mother and several dogs. He had no arrest record. A New Haven police detective who was hospitalized across the hall from me recalled Silva as a socially marginal neighborhood character. He was not, apparently, a drug user. He had told neighbors about much violence in his family—indeed not long before August 7 he showed one neighbor a scar on his thigh he said was from a stab wound.

A week earlier, Silva's 79-year-old mother had been hospitalized for diabetes. After a few days the hospital moved her to a new room; when Silva saw his mother's empty bed he panicked, but nurses swiftly took him to her new location. Still, something seemed to have snapped. Earlier on the day of the stabbings, police say, Silva released his beloved dogs, set fire to his house, and rode away on his bicycle as it burned. He arrived on Audubon Street with a single dog on a leash, evidently convinced his mother was dead. (She actually did die a few weeks after Silva was jailed.)

While I lay in the hospital, the big story on CNN was the federal crime bill then being debated in Congress. Even fogged by morphine I was aware of the irony. I was flat on my back, the result of a particularly violent assault, while Congress eventually passed the anti-crime package I had editorialized against in *The Nation* just a few weeks earlier. Night after night in the hospital, unable to sleep, I watched the crime bill debate replayed and heard Republicans and Democrats (who had sponsored the bill in the first place) fall over each other to prove who could be the toughest on crime.

The bill passed on August 21, a few days after I returned home. In early autumn I actually read the entire text of the crime bill—all 412 pages. What I found was perhaps obvious, yet under the circumstances compelling: Not a single one of those 412 pages would have protected me or Anna or Martin or any of the others from our assailant. Not the enhanced prison terms, not the forty-four new death penalty offenses, not the three-strikes-you're-out requirements, not the summary deportations of criminal aliens. And the new tougher-than-tough anti-crime provisions of the Contract With America, like the proposed abolition of the Fourth Amendment's search and seizure protections, offer no more practical protection.

On the other hand, the mental-health and social-welfare safety net shredded by Reaganomics and conservatives of both parties might have made a difference in the life of someone like my assailant—and thus in the life of someone like me. My assailant's growing distress in the days before August 7 was obvious to his neighbors. He had muttered darkly about relatives planning to burn down his house. A better-funded, more comprehensive safety net might just have saved me and six others from untold pain and trouble.

From my perspective—the perspective of a crime victim—the Contract With America and its conservative Democratic analogs are really blueprints for making the streets even less safe. Want to take away that socialistic income subsidy called welfare? Fine. Connecticut Governor John Rowland proposes cutting off all benefits after eighteen months. So more people in New Haven and other cities will turn to the violence-breeding economy of crack, or emotionally implode from sheer desperation. Cut funding for those soft-headed social workers? Fine; let more children be beaten without the prospect of outside intervention, more Daniel Silvas carrying their own traumatic scars into violent adulthood. Get rid of the few amenities prisoners enjoy, like sports equipment, musical instruments and the right to get college degrees, as proposed by the Congressional right? Fine; we'll make sure that those inmates are released to their own neighborhoods tormented with unchanneled rage.

One thing I could not properly appreciate in the hospital was how deeply many friends, neighbors and acquaintances were shaken by the coffeehouse stabbings, let alone strangers who took the time to write. The reaction of most was a combination of decent horrified empathy and a clear sense that their own presumption of safety was undermined.

But some people who didn't bother to acquaint themselves with the facts used the stabbings as a sort of Rorschach test on which they projected their own preconceptions about crime, violence and New Haven. Some present and former Yale students, for instance, were desperate to see in my stabbing evidence of the great dangers of New Haven's inner city. One student newspaper wrote about "New Haven's image as a dangerous town fraught with violence." A student reporter from another Yale paper asked if I didn't think the attack proved New Haven needs better police protection. Given the random nature of this assault—it could as easily have happened in wealthy, suburban Greenwich, where a friend of mine was held up at an ATM at the point of an assault rifle— it's tempting to dismiss such sentiments as typical products of an insular urban campus. But city-hating is central to today's political culture. Newt Gingrich excoriates cities as hopelessly pestilential, crime-ridden and corrupt. Fear of urban crime and of the dark-skinned people who live in cities is the right's basic text, and defunding cities a central agenda item for the new Congressional majority.

Yet in no small measure it was the institutions of an urban community that saved my life last August 7. That concerned police officer who found me and Kerstin Braig on the street was joined in a moment by enough emergency workers to handle the carnage in and around the coffeehouse, and his backups arrived quickly enough to chase down my assailant three blocks away. In minutes I was taken to Yale-New Haven hospital less than a mile away—built in part with the kind of public funding so hated by the right. As I was wheeled into the E.R., several dozen doctors and nurses descended to handle all the wounded.

By then my abdomen had swelled from internal bleeding. Dr. Gerard Burns, a trauma surgeon, told me a few weeks later that I arrived on his operating table white as a ghost; my prospects, he said, would have been poor had I not been delivered so quickly, and to an E.R. with the kind of trauma team available only at a large metropolitan hospital. In other words, if my stabbing had taken place in the suburbs I would have bled to death.

"Why didn't anyone try to stop him?" That question was even more common than the reflexive city-bashing. I can't even begin to guess the number of times I had to answer it. Each time, I repeated that Silva moved too fast, that it was simply too confusing. And each time, I found the question not just foolish but offensive.

"Why didn't anyone stop him?" To understand that question is to understand, in some measure, why crime is such a potent political issue. To begin with, the question carries not empathy but an implicit burden of blame; it really asks "Why didn't *you* stop him?" It is asked because no one likes to imagine oneself a victim. It's far easier to graft onto oneself the aggressive power of the attacker, to embrace the delusion of oneself as Arnold Schwarzenegger defeating a multitude single-handedly. *If I am tough enough and strong enough I can take out the bad guys.*

The country is at present suffering from a huge version of this same delusion. This myth is buried deep in the political culture, nurtured in the historical tales of frontier violence and vigilantism and by the action-hero fantasies of film and television. Now, bolstered by the social Darwinists of the right, who see society as an unfettered marketplace in which the strongest individuals flourish, this delusion frames the crime debate.

I also felt that the question "Why didn't anybody stop him?" implied only two choices: Rambo-like heroism or abject victimhood. To put it another way, it suggests that the only possible responses to danger are the individual biological imperatives of fight or flight. And people don't want to think of themselves as on the side of flight. This is a notion whose political moment has arrived. In last year's debate over the crime bill, conservatives successfully portrayed themselves as those who would stand and fight; liberals were portrayed as ineffectual cowards.

"Why didn't anyone stop him?" That question and its underlying implications see both heroes and victims as lone individuals. But on the receiving end of a violent attack, the fight-or-flight dichotomy didn't apply. Nor did that radically individualized notion of survival. At the coffeehouse that night, at the moments of greatest threat, there were no Schwarzeneggers, no stand-alone heroes. (In fact I doubt anyone could have "taken out" Silva; as with most crimes, his attack came too suddenly.) But neither were there abject victims. Instead, in the confusion and panic of life-threatening attack, *people reached out to one another.* This sounds simple; yet it suggests there is an instinct for mutual aid that poses a profound challenge to the atomized individualism of the right. Cristina Koning helped the wounded Kerstin Braig to escape, and Kerstin in turn tried to bring Cristina along. Anna and I, and then Martin and I, clung to each other, pulling one another toward the door. And just as Kerstin found me on the sidewalk rather than wait for help alone, so Richard and Emily, who had never met before, together sought a hiding place around the corner. Three of us even spoke with Silva either the moment before or the instant after being stabbed. My plea to Silva may or may not have been what kept him from pushing his knife all the way through my chest and into my heart;

it's impossible to know what was going through his mind. But this impulse to communicate, to establish human contact across a gulf of terror and insanity, is deeper and more subtle than the simple formulation of fight or flight, courage or cowardice, would allow.

I have never been in a war, but I now think I understand a little the intense bond among war veterans who have survived awful carnage. It is not simply the common fact of survival but the way in which the presence of these others, seemed to make survival itself possible. There's evidence, too, that those who try to go it alone suffer more. In her insightful study *Trauma and Recovery*, Judith Herman, a psychiatrist, writes about rape victims, Vietnam War veterans, political prisoners and other survivors of extreme violence. "The capacity to preserve social connection . . ." she concludes, "even in the face of extremity, seems to protect people to some degree against the later development of post-traumatic syndromes. For example, among survivors of a disaster at sea, the men who had managed to escape by cooperating with others showed relatively little evidence of post-traumatic stress afterward." On the other hand, she reports that the "highly symptomatic" ones among those survivors were " 'Rambos,' men who had plunged into impulsive, isolated action and not affiliated with others."

The political point here is that the Rambo justice system proposed by the right is rooted in that dangerous myth of the individual fighting against a hostile world. Recently that myth got another boost from several Republican-controlled state legislatures, which have made it much easier to carry concealed handguns. But the myth has nothing to do with the reality of violent crime, the ways to prevent it or the needs of survivors. Had Silva been carrying a handgun instead of a knife on August 7, there would have been a massacre.

I do understand the rage and frustration behind the crime-victim movement, and I can see how the right has harnessed it. For weeks I thought obsessively and angrily of those minutes on Audubon Street, when first the nameless woman in the window and then the security guard refused to approach me—as if I, wounded and helpless, were the dangerous one. There was also a subtle shift in my consciousness a few days after the stabbing. Up until that point, the legal process and press attention seemed clearly centered on my injuries and experience, and those of my fellow victims. But once Silva was arraigned and the formal process of prosecution began, it became *his* case, not mine. I experienced an overnight sense of marginalization, a feeling of helplessness bordering on irrelevance.

Sometimes that got channeled into outrage, fear and panic. After arraignment, Silva's bail was set at $700,000. That sounds high, but just 10 percent of that amount in cash, perhaps obtained through some relative with home equity, would have bought his pretrial release. I was frantic at even this remote prospect of Silva walking the streets. So were the six other victims and our families. We called the prosecutor virtually hourly to request higher bail. It was eventually raised to $800,000, partly because of our complaints and partly because an arson charge was added. Silva remains in the Hartford Community Correctional Center awaiting trial.

Near the six-month anniversary of the stabbings I called the prosecutor and learned that in December Silva's lawyer filed papers indicating he intends to claim a "mental disease or defect" defense. If successful it would send him to a maximum-security hospital for the criminally insane for the equivalent of the maximum criminal penalty. In February the court was still awaiting a report from Silva's psychiatrist. Then the prosecution will have him examined by its own psychiatrist. "There's a backlog," I was told; the case is not likely to come to trial until the end of 1995 at the earliest. Intellectually, I understand that Silva is securely behind bars, that the court system is overburdened, that the delay makes no difference in the long-term outcome. But emotionally, viscerally, the delay is devastating.

Another of my bursts of victim-consciousness involved the press. Objectively, I know that many people who took the trouble to express their sympathy to me found out only through news stories. And sensitive reporting can for the crime victim be a kind of ratification of the seriousness of an assault, a reflection of the community's concern. One reporter for the daily *New Haven Register*, Josh Kovner, did produce level-headed and insightful stories about the Audubon Street attack. But most other reporting was exploitative, intrusive and inaccurate. I was only a few hours out of surgery, barely able to speak, when the calls from television stations and papers started coming to my hospital room. Anna and Martin, sent home to recover, were ambushed by a Hartford TV crew as they emerged from their physician's office, and later rousted from their beds by reporters from another TV station ringing their doorbell. The *Register*'s editors enraged all seven victims by printing our home addresses (a company policy, for some reason) and running spectacularly distressing full-color photos of the crime scene complete with the coffee bar's bloody windowsill.

Such press coverage inspired in all of us a rage it is impossible to convey. In a study commissioned by the British Broadcasting Standards Council, survivors of violent crimes and disasters "told story

after story of the hurt they suffered through the timing of media attention, intrusion into their privacy and harassment, through inaccuracy,
distortion and distasteful detail in what was reported." This suffering is
not superficial. To the victim of violent crime the press may reinforce
the perception that the world is an uncomprehending and dangerous
place.

The very same flawed judgments about "news value" contribute significantly to a public conception of crime that is as completely
divorced from the facts as a Schwarzenegger movie. One study a few
years ago found that reports on crime and justice constitute 22–28 percent of newspaper stories, "nearly three times as much attention as the
presidency or the Congress or the state of the economy." And the most
spectacular crimes—the stabbing of seven people in an upscale New
Haven coffee bar, for instance—are likely to be the most "newsworthy"
even though they are statistically the least likely. "The image of crime
presented in the media is thus a reverse image of reality," writes sociologist Mark Warr in a study commissioned by the National Academy of
Sciences.

Media coverage also brings us to another crucial political moral: The
"seriousness" of crime is a matter of race and real estate. This has
been pointed out before, but it can't be said too often. Seven people
stabbed in a relatively affluent, mostly white neighborhood near Yale
University—this was big news on a slow news night. It went national
over the A.P. wires and international over CNN's *Headline News*. It
was covered by *The New York Times*, and words of sympathy came to
New Haven from as far as Prague and Santiago. Because a graduate student and a professor were among those wounded, the university sent
representatives to the emergency room. The morning after, New Haven
Mayor John DeStefano walked the neighborhood to reassure merchants
and office workers. For more than a month the regional press covered
every new turn in the case.

Horrendous as it was, though, no one was killed. Four weeks later, a
15-year-old girl named Rashawnda Crenshaw was driving with two
friends about a mile from Audubon Street. As the car in which she was
a passenger turned a corner she was shot through the window and
killed. Apparently her assailants mistook her for someone else.
Rashawnda Crenshaw was black and her shooting took place in the
Hill, the New Haven neighborhood with the highest poverty rate. No
Yale officials showed up at the hospital to comfort Crenshaw's mother
or cut through red tape. *The New York Times* did not come calling;
there were certainly no bulletins flashed around the world on CNN.

The local news coverage lasted just long enough for Rashawnda Crenshaw to be buried.

Anyone trying to deal with the reality of crime, as opposed to the fantasies peddled to win elections, needs to understand the complex suffering of those who are survivors of traumatic crimes, and the suffering and turmoil of their families. I have impressive physical scars: There is a broad purple line from my breastbone to the top of my public bone, an X-shaped cut into my side where the chest tube entered, a thick pink mark on my chest where the point of Silva's knife rested on a rib. Then on my back is the unevenly curving horizontal scar where Silva thrust the knife in and yanked it out, leaving what looks like a crooked smile. But the disruption of my psyche is, day in and day out, more noticeable. For weeks after leaving the hospital I awoke nightly agitated, drenched with perspiration. For two months I was unable to write; my brain simply refused to concentrate. Into any moment of mental repose would rush images from the night of August 7; or alternatively, my mind would simply not tune in at all. My reactions are still out of balance and disproportionate. I shut a door on my finger, not too hard, and my body is suddenly flooded with adrenaline and I nearly faint. Walking on the arm of my partner, Margaret, one evening I abruptly shove her to the side of the road; I have seen a tall, lean shadow on the block where we are headed and am alarmed out of all proportion. I get into an argument and find myself quaking with rage for an hour afterward, completely unable to restore calm. Though to all appearances normal, I feel at a long arm's remove from all the familiar sources of pleasure, comfort and anger that shaped my daily life before August 7.

What psychologists call post-traumatic stress disorder is, among other things, a profoundly political state in which the world has gone wrong, in which you feel isolated from the broader community by the inarticulable extremity of experience. I have spent a lot of time in the past few months thinking about what the world must look like to those who have survived repeated violent attacks, whether children battered in their homes or prisoners beaten or tortured behind bars; as well as those, like rape victims, whose assaults are rarely granted public ratification.

The right owes much of its success to the anger of crime victims and the argument that government should do more for us. This appeal is epitomized by the rise of restitution laws—statutes requiring offenders to compensate their targets. On February 7 the House of Representatives passed, by a vote of 431 to 0, the Victim Restitution Act, a plank of the Contract With America that would supposedly send back to jail offenders who don't make good on their debts to their victims. In my own state, Governor Rowland recently proposed a restitution amendment to the state Constitution.

On the surface it is hard to argue with the principle of reasonable restitution—particularly since it implies community recognition of the victim's suffering. But I wonder if these laws really will end up benefiting someone like me—or if they are just empty, vote-getting devices that exploit victims and could actually hurt our chances of getting speedy, substantive justice. H. Scott Wallace, former counsel to the Senate Judiciary Subcommittee on Juvenile Justice, writes in *Legal Times* that the much-touted Victim Restitution Act is "unlikely to put a single dollar into crime victims' pockets, would tie up the federal courts with waves of new damages actions, and would promote unconstitutional debtors' prisons."

I also worry that the rhetoric of restitution confuses—as does so much of the imprisonment-and-execution mania dominating the political landscape—the goals of justice and revenge. Revenge, after all, is just another version of the individualized, take-out-the-bad-guys myth. Judith Herman believes indulging fantasies of revenge actually worsens the psychic suffering of trauma survivors: "The desire for revenge . . . arises out of the victim's experience of complete helplessness," and forever ties the victim's fate to the perpetrator's. Real recovery from the cataclysmic isolation of trauma comes only when "the survivor comes to understand the issues of principle that transcend her personal grievance against the perpetrator . . . [a] principle of social justice that connects the fate of others to her own." The survivors and victims' families of the Long Island Rail Road massacre have banded together not to urge that Colin Ferguson be executed but to work for gun control.

What it all comes down to is this: What do survivors of violent crime really need? What does it mean to create a safe society? Do we need courts so overburdened by nonviolent drug offenders that Daniel Silvas go untried for eighteen months, delays that leave victims and suspects alike in limbo? Do we need to throw nonviolent drug offenders into mandatory-sentence proximity with violent sociopaths and career criminals? Do we need the illusory bravado of a Schwarzenegger film—or the real political courage of those L.I.R.R. survivors?

If the use of my picture on television unexpectedly brought me face to face with the memory of August 7, some part of the attack is relived for me daily as I watch the gruesome, voyeuristically reported details of the stabbing deaths of two people in California, Nicole Brown Simpson and Ronald Goldman. It was relived even more vividly by the televised trial of Colin Ferguson. (One night recently after watching Ferguson on the evening news I dreamed that I was on the witness stand and Silva, like Ferguson, was representing himself and questioning me.) Throughout the trial, as Ferguson spoke of falling asleep and having someone else fire his gun, I heard neither cowardly denial nor what his first lawyer called "black rage", I heard Daniel Silva's calm, secure voice telling me I killed his mother. And when I hear testimony by the survivors of that massacre—on a train as comfortable and familiar to them as my neighborhood coffee bar—I feel a great and incommunicable fellowship.

But the public obsession with these trials, I am convinced, has no more to do with the real experience of crime victims than does the anti-crime posturing of politicians. I do not know what made my assailant act as he did. Nor do I think crime and violence can be reduced to simple political categories. I do know that the answers will not be found in social Darwinism and atomized individualism, in racism, in dismantling cities and increasing the destitution of the poor. To the contrary: Every fragment of my experience suggests that the best protections from crime and the best aid to victims are the very social institutions most derided by the right. As crime victim and citizen what I want is the reality of a safe community—not a politician's fantasyland of restitution and revenge. That is my testimony.

ALLEGORY OF THE CAVE—EXCHANGE

Arthur C. Danto, Clayton Eshleman, Alexander Cockburn

•

NEW YORK CITY

THE MAIN THING to remember," Alex Cockburn writes in his curious effort to discredit the authenticity of the recently discovered cave paintings in the Ardèche ["Beat the Devil," Feb. 20], "is that experts are mostly worthless, and most 'evidence' open to challenge or fraudulent." He forthwith, without a scrap of skeptical reservation, appeals to the whimsical authority and capricious "evidence" of the painter Alex Melamid, who claims that "these were pictures made by someone who had experience of photography." Melamid's ingeniously garbled argument contends that "when we see the animal running we think we see how its legs move, but we don't; what we see is the image we remember from the photograph." So the paintings cannot predate the photographs that record animals in motion. "Amazed at the zeal to believe," Melamid thus deconstructs the cave paintings that have recently inspired so many of us, and, according to Cockburn, "hits the nail on the head." No: He hits the thumb on the nail. But since Cockburn evidently felt it important enough to turn aside from his usual targets in order to cast doubt upon these marvelous paintings, a few corrective words on this art-historical matter may not be out of place.

It is well known that the unaided eye cannot answer certain questions regarding the locomotion of animals—for example, whether a running

horse ever has all four legs off the ground at once. It was in order to settle this (and decide a bet) that the British-born photographer Eadweard
Muybridge set up a bank of fourteen cameras whose shutters were triggered by a horse running in front of them, tripping attached threads.
These photographs were published in 1878 under the title *The Horse in
Motion*, and it is doubtless to these that Melamid refers. They, and the
subsequent images in *Animal Locomotion*, published in 1887, made
Muybridge famous, and when he projected them by means of his
zoopraxinoscope—a technical forerunner of the modern motion-pic-
ture mechanism—the illusion of motion was quite thrilling. No one
who has seen Muybridge's images, however, which after all are stills
showing arrested motion, would have the slightest temptation to see any
resemblance between them and the running beasts of the Ardèche.

The reason is easy to state. We really *don't* see animals move the way
Muybridge shows them moving, or else there would have been no need
for the photographs in the first place: It was because no one knew the
disposition of horses' feet when they run that Muybridge hit upon his
awkward but authoritative experiments. Muybridge's images had an
impact on artists like Eakins and the Futurists, and especially on
Degas, who sometimes shows a horse moving stiff-legged across the
turf, exactly the way it can be seen in Muybridge's photographs, but
never in life. Far more visually satisfying are the schematisms artists
have evolved down the centuries for representing animals in motion
the way we *feel* they move. And what is striking about the Ardèche
animals is the presence of such schematisms twenty centuries ago.

Muybridge was of course positivistically contemptuous of the use of
schematisms. His photographs showed how differently the horse uses
its legs in the amble, the canter and the gallop: It was, he told audiences, "absurd" to depict a galloping horse with all four feet off the
ground. But a famous painting, which he made merry with—Frith's
Derby Day of 1858—shows no fewer than ten horses in this visually
convincing but locomotively false posture. The animals at Ardèche
dash headlong through space, vastly more like Frith's—or Gericault's
or Leonardo's—than the reality Muybridge's photography disclosed.

This, to be sure, does not establish the authenticity of the Ardèche
pictures. But it kicks the prop from under the argument of the two
Alexes, who may, of course, always fall back on the possibility that
impostors carried a mezzotint of William Powell Frith's masterpiece
into the cave with them as they pre-emptively duped the art critic of
this magazine and countless gullible others.

ARTHUR C. DANTO

Ypsilanti, Mich.

In his article on the recently discovered decorated cave in the French
Ardèche region, Alexander Cockburn offers a list of "suspicious features of the find" that lead him to conclude that the paintings may very
well be fakes. Put in a context that includes other caves, these "suspicious features" are not suspicious at all. Having been in some fifty decorated Ice Age caves over the past twenty years (and followed up my
field trips with a lot of reading), upon reading Cockburn's list, I immediately thought of many examples elsewhere that support an argument
for the authenticity of the new cave.

Lascaux, dated at 17,000 B.C.E., and now considered to be of indis-
putable authenticity, was, until its discovery in 1940, "untouched for
millennia"; and also like the new cave Lascaux has many running animals (a slight space left between a horse's body and the beginning of its
leg, which appears to emphasize perspective and movement). Apparently Cockburn's expert has not considered Lascaux, and if he has not,
then why bother to quote him at all?

There is nothing unique about rhinos in motion; they are depicted
in motion in Lascaux and in Rouffignac. There is nothing *suspicious* in
discovering a new animal, especially a carnivore. While depicted much
less often than bison and horses, carnivores are to be found in all
regions with Ice Age art (Dolni Vestonice and Pavlov are in fact sites
dominated by carnivores).

As for the suspect "altar scene," two other authenticated such scenes
come to mind: At Montespan there is a bear modeled in clay (when
Norbert Casteret discovered the sculpture in 1923 there was the skull
of a bear cub between the model's paws); at El Juyo, in 1981, a scene
that could understandably be described as an altar was discovered. The
"centerpiece" was a stone head, the left side of which portrayed a
bearded man and the right side a carnivore. Below the head was a three-
foot by four-foot trench containing animal bones, shells, spear points
and other coloring material. Above the head, resting on vertical slabs,
was a horizontal limestone slab six feet long and four feet wide, weighing almost a ton. The Spanish and American team inspecting the site
said that it must have taken ten to fifteen people to move the slab and
concluded that the "sanctuary" served "a shared system of group
belief." They also stated that it had not been entered for around 13,000
years because it was "hermetically sealed by a rock fall, and trickling
water had turned the rocks to cement."

Cockburn, on the basis of no support whatsoever, also implies that such "experts" as Jean Clottes are suspect. For whatever it is worth, I have known Clottes for two decades. His credentials are impeccable. He is undoubtedly the most knowledgeable specialist in Ice Age French rock art alive. I sent him Cockburn's article and he wrote back to me as follows: "Many thanks for sending the article and your reply. Every major discovery of rock art since Altamira was challenged as a fake. This had been missing for the Chauvet cave!"

In some of the color photos of images in the Ardèche cave, I have noticed what appears to be whitish calcite covering some or all of certain animals. If my observations are correct, such formations, as in the case of Lascaux, may be used to confirm the authenticity of this new cave.

CLAYTON ESHLEMAN

•

COCKBURN REPLIES
Petrolia, Calif.

I'm quite happy to stipulate that the new find in the Ardèche is "genuine" if that makes people feel better, though I'm fond of the idea that a good many of the French cave paintings "came to light," to put it tactfully, as part of a national heritage program signaled by the famous French Historical Monuments Act of 1887.

The Monuments Act had really been in germination for over fifty years, during which period writers such as Montalembert, Chateaubriand, Guizot and Victor Hugo were preparing the cultural ground. It was Montalembert who said, *"Les longs souvenirs font les grands peuples"*—"long memories make great peoples"—and in his impassioned tract, "Guerre aux Démolisseurs" Hugo writes of a "universal cry that summons the new France to the rescue of the old."

"Better than all books," exclaimed Antonin Proust, Minister of Fine Arts in 1881–82, "the keeps of Coucy and of Gisors, the ramparts of Carcassonne and Avignon instruct us about the power of the feudal regime. In these books of stone we find what Augustin Thierry has called the soul of history." And forty years earlier M. Martin, the Keeper of the Seal, declared in the Chamber of Deputies, "Public utility is not a purely material thing; national traditions, history, art itself, are they not in truth matters of public utility, just as much as bridges and arsenals and roads?"

The question of "genuineness" is pretty moot, even if one doubts Alex Melamid's view—cited in my column—that the Ardèche creatures are painted in accord with the terms of relatively recent Western artistic conventions. Mercifully, perhaps because it is not fungible (at least not yet) in discrete pieces, paleolithic art has been spared Berenson-type ascriptions of individual authorship. But was the sketch on a slab of slate of the Font-de-Gaume bison that turned up 180 miles away, at another cave, the Abri de la Genière, the equipment of an itinerant master, of a "disciple" or of a forger?

The time frames of the proclaimedly "genuine" cave paintings are ample, with variations in estimates ranging from 2,000 or 3,000 years to ten times that number. By such a standard the beautiful little metal crucifix I recently picked out of the earth at my late mother's home in Ireland would be simply "genuine early Christian art" whether it is contemporary with the building of St. Declan's Church, standing in ruins nearby and raised more than a thousand years ago, or was made 500 or fifty or even five years ago.

As I understand him, Alex Melamid doesn't believe in "Art"—in the sense that, for him, the poor Russian reproduction of the Sistine Chapel ceiling that he gazed upon as a boy has as much meaning and authenticity as the twentieth-century restoration now on the chapel's ceiling, which is intended as a "genuine" reflection of what Michelangelo put up in the first years of the sixteenth century. So for Alex M., it would not be a desecration of the numinous affect of certain subterranean and reputedly paleolithic paintings to suppose that they might be of far more recent vintage.

As I also understand him, Alex M. is much influenced by Morozov, a Russian revolutionary who spent long years in prison at the start of this century, emerging to produce a voluminous work disposing a view of history not as a chronological progression—diachrony—but as overlapping synchronies. Thus the French passion for Chinese art in the late nineteenth century, the Mongolian horse type discovered in China in 1880, the evolution of French monumental policy in the 1880s, the discovery of what is called the "Chinese horse" at Lascaux, opened in 1940, and indeed the painting of the Lascaux caves are, so to speak, simultaneous events, although they might appear to vulgar diachronists as widely separated in time.

Unlike those who challenged Altamira in the late nineteenth century, I certainly believe in the ability of our distant ancestors to make such paintings. In questioning the claims about the Ardèche paintings, I was moved not so much by Alex M.'s cosmochrony as by a general antipathy to "experts," particularly in a field in which these same experts so regularly revise their judgments by tens of thousands of years. I fear Arthur

Danto thought that the coincidence of publication of his and my very different responses to the Ardèche pictures was an effort on my part to get at him. Not at all. I presented my own column entirely unaware that he had, that same week, delivered his reflections on Republican philistinism in light of the Ardèche painters. Clayton Eshleman seems to controvert the initial claims for startling originality in the Ardèche work by citing precisely its absence of originality (which proves nothing so far as the "genuineness" issue is concerned). Alex M. is not my "expert" but a painter, who explicitly denies the idea of the "expert."

Piltdown Man was denounced as a forgery in 1953. Charles Dawson, who "discovered" it in the company of Woodward and Chardin in 1912, prospered as an archeologist at a time—through the 1890s and up to World War I—when there was an enormous interest in digging things up and making deductions. I have an article by my father from 1953 noting this and mentioning Flint Jack, who "had learned to cut flints to suit pretty well any theory anyone wanted to hold."

Eoanthropus dawsoni threw some experts in a heap because the reconstructed skull, with scholarly forehead but apelike jaw, ran athwart their notions of human development. So in the end the prevailing group of experts did him in. But even so he still had his defenders, notably the prehistorian and dentist Theophilus Marston, who said that no one in 1912 would have been able to operate on a tooth duct in such a way as to force a conclusion that it was over 20 million years old (his personal view). Maybe *Eoanthropus dawsoni's* time will come again. I conclude with the paleontological reconstruction made by Otto van Guericke, Mayor of Magdeburg and inventor of the air pump, back in the seventeenth century. He found a hoard of enormous bones and teeth and believed them to be the skull and bones of the unicorn mentioned in the Book of Job. The philosopher Leibniz gave his approval, published a copy in his *Protogaea* and all textbooks of the time had to follow suit.

ALEXANDER COCKBURN

BUYING HIS WAY TO A MEDIA EMPIRE

Robert Sherrill

•

BRILLIANT TIMING. WHILE the rest of the bomb-spooked bureau-crats in Washington try to convince a restless and unhappy public that they shouldn't be objects of contempt, the Federal Communications Commission comes out with a ruling—against the N.A.A.C.P. and in favor of journalism's foremost bully-boy, Rupert Murdoch—that shows just how easy it is for folks with big-big money to break the law and get away with it.

The F.C.C. should have stripped billionaire Murdoch of his Fox TV stations. Actually, in its ruling of May 4, the commission acknowledged that he is an outlaw in the industry (we'll get into the details later on) and, in a bit of bureaucratic bluster, gave Murdoch forty-five days to convince the commission that it shouldn't punish him. Don't be fooled by that. They'll do nothing to him. And the upshot of the F.C.C.'s action will ultimately be the approval of his plan to turn Fox into what will become the right wing's principal voice in this country.

Rupert Murdoch has built a global newspaper/TV empire by ped-dling sleaze and piffle; because those commodities have such an appeal to the world's boobocracy, the empire grows apace—most recently through a linkup with telecommunications giant MCI. Many in the media industry despise him. *The Wall Street Journal*, with typical understatement, once wrote that among British and U.S. liberal journalists "he has inspired a hatred and scorn that have seldom been equaled in the history of press ownership." On the other hand, many politicians and bureaucrats seem to like him very much. This is doubtless because he does nice things for them. But just how far does his generosity go? Surely he doesn't stoop to outright bribery. Perish the thought!

Nevertheless, given his reputation for "empire-building on the edge, financial loosey-goosey" (to borrow *Business Week*'s description), it wasn't surprising that when Murdoch's organization was caught trying to slip Newt Gingrich $4.5 million for what would be two ghostwritten books, and given the fact that Gingrich is not exactly known as a bestselling author (his last book netted him $15,000), there were some who just automatically interpreted that as a kind of bribe.

It was a rather natural conclusion to come to, considering that Murdoch had pulled the book contract ploy twice before in ways that cynics might interpret crudely. Margaret Thatcher got more than $5 million from Murdoch's publishing house, HarperCollins, for her memoirs when she stepped down as Britain's Prime Minister, and many felt this was not so much a recognition of her literary skills as it was a payoff— a delayed bribe you might say—for virtually handing over Great Britain to feed Murdoch's bottomless ambitions. With the Tory government suspending the antitrust laws, forgiving the misleading claims he filed with the government, exempting his satellite TV station from regulations that applied to earthbound TV companies, and helping him crush the press unions, etc., Murdoch wound up owning one-third of the national press and operating a satellite TV station that had almost five times as many TV channels as all the terrestrial broadcasters put together. Five million bucks was dirt cheap.

If it worked in Britain, why not try it in Asia? Murdoch's Star TV, based in Hong Kong, beams five channels via satellite free of charge to thirty-nine countries, from Israel to Indonesia. Income is from advertisers. But competition abounds from other satellites and Murdoch was having trouble getting advertisers. He needed subscribers, and that meant going into cable, particularly in the lucrative China market. And *that* meant buttering up its corrupt government. Once again cynical observers thought they smelled a bribe when Basic Books (a subsidiary of HarperCollins) paid an unspecified amount—you can bet that it was plenty—to Xiao Rong for a biography of her father, the bloodthirsty Deng Xiaoping, the guy who ordered the massacre at Tiananmen Square.

We now know why Murdoch would want to buy U.S. Congressmen at this particular moment. For insurance—fire insurance. His file at the F.C.C. was beginning to smoke, and he could have been in deep trouble—trouble that could have cost him as much as half a billion in back taxes and many more billions in the stunting of his global expansion. Mike Royko, who once described Murdoch as "a greedy, money-grubbing, power-seeking, status-climbing cad," puts the $4.5 million in perspective: "Even if the book advance were a legal bribe, Murdoch never got the short end of any deal, and Newt was probably being underbribed."

Underbribed indeed. Murdoch and his family own 46 percent of News Corporation, the Australian company he built and that pays for all his dirty work. It's a gusher, bringing in more than $8 billion in operating revenues a year and a cash flow of at least $1 billion. So why wouldn't it be wise to spend a few million bucks to buy the necessary politicians and bureaucrats to protect the empire's U.S. realm, which includes the Fox TV network of 158 affiliates and the eight stations it owns outright, which generate an astounding 50 percent profit, and the six it's trying to get a piece of?

Fair play (which Washington politics once again smothered) would have put those holdings in jeopardy. Indeed, the F.C.C.'s own staff, after a two-year investigation, recently recommended that because Murdoch had violated foreign ownership laws when he applied back in 1985 to buy his first batch of stations, Fox should be forced to make a drastic corporate restructuring and be hit with a hefty fine and a formal rebuke—all of which would doubtless be used by opponents to challenge any future station purchases. The investigation had been prompted by charges raised by the N.A.A.C.P. (NBC had for a time joined in the accusations, but dropped out when Murdoch bought NBC off by allowing it space on his Asian TV satellite.) The N.A.A.C.P. wanted to block "his" purchase of another TV station in Philadelphia and to make him surrender those he already "owns," including WNYW in New York City. The staff's recommendations were rejected by the full commission, which admitted Murdoch had broken the law but said the "totality" (their word) of evidence didn't prove he had been a total liar on his application.

I put quote marks around the words "his" and "owns" because that was the crucial question: Are they really his, and does he own them—or do they belong to a foreign corporation that has no legal right to own them?

The crux of Murdoch's problem was citizenship. He was accused by the N.A.A.C.P. of "lack of candor" in his application regarding Section 310 (b) (4) of the Communications Act, which prohibits a foreigner from owning more than 25 percent of a television station. To get hung up on the question of citizenship must gall the hell out of Murdoch because he has never shown any desire to be a responsible citizen of any country and holds all governments in contempt. Not long ago he predicted that new technology would soon allow him to overpower broadcasting regulations around the world in order to achieve his ambition to become the Global Mogul of TV. "In the end," he said, "technology can get past the politicians and past the regulators."

Maybe eventually. But in the meantime he has been forced to toe a few lines. And the most important of these has been citizenship.

Isn't he a citizen? Yes. He became a U.S. citizen in 1985, strictly for commercial reasons, as he admits. "A business justification," he says. "Put it that way." Having made a humongous fortune debasing newspaper in Australia (his homeland) and in Britain and in the United States, he wanted to move into television. With the help of anti-regulation Tories he succeeded in a big way in Britain, but he was blocked by Section 310 in this country until he became Citizen Murdoch. President Reagan cut red tape to expedite his becoming a patriot-for-dollars. Since then Murdoch has been awesomely aggressive in pushing the Fox network, and its potential seemed almost limitless, until. . . .

Until the N.A.A.C.P. and others contended that he didn't really own the Fox outfit. They charged that his citizenship was merely a front for the real owner, News Corporation, which is not allowed to own television stations in the United States.

Anyone with common sense would have agreed. To get its hands on a television setup in this country, News Corporation laid out $600 million and assumed $1 billion in debt. For that it got all the common stock. Murdoch owns none of it. But he owns most of the preferred stock (costing $760,000), which he says gives him voting control of the company and therefore qualifies him as the "owner" by F.C.C. standards. He dismisses equity as of no importance.

On that issue, consider this Q. and A., found in a confidential deposition recently obtained by *The Nation*, which the F.C.C. took from Murdoch in January. At one point the F.C.C. attorney read a 1992 statement that had been made by Barry Diller, then Fox's chief executive officer, explaining why he was leaving the corporation. "Rupert Murdoch and I began discussing last summer my growing desire to become an actual principal in the business activities with which I was associated. Clearly, since Fox is a wholly owned unit of News Corp., that was not a practical or possible ambition within the company."

The F.C.C. attorney taking the deposition asked Murdoch if he agreed with Diller's statement. Well, yes, said Murdoch, he had to admit that Fox "is a wholly owned unit of News Corp.," and that "the capital, the losses, the risk was all within News Corporation." All the profits, too, are News Corporation's, he said. But, he argued, Fox is "not a wholly owned subsidiary in terms of voting control. The directors of News Corporation do not control the Fox Television stations or Fox. I did."

Murdoch said he didn't know his exact title, but "I'm the man who gives all the instructions, yes." But giving all the instructions is a far cry from being the owner, as any C.E.O. will tell you. Anyway, it isn't safe to believe anything Murdoch says about corporate operations. Later in the deposition Murdoch reversed himself, saying, "Diller was pretty much the master" of the Fox operation, and "Mr. Diller really ran it very completely."

As for Murdoch's claim that possessing a majority of the preferred stock gave him ownership, I again call your attention to Diller's parting press release, which Murdoch approved before it was released. Diller's chief complaint was that he was not "an actual principal in the business activities" at Fox. Yet he owned 25 percent of the preferred shares, or $250,000 worth (Murdoch owned 51 percent). Why didn't Diller consider that his stake in Fox made him an owner? Well, for one thing, he never received a penny of the corporate profits. Instead, he was paid 12 percent interest on his investment. No matter what Murdoch now claims about the power of preferred shares, Diller obviously didn't feel that his gave him any portion of ownership.

The deposition shows it apparently wasn't job-safe for Murdoch's employees to suggest there was something so fishy about the Fox corporate layout that it might arouse the suspicions of the F.C.C. An attorney wrote a memo containing this paragraph: "Because of the uncertainty, however, of the outcome of a challenge to Fox TV's ownership structure, we have been in agreement that it is paramount to avoid any corporate restructuring which would potentially invite reexamination of Fox TV's ownership structure by the Commission." The guy who wrote that is now off the payroll.

Murdoch has a way of putting the fear of God—or of financial loss into those who work for him, including Diller, who still has a TV production tie to a Murdoch company. When the F.C.C. deposed Diller, an attorney read back to him the departing statement that Fox was a wholly owned unit of News Corp. and asked, "What did you mean when you said that?" Babbling incoherently, in what sounds like panic, Diller replied:

> Well, it has no—there's no distinction other than the fact that what my meaning was, I was simply trying to convey meaning by statements that you're reading from, underlying meaning as to why I was going to leave the company is that while people may have thought that I was a principal in Fox, and Fox company, and, in fact, while I may function as one and to some degree do, in fact its common stock, so to speak, ownership, its equity was owned by NewsCorp.

O.K., O.K., Diller, calm down, get a grip on yourself and try it again, starting with that last mention of "ownership."

Are there good reasons for cursing the bureaucrats for the likelihood that Murdoch will win this fight? Plenty of them. One excellent reason, as the N.A.A.C.P. has argued, is that if the F.C.C. caves in and permits unlimited foreign ownership—or if Congress changes the law to allow it—the big money from abroad (the N.A.A.C.P. claims that 80 percent of the world's telecommunications capital is foreign) will come flooding in and make it even more difficult than it already is for U.S. minority groups to buy into the industry. Another reason the N.A.A.C.P. wants to get Murdoch out of television is the same reason it had for opposing his purchase of the *New York Post* and station WNYW—it believes he panders to racism.

The limit on foreign ownership has been communications law for sixty-one years. Why change it now? In fact, this is exactly the wrong time to change it. News Corporation's dominance of the media in Britain, and the incredibly wretched standards it has brought to that market, are frightening evidence of what Murdoch would do in the United States if the F.C.C. continues to relax its regulations. You may think television is a wasteland now, but if his British operations are any guide when Murdoch really gets rolling, Fox's *Married . . . With Children* will seem, in retrospect, like *Hamlet*.

Murdoch-controlled media have prospered around the world by stressing what William Shawcross, Murdoch's biographer, accurately called "titillation, sensationalism and vulgarity." The Fox network offers nothing that can be called a news program, which may be a blessing, for Murdoch has steadfastly demonstrated in his papers, including the *New York Post*, that he has no interest in delivering news about politics except as it is used for propaganda to promote the politicians who let him have his way. People who have worked for him say he constantly meddles in editorial policy and directs the slanting of political reporting.

Murdoch thought it was a great idea to publish Hitler's diaries, though he had been warned they were phony; when the hoax was exposed he shrugged it off, saying, "After all, we are in the entertainment business." Is there a limit on how much garbage he will sell? As the *Daily Telegraph* pointed out, Murdoch is the guy who tolerated his newspaper's "glorification of 1,200 deaths on the [Argentine cruise ship General] Belgrano; the falsification of memoirs by the widow of a Falklands War hero; the lie that Liverpool supporters had rifled corpses at Hillsborough football stadium." And one of Murdoch's papers, as Anthony Lewis pointed out, carried on a "cruelly irresponsible anti-science" campaign questioning the existence of an AIDS epidemic in Africa.

So much for Murdoch's journalistic "standards." Speaking of which, it is ironic that he recently became a financier for a new right-wing publication to be called *The Standard*. Its editor, William Kristol, promises a magazine that will be "a cross between a conservative *New Republic* and a weekly *Wall Street Journal* editorial page." In other words, politically Ice Age and socially thuggish.

First and last, Murdoch has the soul of a tabloid journalist. He may be, as Auberon Waugh once said, "a hairy-heeled tit-and-bum merchant from Oz," but it pays off. Nude women on page three, sex advice, fabricated news and racial scare stories turned his London tabloid *The Sun* into the largest-selling English-language paper in the world. In this country, his checkout-counter *Star*, with headlines like "Rapist Caught by Own Cat," won the hearts of 2.8 million buyers.

But what he's done with his newspapers is nothing compared with what he sees in the near television future. F.C.C. regulations prohibit any individual or company from owning more than twelve TV stations or reaching more than 25 percent of the country through its stations, but if Murdoch succeeds in his present plans, the Fox network and its business partners will soon push past those limits. If that prospect bothers liberals for ideological reasons, it ought to scare the shit out of the religious right for all the reasons it sums up in the phrase "family values."

Some on the right know what's coming. In his *Wall Street Journal* column Tim Ferguson recently noted that to many, Fox's evening lineup is "replete with vulgar sensationalism." And he quotes William Bennett, the right wing's padre, with this complaint: "It doesn't follow that being libertarian, one has to put on trash for other people's children to watch." To all such criticism, Murdoch responds innocently, "What is taste, what is morality?"

And if Murdoch's right-wing supporters think he's hot to promote democracy around the world, let them remember his most notorious surrender. While setting up his Asian operation he proclaimed that satellite technology posed "an unambiguous threat to totalitarian regimes everywhere." Murdoch's satellite was beaming BBC broadcasts highly critical of China's thuggish leaders. The thugs—with whom Murdoch was eager to do business—complained. So he did what came naturally: He kicked the BBC off the air.

Whatever, if any, corporate juggling the F.C.C. asks for in this charade can be easily handled by Murdoch, who in his deposition boasted that things like equity and ownership are "all semantics" and "you can get a bunch of accountants to give any names" you want to it. Like a lot of bureaucratic interventions aimed at corporations, this one has an enormous loophole. Violators of the alien ownership limits will be driven out of the industry, the law says, only "if the commission finds that the public interest will be served by the refusal or revocation of such license." Uh-oh. Indeed, in its May 4 ruling, the F.C.C. invited Fox to give it cause to justify a waiver, unprecedented in its history.

For some reason, F.C.C. commissioners do not like to displease Murdoch. They have done a number of extraordinary favors for him in the past. In 1993 the F.C.C. made an unprecedented exception to the rule that nobody could own a TV station and a newspaper in the same city—thereby allowing Murdoch, who already owned New York City's WNYW, to buy the *New York Post*. Later, the commissioners exempted Fox from certain key marketing restrictions that applied to other networks. They said they did this because Fox wasn't really a network—although everybody in the industry treats it as a network, the press (including the trade press) calls it a network and Murdoch himself boasts of it as the "fourth network" (or "network," as a Freudian typo in one of the N.A.A.C.P.'s legal briefs aptly put it). On several occasions the F.C.C. commissioners have demanded that he turn over certain files to determine if he is telling the truth; Murdoch (through his lawyers) just laughs at them, saying he'd rather see them in court, and they let him get away with it.

A major reason the F.C.C. will probably do nothing to punish Murdoch is that it knows whatever it did would be swiftly undone by the Republican Congress, which seems in the mood to kill the alien-ownership limit. This, of course, is what Murdoch, accompanied by his

Washington lobbyist, went to see Gingrich about before the book deal was announced. Murdoch's own spokesman acknowledged that Gingrich was only one of the eighteen officials Murdoch cornered in a three-day blitz of Washington. Senate majority leader Bob Dole made no secret of talking with Murdoch about his "problem," nor did most of the others.

Murdoch got what he came for. Several killer bills were proposed, the most important probably being the one introduced by Senator Larry Pressler, the Republican peanut from South Dakota. Its importance stems from the fact that he is the new chairman of the Commerce Committee, which oversees telecommunications legislation. Pressler is a pretty pitiful guy. He was first elected to congress twenty-one years ago as "a Common Cause candidate," vowing to chase all that dirty special interest money out of politics. You guessed it: His re-election kitty is booming. If plenty of Murdoch money doesn't wind up in that kitty, Pressler isn't Pressler.

But if fellows like Murdoch do press money on their benefactors, is that just supporting democracy, or is it a bribe? In the PAC era, it gets harder and harder to tell. John Noonan Jr., the University of California legal scholar who did a landmark study of bribery, says, "The core of the concept of a bribe is an inducement improperly influencing the performance of a public function meant to be gratuitously exercised." But that definition, as he concedes, is maddeningly vague and changes with the times. Making it all the more confusing, "often a society has at least four definitions of a bribe—that of the more advanced moralists; that of the law as written; that of the law as in any degree enforced; that of common practice."

Murdoch was in such a rush to become a citizen and get on with business that perhaps he didn't take time to read the Constitution of his new homeland. If he had done so, he might have had some historical interest in seeing that the founders of this country looked upon bribery as such a loathsome practice that it is one of only two crimes (treason is the other) mentioned by name in the Constitution for which a federal official can be impeached and removed from office.

Or perhaps he did read the Constitution on that point but considered it unimportant because it is quite obvious that the bribing of public officials, by one means or another, has become a commonplace and casual crime, and is usually done without public embarrassment, much less punishment. Not, of course, that Murdoch would consider doing such a thing, or that the members of Congress he deals with would consider taking a bribe if offered.

Still, since temptations do abound, they should all bear in mind that, though most offenders get away with it, the buying and selling of political favors is not a peril-free sport. In the past three decades at least one Vice President, half a dozen or so Congressmen, four governors and hundreds of lesser officials have been convicted of bribery, and some have gone to prison. And the Securities and Exchange Commission forced so many large American corporations into confessions that it produced what Professor Noonan calls "the most abundant documentation of bribe giving known to history."

Bearing in mind the dominant party in Washington today, it may be apropos to note that most of that bribery occurred during periods when Republicans—that illustrious triumvirate Nixon/Reagan/Bush—were setting the moral tone for government.

HIRING QUOTAS FOR WHITE MALES ONLY

Eric Foner

•

THIRTY-TWO YEARS AGO, I graduated from Columbia College. My class of 700 was all-male and virtually all-white. Most of us were young men of ability, yet had we been forced to compete for admission with women and racial minorities, fewer than half of us would have been at Columbia. None of us, to my knowledge, suffered debilitating self-doubt because we were the beneficiaries of affirmative action—that is, favored treatment on the basis of our race and gender.

Affirmative action has emerged as the latest "wedge issue" of American politics. The recent abrogation of California affirmative action programs by Governor Pete Wilson, and the Clinton Administration's halting efforts to re-evaluate federal policy, suggest the issue is now coming to a head. As a historian, I find the current debate dismaying not only because of the crass effort to set Americans against one another for partisan advantage but also because the entire discussion lacks a sense of history.

Opponents of affirmative action, for example, have tried to wrap themselves in the mantle of the civil rights movement, seizing upon the 1963 speech in which Martin Luther King Jr. looked forward to the time when his children would be judged not by the "color of their skin" but by the "content of their character." Rarely mentioned is that King came to be a strong supporter of affirmative action.

In his last book, *Where Do We Go From Here?*, a brooding meditation on America's long history of racism, King acknowledged that "special treatment" for blacks seemed to conflict with the ideal of opportunity based on individual merit. But, he continued, "a society that has done something special *against* the Negro for hundreds of years must now do something special *for* him."

Our country, King realized, has never operated on a colorblind basis. From the beginning of the Republic, membership in American society was defined in racial terms. The first naturalization law, enacted in 1790, restricted citizenship for those emigrating from abroad to "free white persons." Free blacks, even in the North, were barred from juries, public schools, government employment and the militia and regular army. Not until after the Civil War were blacks deemed worthy to be American citizens, while Asians were barred from naturalization until the 1940s.

White immigrants certainly faced discrimination. But they had access to the political power, jobs and residential neighborhoods denied to blacks. In the nineteenth century, the men among them enjoyed the right to vote even before they were naturalized. Until well into this century, however, the vast majority of black Americans were excluded from the suffrage except for a period immediately after the Civil War. White men, native and immigrant, could find well-paid craft and industrial jobs, while employers and unions limited nonwhites (and women) to unskilled and menial employment. The "American standard of living" was an entitlement of white men alone.

There is no point in dwelling morbidly on past injustices. But this record of unequal treatment cannot be dismissed as "vague or ancient wrongs" with no bearing on the present, as Republican strategist William Kristol recently claimed. Slavery may be gone and legal segregation dismantled, but the effects of past discrimination live on in seniority systems that preserve intact the results of a racially segmented job market, a black unemployment rate double that of whites and pervasive housing segregation.

Past racism is embedded in the two-tier, racially divided system of social insurance still on the books today. Because key Congressional committees in the 1930s were controlled by Southerners with all-white electorates, they did not allow the supposedly universal entitlement of Social Security to cover the largest categories of black workers— agricultural laborers and domestics. Social Security excluded 80 percent of employed black women, who were forced to depend for a safety net on the much less generous "welfare" system.

The notion that affirmative action stigmatizes its recipients reflects not just belief in advancement according to individual merit but the older idea that the "normal" American is white. There are firemen and black firemen, construction workers and black construction workers: Nonwhites (and women) who obtain such jobs are still widely viewed as interlopers, depriving white men of positions or promotions to which they are historically entitled.

I have yet to meet the white male in whom special favoritism (getting a job, for example, through relatives or an old boys' network, or because of racial discrimination by a union or employer) fostered doubt about his own abilities. In a society where belief in black inferiority is still widespread (witness the success of *The Bell Curve*), many whites and some blacks may question the abilities of beneficiaries of affirmative action. But this social "cost" hardly counterbalances the enormous social benefits affirmative action has produced.

Nonwhites (and even more so, white women) have made deep inroads into the lower middle class and into professions once reserved for white males. Columbia College now admits women and minority students. Would these and other opportunities have opened as widely and as quickly without the pressure of affirmative action programs? American history suggests they would not.

It is certainly true, as critics charge, that affirmative action's benefits have not spread to the poorest members of the black community. The children of Harlem, regrettably, are not in a position to take advantage of the spots Columbia has opened to blacks. But rather than simply ratifying the advantages of already affluent blacks, who traditionally advanced by serving the segregated black community, affirmative action has helped to create a *new* black middle class, resting on professional and managerial positions within white society.

This new class is much more vulnerable than its white counterpart to the shifting fortunes of the economy and politics. Far more middle-class blacks than whites depend on public employment—positions now threatened by the downsizing of federal, state and municipal governments. The fact that other actions are needed to address the problems of the "underclass" hardly negates the proven value of affirmative action in expanding black access to the middle class and skilled working class.

There is no harm in rethinking the ways affirmative action is implemented—re-examining, for example, the expansion to numerous other groups of a program originally intended to deal with the legacy of slavery and segregation. In principle, there may well be merit in redefining disadvantage to include poor whites. The present cry for affirmative action based on class rather than race, however, seems as much an evasion as a serious effort to rethink public policy. Efforts to uplift the poor, while indispensable in a just society, are neither a substitute for nor incompatible with programs that address the legacy of the race-based discrimination to which blacks have historically been subjected. Without a robust class politics, moreover, class politics, are unlikely to get very far. The present Congress may well dismantle affirmative action, but it hardly seems sympathetic to broad "color-blind" programs to assist the poor.

At a time of deindustrialization and stagnant real wages, many whites have come to blame affirmative action for declining economic prospects. Let us not delude ourselves, however, into thinking that eliminating affirmative action will produce a society in which rewards are based on merit. Despite our rhetoric, equal opportunity had never been the American way. For nearly all our history, affirmative action has been a prerogative of white men.

TO NEWT ON ART

Arthur Miller

•

Near the end of May an eclectic contingent including Wendy Wasserstein, Melanie Griffith, Walter Mosley and Joanne Woodward attended a breakfast to lobby for continued Congressional support of the arts. Among those present was Newt Gingrich, who remarked to the assembled that playwright Arthur Miller represented a counter-argument: After all, he had effected his great works without the benefit of government fellowships. On hearing this, Miller sent the following letter to Gingrich, which we thought worthy of sharing with our readers.

—THE EDITORS

JUNE 6, 1995

Dear Mr. Gingrich:

I write to correct an impression which you seem to have concerning my having created a literary career with no help from government. (This from a member of a writers' delegation who discussed the N.E.A. with you very recently.)

It is true that I was able to survive in my early years by writing radio adaptations of books and plays for the Du Pont Cavalcade of America, and the U.S. Steel program, among others, while working on my stage plays at the same time. I confess I have taken a certain pride in this independence. But I was greatly helped at two points in my life by the Feds.

In 1936, as a student at the University of Michigan, the National Youth Administration paid me $15 a month to feed a couple of thousand mice in a cancer research laboratory. I washed dishes for my meals but without that N.Y.A. money I couldn't have paid my room rent and would no doubt have had to leave school. Jobs in those times were next to impossible to find.

In 1938 when I graduated I managed to get onto the W.P.A. Writers Project—$22.77 a week—for six months until the Project was shut down. In that time I wrote a tragedy for the stage about the conquest of Mexico, and perhaps more important, managed to break into writing for commercial radio. The government's help in both instances was brief but crucial. (Among my colleagues on the W.P.A. was Orson Welles; we were both helped to find our feet by the W.P.A., and I have often wondered whether his and my income taxes in later years hadn't paid for a big part of the Project's costs not only on our behalf but on many others'.)

But I believe there was something more involved than keeping artists financially alive. The country then was in crisis, as you know, and the support of the arts by government was a vital gesture of mutuality between the American people and the artists, and helped sustain a faith in one another and the country's future.

The arts are not going to die in America because Congress turns its back on them—the artist is a weed that can survive in the cracks of a sidewalk. But in the act of supporting its arts, Congress demonstrates a pride in our arts which I know will move most American artists to tap their highest artistic ideals in return.

You are aware I'm sure that we spend far less on the support of our fine arts than almost every other advanced country. To you this indeed may well be a valid expression of the American way, an emphatic reliance on the self rather than others. But as a historian you must recall that over the millennia the nature and function of the arts have been regarded as decisively different from other human enterprises.

Some thirty or so years ago, I spoke at Brandeis College in support of some kind of subsidy for theater in the belief that sooner or later the bottom-line attitude would serve us badly. (And in fact, last year on Broadway there was one non-musical play that survived current astro- nomical production costs—*Angels in America*—and even this much- praised work could not pay back its investment.)

A man rose in the audience: "I manufacture shoes; if the public won't buy enough of them, why shouldn't I demand government sup- port?" Hard to answer that one. I could only think to ask him a ques- tion in reply. "Can you name me one classical Greek shoemaker?"

That sounds like an elitist answer, admittedly, but a work of art does outlast the best-made pair of shoes, probably because it reflects the soul and spirit of a people rather than only its body. Where theater is concerned, it was in fact funded in Greece by donations from the well-to-do (often despite themselves); and in Elizabethan England by the nobility, along with ticket sales; and in Renaissance Italy by the church.

Finally—having traveled in Russia, Eastern Europe and China—I am absolutely opposed to a system of government funding of all the arts and artists. That way lies government control of the arts. But a system of at least helping to fund individual projects over limited periods of time need not do so. The British funding system for their famous subsidized theaters certainly proves this beyond all question, as does the French. Indeed, subsidy has enhanced their freedom to produce the truly great plays of the past and present which very often are taken over by commercial producers for long runs. This symbiosis is extraordinarily fruitful.

The view that culture and the arts are beyond the responsibilities of Congress is a meager one and unhistorical. After all, the land grant colleges of Michigan, Illinois, Wisconsin and the other states were established by order of the federal government as a condition of their later admission into the Union. And the specific mission of these schools was to raise the cultural level of mechanics, farmers and artisans.

We believe most in the reality of what is marketable; this is the hallmark of commercial society and we glory in it. But there is often more enduring value in what is not marketable, or not immediately so. The real question, it seems to me, is whether the American artist is to be alienated from his government or encouraged by it to express the nature and genius of his people. The National Endowment, compared to similar efforts in other countries, is minuscule in scope; but the spirit behind it must not be extinguished. I hope in the end you will agree.

Sincerely yours,
ARTHUR MILLER

IS THERE METHOD IN HIS MADNESS?

Kirkpatrick Sale

•

ANY DAY NOW the powers at *The New York Times* and *The Washington Post* will have to decide whether they will print the full 35,000-word text of the document sent to them in late June by the man the Federal Bureau of Investigation is calling the Unabomber. In the letter that accompanied the text, he gave each paper three months to publish his screed, upon which he promises to "desist from terrorism," but he warned that if they refused he would "start building [his] next bomb." That deadline is September 29.

Naturally the decision has been somewhat complicated for the two papers, since they don't want to seem to "give in to terrorist demands" and don't particularly like giving such publicity to the Unabomber's decidedly anti-establishmentarian opinions. They are especially perturbed by his demand to be allowed to publish additional 3,000-word pieces for the next three years to rebut any critics of the original, thus prolonging the Damoclean threat. And yet they obviously don't want to give the man an excuse to send out more of his mail bombs, two of which have killed and two wounded their recipients in the past three years.

I have read the full text of the Unabomber treatise—the F.B.I. sent along two young female agents with copies of it for me to peruse—and I would recommend that either one of the papers publish it and trust the man will keep his word about ending the mad, unconscionable bombings. They should forget about the "giving in to terrorism" excuse, which is mostly meaningless in this case since there are no grand causes to be satisfied, no hostages to be freed and no reason to think that the threat would be repeated because it then becomes laughable. They needn't worry about the propaganda effect of printing it, since it is a woodenly written term paper, full of academic jargon and pop psychology, repetitive and ill-argued, that will keep only the most dedicated readers awake beyond its opening paragraphs.

Which, I would say, is a shame. Because the central point the Unabomber is trying to make—that "the industrial-technological system" in which we live is a social, psychological and environmental "disaster for the human race"—is absolutely crucial for the American public to understand and ought to be on the forefront of the nation's political agenda.

I say this, of course, as a partisan. The Unabomber stands in a long line of anti-technology critics where I myself have stood, and his general arguments against industrial society and its consequences are quite similar to those I have recently put forth in a book on the people who might be said to have begun this tradition, the Luddites. Along with a number of people today who might be called neo-Luddites— Jerry Mander, Chellis Glendinning, Jeremy Rifkin, Bill McKibben, Wendell Berry, Dave Foreman, Langdon Winner, Stephanie Mills and John Zerzan among them—the Unabomber and I share a great many views about the pernicious effect of the Industrial Revolution, the evils of modern technologies, the stifling effect of mass society, the vast extent of suffering in a machine-dominated world and the inevitability of social and environmental catastrophe if the industrial system goes on unchecked.

We disagree, to be sure, about what is to be done about all this and the means by which to achieve it. In the course of his career, at least as the F.B.I. has reconstructed it, the Unabomber has carried out sixteen bombings, killing three people and injuring twenty-three others, apparently choosing targets in some way connected to modern technology— a technological institute at Northwestern University, the University of Utah business school, a Salt Lake City computer store, a University of California geneticist, and a Yale computer scientist, among others—to try to "propagate anti-industrial ideas and give encouragement to those who hate the industrial system." That strikes me as simple madness. Maiming and killing people does not normally propagate ideas, and in this case no one knew what ideas were in the Unabomber's mind until he started writing letters this past year and then delivered his treatise in

June. As for getting the message across, the only message that anyone got for sixteen years was that some nut was attacking people associated with universities and computers (hence the F.B.I.'s tag, *Una*bomber).*

But the bombings are going to get his document published, right or wrong, one way or another, and sooner rather than later. If the two newspapers don't publish it, *Penthouse* has offered to, and failing that, someone is sure to try to get it out as a pamphlet or send it over the Internet. That is what moves me to try to assess the treatise now, because I believe it would be a good idea to sort out its sound ideas from its errant ones, and to find the areas that ought not be discredited simply because of the agency that puts them forth—and as a service to all those who would fall asleep over the document itself.

"Industrial Society and Its Future" is the modest-enough title, and it is labeled as "by FC," which the author describes as a "terrorist group" though there is no sign from the writing style here that more than one person is behind it, and the F.B.I. believes that the Unabomber is acting alone. (The fact that he has escaped detection for seventeen years—especially during this past year, when he has become the target of the largest manhunt in the agency's history—would tend to support that.) "FC" is variously cited as the initials for "Freedom Club" or "Freedom Collective," although it is popularly thought to stand for a vulgar comment about computers; it is not explained in his text.

The sixty-six pages that follow begin with two pages of trivial typo corrections, showing the kind of fastidiousness ("sovle" should be "solve" "poit" should be "point") one might expect from a craftsman whose bombs the F.B.I. has described as "meticulously" constructed; then come fifty-six pages of argument divided into twenty-four subtitled sections and 232 numbered paragraphs; and it all ends with thirty-six foot-notes, mostly qualifying statements in the text. That form, plus the leaden language and stilted diction, the fondness for sociological jargon and psychobabble, and the repeated use of "we argue that" and "we now discuss" and the like, make it certain that this was written by someone whose writing style, and probably the whole intellectual development, was arrested in college.

The F.B.I. has said that it believes he was a student of the history of science, but on the evidence here he was a social psychology major with

*The "a" stands for "airline" because only one early target was an airline executive, but I remain unconvinced that this was a genuine Unabomber victim. I'd render him "Unibomber," considering nine of the sixteen bombs were aimed at university targets or professors.

a minor in sociology, and he shows all the distressing hallmarks of the worst of that academic breed. He spends twelve pages, for example, on a strange and somewhat simplistic explanation of "something that we will call the power process," consisting of four elements "we call goal, effort and attainment of goal," plus "autonomy," all in an effort to explain why people today are unhappy and frustrated. Only someone trapped in the social sciences would walk that way.

Various professor types have been quoted in the papers saying how "bright" this fellow must be, but the arguments here are never very original and the line of reasoning is often quite convoluted. He has read a lot in certain areas—no poetry, though, I'll bet—and has thought a lot about the particular things that concern him, but aside from a few flashes there is no suggestion of anything more than a routine mind and a dutiful allegiance to some out-of-the-ordinary critics of modern society. I'm sure he makes good bombs, but grading him on his intellect I wouldn't give him more than a C+. I venture to say he didn't make it to his senior year.

The opus isn't helped by the fact that at least a third of it is essentially irrelevant, social-psych padding and scholarly back-and-forthing, one-hand-and-the-othering. Two long sections attacking "modern leftism" and "leftish" academics have nothing to do with his thesis, and I suspect they are offered because he had a bad time with certain sectarian groups in the early 1970s—no surprise—and with certain progress-minded, pro-technology Marxists he met in the academy.* Any good editor would have cut it.

But as near as I can fathom it after three careful readings, the Unabomber's argument would seem to be this:

"Industrial-technological society" has succeeded to the point where, because of its size and complexity, it has constricted human freedom, meaning one's power to "control the circumstances of one's own life." Such freedoms as we do have are those permitted by the system consistent with its own ends—economic freedom to consume, press freedom to expose inefficiency and corruption—and do not in fact give individuals or groups true power, in the same sense that they have control over satisfying "life-and-death issues of one's existence: food, clothing, shel-

---

*The F.B.I. has leaked the idea that the Unabomber is really Leo Frederick Burt, one of the "New Year's Gang" that bombed the Army Math Research Center at the University of Wisconsin in August 1970 and who has been a fugitive ever since. If so, he probably was steeped beyond human endurance in the kind of fractious sectarian stews aboiling in those days and comes by his dislike of what he thinks is leftism legitimately.

ter and defense." "Today people live more by virtue of what the system does FOR them or TO them than by virtue of what they do for themselves. . . . Modern man is strapped down by a network of rules and regulations, and his fate depends on the actions of persons remote from him whose decisions he cannot influence."

Industrial society *must* perform this way in order to succeed—"The system has to regulate human behavior closely in order to function"—and cannot be reformed to work differently. "Changes large enough to make a lasting difference in favor of freedom would not be initiated because it would be realized that they would gravely disrupt the system."

Industrial society must increasingly work to constrict freedom and control behavior since "technology advances with great rapidity" and on many fronts: "crowding, rules and regulations, increasing dependence of individuals on large organizations, propaganda and other psychological techniques, genetic engineering, invasion of privacy through surveillance devices and computers, etc."*

But the problem of "control over human behavior" continues to bedevil this society, and right now "the system is currently engaged in a desperate struggle to overcome certain problems that threaten its survival," primarily social (the "growing numbers" of "rebels," "dropouts and resisters") but also economic and environmental. "If the system succeeds in acquiring sufficient control over human behavior quickly enough, it will probably survive. Otherwise it will break down. We think the issue will most likely be resolved within the next several decades, say 40 to 100 years."

Therefore, the task of those who oppose the industrial system is to advance that breakdown by promoting "social stress and instability in industrial society," which presumably includes bombing, and by developing and propagating "an ideology that opposes technology," one that puts forth the "counter-ideal" of nature "in order to gain enthusiastic support." Thus, when the system becomes sufficiently stressed and unstable, a "revolution against technology may be possible."

Now, this is a reasonable enough argument—the Unabomber is not irrational, whatever else you can say about him—and I think it is even to some extent persuasive. There is nothing wild-eyed or rabble-rousing about it (it could actually use a lot more Paine-ist fomentation and

---

*Oddly, the Unabomber's antipathy toward technology is more in the abstract than the particular. He actually likes certain technologies—"electricity, indoor plumbing, rapid long-distance communications . . . how could one argue against any of these things?"—and argues that revolutionaries should use "some modern technology."

furor) and the points are most often buttressed with careful arguments and examples—though nowhere, interestingly, a single statistic. It is too slow, too plodding, too repetitive; but you have to say its case is made in a competent, if labored, fashion.

His critique of industrial society today is most telling, I think, and reads as if he'd spent a lot of time defending it in the back rooms of bars. (Excerpts presented in the *Times* and the *Post* for some reason concentrate on the treatise's weaker and tangential early parts and give only limited attention to this central message.) Just picking at random, I find these examples:

> The system does not and cannot exist to satisfy human needs. Instead, it is human behavior that has to be modified to fit the needs of the system. This has nothing to do with the political or social ideology that may pretend to guide the technological system. It is not the fault of capitalism and it is not the fault of socialism. It is the fault of technology, because the system is guided not by ideology but by technical necessity.

> If the use of a new item of technology is INITIALLY optional, it does not necessarily REMAIN optional, because new technology tends to change society in such a way that it becomes difficult or impossible for an individual to function without using that technology. . . . Something like this seems to have happened already with one of our society's most important psychological tools for enabling people to reduce (or at least temporarily escape from) stress, namely, mass entertainment. Our use of mass entertainment is "optional" . . . yet mass entertainment is a means of escape and stress-reduction on which most of us have become dependent.

> The technophiles are hopelessly naive (or self-deceiving) in their understanding of social problems. They are unaware of (or choose to ignore) the fact that when large changes, even seemingly beneficial ones, are introduced into a society, they lead to a long sequence of other changes, most of which are difficult to predict. . . . In fact, ever since the industrial revolution technology has been creating new problems for society far more rapidly than it has been solving old ones.

Not inspired, but thoughtful, perceptive enough, when abstracted from its labored context.

What's surprising about all this, though, is that it reads as if the

Unabomber thinks he's the first person who ever worked out such ideas. It is hard to believe, but he seems woefully ignorant of the long Luddistic strain in Western thought going back at least to William Blake and Mary Shelley, and he does not once cite any of the great modern critics of technology such as Lewis Mumford, Jacques Ellul, Paul Goodman, Max Weber, E. F. Schumacher or Rachel Carson, nor any of the contemporary laborers in this vineyard. In one of his letters to the *Times* he does say that "anyone who will read the anarchist and radical environmentalist journals will see that opposition to the industrial-technological system is widespread and growing," so he must know something about the current critics, although he does not mention specific articles or authors or particular periodicals. (If I had to guess which has been most influential on him, I'd say the *Fifth Estate*, a feisty anti-technology paper published out of Detroit for the past thirty years, but he does not name it anywhere.)

That failure to ground himself in the Luddistic tradition, where both utopian and dystopian models proliferate, may be the reason that the Unabomber is so weak on envisioning the future, particularly the kind of revolution he seems to want.

I would agree with the Unabomber's general position that "to make a lasting change in the direction of development of any important aspect of a society, reform is insufficient," and I might even agree that in certain circumstances therefore "revolution is necessary." But I can't figure out at all what kind of revolution this is to be. He says that "a revolution does not necessarily involve an armed uprising or the overthrow of a government," a conviction he is so certain of he repeats it twice more, adding that "it may or may not involve physical violence," and in two footnotes he suggests that it might be "somewhat gradual or piecemeal" and might "consist only of a massive change of attitudes toward technology resulting in a relatively gradual and painless disintegration of the industrial system."

This is a somewhat peculiar position for a man who has been killing and injuring people in service to his dream of a new society, and I'm not sure what he thinks revolutions are or how they are achieved. If he has in mind something more like the Industrial Revolution or the Copernican revolution, he doesn't suggest how that might come about, and the sorts of strategies he ends up advocating—promoting social instability, destroying and wrecking "the system," seeing "its remnants . . . smashed beyond repair"—sound an awful lot like a revolution with a good deal of violence. He even suggests at one point that the models are the French and Russian revolutions, both pretty bloody affairs.

The whole question of violence indeed is confused in the Unabomber's mind, oddly enough after seventeen years during which he must have been thinking about it a little. He never once addresses the reasons for his own string of bombings or explains what he thinks he has been accomplishing, other than to say that this was the way to have "some chance of making a lasting impression." He is critical of "leftists" who commit violence, because it is only "a form of 'liberation' " they justify "in terms of mainstream values . . . fighting against racism or the like," and later is critical of leftists because they are "against competition and against violence." His revolution is not necessarily to be violent, yet he never confronts the idea of a nonviolent revolution or how it would be strategically carried out.

The one task of revolutionaries the Unabomber is clear about is the business of producing an anti-technology "ideology," although he doesn't anywhere concern himself with the hard business of saying what that would consist of. But it doesn't much matter to him, since the primary purpose of this ideology is "to create a core of people who will be opposed to the industrial system on a rational, thought-out basis," an intellectual cadre who can then dish it out "in a simplified form" for the "unthinking majority" who "like to have such issues presented in simple, black-and-white terms." "History is made by active, determined minorities," you see, and "as for the majority, it will be enough to make them aware of the existence of the new ideology and remind them of it frequently." Lenin couldn't have put it better.

The Unabomber's idea of a systemic breakdown is, I think, more plausible than his concept of revolution; one could see how, as the system was breaking down of its own weight and incompetence, unable to manage the problems its technology creates, this might be "helped along by revolutionaries." Just how the breakdown would come about is not spelled out. The Unabomber gives only a passing glance to the multiple environmental disasters the system is producing for itself and never mentions the likelihood, as chaos theory predicts, that the complex industrial house of cards will not hold. At least he does posit a "time of troubles" after which the human race would be "given a new chance."

I should note that the Unabomber, on the evidence here, does not have any special vision of an ecologically based future, as the newspapers have suggested. Indeed, he is no environmentalist, and I'd say he has only the faintest grasp of the principles of ecology. It's true that he refers to nature at one point—"That is, WILD nature!"—as a "positive ideal," but this is almost entirely cynical, nature as a concept that he figures will be useful in propaganda terms because it is "the opposite of technology," because "most people will agree that nature is beautiful" and because "in many people, nature inspires the kind of reverence that is associated with religion." He shows no real understanding of the role of technology in enabling industrial society not only to exploit nature but to pass that off as legitimate, and not one individual environmental problem is addressed here, except overpopulation. (And on that one the Unabomber, though acknowledging that it produces overcrowding and stress, indicates no awareness of its awful consequences for all the other species of the world, whose endangerment and extinctions we are caus- ing by our exploding numbers, or for the natural systems of the world, whose degradation we are causing by our exploding consumption.)

It's clear enough that the Unabomber counts "radical environmen- talists" as among those rightly opposing technology, and his use of wood in some of his bombs and his killing of a timber lobbyist in Cali- fornia suggests a further affinity. But he indicates no sympathy for the kind of biocentric "deep ecology" and bioregionalism espoused by most of them, and his concerns are exclusively anthropocentric, his appreciation of other species and natural systems nil. He also mocks those who believe in the "Gaia theory" of a living earth, common in many environmental groups: "Do its adherents REALLY believe in it or are they just play-acting?"

In short, it feels to me that his appeal to nature is entirely utilitarian (like adding another little mechanism to your bomb to make sure it works) rather than a heartfelt passion, of which he seems to have very few in any case.

But if nature does not inspire his vision of the future, it is hard to tell what does. Presumably he would want, as a self-described anarchist, some kind of world where "people live and work as INDIVIDUALS and SMALL GROUPS," using "small-scale technology . . . that can be used by small- scale communities without outside assistance." But he nowhere bothers to hint at how this future society would operate (other than to say it would burn all technical books), nor does he refer to any in the long line of anarcho-communal writers from Kropotkin to Bookchin who have given a great deal of thought to the configurations of just such a society.

It's true that the Unabomber offers the defense at one point that "a new kind of society cannot be designed on paper" and "when revolu- tionaries or utopians set up a new kind of society, it never works out as planned." That gives him leeway to avoid discussing what kind of world he wants (even in a three-page section called "THE FUTURE"); unfortu- nately, it also leaves a gaping hole in his treatise. Even those who agree that the industrial system should be torn down will want to get some idea of what is supposed to replace it before they are moved to endorse the cause, much less become the revolutionaries the Unabomber wants.

So, in sum, what are we to make of this strange document? So important to its author that he is prepared to kill people (even though he has written that he is "getting tired of making bombs") to get it published in a major newspaper. So embarrassing to those newspapers that they don't know what to do with it.

It is the statement of a rational and serious man, deeply committed to his cause, who has given a great deal of thought to his work and a great deal of time to this expression of it. He is prescient and clear about the nature of the society we live in, what its purposes and methods are, and how it uses its array of technologies to serve them; he understands the misery and anxiety and constriction this creates for the individual and the wider dangers it poses for society and the earth. He truly believes that a campaign of social disorder led by misfits, rebels, dropouts and saboteurs (and presumably terrorists), coupled with the concerted propaganda work of a dedicated intellectual elite, has a chance to cause or hasten the breakdown of industrial society, and this motivates him in his grisly work.

The document is also the product of a limited and tunnel-visioned man, with a careful and dogged but somewhat incoherent mind, filled with a catalogue of longstanding prejudices and hatreds, academically trained, occasionally inventive, purposeful and humorless. He is amoral, not to say coldblooded, about acts of terrorism, which are regarded as an effective tactic in service to the larger cause. He is convinced enough in his cause to have produced this long justification for it, complete with numerous bold assertions and his own "principles of history," but he repeatedly finds qualifications and reservations and indeed ends up calling the article no more "than a crude approximation to the truth," as if to suggest that somewhere within he is not quite confident.

All in all, I think despite its flaws it is a document worth publishing, and not only because that could presumably help stop the killing. There is a crucial message at the core of it for those with fortitude enough to get through it, and unless that message is somehow heeded and acted on we are truly a doomed society hurtling toward a catastrophic breakdown. I can't expect the *Times* and the *Post* to give much credence to that idea—and they can lard it with their own dissents and denials if they choose—but they might just realize that there is a growing body of people these days beginning at last to understand the increasing perils of the technosphere we have created. For, as *The New Yorker* recently put it, there's a little of the Unabomber in all of us.

DIFFERENT DRUMMER
PLEASE, MARCHERS!

Patricia J. Williams

•

BY THE TIME this is published, I imagine it will be a different world; but imagine if you will, Gentle Reader, a time before the Million Man March on Washington. Imagine trying to imagine what will happen, if whatever has already happened hadn't yet.

I am trying to do just that because I am trying to understand the enormous, even passionate, appeal the very idea of this march has among so many of my friends—black men whose opinions I respect, whose values I admire. I guess I also need to confess that I find that appeal somewhat mystifying because I have nothing but misgivings about any venture organized by either Nation of Islam leader Louis Farrakhan or former N.A.A.C.P. executive director, Ben Chavis, never mind the two of them together. From Farrakhan's legendary anti-Semitism to Chavis's legendary sexual transgressions, there have been enough examples of bad judgment, ethnic slurs, extreme misogyny, uncontained homophobia and old-fashioned breach of fiduciary responsibility to make them the media's top Black Leaders Everyone Just Loves to Hate. Add in the media talents of Washington Mayor Marion Barry and the Rev. Al Sharpton, who recently jumped on board the organizational bandwagon, and I start to get extremely anxious.

My anxiety notwithstanding, eighty black religious leaders have declared October 16 a holy day. Both Jesse Jackson and Cornel West have decided to march. Baltimore's thoughtful mayor, Kurt Schmoke, supports the idea of a show of black male "uplift." The Association of Black Psychologists has issued an endorsement of the march as a way to focus on black men's "personal responsibility to arrest self-imposed destructive attitudes, feelings and behavior," and C. DeLores Tucker, head of the National Political Congress of Black Women and crusader against misogynist gangsta rap, has let her approval be known. New York's oldest black-owned paper, *The Amsterdam News*, dismisses critics of the march as those who will "grind their molars into dust."

There are, I realized, a lot of powerful currents swirling underneath this one. So I decided to take a look at the official "Position Statement" of the organizing committee. "We are coming to Washington . . . to repent and atone," it says. Men are urged to come as a way of taking "our place" at the "head of families" and "maintainers" of women and children. Women are urged to attend, but to "stay at home" while remaining "by our side" and are thanked for their patience in "waiting for us to take up our responsibility." The march will be a day of prayer and petition to "the government" that manufacturing jobs need not be "ceded" to "Third World countries." "The Black community . . . in a partnership with government" can unite to form "the salvation army of the world."

The steely-eyed lawyer in me reviews all this and concludes that this is going to be a public relations nightmare. A National Day of Atonement, as the Position Statement puts it—this is a religious enterprise. Why march on Washington? That's not where God lives, last I heard. This basically fundamentalist platform of isolationism, personal responsibility and women-waiting-at-home sounds somewhere between the scripts of the Promise Keepers (a Christian men's movement) and the Contract With America. And while atonement might be a great idea if it were only for the organizing committee, dragging a million black men with them risks buying into the stereotypification of criminality and deviance as exclusively a "black male thing"—and a pathological thing at that. It starts to sound like a day for black men to forgive themselves for the *stereotype* of themselves, even if in the name of "showing the world who we are." And isn't there a risk that all it will take is one sorry indiscretion, one set of loose lips, for the antihero of the march to assume the Willie Horton Crown of Media Thorns and the march to be declared a riot? Then a million others will be deemed the "just likes" of.

Yes, of course that will happen, says a friend who's going. *But that's what happens all the time. It doesn't matter who's in charge. It doesn't matter who says what. It doesn't matter, it doesn't matter. No one sees a difference, nothing makes a difference. Black men are living in a state of despair and distortion. Who cares what the media thinks— this thing could be a communion I need in the worst way.*

It is this kind of passionate hope so many will bring to this event that I hope is not disappointed—this promise of renewal, this potential for affirmation that seems so precariously placed and so bottomlessly expectant. There are friends of mine who would have absolutely nothing to do with the conservative fundamentalism of this platform under any other circumstance who find this call for a coming together irresistible—and they will not argue about it; they do not care to see beyond that Great Coming of togetherness.

And while I understand that longing on many levels—there is a real and dangerous racial crisis facing this nation, and black men are bearing much of the brunt of this country's worst fears and cruelest neglect—I also worry about a "personal responsibility" march, as some of the organizers have called it, on the site of the civil rights marches of the past. The privatizing symbolic catchwords of the day seem to have displaced the broader political battles of the past. If the marches of the past were about all blacks achieving the full benefits of citizenship, this march of atoning black men seems to insist that "We exist!" "We are different!" and "We are good!" And there is something about that vision of a march-of-atonement that I find inestimably sad—a loneliness, an absence at the center, no matter how many voices are lifted to testify and no matter how many millions may show up to be seen.

I'll tell you what I'd like to see. If we're going to have a national day of atonement, what a great occasion to extol inclusiveness as the centerpiece. Why not design a march that Bob Packwood could join, marching side by side with Ben Chavis, both apologizing up a storm? Where Rush Limbaugh and Mark Fuhrman could weep for their sins with Marion Barry; where Pat Buchanan and Louis Farrakhan could jump up shouting with the ecumenical power of divine redemption. In which Clinton came down from his mount and atoned for Lani Guinier, while Jesse Helms climbed up out of his burrow and let Clinton appoint her to the Justice Department. In which Charles Murray and Dinesh D'Souza confronted the Black Child Within and had transformational experiences. And it would be good to see Ricki Lake out there atoning too—quietly, if it's not too great a stretch of the imagination. Shoving the cameras away, muttering those words we all so long to hear: "Enough!"

THE BALLAD OF THE SKELETONS

•

Said the Presidential skeleton
I won't sign the bill
Said the Speaker skeleton
Yes you will

Said the Representative skeleton
I object
Said the Supreme Court skeleton
Whaddya expect

Said the Military skeleton
Buy Star Bombs
Said the Upperclass skeleton
Starve unmarried moms

Said the Yahoo skeleton
Stop dirty art
Said the Right Wing skeleton
Forget about yr heart

Said the Gnostic skeleton
The Human Form's divine
Said the Moral Majority skeleton
No it's not it's mine

Said the Buddha skeleton
Compassion is wealth

Said the Corporate skeleton
It's bad for your health

Said the Old Christ skeleton
Care for the Poor
Said the Son of God skeleton
AIDS needs cure

Said the Homophobe skeleton
Gay folk suck
Said the Heritage Policy skeleton
Blacks're outta luck

Said the Macho skeleton
Women in their place
Said the Fundamentalist skeleton
Increase human race

Said the Right-to-Life skeleton
Foetus has a soul
Said Pro-Choice skeleton
Shove it up your hole

Said the Downsized skeleton
Robots got my job
Said the Tough-on-Crime skeleton
Tear-gas the mob

Said the Governor skeleton
Cut school lunch
Said the Mayor skeleton
Eat the budget crunch

Said the Neo-Conservative skeleton
Homeless off the street!
Said the Free Market skeleton
Use 'em up for meat

Said the Think Tank skeleton
Free Market's the way

Said the S&L skeleton
Make the State pay

Said the Chrysler skeleton
Pay for you & me
Said the Nuke Power skeleton
& me & me & me

Said the Ecologic skeleton
Keep Skies blue
Said the Multinational skeleton
What's it worth to you?

Said the NAFTA skeleton
Get rich, Free Trade,
Said the Maquiladora skeleton
Sweat shops, low paid

Said the rich GATT skeleton
One world, high tech
Said the Underclass skeleton
Get it in the neck

Said the World Bank skeleton
Cut down your trees
Said the I.M.F skeleton
Buy American cheese

Said the Underdeveloped skeleton
Send me rice
Said Developed Nations' skeleton
Sell your bones for dice

Said the Ayatollah skeleton
Die writer die
Said Joe Stalin's skeleton
That's no lie

Said the Petrochemical skeleton
Roar Bombers roar!

Said the Psychedelic skeleton
Smoke a dinosaur

Said Nancy's skeleton
Just say No
Said the Rasta skeleton
Blow Nancy Blow

Said Demagogue skeleton
Don't smoke Pot
Said Alcoholic skeleton
Let your liver rot

Said the Junkie skeleton
Can't we get a fix?
Said the Big Brother skeleton
Jail the dirty pricks

Said the Mirror skeleton
Hey good looking
Said the Electric Chair skeleton
Hey what's cooking?

Said the Talkshow skeleton
Fuck you in the face
Said the Family Values skeleton
My family values mace

Said the N.Y. Times skeleton
That's not fit to print
Said the C.I.A skeleton
Cantcha take a hint?

Said the Network skeleton
Believe my lies
Said the Advertising skeleton
Don't get wise!

Said the Media skeleton
Believe you me

Said the Couch-Potato skeleton
What me worry?

Said the TV skeleton
Eat sound bites
Said the Newscast skeleton
That's all Goodnight

2/12–16/95

Allen Ginsberg

INSIDE THE BUTTS BOX
THE CIGARETTE PAPERS

Jon Wiener

•

W HEN CBS LAWYERS spiked a *60 Minutes* interview with a former tobacco executive who wanted to criticize the industry, a door opened to a story that is only beginning to be told: the way Big Tobacco has silenced critics and manipulated public information about its cancer-causing product. As the *60 Minutes* episode faded into a Morley-is-mad-at-Mike story, several crucial aspects of the power of the tobacco corporations to control the news have gone unexamined. Brown & Williamson (B&W), the company CBS lawyers feared, didn't have to threaten, much less sue, the network to censor a story; but the same company has failed to prevent publication, in a variety of media, of information it desperately wanted to keep secret. Thus while Mike and Morley have bowed to their masters, on another front the tobacco companies seem to have met their match—in a professor, a librarian and a whistleblowing temp.

The odd thing about the big FedEx box that arrived at Dr. Stanton Glantz's office at the University of California, San Francisco, medical school (U.C.S.F.) was the return address: "Mr. Butts," the Doonesbury character who tries to talk kids into smoking. Glantz is one of the best-known researchers in the fight against tobacco; the box arrived in his office in May 1994. "As soon as I opened it, I knew what it was," he said. "To the extent a professor can, I dropped everything."

The box contained 4,000 pages of documents that B&W later claimed were stolen from its files. Brown & Williamson, the nation's third-largest tobacco company, makes Kool, Pall Mall and Lucky Strike, among other brands; 1993 domestic sales were $2.4 billion, worldwide profit, $385 million. The documents, which made a pile four feet high, represented a smoking gun in the debate over the effects of tobacco on health. They showed that "thirty years ago the tobacco industry knew that nicotine was an addictive substance," Glantz says, "and that it caused cancer. And it showed that they withheld this information from the public." That's significant particularly in view of the Congressional testimony by the C.E.O.s of the seven biggest tobacco companies, all of whom had sworn a month earlier that they didn't believe cigarettes were addictive or caused cancer.

In the months that followed, the B&W documents that Glantz received became a landmark not only in tobacco litigation, medical scholarship and government policy but also in the battle against corporate control of information. The tobacco company filed a lawsuit to force the return of what it regarded as its stolen property. But Glantz had already taken a step that resulted in a decisive First Amendment victory: He and the university library had established a site on the World Wide Web to disseminate the documents. The lawsuit eventually ended up at the California Supreme Court, which O.K.'d the Internet posting.

When I asked Glantz about his strategy for defeating the tobacco company's efforts to prevent dissemination of the documents, he replied, "I wish I could say I had it all figured out. But in fact it was all inadvertent. I didn't think about a lawsuit; my only concern was that my office was too crowded."

The box of important documents was "sitting on the floor of my office," Glantz said, which he described as "the size of a broom closet." People from the media were calling, asking to come and look at the materials. In addition to having no room in his office, he was concerned about protecting the integrity of the documents. "So it occurred to me to stick the box in the library, where we had already established an archive on tobacco policy in California in the special collections department." Putting the Butts box in the university library turned out to be a key step in preventing the tobacco company from blocking public access to the documents.

Word spread among journalists and tobacco litigators that Glantz was sharing the B&W documents—the contents of which had just been the subject of a series of articles in *The New York Times* by

Philip Hilts, who had seen about 10 percent of the material sent to Glantz. (Hilts reported receiving documents from an unnamed Congressman, presumably Henry Waxman of Los Angeles, who had read some of the B&W documents into the *Congressional Record* after receiving an anonymous shipment. *The Washington Post* and *The Wall Street Journal* also obtained copies and printed stories.) As a growing stream of people came to San Francisco to look at the documents in the U.C.S.F. library, the librarians concluded there were too many to accommodate in the special collections department. Special collections departments everywhere operate under strict rules that protect their materials from theft, vandalism and loss; generally, an archivist watches over each user. At U.C.S.F. only one person at a time could work on them, so a waiting list was set up, which frustrated people from the press—"and the librarian wasn't getting any work done assembling the rest of the tobacco archive," Glantz recalled.

Karen Butter, deputy director of the library, came up with a practical solution: Scan the documents electronically and put them on a CD-ROM. Later they decided to put them on the Web as well. That would solve the security problem and eliminate the waiting list—people all over the world could gain access to the documents. That decision—also made for purely practical reasons rather than as part of a defensive legal strategy—transformed the case: Now B&W couldn't simply try to recover its "stolen" property from Stanton Glantz; putting out the documents on the Internet and on a CD-ROM was a form of publication, so B&W had to try to persuade the courts to engage in prior restraint of publication—to ask the courts to ignore the First Amendment guarantee of freedom of the press.

The tobacco company didn't find out that Glantz had the documents until January 1995, when an attorney for plaintiffs suing B&W in Mississippi tried to introduce the material into that case. Instead of using the normal discovery procedures to obtain them, he told the court that discovery was unnecessary because the documents were already in the public domain—at the archives of the U.C.S.F. library.

The head of litigation for B&W in San Francisco was a former federal judge named Barbara Caulfield; she showed up at the U.C.S.F. library in early February with a team of investigators. They announced that they had come to examine documents they believed were their property. "Our position was, any member of the public could see them, including attorneys for B&W," said Karen Butter. After seeing them, Caulfield declared the documents had been stolen from B&W; she demanded that the library return them immediately. "That resolved any questions we had about the authenticity of the materials," Glantz observed. B&W made two other demands: Until the documents were returned, it wanted the library to deny public access to them; and it demanded that the library provide B&W with a list of everyone who had seen them. When the library refused all three demands, B&W filed suit.

It's unusual, to say the least, to find private investigators watching library patrons to see what they are reading—but the tobacco company sent investigators into the library, Butter recalled, "to watch anyone who came in or out of the special collections reading room." That room is visible from the library's lobby through glass walls. "We asked them to leave," Butter recalls, "but they didn't. Then the university counsel asked the B&W legal counsel to get them to leave. They refused." This intimidation had some effect: The library eventually agreed to deny the public access to the documents—temporarily—until the suit was settled. In mid-February both sides agreed to move the documents to the campus police office until the court ruled.

When the court finally heard arguments in May, B&W's legal position was "weak," says University of California counsel Christopher Patti, who argued the case. The claim that the documents were "stolen property" had one big problem: Nothing was missing from the B&W files; the company still had possession of its "property." What U.C.S.F. had were simply copies, which had been leaked, not stolen. B&W was really claiming the right to block dissemination of the information in the documents. As Patti put it, "That raised very serious First Amendment issues."

The university's defense would have been considerably weaker if the documents had remained in Glantz's office. Making them accessible to the public at the library, and then preparing to "publish" them on CD-ROM and the Web site, transformed the case, turning Glantz's dissemination of the tobacco documents into something similar to what *The New York Times* did with the Pentagon Papers. "That similarity," Patti said, "became a lot clearer in everyone's mind when we were talking about real publication of the documents." Since the Supreme Court's 1973 Pentagon Papers decision, courts have been reluctant to order prior restraint of publication unless it can be shown to endanger directly national security or the lives of citizens.

The university showed impressive courage in defending the suit. Patti explained: "You had information here that was important to the public and the academic community, and a powerful entity arguing against its distribution. The university felt it shouldn't bend to that kind of pressure." At a time when the major corporations that publish books and run TV networks bow to the wishes of the tobacco companies, the importance of the university's action is even more significant.

On June 29 the California Supreme Court rejected the company's move to suppress the documents, and within twenty-four hours the university started putting the papers on-line at the U.C.S.F. library Web site that had been established for that purpose (http://www. library.ucsf.edu/tobacco). B&W documents that came form Congressman Waxman had already been scanned into electronic form, and were posted first; the new documents were posted daily, over a period of six weeks, until 8,000 pages were on-line. The Web site permits viewers to download their own copies of the documents, including correspondence on company letterhead and internal memos. The CD-ROM went on sale in late November, and is intended primarily for other libraries and institutions.

Lots of people are interested in the documents: journalists and academics; people involved in current lawsuits focusing on tobacco addiction and disease; students; people trying to pass local antismoking ordinances. Robin Chandler, head of archives and special collections at the U.C.S.F. library, said that the library kept statistics for the first five weeks the Web site was available: More than 52,000 documents were requested by computer users, during which time "the system was logging an average of 4,670 requests for information each day. Inquiries come from as far away as Australia, Japan, the United Kingdom and Germany." One of the most popular items: a confidential letter from Sylvester Stallone promising to use Brown & Williamson cigarettes in five of his films in exchange for half a million dollars.

B&W's big worry now is that the documents on the CD-ROM and Web site will be used in court, first of all in the massive smokers' class-action suit against the tobacco industry, which was cleared for trial in February by Judge Okla Jones 2d of Federal District Court in Louisiana. The judge ruled that the tobacco industry could be sued for punitive damages on the grounds that it knowingly addicted 100 million Americans to cigarettes and concealed that fact that cigarettes were addicting. The State of Mississippi's lawsuit seeking reimbursement from the tobacco companies for state Medicare costs is also pending. The key issues in each are what the tobacco companies knew and when they knew it—and the B&W documents provide a pretty definitive answer.

A B&W spokesman commented after the California court ruling, "This decision invites any person to steal documents and launder them through the U.C.S.F. library, where plaintiffs' lawyers can then argue that the documents are public." That's hard to argue with. Nevertheless, it will be up to the judges in each of the cases to decide whether to admit the documents Glantz made public at the U.C. Web site and on CD-ROM.

Although newspapers published articles about the leaked tobacco papers, the Web site for the B&W documents shows how the Internet has made it possible to convey sensitive materials to the public without the help of the news media. Daniel Ellsberg had to convince *The New York Times* to publish the Pentagon Papers; today, he could simply post them on a Web site. A. J. Liebling wrote in 1960 that "freedom of the press is guaranteed only to those who own one." Stanton Glantz and the University of California have shown that is no longer as true as it once was.

THE PUBLISHING STORY

"Publishing" the documents on the World Wide Web and on CD-ROM was only the beginning of the fight against corporate control of tobacco information; Glantz and his associates next wrote a book and a series of articles analyzing the documents. Their efforts to publish their studies reveal both the immense power the tobacco companies have to intimidate publishers and the courage of a few in refusing to submit to that power.

The Cigarette Papers, written by Glantz and four associates (Deborah Barnes, Lisa Bero, Peter Hanauer and John Slade), looked like a hot book to Glantz's literary agent, Jane Dystel, who currently represents five Pulitzer Prize winners. Editors to whom she submitted the proposal were initially enthusiastic; several called it "the Pentagon Papers of tobacco." But at press after press, editors were told by legal departments not to publish the book. "Everybody was afraid of being sued," Dystel said, "even though none of them had any contact with Brown & Williamson."

More than two dozen publishers turned the book down. "I just couldn't imagine I was going to have the problems I had," Dystel recalled. "This was explosive information. I really thought that it was important publishing. It's the reason a lot of us are in this business. I've been in the business for twenty-eight years as a publisher, editor and agent. In that time I've dealt with hundreds and hundreds of books. I've never had this experience before."

Perhaps legal considerations weren't the only ones. The book was a serious analysis by medical researchers; it was not written as a popular exposé. Paul Golob, the editor who turned it down at Basic Books, told me his reason was that "we didn't think it was going to be viable as a trade book." "That's not what I remember," Dystel commented. "Paul had long talks with Stan and he really was interested. He just couldn't convince his bosses. I remember him saying their legal department didn't want to take a chance."

Other editors gave other reasons. Times Books "seemed like a natural publisher for this," Dystel said, but when I asked publisher Peter Osnos why he turned it down, he told me, "I haven't got any recollection of it at all—we turn down nine of ten books we see." Dominick Anfuso at Simon and Schuster simply didn't return my calls asking why they turned the book down. Arnold Dolin, senior vice president and associate publisher at Dutton/Signet Books, said, "I had no legal concerns. I just didn't see it as a book that would work for us commercially." Marion Maneker, editor at Viking Penguin, also denied that legal concerns played a role in their decision ; the book simply "wasn't a strong editorial package," he said. But this was a book whose author would be featured on *60 Minutes*, scheduled for an hourlong *Peter Jennings Reports* on ABC and interviewed by *Newsweek* for December's "Newsmakers of the Year" feature. Ordinarily trade publishers will do almost anything to sign up authors with that kind of media coverage.

Kirk Jensen, an editor at Oxford University Press, seemed more forthright than many of his peers. He admitted that his house was "reluctant to go to battle with the tobacco industry" after "the marketing people said it was too scholarly"—so "there was little reason to stick our neck out." Jensen added, "I wasn't courageous enough. I couldn't get the support the book deserved."

The most disheartening turndown came from the New Press, which prides itself on publishing books considered risky and controversial. Associate director Diane Wachtell explained that "it was a painful decision for me personally. Editorially we were dying to do this book. But ten attorneys in a row said, 'B&W will sue you whether they have grounds or not.' At serious big-league law firms, the consensus was that, although we could probably ultimately show that we have a right to publish, financially we'd be out of business before we had a chance to show anybody anything. If you anger a tobacco company and get into what amounts to a financial war with it—where the issue is who can afford better attorneys for longer—you're going to lose. It's a shame that that's what has to prevail, but I'm not interested in putting the New Press out of business."

Finally one publisher decided to take on the tobacco companies: the

University of California Press. Executive editor Naomi Schneider explained that the press believed the California Supreme Court decision permitting publication of the documents on a university Web site provided them with some legal protection, and the willingness of the university counsel's office to defend publication showed that "in the worst-case scenario they would aggressively defend us."

"We've been given a real opportunity," Schneider says. "Publishing this book is a good thing for the world. As a publisher, I care about that. And we're going to receive a lot of attention for a high-profile book." She predicted that "trade publishers will regret their decision."

U.C. Press will publish *The Cigarette Papers* next April. The book will also be published on the Internet at the U.C.S.F. library tobacco documents Web site. Diane Wachtell says, "I wish U.C. Press the best. I'm delighted someone is publishing it. The public has a right to know this material. I'll be very curious to see whether B&W takes action against U.C. Press."

One other institution was willing to publish Glantz's challenge to corporate control of tobacco information: the American Medical Association. Medical school professors are supposed to publish research articles, so Glantz and his associates turned material from the book manuscript into five articles and submitted all of them to the most prestigious medical journal in the country, the *Journal of the American Medical Association (JAMA)*. "I thought, no way will they take five articles from one research group," he recalled. The journal editors subjected the five submissions to unprecedented peer review, according to Glantz—eight reviewers instead of the usual three—and the editors decided to accept all five articles.

The A.M.A.'s lawyers, Glantz reports, told editor George Lundberg that publishing articles based on the Butts box might provoke serious legal retaliation from B&W. *JAMA* was willing to take the risk, according to deputy editor Drummond Rennie. "Clearly, whenever the tobacco companies are involved one is extremely wary," he explained. "But with these articles, the public had an enormous right to know, because we're talking about the death of people on a huge scale. When you're a doctor, let alone a scientist, let alone a medical editor, that gives you a whole lot of backbone and it makes you extremely persuasive when it comes to arguments with anyone—including lawyers." The editors presented their decision to publish to the A.M.A.'s board of trustees, and the trustees unanimously endorsed publication of all five articles in its July 19 issue.

As if the articles weren't enough, the issue opened with a fierce editorial—as far as can be ascertained, the first editorial co-written by the A.M.A.'s board of trustees in the more than 100-year history of *JAMA*. It declared that the tobacco companies have "managed to remain hugely profitable from the sale of a substance long known by scientists and physicians to be lethal," responsible for a million deaths worldwide each year. The tobacco companies "dissemble, distort, and deceive, despite the fact that the industry's own research is consistent with the scientific community's conclusion that continued use of their product will endanger the lives and health of the public."

"If the industry uses political weapons," the editorial concluded, "so shall we," and it listed a number of such weapons. It called on politicians not to accept money from the tobacco industry and called for the public identification of those who do. The A.M.A. board recommended that medical schools and researchers "should refuse any funding from the tobacco industry," since it purpose is "to convince the public that there still is a controversy about whether tobacco has ill effects, to buy respectability, and to silence universities and researchers." It recommended that "federal funding be withdrawn from cancer research organizations that accept tobacco industry support." And the board declared its support for legal action to force the tobacco companies to reimburse Medicare and Medicaid for the excess medical costs stemming from tobacco-related diseases. " We should force the removal of this scourge from our nation," the editorial concluded, and thereby "set an example for the world." In another unusual move, the entire A.M.A. board, including then-president Robert McAfee and president-elect Lonnie Bristow, signed the editorial.

Never before had the A.M.A. taken such a strong stand against such a powerful antagonist; indeed, for decades the association had served as a loyal ally of the tobacco industry. When the Surgeon General's report condemning smoking was published in 1964, the A.M.A. refused to endorse it, saying instead that "more research" was needed. An A.M.A. research program on tobacco received $18 million from the tobacco companies over the next nine years, during which the association kept silent about the dangers of smoking. For the board to recommend that no one should accept tobacco-company funding for research was thus a significant reversal.

The five articles *JAMA* published went well beyond the health effects of smoking by detailing how B&W controlled information. One showed that medical research sponsored by the tobacco company was controlled by lawyers seeking to protect the companies against liability lawsuits. The articles demonstrated that the company hid its own research (showing that smoking causes cancer) from the public and the courts by sending the most damaging material to its legal department, where B&W lawyers claimed the material was protected from disclosure by the attorney-client privilege. When the tobacco industry funded university research, the selection of projects involved company lawyers and executives, in violation of scientific procedures requiring peer review of proposals by scientists. Professors who received grants reported on their research results to the tobacco industry before seeking publication—one letter Glantz published came from L.S.U. professor Henry Rothschild, who wrote in 1979 to a tobacco company attorney enclosing "the paper we would like to submit to the New England Journal of Medicine" and declaring, "I await your comments prior to submission." This of course is completely in violation of scientific procedures.

DEFUNDING GLANTZ

When JAMA published the five articles on the B&W documents, each of the articles by Glantz and associates carried the same note: "This work was supported in part by grant CA-61021 from the National Cancer Institute." The N.C.I., which is funded by Congress, had awarded Glantz the grant for a three-year project in 1994; thus one year remains to be funded by the institute. The grant is part of an N.C.I. research program in "Tobacco Prevention and Control." The institute had solicited proposals that would "evaluate the effect of advocacy in the development of tobacco control policy." Glantz's proposal had been approved by a peer-review committee of the National Institutes of Health, parent of the N.C.I. Reviewers gave it a score ranking it above 90 percent of the other proposals recommended for funding.

Despite this careful screening, a week after the *JAMA* issue appeared the Republican-controlled House Appropriations Committee took action to cancel Glantz's funding from the N.C.I. A subcommittee report declared that the grant that funded Glantz's work did "not properly fall within the boundaries of the NCI portfolio," and that therefore no further funding should be provided "for this research grant." The staff director for the House Appropriations Committee is James Dyer, a former Philip Morris lobbyist. This is the only case in the history of the N.C.I. in which a grant has been singled out for defunding by Congress.

The tobacco companies had now broadened the fight over corporate control of information by enlisting Congress in its attempts to silence a leading critic. This marked an unprecedented political intrusion into medical research. Heretofore Congress had encouraged the National Institutes of Health to rely on peer review by scientists to determine which grant proposals deserved funding. Indeed, the same House sub-committee report had earlier declared support for allowing the N.I.H. to use its best scientific judgment: "To enhance NIH's flexibility to allocate funding based on scientific opportunity, the Committee has attempted to minimize the amount of direction provided in the report accompanying the bill." The committee declared that while Congress should rightfully "highlight disease areas of interest," the committee "does not intend to impede NIH's flexibility in decision-making."

The Washington Times, an important institution of the right long associated with the Moonies, had started a public campaign to defund Glantz by publishing an ad in March denouncing the N.C.I. for funding him. The ad declared that "the dismal record of the National Cancer Institute to control cancer is forcing it to desperate measures." The ad was signed "the 130/10 Club, a group of citizens who chip in $10 a month to expose government waste." It gave a P.O. box in Holland, Kentucky, as its address; the newsletter of the American Smokers Alliance, which was established by Philip Morris, later took credit for the ad.

The *Times* then ran a front-page story in April criticizing the N.C.I. for funding Glantz. Headlined "Agency Probes Tobacco Politics," it quoted the chairman of the subcommittee that oversees the N.C.I.'s appropriation in the house, Representative John Porter, as saying, "This is not clinical or behavioral research and should not be funded by NCI." The *Times* followed up with an editorial the next month criticizing the N.C.I. for funding Glantz's project.

Then in July the PBS program *TechnoPolitics* attacked the grant. The show is funded in part by Kraft General Foods, a subsidiary of Philip Morris, and was previously funded by R. J. Reynolds. The next assault on Glantz's research funding appeared in the August *National Review* in an article titled "Policing PC: How the government is stacking the deck in the debate over smoking."

All of these attacks on Glantz make the same argument: Cancer research should not examine the political activities of the tobacco companies. Donna Shalala, Secretary of Health and Human Services, responded in July, pointing out that the mandate of the N.C.I. is to fund research into the "cause, diagnosis, prevention and treatment of cancer." She argued that "state and local policies are an essential element of tobacco control," and declared that "Dr. Glantz's research, which analyzes state level tobacco control policymaking, is thus within the NCI legislative mandate." Glantz's grant, she wrote, was "designed to answer critical research questions using the most appropriate scientific methods." She pledged, however, that the grant "will not be used to review campaign contributions to federal lawmakers."

"WARNING: Tobacco Interests Using Budget Process to Block Cancer Control Research"—so read the headline on a public service ad Glantz's supporters placed in *The New York Times* in October. The ad declared that the tobacco companies had "never hesitated to subvert medical science or manipulate the political process for the sake of easy profit"; in attacking Glantz, "the new House majority, intoxicated by its power over America's health research budget, is eager to aid and abet the industry." The ad was signed by twenty-nine leading health advocates, including former Surgeon General C. Everett Koop; Larry Fuller, chairman of the board of the American Cancer Society; Michael Pertschuk, former chairman of the Federal Trade Commission (and a member of *The Nation*'s editorial board); and Joseph Martin, chancellor of the University of California, San Francisco.

The current House appropriations bill for the N.C.I. includes a report that recommends defunding Glantz, while the Senate version does not. After the Senate votes, its version goes to a conference committee, and House members will have a chance to keep their language in the bill that is sent to the President. Even if Glantz is not defunded by Congress, the targeting of a specific grant has already had a chilling effect. Will others who lack Glantz's high public profile and extensive support network be afraid to propose research projects that will earn the displeasure of the tobacco companies—or other powerful corporations, for that matter? Although the tobacco giants may not win this round, they will have made progress toward their larger goal.

THE TEMP

B&W says its papers were stolen in 1989 by Merrell Williams Jr., a 54-year-old unemployed Ph.D. and former paralegal who once worked for Wyatt, Tarrant & Combs, one of B&W's law firms. One of the heroes of the fight against corporate control of information, Williams has paid a heavy price for his actions. A restraining order issued in Kentucky in September 1993 prohibited him from disclosing to anyone, including his lawyer, any information learned in connection with his employment—including, of course, discussing the contents of the documents. His lawyer, J. Fox DeMoisey, told me, "This is the only case where the court has prevented an attorney and his client from discussing the merits of the case. Jeffrey Dahmer killed and ate people. He got counsel. The lesson I am learning is that you can kill and eat people and we'll let you have counsel, but in Kentucky, by God, if you take sensitive tobacco documents, you can't have counsel. What has Merrell Williams done that deserves this kind of treatment?"

Williams was hired in 1988 and assigned, in B&W's words, to "analyze and classify documents in connection with the defense of smoking and health lawsuits." He spent more than four years reading the tobacco company's files. The more he read, the more he became concerned that he was helping conceal a company conspiracy to defraud the public. At the time he was hired, the company says, he signed a confidentiality agreement; now it claims he violated that, and charges him with fraud.

"But what if he disclosed the fact that there is an ongoing fraud by both the tobacco attorneys and the tobacco companies?" DeMoisey asks. Williams says that in his work for B&W's law firm, he discovered that the company was avoiding legal discovery proceedings by funneling the most damaging material in its files to its legal departments, where company lawyers claimed the material was protected from disclosure by the attorney-client privilege and as attorney work product. That is fraud—and "that's never protected by attorney-client work privilege or work product," DeMoisey says.

Williams had smoked Kools, a B&W product, for almost thirty years; after a night of chest pains in 1993, he underwent heart surgery and had a quintuple bypass. He then brought a personal-injury suit against B&W. "We did have some settlement discussions" with B&W, DeMoisey reports, in which Williams would receive a cash settlement in exchange for his agreement to keep the documents secret. One of the tobacco company's conditions was that DeMoisey "would have to agree never to represent any plaintiff cigarette smoker, ever," he says. That's unethical under the American Bar Association's Model Rules of Professional Conduct, adopted in 1983, which prohibit any lawyer from "offering . . . an agreement in which a restriction on the lawyer's right to practice is part of the settlement of a controversy between private parties."

DeMoisey is not a prominent tobacco litigator; in fact, he's never represented a plaintiff against the tobacco companies before Merrell Williams. DeMoisey says, "My response was, I would agree except for one situation: my own case. I smoke Marlboros." He told the B&W attorneys, "I'm not going to waive my right to file a claim of action against the makers of Marlboro, but other than that, I will agree to this provision to help Merrell Williams." The company turned him down, telling him the tobacco companies have a policy of never settling any case. Shortly thereafter the documents were shipped to Stanton Glantz, Congressman Waxman, *The New York Times* and other news media.

B&W continues to pursue Williams in the courts. It is trying to get the Louisville, Kentucky, judge presiding in the case to hold him in criminal contempt for leaking the documents. The penalty is a six-month prison term. "All these documents are now public record everywhere," DeMoisey said. "The only two people in Western civilization as we know it who would like to see these documents but can't are the two counsel for Merrell Williams. It seems a little ludicrous to me. And they want to stick my client in jail for this."

The court eventually saw the logic in DeMoisey's argument. On November 27, Jefferson Circuit Judge Thomas Wine modified the gag order, ruling that Williams may now talk to his lawyers about the documents. But B&W can still get DeMoisey disqualified from representing Williams if the information they talk about falls under the company's attorney-client privilege. That seems to mean they can discuss information they find on the U.C.S.F. Web site.

CONCLUSION

The University of California has done many bad things recently, from abolishing affirmative action to operating nuclear weapons labs. But in this case the university lived up to its ideals and responsibilities. And that wouldn't have happened if a temp in a law firm hadn't decided to bring to the public documents that showed the fraud being perpetrated by his employer. The courage and commitment of the temp, the professor, the librarian, the university press editor and the university counsel—along with that of the American Medical Association—stand in glaring contrast to the spinelessness of the TV networks, CBS/Westinghouse, ABC/Disney (which had earlier buckled under to tobacco company intimidation) and the timidity of the trade publishers.

If the story of Stan Glantz and the Butts box shows it's possible to stand up to the tobacco companies, the capitulation of ABC, CBS and two dozen book publishers has ominous implications—and not just for smoking and health. Big Tobacco's intimidation tactics provide a model for other corporations that don't want the public to find out what they are doing: military contractors, oil firms, drug makers, nuclear power plants—all the companies that make dangerous or unsafe products or do things that are unethical or illegal. Eventually every corporation in the country could require every employee to agree never to talk to any journalist about anything. Then the "news" at CBS and ABC would consist of Mike and Morley and Peter reading aloud from corporate P.R. handouts.

Meanwhile, universities everywhere are cozying up to corporations, desperate for financial support in the face of cuts in public funding. They too can be intimidated or decide not to take risks. The story of the Butts box also demonstrates the importance of fighting corporate domination of the universities—so that they can continue to serve as places where people tell the truth about the crimes of the powerful.

HIP IS DEAD

Tom Frank

•

ABOUT A YEAR ago I published a long essay pointing out that between all the entertainment-industry mergers and acquisitions, the appearance of the new computer and TV technologies and all the glorious developments celebrated weekly in *The New York Times*'s business-section pages devoted to what is euphemistically called "The Information Industries," we have stumbled into a rather alarming cultural crisis. We may be able to pick up more channels now than we could before, but we have also witnessed the rise of a veritable Culture Trust, which in the absence of any countervailing force is naturally expanding its control over as much cultural space as it possibly can. The miracle of the Information Age is not the Web; it is that vast uncharted regions of private life have been opened to corporate colonization.

What's strange now is how little this argument—a fairly obvious one, easy to understand—has caught on. Railing against trusts used to be a commonplace thing, with all sorts of muckraking journalism appearing in national magazines exposing the evil machinations of the beef trust or the sugar trust or the railroad barons or the Standards Oil Company. You'd think this would be an attractive topic, a subject that any journalist would like to sink his teeth into: David Geffen's war on young people, say, or Michael Eisner's wooing of some state legislature somewhere. These developments call for another *Wealth Against Commonwealth*, a *Shame of the Cellphones*, a *Chapters of Geffen*. You'd also think that, since the Culture Trust controls something so much more basic and precious and personal than railroads or oil or string, people would be that much more infuriated by it. But they aren't.

Instead, the only interpretation of the Information Age that you're likely to hear expressed publicly is some rephrasing of the great Myth of the Culture Trust: that this vast concentration of power will, paradoxically, make each of us more autonomous. Every one of us has heard so many variations on this theme that we could probably rattle them off without pulling out our PowerBooks: that English child telling us that, thanks to MCI, there will "be no more there there," or, say, every other article that has ever appeared in *Wired* magazine. The myth goes like this: Thanks to the rapid advances being made by the Culture Trust, you'll have many, many more channels to choose from. More movies, more rockin' video games. You may not have to watch advertisements anymore. You can make your own Web page, contact anybody you want, even in a foreign country, via e-mail. The Culture Trust deals in popular taste; the Culture Trust deals in liberation; the Culture Trust deals in the Will of the People. To disagree with those tastes or defy that will is reactionary and elitist and bad. David Geffen and Michael Eisner aren't an elite, *you are.*

So what's wrong with us? Why haven't these gigantic developments aroused public anger? What happened to that older model of dissent under which trusts were always suspect? And why is the model by which today we all understand liberation so powerless and backward, so susceptible to hijacking by the likes of Geffen and Eisner?

Why are the hippest minds of my generation so puzzled when, dragging through the streets of Wicker Park or North Beach or Greenwich Village at dawn, searching for that angry fix, they invariably find themselves joined by ad executives, network presidents and bankers? Our problem is that we have a fixed idea of what power is, of how power works and of how power is to be resisted. It's an idea called "hip." It holds that the problem with capitalism is that it oppresses us through puritanism, homogeneity and conformity, and that we resist by being ourselves, by pushing the envelope of uninhibition, by breaking all the rules in pursuit of the most apocalyptic orgasm of them all. It's an idea that hasn't changed at all in forty years, even as capitalism has undergone revolution after revolution.

Pick up any recent book of management theory: Today, hip is the orthodoxy of Information Age capitalism. It's being your own dog, Reebok letting U.B.U., Finding Your Own Road in a Saab; it's Ginsberg shilling for the Gap and William Burroughs for Nike; it's business texts quoting Gurdjieff and Bob Dylan and bearing titles like *Thriving on Chaos* and *The Age of Unreason.*

The problem isn't that hip has been co-opted but that it isn't adversarial in the first place. That it's toothless even before Mr. Geffen's boys discover it angsting away in some bar in Lawrence, Kansas. Hip is no longer any different from the official culture it's supposed to be subverting. The basic impulses of hip, as descended from Norman Mailer and the holy Beats, are about as threatening to the new breed of information businessmen as casual-dress days are to worker efficiency.

These people aren't Babbitts. They don't correspond to any of the old symbols by which we understand the problems of the corporate world. The people who staff the Combine aren't like Nurse Ratched. They aren't Frank Burns, they aren't the Church Lady, they aren't Dean Wormer from *Animal House,* they aren't those repressed old folks in the commercials who want to ban Tropicana Twisters. They're hipper than you can ever hope to be because hip is their official ideology, and they're always going to be there at the poetry reading to encourage your "rebellion" with a hearty "right on, man!" before you even know they're in the auditorium. You can't outrun them, or even stay ahead of them for very long; it's their racetrack, and that's them waiting at the finish line to congratulate you on how *outrageous* your new style is, on how you *shocked* those stuffy prudes out there in the heartland.

Hip is false populism on a par with Pat Buchanan, the same bogus MTV individualism as that of business writers Charles Handy and James Champy. Hip is the faith of the marketplace, simultaneously the blank blue stare of TV passivity and the howl of unreflective consumerism, caught up in the endless search for an ever-more-efficient machinery of instant obsolescence. The Man isn't who you think he is. He wears Henry Rollins tattoos, not gray flannel. He's Tom Peters, screeching antinomian of the boardroom; he's Ben Nighthorse Campbell, new convert to the Contract With America, in ponytail, on motorcycle, decked out and proclaiming his Capitol nonconformity from Banana Republic ads all over town. Not only is he going to gut labor law, workplace safety and what remains of the welfare state but he's going to convince the public that it's the rebel thing to do.

It's time to acknowledge that new hairstyles aren't going to change the relations of power in America. Nor is buying soda X instead of soda Y, no matter how subversive you believe the decision to be. Hip is the clanking strategy of forty years ago, something that was fresh and menacing when *Organization Man* was on bookstore shelves, maybe, but whose only use now is to sidetrack popular discontent. Mutating constantly and obsoleting itself instantly, business has long since captured the antinomian language of hip to express its love of perpetual instability.

Clearly, hip is exhausted as a mode of dissent. As the affluent society amid which it once made some sense drains away, we need to recover that much more powerful strain of dissent that built the affluent society in the first place, to rediscover the language of class, the non-market-friendly concept of industrial democracy. Leave hip to the M.B.A.s.

The shiny capitalism of the Third Wave is turning out to be little more than the ugly exploitative capitalism of a hundred years ago—available in stone-washed easy-fit, with an electric guitar soundtrack. The Culture Trust not only controls the country's most important industry but its conception of dissent as well. Resisting it is going to take much more than dissing the squares, reviving lounge music or finally getting MTV interviews with the candidates. It's going to require Information Age muckraking. And if *The New York Times* won't publish *Chapters of Geffen,* do it yourself.

DOES MAUREEN DOWD HAVE AN OPINION?

Susan Faludi
•

IN THE NINE months since she's replaced Anna Quindlen as the only female columnist on the *New York Times* Op-Ed page, Maureen Dowd has taken us to Barneys to inspect Gaultier tuxedo jackets and Clinique scruffing lotions, ruminated about whether to sponge Golden Campine paint on her wall and agonized over tossing her old *Flashdance* album. But she's yet to take a stand on a social or political issue of any importance. She snickers at silly government hearings and rebukes public figures for dorkiness, but when it comes to moral convictions, Maureen Dowd seems at a loss. It's as if we've gone from Anna Quindlen to Anna Quibbler.

Since women first broke into press punditry, they've had to play either the primly principled commentator or the wickedly frivolous disher. They could care too much to be perceived as the life of the party, like Margaret Fuller—or they could be carelessly catty like Hedda Hopper or Eleanor (Cissy) Patterson, who took over the Washington *Herald* in 1930 and filled its pages with gossip. Columnists like Molly Ivins, Barbara Ehrenreich, Katha Pollitt and Anna Quindlen have been breaking down these molds by voicing passionate beliefs— particularly on women's rights—with wit and impudence. But at the *Times*, we seem to have been returned to the days of Jennie June's shopping and gossip columns—and, ironically, by a columnist who is perceived as too harsh by media critics.

A few weeks ago, Dowd finally showed real outrage (albeit only on her own behalf) over charges by press analyst James Fallows that her cynical treatment of pols was damaging democracy. An indignant Dowd fired back that it was not a Washington journalist's job to be nice but to explore the realities of government, warts and all. But Dowd's explorations are only skin-deep. She condemns the White-water transactions not on the underlying (and debatable) facts but for their "cheesiness"; she finds Bob Dole's first name "bland"; she's miffed that Hillary Clinton "wore pink" to a press conference. Surface is everything. Indeed, in one of two columns on proper dressing (school uniforms—thumbs up; casual dress at the office—thumbs down), she insists that the "central fact of American life" is this: "Appearances matter." This must be why she's written not one but two columns on mail-order catalogues, and not one but *three* columns on Barneys. "Sartorial" is her favorite adjective.

Dowd's decorative approach would be harmless, even fun, if she didn't bear the onus of being the *Times*'s only female columnist. Quindlen dignified her post with strong, well-argued stands on social issues from abortion to rape to the rights of single mothers. "I'm a feminist, first and foremost," Quindlen told me. She saw her role as "a crusader for the voiceless," especially voiceless women. "Now there's a newer pundit role emerging," Quindlen said: "to illuminate the absurdity of modern life." She demurred from criticizing Dowd, whom she helped get her first *Times* job as a city reporter, but Quindlen said it troubles her that "I don't remember a column on abortion" by Dowd.

That's because there hasn't been one. Dowd appears to have no interest in addressing women's rights—and she seems only to write about individual women when she can make fun of them, sometimes brutal fun, as she did when alluding to "the nervous retreat of the way-overweight Shannon Faulkner." (What did she think of the misogynous Citadel's treatment of Shannon? She never says.) The woman whose surface she derides with the most regularity is Hillary Clinton. Dowd sneers at the First Lady's "latest fluffer-nutter make-over," and then, after dubbing her "Earth Mother meets Mommie Dearest," she scoffs that it's "hard to believe" that Hillary Clinton gets a lot of flak because she's a strong woman.

One column does start out as if Dowd might be about to comment on women's status, albeit dubiously: "I have passed several anxious days pondering the sensibility of feminism. I feel as flustered as a

dowager with an unruly poodle." But it turns out to be only a pretext
for sniffing at *The New Yorker*, the hallowed "magazine of Dorothy
Parker and Hannah Arendt," for "joining forces with the boorish TV
star" Roseanne. Dowd's acidic style is often compared to Dorothy
Parker's. But underneath Parker's caustic wit boiled political outrage,
most particularly at women's lousy lot. As Christopher Hitchens, who
profiled Dowd in *Vanity Fair* and suspects her role model is Parker,
said to me, Parker feigned detachment but was driven by "strong feelings about social injustice."

Maybe Dowd's true role model dates from another era—fifties
sweater girl. A friend of mine says she stopped reading Dowd's column
because it was like listening to a bobby-soxer in a soda shop tossing her
hair cutely as she rates the passing boys. Dowd eyes male politicians as
if they were pimply teens or prospective suitors. She tells us that Bill
Clinton admired her pin while "smiling dreamily" at her. She yearns
for a "father figure" in a President, but Bill is just a "gifted teenager."
And while "Newt is cute," Dowd sighs, he acts like "a chubby little boy
with chocolate pudding smeared on his face." Only Colin Powell is man
enough to make a poodle-skirted girl's heart go pitter-pat—but, in teen
beach movie fashion, he must slip away, leaving her heart broken but
her virginity intact. "The graceful, hard male animal," she writes,
"who did nothing overtly to dominate us yet dominated us completely,
in the exact way we wanted that to happen at this moment, like a fine
leopard on the veld, was gone . . . 'Don't leave, Colin Powell,' I could
hear myself crying from somewhere inside."

After Cissy Patterson spent years penning snotty front-page editori-
als—most attacking her social rival, Alice Roosevelt Longworth—
something befell her. The Depression hit, and she disguised herself as
a homeless woman and applied for maids' jobs, for a story about the
unemployed. The experience changed her from a socialite to a social
crusader, investigating the lot of poor veterans, demanding hot lunches
for hungry schoolchildren.

After Dowd wrote her first column on Barneys, the store's publicist
offered her a $10 gift certificate for a return visit. I'd like to make a dif-
ferent kind of offer: I'll pay the fare, Maureen, if you'll only go somewhere and find something you care about. Your readers will thank you
for your strong words.

HOW NEWS BECOMES OPINION, AND OPINION OFF-LIMITS

Salman Rushdie

•

I WAS WONDERING what, if any, common ground might be occupied by novelists and journalists when my eye fell upon the following brief text in a British national daily:

"In yesterday's *Independent*, we stated that Sir Andrew Lloyd Webber is farming ostriches. He is not."

One can only guess at the brouhaha concealed beneath these admirably laconic sentences: the human distress, the protests. As you know, Britain has been going through a period of what one might call heightened livestock insecurity of late. As well as the mentally challenged cattle herds, there has been the alarming case of the great ostrich-farming bubble, or swindle. In these overheated times, a man who is not an ostrich farmer, when accused of being one, will not take the allegation lightly. He may even feel that his reputation has been slighted.

Plainly, it was quite wrong of the *Independent* to suggest that Sir Andrew Lloyd Webber was breeding ostriches. He is, of course, a celebrated exporter of musical turkeys. But if we agree for a moment to permit the supposedly covert and allegedly fraudulent farming of ostriches to stand as a metaphor for all the world's supposedly covert and allegedly fraudulent activities, then must we not also agree that it is vital that these ostrich farmers be identified, named and brought to account for their activities? Is this not the very heart of the project of a free press? And might there not be occasions on which every editor would be prepared to go with such a story—leaked, perhaps, by an ostrich deep throat—on the basis of less-than-solid evidence, in the national interest?

I am arriving by degree at my point, which is that the great issue facing writers both of journalism and of novels is that of determining, and then publishing, the truth. For the ultimate goal of both factual and fictional writing is the truth, however paradoxical that may sound. And truth is slippery, hard to establish. Mistakes, as in the Lloyd Webber case, can be made. And if truth can set you free, it can also land you in hot water. Fine as the word sounds, truth is all too often unpalatable, awkward, unorthodox. The armies of received ideas are marshaled against it. The legions of all those who stand to profit by useful untruths will march against it. Yet it must, if at all possible, be told.

But, it may be objected, can there really be any connection between the truth of the news and that of the world of the imagination? In the world of facts, a man is either an ostrich farmer or he is not. In fiction's universe, he may be fifteen contradictory things at once.

Let me attempt an answer.

The word "novel" derives from the Latin word for *new*; in French, *nouvelles* are both stories and news reports. A hundred years ago, people read novels, among other things, for information. From Dickens's *Nicholas Nickleby*, British readers got shocking information about poor schools like Dotheboys Hall, and such schools were subsequently abolished. *Uncle Tom's Cabin*, *Huckleberry Finn* and *Moby-Dick* are all, in this newsy sense, information-heavy.

So: Until the advent of the television age, literature shared with print journalism the task of telling people things they didn't know.

This is no longer the case, either for literature or for print journalism. Those who read newspapers and novels now get their primary information about the world from the TV news and the radio. There are exceptions, of course. The success of that excellent, lively novel *Primary Colors* shows that novels can just occasionally still lift the lid on a hidden world more effectively than the finest reporting. And of course the broadcast news is highly selective, and newspapers provide far greater breadth and depth of coverage. But many people now read newspapers, I suggest, to read the news *about* the news. We read for opinion, attitude, spin. We read not for raw data, not for Gradgrind's "facts, facts, facts," but to get a "take" on the news that we like. Now that the broadcasting media fulfill the function of being first with the news, newspapers, like novels, have entered the realm of the imagination. They both provide versions of the world.

Perhaps this is clearer in a country like Britain, where the press is primarily a national press, than in the United States, where the great proliferation of local papers allows print journalism to provide the additional service of answering to local concerns and adopting local characteristics. The successful quality papers in Britain—among dailies, the *Guardian*, *Times*, *Telegraph* and *Financial Times*—are successful because they have clear pictures of who their readers are and how to talk to them. (The languishing *Independent* once did, but appears lately to have lost its way.) They are successful because they share with their readers a vision of British society and of the world.

The news has become a matter of opinion.

And this puts a newspaper editor in a position not at all dissimilar from that of a novelist. It is for the novelists to create, communicate and sustain over time a personal and coherent vision of the world that entertains, interests, stimulates, provokes and nourishes his readers. It is for the newspaper editor to do very much the same thing with the pages at his disposal. In that specialized sense, we are all in the fiction business now.

One of the more extraordinary truths about the soap opera that is the British royal family is that to a large extent the leading figures have had their characters invented for them by the British press. And such is the power of the fiction that the flesh and blood royals have become more and more like their print personae, unable to escape the fiction of their imaginary lives.

The creation of "characters" is, in fact, rapidly becoming an essential part of print journalism's stock in trade. Never have personality profiles and people columns—never has gossip—occupied as much of a newspaper as they now do. The word "profile" is apt. In a profile, the subject is never confronted head-on but receives a sidelong glance. A profile is flat and two-dimensional. It is an outline. Yet the images created in these curious texts (often with their subjects' collusion) are extraordinarily potent—it can be next to impossible for the actual person to alter, through his own words and deeds, the impressions they create—and thanks to the mighty clippings file, they are also self-perpetuating.

A novelist, if he is talented and lucky, may in the course of a lifetime's work offer up one or two characters who enter the exclusive pantheon of the unforgotten. A novelist's characters hope for immortality; a profile journalist's, perhaps, for celebrity. We worship, these days, not images but Image itself: And any man or women who strays into the public gaze becomes a potential sacrifice in that temple. Often, I repeat, a willing sacrifice, willingly drinking the poisoned chalice of Fame. But for many people, including myself, the experience of being profiled is perhaps closest to what it must feel like to be used as a writer's raw material, what it must feel like to be turned into a fictional character, to have one's feelings and actions, one's relationships and vicissitudes, transformed, by writing, into something subtly—or unsubtly—different. To see ourselves mutated into someone we do not recognize.

For a novelist to be thus rewritten is, I recognize, a case of the biter bit. Fair enough. Nevertheless, something about the process feels faintly—and I stress, *faintly*—improper.

In Britain, intrusions into the private lives of public figures have prompted calls from certain quarters for the protection of privacy laws. It is true that in France, where such laws exist, the illegitimate daughter of the late President Mitterrand was able to grow up unmolested by the press; but where the powerful can hide behind the law, might not a good deal of covert ostrich farming go undetected? My own feelings continue to be against laws that curtail the investigative freedoms of the press. But speaking as someone who has had the uncommon experience of becoming, for a time, a hot news story—of, as my friend Martin Amis put it, "vanishing into the front page"—it would be dishonest to deny that when my family and I have been the target of press intrusions and distortions, those principles have been sorely strained.

However, my overwhelming feelings about the press are ones of gratitude. In the long unfolding of the so-called Rushdie affair, American newspapers have been of great importance in keeping the issues alive, in making sure that readers have kept sight of the essential points of principle involved, and even in pressuring America's leaders to speak out and act. But I am grateful for more than that. I said earlier that newspaper editors, like novelists, need to create, impart and maintain a vision of society to readers. In any vision of a free society, the value of free speech must rank the highest, for that is the freedom without which all other freedoms would fail. Journalists do more than most of us to protect those values; for the exercise of freedom is its best defense.

It seems to me, however, that we live in an increasingly censorious age. By this I mean that the broad, indeed international, acceptance of First Amendment principles is being steadily eroded. Many special-interest groups, claiming the moral high ground, now demand the protection of the censor. Political correctness and the rise of the religious right provide the procensorship lobby with further cohorts. I would like to say a little about just one of the weapons of this resurgent lobby, a weapon used, interestingly, by everyone from anti-pornography feminists to religious fundamentalists: I mean the concept of "respect."

On the surface of it, "respect" is one of those ideas nobody is against. Like a good warm coat in winter, like applause, like ketchup on your fries, everybody wants some of that. *Sock-it-to-me-sock-it-to-me,* as Aretha Franklin has it. But what was used to mean by respect, what Aretha meant by it—that is, a mixture of good-hearted consideration and serious attention—has little to do with the new ideological usage of the word.

Religious extremists, these days, demand "respect" for their attitudes with growing stridency. Few people would object to the idea that people's rights to religious belief must be respected—after all, the First Amendment defends those rights as unequivocally as it defends free speech—but now we are asked to agree that to dissent from those beliefs, to hold that they are suspect or antiquated or wrong, that in fact they are *arguable*, is incompatible with the idea of respect. When criticism is placed off-limits as "disrespectful," and therefore offensive, something strange is happening to the concept of respect. Yet in recent times both the American N.E.A. and the very British BBC have announced that they will employ this new perversion of "respect" as a touchstone for their funding and programming decisions.

Other minority groups—racial, sexual, social—have also demanded that they be accorded this new form of respect. To "respect" Louis Farrakhan, we must understand, is simply to agree with him. To "dis" him is, equally simply, to disagree. But if dissent is also to be thought a form of "dissing," then we have indeed succumbed to the Thought Police.

I want to suggest that citizens of free societies do not preserve their freedom by pussyfooting around their fellow citizens' opinions, even their most cherished beliefs. In free societies, you must have the free play of ideas. There must be argument, and it must be impassioned and untrammeled. A free society is not a calm and eventless place—that is the kind of static, dead society dictators try to create. Free societies are dynamic, noisy, turbulent and full of radical disagreements. Skepticism and freedom are indissolubly linked, and it is the skepticism of journalists, their show-me, prove-it unwillingness to be impressed, that is perhaps their most important contribution to the freedom of the free world. It is the *disrespect* of journalists—for power, for orthodoxies, for party lines, for ideologies, for vanity, for arrogance, for folly, for pretension, for corruption, for stupidity, maybe even for editors—and the disrespect of every citizen, in fact, that I would like to celebrate, and that I urge all, in freedom's name, to preserve.

CENTRISM, POPULIST STYLE

Richard Parker

•

As this is written, American liberals have made scarcely a new proposal for reform in twenty years. It is not evident that they have any important new ideas. Reputations for liberalism or radicalism continue to depend almost exclusively on a desire to finish the unfinished social legislation of the New Deal . . .

•

A QUICK TEST: Who's the pundit here? George Will, with a self-satisfied sneer in his voice? E. J Dionne, lamenting progressives' midnineties dilemma? Or is it Al From, about to tell us why the Democratic Leadership Council represents the future? Answer: None of the above. It's John Kenneth Galbraith, and the year is 1952.

A second quick test: What are the measures of progressive electoral success since 1952? There were Johnson's three years of domestic victories thirty years ago, but look back at the Galbraith quote. Then consider: Republicans have controlled the White House nearly two-thirds of the time since 1952, and conservatives haven't done badly with Congress, even when they've lacked formal control. If Bill Clinton wins in November, he'll be only the second elected Democratic President reelected since Franklin Roosevelt.

Question: What should those of us who label ourselves progressive, or radical, or left-liberal, or social democrat, or democratic socialist, or whatever other term suggests the typical *Nation* reader be doing about not just Clinton's reelection campaign but the larger future of the Democratic Party?

For me the answer comes in two stages. Between now and November, I intend to support Clinton's re-election with my voice, my time and my money. Frankly, I'll hate every minute of it, but I'm going to do it. Back in 1968, I was one among hundreds of thousands in the student left who claimed to see no difference between Richard Nixon and Hubert Humphrey; we were right about a lot of things, but on that one we were wrong—and all of us have paid a heavy price.

But starting November 6, it's no more Mr. Clintonite for me. Between now and the year 2000, I want the D.L.C. reduced to utter fecklessness. I'll push to see corporate and big-money PAC financing deeply curtailed and I hope to celebrate a reconstituted Democratic Party able to run successfully without the albatross of the old Democratic South around its neck.

My bet is that Clinton will win—without the South as his core, without major Republican crossover, but with minorities, women, blue-collar voters and a big chunk of the Northeast and Western middle class behind him. Most important will be a revitalized union movement that will have poured millions of dollars and hours into this campaign, and that hankers for the voice inside the party it hasn't had for years.

Clinton's victory, with left-liberal support, is key here, because it's needed to upbraid not just Newt Gingrich and his allies in the House but the Washington and New York chattering classes, which for the past two decades have bemoaned the "ultraliberal" and "special-interest" groups (read you-know-who, friends) that allegedly control the Democratic Party. It's they who've trumpeted the realignment of U.S. politics, the durability of the Reagan "revolution" and the "brilliant new" politics of the lobbyist-financed D.L.C.

Now, the Dickie Morris-guided Clinton, as we all know, is a President of the polls, not the people—at least if we mean "people" in its best Jeffersonian-Capraesque sense. Plus, he'll have lots of Republicans in Congress (some of them nominal Democrats), a nervous stock and bond market and a Washington media corps dedicated to interpreting his victory as proof that only center-right politics works in this country.

But Clinton's also going to be facing the nastiest trend in twentieth-century U.S. politics—and ever-widening gulf between not just the rich and the poor but the rich and everyone else in the country. And that means running room for the rest of us. To take advantage of the opportunity, we need a progressive politics that rethinks its constituency and purpose—not just to pressure Clinton from the left but to establish grounds on which to win back lasting and meaningful political power.

The first issue before us is the terrain of battle: *We need to make American politics a fight over the economy and who wins or loses in it, not a fight over government.*

The second is the terms of combat: We need to regroup around a forceful new conception of whom we are fighting for—not the poor, not the downtrodden, not the excluded but the American middle class. To those of you shocked or appalled by what I've just written, let me twist the knife further: I mean that as a central political precept, not as a tactical or strategic move. *I am proposing that we define progressive politics—clearly, bluntly and without compromise—as being about the permanent enlargement of the middle class.*

A century ago, progressive thinking centered on two, often overlapping, groups: the working class and the poor. Those focused on the former ranged from Gomperites to socialists or communists, but they all saw the identity of the working class as distinct not only from capitalists but from the then-small middle class (whose support for labor seemed ambivalent at best). The labor movement quarreled for fifty years about direction, the socialists lost to the Gomperites—and then over the past thirty years, unions have lost much of their power.

The poor represent a different notion of agency, one often favored by progressive professionals, who took it as their role to relieve the poor (which sometimes included but wasn't equivalent to the working class). In the sixties, when poverty was "rediscovered," the war against it focused heavily on race and regions (the South and inner cities), on the unemployed or marginally employed—in such a way that, as the Reagan years painfully taught us, a major political gulf opened between, on one side, middle-class and blue-collar voters and, on the other, the Democrats and progressive politics generally.

I'm proposing that we abandon both these conceptions and replace them with explicit loyalties to the middle class for the following very concrete reasons: Most working-class people now identify with the middle class; most poor people would prefer to be middle class rather than poor. Insisting that "our politics speaks for the working class" sounds antiquated and out of touch; insisting that "we are for the poor," without centrally affirming that we are also for the much larger middle class and want to see it prosper—and want to see the poor *become* middle class, rather than semipermanent public wards—intolerably isolates us (and the poor).

The rich represent a challenge in their own right, given the Democratic Party's shift to a pro-business rhetoric and practice in the past fifty years. The top 2 percent who control nearly half the nation's private wealth once had a plausible function in economic life: They provided the savings for investment and the corporate management that together trickled down into middle-class prosperity and provided the jobs that eventually reduced the ranks of the poor.

Nowadays the rich don't really do either. The massed savings of the middle class—in pension funds, mutual funds, I.R.A.s and the like, along with undistributed corporate profits—provide the most prominent source of investable funds. And business schools churn out competent managers by the hundreds of thousands from the raw material fed to them by the same middle class.

What the rich pass along instead are the costs of their greed—the savings-and-loan cleanup, the unemployment and dislocation of downsizing inspired by corporate raiders, the devastation of entire industries and communities caused by capital flight to low-wage countries.

James Carville got it partly right in 1992 when he said, "It's the economy, stupid." It *is* the economy—not the government—that today poses the greatest threat to Americans' well-being and future security. But only partly right because the phrase remained rhetorical, not programmatic. It's control of the economy that we must contest in order to create a middle-class life that works for the overwhelming majority. A progressive campaign would set as its goals the following three visions:

- *Fair earnings*: A new middle-class vision would set both a floor and ceiling to wealth and income. The floor might be half the median income, the ceiling ten or fifteen times the median— plenty of room for ambition, no room for poverty.
- *Basic security*: A new middle-class vision would include universal retirement income, health care and child care, financed through progressive taxes on total income, not regressive taxes on wages.
- *A new notion of private property*: A new middle-class vision would expand middle-class ownership and control of corporations in new ways, in lieu of insisting on public ownership, which is widely seen as state or bureaucratic control.

Here we aren't assaulting the institution of property itself (as conservatives would like to believe) but simply doing what our ancestors have always done. Slaves were legal property for 5,000 years; people's rights to work for any but feudal masters were likewise proscribed. As views change, so do definitions of property.

In the early nineteenth century, 90 percent of us were self-employed. Government then created new protections and rights for corporations, while for many decades mostly denying equal protections and rights to workers. Skip over the familiar history of how that changed to today, when corporations define economic life and employ most of us; the top 1–2 percent of them control a greater share of G.D.P. than the government.

This situation requires that we go on to something new, creating new concepts of corporate ownership and obligation to achieve a stable and democratic middle-class economy that has elsewhere been called a "stakeholder society." We should support legislation that would increase significantly employee and community involvement in and control of corporations, and reward those that profit-share aggressively and that invest in the U.S. economy and in workers' training, health and pensions. New legislation could democratize financial markets' leverage over corporate behavior and the distribution of their gains, which currently reward shareholders disproportionately compared with other stakeholders in the company and the society.

But what about the near term? What about Clinton's horrific welfare bill? What about health care reform and gay rights and the unholy sanctity of the military budget? The most important issue here is not whether we ought to be "doing" something about those things but the larger terms and visions through which we will build the support that will do something in fact.

The Republicans famously know that ideas matter in politics, and they have framed a debate in which we are prisoners and they the jailers. Their two most powerful claims are that government is the problem (and progressives are its guardians) and that the economy is undergoing inexorable changes, and the pain will end only after more sacrifice. The first is a fraud and the second a myth, but the Republicans have done well with them, and show no signs of abandoning them.

Either we argue on their terms or get a new set of arguments; I prefer the latter. Fifty-nine percent of Americans, according to a recent poll, are "very concerned" about not having enough money for retirement, 47 percent are very concerned about losing their job or taking a pay cut, and two-thirds fear their children won't have decent job opportunities. My bet is that they might listen to what a progressive middle-class vision could offer.

'TRANSITION' OR TRAGEDY?

Stephen F. Cohen

•

A TERRIBLE NATIONAL tragedy has been unfolding in Russia in the 1990s, but we will hear little if anything about it in American commentary on this fifth anniversary of the end of the Soviet Union. Instead, we will be told that Russia's "transition to a free-market economy and democracy" has progressed remarkably, despite some "bumps in the road." Evidence alleged to support that view will include massive privatization, emerging financial markets, low inflation, "stabilization," and impending economic "takeoff," last summer's presidential election, a sitting Parliament and a "free press."

Few if any commentators will explain that Russia's new private sector is dominated by former but still intact Soviet monopolies seized by ex-Communist officials who have become the core of a semi-criminalized business class; that inflation is being held down by holding back salaries owed to tens of millions of needy workers and other employees; that a boom has been promised for years while the economy continues to plunge into a depression greater than America's in the 1930s; that President Yeltsin's re-election campaign was one of the most corrupt in recent European history; that the Parliament has no real powers and the appellate court little independence from the presidency; and that neither Russia's market nor its national television is truly competitive or free but is substantially controlled by the same financial oligarchy whose representatives now sit in the Kremlin as chieftains of the Yeltsin regime.

In human terms, however, that is not the worst of it. For the great majority of families, Russia has not been in "transition" but in an endless collapse of everything essential to a decent existence—from real wages, welfare provisions and health care to birth rates and life expectancy; from industrial and agricultural production to higher education, science and traditional culture; from safety in the streets to prosecution of organized crime and thieving bureaucrats; from the still enormous military forces to the safeguarding of nuclear devices and materials. These are the realities underlying the "reforms" that most U.S. commentators still extol and seem to think are the only desirable kind.

Fragments of Russia's unprecedented, cruel and perilous collapse are reported in the U.S. mainstream media, but not the full dimensions of insider privatization, impoverishment, disintegration of the middle classes, corrosive consequences of the Chechen war or official corruption and mendacity. Why not? Why don't American commentators lament the plight of the Russian people as they did so persistently when they were the Soviet people? The United States has thousands of professed specialists on Russia. Why have so few tried to tell the full story of post-Soviet Russia? Indeed, why, despite incomparably greater access to information, do most reporters, pundits and scholars tell us less that is really essential about Russia today than they did when it was part of the Soviet Union?

There are, it seems, several reasons, all of them related to the American condition rather than to Russia's. As during the cold war, most U.S. media and academic commentators think (or speak) within the parameters of Washington's policies toward Russia. Since 1991, Russia's purportedly successful transition, and the U.S. "strategic" role in it, have been the basic premise of White House and Congressional policy.

American business people, big foundations and academics involved with Russia also have their own stake in the "transition." For the business community, it is the prospect of profits; for foundations, another frontier of endowed social engineering; for academia, a new paradigm ("transitionology") for securing funds, jobs and tenure. Confronted with the fact that the results of Russia's "transition" continue to worsen and not improve, most of its U.S. promoters still blame the "legacy of Communism" rather than their own prescriptions, or insist that robber baron capitalism will surely reform itself there as it did here, even though the circumstances are fundamentally different.

More generally, Americans have always seen in Russia, for ideological and psychological reasons, primarily what they sought there. This time it is a happy outcome of the end of Soviet Communism and of our "great victory" in the cold war. How many of us who doubt that outcome, who think the world may be less safe because of what has happened in the former Soviet Union, who believe that ordinary Russians (even those denigrated "elderly" Communist voters) have been made to suffer unduly and unjustly, who understand that there were less costly and more humane ways to reform Russia than Yeltsin's "shock" measures—how many of us wish to say such things publicly knowing we will be accused of nostalgia for the Soviet Union or even of pro-Communism? Crude McCarthyism has passed, but not the maligning of anyone who challenges mainstream orthodoxies about Soviet or post-Soviet Russia. And the presumed "transition to a free-market economy and democracy" is today's orthodoxy.

But does it even matter what Americans say about Russia today? Those of us who oppose the Clinton Administration's missionary complicity in the "transition," and its insistence that Russia "stay the course," may wish the United States would say and intervene less. In one respect, however, U.S. commentary matters greatly. Eventually, today's Russian children will ask what America felt and said during these tragic times for their parents and grandparents, and they will shape their relations with our own children and grandchildren accordingly.

HANS CHRISTIAN OSTRO*

Even today there are no trains into the Vale of Kashmir.

And those defunct trains—Kashmir Mail,
Srinagar Express—took
pilgrims only till the last of the plains.
There, in blue-struck buses, they forsook
the monsoon. What iron could be forged to rail
like faith through mountains

star-sapphired, by dawn amethyst?
It's not a happy sound . . .
There is such pathos in the cry of trains:
Words breathed aloud but inward-bound.
Bruised by trust O Heart bare amidst
fire arms turquoise with veins

from love's smoke-mines bléssed infidel
who wants your surrender?
I cannot protect you: these are my hands.
I'll wait by the deep-jade river;
you'll emerge from the mist of Jewel Tunnel:
O the peaks one commands—

---

*Twenty-seven-year-old Norwegian hostage killed in Kashmir by the Al-Faran militants in August 1995.

A miracle!—from there . . . Will morning
suffice to dazzle blind
beggars to sight? *Whoso gives life to a soul*
shall be as if he had to all of mankind
given life. Or will your veins' hurt lightning—
the day streaked with charcoal—

betray you, beautiful stranger
sent to a lovelorn people
longing for God? Their river torn apart,
they've tied waves around their ankles,
mourning the train that save its passenger
will at night depart

for drowning towns. And draped in rain
of the last monsoon-storm,
a beggar, ears pressed to that metal cry,
will keep waiting on a ghost-platform,
holding back his tears, waving every train
Goodbye and Goodbye.

Agha Shahid Ali

JOURNALS OF THE PLAGUE YEARS

Edmund White

•

AN OCEAN OF ink has been spilled since 1981 and the beginning of the AIDS epidemic. The most memorable plays of the past fifteen years, including Larry Kramer's *The Normal Heart*, William Hoffman's *As Is* and Tony Kushner's *Angels in America*, have dealt with this subject—perhaps AIDS has even been specially suited to the public forum of the theater. Since Greek times the theater has been a place for religious commemoration and the debate over public values, and even today plays can memorialize as well as polemicize.

But poetry—lyric, personal, a way of reading the most intimate feelings off the transcript of nature—has also called on our greatest talents. Paul Monette memorialized the death of his lover Rog in *Love Alone*, just as Mark Doty recorded in *My Alexandria* all his thoughts and half-thoughts on this impossible subject. I recall specially his poem "Brilliance," in which at first a dying man refuses a gift of goldfish, saying, "*I can't love/anything I can't finish.*" Later he leaves the message: "*Yes to the bowl of goldfish.*/Meaning: let me go, if I have to,/ in brilliance." Poetry, with its shocking, playful and sudden shifts in registers, its abhorrence of cant and insistence on exactitude, is the most honest art form. For that reason it has perhaps best resisted what can only be called AIDS kitsch, the often well-meaning but sentimental recourse to heart-tugging clichés. Some of my favorite collections of poetry have been Michael Lynch's *These Waves of Dying Friends*, Richard

Howard's *Like Most Revelations*, Marilyn Hacker's *Winter Numbers* and, especially, Thom Gunn's *The Man With Night Sweats*.

When I say poetry is the most honest art form, I'm thinking of Gunn's "Lament," in which the poet recalls step-by-step the death of a friend or lover. Gunn has always been famous for his dry, hard language, shorn of all rhetorical flourish, and for his flinty rhymes, but here his style has at last found its perfect subject, one that requires a matter-of-factness to match the horror.

> In hope still, courteous still, but tired and thin,
> You tried to stay the man that you had been,
> Treating each symptom as a mere mishap
> Without import. But then the spinal tap.
>   . . .
> That frown, that frown:
> I'd never seen such rage in you before
> As when they wheeled you through the swinging door.
> For you knew, rightly, they conveyed you from
> Those normal pleasures of the sun's kingdom
> The hedonistic body basks within
> And takes for granted—summer on the skin,
> Sleep without break, the moderate taste of tea
> In a dry mouth.
>   . . .
> How thin the distance made you. In your cheek
> One day, appeared the true shape of your bone
> No longer padded. Still your mind, alone,
> Explored this emptying intermediate
> State for what holds and rests were hidden in it.
>   . . .
> Outdoors next day, I was dizzy from a sense
> Of being ejected with some violence
> From vigil in a white and distant spot
> Where I was numb, into this garden plot

I've given just a few sample stanzas, but I think they show the intensity of the feeling—the way that AIDS poetry at its best benefits from almost imperceptible formal constraints and pushes right on through to the most rigorous sincerity.

AIDS has also inspired countless essays and memoirs—Abraham Verghese's *My Own Country*, Larry Kramer's *Reports From the Holo-*

caust, Paul Monette's *Borrowed Time*, Mark Doty's *Heaven's Coast*,
George Whitmore's *Someone Was Here*, David Wojnarowicz's *Close to
the Knives*, Clifford Chase's *The Hurry-Up Song*. Essex Hemphill
alternated prose and poetry in his book *Ceremonies*; Andrew Holleran
collected his stunning first-person essays in 1988 in *Ground Zero*.
There have been celebrity biographies and autobiographies of Rock
Hudson, Arthur Ashe, Perry Ellis, Magic Johnson, Robert Mapplethorpe, Liberace and Bruce Chatwin. There have been works of
penetrating social criticism such as Diane Johnson's pioneering AIDS
reportage in *The New York Review of Books* and Simon Watney's
Policing Desire and *Practices of Freedom*.

Of course, I haven't even begun to mention the enormous proliferation of fiction. I could mention Allen Barnett's *The Body and Its Dan-
gers and Other Stories*; Ann Beattie's story "Second Question"; Peter
Cameron's *The Weekend*; Christopher Coe's *Such Times*; Michael Cun-
ningham's *A Home at the End of the World*; Larry Duplechan's *Tan-
gled Up in Blue*; David Feinberg's *Eighty-Sixed* and *Spontaneous
Combustion*; Robert Ferro's *Second Son*; Paul Gervais's *Extraordinary
People*; James Earl Hardy's *B-Boy Blues*; Andrew Holleran's *The
Beauty of Men*; Alan Hollinghurst's *The Folding Star*; Bo Huston's
The Listener; Kevin Killian's *Bedrooms Have Windows*; Harry Kon-
doleon's *Diary of a Lost Boy*; Stan Leventhal's *Skydiving* on *Christo-
pher Street*; Adam Mars-Jones's *The Waters of Thirst*; Joseph Olshan's
Nightswimmer; Dale Peck's *Martin and John*; Patricia Powell's *A
Small Gathering of Bones*; James Purdy's *Garments the Living Wear*;
Lev Raphael's *Dancing on Tisha B'Av*; Joel Redon's *Bloodstream*;
Paul Russell's *Sea of Tranquility*; Sarah Schulman's *Empathy, People
in Trouble and Rat Bohemia*; John Weir's *The Irreversible Decline of
Eddie Socket*. When I looked through a recent gay book catalogue, I
learned that Reynolds Price has written an AIDS novel, *The Promise
of Rest*, and that a collection of poetry, essays and performance pieces
by the late Assotto Saint, *Spells of a Voodoo Doll*, was published not
long ago. This list is a random one and just includes those novels I
know something about. I've also left out AIDS novels I've read in
French and Italian and Spanish.

Do I want to say that I'd be willing to vouch for this art, or even that
I considered it all art?

That question makes me uncomfortable whenever it's raised, especially about the work of living writers, but it is exacerbated when the
subject matter is AIDS and even more so when the writer has AIDS or
has died from AIDS complications. I can scarcely defend my feeling

beyond saying that it strikes me as indecent to hand out grades to men and women on the edge of the grave. Who are we to judge them? Who are sero-negative critics to judge us? It sometimes seems strange to me that now, at a moment when literary fiction is being challenged for its very right to exist, people are still squabbling over questions of artistic rank and precedence. Elsewhere I have argued that the whole concept of the canon—of any canon, no matter how up-to-date and carefully revised and balanced—is unsuitable to our society. To me the idea of multiculturalism is incompatible with a canon; now I'd go even further and say multiculturalism is incompatible with the whole business of handing out critical high and low marks.

AIDS literature has challenged the fundamental notion of artistic discrimination since it is often written out of a burning desire for, if not immortality, at least remembrance. Susan Sontag once said that camp, which is a characteristically gay aesthetic response, is a way of endorsing failed glamour; perhaps a similarly generous impulse is behind our desire to welcome all AIDS works of literature, even the artistic failures, onto Mount Parnassus. Whereas most critics have a Platonic view of art, as though every book is struggling to approximate The Book hovering above us in the paradise of ideas, most working writers operate out of a very different aesthetic principle: the notion that each person is unique and contains his or her own music, which it is his or her job to learn to release. From that point of view, all books put together are like those household objects that a xylophonist might line up to play, eliciting a bright, high ping from a glass or a dull thud from an earthenware jug. We each possess our special note, and literature would be impoverished if even a single instrument were stilled.

Yes, but we must choose, we must know which are the crucial books to read, people say. But I would ask, Why? Read the books that come your way, let serendipity be your guide, buy street poetry that's been photocopied, study what someone has scrawled on his paper placemat. When I look at the usual debates about art I feel quite alienated from them. The other day, for instance, I was reading a brilliant discussion by a contemporary philosopher about whether literature should conform to Stendhal's idea that art is a "promise of happiness" or whether it should conform to Kant's idea of purely "disinterested contemplation"; obviously, happiness can never be disinterested, so we must choose between Stendhal and Kant, this philosopher was suggesting.

Not me. I had to smile. I can remember when I used to worry about such debates, though I imagine very few people could really get it up for these issues now. Of course they are "eternal" questions, but I think anyone who has lived with or through AIDS and its devastations knows that art is not about the promise of happiness or disinterested contemplation but rather about leaving stones behind us as we enter the dark forest to mark the path back to safety or just to show where we lost our way. There is an urgency about AIDS writing, a desire to get it all down, to crowd even the margins with necessary details, recollected words, horrifying events—all of it unspeakable, although we are precisely the people who must speak about it.

If you are facing your own imminent death or the death of your lover or friend or brother, you snatch a few moments a day to write, just to scrawl down something; if you're fighting to survive for another day, you have time only to jot a message down and put it in a bottle and cast it out to sea before you go back to the work, the hard work, of dying or getting someone else ready to die.

Whereas most writers—the healthy ones—nibble on their pencils and wonder what to write about next, fuss over point-of-view problems and the proportion of direct to indirect discourse, we are being pushed around by our subject matter, which is like a big bully growing steadily bigger, and we grab for any technique that will convey all we are feeling and thinking and doing. And what we are feeling has little to do with the promise of happiness or any form of disinterestedness. Our suffering has returned us to an earlier period of art, before the invention of the idea of good taste and the development of aesthetics as a branch of philosophy. We have been taken back to a time when griots told stories in Africa, when old wives invented fairy tales, when audiences felt pity and terror.

I'm not trying to invoke primitivism or suggest that we are inspired but unconscious writers. I'm merely saying that since the early nineteenth century a strange divergence has been growing between writers and readers. Whereas writers have felt that they were living more and more on nerve, risking their very sanity as they explored new areas of experience, readers were priding themselves on their objectivity, their coolness, yes, on their good taste. AIDS as a subject calls for an end to this divergence. We will not permit our readers to evaluate us; we want them to toss and turn with us, drenched in our night sweats. Just as AIDS has struck enormous numbers of black and white people, drug users, prostitutes, Africans and Asians, babies born to infected mothers—it is the ultimate equal-opportunity disease—in the same way, AIDS literature is the literature of everyone. Through its powerful prism every color and coloration of experience have been projected.

Look at some of the books I've named. A few are by women, both straight and lesbian, most are by gay white men, three are by black gay men, one by a black lesbian from the Caribbean, one is by a religious Jew who has sought a place for his lover and himself in Judaism and who created a major scandal not long ago when he attempted to acknowledge in Jerusalem, at the Wailing Wall, the persecution of gays during the Holocaust. Several writers are English. They come from every region; they represent every religion. Some have also been politically militant, some were cross-dressers, a few are dead, some are old and some are young. A few of the books I mentioned are first novels. And they fall into every genre—in fact, they have done much to break down the distinctions between genres, especially to confuse the separation between fiction and memoir, even between poetry and prose. "It has been suggested," writes Soshana Felman, "that testimony is the literary—or discursive—mode par excellence of our times." By that token, AIDS literature has borne witness with more fidelity and energy than any other since Holocaust literature—with this difference: Most Holocaust literature was written long after the event, whereas AIDS literature is flowing directly out of the magma.

Above all, works of AIDS literature give us living, suffering individuals. Randall Jarrell once complained that too many of the poems he received through the mail were like a sawed-off leg on which the writer had scrawled in lipstick, "This is a poem." I never understood his objection; I'd like to get something that exciting through the mail, and since the advent of AIDS literature I feel I've signed for several severed, bleeding limbs, and I have known what to make of them. I had dinner recently with a young heterosexual writer who told me he'd set aside his latest book because he felt it was about things that have occurred too recently, about which he wasn't sufficiently objective. I said to him, "Your hesitation sounds to me very old-fashioned. Why wait? Why be objective?"

Many of the aesthetic and political debates of our day have been restaged by AIDS literature and literary criticism. Should gays become assimilated by the general society and disappear as a special group now that, presumably, their rights are subsumed under a general ethic of shared human freedom? This is what Bruce Bawer and Andrew Sullivan are suggesting. Or should gay culture retain its individuality not only because our rights are far from being assured but also because we have something to teach other people about friendship, about throwing off the constraints of jealousy and sexual exclusiveness, about the creative energy that can be released by the realization of sexual identity?

Of course, it could be said that most of AIDS literature has been assimilationist—the sick son is received back into the bosom of his family. If family members must accept his homosexuality, he must accept their love and all it entails. The gay man is no longer perceived as a sinner but as a sufferer, no longer as a high-flying hedonist, more handsome and sophisticated than his stay-at-home heterosexual siblings, but rather as the pathetic prodigal who has come crawling home, longing for acceptance, sometimes even bitterly renouncing his former life of promiscuity. If this is the stuff of many AIDS novels and most stage and screen melodramas, it is also a scenario that many of our more careful writers and thinkers have sought to modify or defy.

Sometimes the defiance has been on the level of form. For the prodigal-son story to work it must follow a clear-cut trajectory in time. It must have a beginning, middle and end, in which the middle is illness and the end death; all the moralizing about AIDS in art depends on this form. But that form inheres primarily in the novel; short-story writers such as Adam Mars-Jones have chosen that abbreviated form because it allows the narrative to cut into and out of the story without conforming to the fatal trajectory. Even the novel can take a new form. As Richard Hall commented, with the ironically titled *The Irreversible Decline of Eddie Socket* in mind:

> Something is happening to the surfaces of the new novels. Thoughts, events, relationships are speeding up. Time, a sense of leisure and the inevitable, the only protection we have against everything happening at once, is disappearing. . . . The words spin by, a few daubs in the darkness, which we collect and reformulate to produce mental images, connections. Ezra Pound's remark, "Narrative is a form cut into time," no longer holds. Narrative is condensing; simultaneity is desired.

Another fictional strategy for defeating the cliché of the personal AIDS narrative, which is usually documentary and autobiographical, is what critic Steven Kruger calls the "epidemiological" or "population narrative," a dystopia or science fiction subgenre that might be stretched to include such serious literary works as Monette's *Afterlife* or Schulman's *People in Trouble*. In any event, contemporary writers are turning to marginal fictional genres such as science fiction, political thrillers, detective stories, erotica and pornography and often elevating them by infusing them with wry, ingenious, deeply felt content. The Spanish novelist Juan Goytisolo has perhaps been the most striking innovator in mixing genres while writing about AIDS and the political dangers facing contemporary society.

Even hagiography is not safe as a genre. Take Robert Glück's novel *Margery Kempe*. The narrator, Bob, is in love with an absent and ultimately rejecting man named L. Discussions of the Bob-L. affair are interwoven with scenes from the life of the fifteenth-century English wannabe saint Margery Kempe, who is believed to have written the first autobiography. The real Kempe sobbed so continually as she contemplated Christ's Passion that she annoyed everyone she ever encountered, especially during her long voyage to the Holy Land. Glück draws a parallel between Bob's excessive suffering over L. and Margery's over-the-top suffering over Christ, but the parallel works for us because the implied subject is AIDS. Close to the beginning of the novel, the narrator declares: "His naked skin expresses mortality and compassion. My last word when I die will be his name." Just as "Margery turns the cosmos into the witness of her love," the narrator plagues all his friends by endlessly discussing his love for L.

The narrator appropriates the Passion of our Lord (the original symbol of the excruciated, suffering young male dying and dead) through the agency of a ridiculous woman, despised by everyone for her lachrymose claims on their attention. Margery suffers just as we all suffer when we foist our tragedies on healthy, prosperous people. Like Margery, like the besotted narrator, like the AIDS scribe, hooked to a gurgling machine and writing in his journal, we are all attempting to talk ourselves into existence.

Now all this seems to be changing. With the miraculous success of protease inhibitors for those who have the money to buy them and the livers healthy enough to process them, AIDS as a death sentence may become a thing of the past for the writing classes. At least in the States. At least among affluent whites. I keep thinking that if I were a clever writer I'd dash off a short story for *The New Yorker* about a young man who has run up an impossibly high bill on his charge cards, quit his job, sold his apartment, told off his friends, spent his last penny on a round-the-world death trip—and now, suddenly, he discovers he's condemned to live. Thanks to the triple therapy he must start worrying about paying his debts, working out a retirement plan, finding new friends and landing a new job.

Will AIDS and AIDS literature soon be forgotten in our speeded-up society? Will we turn our backs once again on the poor of our own society and on the Third World? Or will we admit that the virus and the fiction and poetry and memoirs and plays and essays it has inspired are inescapable, ineradicable, unforgettable?

The challenge is a knotty one. Larry Kramer, our great political leader, has likened the AIDS epidemic to the Holocaust. That parallel has often been questioned, but it is a suggestive one at least in certain incontrovertible ways. As Phillip Lopate has pointed out, for centuries rabbis scorned writing contemporary history beyond a few sketchy notes since the Bible was "sacred history," and anything more recent would be considered impious. Then the slaughter of 6 million Jews pushed aside this anti-historical bias and became the new defining event in the consciousness of Jews and gentiles alike. The number of Holocaust museums that keep opening in America, Europe and Israel, the high visibility of Holocaust films and novels, the pressure to keep the memory of the event alive in schools everywhere—all this points to the defining importance of the Holocaust to a Jewish culture that is increasingly secular and political.

Before AIDS, lesbian and gay artistic history could work out distinguished genealogies that began with Plato and included Michelangelo and came down to Genet. Or queer historians could single out gay martyrs such as Oscar Wilde or reconstruct the penal record in various countries or delve into the diaries of ordinary women and men who lived out their forbidden desires. Modern lesbian and gay history, however, began in 1969 with Stonewall; the political movement grew for a few years, then sagged, until it was reinvigorated at the end of the seventies by the hostility of the Christian right. It was AIDS, though, that made homosexuals visible, that showed that if you prick us we bleed, that convinced famous actresses and politicians to fundraise for us, that united the gay community, often in fury, that put us in the headlines week after week and that, ultimately, led many powerful people to come out, everyone from David Geffen to Newt Gingrich's sister.

Whereas before AIDS the gay male community had been perceived as hedonistic, self-indulgent, selfish, the disease changed all that. The split between lesbians and gays was healed, a powerful and funded political movement sprang up, the public and the media no longer focused on drag queens and leather boys but also saw the human face contorted in pain behind the exotic feathered mask or zippered hood.

Now what? Will all those people who died be forgotten? Will the quilt be stored somewhere until it rots away from neglect? Will the old rancor and divisiveness reappear? Lesbians and gays seldom hand their sexual identity down to their children; in that way they are not like Jews or African-Americans or Latinos. Will what we are suffering be lost? Will we continue our fight to help the poor suffering from AIDS here and abroad? Or will we succumb to instant amnesia, pop an Ecstasy and return to the dance floor?

OCTOBER 6, 1997

HEART OF WHITENESS
MILTON FRIEDMAN, GARY BAUER, WILLIAM F. BUCKLEY. COULD WE ASK MORE OF A CRUISE?

Eric Alterman

•

Going up that river was like travelling back to the earliest beginnings of the world, when vegetation rioted on the earth and the big trees were kings. An empty stream, a great silence, an impenetrable forest. The air was warm, thick, heavy, sluggish. There was no joy in the brilliance of sunshine. The long stretches of the waterway ran on, deserted, into the gloom of overshadowed distances.

—JOSEPH CONRAD, HEART OF DARKNESS

SUNDAY AFTERNOON: I am worried and you would be too. I am en route to Alaska, where my editors have instructed me to submit myself to a cruise through the state's inland passage with the likes of Bill Buckley, Milton Friedman and Gary Bauer, sponsored by *National Review* magazine. Upon landing in Juneau I am immediately assaulted near the baggage counter by a woman handing out photos of herself beside a smiling Newt Gingrich. "Character!" she screeches over and over. The bus to port features an endless tape loop of what must be the world's only female Republican folk singer. And I am going to be stuck on a boat with these people for an entire week! Sartre did not know the meaning of "No Exit."

My mood improves mightily upon arrival at our boat, the M. S. Ryn-dam, a vessel the size of Times Square. On the gangplank, I am enthu-siastically greeted by various *National Review* staff members, who appear to have been handed my photo in advance with instructions to kill me with kindness. They take my picture, hand me an *N.R.* sweat-shirt and send a bottle of champagne to my room. Inside my room fresh fruit grows out of the glass bowl on the coffee table every time I bite an apple. And this is in the cheap seats—no balcony, no porthole. I shudder to think of the freebies the Buckleys must be scarfing down floors above in their 1,126-square-foot penthouse. Before I have time to unpack, alarms start blaring and we are herded toward a lifeboat drill on the lower promenade deck, where we line up in our state-of-the-art life preservers to watch the crew lower the boats into the water while we consider the merits of a watery grave. The conversation is nervous and joking, as people meditate on just how we each would react if it were them or me. I wonder if, in extremis, I would eat Robert Novak. We have not yet been given our dining assignments, so I eat dinner alone. There is no sign of the Buckleys or any of the other muckety-mucks at dinner. I am horrified to learn that while the food is plentiful and ter-rific, the drinks cost money. Heading back to my cabin, I make the no less astonishing discovery that room service is free. I order chocolate cake, even though I'm not hungry, to make up for the drinks. Falling asleep to *A Very Brady Sequel*, I'm wondering how Gary Bauer, whose Family Research Council has parlayed the nuclear American family into one of Washington's most potent new-right political machines, is handling the semi-incest subplot between Marcia and Greg.

Monday: *N.R.* seminar sessions are held in the ship's Vermeer Show Lounge, which is decorated with a three-dimensional tulip motif that somehow calls to mind not flowers but nuclear-tipped missiles. Our subject for today is "The State of the G.O.P." The crowd, about 475 strong, is dressed down, with about half sporting our new gray-hooded *National Review* sweatshirts. They are also mad as hell. It seems Newt Gingrich, the star of this cruise just two years ago, has metamorphosed into one of "them." Seduced by the siren song of Beltway bewitch-ment, he has sacrificed his principles and caved in to Clinton on the recent so-called balanced budget. I imagine the siren of "Character" eating her snapshots, as rough seas and hard rain rock the room back and forth, sending chairs rolling across the stage and coffee cups into the laps of their erstwhile consumers. Buckley chairs the session, which is staged as a kind of floating *Firing Line*. The deal "wouldn't be so objectionable," Milton Friedman huffs, "if the Republicans weren't going around boasting about it." *N.R.* Washington editor Kate O'Beirne suggests self-esteem classes for the majority. Bob Novak says he hardly recognizes Dick Armey anymore. *N.R.* senior editor Richard Brookhiser piles on with a nasty story about House budget committee chairman John Kasich, who admitted to one of the magazine's young star reporters how "absolutely incredible" he found the new Toad the Wet Sprocket album. Such regard from a Republican committee chairman for this third-generation Dead knockoff, fumes Brookhiser, "is a symbol of the intellectual darkness in which Kasich wanders and stumbles." What's next? Rat Dog? Phish? The Spice Girls?

Despite the impressive capacity of the auditorium, we are seated on leather club chairs and comfy upholstered couches, as if this were one big Buckley living room. While the purpose of a conservative political gathering may be to complain, luxury cruise ships are designed—at least ostensibly—for relaxation and enjoyment. So the Ryndam travels on a kind of undertow of cognitive dissonance. With a staff-to-passenger ratio of roughly one-to-two, it is a challenge to do anything for yourself on this boat outside the bathroom. In the all-you-can-eat dining room, there is a man who stands by the coffee dispenser so you don't have to move the lever up and down with your index finger. Another man stands by the food-tray line, carefully placing a knife, fork, spoon and napkin on each one, lest it prove too much of a strain for the rest of us. The busboys and waiters smile and agree with everything, regardless of whether they understand it.

The great thing about being a right-winger, so far as I can tell, is that you get to exploit people and feel good about it. Any self-respecting liberal would feel guilty being so well served by so many apparent Third Worlders. But the *National Review* cruisers don't feel guilty about anything, and it seems to make them nicer people. They are polite. They don't sneer. They seem to really care when they ask how you feel, how you slept or how you can possibly believe what you read in the "liberal media." The young female guards posted outside the auditorium to keep out the nonpaying riffraff are warm and friendly. Just think of the angst any decent-minded liberal would experience at the thought of refusing entry to a seminar on how to save the country.

Following the seminar, we have a short break and then it's time to get dressed for the magazine's introductory cocktail party, also amid Vermeer's missiles. *N.R.*publisher Ed Capano takes the liberty of introducing me to the crowd as *The Nation*'s "resident spy." My status on the cruise is akin to that of a llama in a petting zoo. Everyone is as friendly as can be, and their curiosity is boundless and uncontainable. I happen to be talking to Friedman when the introduction takes place, arguing about whether capitalism is "good for the Jews." ("It's been good for all three of us," he playfully points out, meaning himself, his wife, Rose, and me. "And we're all the Jews here.") We are regularly interrupted by a stream of elderly, cleavage-enhanced older women, who beg the diminutive neo-classicist to pose for the photographer. The results are particularly picturesque because the economist's bald pate is just high enough to reach the height of the women's breasts. Once the crowd sees I have been addressed by the great Yoda, my stock rises precipitately, as most assume that my political salvation is only a matter of time. "Converted yet?" they ask, with no discernible irony.

Spying into the private room that contains the captain's table, I notice with some resentment that Buckley has excused himself from the ship's explicit orders regarding formal wear, even with the easily available rentals, while I have shlepped my tuxedo thousands of miles, going so far as to pony up thirty bucks in the jewelry shop to replace forgotten cufflinks, out of misplaced respect for the conservative order of things. I try to approach him, to inquire whether casual dress at formal affairs might not be a formula for chaos and anarchy, but am stymied by the moon-faced bar mitzvah line that materializes every time the Master shows his well-tanned face.

Buckley and Friedman are the trip's biggest draws. The degree of hero worship that conservatives practice toward their leaders is truly something to behold. Richard Brookhiser and his wife cannot enjoy a cup of coffee on deck without being immediately engaged on the question of whether the liberal infiltration of the Catholic Church is irreversible. Haley Barbour is accosted poolside and asked whether *The New York Times* is trying to set him up by being so nice about his recent appearance before Fred Thompson's investigative committee. Even the throng around Pat Sajak, all-purpose conservative celebrity, is three deep at any given moment. Earlier that day, as the boat motored toward prehistoric glaciers, *N.R.* editor John O'Sullivan and I stood on deck and mused on the awesome beauty of these timeless mountains of snow and ice. We were soon interrupted by a middle-aged fan with a camera who explained that he felt like he was meeting his favorite rock stars.

Dinner generally involves at least five courses, which leaves plenty of time for philosophical disputation after pleasantries. The *N.R.* staff has elected to move me around from table to table as a means, I imagine, of entertaining the guests.

Tonight I am seated with three generations of the Napiers, who live an all-American life in suburban Ohio. They are a charming family, and the parents, Jim and Kristine, are both curious, and a bit saddened, by the extent of my commitment to Satan. But they are also a bit concerned that their two children, aged about 10 and 15, might catch whatever it is I'm carrying. So they speak in perpetually hushed voices, and ask me question questions like "How could you possibly oppose abstinence-only sex education?" Jim is already a little frustrated that he cannot convince his teenage daughter to attend any *National Review* sessions, but it's only fair, as he won't even let her watch *The Simpsons*.

The Napiers finally give up on me, more in sorrow than in anger. We bid one another good night, but not before I suggest to the kids that they check out the nice, wholesome Brady movie on TV. In the evening, the ship's entertainment features chintzy magic shows and third-rate summer stock. There's also a karaoke bar, but *The Nation* does not pay me enough to watch drunken right-wingers strangle Sinatra in this fashion, so you will have to use your imagination. Instead I retire to the casino, where I seem to be in favor with the conservatives' favorite legislator, as the blackjack dealer busts four times in a row.

Tuesday: The weather is no better today and the mood on board turns ugly. Glacier Bay National Park is out there somewhere, but we might as well be in Queens. It's freezing cold in the middle of August, and the sun is a distant memory. There is only so much Scrabble and bridge a person can play. And having an underpaid Indonesian lay out one's silverware and fill one's coffee cup loses its romance rather quickly. Moreover, the ship's activities appear to have been designed with a dogged commitment to enforced boredom and self-mockery. We are offered a "Bad Hair Day" workshop, "The Art of Napkin-Folding and Dining Etiquette," ice- or vegetable-carving and scarf-tying demonstrations, in addition to what appears to be round-the-clock Snowball Bingo. For art lovers, the ship's gallery features LeRoy Neiman prints; for bibliophiles, the library boasts an extensive collection of *Reader's Digest* condensed fiction.

Following four courses and 10,000 calories of lunch, it's time for Part II of the "It's Our Party and We'll Cry if We Want To" session. By now, yesterday's polite, well-behaved audience has grown tired of Buckleyesque high-mindedness. The grouchiness builds as the subject turns to Bill Clinton. If right-wingers are disgusted by their own, they tremble in awe at the President's supernatural ability to trump them on *their* issues. "He embraced our agenda in general, and attacked it in detail," cries Barbour. "He is the only man alive who can cry with just one eye." At one point, Brookhiser tries to convince the assembled faithful that if Clinton had chosen to vacation with them, rather than on Martha's Vineyard, "a lot of you would leave this room thinking he wasn't so bad." The audience gasps in horror. If this had been a movie, we would have been engulfed by a tidal wave.

Leaving aside its accouterments—like first-rate food, bonechina coffee cups and leather recliners, to say nothing of the rolling seas—well-fed, luxuriously located conservative anger is difficult to distinguish from the undernourished, folding-chair liberal variety, at least by sound alone. Like the denizens of any Grace Paley story planning a boycott of the grapes at a West Village supermarket, gray-haired ladies and balding men stand up at the mike and demand to know: "Where are our leaders today?" and "Where is our vision?" and "What can we, the people who are in this room, do about this terrible problem?" The answer was always the same: Return to the principles that made us great, the principles of Ronald Reagan.

Reagan nostalgia engulfs this gathering like the goddamn fog and rain outside the boat. Gary Bauer brings the audience almost to tears with a sappy story about watching Reagan give Barry Goldwater's 1964 nominating speech and promising his dad that he would work for that man "someday, when he's President." The *N.R.* guest who makes the best use of this affection by wrapping himself in its mantle is California Attorney General Dan Lungren. The boyishly handsome, ex-Little League coach speaks wistfully about Reagan to the enraptured audience. Instead of joining the collective kvetch about Republican failures of nerve, Lungren outlines a rhetorical package of "rights and responsibilities" around which a new post-Reagan conservatism could coalesce, a package that contains pretty much the same unpleasantness that animates California conservatism today: antiwelfare, anti-affirmative action, anti-immigration, tough-guy crime packages and allergies to most forms of legitimate taxation. But Lungren comes across as not constipated like Pete Wilson, nor hysterical like Pat Buchanan, but next-door-neighborly, like Reagan without the attendant goofiness. Today Lungren calmly points out that while it is illegal for a 17-year-old girl to sign up for a tanning session or receive a tattoo without her parents' permission, those same parents have no right "to know what's up" when she asks for an abortion. He's just a likable, suburban Everydad, and here's what happens to be on his mind. Among the cruisers, the buzz on Lungren builds all weeks long. By its end, people start wondering if Lungren will feel a need to serve out his entire governorship, which he expects to win next year, before going all the way. Democrats should be very afraid.

Dannymania calms down a bit after the session, and, following more downtime to stare into rainy mist, there's another cocktail party scheduled, this one by the pool. Women with big diamonds and big hair; men with big diamonds and big bellies, though none quite as substantial as Bob Novak's. Not even Haley Barbour's is as substantial as Novak's, which is helpful, I imagine, during those inevitable moments when decent-hearted people fantasize about sending him hurtling overboard into the frozen fjords. Tonight, dress is casual, and the room becomes a sea of polyester. Mentally adding up all the black, Latino and Asian *National Review* cruisers, I come to an informal tally of zero.

Openly gay cruisers, so to speak, number two: conservative Boston talk-radio personality David Brudnoy and his dashing friend, Ward Cromer. Since the frumpy, self-loathing Whittaker Chambers continues to provide the model for how a gay conservative is supposed to conduct himself, to admit that one is happily gay on an *N.R.* cruise is a faux pas on a Napoleonic scale. Forming a tactical alliance, Brudnoy and I sally over to Gary Bauer to try to make sense of why Christian right-wingers get so *verklempt* over gay marriage. Bauer is yet another case of "when-bad-politics-happens-to-nice people," and, like Ralph Reed, he looks like he could be a member of the graduating class of Beaver Cleaver's junior high; but his arguments turn out to be a massive letdown. "If we let two men or two women marry," Bauer politely asks, "then why shouldn't a man be allowed to marry two women? Why shouldn't I be allowed to marry my own daughter?" It's a war against sexual anarchy, in other words, and gay marriage is just the perverts' plan to annex the Sudetenland. Asked why he wants to hang around with so many homophobes, Brudnoy explains that they are preferable to the gay left, who "read him out of the human race for not adhering to their line." "These people," he insists, "can be educated."

Tonight I have the misfortune to be seated next to—but not at—the captain's table, in the little room where Captain Buckley and his wife, Pat, host from opposite ends. I imagine the dry wit is flowing as generously as what looks to be the free liquor, while consoling myself with my own decidedly unwitty and uncharming dinner companions. One guy next to me blows a ceaseless stream of cigarette smoke onto my lobster while explaining in excruciating detail how he discovered all the oil in the North Sea, and Maggie Thatcher still owes him money for it. Another elderly gentleman grows exasperated with the lack of progress in my conversion to Friedmanism and screams: "If it weren't for capitalism, there wouldn't be a *Nation* magazine to pay you to tell people how awful it is, young man!" (Little does he know . . .) I forgive the dumb bastard, however, when, feeling guilty, he orders me a couple of drinks and I retire, two-fisted, to the casino once again, where Bauer's boss dances on my shoulder, throwing thunderbolts on the hands of the dealer.

Wednesday: The ship docks in a nowheresville called Sitka. The cold rain and mud make the place feel hellish, with nothing but redneck bars, depressing pawnshops, tourist-trap stores and long rain-soaked lines in front of the town's few working pay phones. Back on board, cruisers are wondering aloud why the hell *National Review* didn't stick with its previous winning formula and take everybody to the Caribbean, where the sun tends to shine in August and the thermometer occasionally spurts past 50 degrees. There's a post-dinner "smoker" that night by the pool, and the magazine provides cognac, cigars and young Dutch women to light them in grand ceremony. Ed Capano asks me whether I've had much time to hang with the Buckleys. I reply that I am waiting for the bar mitzvah line to die down. The following morning, I am greeted by a hand-scribbled note from the Man Himself that "the line isn't that long." I am among the first to admit to being charmed by Buckley's Lord of the Manor act. But I can wait until Friday night, when I am scheduled to sit at the captain's table.

Thursday: We dock in the early morning in Juneau, Alaska's capital. The sun is finally out and the city is beautiful. Alaska's conservative political leadership talks free-enterprise tough but lives off the fat of its oil-rich public lands. Residents like to think of themselves as hardy pioneers, but three-quarters of them live in metropolitan areas with cable TV, cell phones and sport-utility-vehicle traffic jams. They pay no sales tax and no income tax, and spout aggressive antigovernment rhetoric. At Republican Governor Tony Knowles's reception for Buckley and company that afternoon, the festivities commenced with a musical performance of "The Star-Spangled Banner." Buckley later chuckled that this was indeed preferable to "Hound Dog," the tune on the lips of the rest of the nation, on this, the twentieth anniversary of Elvis's death. Buckley should be more respectful. Given Elvis's politics, he might one day decide to show his face again—on a *National Review* cruise.

Like the rest of the fare-paying paparazzi, I am not invited to the governor's house, so I have the day to do what one does as an Alaskan tourist. Salmon fishing, salmon-baking, salmon-watching, salmon-farming and the like, however, do not inspire. Instead, I fly over the spectacular Mendenhall glacier in a six-seat floatplane. Alaska is filled with such natural wonders, including the Tongass National Forest, which the conservatives on board are trying to destroy. They will accomplish this, no doubt, just minutes after the Clinton-Gore photo op announcing its salvation.

Back on board, my dinner arrangements appear to have been scheduled by Pat Robertson. The appointed subject matter for our conversation tonight appears to be "Why Don't You Jews Just Give It Up, Already?" The most pleasant of my inquisitors is a middle-aged Northern California lay preacher who is genuinely interested in discussing theology. Our conversation is illuminating until he says he wishes he could introduce me to his friends who are "completed Jews"—that is, the pro-Jesus kind. I try to get back to my fillet but suddenly the rest of the table wants to join in the conversation. "Why have the Jews been at war with Christianity for 2,000 years?" asks one of them. "Did you know that some people say the Holocaust never happened?" inquires another. My friend with the completed Jews at home apologizes with his eyes. Thanks, Bud. To add an appropriate note of surrealness, the boat has instructed its blonde female staff members to cruise the hall dressed in Canadian Mountie uniforms and swoop down on unsuspecting diners in the hopes that people will pay $9.95 for a photo commemorating this weird event. I hear the call of the casino and excuse myself. For the third night in a row, The Big Guy stays just where He belongs on the blackjack table.

Friday: This morning's seminar topic is "The Future of School Choice," but it features no teachers or other professional educators. Friedman argues the issue, as he does every issue, strictly on the grounds of the right of individual choice. Bauer views school choice as yet another front in the ongoing culture war. Sixties radicals have taken over the education establishment much as they have the news media. "For the schools to work," he insists, "they ought to teach our children to love the things we love, and care about the things we care about—and that's why we need vouchers." Buckley gently raises objections he's heard from his "Jewish friends," to whom right-wingers should listen, because they are all neoconservatives and no longer among the "the compassionate people." Even neocons, Buckley instructs his audience, worry about having a Christian education foisted on their children by the likes—though he does not say this—of Gary Bauer. Gary himself seeks me out on deck one day to tell me that, under a voucher plan, I would be free to send my children to whatever school I chose. I find this quite decent of him, since any school I would pick would be one that teaches children to fight the narrow-minded intolerance being taught to Gary's kids.

The spectators, now finished behaving themselves, are ready to vent. "Shouldn't we be demonizing the already criminalized Democratic Party?" asks one of those people who always end up at audience microphones. The panelists tell the lunatic that conservative politicians need Democratic votes and suggest instead that they focus their anger exclusively on the true villains, the teachers' unions. The applause is thunderous. There is no fatter target than a teachers' union on a conservative luxury cruise.

All I remember about Ketchikan, where we docked that afternoon, is that the Dow dropped 247 points just as we got off the boat. I am not the kind of person who takes these things in stride, and so I canceled my reservation on yet another tiny $200-per-hour fjord-cruising plane, as I no longer had the disposable income to pay for it. Upon returning to my cabin to dress for my formal dinner engagement at the captain's table, I discover a note under the door informing me that arrangements have been changed and I am now back with the decidedly-ambivalent-about-incomplete-Jews table of last night. Fuck that. I put on my tux, sit down at the captain's table anyway and wait to be ejected. Of course this never happens, but neither do the Buckleys show. I spend most of dinner trying to figure out if I was moved because Buckley wasn't showing or whether he didn't show because I didn't move. I wave to him at a tiny little table outside the private room and he waves back, not a clue on his face. This will always remain a mystery. I retire to the casino and lose all the money I've won so far, having doubled my usual bet to make up for the goddamn Dow. Sorry, Gary, the S.O.B. *is* dead!

That night, around midnight, my phone goes off and I am invited upstairs by some *National Review* staff members for a nightcap. I was in my room watching the bloody scenes in *Michael Collins*, where every surprise phone call leads to brutal assassination. Naturally I wonder about being set up. I go anyway, and end up drinking and playing Ping-Pong—killing them in Ping-Pong if you must know—until about 3. Each time we hear footsteps, however, the three of them start rushing in the other direction. I am deeply touched by the risks undertaken for this unauthorized fraternization and will not reveal their identities on pain of forced karaoke.

* * *

Saturday: Perhaps I was set up. Staying up till 3 means I sleep through a healthy portion of the forum on racial quotas, which, of course, features only Caucasian discussants. The panel members expend a great deal of moral outrage, speaking of "official racism" and "media intimidation." Dan Lungren was supposed to sit this one but he has ascended the dais, I later learn, owing to popular demand, and is introduced as "the next governor of California" to loud cheers. Lungren, looking ahead no doubt to that election, tells the audience that it's time for conservatives to reach out to black Americans, particularly through black churches, which ought to be their natural allies.

After the seminar I sit down with the guy for a formal interview. When I ask what positions he holds that might piss off those on the boat, Lungren avers that, just between us, he rather likes the Brady bill rather more than Charlton Heston does, and believes it extremely important, when in Congress, to convince his fellow conservatives to support a national holiday in honor of Martin Luther King Jr. Lungren's politics are well to the right of those of most Americans', but not as far as Ronald Reagan's were in 1980. Like Reagan, there is no hatred in his voice, and he emits no scary vibes. At 51, he's debate-team smart, aging-Beach Boy handsome and Eagle Scout sincere. Though he has spent most of his adult life in politics—he was a five-term Congressman from Long Beach—he does not hesitate for a second to tell you what he believes. In a one-on-one debate with a robotic politician like Al Gore, I fear Lungren would likely tear the wooden man apart limb by limb.

That afternoon, we convene for the final seminar of the tour, on the future of the conservative agenda. Ed Capano, my nemesis, promises to fax a copy of this article to everyone on board so as not to artificially jack up *The Nation's* circulation figures. This is considered hilarious. The issue that really gets juices flowing is affirmative action—which appears to be the ultimate stimulant to the trigger-happy crowd. "We are the party of the American Nation. They are the party of balkanization," announces *N.R.* editor and British citizen John O'Sullivan. "Either we remain a society that is essentially free or we have a small number of left-wing bureaucrats use one group against another and create a managed, caste-oriented, bureaucratic socialistic society." Wrapping up, Milton Friedman makes one of the stranger and more interesting comments of the week when he argues that Norman Thomas's Socialist Party has been "the most influential party in the history of this country," as "every one of its 1928 platform planks" was later enacted. The crowd murmurs uncomfortably about this, until a light goes on: Friedman is saying they're living in a socialist country. *Well, shit, they knew that.* So Norman Thomas is the father of the American twentieth century. You heard it here first.

At cocktails, just before dinner, I seek out my new comrade, fellow Norman Thomas devotee Dr. Friedman. Rather than doing what I should have done, which was ask him what the hell was going to happen with the Dow, I listen to him expound on the great equalizing forces of the "invisible hand." "Is anyone forcing those Vietnamese to work in Nike factories at the point of a gun?" he demands.

Dinnertime: I try to scam myself back into the captain's table. But it's full of people who are supposed to be sitting there. Pat Buckley and I share a few laughs about how strange these Kennedy boys have turned out. I grab a drink, head out to watch the sun set on the veranda deck and wonder, once again, how it is that some people can be so smart, so decent and so wrong all at the same time. Here's something upon which I'm sure all my fellow cruisers can agree: After a week with them cruising Alaska's inland passage, I still don't have a clue.

WHEN GOVERNMENT GETS MEAN
CONFESSIONS OF A RECOVERING STATIST

Barbara Ehrenreich

•

CALL THIS THE confessions of a recovering statist—at least that's how the right will probably view it. In the past fifteen or so years, I've ended hundreds of speeches with the words "cut military spending and expand social spending," or some euphonious version thereof, implicitly identifying government as the only appropriate focus for activism. In these predilections I have hardly been alone: Progressivism is almost defined, in our times, by its advocacy of an "activist government."

A couple of decades ago, it made sense to pin our hopes on the federal government as a positive instrument for social change. In the sixties and seventies—pressured by the civil rights movement, the nascent feminist movement and a still-muscular labor movement—the federal government expanded both its economic protections and its guarantees of civil liberties. We gained, in little more than a decade, Medicare and Medicaid, workplace safety and environmental regulations, cost-of-living increases in Social Security and laws against race- and sex-based discrimination, as well as the right to birth control and abortion. To many of us who came together in the early eighties to form the Democratic Socialists of America, for instance, it seemed possible that we would achieve our goal of an economically socialist and socially libertarian society by building on the programs and guarantees already offered by the federal government. At the very least, that government seemed to embody, in however imperfect a form, some defense against corporate banditry.

So when a populist right emerged to challenge "big government" and the legitimacy of government-based reforms in general, we valiantly leapt to its defense. At the time, this seemed like the only reasonable and principled response: We knew the right was not so much "against government" as it was against the meager protections government provides for the low-and middle-income majority. But ineluctably we, the erstwhile radicals, became far better defenders of government than any of its elected functionaries. As the right escalated its attacks, we escalated our defense, to the point, all too often, of seeming to abandon our own antistatist tradition and critiques of existing government programs. I realized how much our image had changed—from "radical" to "defenders of government"— in discussions with some of the rural right-wingers I regularly talk to. To my surprise, they were surprised to discover that I share their outrage over random drug searches and similar intrusions: It was their impression that "liberals" thought the government could do no wrong!

I'm not sure whether we should have responded differently to the right's antigovernment rhetoric from the start. But surely today, after nearly two decades of conservative national governance, Reagan through Clinton, we can no longer let progressivism be understood as the defense of government—this government anyway—against the antigovernment forces of the right. The federal government of 1997 is a very different creature from that of, say, 1977—more egregiously corrupt and sycophantic toward wealth, more glaringly repressive and even less responsive to the needs of low-and middle-income people. By setting ourselves up as the defenders of government (or, colloquially speaking, "big government") against the neo-anarchists of the right, progressives have boxed themselves into a pragmatically and morally untenable position.

Pragmatically, the problem is that hardly anyone out there wants to hear about more government or bigger government. Even the constituency for better government is tepid: Witness the non-response to our current campaign finance scandals. It is, unfortunately, the federal government—long favored by the left because of its relative ability to rise above the racism and corporate caprices that typically dominate the statehouses—that has been the most thoroughly discredited as a potential agency of positive change. Maybe that will change—as, for example, people notice that it is the federal government and not the Chamber of Commerce that tends to organize disaster relief and that has brought us such innovations as the Internet. But for the time being, we're not going to get anywhere with a progressive agenda consisting of wonderful new government initiatives. Believe me, I have tried, and found again and again that the enthusiasm for, say, national health insurance or stricter environmental regulation quickly ebbs when I point out that the only source of such improvements is likely to be the federal government. Socialism is, of course, completely out of the question as long as it is conceived as a hypertrophied version of the government we now have, or, in the paranoid fantasy of the populist right, Hillary running everything.

Americans did not always hate their government. The proportion who say they "trust the government in Washington" only "some of the time" or "none of the time" has shot up only recently, rising from 30 percent to 70 percent just in the years between 1966 and 1992. We usually explain this shift in outlook as a brilliant propaganda coup for the right, which, by the mid-seventies, was raking in enough corporate money to create a lush intellectual infrastructure of think tanks and new media outlets. We understand that racism also played its part in the turn against government, helping foster the peculiar perception that people of color have been the chief, if not the sole, beneficiaries of government activism. But we also should understand that the discrediting of government was not accomplished solely through propaganda and prejudice: There are legitimate grounds for distrusting government, and these grounds have been expanding. Through its power over the government it professes to hate, the right has put itself in a position to create a government that is ever more deserving of hatred.

It is, first of all, a government that offers far too little to its average citizens. Thanks to the efforts of the right over the past several decades and especially the past decade and a half, we have a government that does not provide the kinds of services that, in other nations, have helped create a mass constituency for government activism—things like universal health insurance, child care, college tuition, paid parental leave and a reliable safety net. In fact, middle-class, non-elderly Americans encounter their government chiefly in the form of petty-minded bureaucracies like the I.R.S. and the D.M.V. Hence the vicious cycle that has been powering the rightward march of U.S. politics. The less the government does for us, the easier it is to believe the right's antigovernment propaganda; and the more we believe it, the less likely we are to vote for anyone who might use government to actually improve our lives.

The result has been a near-total ideological roadblock for the left. We say "Child care! Health care!" and all the rest, and they say, "Aha, you mean more government!" End of discussion. We have no trouble imagining the kind of polity and social protections we would like, but one of the most venerable instruments for achieving them—government—has been ruled out of order by the ideologues of the right. Now we could of course doggedly continue our defense of government activism against the celebrants of the "free market" economy—pointing out, for example, that government still offers some useful things like Medicare and Head Start, that taxes are actually quite low here compared with other nations, that it is still, despite the ever-tightening rule of wealth, in some vague sense "our" government.

But there is another reason we can no longer let progressivism be defined as the defense of government activism, and this is a moral one. While government does less and less for us, it does more and more *to* us. The right points to the appalling firebombing at Waco; we should be just as noisily indignant about the ongoing police war against low-income Americans of color, not to mention teenagers, immigrants and other designated misfits. If there is any handy measure of a government's repressiveness, it is the proportion of its citizenry who are incarcerated, and at least by this measure the United States leads the world. Furthermore, prison conditions in this country are steadily worsening: Children are incarcerated with adults; efforts at rehabilitation are being discarded as overly indulgent amenities; arbitrary brutality and systematic deprivation are common. We don't, in other words, have a soft, cuddly government of the kind that could be derided as a "nanny state." We have a huge and heavily armed cop.

So government has not been shrinking, as promised, on the Clinton-Gingrich watch. Only the helpful functions of government are shrinking, while the repressive ones are expanding without foreseeable limit and increasingly threaten all Americans. Clinton, in particular, has revealed a boundless appetite for surveillance in the name of the drug war and antiterrorism—proposing, at various times, drug tests for young people seeking driver's licenses, government-accessible "clipper chips" within our PCs and the examination of air travelers' life histories for "suspicious travel patterns." Anthony Lewis has concluded that Bill Clinton "has the worst civil liberties record of any President in at least 60 years." He also has the most flamboyant record—surpassing even Reagan's—for the destruction of government services.

We are not yet a police state, of course. You may disagree with me as to how far we have gone in that direction, but you will surely agree that there is *some* point when the ratio of the repressive to the helpful functions of government will become so top-heavy that it will be masochistic to regard government as a potential ally and friend. Maybe for you that will be when Social Security is abolished (or privatized) and when 10 million, instead of a mere 5 million, Americans are trapped in the criminal justice system. For me that point was passed with the repeal of welfare in 1996, after which I could no longer imagine that my federal taxes served any compassionate function—or, more generally, that the government plays any redistributive role other than to promote the ongoing upward redistribution of wealth.

Our entire outlook has to change. Most fundamentally, given the nature of our real and existing government, we can no longer allow ourselves to be seen as mere cheerleaders for government activism. The power to levy taxes, for example, is increasingly deployed to tithe low- and middle-income people to subsidize the state functions—such as corporate welfare and the military—favored by the corporate elite. Even the few remaining services for the poor are tainted by the repressive agenda of the right, which has budgeted funds for "chastity education" for welfare recipients and favors ever more intimate monitoring of the lifestyles of public housing occupants. When this government gets "active," it may very well act against us.

Yes, we should continue to defend the idea, meaning really the vision, of a truly progressive and robustly democratic form of governance. My point is that we can no longer advance that vision by acting as if the existing government prefigures it in any serious way. We can, of course, continue to try to reform the existing government: by electing progressives to office, for example, and by working to change the rules that make it almost impossible to do so. But these efforts have so far been both arduous and disappointing. Procedural tinkering, such as campaign finance reform and the New Party's unsuccessful effort to legalize fusion tickets, is usually too abstract and complex to generate much excitement. And progressive elected officials only rarely remain so, being quickly absorbed into an insiders' world of corruption and compromise.

In the meantime, though, the progressive agenda cannot be put on hold until we have a government that is worthy and capable of carrying it out. There are plenty of things we can do, right now and even with the existing rules and cast of miscreants. We have to begin, though, by acknowledging that the struggle for economic justice can no longer be conceived simply as a campaign to build support for our wish list of government services. We need a greater emphasis on strategies and approaches that do not depend on the existing government, that in fact bypass it as irrelevant or drownright obstructionist. Some of these approaches are obvious and uncontroversial. First, we can support efforts to organize the 90 percent of American workers who are unorganized, including, most urgently, the former recipients of welfare. Historically, there have been two approaches to economic justice: (1) demanding services and income support from government, and (2) directly confronting private capital by organizing unions. Since the first option has been foreclosed for the time being, there must be an all-out emphasis on the second. A major obstacle, sadly, is union leadership itself, which, even in its recently reinvigorated form, has insisted on funneling millions to Democratic candidates (or, worse, their own re-election campaigns) while strike funds go lacking. Fortunately, though, union organizing does not have to wait for the existing union leadership. The ongoing efforts to organize workfare recipients, for example, are being led by groups like ACORN and the recipients themselves; once the hard work of organizing has been accomplished, the unions will no doubt be happy to incorporate the new members.

Second, we can launch a citizen initiative against corporate crime. In the past couple of years, there have been dozens of demonstrations at the retail outlets of sweatshop-dependent corporations like Nike, Guess and Disney. In the absence of effective regulation against abusive corporations, we have no choice but to pressure them ourselves.

More controversially, I propose that we put greater emphasis on projects that both give people concrete assistance and serve as springboards for further political activism. Examples might include squats, cooperatives of various kinds, community currency projects and some of the less costly types of "alternative services," like those offering information, contacts, referrals and a place for people to gather. Such projects can't provide a substitute for government services since, numerically speaking, their impact is only a drop in the bucket, but they can serve as a "cultural core," in Frances Fox Piven's phrase, of a movement that may eventually be strong enough to win services that are tax-funded and distributed as a matter of right. The feminist health centers, for example, that flourished in the seventies and are still in operation in a number of cities around the country cannot make up for the lack of national health insurance. But they have given many thousands of women the subversive idea that low-cost, high-quality health care is a right—while at the same time serving as organizing centers for the defense of reproductive rights.

There are several reasons for an emphasis on projects that create alternatives. First, they may be necessary for organizing low-income workers, who are often dispersed among many small employment sites that are almost impossible to organize one by one. Such workers may be easier to reach through neighborhood-based centers offering, for example, employment counseling along with information on workers' rights and unions—as some organizers of workfare recipients are currently proposing. Second and more generally, bold and visible alternatives may help break through the hopelessness and passivity engendered by years of right-wing campaigning against public services. Successful projects might inspire the kind of can-do spirit that is so lacking today: If government won't do it, then let government get out of the way, because we're not waiting around!

But for me, the most powerful argument for projects that create alternatives is, ultimately, the scary fact that there is less and less for them to be alternative to. Consider the plight of the people who are being tossed off welfare. Do we simply wait around until the government changes its mind? Applaud the efforts of the Ford Foundation to track the fate of former welfare recipients as they stumble through low-wage jobs and perhaps into homelessness, all the while trying to publicize the horror stories as they unfold? Better to do something that actually helps a few people, or gets them started helping themselves—while at the same time dramatically underscoring the need for economic justice for all. And if our activism is bold and visible enough, it may help prod the existing government in a progressive direction: banning the products of sweatshops, for example, or replacing workfare with the option of adequately paid public-sector jobs.

But economic justice is not the only thing on our agenda. We have to be ready to defy a government that has become an active repressor, and this means putting a greater emphasis on civil libertarian issues. Some progressive have responded to the right's successes with a narrowing focus on economic justice, arguing that the "social issues"—like gay rights, abortion, drug-law reform, even police brutality—are just too divisive. True, most Americans are far more amendable to economic goals like national health insurance than to drug-law reform (which would empty out most of the prison cells overnight). Morally, though, we have no choice but to oppose the steady erosion of individual liberties and the growth of the punishment industry. It might even improve, or at least clarify, our image if we were more forthright and militant about our own brand of libertarianism.

Tragic realities impel us to move beyond our emotional co-dependency on government as the only available instrument for social change, but there are opportunities beckoning us in that direction, one is the need to develop a meaningful internationalism. Rhetorically, most progressives agree that it is the transnational corporations, far more than the nation-states, that rule the world, and that the future depends on our ability to build transnational forms of resistance. In practice, though, it's hard to do this when almost all our efforts are addressed to our own particular nation-state. We might free our imaginations to conceive of truly international strategies if our mission were no longer defined so provincially in terms of our immediate impact on the existing national government.

Finally, there is the opportunity to clarify to the American public what we stand for. We cannot let ourselves be defined or perceived as the defenders of a government that has become, under the tutelage of right-wing Republicans and Democrats alike, outrageously corrupt, loathsomely repressive and socially callous. Our goal is, as it has always been, full freedom and economic security for all. At one point it looked like our government might help us achieve this. But that government is no longer "ours," nor will it be anything we would want to claim as ours without a massive downward transfer of power. For now, it looks like we are on our own, although—if you count the world's oppressed and underpaid majority—we are hardly alone.

IS THE LEFT NUTS? (OR IS IT ME?)

Michael Moore

•

IS IT ME, or is the left completely nuts? I won't bore you with the details of October's Media and Democracy Congress, but suffice it to say that the left is still in fine form, completely ignoring anything that really matters to the American public. I'm convinced there's a good number of you who are simply addicted to listening to yourselves talk and talk and talk—MUMIA! PACIFICA! CUBA! ENOUGH ALREADY!

Speaking of talking to ourselves—just who the hell is reading this? Who *is* the *Nation* readership? Is it my brother-in-law, Tony, back in Flint, who last night was installing furnace ducts until 9 o'clock? Is it the bus driver at the airport who told me he's been cut back to a thirty-hour week so the airport commission won't have to pay the health insurance for his asthmatic daughter? Is it the woman at Sears who sells blouses by day and then waitresses at Denny's from 8 P.M. to midnight?

No. The person reading this would probably sympathize with the one who wrote the flier I saw at the media congress announcing a "Stop Police Brutality Demonstration." The flier promised a rally "from 4 P.M. UNTIL THE TRUTH COMES OUT!" Until the truth comes out? Let me tell you, friend, the truth ain't ever coming out to your rally, and neither is Tony the furnace installer, 'cause he's got mouths to feed. But you don't really want him there anyway, do you? What you really mean by saying that the demonstration is going to last "until the truth comes out" is that it will go deep into the night, until all self-serving, attention-starved "lefties" have had their hour and fifteen minutes at the podium. Get a clue! Go away!

Is it true what they say about "the left"—that it loves humanity but loathes people? I want to let you in on a little secret I've discovered: "The people" are already way ahead of "the left." After years of being downsized, rightsized, re-engineered and forced to work longer hours for less pay and fewer benefits, they already know from *their personal experience* that our economic system is unfair, unjust and undemocratic. They know the evil it does and the havoc it wreaks on their lives. They know that corporate America is the enemy, that the media are telling them lies and that the Democrats and the Republicans are actually the same party, and that neither is worth voting for. Look at any Gallup poll and you'll see that the public is very "left" on all the issues—the majority are pro-choice, pro-environment, pro-labor.

Yet they despise liberals. If they knew where to find the nutty left, they'd despise them, too. They see liberals, progressives and lefties as arrogant, self-righteous and dreadfully predictable. They know you won't ever go have a beer with them, or talk to them about how the Indians did in the Series. Christ, can you even name a single Cleveland Indian?

And why should you? You've got *The Nation* and Pacifica, the food co-op and your Working Assets credit card. Don't get me wrong—I love *The Nation* and Pacifica and food co-ops and not supporting Citibank. But if you stop there and refuse to participate in the real world, how are you ever going to effect change? Back in the eighties thousands of you went to Nicaragua in Sandinista brigades. Yes, that was important work; our government was killing innocent people. But I never saw a single one of you come to Flint while the world's largest company was destroying the lives of 30,000 families. Where were you when we needed you? The people in Flint were ready—Jesse Jackson beat Dukakis by a 9-to-1 margin there. In the white suburbs, Jackson beat him by a 4-to-1 margin! You should have come! The right wing did. They organized the Michigan Militia. It's no accident that Terry Nichols is from the Flint area.

Here's the part I don't get. Remember the antiwar movement, when we didn't have the American public on our side and actually had to go out and *convince* people the war was wrong? That was tough, but we did it. These days, the difficult organizing work has already been done for us by Big Business. It has spent the past decade destroying the middle class and brutalizing the poor. Beating up on the poor. I get—that's the way it's always been. But the middle class? What a stupid error in judgment—and now there are millions of Americans waiting to vent their anger and frustration.

And where are *we*? Inside New York's Cooper Union chanting for Mumia! I want Mumia to live, I've signed the petitions, I've helped pay for the ads—hell, I'll personally go and kick the butt of the governor of Pennsylvania! But, for chrissakes, the woman working at Sears just wants to be able to spend an hour with her kids before she heads off to Denny's. Can't we help her? Do you *want* to help her?

It's taken me a while to figure it all out, and after last month's Media and Democracy Congress I think I have the answer: Because "the left" has lost so many battles, it now doesn't know how to live any other way. It's kind of scary, isn't it, to think that we could actually reach a mass audience. Or that after all these years of failure, real change could actually occur in our lifetime. Better to fight among ourselves! It's an uncomfortable, unfamiliar feeling, isn't it, to get a whiff of a real populist progressive movement taking shape. Better that we keep those furnace installers and bus drivers away from us—they don't read Chomsky anyway!

The signs are everywhere, but "the left" can't read a road map. There's a whole New Politics taking place, and it's being led by U.P.S. drivers and Borders bookstore workers. I say, with all due affection and appreciation for all of you and your causes, get over yourselves, start talking like a real person, then start talking to real people. You could begin by hitting 0 every time you get a robot when you call 411. Have a chat with the human operator—the phone company will eventually have to hire more of them. Or sponsor a bowling team and put the name of your local Labor Party or environmental group on their shirts. Or try bowling yourself. It's where you'll meet Americans.

FIRST PROJECTS, THEN PRINCIPLES

Richard Rorty

•

WHEN I FIRST went into philosophy, I was looking for first principles. I thought that if you could get the right principles, everything else
would fall into place. I was wrong. I gradually realized that it is only
when things have already fallen into place that you can figure out what
principles you want. Principles are useful for summing up projects,
abbreviating decisions already taken and attitudes already assumed.
But if you are undecided between alternative projects, you are not
going to get much help from contemplating alternative principles.
(Consider, for example, the unexceptionable but conflicting moral
principles cited by each side in the abortion debate.)

Plausible principles are usually too uncontroversial to help one
decide which projects to support. I suspect that anybody who thinks
of him or herself as leftist would be happy with the most famous
principle put forward by a political philosopher in recent decades,
John Rawls's Difference Principle: "Social and economic inequalities are to be arranged so that they are both (a) reasonably expected
to be everyone's advantage, and (b) attached to positions and offices
open to all." The trouble is that most people on the right are happy
with it too.

You do not encounter many Republicans who tell you that we shall
always have the poor with us, that deep inequalities are necessary for
the successful functioning of the economy. Rather, Republicans argue
(and most of them actually believe) that since the best poverty program
is a thriving economy, and since such an economy requires that people
who have money send it to their stockbrokers rather than to the gov-

ernment, redistributionist measures will not be to the advantage of the least advantaged. Such measures, they say, even though adopted with the best of intentions, turn out to violate Rawls's principle.

When we on the left argue with Republicans who take this line, it is not about principles. Rather, we insist that a thriving economy can afford redistributionist measures, and that a rising tide will raise all boats only if the government constantly interferes to make sure it does. All the fruitful arguments are about facts and figures, about the concrete consequences of the passage of specific pieces of legislation.

A political left needs agreement on projects much more than it needs to think through its principles. In a constitutional democracy like ours, leftist projects typically take the form of laws that need to be passed: laws that will increase socioeconomic equality. We need a list of First Projects—of laws that will remedy gaping inequalities—much more than we need agreement on First Principles.

If most of the leftist magazines and organizations, and most of the labor unions, could agree on a short list of laws that urgently need passage—bills that had been, or were about to be, put before Congress or the state legislatures—maybe the term "American left" would cease to be a joke. If the Americans for Democratic Action, Common Cause, the New Party, the Democratic Socialists of America, the Gay and Lesbian Alliance Against Defamation, NOW, the N.A.A.C.P. and all the others could get together behind a short but far-reaching People's Charter, the resulting alliance might be a force to reckon with.

Once upon a time, everybody who thought of themselves as being on the left could tell you what laws were most needed: an anti-lynching law, an anti-poll tax law, the repeal of the Taft-Hartley Act, Ted Kennedy's national health insurance law and so on. Nowadays, my leftist students are hard put to it to name *any* laws whose passage they think urgent. They do not seem interested in what bills are before Congress or the state legislatures. Their minds are elsewhere: on what they call "cultural politics." It's easy to talk to them about individualist versus communitarian values, or multiculturalism versus monoculturalism, or identity politics versus majoritarian politics, but it is not easy to get them excited about, for example, a proposed law that would remove obstacles the federal government now places in the way of union organizers.

Unless the American left can pull itself together and agree on a concrete political agenda, it is not likely to amount to much. Most leftist journals of opinion, and most leftist professors and students, share the tacit conviction that nothing can be done, that "the system" is hopeless. The idea that the trade union movement might be revived and become the center of leftist politics strikes them as farfetched. The suggestion that the country is still in basically good shape, and still has a fighting chance to break the power of the rich and greedy, seems to them naïve.

We need to stop airing these doubts about our country and our culture and to replace them with proposals for legislative change. For our only chance of making either the country or the culture better is to do what our forebears did: Keep trying, despite the lethargy and the selfishness, for a classless and casteless society.

This is what the left did, in fits and starts, from the Progressive Era up through the social legislation that Lyndon Johnson shoved through Congress in the mid-sixties. It has not succeeded in doing much along these lines in the past thirty years. Unless the left achieves a few successes, it will never recover its morale and will gradually become even more of a joke that it is now.

The only way to achieve such successes is to retrieve the votes of the Reagan Democrats, the bubbas and the high school graduates and dropouts who resent and despise the colleges and universities as much as they resent and despise the politicians. These people, male and female, black and white, are trying desperately to support households on (if they have enough luck to achieve the national average) $32,000 a year. They need help. They need, for example, unbribed elected officials, health insurance and better schools for their kids. They know perfectly well that they need these things. The left could make itself useful by offering some detailed advice on how to get them.

Those three needs are good candidates for the first three items on a list of First Projects. The first of them should top that list, since most of the present socioeconomic inequities are held in place by bribes paid by the rich to politicians, bribes that the poor will never be able to match. What is delicately called "campaign finance reform" is the issue on which there is most agreement among all sorts and conditions of Americans: rage at unashamed bribe-taking unites the dropout and the doctor, the plumber and the professor. Most of their cynicism about our system comes from the knowledge that bribery is a way of life inside the Beltway—as taken for granted by the unions and the leftist lobbyists as it is by the Christian Coalition.

Suppose somebody like Paul Wellstone or Barbara Boxer introduced a discarded section of the McCain-Feingold Act—the one stipulating that a candidate cannot appear on TV except during free time provided by the networks, which is mandated in exchange for the broadcasters' license over chunks of the electronic spectrum. Suppose he or she titled it "An Act to Prevent the Bribing of Candidates." Suppose the unions proclaimed that from now on they would pay bribes only to politicians who supported this measure—candidates who would help insure that unions would no longer need to spend their members' dues on bribes. Suppose the unions promised, once that measure was passed, to spend the money previously used for bribery on getting out the votes of their rank and file in favor of the legislation that would do their membership the most good.

Another obvious candidate for such legislation is universal health insurance—the issue that Clinton rode to victory, played around with and then forgot about. The poorest fifth of the country still has no medical insurance, and the rest of us are supporting hordes of insurance-company employees—people hired to deny us as much care as they possibly can. Despite retrenchments made in Britain, Scandinavia and elsewhere, no other industrialized democracy would even contemplate dropping universal health insurance. Visitors from Europe and Canada simply cannot believe what happens when uninsured Americans get sick.

Clinton's failure to get his medical care plan through Congress is being treated like a $300 million movie that flopped ludicrously at the box office, rather than as the national tragedy it was. At this point, the details of a new proposal do not much matter—the old Kennedy single-payer bill might do as well as any. If the left would pick such a bill, drag it into every political conversation and demand to know the position of every candidate for national office on it, we might finally be able to do what Truman hoped to do: Make sure there are no charity cases, that anybody who walks into a hospital has the same rights to the same treatments.

What should be the third item on a list of First Projects? Perhaps it should be the equalization of opportunity in primary and secondary education—something that can only be had if we drop the absurd institution of local financing of schools. If ever an arrangement flew in the face of the Difference Principle, that system of financing does. It insures that the quality of a child's education is proportional to the price of her parents' home. The courts of New Jersey and Texas have tried to get the suburbs to kick in some money to repair and staff the schools in the urban ghettos and the rural slums, but without much success.

If a kid grows up in a house with some books and a pervading sense of economic security, she already has quite enough of an educational advantage. She does not deserve the additional boost of cleaner, newer and safer school buildings, or better-paid and less-harassed teachers, than are enjoyed by students in the ghettos. There is no widely disseminated comprehensive plan for equalizing educational opportunity in this country, but we desperately need one.

So much for my suggestions about items that might head the list of First Projects for the U.S. left. Maybe they are the wrong items or are arranged in the wrong order. But at least they share one feature: They are all projects designed to bring the United States up to the level of socioeconomic equality enjoyed by most of the citizens of the other industrialized democracies.

Lots of countries, long ago, adopted laws along the lines of the three I have outlined. In those countries, candidates get radio and TV time for free, during relatively short campaign periods. There are no medical charity cases; medical care is the right of all citizens. To them, the vast disparities between America's suburban and inner-city schools are unimaginable.

These countries have problems, and their citizens are worried. But they have done what we haven't done. They have conceded, grudgingly but steadily, that the best use to make of a thriving economy is to use tax money to increase socioeconomic equality; to make it easier for poor children to get the same life chances as rich children. If the left would unceasingly offer invidious comparisons between Canadian and U.S. health care, between the French *écoles maternelles* and our lack of daycare, between British political campaigns and ours, maybe some headway could be made.

John Dewey hoped that democratic politics would cease to be a matter of batting plausible but contradictory principles back and forth. He hoped that it would become a matter of discussing the results, real or imagined, of lots of different social experiments. The invidious comparisons I am suggesting amount to saying: Look, a lot of good experiments have been run, and some of them have been pretty successful. Let's give them a try. This rhetoric, when combined with a short, easily memorizable list of laws that need to be passed, might give my students a rallying point. It might help some candidates for the Democratic nomination resist the steady shift of the political center toward the right.

That shift toward the right is likely to continue—and the poor will keep right on getting poorer—despite the fact that all our politicians subscribe to all the good old egalitarian principles. New principles will not help reverse this shift, but the success of a few key experiments might.

MICHAEL MOORE'S MAILBAG— EXCHANGE

•

The mail poured in—enraged, delighted, heartfelt, hurt—in response to Michael Moore's November 17 offering. "Is the Left Nuts? (Or Is It Me?)." The article was hailed as "wonderfully passionate," "a lonely voice of sanity"—and as "despicable arrogance" and "pseudo-populist drivel." It caused readers to point out that "the only way the left will win is by boring the right to death," "the intellectuals and the activists of the left need each other—it's been that way since the French Revolution," "the left is afraid of the people it claims to represent" and "frankly some of us worker types [a roofer for thirty years] don't give a fuck who's playing for the Cleveland Indians." A sampling follows.

Los Angeles

In fact, I *can* name one person on the Cleveland Indians—Casey Candaele.

KELLY CANDAELE

Hackettstown, N.J.

Hurrah! Michael Moore should visit the college where I once taught. A cadre of leftists teach history, sociology, political science, and English. They are elitist, boring and dogmatic I often thought they were deliberately put in the classrooms to alienate students from any appreciation for the left.

TERENCE M. RIPMASTER

Brookline, Mass.

O.K. Michael. Maybe you and the little lady from Sears should think on this. The arrogant, clueless left you affect to despise were a step or two ahead of regular folks on the issues. When our government was making Central America safe for U.S. multinationals, who was out protesting? When right-wingers were spreading lurid tales of black criminals while quietly shifting money from schools to prisons, who stood up against the police state? I love the people, too. Unfortunately, the ordinary folks from Flint didn't notice what was going on in this country until their jobs were gone and their schools were rotting. Maybe they were too busy bowling.

Yes, lefties can be a mite out of touch and more than a mite obnoxious, but someone has to keep an eye on the big picture. God knows, the right-wingers don't dis their intellectuals—they set them up in style at the Cato Institute. You want the left to bench Chomsky so Charles Murray can run with the ball?

ELLEN FRANK

New York City

My friends on the left, of varying bowling habits, are working in black communities fighting companies that target them to host toxic chemical plants, with Native American nations threatened with more radioactive waste, with fisherfolk whose livelihoods are under attack by food conglomerates.

I hope Michael Moore keeps pointing the finger, in his wonderfully wacky way, at corporate predators. But if he's going to be pointing at the left, let him also point to those who are practicing precisely what he is preaching. I'm sure he'll find a way to make it amusing.

KENNY BRUNO

San Francisco

Poor Michael Moore. The guy is just looking for love in all the wrong places. Whatever gave him the idea that he could go to the Media & Democracy Congress and find out what the left is up to? Come on, Michael. This was an expensive gathering of media people, most with little or no experience with left political parties, social movements, community or labor-organizing campaigns. It's like attending a gathering of the Salvation Army and then complaining that it seems to lack a real understanding of modern warfare.

There are many social justice organizations that are successfully working with people just like your brother-in-law Tony, the furnace duct installer. Funny thing, though. It's pretty rare that these organizations are attended by the left media celebrities, or even reporters. Maybe that's why nobody has heard of them.

JOHN ANNER
INDEPENDENT PRESS ASSOCIATION

Fremont, Calif.

Thanks to *The Nation* for having the courage to publish Michael Moore, but especially to Mr. Moore. All too often after reading your ivory-towered, egomaniacal, cynical, rude, pompous theorists, we have to turn to something that will raise our spirits, our faith in God (yes!), in our family, in the political process. We don't find that often in *The Nation*.

STEVE AND PAT GALLAGHER (AND FAMILY)

Solana Beach, Calif.

Moore hits the nail on the head in pointing out the palpable, growing sense of anger, frustration and hopelessness among the downwardly mobile working poor who, despite the corporate propaganda flooding our living rooms, absolutely understand what is happening to them. Perhaps the wonks are upset that those who pay scant attention to them are better versed on these issues than the think tankers will ever be. We really can do without trust-fund liberals and elitist socialists who have benefited rightist elements by offering nothing to the angry.

Having grown up just north of Flint, I applaud Moore for his efforts on behalf of those whose experiences should be of supreme study: the poor who get screwed by the right and ignored by the left. Paternalistic lefties should speak to Flint folks about Moore to get a flavor of how a relevant progressive can impact people's lives. If we continue our failure to translate the hopelessness and anger into a tangible political segment, we on the left will again have only ourselves to blame.

ROBERT T. BOWEN

Walnut Creek, Calif.

Michael Moore, baby, we nutty lefties who think our country should stop embarrassing itself with its idiotic embargo against Cuba (last U.N. vote, 136–3 against us) do *so* know the name of a Cleveland Indians player: Hal Trosky (or was it Leon Trotsky?).

Your "enough already" to those campaigning to end the embargo wins the Jesse Helms Seal of Approval, with added applause from Madeleine Albright, Robert Torricelli and the late Jorge Mas Canosa, as well as the famous odd-couple comedy team of Israel and Uzbekistan, the two who kept Washington from being all alone in the world.

LESTER RODNEY

Bloomington, Ill.

How dare Michael Moore cause such consternation! I can hear the gnashing of teeth, the rending of berets, the angry rattle of latte cups.

He had this crazy notion that lefties should actually go and talk with the working class. Even more outrageous, he believes blue-collar Americans have something to teach us—and they haven't even sat through a class on post-structuralist symbolic analysis in mid-nineteenth-century proto-Marxist French literature!

What do blue-collar Americans have to teach us? First is their dogged tenacity, even when their teeth are kicked in and the American Dream dries up before their eyes. The great American dilemma of race, and now gender, is being haltingly negotiated and redefined on the job, sometimes in healthy ways, sometimes not. The only positive of the NAFTA debate was helping many workers realize it isn't the brown-skinned worker across the border who's causing their problems but the corporate monolith that's pitting one worker against the other.

Does the left have anything to offer the average working American? Of course it does. Through all its intensive involvement in identity politics, perhaps it can help build respectful bridges across those identity gulfs. It can help develop global solidarity by using research, connections and organizing to help working folk see their common dilemma. Just eating at ethnic restaurants or wearing batik won't cut it. Picketing in front of Wal-Mart and talking to consumers about 15-years-old Honduran workers in sweatshops for Wal-Mart will.

And get over that longstanding class prejudice that the white working-class male is the enemy. Yep, there are white folk out there who listen to country music, don't always use the politically correct word and sometimes have a Confederate flag decal on their pickup. On Saturday they don camouflage and go out and shoot Bambi. And the only person talking their language is Rush and his militia, offering a convenient enemy one step down the pecking order. We should talk to them in plain everyday language about corporate power, big money and solidarity. Help build a practical way to reach across those barriers of race and gender.

Moore tells us to visit the bowling alley. That's a start. Next time there's a picket line in your neighborhood, ask if you can join. Walk beside a worker and ask some questions. Ask that worker about his or her childhood, home, family, children. Ask how the boss treats them. Ask them what future they think their children will have. They'll probably give you an insightful analysis that will blow you away. Folks know what's going on—what they're lacking is ways to fight it. Let's listen instead of preaching, and perhaps, just perhaps, we can contribute to finding that answer.

Mike Matejka

Houston, Minn.

Yes, Michael, you are right as far as you go, but it's much worse than you think. In your little jeremiad you didn't once mention farmers, so we folks in the rural hinterland know how urban you are.

We lose at least 1 million acres of farmland every year to developers and transportation departments (read: auto industry). One of the best mechanics I've ever known works by himself in a little shop in his mother's backyard. He was angry when a whole lot of cornfield up the road turned almost overnight into a housing development. "Maybe when they're hungry they'll understand what they've done," he said. He's farther left than you, Michael.

The great state of Minnesota sent $630,000 of sin money (from gambling and cigarette taxes) down here in response to grants written by local tourist and development boosters. For two years good citizens sat obediently on committees and were told by "facilitators" and a university "landscape architect" how they might be able to develop luxury housing for rich city folks and tourism for less affluent ones. The money went to the facilitators, the professor and the tourist people.

As my mechanic friend said: "Look what that money could have done for our schools, for local business development, for guys to buy farms!" Now rich folks from the city *are* buying choice ag land for their "getaways" and summer homes—the price of an acre has gone up, local folks can't afford to buy homes in their own townships and our real estate taxes are creeping up.

Many of the guys and their wives who own farms around here "work out." That is, they take jobs in a nearby large city to *subsidize* the farm. Many farmers see their farms disappearing into the maw of corporate landowners and they know, they *know*, their own small farms are more efficient and less polluting and that they are more socially responsible.

Michael, you don't know *zip* about participatory democracy until you've been to a township council meeting where a half-dozen farmers— council members—go over the township budget item by item while a dozen or so farmers listen attentively. Folks speak up freely in sober consideration of all the issues, from road maintenance to bounties for rattlesnakes—a bounty that's been discontinued as the rattlers joined the endangered species list to which smallholders also now belong. There is no rhetoric, no power play. It is this country's best hope.

There aren't many people around here who have time to read *The Nation*. They *are* the nation.

PETER W. DENZER

MOORE REPLIES
New York City

Thanks to everyone who wrote (especially you, Ellen Frank—you sure got us Flint bowlers figured out!). In the spirit of the season, I'd like to share with all of you my favorite recipe for holiday crackers, called "Rudolph's Romp."

You'll need:

- 1 box of Nabisco Sociables triangle-shaped crackers
- 2 pints of Kraft cream cheese
- 1 jar of red pimento strips
- 6 green peppers
- 1 box of pretzel twists (any brand)

Cut the pimento strips into small triangle pieces. Cut the green peppers into small square pieces. Spread a dab of the cream cheese on the cracker. Gently place a triangle of pimento in the corner of the cracker for Rudolph's nose. Put two green pepper squares on the cracker for Rudolph's eyes. Carefully place the pretzel twist on as Rudolph's antlers. Repeat to make as many as desired.

Simple, yet festive—and delicious! Happy holidays!

MICHAEL MOORE

66 Things to Think About When Flying into Reagan National Airport

David Corn

•

The firing of the air traffic controllers, winnable nuclear war, recallable nuclear missiles, trees that cause pollution, Elliott Abrams lying to Congress, ketchup as a vegetable, colluding with Guatemalan thugs, pardons for F.B.I. lawbreakers, voodoo economics, budget deficits, toasts to Ferdinand Marcos, public housing cutbacks, red-baiting the nuclear freeze movement, James Watt.

Getting cozy with Argentine fascist generals, tax credits for segregated schools, disinformation campaigns, "homeless by choice," Manuel Noriega, falling wages, the HUD scandal, air raids on Libya, "constructive engagement" with apartheid South Africa, United States Information Agency blacklists of liberal speakers, attacks on OSHA and workplace safety, the invasion of Grenada, assassination manuals, Nancy's astrologer.

Drug tests, lie detector tests, Fawn Hall, female appointees (8 percent), mining harbors, the S&L scandal, 239 dead U.S. troops in Beirut, Al Haig "in control," silence on AIDS, food-stamp reductions, Debategate, White House shredding, Jonas Savimbi, tax cuts for the rich, "mistakes were made."

Michael Deaver's conviction for influence peddling, Lyn Nofziger's conviction for influence peddling, Caspar Weinberger's five-count indictment, Ed Meese ("You don't have many suspects who are innocent of a crime"), Donald Regan (women don't "understand throw-weights"), education cuts, massacres in El Salvador.

"The bombing begins in five minutes," $640 Pentagon toilet seats, African-American judicial appointees (1.9 percent), *Reader's Digest*, C.I.A.-sponsored carbombing in Lebanon (more than eighty civilians killed), 200 officials accused of wrongdoing, William Casey, Iran/*contra*.

"Facts are stupid things," three-by-five cards, the MX missile, Bitburg, S.D.I., Robert Bork, naps, Teflon.

GENERAL PINOCHET STILL RULES
TWENTY-FIVE YEARS AFTER ALLENDE
AN ANTI-MEMOIR

Marc Cooper

•

SANTIAGO

MEMORY, IN A country like Chile, in a country that has survived its own massacre, is always unpleasant, and certainly, nowadays, unpopular. And yet the raucous demonstrations I witness unfolding in front of the now-reconstructed La Moneda Presidential Palace this winter can't help but remind me of some of the more glorious moments I witnessed here twenty-five years ago when I worked inside the palace as a young translator to Socialist President Salvador Allende.

The immense Constitution Plaza, which yawns in front of the Moneda, was back then very often the stage upon which tens and sometimes hundreds of thousands of Chileans would march and rally around the ideas and programs that then seemed the touchstones of a new and still unfolding era: a nation taking control of its destiny, breaking free from dependence, reclaiming its natural resources, empowering and transferring wealth to the poor, daring to construct a democratic socialism. For me and for many of my generation, what we saw in the plazas and streets of Allende's Chile, coming in the wake of the French '68, the hot Italian autumn of '69, the American post-Kent State student strikes of 1970, promised to ignite a new time of optimism and radical renewal.

We were, of course, wrong. The last massive demonstration I attended in this plaza was on September 4, 1973, the third anniversary of Allende's election, when a half-million Chilean workers, knowing the end was near, marched in front of a somber-looking president and vociferously pleaded for weapons. But it was far too late. Only seven days later, backed by the Nixon White House and bankrolled by the C.I.A., the Chilean military made its move. Within hours, the Moneda was rocketed and burned by Hawker Hunter jets, Allende was dead, Congress was padlocked, tens of thousands of civilians were being hunted down and arrested, and Gen. Augusto Pinochet was in power. A week after that I was forced to leave Chile as a U.N.-protected refugee.

Chile was not the prelude to my generation's accomplishments. Rather, it was our political high-water mark. The Chilean military coup of 1973 was merely overture to the massacres in East Timor and in the Khmer Rouge's Cambodia, the Argentine dirty war, the scorched-earth campaigns in Guatemala and El Salvador, the C.I.A. orchestrated *contra* destabilization of Nicaragua, the rise of Thatcherism in Europe, the Reagan/Bush counterrevolution in the United States.

That's why I am at first so intrigued by the crowds of up to 5,000 Social Security workers who have been regularly flooding downtown Santiago this winter, throwing leaflets into the air, chanting, stomping and whistling, chaining themselves to lightposts and church pews, blocking traffic and standing up to riot-police water cannons and tear-gas barrages. It certainly looks like the same gumption that drove Chilean workers to demand guns from Allende to face down the military.

But there's an ugly glitch in this scenario. This is the Chile of 1998. And like so much in modern Chile, this demonstration is an illusion. These workers aren't fighting for a free pint of milk for every Chilean infant, for nationalization of the copper mines, for a higher minimum wage or for union control of the workplace. No, these workers—men and women alike— are the salaried and commissioned sales force of Chile's privatized pension system. And they are infuriated by a very mild proposed government rule change aimed at curbing the fraud that riddle the system. If approved, the new rule would add a thin layer of protection to all Chilean workers. But it would also directly bite into the monthly commissions the protesting workers have been earning by juggling others' pension funds. Indeed, these workers in the streets today are battling for the right to keep ripping off their fellow workers. It's a long road to have come down in twenty-five years. Since I first arrived here just weeks after Allende's 1970 election, my life has become ever more entwined with Chile, first as a student, then as a researcher in a government publishing house and later as Allende's translator, husband of a Chilean and member of a large Chilean family. But the more profound my involvement, the less I recognize this country.

Allende triumphed in Chile precisely because, long before his election, a century-old tradition of parliamentary democracy and advanced social legislation had forged a society that prided itself on high public discourse, a national commitment to mutual aid and solidarity, and what seemed—even under conservative administrations—a permanent sense of social justice. But that's a Chile that has vanished into collective amnesia. Today—after seventeen years of military dictatorship, and eight years of "democracy" in which what passes for the left is complicit as co-manager of a grotesque system that allows murderers to walk free and torturers to be elected to national office, that boasts one of the most unequal economies in the world, where education is essentially privatized—Chile is perhaps the one place on earth where idolatry of the market has most deeply penetrated.

Chile hardly holds the patent on a pullback from politics, a reflex now rampant from Peoria to Poland. But few countries in recent decades have traveled quite the distance backward that Chile has. In Eastern Europe the economic systems were stood on their heads, but decades of Stalinist cynicism and duplicity served to grease the way for the savageries of frontier capitalism. Chile was different, though. In 1970, on the eve of Allende's election, one U.S. researcher found Chilean teenagers—along with their Israeli and Cuban counterparts—to be among the three least alienated, most optimistic groups of youth in the world. But years of military dictatorship and a quarter-century now of the most orthodox application of sink-or-swim social policy has imposed a sort of collective neurosis on Chileans—it has driven them crazy, driven them to market.

Chilean millworkers now assiduously follow daily stock quotes to make sure their private pensions will be there when they retire. When their children leave the school gates, they plop Velcro-backed insignias from elite academies onto their uniforms, lest the other subway riders guess they go to more downscale institutions. Bookstores that once brimmed with political classics now stock huge piles of translations of Anthony Robbins and other quick-road-to-success gurus. National "educational" TV features training films in entrepreneurship and good customer relations. Prime-time infomercials beam dubbed-over blue-eyed gringos blissfully hawking vegetable Smart Choppers and Sure Fire bass lures to the rural and fishing villages of the Chilean south, where horses are still sometimes a preferred means of transportation.

A recent police checkpoint in the posh Vitacura neighborhood found that a high percentage of drivers ticketed for using their cell phones while in motion were using toy—even wooden—replicas. Other middle-class motorists, pretending they have air-conditioning, bake with their windows closed. Workers at the ritzy Jumbo supermarket complain that on Saturday mornings, the dressed-to-kill clientele fill their carts high with delicacies, parade them in front of the Joneses and then discreetly abandon them before having to pay. In the tony La Dehesa neighborhood, Florida palm trees are the landscaping fashion à la mode and black butlers are all the rage. But they better be stocky six-foot Dominicans, as the first wave of imported help, from Peru, turned out to be unfashionably short-statured. In the rickety shantytowns around Santiago, readily available Diners Club cards are used to charge potatoes and cabbages, while Air Jordans and WonderBras are bought on a twelve-month installment plan.

Yes, a few lonely souls still protest the disappearances, murders and thousands of unprosecuted barbarities of the past two and a half decades. But they are denounced as threats to stability, provocateurs, losers, dinosaurs—as is nearly any reminder of how Chile's new commercial culture was grafted onto a political body charred to the bone.

And yet, for all the striving to forget, for all the frenzied talk about being an "economic Jaguar," about modernization and a global future, Chile cannot escape its past. On March 11 the man who embodies Chile's darkest history, 82-year-old Gen. Augusto Pinochet, gives up his post as Commander of the Army and takes up his new seat as unelected but fully empowered "Senator for Life." Indeed, under a Constitution his regime wrote in 1980, which allows for a certain number of appointed senators, former military commanders will now constitute the single biggest "party" caucus in the Senate. And with a two-thirds Congressional vote necessary to enact serious reforms, Senator Pinochet will, until he dies, hold the power of political veto in his hands.

Pinochet's continuing prominence in Chile is more emblematic than aberrational. His dictatorship may have been voted out of office by the plebiscite of 1988, but it is his economic and political model that has triumphed. For the U.S. media, the Chile story is, as always, a neat and simple tale: Bloody dictator forced by history to wipe out communism gets voted out and a civilian government leads the transition to democracy while retaining a free-market economic system. But reality is more complicated. In Chile there has been no transition, nor will there be one in the foreseeable future. What we are seeing instead is the *consolidation* of a new global model—a model imposed here twenty-five years ago at the point of a bayonet and since then ever more refined and better marketed. It is a model that, in some form or another, is being proposed for all of us. "Chile is what I call a transvestite democracy," says radical Chilean sociologist Tomás Moulian. "She looks like a nice friendly young lady. But lift up her skirts, and you're in for a big surprise."

THE CHILEAN MIRACLE

The New York Times recently celebrated this state of affairs by crediting Pinochet with a "coup that began Chile's transformation from a backwater banana republic to the economic star of Latin America," and the Clinton Administration wants Chile to be the next member of NAFTA. Putting aside the fact that the pre-Pinochet "banana republic" produced a bumper crop of world-renowned artists, scientists and other intellectuals, including the winners of two Nobel Prizes in Literature, the *Times* also got it wrong on the economy. The 7 percent annual growth since 1986 cited by enthusiastic supporters of the Chilean economy obscures several other less attractive figures: There was *no* growth between 1973 and 1986; real salaries have declined 10 percent since 1986; and salaries are still 18 percent lower than they were during the Allende period. One-fourth of the country lives in absolute poverty, and a third of the nation earns less than $30 a week.

A recent World Bank study of sixty-five countries ranked Chile as the seventh-worst in terms of most unequal income distribution, tied with Kenya and Zimbabwe. To get a notion of just how skewed this is, consider the following: In the United States—hardly a paragon of wealth sharing—60 percent of national income goes to workers and 40 percent to capital; in Chile, 40 percent goes to workers and 60 percent to capital. The top 10 percent of the Chilean population earns almost half the wealth. "The 100 richest people in Chile earn more than the state spends on all social services," says Christian Democratic Senator Jorge Lavandero.

Chile is a case of rapid growth with little development—growth concentrated in the export of natural resources. Neither a solid middle class nor a well-paid working class has emerged. In the past, Chile suffered from a chronic job shortage, and the poor subsisted on a network of welfare and social solidarity. The new economy has dismantled welfare and dismembered community aid while at the same time making low-wage jobs plentiful. The result? There are just as many poor people as ever. The only difference is that now they have to work hard to attain even that standing. Therefore, "economic growth by itself will not solve problems of poverty and inequality," says Canadian economist Philip Oxhorn. "It will only reproduce them."

Defenders of the Chilean model say these inequalities are a small and acceptable price to pay for a system that rewards individual initiative. "We have extraordinary success because this system was applied without any political opposition," says Jaime Vargas, a U.S.-trained economist who works for a private think tank. "People know the rules of the game and have to believe in themselves. People are not into politics and not into any groups of any kind—unions, clubs, whatever." Chile, he says proudly, "is a world of incredible individualism."

Orlando Caputo, one of the best-known opposition economists in the country, has a more clinical view: "The Chilean system is easy to understand. Over the past twenty years $60 billion has been transferred from salaries to profits."

THE CHILEAN DREAM

The belt of tin-roofed shantytowns that house a quarter of Santiago's 4 million residents seethed with Allende supporters during his brief tenure and then became a fiery necklace of resistance to the dictatorship. The military bulldozed the Che Guevara and New Havana settlements. And Pinochet "uprooted" 200,000 shantytown dwellers and relocated them to new slums in the chilly Andean foothills. But other neighborhoods took up the mantle of intransigent opposition: La Bandera, La Legua, Pudahuel and especially La Victoria.

Since its birth in a land squat in 1957, La Victoria has incubated two generations of radical activists and revolutionaries. During the protests and confrontations of the mid-eighties, La Victoria was on the front lines. When armed troops opened fire on a group of reporter friends of mine, they shot dead the community priest, Andres Jarlan. His successor, Pierre Dubois, was deported to France. Often during those years, and in defiance of military rule, La Victoria's main artery, Avenida 30 de Octubre, would be covered with proletcult murals denouncing the regime's soldiers as assassins. On the eve of planned protests, the dictatorship would ring La Victoria with thousands of troops, and if confidence was high enough, they would rip the neighborhood apart in house-to-house searches.

Usually standing at the eye of these hurricanes was "Red Olga," the obstreperous, square-shouldered, white-haired Communist matriarch of La Victoria. Arrested in 1974 and held in the notorious Teja Verde concentration camp for two months, Olga returned to La Victoria and turned her tiny home into the "Olla Comun"—the community soup kitchen that not only fed 200 families a day but also served as command-and-control center for the local anti-Pinochet resistance.

When caught by the curfew in La Victoria, when seeking the latest hard information on anything from troop movements to the price of hamburger, or when just simply seeking refuge from a tear-gas cloud in the eighties, I would always retreat to Olga's.

But when I call her up now after not seeing her in ten years she warns, "Don't come in on the main street. You'll get robbed by the drug addicts. Come in the back way." When I finally meet up with her, she seems not to have aged. The same picture of Soviet cosmonaut Yuri Gagarin and straw hat from Cuba hang on her dingy wall. She closed down the soup kitchen in 1990 and soon saw the political tide recede around her. Many of La Victoria's problems are the same as they were a decade ago: high unemployment, inadequate health care, alcoholism and a raging crack epidemic.

"The big difference now," she says, "is we no longer have any organization." The block committees, the community boards, the rank-and-file political groups, have all but evaporated in the ether of modernity. "Now, it's everyone for himself," she sighs. "People live only for the moment. They remember nothing. They vote for anybody. We didn't have to get all the way to socialism, but we should have gotten more than this."

Olga now squeaks by on a pension of $95 a month. Her only luxury is her telephone, which eats up a fifth of her monthly income. "You try to talk to the people about changing their lives," she says. "And all they do is shrug their shoulders." As for today's politicians, so many of whom now claim to have led the opposition to the military, she has no time for them. "Funny, isn't it," she says laughing. "After the war, there sure are a lot of heroes."

A couple of miles down the smog-choked Pan-American Highway and across from the plebeian metropolitan cemetery, I visit my aging Uncle Germain and Aunt Manuela. Their shanty-town, Rio de Janeiro, couldn't have been named for anything to do with that Brazilian city except its infamous *favelas*—the teeming hillside slums. Germain and Manuela are among that bottom third of Chileans getting by on a few dollars a week. There have been changes—some for the better, some just changes—since the early days of the dictatorship. Pavement now covers the dirt road in front of their shack, glass has replaced the heavy plastic in their windows and Manuela's loyalties have drifted from Marx toward Jehovah. Germain has moved from a welfare program in which he swept the steps of public buildings to being a night watchman for $3 a shift. Meat can be eaten two or three times a week instead of once, and a twenty-five-inch Sanyo color TV (a gift from a son) dominates their tiny sleeping quarters and seems to be permanently aglow.

But some things remain the same. None of their grandchildren can dream of paying for university. Doctor's visits—even those subsidized by the tattered state health care system—are considered a luxury, to be indulged in only in emergencies. Medicine—indeed, the ability to stay afloat at all—would be impossible if it weren't for regular help from family living abroad. Also unchanged is an unshakable class consciousness. My aunt swears blue at the mention of the military or those they protect. But old age and decades of defeat make any political response seem like folly to her.

Among Chile's bottom two-thirds of the population, the political center of gravity has shifted increasingly away from places like La Victoria and toward newer communities like La Florida. Situated at the very end of the north-south subway line, a forty-five-minute commute from downtown, composed of cracker-box highrises and cramped single-family houses with postage-stamp-sized patios and iron fences, La Florida is an oasis for working-class and lower-middle-class families who nowadays are putting in twelve-hour workdays. La Florida's own mall, Shell station and McDonald's sit like three sacred pyramids at the gates of the community and are a popular tourist destination for amazed working-class day trippers. A decade ago, such a trio of consumerist temples could be found only in the most exclusive neighborhoods.

Today, La Florida looms as The Chilean Dream. Scrape together a few thousand bucks and buy your own house in the Chilean version of Levittown. No matter that you are twenty miles from nowhere, that the housing stock looks vaguely Bulgarian, that the smog and the traffic are noxious. This is all about feeling rich in miniature. This is about a concept new to Chile: Individual Lifestyle.

When I enter the living room of 35-year-old Cecilia's three-bedroom, 950-square-foot home, I feel like I'll need a coat of Vaseline to squeeze in. Her house, microwave, stereo, used car and private-school tuition for her three kids are all leveraged on several lines of credit. Her husband makes only a couple of hundred dollars a month working in a government highway toll booth.

Cecilia is the main breadwinner. She never talks about politics unless asked. But she's a staunch leftist, coming from a family of Communists and supporters of M.I.R.—the extreme left quasiguerrilla group pulverized by Pinochet. Until recently, Cecilia was one of those Social Security salespeople. After three years of solid performance, she was summarily booted from her job for not having met her monthly quota of sales. "No matter how long you work for these pension agencies," she says over a cup of tea, "you can only come in under quota one month. Two months in a row and kaput."

She explains in surreal detail the corruption and unfairness of Chile's privatized Social Security system. Thanks to "pension reform" imposed by Pinochet in 1981, all workers in Chile, whether employed or self-employed, must contribute a percentage of their income every month to a private retirement fund managed by one of a half-dozen investment companies known as A.F.P.s. Unlike in the United States, where both worker and employer pay 7.5 percent each into Social Security through payroll deductions, Chilean employers no longer make any contribution at all toward worker pensions. They retain, however, the right to withhold employee contributions from workers' paychecks, and news stories are legion of this or that company that "forgets" for months and sometimes years to deposit workers' funds into A.F.P.s. And because so many Chileans are self-or marginally employed, almost half the fundholders don't keep their own required contributions up-to-date. An equal number have been revealed to have less than a $1,000 balance—hardly enough to support retirement.

Because the fund managers invest in bonds and Chilean stocks, each fund closely mirrors the others in terms of investment choice and performance. So while there's tremendous competition among the A.F.P.s. to get as much money into their own investment pools as possible, there's little incentive for workers to transfer from one fund to another. "But that's where we salespeople come in," says Cecilia. "We work on commissions based on the new accounts we recruit. So we get all our friends and say, 'Give me your account and I will give you a gift'—a bottle of whiskey, a cordless phone, a stereo. Right now the hot gift is a mountain bike." As a result, about half of Chilean account holders switch A.F.P.s once every six months. About a third of those transfers, says the government, are "irregular," suggesting considerable fraud.

"My biggest deal was a factory in Valparaiso," remembers Cecilia. "The union there pooled thirty-four workers who offered to transfer their accounts all at once. I closed the deal. I gave the union a big-screen TV, a steam iron and a juicer, which it raffled off to the workers."

Cecilia worries little about being unemployed. She has a thriving side business representing several banks. Like an Avon lady, she goes door to door in the neighborhood selling lines of credit. "All you need to show is six months' worth of pay stubs," she says. Then she can get you an immediate loan equivalent to four months' salary. Payable over twenty-four months, the interest rate is 75 percent a year. "My father would die if he knew what I was doing. I grew up with him reading me Marx and Lenin," she says. "I still believe in all that. But I have no choice. It's sink or swim."

PING-PONG POLITICS: 'EXCESSIVE REALISM'

The same Pinochet who oversaw summary executions, whose political police tortured opponents to death and hid their bodies in pits of lye, who "disappeared" more than a thousand citizens, who ran scores of thousands through his jails and prisons—the same Pinochet can become Senator for Life this month because absolute impunity reigns in Chile. This is not only because of an amnesty law the military regime passed to protect itself but also because of the deal cut between the military and politicians of the center *and* left.

After a decade of slaughter, the Chilean left vigorously surfaced in a wave of massive and sometimes violent protests in the early eighties. But by the end of the decade, confrontation with the military was supplanted by negotiation. By 1988, the civilian opposition agreed to participate in the plebiscite designed by Pinochet's regime. It was win-win for the dictator: A Yes vote would give him eight more years in power; a No vote would allow him to hang on as military commander and would allow a civilian government to be elected but under the terms of his rewritten Constitution. By the time of the plebiscite campaign, the center-left opposition, known as La Concertacion, dropped from its program state intervention in the economy and any questioning of property rights. A vague call for "reconciliation" pushed justice for the military criminals off the political agenda.

The civilian opposition won the plebiscite, but that in no way meant the end of Pinochet's model. In the months following the plebiscite and before the first civilian election, the Christian Democrats and the Socialists—Allende's old party—held extended talks with the regime to plan the "transition," and in so doing almost fully accepted the military's terms: The Senate would continue to be packed with appointees; the secret police and the military would remain protected by amnesty; the archaic and pro-military judicial system would be left intact. The military budget would remain autonomous and untouchable. The new elected president would not be able to remove any top military com-

mander for eight years. As one former army captain told me, "This was
the only transition in Latin America where the military came out not
only untarnished but downright virgin."

The demand voiced by thousands who celebrated in the streets on
the morrow of the plebiscite—that Pinochet resign from the army—
was never echoed by the civilians who took over the government. "How
embarrassing for us," says dissident Senator Lavandero. "We could
have defeated Pinochet in '83, and again in '88, but lamentably my own
party negotiated democracy away with him."

The past eight years of civilian rule have been what some call a time
of "excessive realism." And as the junior partners in this arrangement,
the Socialists have moved from a position of expediency to one of complicity as co-administrator of the hemisphere's most rigidly orthodox
neoliberal economy.

In giving legitimacy to a system designed by their enemies, the
Socialists trivialize politics and generate a vast cynicism. "Young people who are idealists, who had so many hopes when Pinochet lost the
plebiscite, are finding out we are being betrayed, that a deal was cut
over our heads," says Pablo Bussemius, the 25-year-old Socialist student body president at the University of Chile's law school. "Now with
Pinochet headed for the Senate, there's an ever greater disillusionment
and withdrawal from politics."

That disillusionment was measurable in the campaign for last
December's mid-term Congressional elections. When the nightly fifteen minutes of free airtime for political parties came on the TV, ratings plummeted; a full 20 percent of TVs were simply turned off. This
in a country where, traditionally, politics has been the main talk at the
dinner table. No surprise this time around. The right ran a campaign as
defenders of the poor! And the center/left government parties broadcast a campaign that would have tingled Dick Morris's toes. "Love Is
Better in a Democracy," Chileans were told as the tube flashed images
of couples hugging and kissing.

Perhaps one political TV talk show best encapsulated the bank-
ruptcy of modern Chilean politics. As a panel of the four men running
for senator from Santiago fielded inane questions from a clearly
deranged host, tuxedoed waiters walked on-camera and served them
cakes and pastries, while on the corner of the stage two teenage girls
(described by the host as "journalists") sat in skimpy miniskirts and
noted down questions called in from the audience. After a commercial
break, the scenario shifted to the outdoor patio of the TV studio. The
host then encouraged the Socialist candidate to play ping-pong against

the candidate from the hard-right U.D.I.—a party founded by Pinochet's dreaded secret police. As torturer and tortured batted the ball between them and simultaneously answered questions from the host, what could the audience have been thinking?

When the votes came in on December 11, generalized panic set in, and not because the ruling coalition had lost 5 percent of its vote or because the hard right displaced its more moderate allies. A full 41 percent of the eligible electorate either didn't register to vote, abstained, defaced the ballot or left it blank. A million voters under age 25 failed to register. These are predictable results for Americans, but earth-shaking for Chileans, who have been accustomed to 95 percent and higher turnout rates. In Chile's second city of Valparaiso, the winner in the multiparty vote went effectively to "none of the above"—20 percent of the ballots defaced. In Santiago, the Communists, running in opposition to the government, doubled their vote to nearly 10 percent.

The contours of the balloting reveal a barely submerged discontent. Notwithstanding the government's reluctance to take on Pinochet, or the hard-core 30 percent or so of the population who in some measure or another still revere him, the other 70 percent have a visceral hatred for the dictator. He cannot appear unprotected in public, and always provokes catcalls and boos. Polls have consistently shown two-thirds or more of the population in favor of his resignation.

A courageous judge in Spain is currently hearing testimony on Pinochet for "alleged crimes against humanity," including the murder of Spanish citizens in Chile. The Chilean "democratic" government has denounced the inquiry, President Eduardo Frei has tried to block an attempt by a few young Christian Democratic Congressmen to go forward with their own impeachment of Pinochet and the Chilean foreign minister has called the proposed impeachment "profoundly inconvenient." Nonetheless, a large number of Chilean social and cultural leaders have given their public support to the Spanish investigation.

Perhaps even more significant, a Chilean appeals court judge sent shock waves through the political establishment in mid-January when he agreed to hear a case brought by Communist Party leader Gladys Marín. Marín, whose husband was disappeared by the military, is trying to block Pinochet from taking his Senate seat by formally charging him with "genocide, kidnapping and illegal burying of bodies." It's the first time any Chilean court has accepted a direct charge against the dictator.

So far, the much-touted reconciliation in Chile has been one-sided. The military has never been asked to atone or even apologize for its crimes, so the reservoirs of popular resentment run deep even if they are rarely given public voice. But on a recent bus commute through downtown Santiago I witnessed a moving scene. A street troubadour boarded the bus to sing for his supper. This all-too-common occurrence has driven Chilean commuters beyond boredom, so barely anybody made eye contact with the poorly dressed middle-aged singer. But while most of these beggars scratch out three or four tunes before passing the cup, this fellow sang only one song. "*Tu, no eres nada, ni chicha ni limonada,*" he crooned, reviving the signature song of Victor Jara, the leftist folk singer whose hands were smashed and who was then killed by Pinochet's military in the weeks following the coup. "You are nothing, neither hard cider nor lemonade. Get out of the middle of the road, join up and save your dignity. . . ." Two or three young people clapped their Walkman earphones on as soon as he strummed his first chord. The thirty or so others on the packed bus listened quietly as they stared ahead or out the window. But when he finished, almost all went out of their way to give him some coins.

'CONSOLIDATION OF A MODEL'

Strolling through downtown Santiago, one is offered a reminder of how mesmerizing and paralyzing mass consumer culture is when newborn. In our own case, at least American consumerism sprang up as a natural outgrowth of booming economic development. In Chile, mass credit consumerism substitutes for development. Worse, before 1973, conspicuous consumption was taboo in a country still infused with a sense of social solidarity. Television didn't arrive here until 1962. There was no mall until the early eighties, and no fast food till a few years later.

Imagine the *frisson* the average Chilean feels today when he or she walks the Alameda, the main downtown thoroughfare, and sees *all* the world's baubles for sale on easy credit. At the entrance to every department store, every shoe store, every pharmacy, there is the ubiquitous young girl on a podium offering instant credit. Air Nikes? Cash price 29,000 pesos—or twelve payments of 2,900 pesos, the equivalent of $6. A bottle of Shalimar? Cash price 16,000 pesos—or ten payments of 2,200 pesos.

Sociologist Tomás Moulian points to the spread of credit to the masses as only the latest step in implementing the neoliberal economic model. In one of Chile's sweetest ironies, his book on the subject, *The Real Chile: Anatomy of a Myth*, stayed on the country's bestseller list through all of 1997. "What we have in Chile," he says in an interview, "is the marriage of a neoliberal economy with a neodemocracy, a simulated democracy. The end result is a neoliberal system defended now by its historic Socialist adversaries. Pinochet, for his part, is a symbol of this capitalist counter-revolution, which profoundly changed our culture and even the capitalism we had before him."

Moulian's thesis runs something like this: The first two years of military rule merely reversed the Allende-era reforms, liberalized prices, lowered salaries and subjected the working class to the now familiar nostrums of economic "shock therapy." The Chicago Boys period of 1975–81, shaped by Milton Friedman and Arnold Harberger, introduced structural "reforms," increasing exports and creating new economic groups indebted to international banks. A draconian labor law clamped down on workers, and a wave of privatization (including Social Security) atrophied the state. That phase fizzled in 1982, leading to a mini-depression that liquidated national industry and drove half the population below the poverty level.

"But a sense of direction was recovered immediately," says Moulian. "A re-ordering, a re-privatization of everything, commenced under a neoliberal pattern. The new economic groups that emerged were much stronger than the older ones. Not indebted to foreign capital, they were interwoven with it. And the tremendous pools of private money generated by the private pension funds were used to fuel these new groups. It was the workers' money that built such prosperity for the elite." This Chilean model, says Moulian, "anticipated Reagan and Thatcher. Because of the neoliberal intellectual sway over the military, Chile started out early on the road that everybody is now on."

He adds: "In this sense the Chilean terror was rational. This whole model is frankly impossible without a dictatorship. Only the dictatorship could have disciplined the working class into submission while their salaries were lowered and their pensions used to accumulate wealth for others. Only a dictatorship can keep a country quiet while education, universities and health care are privatized, and while an absolute marketization of the labor force is imposed. Today, under this simulated democracy, the work force is too fragmented to recover and the population is distracted by consumerism and disciplined by credit obligations."

WORDS FROM THE COLONEL: "TO BUY OR NOT TO BUY"

Drive around the "Little Manhattan" section of Santiago's Barrio Alto—its lavish "High Neighborhood"—and you'll come face to face with the few who are perched atop the steep pyramid of Chilean social class. Fifty percent of all national construction in the past decade has taken place in just the two wealthy suburbs of Vitacura and Las Con-

des. In the hillside La Dehesa neighborhood, the family house that is a
replica of Tara pales beside the reproduction of Versailles. It seems
there are only two kinds of vehicles up here, Mercedes sedans and shut-
tle buses that cart the domestic help to and from the shantytowns—the
same sort of shuttles that scurry between Soweto and the Johannes-
burg suburb of Bird Haven.

A little closer to downtown but only a half-notch down the social
scale, the municipality of Providencia is a delight of lush gardens and
colonial mansions. Its city hall is a converted Tuscan villa replete with
marble columns, stained glass and crystal chandeliers. Its manicured
rose garden is a favorite meeting place for uniformed nannies taking
their stroller-bound charges for an afternoon airing.

I've come to meet the elected Mayor of Providencia, former army
Col. Cristian Labbe. I knew his father, also a colonel—that is, until
Allende sacked Labbe senior when he refused to salute a visiting Fidel
Castro back in 1971. The young Labbe followed his dad's footsteps into
the military, and Pinochet became his mentor. Rising from the dictator's security apparatus, Labbe became one of his trusted political
advisers, eventually serving as government secretary general in the last
years of the regime.

Outfitted in a white shirt with two Mont Blanc pens in his pocket, his
blond hair greased straight back in the preferred style of the Chilean
aristocracy, Labbe receives me with tea in his personal office. There is
an air of immediate hostility on his part. Not because of my association with Allende, which I purposely avoid mentioning, but because, of
all things, I am an American. In the bizarre ideological universe of
extreme nationalism and latent neo-Nazism that Labbe inhabits, Americans are viewed as busybody socialists. He tells me right off that he's
still angry over the pressure the United States exerted on Pinochet to
stage his 1988 plebiscite. "We carried out each one of our promises
even though no one believed us," Labbe says with a red face. "Not even
you gringos believed us. We had every organ of the U.S. government
down here acting as if they owned us."

For reasons of journalistic efficacy I let the remark pass. Instead I
ask him to reflect on Pinochet's legacy. "We live in democracy today
only because of the work of the military government," he fires back.
"Chileans today recognize the morality of merit and incentives.
Chileans know that if you want to do something, you can. Today, if you
do well, you are respected, not scorned. A Mercedes today is a symbol
of success. Now we have freedom of choice, as Milton Friedman says.
Man is free to buy or not to buy. Once we had two universities. Now we

have 300. Once we had one type of car. Now there are twenty or thirty. That is freedom."

When I ask about the social cost of such liberation, about a certain legacy of human rights abuse, Labbe cuts me off with a condescending smile. "Look, let me tell you a parable," he says, taking a sip of imported Earl Grey. "There's a terrible auto accident. The victim has no vital signs and is barely breathing. He's rushed to the emergency room and his whole family begins *demanding* that everything and anything be done to save him. The surgeons start cutting and operating. The patient revives slowly. First he goes to urgent care. Then he's put on a restricted diet. Some of his activities are also restricted. With careful treatment over years he fully recuperates. He's even free now to choose another doctor if he wants. And one day he goes to the beach. When he takes his shirt off, his brother sees a bunch of scars and stitch marks. And the brother is scandalized! Shocked! 'My God,' he says, 'you are a victim of human rights abuses!' "

At least Labbe, in his roundabout way, recognizes the scars. That's more than a lot of his constituents will do. I know because some of those who say "nothing really happened in Chile" are in my own family. After tea with the colonel I walk a few blocks to my fiftysomething cousin Sonia's gate-guarded Providencia apartment. I dine with her and a 35-year-old third cousin, Lisette, the fair-skinned daughter of a wealthy businessman. Both women are what are called in popular lingo *momias*, reactionary mummies. But even I am not prepared for the dialogue that unfolds.

"What a catastrophe these past eight years of [civilian] government have been," says Sonia. "We are back to strikes, disorder, corruption. Pinochet was grand. He brought order and depoliticized the country."

I answer. "Well, he is also responsible for killing and torturing a lot of people."

"Outside of Chile that's what they say happened," interrupts Lisette. "But it's not true. I've always said if you weren't doing anything wrong, nothing would happen to you. Nothing happened to me. I never saw anyone killed. Though I will say this, these eight years haven't been as bad as I thought they were going to be. Democracy isn't as bad as everyone said it would be."

Ignoring that last remark, I return to death and disappearance. I recount the murder of Orlando Letelier by Chilean secret police in Washington, D.C., the bombing murder of former Gen. Carlos Prats in Buenos Aires, the approximately 3,000 dead—including 1,000 disappeared—listed by the government-named Truth Commission and, finally, my own experience of narrowly escaping Chile alive a week after the coup and the fact that so many of their own family members, including my wife, were forced into exile.

"I don't know about this or that fact," answers Sonia, totally unfazed. "All I know is what I have lived through personally. And personally I was much happier, I felt much safer with Pinochet."

And there you have what Tomás Moulian calls "The Great Psychotic Denial." When there's never been an acknowledgment from the armed forces of any wrongdoing, when the civilian government—including the Socialists—demands no such recognition, when the right and left trumpet Chile as the model of the future, when the dictator remains free to become senator, when torturers and assassins are exempted from prosecution, then anything said to the contrary must be a lie. To admit otherwise would be to acknowledge the horrible price paid for the privileges of Providencia.

BIRTHDAYS AND BARRICADES

The Chilean military can no longer afford to live in the economy it created. During the dictatorship its members took on huge mortgages and big car payments; now removed from direct power, they are struggling to pay the bills in a rampant free-market economy. "They are very worried," says longtime military affairs commentator Raúl Sohr. "The military is the child of the state. And to the state they have returned. While the rest of the country has to put up with privatized everything, the military now has its own schools, its own hospitals, its own vacation camps, its own subsidized housing, transportation and universities. It even has its own state pensions. They have their own private socialism." Beyond the irony in this anecdote, there's also a caveat about Chile's future. Chilean soldiers aren't the only citizens poised on the economic razor's edge. The country's economic stability is leveraged on continuing exports and expanding consumer credit—two pillars easily knocked out by fluctuations in the world market. Already, the Asian economic crisis caused one Chilean stock market dive this year as well as an unprecedented but to date still-controllable dip in the peso. The last time the Chilean economy took a dive, in 1983, the country went to the brink of rebellion—and that was under the heel of military rule.

"The greatest enemy to future stability is a sort of generalized ignorance and arrogance that comes with triumphalism," says Ricardo Israel, director of the University of Chile's Political Sciences Institute. "People are satisfied saying we now have the same products you can buy in New York or London. We are also laden with the tremendous ideological weight of the church and the armed forces. We are still way behind in Chile. Yet so many Chileans have deluded themselves into thinking we are the vanguard. Hardly. Maybe a vanguard in duty-free shops. Nothing more."

There have been some intriguing symptoms of political restlessness of late. The eviscerated labor movement has finally started to distance itself from its "partners" in government. Last October, 80,000 young people jammed the National Stadium—one of the dictatorship's infamous killing fields—for a concert to commemorate the thirtieth anniversary of Che Guevara's death. The hard antigovernment left won student body elections in two of the country's three main universities. And when in November it won in the third, in the fiercely conservative Catholic University, the shock waves battered both the right and the official pro-government left. "When the children of the elite vote for the hard left, you better believe something is happening," says Sohr. Says Colonel Labbe: "I tell you I just can't understand it. Why would the students of La Catolica vote Communist?"

Augusto Pinochet is celebrating his 82nd birthday the evening I leave Chile. His morning starts with civilian supporters lining the sidewalk in front of his Barrio Alto mansion to applaud him. Then come the official visits of the entire army brass. With what one newspaper later calls a "visibly emotional" Pinochet looking on from his balcony, the official army band serenades him with the "Happy Birthday" song. Then the general and future Senator for Life requests a rendition of the "Erika" march, followed by his favorite tune, the old Nazi favorite "Lili Marlene."

An editorial by Cristian Labbe lauding "the vision of a statesman" appears in the leading daily, *El Mercurio* (a former beneficiary of C.I.A. funding).

At twelve noon, a few dozen student leaders gather in front of the downtown Defense Ministry and unfurl a banner offering Pinochet a one-way ticket to Spain for his birthday. Seconds later, squads of national police attack the students and several journalists, clubbing, tear-gassing and arresting them. No one knows what the charges are.

By 8 P.M. Pinochet has arrived at the army's so-called Rock House, where he is feted by 1,300 guests, including several top industrialists, army officers, TV personalities and a former Miss Universe. The President Pinochet Foundation is transmitting the event by closed-circuit TV to thirty-six other banquets in Pinochet's honor across the country. Three of Chile's private TV networks are also transmitting the entire event. As I head to the airport I hear Pinochet's crackly voice over the radio telling his supporters that he is "perfectly aware" of the "destructive ambitions" harbored by those who criticize the military. Suggesting that any effort to hold him personally responsible for the past would be tantamount to treason, he goes on to warn that "anything that affects a single member of the army affects the whole army."

When my taxi crosses into downtown we are snarled in traffic. Some 5,000 mostly young protesters are in the streets blocking traffic, singing and wishing the general a "very unhappy birthday and all the sorrow in the world." To make my flight I have to dodge the water cannons, the barricades, the bonfires and tear gas. But I do so with pleasure. This evening Chile seems much like the country I knew twenty-five years ago. This demonstration is far different from the skirmishes staged all month by the Social Security sales force. These students are fighting for much more than their narrow personal interest. Those of us who lived through the promise of the Allende period hope they are not the last rattle on the snake of rebellion and liberation, that they are instead—and against the odds—the catalyst that will spur millions of others to remember a future.

SOME PEOPLE

•

Some people flee some other people.
In some country under a sun
and some clouds

They abandon something close to all they've got,
sown fields, some chickens, dogs,
mirrors in which fire now preens.

Their shoulders bear pitchers and bundles.
The emptier they get, the heavier they grow.

What happens quietly: someone's dropping from exhaustion.
What happens loudly: someone's bread is ripped away,
someone tries to shake a limp child back to life.

Always another wrong road ahead of them,
always another wrong bridge
across an oddly reddish river.
Around them some gunshots, now nearer, now farther away,
above them a plane seems to circle.

Some invisibility would come in handy,
some grayish stoniness,
or, better yet, some nonexistence
for a shorter or a longer while.

Something else will happen, only where and what.
Someone will come at them, only when and who,
in how many shapes, with what intentions.
If he has a choice,
maybe he won't be the enemy
and will let them live some sort of life.

Wislawa Szymborska
TRANSLATED FROM THE POLISH
BY STANISLAW BARANCZAK AND CLARE CAVANAGH

WE NEED A RADICAL LEFT

Ellen Willis

•

THE *NATION'S* INTRODUCTION to its "First Principles" series conveys a revealing double message. On the one hand we are called on to think about "fundamental questions," to ask what we believe, what kind of society we want and how we can build it. Yet at the same time we are informed that the left has contributed to its current weakness by "failing to unite around economic issues of fairness that join together the interests of all but the wealthiest Americans." In other words, we believe in economic fairness, and the way to achieve it is through appealing to the majority's economic interests while (it is implied) avoiding other issues that are potentially divisive. But why bother to ask fundamental questions if we already know the answers? What's left to discuss except details?

In my view it's exactly this kind of thinking that needs to be challenged if the left is to revive. While I regard economic inequality as a national emergency and a priority on any serious left agenda, I don't agree that "fairness," in itself, is a principle that can successfully combat right-wing ideology and mobilize an effective movement for change. Nor do I think the way to build such a movement is to look for issues that "unite" people. By definition, the project of organizing a democratic political movement entails the hope that one's ideas and beliefs are not merely idiosyncratic but speak to vital human needs, interests and desires, and therefore will be persuasive to many and ultimately most people. But this is a very different matter from deciding to put forward only those ideas presumed (accurately or not) to be compatible with what most people already believe.

When Ronald Reagan was elected in 1980, a wide assortment of liberals and leftists called for unity around a campaign for economic justice. Since then, as the country has moved steadily rightward, I have heard this call repeated countless times, along with many hopeful announcements of projects designed to put it into practice. Each time the right wins an egregious victory (as in the Congressional elections of 1994), dozens of lefty commentators rush into print with some version of this proposal as if it were a daring new idea. You would think that if economic majoritarianism were really a winning strategy, sometime in the past eighteen years it would have caught on, at least a little. Why has it had no effect whatsoever? Are people stupid, or what?

The culprit the majoritarians seem to have settled on is cultural politics. The cultural left, they argue, has given left politics a bad name because of its divisive obsession with race and sex, its arcane "elitist" battles over curriculum, its penchant for pointy-headed social theory and its aversion to the socially and sexually conservative values most Americans uphold. As a result, the right has been able to distract American workers with the culture war, while pursuing class war with impunity. Some anti-culturalists further claim that cultural radicalism is the politics of an economic elite that itself has a stake in diverting the public from the subject of class to, as Michael Lind put it, "inflammatory but marginal issues like abortion." But note the elitist, condescending assumptions embodied in these very arguments: that for two decades most Americans have been manipulated into abandoning their true interests for a cultural sideshow; that they don't have the brains to tell one kind of leftist from another, let alone come up with their own ideas about what kind of politics might improve their condition.

I'd suggest a different explanation for the majoritarians' failure: Their conception of how movements work and their view of the left as a zero-sum-game—we can do class or culture, but not both—are simply wrong. People's working lives, their sexual and domestic lives, their moral values, are intertwined. If they are not ready to defend their right to freedom and equality in their personal relations, they will not fight consistently for their economic interests, either.

In any case, class is itself a cultural as well as an economic issue. The idea that a heterogeneous population is naturally inclined to band together on the basis of its declining share of income relative to the rich makes sense only on the same bonehead premise advanced by the right's "rational choice" theorists: that human beings are economic calculating machines. In fact, a powerful ideology of meritocracy divides people of different socioeconomic strata as effectively as (and usually in combination with) racism or sexism. While large percentages of the working and middle classes may tell pollsters they think CEOs make too much, on a deeper level most people tend to admire the rich, to see them as somehow smarter or better, just as they tend to despise the very poor. Nor is class politics less susceptible than racial or sexual politics to the temptations of cultural nationalism, which is why blue-collar unions have been reluctant to organize white-collar workers, and why in certain circles preference for beer and pretzels over wine and cheese is elevated to a political badge of honor. To argue for a solidarity that transcends these divisions is to challenge deeply ingrained cultural patterns.

No mass left-wing movement has ever been built on a majoritarian strategy. On the contrary, every such movement—socialism, populism, labor, civil rights, feminism, gay rights, ecology—has begun with a visionary minority whose ideas were at first decried as impractical, ridiculous, crazy, dangerous and/or immoral. By definition, the conventional wisdom of the day is widely accepted, continually reiterated and regarded not as ideology but as reality itself. Rebelling against "reality," even when its limitations are clearly perceived, is always difficult. It means deciding things can be different and ought to be different; that your own perceptions are right and the experts and authorities wrong; that your discontent is legitimate and not merely evidence of selfishness, failure or refusal to grow up. Recognizing that "reality" is not inevitable makes it more painful; subversive thoughts provoke the urge to subversive action. But such action has consequences—rebels risk losing their jobs, failing in school, incurring the wrath of parents and spouses, suffering social ostracism. Often vociferous conservatism is sheer defensiveness: People are afraid to be suckers, to get their hopes up, to rethink their hard-won adjustments, to be branded bad or crazy.

It's not surprising, then, that those who stick their necks out to start social movements tend to be in certain respects atypical. Paradoxically, they are likely to have economic and social privileges that free them from an overwhelming preoccupation with survival, that make them feel less vulnerable and more entitled. Or, conversely, they may already be social outcasts or misfits in one way or another and so feel they have little to lose. Often they have been exposed to alternative worldviews through a radical parent or an education that encouraged critical thinking. Such differences are always invoked to attack radicals on the grounds that they are not "ordinary people" but middle-class intellectuals, cultural elitists, narcissists, weirdos, outside agitators. Yet rebellious minorities are really just canaries in the mine. When their complaints speak to widespread, if unadmitted, disappointments and desires, it's amazing how fast "ordinary people's" minds and the whole social atmosphere can change, as happened between the fifties and the sixties.

My experience as an early women's liberation activist was dramatic in this regard. At first we were a small and lonely bunch; our claim that heterosexual relations were unequal everywhere from the office to the kitchen to the bedroom was greeted with incredulity, laughter and blunt aspersions on our sexual and emotional balance. I had many passionate arguments with women who insisted they loved to cook and cater to men. What was I doing, they demanded—trying to destroy sex and love? Two years later feminist groups were erupting all over the country, and it was not unusual to see women turn up at demonstrations who had once denounced the whole enterprise in the most withering terms. Suppose we had reacted to that first wave of hostility (as of course many liberal feminists urged us to do, and many liberal men no doubt wish we had) by concluding, "This will never fly—let's stick to 'equal pay for equal work' "?

It's not necessary, as many leftists imagine, to round up popular support before anything can be done; on the contrary, the actions of a relatively few troublemakers can lead to popular support. The history of movements is crowded with acts of defiance by individuals and small groups—from the 1937 sit-in of workers in a Flint, Michigan, auto plant to Rosa Parks's refusal to get up to radical feminists' disrupting an "expert hearing" on abortion reform—that inspired a wave of similar actions and a broader revolt. When militant minorities also have radical ideas, they capture people's imaginations by presenting another possible world that appeals to the secret hopes of even the resigned and cynical. They mobilize people by providing the context in which winning small changes is worth the time and effort because it is part of a larger project. They attract publicity and make it difficult for the authorities to keep on telling the lies whose credibility depends on uncontradicted repetition. The people in power know all this and are quite wary of the potential threat posed by an organized minority; their impulse is to make concessions (albeit as few as they can get away with). As a result, radical movements that articulate a compelling vision have an impact far beyond their core of committed activists.

American left politics generally works this way: As radical ideas gain currency beyond their original advocates, they mutate into multiple forms. Groups representing different class, racial, ethnic, political and cultural constituencies respond to the new movement with varying degrees of support or criticism and end up adapting its ideas to their own agendas. With these modifications the movement's popularity spreads, putting pressure on existing power relations; liberal reformers then mediate the process of dilution, containment and "co-optation" whereby radical ideas that won't go away are incorporated into the system through new laws are incorporated into the system through new laws, policies and court decisions. The essential dynamic here is a good cop/bad cop routine in which the liberals dismiss the radicals as impractical sectarian extremists, promote their own "responsible" proposals as an alternative and take the credit for whatever change results.

The good news is that this process does bring about significant change. The bad news is that by denying the legitimacy of radicalism it misleads people about how change takes place, rewrites history and obliterates memory. It also leaves people sadly unprepared for the inevitable backlash. Once the radicals who were a real threat to the existing order have been marginalized, the right sees its opportunity to fight back. Conservatives in their turn become the insurgent minority, winning support by appealing to the still-potent influence of the old "reality," decrying the tensions and disruptions that accompany social change and promoting their own vision of prosperity and social order. Instead of seriously contesting their ideas, liberals try to placate them and cut deals, which only incites them to push further. Desperate to avoid isolation, the liberal left keeps retreating, moving its goal post toward the center, where "ordinary people" supposedly reside; but as yesterday's center becomes today's left, the entire debate shifts to the right. And in the end, despite all their efforts to stay "relevant," the liberals are themselves hopelessly marginalized. This is the sorry situation we are in right now.

Yet despite defeat after defeat, liberals retain a touching faith in their modus operandi. In the thrall of historical amnesia, they seem to have the impression that both the post-New Deal welfare state and the post-World War II era of high wages, job security and an expanding middle class came about because voters elected liberal Democrats who enacted government social programs, union organizing rights and so on. In fact, the corporate elite actively collaborated in the creation of welfare state liberalism and mass prosperity in order to stave off the threat to its very existence posed by the crisis of the Depression, the strength of the labor movement and of radical movements domestic and foreign and, crucially, the Soviet Union. (I don't want to be misunderstood as defending the gulag, but there is no denying the irony: By showing that another system was not only possible but able to complete for world dominance, the Soviet regime forced Western capitalists to adopt more humane policies.)

At present, capital faces no significant left opposition to its expansion and consolidation all over the world, and so has no incentive to embrace liberal constraints. With their enormous resources and their power to invest or disinvest, give or withhold credit, transnational corporations are more powerful than any national government and have shown their readiness to retaliate against any government that defies them. The states of Western Europe, which have much more developed social democratic traditions than ours, are still under relentless pressure to reduce their social benefits and worker protections. American leftists who imagine that we can reverse growing income inequality simply by passing laws—that we can somehow force the corporations to be "fair" in the absence of any broader attack on their power—are suffering from a serious confusion between tail and dog.

Instead, we need to think about how we can confront the power of capital at a time when state socialism in all its versions has proved a dead end. The way to start, I believe, is by forming a radical labor movement that claims as its constituency everyone subjected to corporate domination—from "workfare" recipients to well-paid but regimented professionals—and organizes wherever possible across national boundaries. Such a movement would demand an active role for workers in all corporate decisions that affect our daily working lives and the entire social landscape, including decisions about investment, trade, technology, production, hiring, the structure and conditions of work. It would challenge not only low wages and insecurity but the repressiveness of long hours, authoritarian work rules, hierarchical management and women's "double shift." In short, it would be a movement not merely about fairness but about democracy, freedom and the pursuit of happiness. As such it would transcend the majoritarians' untenable distinction between economics and culture and regard movements for black, women's and gay liberation as its natural allies rather than competitors and antagonists.

The real political function of majoritarianism is maintaining that distinction without having to defend it on its merits. Some majoritarians are cultural conservatives who are sympathetic to much of the right's pro-family, nose-to-the-grindstone program but don't want to be attacked for saying so. Others are satisfied with the cultural status quo—OK, it's not perfect, but hey, what is?—and are baffled and irritated that these "marginal issues" should steal attention from what matters to *them*. (In this vein, Richard Rorty lectures *Nation* readers, "We need to stop airing these doubts about our country and our culture"—in other words, have your damn doubts, but don't frighten the horses. Apparently he has decided, like former Speaker of the House Tom Foley on the occasion of the 1989 invasion of Panama, that "this is not the time for a lot of complicated debate.") Still others have concluded that in light of past crimes committed in the name of utopia, raising the possibility of social transformation is out of the question. I can't help detecting in this cluster of stances something that might be called a comfortable-white-male syndrome. Who else, after all, would project their own straitened worldview onto "the American people," instead of simply speaking for themselves?

THE DEVIL'S BALL

•

Because someone could sit
In China for so long, maybe
Imagining one hundred wild days
Of lovemaking beside a green river,

As his blade carved ivory spheres
One inside another, we named it
After the contours of our own minds.
The patience of seeds in a pod

Seldom enters the metal & wood
Of our tools, & we whisper
To the stars time is money.
Maybe the delicate faces,

Houses, & senses were whittled
While he watched a gingko
Measure the summer skies
& a lotus open three mouths of praise.

Yusef Komunyakaa

DIALECTICAL MCCARTHYISM(S)

A REVIEW OF MANY ARE THE CRIMES: MCCARTHYISM IN AMERICA BY ELLEN SCHRECKER

Victory Navasky

•

IN *MANY ARE the Crimes: McCarthyism in America*, Ellen Schrecker undertakes a double deconstruction: Of the anti-Communist crusade that became known as McCarthyism and of the American Communist Party (and the communist movement) at which it was ostensibly directed. Her most valuable and original contribution is her analysis of the interplay between the two.

On McCarthyism—which took its name from its most notorious practitioner despite the fact that it began before Joseph McCarthy arrived on the scene and its legacy persists to this day—she correctly observes that there was not one but many McCarthyisms, each with its own agenda and modus operandi: There was the ultra-conservative version peddled by patriotic groups (campaigns to purge textbooks of favorable references to the United Nations, etc.). There was the mainstream version ("we agree with his goals but we object to his methods"). There was the liberal version, which supported sanctions against Communists but not against non-Communists. There was a partisan version: Republican politicians like Richard Nixon and McCarthy and Democrats like Senator Pat McCarran used it to boost their careers. And there was the obsessive and bureaucratic version of J. Edgar Hoover, which came to dominate the political culture, so much that

Schrecker appropriately proposes that the phenomenon should be renamed Hooverism. All these versions purported to protect the nation from the threat of domestic communism (especially espionage), and they all "subscribed to a set of assumptions that placed national security above the Constitution and Communism below it." While McCarthyism in virtually all its manifestations was aimed at destroying the left, it ended up inflicting legal, political, cultural and personal devastation on the country.

Unlike such earlier students of McCarthyism as sociologist Daniel Bell, who saw it as a populist aberration, Schrecker believes "McCarthyism was primarily a top down phenomenon." And unlike such historians as, say, Ronald Radosh, who argued in a recent *New Republic* that the US Communist Party was an organization controlled, financed and run "entirely" by the leadership of the Communist Party of the Soviet Union, Schrecker believes that the party "was both subservient to the Kremlin and genuinely dedicated to a wide range of social reforms."

Thus even as she describes how the McCarthyite ultras ultimately sold their program to the nation's elites, who put it into practice, Schrecker shows that at the top of the party was responsive to the Soviet-led international apparat, with all its arbitrary twists and turns. Yet simultaneously, at the bottom and in the middle—which is where, after all, most of its members were—it was a progressive reform movement. Moreover, she is careful to distinguish the US Communist Party from the wider communist movement, and in the process she demystifies both the CPUSA and communism, an impressive feat given the pervasive mis- , dis- and noninformation that has prevailed with reference to large-and small-c communism from the earliest days of the cold war to the present.

Schrecker acknowledges that the CP's rigid discipline kept the organization united in the face of repression and of the frequent changes in line, but at the same time she is perceptive and persuasive in her account of the dialectical relationship between the reds and the red hunters—the ways in which party secrecy and other of the CP's most damaging political characteristics were a response to the official and unofficial harassment it often faced.

She shows that during the red scare (*aka* the Palmer raids) of 1918–20—coming after the Espionage Act (1917), which made it illegal to interfere with the draft and led to the imprisonment of thousands of citizens, including Eugene V. Debs; the Sedition Act (1918), which criminalized "disloyal, profane, scurrilous or abusive language"; and the Immigration Act (1918), which codified guilt by association—when the Feds rounded up thousands of foreign-born radicals for deportation, "official repression forced the fledgling party underground."

Although some mainstream reviewers have already taken exception to Schrecker's pluralist view of the party, they can't fault her study, as they did earlier ones of anti-Communism and its victims, for failing to make it sufficiently clear that it was possible to be anti-Communist and anti-McCarthy at the same time. Schrecker understands that social democrats like Irving Howe and cold war liberals like Arthur Schlesinger Jr., the Harvard historian who valorized *The Vital Center* (between the competing totalitarianisms of Communism and Fascism), were fierce critics of Stalinism but had no use for the Wisconsin Senator and his ilk either. She also shows how the anti-Communist formulations crafted by such New York intellectuals "helped to structure the way in which the anti-communist political repression of the McCarthy years functioned."

Consider, for example, Schrecker's fascinating discussion of the *Partisan Review* intellectuals. She treats *Partisan Review*, founded in 1934 as a literary outlet of the New York City branch of the John Reed Club, as emblematic. Its main editors, Philip Rahv and William Phillips, broke with Communism in 1936, then flirted with Trotskyism before becoming cold war liberals in the forties (and I would add, in Phillips's case, neoconservative in the eighties). She shows how throughout its history, the magazine defined its identity in terms of its relationship to Communism.

What is new is her contention that the notion that the CPUSA always did Moscow's bidding arose in part because "on the issue of Trotsky, Stalin demanded and largely received the unquestioning obedience of his American supporters." (In fact, as I indicate below, although many directives and much gold may have flowed from Moscow, any serious understanding of the US party's agenda also requires an analysis from the bottom up.) In a fascinating aside, Schrecker reports that in October 1939 Trotsky accepted an invitation to testify before the House Un-American Activities Committee. He postponed his appearance only because of the State Department's refusal to give him a visa. He was about to give a deposition to a member of the HUAC staff when he was assassinated.

Schrecker does not pretend to provide a comprehensive account of the anti-Communist crusade, claiming that her subject is too large and complex for that. Rather, her method is to give us vivid case studies from those sectors of American society that "took the main hits: organized labor, the civil rights movement, the federal government, and the cultural world." But in the course of her account, the reader gets a panoramic sense of the epidemic. Although there was no single right-wing conspiracy as such, there might as well have been, for the anti-Communist crusade touched all the bases. To emphasize the threat of Communists in government from the Eastern Establishment elite, there was the Alger Hiss case. To show how profound was Communist influence on postwar international economic policy there were the charges against Harry Dexter White, Assistant Treasury Secretary. To dramatize the danger of atomic espionage there was the Rosenberg case (which had the added advantage of speaking to nativist fears of Jewish immigrants). To prove that the CPUSA was dedicated to the overthrow of the government by violence there were the Smith Act cases. To suggest how sabotage would undermine national security in war-time there were the attempts to deport Harry Bridges, the labor leader said to control the West Coast waterfront. To show how the Communists were propagandizing us to death in peacetime there were the HUAC hearings into Communist infiltration of the motion picture industry. To illustrate Moscow's control of the CPUSA there was the demonization and persecution of Gerhart Eisler as "the man who transmitted Stalin's orders to the party faithful." To exploit suspicion of the foreign-born at all levels there were cases like the denaturalization proceedings against CP leader Steve Nelson, his prosecution for contempt of Congress and for sedition against the State of Pennsylvania.

Her point is not that there was no basis in fact for any or all of these. In fact, she picks and chooses among the various charges. On the Rosenbergs she finds that Ethel was a "lever" (to get at Julius) who was guilty only of "standing by her man," and that the prosecution "fixed" the case. On Julius she says that although he was not guilty of stealing the secret of the atom bomb (because there was no secret to steal), the recently released decoded cables from the Soviets to their US spies (the Venona decrypts) "reveal that some of the people recruited by Julius Rosenberg transmitted what the KGB considered to be 'highly valuable' information about radar, jet planes, and other advanced weapons systems."

On Harry Dexter White she says the decrypts are cryptic and that what might have been small talk could have been blown out of proportion by Soviet agents as spy talk. She shows that the government in the Smith Act cases tried to portray the CP as more united, subversive and revolutionary than it was, misrepresenting the classics of Communist literature and imputing positions to the party leadership that it hadn't taken. On the prosecution of Harry Bridges she finds that "security was subsidiary to the [waterfront] program's real objective: destroying the Communist-led . . . unions."

She says the Hiss case "has yet to be resolved" but, oddly, she takes her narrative of the case from Allen Weinstein's *Perjury*, which she identifies as "the most important book on the Hiss case" without letting the reader know that a half-dozen of his key sources (including one who sued and won a settlement and retraction) have disputed the accuracy of his account [see Navasky, "Allen Weinstein's Docudrama," November 3, 1997].

She quotes the Communist lawyer John Abt as providing "further substantiation" of Hiss accuser Whittaker Chambers in the sense that he "admitted that his secret group of federal officials had sometimes sent information to the CP's New York headquarters." Elsewhere Schrecker is careful to make the distinction between "the routine collection of political intelligence," on the one hand, and "the kind of espionage that involved the transmission of sensitive military secrets" on the other, making the point that the former is too often confused with the latter. She even quotes Abt's memoir, in which he says that his group was not an espionage ring but rather that they

> mainly talked about our work in the various agencies where we were employed, what this indicated about the drift and policies of the Roosevelt Administration. If there were developments we thought were particularly interesting, someone would be asked to draft a report to be given to Hal [Ware, the unit's party contact], who presumably passed it on to the national leadership in New York for its consideration in estimating the direction of the New Deal and what might be done to influence it.

Schrecker's bottom line, with which I tend to agree, is that "it is clear that some sort of espionage took place in the 1930s and 1940s" but because the data are incomplete, "it is hard to assess how extensive the spying was."

But if Schrecker is right and the US Communist movement was involved in both espionage and reform, it becomes important to know in what proportions. First, because differences in quantity can make for differences in quality. Such data can also help resolve long-running historical disputes—between the cold war historians and the revisionists, the right and the left, the social historians and the traditionalists—on what it meant to be a Communist in those troubled years. It may also contribute to our political wisdom in dealing with such questions as when, if ever, it is permissible to intrude on bedrock political rights and liberties in the interests of national security.

Here, *Many Are the Crimes* is incomplete. To answer the question of whether the spy rings described by Whittaker Chambers in *Witness* and Elizabeth Bentley in *Out of Bondage* and allegedly confirmed by the Venona decrypts were indeed spy rings or, as John Abt suggests, were primarily progressive caucuses and study groups working for a better world requires scrupulous sifting of the evidence and careful analysis of the new materials made available via Venona and other cold war archives. This Schrecker does not provide. Although she appears to do a good job of parsing the material on Bentley (who fabricated and came up with too much "convenient" information), she seems inexplicably casual in her handling of the matter of Alger Hiss, one of the two great cold war political cases. For example, she says that only one Venona document mentioned Hiss when in fact there there were two (one of them arguably exculpatory); and while she rejects the Chambers narrative as not yet proved, she nevertheless seems to have internalized it. Thus she refers to the entity she has already told us Abt says was not involved in espionage as "the ring of agents . . . led by Victor Perlo." Because so many cold war historians have already rushed to invoke fragmentary new Venona data as "proof" that they were right all along, it is particularly regrettable that Schrecker, who seems fair and sophisticated in her handling of so much of the mountainous materials from the McCarthy era and who herself warns against leaping to premature conclusions based on Venona, does not give us a more systematic analysis of the new evidence.

Historians like Harvey Klehr argue that the newly released Venona materials prove that top party leaders like Earl Browder were on notice as to, and perhaps even complicit in, Communist espionage. For me, the Venona documents come freighted with so many mysteries, surface contradictions and inaccuracies, anonymous footnotes based on questionable assumptions, and the possibility of internal misinformation and inflated claims that serious historians should be wary of drawing factual conclusions from them. Even assuming, for the purposes of argument, that Klehr and Co. are right about what the party's leadership knew, there is no evidence at all that the millions of Americans who passed through the CP were privy to such information or engaged in such activities. To the contrary, books like Michael Denning's *The Cultural Front* would seem to support Schrecker's view that they and the millions of others who operated in its milieu ("fellow travelers," as their critics would have it) were activists publicly involved in the social struggles of their day. That some of them joined because they wanted to put their idealistic commitment in the service of a disciplined international movement centered in Moscow doesn't change that. Indeed, any number of historians have documented that Communism was more complicated than the demonizing stereotypes suggested by the party-as-espionage-front. For example, Mark Naison's illuminating *Communists in Harlem During the Depression* shows how the social and cultural atmosphere of one of the largest black communities in the nation overtook party "theory" in ways the party line could never anticipate, and makes clear that long before the Seventh Comintern Congress in 1935 adopted the Popular Front, the CP in Harlem was working with non-Communists on rent strikes and social issues across the board.

What is missing from Schrecker's book—and, with the exception of Abt's brief reference in his memoir, from domestic cold war literature at large—is a credible counternarrative to the self-contradictory and sensational stories of life in the so-called Communist underground told almost fifty years ago by Whittaker Chambers, Elizabeth Bentley and others Schrecker calls "professional witnesses." This is not Schrecker's fault, because the handful of interested parties who are still very much with us and could put these matters (or nonmatters) in context have declined to tell their tales. As Schrecker reports:

> When I tried to get information from these people, some of them . . . simply refused to talk. Others, like Harry Magdoff, a highly respected Marxist economist named by Elizabeth Bentley, said that they did not want to reopen old wounds.

Victor Perlo, the New Deal economist who went on to write an interesting column for the *People's Weekly World* and a serious book analyzing race and capitalist society, takes the same position.

Given the suffering, hardship and social, political and economic stigma suffered by the victims of McCarthyism, it is difficult for those of us who weren't there to claim that McCarthy's victims have any sort of obligation to put their activities—whatever they were—in context. But unless and until these witnesses to history tell their tale, we may never know what happened. In the absence of such alternatives, all we have is the Chambers narrative, as adumbrated by Bentley; historians like Allen Weinstein, Harvey Klehr and Ron Radosh; former HUAC staffers like Herbert Romerstein; and journalists like Sam Tanenhaus and the late neoconservative Eric Breindel.

Twenty years ago, in *The Great Fear* the British writer David Caute gave us a sector-by-sector rundown of McCarthyism's impact on the lives of its victims. Ellen Schrecker's *Many Are the Crimes* deepens our understanding of the ways in which this particular episode in political hysteria lives on beyond its immediate victims. Among other legacies, it destroyed the left, cut off political and cultural possibilities, robbed left-liberalism of its post-World War II moment of opportunity, ushered in a generation of self-censorship (the anti-Communist ground rules of television were set during those years), purged the State Department of the China hands whose expertise and dissenting cables might have spared us the Vietnam War, decimated the ranks of organized labor, killed national health insurance by branding it "socialized medicine" inconsistent with free enterprise and depoliticized the academy in ways that bureaucratized scholarship and generally diminished the national conversation.

Schrecker's nuanced explication of such matters and her sophisticated rendering of the interaction between anti-Communism and Communism make her book a valuable contribution for anyone who would understand the dynamics of the domestic cold war.

She has provided an alternative, analytic framework that does much to put McCarthyism in America in perspective. But it also poses a challenge: that those previously silent witnesses to history who are able to do so come forth to fill in the missing parts of the picture.

UNCHAINED MELODY

A REVIEW OF THE COMMUNIST MANIFESTO: A MODERN EDITION BY KARL MARX AND FREDERICK ENGELS. WITH AN INTRODUCTION BY ERIC HOBSBAWM

Marshall Berman

•

THE BEST STORY I've ever heard about *The Communist Manifesto* came from Hans Morgenthau, the great theorist of international relations who died in 1980. It was the early seventies at CUNY, and he was reminiscing about his childhood in Bavaria before World War I. Morgenthau's father, a doctor in a working-class neighborhood of Coburg, often took his son along on house calls. Many of his patients were dying of TB; a doctor could do nothing to save their lives, but might help them die with dignity. When his father asked about last requests, many workers said they wanted to have the *Manifesto* buried with them when they died. They implored the doctor to see that the priest didn't sneak in and plant the Bible on them instead.

This spring, the *Manifesto* is 150 years old. In that century and a half, apart from the Bible, it has become the most widely read book in the world. Eric Hobsbawm, in his splendid introduction to the handsome new Verso edition, gives a brief history of the book's reception. It can be summed up fast: Whenever there's trouble, anywhere in the world, the book becomes an item; when things quiet down, the book drops out of sight; when there's trouble again, the people who forgot remember. When fascist-type regimes seize power, it's always on the short list of books to burn. When people dream of resistance—even if they're not Communists, even if they distrust Communists—it provides music for their dreams. Get the beat of the beginning and the end. First line: "A spectre is haunting Europe—the spectre of Communism." Last lines: "The proletarians have nothing to lose but their chains. They have a world to win. WORKING MEN OF ALL COUNTRIES, UNITE!" In Rick's bar in *Casablanca*, you may or may not love France, but when the band breaks into "La Marseillaise," you've got to stand up and sing.

Yet literate people today, even people with left politics, are amazingly ignorant of what's actually in the book. For years, I've asked people what they think it consists of. The most popular answers are that it's (1) a utopian handbook on how to run a society with no money or property, or else (2) a Machiavellian handbook on how to create a Communist state and keep it in power. People who were Communists didn't seem to know the book any better than people who were not. (At first this amazed me; later I saw it was no accident. Classical Communist education was Talmudic, based on a study of commentaries, with an underlying suspicion of sacred primary texts. Among Orthodox Jews, the Bible is a sort of adult movie—a *yeshiva-bucher* is exposed to it only after years of Talmudic training, to insure that he will respond in orthodox ways. Similarly, a trainee at a party school would begin with Stalin, until 1956; then the great indoctrinator Lenin; then, with some hesitation, Engels; Marx came in only at the very end, and then only for those with security clearance.)

Now that security is gone. In just a few years, so many statues and magnifications of Marx have vanished from public squares; so many streets and parks named for him are going under other names today. What does it all mean? For some people, like our Sunday morning princes of the air, the implosion of the U.S.S.R. simply confirmed what they had believed all along, and released them from having to show respect. One of my old bosses at C.C.N.Y. said it concisely: "Nineteen eighty-nine proves that courses in Marxism are obsolete." But there are other ways to read history. What happened to Marx after 1917 was a disaster: A thinker needs beatification like a hole in the head. So we should welcome his descent from the pedestal as a fortunate fall. Maybe we can learn what Marx has to teach if we confront him at ground level, the level on which we ourselves are trying to stand.

So what does he offer? First, startling when you're not prepared for it, praise for capitalism so extravagant, it skirts the edge of awe. Very early in the *Manifesto*, he describes the processes of material construction that it perpetrates, and the emotions that go with them, especially the sense of being caught up in something magical and uncanny:

> The bourgeoisie has created . . . more massive and more colossal productive forces than have all preceding generations together. Subjection of nature's forces to man, machinery, application of chemistry to industry and agriculture, steam navigation, railways . . . clearing of whole continents for cultivation, canalization of rivers, whole populations conjured out of the ground—what earlier century had even a presentiment that such productive powers slumbered in the lap of social labour?

Or a page before, on an innate dynamism that is spiritual as well as material:

> The bourgeoisie cannot exist without constantly revolutionizing the instruments of production, and thereby the relations of production, and with them the whole relations of society. . . . Constant revolutionizing of production, uninterrupted disturbance of all social conditions, everlasting uncertainty and agitation distinguish the bourgeois epoch from all earlier ones. All fixed, fast-frozen relations, with their train of ancient and venerable prejudices and opinions, are swept away, all new-formed ones become antiquated before they can ossify. All that is solid melts into air, all that is holy is profaned, and man is at last compelled to face with sober senses, his real conditions of life, and his relations with his kind.

Part 1, "Bourgeois and Proletarians," contains many passages like these, asserted in major chords with great dramatic flair. Somehow, many readers seem to miss them. But Marx's contemporaries didn't miss them, and some fellow radicals—Proudhon, Bakunin—saw his appreciation of capitalism as a betrayal of its victims. This charge is still heard today, and deserves serious response. Marx hates capitalism, but he also thinks it has brought immense real benefits, spiritual as well as material, and he wants the benefits spread around and enjoyed by everybody rather than monopolized by a small ruling class. This is very different from the totalitarian rage that typifies radicals who want to blow it all away. Sometimes, as with Proudhon, it is just modern times they hate; they dream of a golden-age peasant village where everyone was happily in his place (or in her place behind him). For other radicals, from the author of the Book of Revelation to the Unabomber, it goes over the edge into something like rage against reality, against human life itself. Apocalyptic rage offers immediate, sensational cheap thrills. Marx's perspective is far more complex and nuanced, and hard to sustain if you're not grown up.

Marx is not the first communist to admire capitalism for its creativity; that attitude can be found in some of the great utopian socialists of the generation before him, like Saint-Simon and Robert Owen. But Marx is the first to invent a prose style that can bring that perilous creativity to life. His style in the *Manifesto* is a kind of Expressionist lyricism. Every paragraph breaks over us like a wave that leaves us shaking from the impact and wet with thought. This prose evokes breathless momentum, plunging ahead without guides or maps, breaking all boundaries, precarious piling and layering of things, ideas and experiences. Catalogues play a large role in Marx's style—as they do for his contemporaries Dickens and Whitman—but part of the *Manifesto*'s enchantment comes from our feeling that the lists are never exhausted, the catalogue is open to the present and the future, we are invited to pile on things, ideas and experiences of our own, to pile ourselves on if we can. But the items in the pile often seem to clash, and it sounds like the whole vast aggregation could crash. From paragraph to paragraph, Marx makes readers feel that we are riding the fastest and grandest nineteenth-century train through the roughest and most perilous nineteenth-century terrain, and through we have splendid light, we are pressing ahead where there is no track.

One feature of modern capitalism that Marx most admires is its global horizon and its cosmopolitan texture. Many people today talk about the global economy as if it had only recently come into being. The *Manifesto* should help us see the extent to which it had been there all along:

> The need of a constantly expanding market chases the bourgeoisie over the whole surface of the globe. It must nestle everywhere, settle everywhere, establish connections everywhere.
>
> The bourgeoisie has through its exploitation of the world market given a cosmopolitan character to production and consumption in every country. All old-established national industries have been destroyed or are being daily destroyed. They are dislodged by new industries, whose introduction becomes a life and death question for all civilized nations, by industries that no longer process indigenous raw material, but raw material drawn from remotest zones; industries whose products are consumed, not only at home, but in every quarter of the globe . . .
>
> The cheap prices of its commodities are heavy artillery with which [the bourgeoisie] batters down all Chinese walls, with which it forces the

barbarians' intensely obstinate hatred of foreigners to capitulate. It compels all nations, on pain of extinction, to adopt the bourgeois mode of production; it compels them to introduce what is called civilization into their midst, i.e. to become bourgeois themselves. In one word, it creates a world after its own image.

This global spread offers a spectacular display of history's ironies. These bourgeois are banal in their ambitions, yet their unremitting quest for profit forces on them the same insatiable drive-structure and infinite horizon as that of any of the great Romantic heroes—as Don Giovanni, as Childe Harold, as Goethe's Faust. They may think of only one thing, but their narrow focus leads to the broadest integrations; their shallow outlook wreaks the most profound transformations; their peaceful economic activity devastates every human society like a bomb, from the most primitive tribes to the mighty U.S.S.R. Marx was appalled at the human costs of capitalist development, but he always believed that the world horizon it created was a great achievement on which socialism must build. Remember, the grand appeal to Unite with which the *Manifesto* ends is addressed to "WORKING MEN OF ALL COUNTRIES."

A crucial global drama was the unfolding of the first-ever world culture. Marx, writing when mass media were just developing, called it "world literature." I think it is legitimate at the end of this century to update the idea into "world culture." The *Manifesto* shows how this culture will evolve spontaneously from the world market:

> In place of the old wants, satisfied by the production of the country, we find new wants, requiring for their satisfaction products of distant lands and climes. In place of the old local and national seclusion and self-sufficiency, we have intercourse in every direction, universal interdependence of nations. And as in material, so also in intellectual [or spiritual—*geistige* can be translated either way] production. The intellectual [spiritual] creations of individual nations become common property . . . and from the numerous national and local literatures, there arises a world literature.

This vision of world culture brings together several complex ideas. First, the expansion of human needs: the increasingly cosmopolitan world market at once shapes and expands everybody's desires. Marx doesn't elaborate on this in detail; but he wants us to imagine what it might mean in food, clothes, religion, music, love and in our most intimate fantasies as well as our public presentations. Next, the idea of culture as "common property" in the world market: Anything created by anyone anywhere is open and available to everyone everywhere. Entrepreneurs publish books, produce plays and concerts, display visual art and, in our century, create hardware and software for movies, radio, TV and computers in order to make money. Nevertheless, in this as in other ways, history slips through the owners' fingers, so that poor people get to possess culture—an idea, a poetic image, a musical sound, Plato, Shakespeare, a Negro spiritual (Marx loved them)—even if they can't own it. Culture stuffs people's heads full of ideas. As a form of "common property," modern culture helps us to imagine how people all around the world could share all the world's resources someday.

It's a vision of culture rarely discussed, but it is one of the most expansive and hopeful things Marx ever wrote. In our century, the development of movies, television and video and computers has created a global visual language that brings the idea of world culture closer to home than ever, and the world beat comes through in the best of our music and books. That's the good news. The bad news is how sour and bitter most left writing on culture has become. Sometimes it sounds as if culture were just one more Department of Exploitation and Oppression, containing nothing luminous or valuable in itself. At other times, it sounds as if people's minds were empty vessels with nothing inside except what Capital put there. Read, or try to read, a few articles on "hegemonic/counterhegemonic discourse." The way these guys write, it's as if the world has passed them by.

But if capitalism is a triumph in so many ways, exactly what's wrong with it? What's worth spending your life in opposition? In the twentieth century, Marxist movements around the world have concentrated on the argument, made most elaborately in *Capital*, that workers in bourgeois society had been or were being pauperized. Now, there were times and places where it was absurd to deny that claim; in other times and places (like the United States and Western Europe in the fifties and sixties, when I was young), it was pretty tenuous, and Marxist economists went through strange dialectical twists to make the numbers come out. But the problem with that discussion was that it converted questions of human experience into questions of numbers: It led Marxism to think and talk exactly like capitalism! The *Manifesto* occasionally makes some version of this claim. But it offers what strikes me as a much more trenchant indictment, one that holds up even at the top of the business cycle, when the bourgeoisie and its apologists are drowning in complacency.

That indictment is Marx's vision of what modern bourgeois society forces people to be: They have to freeze their feelings for each other to adapt to a coldblooded world. In the course of "pitilessly tear[ing] asunder the motley feudal ties," bourgeois society "has left remaining no other nexus between man and man than naked self-interest, than callous 'cash payment.' " It has "drowned" every form of sentimental value "in the icy water of egotistical calculation." It has "resolved personal worth into exchange-value." It has collapsed every historical tradition and norm of freedom "into that single, unconscionable freedom—free trade." The worst thing about capitalism is that it forces people to become brutal in order to survive.

For 150 years, we have seen a huge literature that dramatizes the brutalization of the bourgeoisie, a class in which those who are most comfortable with brutality are most likely to succeed. But the same social forces are pressing on the members of that immense group that Marx calls "the modern working class." This class has been afflicted with a case of mistaken identity. Many readers have always thought that "working class" meant only factory workers, or industrial workers, or manual workers, or blue-collar workers, or impoverished workers. These readers then note the changing nature of the work force over the past half-century or so—increasingly white collar, educated, working in human services, in or near the middle class—and they infer the Death of the Subject, and conclude that all hopes for the working class are doomed. Marx did not think the working class was shrinking: In all industrial countries it already was, or was in the process of becoming, "the immense majority"; its swelling numbers would enable it to "win the battle of democracy." The basis for his political arithmetic was a concept that was both simple and highly inclusive:

> The modern working class, developed . . . a class of labourers, who live only so long as they find work, and who find work only so long as their labour increases capital. These labourers, who must sell themselves piecemeal, are a commodity, like every other article of commerce, and are consequently exposed to all the vicissitudes of competition, to all the fluctuations of the market.

The crucial factor is not working in a factory, or working with your hands, or being poor. All these things can change with fluctuating supply and demand and technology and politics. The crucial reality is the need to sell your labor to capital in order to live, the need to carve up your personality for sale—to look at yourself in the mirror and think, "What have I got that I can sell?"—and an unending dread and anxiety that even if you're O.K. today, you won't find anyone who wants to buy what you have or what you are tomorrow, that the changing market will declare you (as it has already declared so many) worthless, that you will find yourself physically as well as metaphysically homeless and out in the cold. Arthur Miller's *Death of a Salesman*, a twentieth-century masterpiece, brings to life the consuming dread that may be the condition of most members of the working class in modern times. The whole existentialist tradition dramatizes this situation with great depth and beauty, yet its visions tend to be weirdly unembodied. Its visionaries could learn from the *Manifesto*, which gives modern anguish an address.

A great many people are in the working class but don't know it. Many are the people who fill up the huge office buildings that choke all our downtowns. They wear elegant suits and return to nice houses, because there is a great demand for their labor right now, and they are doing well. They may identify happily with the owners, and have no idea how contingent and fleeting their benefits are. They may not discover who they really are, and where they belong, until they are laid off or fired—or deskilled, outsourced, downsized. (It is fascinating how many of these crushing words are quite new.) And other workers, lacking diplomas, not dressed so nicely, working in cubicles, not offices, may not get the fact that many of the people who boss them around are really in their class. But this is what organizing and organizers are for.

One group whose working-class identity was crucial for Marx was the group to which he himself belonged: intellectuals.

> The bourgeoisie has stripped of its halo every occupation hitherto honoured and looked up to in reverent awe. It has transconverted the physician, the lawyer, the priest, the poet, the man of science, into its paid wage labourers.

Marx is not saying that in bourgeois society these activities lose their human meaning or value. If anything, they are more meaningful and valuable than ever before. But the only way people can get the freedom to make discoveries, or save lives, or poetically light up the world, is by working for capital—for drug companies, movie studios, boards of education, politicians, H.M.O.s, etc., etc.—and using their creative skills to help capital accumulate more capital. This means that intellectuals are subject not only to the stresses that afflict all modern workers but to a dread zone all their own. The more they care about their work and want it to mean something, the more they will find themselves in conflict with the keepers of the spreadsheets; the more they walk the line, the more they are likely to fall. This chronic pressure may give them a special insight into the need for workers to unite. But will united workers treat intellectual and artistic freedom with any more respect than capital treats it? It's an open question; sometime in the twenty-first century the workers will get power somewhere, and then we'll start to see.

Marx sees the modern working class as an immense worldwide community waiting to happen. Such large possibilities give the story of organizing a permanent gravity and grandeur. The process of creating unions is not just an item in interest-group politics but a vital part of what Lessing called "the education of the human race." And it is not just educational but existential: the process of people individually and collectively discovering who they are. As they learn who they are, they will come to see that they need one another in order to be themselves. They will see, because workers are smart: Bourgeois society has forced them to be, in order to survive its constant upheavals. Marx knows they will get it by and by. (Alongside his fury as an agitator, the *Manifesto*'s author also projects a brooding, reflective, long patience.) Solidarity is not sacrifice of yourself but the self's fulfillment. Learning to give yourself to other workers, who may look and sound very different from you but are like you in depth, gives a man or woman a place in the world and delivers the self from dread.

This is a vital part of the moral vision that underlies the *Manifesto*. But there is another moral dimension, asserted in a different key but humanly just as urgent. At one of the book's many climatic moments, Marx says that the Revolution will end classes and class struggles, and this will make it possible to enjoy "an association, in which the free development of each is the condition for the free development of all." Here Marx imagines communism as a way to make people happy. The first aspect of this happiness is "development"—that is, an experience that doesn't simply repeat itself but that goes through some sort of change and growth. This model of happiness is modern, and informed by the incessantly developing bourgeois economy. But bourgeois society, although it enables people to develop, forces them to develop in accord with market demands: What can sell gets developed; what can't sell gets repressed, or never comes to life at all. Against the market model of forced and twisted development, Marx fights for "*free* development," development that the self can control.

In a time when crass cruelty calls itself liberalism (we're kicking you and your kids off welfare for your own good), it is important to see how much ground Marx shares with the best liberal of all, his contemporary John Stuart Mill. Like Marx, Mill came to see the self's "free development" as a fundamental human value; like Marx, he believed that modernization made it possible for everybody. But as he grew older, he became convinced that the capitalist form of modernization—featuring cutthroat competition, class domination, social conformity and cruelty—blocked its best potentialities. He proclaimed himself a socialist in his old age.

Ironically, the ground that socialism and liberalism share might be a big problem for both of them. What if Mister Kurtz isn't dead after all? In other words, what if authentically "free development" brings out horrific depths in human nature? Dostroyevsky, Nietzsche and Freud all forced us to face the horrors, and warned us of their permanence. In response, both Marx and Mill might say that until we have overcome social domination and degradation, there is simply no way to tell whether the horrors are inherent in human nature or whether we could create benign conditions under which they would wither away. The process of getting to that point—a point where Raskolnikovs won't rot on Avenue D, and where Svidrigailovs won't possess thousands of bodies and souls—should be enough to give us all steady work.

The nineties began with the mass destruction of Marx effigies. It was the "postmodern" age: We weren't supposed to need big ideas. As the nineties end, we find ourselves in a dynamic global society ever more unified by downsizing, de-skilling and dread—just like the old man said. All of a sudden, the iconic looks more convincing than the ironic; that classic bearded presence, the atheist as biblical prophet, is back just in time for the millennium. At the dawn of the twentieth century, there were workers who were ready to die with the *Communist Manifesto*. At the dawn of the twenty-first, there may be even more who are ready to live with it.

PERFORMANCE AND REALITY: RACE, SPORTS AND THE MODERN WORLD

Gerald Early

•

LAST YEAR'S CELEBRATION of the fiftieth anniversary of Jackie Robinson's breaking the color line in major league baseball was one of the most pronounced and prolonged ever held in the history of our Republic in memory of a black man or of an athlete. It seems nearly obvious that, on one level, our preoccupation was not so much with Robinson himself—previous milestone anniversaries of his starting at first base for the Brooklyn Dodgers in April 1947 produced little fanfare—as it was with ourselves and our own dilemma about race, a problem that strikes us simultaneously as being intractable and "progressing" toward resolution; as a chronic, inevitably fatal disease and as a test of national character that we will, finally, pass.

Robinson was the man white society could not defeat in the short term, though his untimely death at age 53 convinced many that the stress of the battle defeated him in the long run. In this respect, Robinson did become something of an uneasy elegiac symbol of race relations, satisfying everyone's psychic needs: blacks, with a redemptive black hero who did not sell out and in whose personal tragedy was a corporate triumph over racism; whites, with a black hero who showed assimilation to be a triumphant act. For each group, it was important that he was a hero for the other. All this was easier to accomplish because Robinson played baseball, a "pastoral" sport of innocence and triumphalism in the American mind, a sport of epic romanticism, a sport whose golden age is always associated with childhood. In the end, Robinson as tragic hero represented, paradoxically, depending on the faction, how far we have come and how much more needs to be done.

As a nation, I think we needed the evocation of Jackie Robinson to save us from the nihilistic fires of race: from the trials of O. J. Simpson (the failed black athletic hero who seems nothing more than a symbol of self-centered consumption), from the Rodney King trial and subsequent riot in Los Angeles and, most significant, from the turmoil over affirmative action, an issue not only about *how* blacks are to achieve a place in American society but about the perennial existential question: *Can* black people have a rightful place of dignity in our realm, or is the stigma of race to taint everything they do and desire? We know that some of the most admired celebrities in the United States today—in many instances, excessively so by some whites—are black athletes. Michael Jordan, the most admired athlete in modern history, is a $10 billion industry, we are told, beloved all over the world. But what does Michael Jordan want except what most insecure, upwardly bound Americans want? More of what he already has to assure himself that he does, indeed, have what he wants. Michael Jordan is not simply a brilliant athlete, the personification of an unstoppable will, but, like all figures in popular culture, a complex, charismatic representation of desire, his own and ours.

Perhaps we reached back for Jackie Robinson last year (just as we reached back for an ailing Muhammad Ali, the boastful athlete as expiatory dissident, the year before at the Olympics) because of our need for an athlete who transcends his self-absorbed prowess and quest for championships, or whose self-absorption and quest for titles meant something deeper politically and socially, told us something a bit more important about ourselves as a racially divided, racially stricken nation. A baseball strike in 1994–95 that canceled the World Series, gambling scandals in college basketball, ceaseless recruiting violations with student athletes, rape and drug cases involving athletes, the increasing commercialization of sports resulting in more tax concessions to team owners and ever-more-expensive stadiums, the wild inflation of salaries, prize money and endorsement fees for the most elite athletes—all this has led to a general dissatisfaction with sports or at least to some legitimate uneasiness about them, as many people see sports, amateur and professional, more and more as a depraved enterprise, as a Babylon of greed, dishonesty and hypocrisy, or as an industry out to rob the public blind. At what better moment to resurrect Jackie Robin-

son, a man who played for the competition and the glory, for the love of
the game and the honor of his profession, and as a tribute to the dignity and pride of his race in what many of us perceive, wrongly, to have
been a simpler, less commercial time?

What, indeed, is the place of black people in our realm? Perhaps, at
this point in history, we are all, black and white, as mystified by that
question as we were at the end of the Civil War when faced with the
prospect that slave and free must live together as equal citizens, or must
try to. For the question has always signified that affirmative action—a
public policy for the unconditional inclusion of the African-American
that has existed, with all its good and failed intentions, in the air of
American racial reform since black people were officially freed, even,
indeed, in the age of abolition with voices such as Lydia Maria Child
and Frederick Douglass—is about the making of an African into an
American and the meaning of that act for our democracy's ability to
absorb all. We were struck by Jackie Robinson's story last year because
it was as profound, as mythic, as any European immigrant's story about
how Americans are made. We Americans seem to have blundered about
in our history with two clumsy contrivances strapped to our backs,
unreconciled and weighty: our democratic traditions and race. What
makes Robinson so significant is that he seemed to have found a way to
balance this baggage in the place that is so much the stuff of our
dreams: the level playing field of top-flight competitive athletics. "Athletics," stated Robinson in his first autobiography, *Jackie Robinson:
My Own Story* (ghostwritten by black sportswriter Wendell Smith),
"both school and professional, come nearer to offering an American
Negro equality of opportunity than does any other field of social and
economic activity." It is not so much that this is true as that Robinson
believed it, and that most Americans today, black and white, still do or
still want to. This is one of the important aspects of modern sports in
a democratic society that saves us from being totally cynical about
them. Sports are the ultimate meritocracy. Might it be said that sports
are what all other professional activities and business endeavors, all
leisure pursuits and hobbies in our society aspire to be?

If nothing else, Robinson, an unambiguous athletic hero for both
races and symbol of sacrifice on the altar of racism, is our most magnificent case of affirmative action. He entered a lily-white industry
amid cries that he was unqualified (not entirely unjustified, as Robinson had had only one year of professional experience in the Negro
Leagues, although, on the other hand, he was one of the most gifted
athletes of his generation), and he succeeded, *on merit*, beyond any-

one's wildest hope. And here the sports metaphor is a perfectly literal expression of the traditional democratic belief of that day: If given the chance, anyone can make it on his ability, with no remedial aid or special compensation, on a level playing field. Here was the fulfillment of our American Creed, to use Gunnar Myrdal's term (*An American Dilemma* had appeared only a year before Robinson was signed by the Dodgers), of fair play and equal opportunity. Here was our democratic orthodoxy of color-blind competition realized. Here was an instance where neither the principle nor its application could be impugned. Robinson was proof, just as heavyweight champion Joe Louis and Olympic track star Jesse Owens had been during the Depression, that sports helped vanquish the stigma of race.

In this instance, sports are extraordinarily useful because their values can endorse any political ideology. It must be remembered that the British had used sports—and modern sports are virtually their invention—as a colonial and missionary tool, not always with evil intentions but almost always with hegemonic ones. Sports had also been used by their subjects as a tool of liberation, as anti-hegemonic, as they learned to beat the British at their own games. "To win was to be human," said African scholar Manthia Diawara recently, and for the colonized and the oppressed, sports meant just that, in the same way as for the British, to win was to be British. Sports were meant to preserve and symbolize the hegemony of the colonizer even as they inspired the revolutionary spirit of the oppressed. Sports have been revered by fascists and communists, by free-marketers and filibusters. They have also been, paradoxically, reviled by all those political factions. Sports may be among the most powerful human expressions in all history. So why could sports not serve the United States ideologically in whatever way people decided to define democratic values during this, the American Century, when we became the most powerful purveyors of sports in all history?

Both the left and the right have used Jackie Robinson for their own ends. The left, suspicious of popular culture as a set of cheap commercial distractions constructed by the ruling class of post-industrial society to delude the masses, sees Robinson as a racial martyr, a working-class member of an oppressed minority who challenged the white hegemony as symbolized by sports as a political reification of superior, privileged expertise; the right, suspicious of popular culture as an expression of the rule of the infantile taste of the masses, sees him as a challenge to the idea of restricting talent pools and restricting markets to serve a dubious privilege. For the conservative today, Robinson is the *classic, fixed* example of affirmative action properly applied

as the extension of opportunity to all, regardless of race, class, gender
or outcome. For the liberal, Robinson is an example of the *process* of
affirmative action as the erosion of white male hegemony, where outcome is the very point of the exercise. For the liberal, affirmative action
is about the redistribution of power. For the conservative, it is about
releasing deserving talent. This seems little more than the standard difference in views between the conservative and the liberal about the
meaning of democratic values and social reform. For the conservative,
the story of Robinson and affirmative action is about conformity:
Robinson, as symbolic Negro, *joined* the mainstream. For the liberal,
the story of Robinson and affirmative action is about resistance:
Robinson, as symbolic Negro, *changed* the mainstream. The conservative does not want affirmative action to disturb what Lothrop Stoddard
called "the iron law of inequality." The liberal wants affirmative action
to create complete equality, as all inequality is structural and environmental. (Proof of how much Robinson figured in the affirmative action
debate can be found in Steve Sailer's "How Jackie Robinson Desegre-
gated America," a cover story in the April 8, 1996, *National Review*,
and in Anthony Pratkanis and Marlene Turner's liberal article, "Nine
Principles of Successful Affirmative Action: Mr. Branch Rickey, Mr.
Jackie Robinson, and the Integration of Baseball," in the Fall 1994
issue of *Nine: A Journal of Baseball History and Social Policy Perspectives*.) Whoever may be right in this regard, it can be said that inasmuch as either side endorsed the idea, both were wrong about sports
eliminating the stigma of race. Over the years since Robinson's arrival,
sports have, in many respects, intensified race and racialist thinking or,
more precisely, anxiety about race and racialist thinking.

Race is not merely a system of categorizations of privileged or discredited abilities but rather a system of conflicting abstractions about
what it means to be human. Sports are not a material realization of the
ideal that those who succeed deserve to succeed; they are a paradox of
play as work, or highly competitive, highly pressurized work as a form
of romanticized play, a system of rules and regulations that govern
both a real and a symbolic activity that suggests, in the stunning complexity of its performance, both conformity and revolt. Our mistake
about race is assuming that it is largely an expression of irrationality
when it is, in fact, to borrow G. K. Chesterton's phrase, "nearly reasonable, but not quite." Our mistake about sports is assuming that they are
largely minor consequences of our two great American gifts: marketing and technology. Their pervasiveness and their image, their evocation of desire and transcendence, are the result of marketing. Their

elaborate modalities of engineering—from the conditioning of the athletes to the construction of the arenas to the fabrication of the tools and machines athletes use and the apparel they wear—are the result of our technology. But modern sports, although extraordinary expressions of marketing and technology, are far deeper, far more atavistic, than either. Perhaps sports, in some ways, are as atavistic as race.

THE WHITENESS OF THE WHITE ATHLETE

In a December 8, 1997, *Sports Illustrated* article, "Whatever Happened to the White Athlete?" S. L. Price writes about the dominant presence of black athletes in professional basketball (80 percent black), professional football (67 percent black) and track and field (93 percent of gold medalists are black). He also argues that while African-Americans make up only 17 percent of major league baseball players, "[during] the past 25 years, blacks have been a disproportionate offensive force, winning 41 percent of the Most Valuable Player awards." (And the number of blacks in baseball does not include the black Latinos, for whom baseball is more popular than it is with American blacks.) Blacks also dominate boxing, a sport not dealt with in the article. "Whites have in some respects become sports' second-class citizens," writes Price. "In a surreal inversion of Robinson's era, white athletes are frequently the ones now tagged by the stereotypes of skin color." He concludes by suggesting that white sprinter Kevin Little, in competition, can feel "the slightest hint—and it is not more than a hint—of what Jackie Robinson felt 50 years ago." It is more than a little ludicrous to suggest that white athletes today even remotely, even as a hint, are experiencing something like what Robinson experienced. White athletes, even when they play sports dominated by blacks, are still entering an industry not only controlled by whites in every phase of authority and operation but also largely sustained by white audiences. When Jackie Robinson departed the Negro Leagues at the end of 1945, he left a sports structure that was largely regulated, managed and patronized by blacks, inasmuch as blacks could ever, with the resources available to them in the 1920s, '30s and '40s, profitably and proficiently run a sports league. Robinson's complaints about the Negro Leagues— the incessant barnstorming, the bad accommodations, the poor umpiring, the inadequate spring training—were not only similar to white criticism of the Negro Leagues but they mirrored the criticism that blacks tended to levy against their own organizations and organizational skills. As Sol White makes clear in his seminal 1907 *History of Colored Base Ball*, black people continued to play baseball after they were banned by white professional leagues to show to themselves and to the world that they were capable of *organizing* themselves into teams and leagues. When Robinson left the Kansas City Monarchs, he entered a completely white world, much akin to the world he operated in as a star athlete at UCLA. It was, in part, because Robinson was used to the white world of sports from his college days that Branch Rickey selected him to become the first black man to play major league baseball. Today, when white athletes enter sports dominated by blacks, they do not enter a black *organization* but something akin to a mink-lined black ghetto. (My use of the word "ghetto" here is not meant to suggest anything about oppression, political or otherwise.) Although blacks dominate the most popular team sports, they still make up only 9 percent of all people in the United States who make a living or try to make a living as athletes, less than their percentage in the general population.

What I find most curious about Price's article is that he gives no plausible reason for why blacks dominate these particular sports. He quotes various informants to the effect that blacks must work harder than whites at sports. "Inner-city kids," William Ellerbee, basketball coach at Simon Gratz High in Philadelphia, says, "look at basketball as a matter of life or death." In a similar article on the black makeup of the NBA in the *Washington Post* last year, Jon Barry, a white player for the Atlanta Hawks, offers: "Maybe the suburban types or the white people have more things to do." Much of this is doubtless true. Traditionally, from the early days of professional baseball in the mid-nineteenth century and of professional boxing in Regency England, sports were seen by the men and boys of the poor and working classes as a way out of poverty or at least out of the normally backbreaking, low-paying work the poor male was offered. And certainly (though some black intellectuals may argue the point, feeling it suggests that black cultural life is impoverished) there probably is more to do or more available to amuse and enlighten in a middle-class suburb than in an inner-city neighborhood, even if it is also true that many whites who live in the suburbs are insufferably provincial and philistine.

Nonetheless, these explanations do not quite satisfy. Ultimately, the discussion in both articles comes down to genetics. There is nothing wrong with thinking about genetic variations. After all, what does the difference in human beings mean and what is its source? Still, if, for instance, Jews dominated football and basketball (as they once did boxing), would there be such a fixation to explain it genetically? The fact of the matter is that, historically, blacks have been a genetic wonder, monstrosity or aberration to whites, and they are still burdened by this implicit sense that they are not quite "normal." From the mid-nine-teenth century—with its racist intellectuals like Samuel Cartwright (a Southern medical doctor whose use of minstrel-style jargon, "Dyses-thaesia Ethiopica," to describe black people as having thick minds and insensitive bodies is similar to the talk of today's racist geneticists about "fast-twitch" muscles) and Samuel Morton (whose *Crania Amer-icana* tried to classify races by skull size), Louis Agassiz, Arthur de Gobineau and Josiah Nott (who with George Gliddon produced the extremely popular *Types of Mankind* in 1854, which argued that races had been created as separate species)—to Charles Murray and Richard Hernstein's most recent defense of intelligence quotients to explain economic and status differences among racial and ethnic groups in *The Bell Curve*, blacks have been subjected to a great deal of scientific or so-called scientific scrutiny, much of it misguided if not outright mali-cious, and all of it to justify the political and economic hegemony of whites. For instance, Lothrop Stoddard, in *The Revolt Against Civi-lization* (1922), a book nearly identical in some of its themes and polemics to *The Bell Curve*, creates a being called the Under-Man, a barbarian unfit for civilization. (Perhaps this is why some black intel-lectuals loathe the term "underclass.") "The rarity of mental as com-pared with physical superiority in the human species is seen on every hand," Stoddard writes. "Existing savage and barbaric races of a demonstrably low average level of intelligence, like the negroes [sic], are physically vigorous, in fact, possess an animal vitality apparently greater than that of the intellectually higher races." There is no escap-ing the doctrine that for blacks to be physically superior biologically, they must be inferior intellectually and, thus, inferior as a group, Under-People.

But even if it were true that blacks were athletically superior to whites, why then would they not dominate all sports instead of just a handful? There might be a more plainly structural explanation for black dominance in certain sports. This is not to say that genes may have nothing to do with it but only to say that, at this point, genetic arguments have been far from persuasive and, in their implications, more than a little pernicious.

It is easy enough to explain black dominance in boxing. It is the Western sport that has the longest history of black participation, so there is tradition. Moreover, it is a sport that has always attracted poor and marginalized men. Black men have persistently made up a dispro-portionate share of the poor and the marginalized. Finally, instruction is within easy reach; most boxing gyms are located in poor neighborhoods, where a premium is placed on being able to fight well. Male fighting is a useful skill in a cruel, frontierlike world that values physical toughness, where insult is not casually tolerated and honor is a highly sensitive point.

Black dominance in football and basketball is not simply related to getting out of the ghetto through hard work or to lack of other amusements but to the institution most readily available to blacks in the inner city that enables them to use athletics to get out. Ironically, that institution is the same one that fails more often than it should in fitting them for other professions: namely, school. As William Washington, the father of a black tennis family, perceptively pointed out in an article last year in the *New York Times* discussing the rise of tennis star Venus Williams: "Tennis, unlike baseball, basketball or football, is not a team sport. It is a family sport. Your immediate family is your primary supporting cast, not your teammates or the players in the locker room . . . The experiences [of alienation and racism] start soon after you realize that if you play this game, you must leave your neighborhood and join the country club bunch. You don't belong to that group, and they let you know it in a variety of ways, so you go in, compete and leave."

In short, because their families generally lack the resources and connections, indeed, because, as scholars such as V. P. Franklin have pointed out, black families cannot provide their members the cultural capital that white and Asian families can, blacks are at a disadvantage to compete in sports where school is not crucial in providing instruction and serving as an organizational setting for competition. When it comes to football and basketball, however, where school is essential to have a career, not only are these sports played at even the poorest black high schools, they are also the dominant college sports. If baseball were a more dominant college sport and if there were no minor leagues where a player had to toil for several years before, maybe, getting a crack at the major leagues, then I think baseball would attract more young black men. Because baseball, historically, was not a game that was invented by a school or became deeply associated with schools or education, blacks could learn it, during the days when they were banned from competition with white professionals, only by forming their own leagues. Sports, whatever one might think of their worth as activities, are extremely important in understanding black people's relationship to secular institutions and secular, non-protest organizing: the school, both black and white; the independent, nonprofessional or semiprofessional league; and the barnstorming, independent team, set up by both whites and blacks.

Given that blacks are overrepresented in the most popular sports and that young black men are more likely than young white men to consider athletics as a career, there has been much commentary about whether sports are bad for blacks. The March 24, 1997, issue of *U.S. News & World Report* ran a cover story titled "Are Pro Sports Bad for Black Youth?" In February of that year Germanic languages scholar John Hoberman published *Darwin's Athletes: How Sport Has Damaged Black America and Preserved the Myth of Race*, to much bitter controversy. *The Journal of African American Men*, a new academic journal, not only published a special double issue on black men and sports (fall 1996/Winter 1997) but featured an article in its Winter 1995/96 number titled "The Black Student Athlete. The Colonized Black Body," by Billy Hawkins. While there are great distinctions to be made among these works, there is an argument about sports as damaging for blacks that can be abstracted that tends either toward a radical left position on sports or, in Hawkins's case, toward a militant cultural nationalism with Marxist implications.

First, Hoberman and Hawkins make the analogy that sports are a form of slavery or blatant political and economic oppression. Superficially, this argument is made by discussing the rhetoric of team sports (a player is the "property" of his team, or, in boxing, of his manager; he can be traded or "sold" to another team). Since most relationships in popular culture industries are described in this way—Hollywood studios have "properties," have sold and swapped actors, especially in the old days of studio ascendancy, and the like—usually what critics who make this point are aiming at is a thorough denunciation of popular culture as a form of "exploitation" and "degradation." The leftist critic condemns sports as a fraudulent expression of the heroic and the skilled in capitalist culture. The cultural nationalist critic condemns sports as an explicit expression of the grasping greed of white capitalist culture to subjugate people as raw resources.

On a more sophisticated level, the slavery analogy is used to describe sports structurally: the way audiences are lured to sports as a false spectacle, and the way players are controlled mentally and physically by white male authority, their lack of access to the free-market worth of their labor. (This latter point is made particularly about college players, since the breaking of the reserve clause in baseball, not by court decision but by union action, has so radically changed the status and so wildly inflated the salaries of many professional team players, regardless of sport.) Probably the most influential commentator to make this analogy of sport to slavery was Harry Edwards in his 1969 book, *The Revolt of the Black Athlete*. Richard Lapchick in his 1984 book, *Broken Promises: Racism in American Sports*, extends Edwards's premises. Edwards is the only black writer on sports that Hoberman admires. And Edwards is also cited by Hawkins. How convincing any of this is has much to do with how willing one is to be convinced, as is the case with many highly polemical arguments. For instance, to take up Hawkins's piece, are black athletes more colonized, more exploited as laborers at the university than, say, graduate students and adjunct faculty, who teach the bulk of the lower-level courses at a fraction of the pay and benefits of the full-time faculty? Are black athletes at white colleges more exploited than black students generally at white schools? If the major evidence that black athletes are exploited by white schools is the high number who fail to graduate, why, for those who adopt Hawkins's ideological position, are black students who generally suffer high attrition rates at such schools not considered equally as exploited?

What is striking is the one analogy between slavery and team sports that is consistently overlooked. Professional sports teams operate as a cartel—a group of independent entrepreneurs who come together to control an industry without giving up their independence as competitive entities. So does the NCAA, which controls college sports; and so did the Southern planters who ran the Confederacy. They controlled the agricultural industry of the South as well as both free and slave labor. The cartelization of American team sports, which so closely resembles the cartelization of the antebellum Southern planters (the behavior of both is remarkably similar), is the strongest argument to make about slavery and sports or about sports and colonization. This is what is most unnerving about American team sports as an industry, and how the power of that industry, combined with the media, threatens the very democratic values that sports supposedly endorse.

The other aspects of the sports-damage-black-America argument, principally made by Hoberman, are the blacks are more likely to be seen as merely "physical," and thus inferior, beings; that society's promotion of black sports figures comes at the expense of promoting any other type of noteworthy black person; that black overinvestment in sports is both the cause and result of black anti-intellectualism, itself the result of virulent white racism, meant to confine blacks to certain occupations. Implicit in Hoberman's work is his hatred of the fetishization of athletic achievement, the rigid rationalization of sports as a theory and practice. He also hates the suppression of the political nature of the athlete, and hates, too, both the apolitical nature of sports, mystified as transcendent legend and supported by the simplistic language of sportswriters and sports-apologist intellectuals, and the political exploitation of sports by ideologues and the powerful. As a critical theorist, Hoberman was never interested in proving this with thorough empiricism, and, as a result, was attacked in a devastatingly effective manner by black scholars, who blew away a good number of his assertions with an unrelenting empiricism. But he has got into deep trouble with black intellectuals, in the end, not for these assertions or for the mere lack of good empiricism. Hoberman, rather, has been passionately condemned for suggesting that blacks have a "sports fixation" that is tantamount to a pathology, a word that rightly distresses African-Americans, reminiscent as it is of the arrogance of white social scientists past and present who describe blacks as some misbegotten perversion of a white middle-class norm.

There is, however, one point to be made in Hoberman's defense. Since he clearly believes high-level sports to be a debased, largely unhealthy enterprise and believes that the white majority suffers a sports obsession, he would naturally think that blacks, as a relatively powerless minority and as the principal minority connected to sports, would be especially damaged by it. The black intellectual who most influenced Hoberman was Ralph Ellison; and, as Darryl Scott pointed out in a brilliant analysis delivered at a sports conference at New York University this past April that dealt almost exclusively with Hoberman's book, Ellison might rightly be characterized as "a pathologist" and "an individualist." But he was, as Scott argued, "a pathologist who opposed pathology as part of the racial debate." Yet one of the most compelling scenes in *Invisible Man* is the Battle Royal, a surreal perversion of a sports competition in which blacks fight one another for the amusement of powerful whites. Although racism has compelled blacks to participate in this contest, the characters come willingly, the winner even taking an individualistic pride in it. Such participation in one's own degradation can be described as a pathology. How can an Ellison disciple avoid pathology as part of the debate when Ellison made it so intricately serve the artistic and political needs of his novel? Ellison may have loved jazz, and growing up black and poor in Oklahoma may have been as richly stimulating as any life, just as going to Tuskegee may have been the same as going to Harvard—at least according to Ellison's mythologizing of his own life—but he found black literature generally inadequate as art and thought that blacks used race as a cover to avoid engaging the issues of life fully. For Ellison, black people, like most oppressed minorities, intensely provincialized themselves.

This is not to say Hoberman is justified in adding his own pathologizing to the mix, but his reasoning seems to be something like this: If racism is a major pathology and if we live in a racist society, one might reasonably suspect the victims of racism to be at least as pathologized by it as the perpetrators. If the victims are not pathologized at all by it, why single out racism as a particularly heinous crime? It would, in that instance, be nothing more than another banal example of man's inhumanity to man.

In response to an article like *SI*'s "Whatever Happened to the White Athlete?" blacks are likely to ask, Why is it whenever we dominate by virtue of merit a legitimate field of endeavor, it's always seen as a problem? On the one hand, some blacks are probably willing to take the view expressed in Steve Sailer's August 12, 1996, essay in *National Review*, "Great Black Hopes," in which he argues that black achievement in sports serves very practical ends, giving African-Americans a cultural and market niche, and that far from indicating a lack of intelligence, blacks' dominance in some sports reveals a highly specialized intelligence: what he calls "creative improvisation and on-the-fly interpersonal decision-making," which also explains "black dominance in jazz, running with the football, rap, dance, trash talking, preaching, and oratory." I suppose it might be said from this that blacks have fast-twitch brain cells. In any case, blacks had already been conceded these gifts by whites in earlier displays of condescension. But black sports dominance is no small thing to blacks because, as they deeply know, to win is to be human.

On the other hand, what the *SI* article said most tellingly was that while young whites admire black athletic figures, they are afraid to play sports that blacks dominate, another example of whites leaving the neighborhood when blacks move in. This white "double-consciousness"—to admire blacks for their skills while fearing their presence in a situation where blacks might predominate—is a modern-day reflection of the contradiction, historically, that has produced our racially stratified society. To be white can be partly defined as not only the fear of not being white but the fear of being *at the mercy* of those who are not white. Whiteness and blackness in this respect cease to be identities and become the personifications not of stereotypes alone but of taboos, of prohibitions. Sports, like all of popular culture, become the theater where the taboos are simultaneously smashed and reinforced, where one is liberated from them while conforming to them. Sports are not an idealization of ourselves but a reflection.

THE PRINCE AND HIS KINGDOM

Arguably the most popular and, doubtless, one of the most skilled boxers in the world today is the undefeated feather-weight champion, Prince Naseem Hamed of England. (The "Prince" title is a bit of platonic self-romanticism; Naseem, of lower-middle-class origins—his father a corner-store grocer—has no blood tie to any aristocracy.) When he was boy, Hamed and his brothers fought all the time in the street, usually against white kids who called them "Paki." "I'd always turn around and say, 'Listen, I'm Arab me, not Pakistani,'" said Hamed in an interview some years later. "They'd turn round and say you're all the same." Indeed, Hamed was discovered by Brendan Ingle, his Irish manager, fighting three bigger white boys in a Sheffield schoolyard and holding his own very well. The fight was probably instigated by racial insult. Although his parents are from Yemen and Naseem is worshiped nearly as a god among the Yemeni these days, he was born in Sheffield, is a British citizen, never lived in Yemen and, despite his Islamic religious practices, seems thoroughly British in speech, taste and cultural inclination. Yet when Naseem was fighting as an amateur, he was sometimes taunted racially by the crowd: "Get the black bastard." Even as a professional he has sometimes been called "Paki bastard" and "nigger." He was once showered with spit by a hostile white audience. But Naseem was far more inspired than frightened by these eruptions, and was especially impressive in winning fights when he was held in racial contempt by the audience, as he would wickedly punish his opponents. For Hamed, these fights particularly became opportunities to rub white Anglo faces in the dirt, to beat them smugly while they hysterically asserted their own vanquished superiority. But his defiance, through his athleticism, becomes an ironic form of assimilation. He is probably the most loved Arab in England, and far and away the most popular boxer there. As he said, "When you're doing well, everyone wants to be your friend."

On the whole, these displays of racism at a sporting event need to be placed in perspective. For what seems a straightforward exhibition of racialist prejudice and Anglo arrogance is a bit more complex. And deeper understanding of the Naseem Hamed phenomenon might give us another way to approach the entangled subject of race and sports.

It must be remembered that professional boxing has been and

remains a sport that blatantly, sometimes crudely, exploits racial and
ethnic differences. Most people know the phrase "Great White Hope,"
created during the reign (1908–15) of the first black heavy-weight boxing champion, Jack Johnson, when a white sporting public that had, at
first, supported him turned against him in part because he flaunted his
sexual affairs with white women; in part because he seemed to be so far
superior to the white opponent, Tommy Burns, from whom he won the
title. The advent of Johnson did not, by any means, invent the intersection of race and sports but surely heightened it as a form of national
obsession, a dark convulsion in an incipient American popular culture.
The expression "Great White Hope" is still used today, in boxing, track
and field, and professional basketball, whenever a white emerges as a
potential star.

But ethnicity and racialism in boxing has a more intricate history
than white against black. Boxers have often come from racially and ethnically mixed working-class urban environments where they fought
racial insults as street toughs. This was particularly true of white ethnic fighters—Jews, Italians and Irish—in the United States from the
turn of the century to about the fifties, when public-policy changes
widened economic and educational opportunities, and suburbanization
altered white ethnic urban neighborhoods, changing the character of
boxing and big-city life. John L. Sullivan, the last great bare-knuckle
champion, may have been "white" when he drew the color line and
refused to fight the great black heavyweight Peter Jackson (at nearly
the same time that Cap Anson refused to play against blacks in baseball, precipitating a near-sixty-year ban on blacks in professional baseball), but to his audience he was not merely white but Irish. Benny
Leonard was not just a white fighter but a Jewish fighter. Rocky
Graziano was not merely a white fighter but an Italian fighter. Muhammad Ali, reinventing himself ethnically when the fight game became
almost exclusively black and Latino, was not just a black fighter but a
militant black Muslim fighter. Fighters, generally, as part of the show,
tend to take on explicit ethnic and racial identities in the ring. One
needn't be a deconstructionist to understand that race *aspires* to be a
kind of performance, just as athletic performance aspires to be something racial. This is clear to anyone who has seriously watched more
than, say, a half-dozen boxing matches. Today, basketball is a "black"
game not only because blacks dominate it but because they have developed a style of play that is very different from the style when whites
dominated the pro game back in the fifties. It is said by scholars, writers and former players that Negro League baseball was different from

white baseball and that when Jackie Robinson broke the color line, he introduced a different way of playing the game, with more emphasis on speed and aggressive base-running. In the realm of sports, this type of innovation becomes more than just performance. The political significance of race in a sporting performance is inextricably related to the fact that sports are also contests of domination and survival. It should come as no surprise that the intersection of race and sports reached its full expression at the turn of the century when social Darwinism was the rage (Charles Murray is our Herbert Spencer); when sports, imitating the rampant industrialism of the day, became a highly, if arbitrarily, rationalized system; when business culture first began to assimilate the values of sports; when it was believed that blacks would die out in direct competition with whites because they were so inferior; when Euro-American imperialism—race as the dramaturgy of dominance— was in full sway.

In most respects, the racialism displayed at some of Naseem Hamed's fights is rather old-fashioned. This racialism has three sources. First, there is the old Anglo racism directed against anyone nonwhite but particularly against anyone from, or perceived to be from, the Indian subcontinent. (Hamed is insulted by being called a "Paki," not an Arab, a confusion that speaks to something specific in white British consciousness, as does the statement "they are all the same.") In short, in British boxing audiences, we see Anglo racism as a performance of competitive dominance as well as a belief in the superiority of "whiteness."

Second, there is the way that Hamed fights. "Dirty, flash, black bastard," his audience shouts, meaning that Hamed has stylish moves, is very fast, but really lacks the heart and stamina to be a true boxer, does not have the bottom of a more "prosaic" white fighter. Hamed is derided, in part, because his showy, flamboyant style seems "black," although there have been several noted white fighters in boxing history who were crafty and quick, like Willie Pep. Hamed is immodest, something the white sporting crowd dislikes in any athlete but particularly in non-white athletes. He fights more in the style of Sugar Ray Leonard and Muhammad Ali than in the mode of the traditional stand-up British boxer. To further complicate the ethnicity issue, it must be remembered that famous black British boxers such as Randy Turpin, John Conteh and Frank Bruno have been very much accepted by the British sporting public because they fought in a more orthodox manner.

Third, traditional working-class ethnocentrism is part of most boxing matches, as it is a seamless part of working-class life. Hamed calls his manager "Old Irish," while Ingle calls him "the little Arab." A good deal of this ethnocentrism is expressed as a kind of complex regional chauvinism. Below the glamorous championship level, boxing matches are highly local affairs. Hamed has received his most racist receptions when fighting a local boy on that boy's turf. This almost always happens, regardless of ethnicity, to a "foreign" or "alien" boxer. In international amateur competitions, Hamed himself was constantly reminded that he was "fighting for England." It is all right if Hamed is a "Paki" as long as he is "our Paki."

What we learn from the example of Hamed is that race is a form of performance or exhibition in sports that is meant, in some way, for those at the bottom, to be an act of assertion, even revolt, against "how things are normally done." But also, in boxing, ethnic identities are performances of ethnic hatreds. As Jacques Barzun wrote, "In hatred there [is] the sensation of strength," and it is this sensation that spurs the fighter psychologically in the ring, gives him a reason to fight a man he otherwise has no reason to harm. So it is that within the working-class ethnic's revolt there is also his capitulation to playing out a role of pointless, apolitical resentment in the social order. This is why boxing is such an ugly sport: It was invented by men of the leisure class simply to bet, to make their own sort of sport of their privilege; and it reduces the poor man's rightful resentment, his anger and hatred, to a form of absurd, debased, dangerous entertainment. The Hameds of the boxing world make brutality a form of athletic beauty.

Postscript: O Defeat, Where Is Thy Sting

She: Is there a way to win?
He. Well, There is a way to lose more slowly
> —*Jane Greer and Robert Mitchum*
> in Out of the Past

I'm a loser
And I'm not what I appear to be.

> —*Lennon and McCarthy*

It is certainty that sports teach us about defeat and losing, for it is a far more common experience than winning. It might be suggested that in any competition there must be a winner and a loser and so winning is just as common. But this is not true. When a baseball team wins the World Series or a college basketball team wins a national title or a tennis player wins the French Open, everyone else in the competition has lost: twenty-nine other baseball teams, sixty-three other basketball teams, dozens of other seeded and unseeded tennis players. Surely, all or nearly all have won at some point, but most sports are structured as elaborate eliminations. The aura of any sporting event of season is defeat. I am not sure sports teach either the participants or the audience how to lose well, but they certainly teach that losing is the major part of life. "A game tests, somehow, one's entire life," writes Michael Novak, and it is in this aspect that the ideological content of sports seems much like the message of the blues, and the athlete seems, despite his or her obsessive training and remarkable skill, a sort of Everyperson or Job at war, not with the gods but with the very idea of God. Sports do not mask the absurdity of life but rather ritualize it as a contest against the arbitrariness of adversity, where the pointless challenge of an equally pointless limitation, beautifully and thrillingly executed, sometimes so gorgeously as to seem a victory even in defeat, becomes the most transcendent point of all. Black people have taught all of us in the blues that to lose is to be human. Sports, on any given day, teaches the same.

My barber is a professional boxer. He fights usually as a light-heavyweight or as a cruiser-weight. He is 34 and would like to fight for a championship again one day, but time is working against him. He has fought for championships in the past, though never a world title. It is difficult to succeed as a boxer if you must work another job. A day of full-time work and training simply leaves a fighter exhausted and distracted. I have seen him fight on television several times, losing to such world-class fighters as Michael Nunn and James Toney. In fact, every time I have seen him fight he has lost. He is considered "an opponent," someone used by an up-and-coming fighter to fatten his record or by an established fighter who needs a tune-up. An opponent does not make much money; some are paid as little as a few hundred dollars a fight. My barber, I guess, is paid more than that. This is the world that most boxers occupy—this small-time world of dingy arenas and gambling boats, cramped dressing rooms and little notice. It is the world that most professional athletes occupy. He last fought on June 2 against Darryl Spinks for something called the MBA light-heavyweight title at the Ambassador Center in Jennings, Missouri. Darryl Spinks is the son of notorious St. Louis fighter and former heavyweight champion Leon Spinks. Spinks won a twelve-round decision, and my barber felt he was given "a hometown decision" in his own hometown, as he felt he decisively beat young Spinks. But Spinks is an up-and-coming fighter, and up-and-coming fighters win close fights. When I talked to my barber after the fight, he seemed to accept defeat with some equanimity. What upset him was that the local paper, or the local white paper, as it is seen by most blacks, the *St. Louis Post-Dispatch*, did not cover the fight. It was prominently covered by the *St. Louis American*, the city's black paper. I told him I would write a letter to the editor about that; he appreciated my concern. As things turned out, the fight was mentioned in the *Post-Dispatch* ten days later as part of a roundup of the local boxing scene. My barber's fight earned three paragraphs. It probably wasn't quite what he wanted, but I am sure it made him feel better. After all, a local fighter has only his reputation in his hometown to help him make a living. Nonetheless, I admired the fact that he took so well being unfairly denied something that was so important to him. Most people can't do that.

I might quarrel a little with my good friend Stanley Crouch, who once said that the most exquisite blues statement was Jesus, crucified, asking God why he had been forsaken. It's a good line Jesus said on the old rugged cross. But for us Americans, I rather think the most deeply affecting blues statement about losing as the way it is in this life is the last line of a song we learned as children and we sing every time we go to the park to see our favorite team: " 'Cause it's one, two, three strikes you're out at the old ball game."

ALL THE WORLD'S A BALL

Eduardo Galeano

•

THANKS TO WORLD Cup 1988, we learned or confirmed a few things:
- MasterCard is a muscle toner, and a good athlete needs plenty of Coca-Cola and McDonald's hamburgers.
- In the final, France shocked Brazil, and Adidas beat Nike. A lover of Brazilian soccer, Nike shelled out a reported $400 million to the team plus another fortune to its star Ronaldo. Well-placed sources say Nike insisted that Ronaldo play the final match even though he was seriously ill. Yanked out of the hospital, he played but he didn't play.
- The winning side was a team of immigrants. Opinion polls say half of France would like to toss out such interlopers, but all of France celebrated as if these victorious blacks and Arabs were the sons of Joan of Arc.
- Soccer miraculously retains its capacity for surprise. Nobody gave 2 cents for Croatia, but their grit took them to third place.
- Miraculously, soccer retains its capacity for beauty. I saw every match and don't regret it. Defensive and calculating, end-of-the-century soccer is chary with its splendor, but splendor there was.

St. Denis reminded us, once again, that today the stadium is a gigantic TV studio. The game is played for television so you can watch it at home. And television rules.

Twelve years ago, at the 1986 World Cup, Valdano, Maradona and other players protested because the big matches were played at noon under a sun that fried everything it touched. Noon in Mexico, nightfall in Europe, the best time for European television. The German goalkeeper, Harald Schumacher, told the story: "I sweat. My throat is dry. The grass is like dried shit: hard, strange, hostile. The sun shines straight down on the stadium and strikes us right on the head. We cast no shadows. They say this is good for television."

Was the sale of the spectacle more important than the quality of play? The players are there to kick, not to cry, and Jean Marie Faustin de Godefroid Havelange, head of FIFA, the International Federation of Football Associations, put an end to that maddening business: "They should play and shut their traps," he decreed.

Who ran the '86 World Cup? The Mexican Soccer Federation? No, please, no more intermediaries: It was run by Guillermo Cañedo, vice president of Televisa and president of the company's international network. That World Cup belonged to Televisa, the monopoly that owns the free time of all Mexicans and also owns Mexican soccer. When a Mexican journalist had the insolence to ask about the costs and profits of the World Cup, Cañedo cut him off cold: "This is a private company and we don't have to report to anybody."

Throughout the world, by direct and indirect means, television decides where, when and how soccer will be played. The game has sold out to the small screen in body and soul—and clothing, too. Players are now TV stars. The program that had the largest audience in France and Italy in 1993 was the final of the European Champions Cup between Olympique de Marseille and Milan. Milan, as we all know, belongs to Silvio Berlusconi, the czar of Italian television. Bernard Tapie was not the owner of French TV, but his club, Olympique, received from the small screen that year 300 times more money than in 1980.

Now millions of people can watch matches, not only the thousands who fit into stadiums. But unlike baseball and basketball, soccer is a game of continuous play that offers few interruptions for showing ads. A half-time isn't sufficient. American television has proposed to correct this unpleasant defect by dividing matches into four twenty-minute periods—and Havelange agrees . . .

Who are the players? Monkeys in a circus? They may dress in silk, but aren't they all still monkeys? They are never consulted when it comes to deciding when, where and how they play. The international bureaucracy changes rules at its whim. The players can't even find out how much money their legs produce, or where those fugitive fortunes end up.

The fact is, professional players offer their labor power to the factories of spectacle in exchange for a wage. What about the thousands upon thousands of players who are not stars? The ones who don't enter the kingdom of fame, who get stuck going round and round in the revolving door? Of every ten professional soccer players in Argentina, only three manage to make a living from it.

Here is the itinerary of a player from the southern reaches of the globe who has good legs and good luck: From his home town he moves to a provincial city, then from the provincial city to a small club in the country's capital. The small club has no choice but to sell him to a large one; the large club, suffocated by debt, sells him to an even larger club in a larger country. And the player crowns his career in Europe.

All along this chain, the clubs, contractors and intermediaries end up with the lion's share of the money. Each link confirms and perpetuates the inequality among the parties, from the hopeless plight of neighborhood clubs in poor countries to the omnipotence of the corporations that run European leagues.

In Uruguay, for example, soccer is an export industry that scorns the domestic market. The continuous outflux of good players means mediocre professional leagues and ever fewer, ever less fervent fans. People desert the stadiums to watch foreign matches on television. When the world championships come around, our players gather from the four corners of the earth, meet on the plane, play together for a short while, and bid each other good-bye without ever having the time to become a real team—eleven heads, twenty-two legs, a single heart.

When Brazil won its fourth World Cup, in 1994, only a few of the celebrating journalists managed to hide their nostalgia for the marvels of days past. The team of Romario and Bebeto played an efficient game, but it was stingy on poetry: a soccer much less Brazilian than the hypnotic play of Garrincha, Didí, Pelé and their teammates in '58, '62 and '70. More than one reporter noted the shortage of talent, and several commentators pointed to the style of play imposed by the coach, successful but lacking in magic. In 1998 it wasn't even successful. Brazil sold its soul to modern soccer. But there was another point that went practically unmentioned: The great teams of the past were made up of Brazilians who played in Brazil. On the '94 team, eight of them played in Europe. Romario, at that time the highest-paid Latin American player in the world, was earning more in Spain than all eleven from

Brazil's '58 team put together, who were some of the greatest artists in the history of soccer.

The ball turns, the world turns. People suspect the sun is a burning ball that works all day and spends the night bouncing around the heavens while the moon does its shift, though science is somewhat doubtful. There is absolutely no question, however, that the world turns around a spinning ball: The final of the '98 World Cup was watched by the largest crowd ever of the many that have assembled in this planet's history. It is the passion most widely shared: Many admirers of the ball play with her on fields and pastures, and many more have box seats in front of the TV and bite their nails as they watch the show performed by twenty-two men in shorts who chase a ball and kick her to prove their love.

At the end of the '94 World Cup every child born in Brazil was named Romario, and the turf of the stadium in Los Angeles was sold off like pizza, at $20 a slice. A bit of insanity worthy of a better cause? A primitive and vulgar business? A bag of tricks manipulated by the owners? I'm one of those who believe that soccer might be all that, but it is also much more: a feast for the eyes that watch it and a joy for the body that plays it. A reporter once asked the German theologian Dorothee Sölee: "How would you explain to a child what happiness is?"

"I wouldn't explain it," she answered. "I'd toss him a ball and let him play."

Professional soccer does everything to castrate that energy of happiness, but it survives in spite of all the spites. And maybe that's why soccer never stops being astonishing. As my friend Angel Ruocco says, that's the best thing about it—its stubborn capacity for surprise. The more the technocrats program it down to the smallest detail, the more the powerful manipulate it, soccer continues to be the art of the unforeseeable.

And afterward? Perhaps, just a source of melancholy, that melancholy we all feel after making love and at the end of the game.

WRITING ROBESON

Martin Duberman

•

IT WAS PAUL Robeson Jr. who invited me, back in 1981, to be his father's biographer. He had offered me exclusive access for seven years to the vast family archives long closed to scholars, and had stressed at our very first meeting that he wasn't looking for a "Saint Robeson" but rather a tell-it-like-it-was account that would make his father an accessible human being rather than a pedestalized god.

Impressed, flattered and eager as I was to accept Paul Jr.'s offer, it also puzzled me. "You can see that I'm white," I said to him during that first meeting, "but do you also know that I'm gay, and that I've been actively involved in the gay political movement for years?" He casually replied that he did, that he had had me "thoroughly checked out." He had become convinced that I was the right biographer for his father because (as I recorded his words in my diary) of my "nuanced prose," my "complex understanding of personality," my left-wing politics and my experience in the theater.

Since I was not the only historian with left-wing views who wrote "nuanced" prose, I remained skeptical that Paul Jr.'s stated reasons for inviting a white gay activist to become his father's biographer exhausted the range of his motives. But wanting to believe him, I kept my skepticism to myself and accepted his invitation.

I did set one condition. I told him that I could comfortably undertake the biography only if we drew up a legal agreement in which he formally gave up all control over what I might ultimately choose to write. No self-respecting scholar, I explained, could work with someone looking over his shoulder—and especially not a son, deeply invested emotionally, and with his own pronounced views and agenda. Paul Jr. said he had expected me to set those conditions and was willing to sign such an agreement. "As we move ahead," he added with a sly grin, "I'll doubtless backslide." (Oh Lord, would he backslide!)

And so we were launched. Paul Robeson Jr. had given me the necessary assurances, had insisted he wanted a wholly truthful—not a plaster cast—portrait, and was soon, moreover, introducing me to some of his father's closest friends. But as I set to work on the mountainous source materials, a sense of unease lingered. *Was* this, I asked myself, a case of bizarre miscasting, a grotesque mismatch of author and subject—as some were quick to charge as soon as the project was publicly announced?

To quiet my discomfort, I tried putting the issue in a large context: What, after all, *are* the essential qualities in a given biographer that heighten the chances for understanding a given life? Who is best qualified to write about whom—and why? Are there certain unbreachable guidelines that must be followed, certain fundamental boundaries that must not be crossed? Do we want to argue, for example, that no man should attempt to write about a woman, no younger person about an older, no adult about a child, no straight person about a gay one, no white person about a person of color (or vice versa)?

Even the most committed essentialists, I feel sure, would balk at strictures this severe: We have become too aware of how reductive the standard identity categories of gender, class, race and ethnicity are when trying to capture the actual complexities of a given personality. (Paul Robeson cannot simply be summarized as "a black man," nor Martin Duberman as "a gay man.") Besides, many people have overlapping identities that compete for attention over time; and how we rank their importance in shaping our personalities can shift, which in turn leads to a re-allocation of political energies.

But why is the assumption to widespread in the first place that a matchup between author and subject in regard to standard identity categories *is* the best guarantor of understanding? Indeed, why do we lazily assume that these categories are, in every case, the critical ones, while ignoring any number of other commonalities between biographer and subject that might provide critical insights—matters such as having been raised in comparable family or regional cultures or sharing similar psychologies of self, professional experience or religious affiliations.

Which of the affiliative links, standard or otherwise, between biographer and subject are likely to prove the most trenchant pathways to understanding? Perhaps—heresy!—the answer is *none*, or none that can be presumed in advance to guarantee access into the furthest recesses of personality. Perhaps what will turn out to matter most is that which is least visible and hardest to define: something to do with an elusive empathy of the spirit between biographer and subject, a shared if shadowy sense of how one should best navigate through life, treat other people, leave a mark and make a contribution without succumbing to self-importance—or self-destruction. How one positions oneself in the world will always reflect to some degree the seminal experience and indoctrinations of class, race and gender, but may also, perhaps even to a greater degree, float above them, wondrously unanchored in categorical imperatives, mysteriously untraceable in derivation.

The simplifications currently at work are easily enumerated. Whether, for example, one defines "working class" in terms of income, job status or educational level, it should be obvious that not all working-class people have had an interchangeable set of experiences; being on an assembly line cannot be equated with cooking hamburgers at McDonald's, nor illiteracy with a high school education, nor life in a trailer park with life in a slum. A historian with a "working class" background cannot assume that that fact alone will open the gates of understanding to his or her working-class subject.

As for race, surely whites now realize that there is no homogeneity of lifestyle or opinion among members of a minority group. African-Americans, for example, vary widely in their views on everything from parenting to education to politics to white people. As for gender, the mere fact of being a woman not in itself prepare a university-trained PhD doing the biography of, say, Grandma Moses, to understand a rudimentary rural life, the techniques of primitive painting, the process of aging or the morass of celebrity-hood.

To take as a given that no white person is able (or morally entitled) to write about someone black can itself be seen as a form of racism—a particularly simplistic form, of it is based on the insidious assumption that fellow-feeling hinges on the color of one's skin and that an individual's character can be accurately prejudged on the basis of his or her membership in a particular group.

Since no biographer can duplicate in his or her person the full range of the subject's experience—or *exactly* duplicate any of it—every biographer will be found wanting in some areas. And, yes, the disability can sometimes be directly linked to racial (or class or gender) dissonance. I do not doubt, for example, that as a white person I failed to capture some of the nuances of what it meant for Robeson to grow up in the black church (his father was a minister). Yet, oppositely, my own second career in the theater gave me a background few if any scholars could bring to bear in evaluating Robeson's stage experience.

Which brings us to the "gay issue." Soon after my biography of Robeson had been published, in February 1989, I was in San Francisco on the final leg of the book tour. Between the usual signings and readings, I made time to pay a return visit to Lee and Revels Cayton. Both had been helpful during the seven years I spent on the biography, and Revels, a radical veteran of the trade union wars and one of Robeson's closet friends, had at several points given me crucial information and advice.

I had sent the Caytons an early copy of the book, and Revels greeted me with a bear hug, effusive with congratulations for having "gotten it right." Later, over coffee, he made a comment that started me: "you know, I've been thinking about it and I believe that only a gay man could have understood Paul's sex life."

I had been thinking about that too—for a long time—and thought I knew what Revels meant: Most heterosexual scholars, a conservative breed not known for their erotic capers, would be likely to share the mainstream view that lifetime, monogamous pair-bonding is the optimal path to human happiness—not to say moral decency. That assumption, in turn, would incline them, when confronted with the unconventional erotic history of someone like Robeson, to evade, minimize, condemn or apologize for his robust sexuality.

A legion of heterosexual scholars strenuously believe in their hearts, not merely in their public pronouncements, that sexual "restraint" is one of the admirable moral cornerstones of our national character. (It took DNA, remember, finally to break down their adamant denial of a sexual liaison between Thomas Jefferson and Sally Hemings.)

Confronted with Robeson's many sexual adventures, such scholars would most likely characterize them as "womanizing" or "Don Juanism." Additionally, they would probably "explain" the fact that Robeson's most intense, long-lasting affairs were nearly all with white women by regurgitating hoary, simplistic formulas about his need to prove himself to the white world—or to work out his anger toward it.

By the time I visited the Caytons, Revels's view that most heterosexual scholars would react uneasily to Robeson's sexuality had already been borne out in some of the early reviews. The critic in the *San Francisco Chronicle* had referred to Robeson's "compulsive womanizing." The *Village Voice* reviewer had wondered about "the unquenchable need that lay behind his behavior." Ishmael Reed, while praising my "fine" biography, had taken me to task for the book's "excessive and voyeuristic detail" about Robeson's romantic and sexual encounters. And Paul Robeson Jr. would soon issue a formal statement, printed in the *Amsterdam News*, characterizing my biography as "prurient." When I later told Revels about that, he shook his head in disbelief, chuckling over what he called my "restrained" account of Robeson's erotic activities.

Was Revels Cayton right in seeing my homosexuality as an *asset* in writing Robeson's biography, or was it—as many more have asserted—an offensive liability? Lloyd Brown, who collaborated with Robeson in the fifties on his autobiographical manifesto, *Here I Stand*, has been among the more publicly outraged. When my editor at Knopf sent Brown an early copy of the biography, he wrote back that I was "a sick writer" whose "homosexual values" were asserted throughout the book. Down to the present day, Brown continues to denounce my "preoccupation with the bedroom aspects of Robeson's life."

One of the ironies in all this is that my biography is, if anything, a rather truncated—one might even say chaste—rendering of Robeson's highly charged erotic life. Only Robeson's half-dozen significant romantic attachments are discussed in any detail, and his many short-term encounters are barely mentioned. Nor do I ever describe, let alone itemize, his actual sexual behavior—his preferences and performances in bed.

Moreover, as I made clear in the biography, Robeson's wife, Essie, had early on understood that her husband was not cut out for monogamy and domesticity; wanting to remain Mrs. Robeson, she had made her peace with his extramarital pleasures. That Essie was knowledgeable about Paul's sexual adventures would not, of course, make them more palatable to traditional moralists—including many church-going African-American adherents of mainstream sexual mores.

White conservatives, long since enraged at Robeson's political militancy, gleefully latch on to his erotic history as an additional weapon in portraying him as a "moral transgressor." For white racists, moreover,

Robeson's exuberant sexuality can usefully be made to play into the longstanding, vicious stereotype of the black man as a "rampaging lustful beast." That almost all of Robeson's major affairs were with white women, finally, can be used to diminish his stature even among those who otherwise deeply admire his unyielding struggle against racism and colonialism. (After my biography was published, Paul Robeson Jr. claimed that I had deliberately omitted a "list" he had given me of his father's black female lovers. If there is such a list, I was never shown it. Besides, the evidence of Paul Sr.'s preference for white lovers is overwhelming and incontestable.)

The biographer's job is to tell the truth—to the extent that inevitable gaps in the evidence and subjective distortion will allow for it. The biographer is not responsible for how others manipulate that truth to serve agendas of their own. Those who despise Robeson's socialism will always manage to find grounds for justifying their hostility; neither the inclusion nor the omission of evidence about his sexual life will dislodge their underlying animus toward his politics.

Yet even some who feel deeply sympathetic to Robeson's politics experience discomfort over his troubled marriage and his frequent extramarital affairs—and especially traditional socialists of the older generation, for whom economic, not sexual or gender, liberation remains the one legitimate issue of abiding importance.

This discomfort needs to be directly addressed, along with the underlying assumption that feeds it: namely, that monogamous, lifetime pair-bonding is, for everyone, the only defensible, natural, moral path. But how much sex *is* too much sex? Does the answer hinge on the number of different partners involved, the number of encounters with the same partner, particular configurations (three-way or group sex, say) or particular sexual acts (anal intercourse, say, or sadomasochism)? The answers will hinge on individual assumptions about what is "normal," "healthy" or "moral." In this country numbers alone are likely to settle the argument: The higher the figure, the more brows start to furrow—even when we are talking about consenting adults.

We need to take a closer look as well at what most people in our culture mean when using the designation "womanizer"—the charge Robeson's detractors most often level at him (that is, when they are not denouncing his "Stalinism"). Three definitions currently predominate: A "womanizer" is someone whose self-regard hinges on multiple conquests; is someone incapable of love and, to disguise that fact (not least from himself), pursues multiple sexual encounters; and, finally, is someone who treats his partners as exploitable objects, to be used disdainfully and discarded cavalierly.

None of those definitions, I would submit, apply to Paul Robeson. That is the overwhelming testimony of both his lovers and his psychiatrists. Every woman I spoke to who had been involved with Robeson for an extended period emphasized that he treated her as an equal, not a mere convenience or appendage. He could be difficult, neglectful and secretive, but was much more often tender, considerate and loving. As if in confirmation, one of Robeson's psychiatrists described him to me as a man whose "motivational spring was compassion, not ego."

And so when I hear Robeson described as a "womanizer," I've learned to take it as a rule of thumb that I'm listening to someone who despises the man politically and wishes to discredit him—as nothing can do more powerfully in our sex-negative culture than the accusation of "philanderer."

Unless it be, of course, to spread rumors that he was to some degree erotically involved with men. Such rumors, as I learned to my astonishment, were already in circulation when I began Robeson's biography. In a 1981 issue of the left-wing magazine *WIN* (now defunct), an article on Robeson had referred to his bisexuality as if it were a well-established fact. Some years later *The Advocate* (a national gay magazine) printed the claim that Robeson had recently "[been] revealed to have been gay." I protested both pieces and in the biography wrote that, "I had found absolutely no evidence of Robeson's erotic interest in men."

While I was working on the book, the candidate most often urged on me as Robeson's male lover was the Russian filmmaker Sergei Eisenstein. When I discussed that possibility with, among others, Zina Voynow, Eisenstein's sister-in-law, she scoffed at the notion of such an affair—though she did not, as some of his biographers have, deny Eisenstein's homosexuality.

Nevertheless, even after my biography was published, the rumor surfaced yet again (in a 1990 article by one Hugh Murray) that insisted—at length, and based on a fatuous twisting of suspect scraps of "evidence"—that the matter of Robeson's bisexuality remained "an open question." It does not. Barring the (almost unimaginable) surfacing of new evidence to the contrary, Robeson was—as I wrote in the biography and as I have repeatedly said in response to ongoing queries—singularly, rigorously, contentedly heterosexual.

For merely insisting on scholarly standards of evidence, I expected no medal for Meritorious Resistance to Political Correctness. But I *was* surprised that among the several critics who denounced Robeson as "oversexed" and my biography of him as "prurient," only one—in *Commentary*, no less—so much as mentioned that my book had put to rest the longstanding rumors of Robeson's bisexuality. Not even the *Commentary* reviewer thought to mention that I had done so as a gay man who might have been expected to maximize every remote innuendo or shard of evidence that could have left open the opportunity to claim Robeson for Our Side.

When nongays credit anything of value in the gay perspective—and only a few leftists ever do—they usually cite its iconoclasm, its insistent challenge to "regimes of the normal," especially in regard to gender and sexuality. In writing Robeson's biography, iconoclasm stood me in good stead. Yet ultimately I came to feel that it was less important in helping me get beneath the layers of his personality than what I would call our shared status as outsiders—outsiders who to a significant degree had been "let in," had been treated by the mainstream as an acceptable representative of an otherwise despised group.

Years into researching the book, I continued to mull over the question of whether I was an appropriate biographer for Robeson. I finally came to the conclusion that a strong argument could be made—just as Revels Cayton would later suggest—that far from disqualifying me as an effective interpreter of Robeson's life, my being gay had in fact given me some important advantages. Here is how I ultimately summed it up in a diary entry:

Like Robeson, I know about the doublebind of being accepted and not accepted.

I know about the outsider's need to role-play (the uses of theater off-stage).

I know about the double-vision of the outsider who is let inside; about being a "spy" in the culture.

I know some of the strategies for concealing pain, including from oneself.

I know about the exuberant investment of hope in a "liberation" movement—and the attendant despair when it falls short.

I know about the seductive double-talk employed, when considered serviceable, by the white male power structure.

I know about the tensions of trying to be a "good" role model.

I know about the conflict between the yearnings of lust and the demands of a public image.

I know about the tug-of-war between the attractions of career and of doing "good works."

I know about the disjunction between the desire to be liked (and knowing one has the necessary social skills to accomplish that) and feeling disgust at the neediness of the desire.

I know about stubbornness—and about the need to sometimes play the supplicant.

I know about the counterpulls of feeling gregarious and longing for—requiring—solitude.

I know about concealment.

I know about buried anger.

I know about politeness substituting for anger, about anger eating up one's vitals, distorting one's judgment.

I know about loneliness.

Once the biography was published, it came as an enormous relief to me that many African-American intellectuals—including Herb Boyd, Nathan Huggins, David Levering Lewis, Nell Irvin Painter and Arnold Rampersad—hailed it. The review that perhaps pleased me most was Painter's. Some years earlier, she had rather sharply attacked me and other white historians (during an American Historical Society panel on "Black Biography") for "wrongheadedly" undertaking biographies of African-Americans. Yet reviewing my biography in the *Boston Globe*, she reversed fields, writing that the book especially "rates high marks for having seen much that white biographers of African-American subjects frequently disregard, notably anger and strategies for its management. . . ."

Nell Painter did not suggest that my being gay might have been importantly connected to my ability to see "much that white biographers . . . frequently disregard." But after years of inner debate, I have come to hold that view decisively. To whatever extent my biography of Robeson does represent an empathy of the spirit, I believe the sensitizing factor of critical importance was precisely my homosexuality.

HISTORIC QUESTION DEPARTMENT, 11TH GRADE DIVISION

·

In every century, it seems,
The Constitution's put to test.
Important questions must be asked,
And ours is, "Did he touch her breast?"

Calvin Trillin, January
11/18, 1999

THE FALSE DAWN OF CIVIL SOCIETY

David Rieff

•

WHEN WE PUT our faith in civil society, we are grasping at straws. Apart from a few principled nationalists, libertarians and Marxists, most well-intentioned people now view the rise of civil society as the most promising political development of the post-cold war era. By itself, that fact only points to how desperate we are, on the cusp of the millennium, to identify any political paradigm offering some realistic prospect of a more humane future. Such hopes give credit to those who entertain them, but they also perfectly illustrate J. D. Bernal's insight that "there are two futures, the future of desire and the future of fate, and man's reason has never learned to separate them."

Civil society is just such a projection of our desires. Worse, it gravely misdescribes the world we actually confront. As a concept, it has almost no specific gravity. It is little better than a Rorschach blot, the interpretations of which have been so massaged and expanded over the past fifteen years that the term has come to signify everything— which is to say nothing. Conventionally, we use civil society to apply to groups, societies and social trends of which we approve: societies based on diversity and tolerance, in which mutual assistance and solidarity are deeply established and the state is responsive rather than repressive.

Civil society is often described as a return to mutuality in political and social arrangements, and as the third force through which the traditional hierarchy of state and subject can be unseated. The term is used somewhat more rigorously by political scientists to encompass all those elements of society, and all those arrangements within it, that exist outside the state's reach or instigation. But in our time, the most general understanding of civil society is as the vehicle for a range of political and social goals. It has become a shorthand way of referring to all those democratically minded groups that have opposed and sometimes brought about the overthrow of repressive regimes in countries as varied as Marcos's Philippines, Abacha's Nigeria and Husak's Czechoslovakia. Where civil society is absent, repressive, tyrannical, even genocidal forces are supposed to have a freer hand; where it is present, it is supposed to constitute a firebreak against war, exploitation and want.

In short, civil society has come, simultaneously, to be thought of as encompassing everything that is not the state and as exemplifying a set of inherently democratic values. That is why those who tout it as the silver bullet both to "open" repressive societies and to guarantee or deepen democratic liberties and curb state power move with feline grace between using civil society as a descriptive term and as a prescriptive one. To which it might be added that the dogma holding that strengthening civil society is the key to creating or sustaining a healthy polity has come to dominate the thinking of major charitable foundations, as well as human rights and humanitarian organizations.

Those disposed to accept the claims of these groups for the emancipatory potential of civil society should note that the term has been enthusiastically embraced by many government officials in the United States and the countries of the European Union. In the framework of development aid in particular, the shift from channeling assistance to governments, as had been the case well into the eighties, to offering it to local nongovernmental organizations (NGOs) has been justified not simply as the inevitable prudential response to states misusing aid but as a way of building civil society.

That this emphasis on local capacity building, to use the bureaucratic term of art, and on fostering civil society arose at exactly the moment when development aid from most major donor countries was plummeting (in many countries, including the United States, they are now at historic lows) may, of course, be coincidental. But in the development sphere, at least, ideological commitment to making states "responsive" to civil society seems to have been accompanied by a determination to cut funding. When pressed, development specialists who favor this new approach insist that a robust civil society will open the way for the integration of the poor world into the global economy—supposedly the first step toward prosperity.

Viewed from this angle, the idea of civil society begins to look less like a way of fostering democratic rights and responsive governments and more like part of the dominant ideology of the post-cold war period: liberal market capitalism. A perfect example of this synthesis of emancipatory sentiments and faith in free markets can be found in the Executive Summary of the 1997 Carnegie Commission on Preventing Deadly Conflict. Civil society is assigned a pivotal role. "Many elements of civil society," the report states, "can work to reduce hatred and violence and to encourage attitudes of concern, social responsibility and mutual aid within and between groups. In difficult economic and political transitions, the organizations of civil society are of crucial importance in alleviating the dangers of mass violence." The paragraph then segues, without break or transition, into the following assertion: "Many elements in the private sector around the world are dedicated to helping prevent deadly conflict."

Obviously, the communitarians, human rights activists and liberal foundation executives who first raised the banner of civil society were no more interested in helping refurbish liberal capitalism's ideological superstructure than was the human rights movement in making its cause the quasi-religious faith of the international new class, but this is nonetheless exactly what they have done. Surely, it is a safe assumption that any term that can be embraced as warmly by the Clinton Administration and the European Commission as "civil society" has been threatens no important vested interests in the rich world.

Again, there is no question of a subterfuge. The idea of civil society simply coincides with the tropism toward privatization that has been the hallmark of these post-cold war times. Far from being oppositional, it is perfectly in tune with the *Zeitgeist* of an age that has seen the growth of what proponents like Bill Clinton and Tony Blair are pleased to call the "Third Way" and what might more unsentimentally be called "Thatcherism with a human face." As we privatize prisons, have privatized development assistance and are in the process, it seems, of privatizing military interventions into places like New Guinea, Sierra Leone and Angola by armies raised by companies like Sandline and Executive Outcomes, so let us privatize democracy-building. Let's give up on the state's ability to establish the rule of law or democracy through elections and legislation, and instead give civic associations— the political equivalent of the private sector—a chance to do their thing.

The fact that all this comes couched in the language (and the imaginative framework) of emancipation does not, in and of itself, make it emancipatory. Indeed, there are times when it seems as if the advocates of civil society are the useful idiots of globalization. In further undermining the state, they undermine the only remaining power that has at least the potential to stand in opposition to the privatization of the world, commonly known as globalization.

Making the world safe for global capitalism may be one of the effects of the triumph of the ideal of civil society, but it is not, of course, the sole or even the principal reason for its prominence. The ideal of civil society responds to a deeper problem—an intellectual, not to say a moral, void. The most profound legacy of the post-cold war era may prove to be the ideological hollowing-out that all developed countries and many poor ones have experienced. The disappointments, for liberals and leftists, respectively, of nationalism and communism were already largely assimilated well before the collapse of the Soviet empire. What was unexpected was that the end of the superpower rivalry and the victory of market capitalism over state socialism would also reveal just how diminished the nation-state had become over the half-century since the end of the Second World War, and just how ineffectual the international institutions—above all the United Nations and the Bretton Woods organizations—that were established in its wake.

This is the revelation that has come in the package marked "globalization." The cold war had been an era of alliances and battlegrounds. Every nation had its place, whether it wanted one or not. It was above all a militarized environment, and, because only nations could afford modern armies, the nation-state still appeared to be quite strong. But this only shows how the transformation of the world economy could take place without sufficient notice being taken of the implications of those changes.

For all the bluff talk of the United States being "the indispensable nation" or the "only remaining superpower," it is less able to impose its will than it was during the cold war, and internationally, no national project with the unifying force of anti-Communism is anywhere to be found. Multiculturalism, global capitalism's consumerist ideological adjunct, has further fragmented any unitary cultural conception of the nation except in its most debased, commodified form.

All the major nations seem to have emerged from the cold war weaker and more incoherent than they were when they entered it. And for good reason. The course of the world economy has been deeply subversive of the established structures of power. But as Robert Hormats, the vice chairman of Goldman, Sachs & Co. International, observed, nobody controls globalization—certainly not national governments, as was demonstrated by the inability of the British government in 1992 to protect the value of the British pound against speculators led by George Soros.

Such perceived and real loss of power has been followed by a loss of legitimacy. It is now politicians who are the supplicants and corporate executives who are viewed as the dispensers of wisdom and authority and the holders of real power. The European Union countries were not able to muster the resolve to end the Bosnian war, but they were able to launch European monetary union at the behest of corporate Europe—an event that in many ways was European capitalism's end run around a half-century-old social contract between capital and labor, now seen to be interfering with the corporate bottom line.

In the United States, a renewed ethnic consciousness has led to what seems like a flowering of a multiplicity of allegiances; in Western Europe, the subsumption of nation-states in the project of the European Union, as well as the arrival of large numbers of nonwhite immigrants for the first time in several centuries, has produced similarly subversive effects on the legitimacy of the nation.

Faced with such confusions, is it any wonder that the ideal of civil society, which does not seek to oppose this fragmentation but rather to capitalize on it, should have become so important? Add to this civil society's seeming moral dimension, and the stew becomes well-nigh irresistible.

Furthermore, this blend of economic and democratic determinism has combined easily with a deep fatalism about the future of the nation-state. Political scientists constantly assure us that we have been going through the most profound change in international relations since the establishment of the Westphalian order in the seventeenth century. Nations have been clearly less and less able to affect investment flows and have thus been judged to be turning into hollow shells. And the future of supranational institutions like the UN system is seen as being, if anything, bleaker still. Better make a virtue of necessity and insist that the new medievalism of civil society, with the NGOs playing the role of the guilds in fourteenth-century Italy, would be an improvement over a world of etiolated nation-states in which even that sine qua non of state power, a monopoly on violence, is in many cases no longer assured.

A world in which the Enlightenment project of universal values seems to have been reduced to human rights of activists' demands for more stringent and binding international legal regimes was bound to be drawn to a faith in localism and single-issue activism. In fairness, the perception of the weakening of the nation and of the impotence of international organizations has not been mistaken. What has been misplaced is the belief that a network of associations could accomplish what states could not.

Proponents of the effectiveness of civil society point to examples of the successful opposition of popular action to repressive regimes or state policies. People power in the Philippines, the Velvet Revolution in what was then Czechoslovakia, the recent campaign to ban landmines—these are the great success stories of civil society. But it was always an empirical stretch to claim that these historic events were proof that human betterment would henceforth mainly be the product of the struggles of dissidents and grassroots activists.

The idea of civil society has been most coherent when applied to nations where civil citizens needed protection from a repressive state, as was the case in the Soviet empire. But in other parts of the world this paradigm is either irrelevant or of distinctly secondary importance. There are parts of Africa where a stronger state, one that could bring the various bandits and insurgents to heel, might be of far greater value. It's tempting to add that the United States, after more than two decades of seemingly inexorable privatization, is a country where strengthening the state's role would be preferable to hoping that NGOs will somehow be able to take up the slack.

The suggestion that civil society can cope where nations have failed is, in fact, a counsel of despair in such instances. Without a treasury, a legislature or an army at its disposal, civil society is less equipped to confront the challenges of globalization than nations are, and more likely to be wracked by divisions based on region and the self-interest of the single-issue groups that form the nucleus of the civil society movement.

Why should fragmented groups of like-minded individuals be more effective in, say, resisting the depredations of environmental despoilers than a national government? Remember, the ideal of civil society is being advanced not simply for the developed world, where to a large extent it exists already, but for the world as a whole. And yet, as we know from bitter experience, the leverage of grassroots activists even in the United States, where there are courts to turn to and media to beguile, is not enormous. One can admire the efforts and sacrifices of activists in the poor world without losing sight of the fact that their countries would be better off with honest and effective governments and legal systems, and with militaries that stay in their barracks, than with denser networks of local associations, which may stand for good values or hideous ones.

This last point is essential. Viewed coldly, the concept of civil society is based on the fundamentally apolitical, or even anti-political, concept of single-issue activism. And yet surely one person's civil society group is another person's pressure group. The assumption of the advocates of civil society is that somehow locally based associations are always going to stand for those virtues the authors of the Carnegie Commission associated them with. When it is said that civil society must be recognized as a new force in international politics, what is meant is a certain kind of civil society—in other words, a certain kind of political movement. But why should this be the case? It is only because what is properly a descriptive term is being misused as an ideological or moral one.

Why, for example, is the International Campaign to Ban Landmines viewed as an exemplar of civil society instead of, say, the National Rifle Association, which, whatever one thinks of its politics, has at least as good a claim to being an authentic grassroots movement? The UN bitterly resisted having to recognize the NRA as a legitimate NGO. And yet if we think of NGO as a description and not a political position, the NRA obviously qualifies.

In any case, to make the claim that civil society is bound to be, or is even likely to be, a force for good is roughly akin to claiming that people, at least when left to their own devices, are good. In contrast, proponents of civil society are often mesmerized by the depredations of states and seem to assume that states, by their nature, are malign or impotent or both. But there are other predators besides government officials, other ills besides those unleashed by untrammeled state power. An example might be the Bosnian Serbs under Radovan Karadzic. During the Bosnian war, it was a liberal conceit that the Serbs acted as they did because of fear or media manipulation. The idea, say, that people are capable, without manipulation, of great evil was dismissed out of hand. And yet as one who spent a good deal of time covering the war in Bosnia, my view is that Karadzic represented the aspirations of ordinary Serbs in that extraordinary time all too faithfully, and could rightfully lay just as great a claim to being an exemplar of civil society as Vaclav Havel.

That Karadzic is an evil man and Havel a good one should go without saying. But where the question of civil society is concerned, it is beside the point, unless, of course, you accept the claim that civil society exists only when the ideals or interests being expressed are good, peace-loving and tolerant. At that point civil society becomes, as it has for its more unreflective advocates, a theological notion, not a political or a sociological one. The example of Rwanda, which, as Peter Uvin has shown in his extraordinary book *Aiding Violence*, was viewed by development experts before the genocide as having one of the most developed civil societies in Africa, should be a warning to anyone who assumes it is a sure measure of a nation's political health or a buffer against catastrophe.

Finally, there is the problem of democracy. Leaders of associations, pressure groups and NGOs—unlike politicians in democracies—are accountable to no one except their members and those who provide them with funds. That may seem a minor question to adherents of a particular cause. Does it matter that Jody Williams was never elected to lead the campaign against landmines? Perhaps it doesn't. But proponents of civil society are claiming that it offers a better alternative, or at least an important additional voice, to that of governments and parliaments, not just on a single issue but on all the pressing questions of our time. And leaders of such groups, unlike politicians, do not have to campaign, hold office, allow the public to see their tax returns or stand for re-election. It is, indeed, the new medievalism, with the leaders of the NGOs as feudal lords.

This, of course, is hardly what most advocates of civil society have in mind. And yet as things stand, it is this unaccountable, undemocratic congeries of single-interest groups that is being proposed as the only viable alternative to the nation-state. It seems to me that were they to achieve the kind of prominence and centrality that is being predicted for them, we would all be far worse off than we are today. And things are gloomy enough already. The premise on which the advocates of civil society have been operating is simply wrong. The nation-state has been weakened, but it is not a spent force. And those who aspire to the better world the magic bullet of civil society is supposed to engineer would do better to fight the political battles they believe need fighting in the full knowledge that we do not all agree on what should be done or how societies should be organized, and we never will.

SEXTUPLE JEOPARDY

Jonathan Schell

•

IN THE SPIRIT *of the Laws*, Montesquieu draws a distinction that is useful in thinking about the impeachment of Bill Clinton. Montesquieu distinguishes between the structure of government, which he calls its "nature"—for example, monarchy, republicanism, tyranny—and the spirit that animates it, which he calls its "principle." For monarchy the principle is honor; for a republic it is virtue; and for tyranny it is fear. The structure, to use a simple analogy, is like the type of a vehicle—for instance, bicycle, car or train—and the principle is the fuel that makes it go (leg-power, gas or electricity).

The "principle" that has fueled the assault on Clinton has been constant throughout and is easily identified. It has been the zeal of the political right in general and of the Republican Party in particular to damage or destroy the presidency of Bill Clinton. The structures of the campaign, however, have been many. They include sexual harassment law, an independent prosecutor and the impeachment provision in the Constitution.

This restless search by an implacable faction for a variety of weapons to use against the President has resulted in a novel situation. The law forbids double jeopardy, but Clinton now faces, if my count is correct, sixfold jeopardy.

The first, of course, is the Senate trial, in which Clinton is likely to be acquitted because the Founders required a two-thirds majority to convict and the attacking party holds only fifty-five of the Senate's hundred seats. This insufficiency has sent the Republicans in search of forms of punishment within its reach.

The second is impeachment itself (as distinct from conviction and removal), which Republicans wish to interpret as condemnation, as if it were now enough to accuse someone of a crime in order to brand him guilty. The problem is that the public, according to every measure of its opinions, condemns Congress for impeaching the President much more harshly than it condemns the President for his misdeeds.

The third is censure, favored by the Democrats, who want to register their disapproval of the President without removing him from office.

The fourth, which has been invented more or less on the spot, is the idea of voting in the Senate on a so-called "finding of fact," by which the Senate would formally define the President's bad behavior even as, in a second vote, it would acquit him. Inasmuch as this "finding of fact"—more accurately named a "finding of conclusions" or a "finding of guilt" (inasmuch as the relevant facts were all found long ago)—can be passed by a simple majority, it amounts to an end-run around the inconvenient two-thirds rule.

Some Republicans, though, are unsatisfied with this innovation. Senator Orrin Hatch, for one, worries that if the Senate "finds that perjury and obstruction of justice are not removable" it would send the message that the Senate does not take these offenses seriously. He accordingly invented a variation of the fourth form of jeopardy, in which, after voting the censorious finding, the Senate would simply suspend the trial permanently, depriving Clinton of his acquittal. As part of this now-final judgment, Hatch would buttress the punishment value of impeachment by having the Senate go on record to the effect that "Impeachment Without Removal" (the apotheosis of this sanction through the use of capital letters is Hatch's own) would be designated "the highest form of censure." Here, in a perfect inversion of the rule that a person is innocent until proven guilty, mere accusation (impeachment) is formally transmuted by senatorial declaration not only into conviction but into the sentencing as well.

While all these constitutional novelties were being considered in the Senate, the never-sleeping Ken Starr was concocting a fifth form of punishment—indictment of the President even while he remains in office (as he will for two years after a failure to convict him in the Senate). Taking upon himself the power of judging Presidents that the Constitution gives to Congress, he was in effect saying to the Senate, "If you don't convict him, I will."

The sixth—and, perhaps, most keenly desired—form of punishment is the public humiliation of the President, not only before today's citizens but before all history. With this demand, we leave the realm of law and politics behind and approach the psychosexual substrate—the smoldering, sulfurous, hidden core—of the scandal. Is there any pejorative in the English language that has not been applied to Clinton? Not since Hitler finished himself off in his bunker, it sometimes seems, has a public figure been excoriated as Clinton has. Just last week, Senator Robert Byrd, heaping up damning modifiers and metaphors with a repetitiousness that betrays obsession, announced that he sought a censure that would be "indelibly seared into the ineffaceable record of history for all future generations to see and to ponder"—a condemnation that "can never be erased" and, "like the mark that was set upon Cain, it will follow even beyond the grave." And A. M. Rosenthal, outdoing in promiscuous fury even this verbal flogging, demanded, vampire-like, a judgment on Clinton that would leave a "bite mark" on him "through history." To which one can only add that if the teeth marks are Rosenthal's, poor Clinton will be at risk of rabies.

However, the main instrument of humiliation was the insistence by the House managers that the Senate either hear live witnesses or release videotapes of their depositions. Defending this demand, manager Asa Hutchinson commented that "only people who have been affected by this real-life drama, speaking from the heart," can sway the senators' "judgment." And Hutchinson's fellow manager Ed Bryant has famously declared, "Wouldn't you want to observe the demeanor of Miss Lewinsky and test her credibility? Look into her eyes?"

Did the managers unconsciously remember, perhaps, that the entire scandal began with Clinton looking into Lewinsky's eyes? Perhaps they had been afflicted by a similar longing. Like psychoanalysts, it seems, they wished to revisit—indeed, to re-enact—the scene that caused the trauma. Isn't it somehow the measure of the folly of this crisis that, in obedience to a pathology we cannot quite put our finger on, the trial perhaps cannot end until almost the entire US government—the House managers, the full Senate, the Chief Justice of the United States—has, following in the misguided, reckless footsteps of Bill Clinton, gazed into the vacant eyes of Monica Lewinsky?

NATO: AT 50, IT'S TIME TO QUIT

Benjamin Schwarz and Christopher Layne

•

THE WAR AGAINST Serbia is the Banquo's ghost of NATO's fiftieth-anniversary celebration in Washington. Disappointing partygoers and policy wonks alike, it has dampened plans for the gala (no black tie, no Barbra Streisand) and prompted the alliance to postpone decisions about new members. The war has, however, answered concretely the important issue the summit was to address: when and if the alliance would be intervening outside the territory of its members. Still, two crucial questions remain unanswered. The first—why is NATO still in business?—leads inevitably to the second—why do US policy-makers still think American leadership in Europe vital? After all, the Soviet threat has vanished, and the Western Europeans certainly have the resources to provide for their own security.

With the Warsaw Pact's collapse, both NATO and US leadership in Europe would seem to have outlived their usefulness. Yet, far from disappearing, at Washington's prompting NATO has both expanded geographically (adding Poland, Hungary and the Czech Republic) and redefined its strategic mission. The "new" NATO is being tested in Kosovo—where US and alliance officials have declared that the alliance must prevail to establish its credibility, lest a pall be cast over its golden anniversary gala. Rather than celebrating the alliance's fiftieth birthday as a prelude to NATO's second halfcentury, it is long past time for Americans to ask whether a continued US military role in Europe is either necessary or justifiable. To answer these questions, we have to examine the assumptions, spoken and otherwise, that underlie America's European strategy.

In the early cold war years, the United States, through its dominant role in NATO, assumed responsibility for defending Western Europe from the Soviet Union because immediately after World War II that area was clearly incapable of protecting itself. Yet, by the mid-sixties, the Western Europeans had staged a vigorous economic recovery, and the Soviet Union's objective in Europe was obviously to maintain, rather than overthrow, the post-1945 status quo. Indeed, even the hawkish former Reagan Administration Pentagon official Fred Ikle has suggested that any serious likelihood of Soviet aggression against Western Europe had already vanished by the end of the fifties. So why then did the United States persist in its strategy long after it was apparent that, if indeed really threatened at all, Western Europe was capable of providing for its own security? And why did the United States continue to insist—as it still does—that a US-led NATO was the indispensable foundation of any European security architecture, thus consistently blocking proposals that would have given Western Europe the responsibility for its own defense?

Although the continuity and fundamental goals of America's role in Europe are in many ways obscured by focusing on the containment of its cold war enemy, they are illuminated by examining the containment of its allies. By providing for Germany's security and by enmeshing its military and foreign policies into an alliance that it dominated, the United States contained its erst-while enemy, preventing its "partner" from embarking upon independent foreign and military policies. This stabilized relations among the states of Western Europe, for by controlling Germany, the United States—to use a current term in policy-making circles—"reassured" Germany's neighbors that they would not be threatened by the resurgence of German power (a resurgence that was necessary both to contain the Soviet Union and to insure a prosperous Western European and world economy). The leash of America's security leadership thereby reined in the dogs of war. By, in effect, banishing power politics, NATO protected the states of Western Europe from themselves.

To US policy-makers, America's "leadership" through NATO in ameliorating the security concerns of the Europeans continues to be vital despite the Soviet Union's demise. After all, the now-infamous draft of the Pentagon's 1992 "post-cold war" Defense Planning Guidance argued that the United States should still do this by "discouraging the advanced industrialized nations from challenging our leadership or even aspiring to a larger global or regional role," thereby dominating the international system.

To accomplish this, Washington must keep the former great powers of Western Europe, as well as Japan, firmly within the constraints of the US-created postwar system by providing what one of the guidance's authors terms "adult supervision." It must protect the interests of virtually all potential great powers for them so that they need not acquire the capabilities to protect themselves—that is, so that they need not act like great powers. (No wonder the United States must spend more on its "national security" than the rest of the world's countries combined.) The very existence of truly independent actors would be intolerable, for it would challenge US hegemony, which Washington says is the key to a prosperous and stable international order.

Thus, in 1990 Deputy Assistant Secretary of State for European Affairs James Dobbins—now ambassador and one of Madeleine Albright's closest advisers—explained America's post-cold war role in Europe. Testifying before Congress, Dobbins argued that "we need NATO now for the same reasons NATO was created." The danger, he asserted, was that without the "glue" of US leadership in NATO, Western Europeans would revert to their bad ways, that is, "re-nationalizing" their armed forces, playing the "old geopolitical game," and "shifting alliances." According to Dobbins, without the United States acting as the stabilizer, jockeying among the states of Western Europe would "undermine political and economic structures like the EC" and even lead to a resumption of "historic conflicts" like the two world wars. President Clinton has maintained NATO's central role, asserting that since the late forties the US-led alliance has prevented "a return to local rivalries" in Western Europe. More important, this thinking has impelled NATO's two most dangerous and controversial post—cold war actions: its eastward expansion and its interventions in the Balkans.

The argument that NATO's security umbrella must be expanded to Eastern (and now southeastern) Europe is merely an extension of the argument that the United States must provide "adult supervision" by leading in European security affairs. In the view of the proponents of NATO enlargement, if a US-dominated NATO demonstrates that it cannot or will not address the new security problems in post—cold war Europe (for instance, the "spillover" of ethnic conflict, refugee flows into Western Europe and the possibility that these could ignite ultranationalist feelings in, for example, Germany), then the alliance will be rendered impotent. Should that happen, policy-makers fear, the post-cold war continent will lapse into the same old power politics that the alliance was supposed to suppress, shattering economic and political cooperation in Western Europe.

So, as Senator Richard Lugar—the leading Republican foreign policy spokesman—has argued, since European stability is now threatened by "those areas in the east and south where the seeds of future conflict in Europe lie," the US-led NATO must stabilize both halves of the continent. The important point is that the logic of US global strategy does indeed dictate that the US-led NATO move eastward. While NATO expansion is often described as a "new bargain," it is in fact only the latest investment, made necessary by changing geopolitical circumstances, in a pursuit begun long ago. Since the logic of US policy won't allow America's Western European "partners" to assume responsibility for stabilizing their own neighborhood, US responsibilities must multiply. As Lugar explained, "The only mechanism capable of this task is NATO; not the European Community, not CSCE, not the WEU. . . . if NATO does not deal with the security problems of its members, they will ultimately seek to deal with these problems either in new alliances or on their own." This thinking leads inevitably to dangerously open-ended commitments.

Military involvement in Kosovo—or someplace like it—was foreshadowed by NATO expansion. As Deputy Secretary of State Strobe Talbott stated in arguing the case for an enlarged NATO, "The lesson of the tragedy in the former Yugoslavia is not to retire NATO in disgrace but to develop its ability to counter precisely those forces that have exploded in the Balkans."

And as NATO's war against Serbia demonstrates, there is no logical stopping point for US commitments in Europe according to the calculus driving America's European strategy. For example, now that Poland, Hungary and the Czech Republic have been admitted to NATO, instability arising in the regions to the east of the expanded alliance will threaten those states and ultimately Western Europe, or so it will inevitably be argued. The need to defend already extant security interests will be invoked to support subsequent enlargement, thus incurring new strategic responsibilities for the alliance and entangling it even more deeply in a geopolitically volatile region. After all, Lugar argues that the US-led NATO must "go out of area" because "there can be no lasting security at the center without security at the periphery." Of course, to follow this logic means that the ostensible threats to US security will be nearly endless.

American policy-makers believe that perpetuating US hegemony in Europe (and globally) will enhance US security and maintain stability on the continent. But this belief rests on a misreading of history's lessons and betrays a naïveté about the nature of international relations. This is especially apparent with respect to Washington's relations with Moscow, which have been badly damaged by NATO expansion and by the US-led intervention in Kosovo. American policy-makers can tell Moscow that it should not perceive US policies as a threat. But in a "unipolar" world—today's world in which the United States is the only great power—it should come as no surprise that Russia (and others) assign more weight to America's unchecked power than to its assurances that it doesn't constitute a threat to any other state.

Hidden by all the lofty (and misleading) rhetoric about NATO and transatlantic partnership is a simple fact: US policy in Europe aims not to counter others' bids for hegemony but to perpetuate America's own supremacy. American policy-makers seem not to understand that while hegemons love themselves, other states inevitably fear them and therefore form alliances to balance against them. Russia, the state most obviously threatened by US policy in Europe, has responded predictably, countering NATO expansion by bolstering its security ties with Belarus and Iran in an attempt to create counterweights to an expanded, US-led alliance. More ominously for the longer term, NATO expansion has provoked a strategic rapprochement between the Russians and Chinese, based on their anxiety about a world dominated by a single great power—the United States. And as the Kosovo conflict has deepened, Moscow's concerns about NATO action in a historically Russian sphere of influence have, of course, only intensified. Over time, NATO expansion could provoke the very Russian threat it ostensibly seeks to deter. Indeed, NATO expansion may prove to be a diplomatic blunder on a par with the 1919 Versailles Treaty, which, by humiliating Germany, fanned the flames of German revanchism and sowed the seeds for Hitler and World War II.

Forty-nine years ago the French commentator J. J. Servan Schreiber defined America's role in Europe: "When a nation bears the responsibility for the military security and the economic stability of a geographic zone, that nation is in fact—whether it wants it or not—the head of an empire." Fifty years after NATO's founding, as the post–cold war alliance finds itself at war, the time has come to reassess US imperial policy in Europe.

The war in Yugoslavia is a watershed in NATO's history. Today, the

United States has expanded the alliance's geographical scope and created a new role for it: intervention in the internal affairs of sovereign states whose domestic policies offend NATO's "values"—even when such states pose no security threat to the alliance's partners. If the United States is to avoid the risks and costs that inevitably accompany defending and expanding imperial frontiers, then a new debate must begin. Rather than focus on such narrow issues as the proper military "burden sharing" formula for the United States and its allies, this debate must assess underlying assumptions; it must stop revolving around how the Pax Americana should be administered and instead examine whether there should be a Pax Americana at all.

Arguing for the maintenance of Washington's leftover "cold war" alliances, a high-ranking Pentagon official asked, "If we pull out, who knows what nervousness will result?" The problem is, we can never know, so, according to this logic, we must always stay. Instead of persisting in this open-ended, permanent and hazardous imperial policy, we should finally, fully and in an orderly way devolve to a thriving and democratic Europe the task of insuring its own stability and prosperity. In the West European Union, Western Europe possesses an embryonic strategic identity, and the European Union is committed to implementing a unified, independent foreign and security policy. To be sure, many US policy-makers have argued that in the Balkan crises Western Europeans have demonstrated that they are incapable of acting effectively without US "leadership." But these protests are hypocritical—who can blame the Europeans for their inability to assert themselves in security affairs when Washington has for decades repeatedly squelched European initiatives that would have made that assertion possible?

It's time to stop infantilizing our "partners." Such astute US statesmen as Kennan, Marshall, Eisenhower and Fulbright did not intend for NATO to establish a permanent US protectorate over the continent, and they worried that if it became permanent, the US presence would have the ironic consequence of under-mining the emergence of an independent Western Europe. A decade after the cold war's end, the continuing US military preponderance on the continent is doing just that, and thereby crippling the sine qua non of a healthy transatlantic relationship in the twenty-first century. America's strategic interest in Europe does not demand that it insure against every untoward event there.

Certainly, disorder in Kosovo and other places on Europe's fringes should be a matter for Europeans, who have the where-withal and the maturity to combat it, quarantine it or, if they choose, ignore it. Western Europe today is capable of standing on its own and looking after itself. If it is in Western Europe's interest—and America's—that it do so.

UNFINISHED BUSINESS
CLINTON'S LOST PRESIDENCY

William Greider

•

AS HE TRAVELS around the country, musing aloud on his hopes for the future, Bill Clinton inspires an unintended melancholy about his presidency. He has big dreams for the country, bold convictions about reforming this and that, and he states them passionately, as always. He wants to bring Americans together. He embraces "fair trade" for the global economy and insists it can be reconciled with "free trade." He worries about global warming and warms that America must confront the problem, and that it can by employing already available technologies.

Last summer, Clinton chose the University of Chicago, mother church of laissez-faire economics, as the place to deliver a cogent rebuttal to Milton Friedman's utopian claim that an unfettered marketplace governs best. The free market, Clinton argued, needs strong social institutions to thrive—"a legal framework of mutual responsibility and social safety."

"All of us know that the problem with the new global economy is that it is both more rewarding and more destructive," Clinton told the graduates. "So the question is, how can we create a global economy with a human face—one that rewards work everywhere, one that gives all people a chance to improve their lot and still raise their families in dignity, and supports communities that are coming together, not being torn apart?" The media largely ignored his remarks, and why not? Clinton, as President, consigned the malfunctioning global economy to the reform energies of the Business Roundtable and Wall Street. His Administration led cheers for multinational commerce, opened fragile economies to the manic surges of global capital and created the World Trade Organization to judge whether new social standards are, in fact, barriers to trade and therefore forbidden.

When Bill Clinton recites the big challenges, he reminds us of all he danced away from as President. The spirited reformer is the young man we met back in 1992, brimming with big ideas, but he is utterly unconvincing now. One feels sadness for the lost promise of this extraordinarily skillful politician. One also suspects that Clinton is trying to revise the public memory of his presidency, polishing his reformer image so that when future President actually do take up these big ideas and confront the challenges, he will be able to claim parentage. Clinton has taught Democrats to think small. And it works as politics in this media age, given his talent for emotive communication. Republicans are learning from him too, smoothing over their big ideas with more charm, less snarl. Clinton's many retreats from large purpose—accompanied always by small, symbolic gestures—were supposed to restore faith in government, bit by bit, and raise public expectations for genuine action. Instead, his political success has deepened the skepticism. For the cynical and disengaged, he confirms their assumption that politics is not real. For idealistic young people, who feel Clinton did the best he could, the message is that large ideas are simply impossible to achieve in this era.

Clinton's shrewd politics did lead the Democratic Party onto new ground, but it looks like a trap. When the President was elected in 1992, the Democrats had fifty-seven senators; now they have forty-five. They controlled Congress, with a House majority of 266; now they have a minority of 211. They held twenty-eight governorships and a majority of state legislatures; now Democrats have seventeen governors and a minority of the state assemblies. Republicans have their own problems in establishing a stable majority, but for the moment, their guy is running ahead in presidential polls despite a glowing prosperity that ought to insure easy victory for White House Democrats.

The "New Democrat" straddle—the money comes from business and finance, the votes from ordinary people—worked for Clinton, but it is a cul-de-sac for the party that claims to speak for the working class and poor, that built its reputation by leading bravely on the toughest questions of reform. The Clinton success actually confines Election

2000, limiting what his party's candidates can say and think. One important subtext of this election is whether the Democrats will find a way out of the dilemma or simply become smaller in number, weaker in purpose.

While the good times roll forward with a general sense of rising prosperity, it is impossible for any Democrat to speak bluntly, honestly, about the true nature of the Clinton legacy. Clinton's robust approval ratings reflect the supposed triumph of his economics, and his party's main voting constituencies still support him. An old friend, a liberal labor lawyer who now works on the other side of the street, summarized the Democrats' predicament: "Clinton made a deal with the devil, and the devil kept his part of the bargain—low unemployment and good times."

The deal with the devil required Clinton to keep his mouth shut while a conservative Federal Reserve ran the economy, with a cautious foot on the brake during most of the decade. The Administration, meanwhile, devoted itself to a doctrine of fiscal rectitude, balancing the federal budget. The President embraced major objectives of big business and finance as his own—promoting globalization, further deregulation, the managerial values of efficiency and continued shredding of the old social contract. Leave aside the arguments over whether politics and historic developments made this course unavoidable. The logical results of these policy choices were never a mystery: They would encourage deepening inequality in both wealth and wages and steady concentration of power for corporations and finance. And that is what occurred, probably more dramatically than Clinton envisioned.

That outcome describes the Clinton legacy. Rather than bring Americans together, his presidency deepened the economic fault line that separates the many from the few. Bottom line: The folks who twice supported him for President are worse off in fundamental terms, despite the currently improving conditions. The median family income did not get back to its 1989 level until 1998 (a slower postrecession recovery of lost ground than occurred in the Reagan years). Real wages for nonsupervisory production workers remain at early seventies levels. The maldistribution of wealth—ownership of property and financial assets—has accelerated; its impact is reflected in the negative savings rate for households. In these best of all possible times, how come typical Americans are still spending more than they earn to keep up?

Recent headlines, based on the Federal Reserve's new survey of family finances, heralded the robust 17 percent increase in the median net worth of US households, driven mainly by booming stock prices from

1995 to 1998. The real news in the study is not so cheerful: Among families in debt, median outstanding debt also grew in the same period by an astonishing 42 percent and is now 73 percent above a decade earlier. Alas, the statistical medians are deeply misleading because the people with surging financial assets are generally not the same people who have surging debts.

Under closer scrutiny, the Fed statistics confirm the widespread anxieties felt by the broad middle class, not to mention the poor. Since Clinton was first elected in 1992, every income class except families earning $100,000 or more has experienced a worsening ratio of debt payments to income. One-fifth to one-third of the families earning less than $25,000 are in real trouble—40 percent of their income is now owed in debt. "If events are sufficiently contrary to their assumptions," the survey dryly observes, "the resulting defaults might induce restraint in spending and a broader pattern of financial distress in the economy." That sounds like Fedspeak for "look out below!"

The supposed democratization of wealth in the stock market is utter myth—and another trap for anxious families living beyond their means. Edward Wolff of New York University explains the illusion in a forthcoming article for The Century Foundation, "Why Stocks Won't Save the Middle Class." What occurred, he says, is that families typically shifted modest nest eggs from bank savings accounts to mutual funds, so the number of families owning stock did indeed rise steadily, to 49 percent. Nevertheless, most families own very few shares or none. Wolff found that among the bottom three quintiles of the population, as of 1997, only about 25 percent own any stock at all. And only 6–7 percent of them own more than $10,000. The new Fed study may improve these numbers slightly, he said, but not enough to change the big picture. Despite the boom, rising wages and lower unemployment, the middle class is still digging a deeper hole for itself.

If this had occurred under a Republican President, Democrats would be howling righteously about the inequities, as they did when a very similar shift in income shares and wealth occurred during the Reagan/Bush years and for approximately the same reasons. Professor Wolff offers straightforward suggestions about how government could begin correcting the imbalances—a modest tax on wealth, restoration of much steeper progressivity to income-tax rates and reduction of the Social Security payroll tax, which is very regressive, since it exempts all income above $76,200 and imposes the greatest tax burden for most working Americans. Does anyone imagine the Democratic nominee will espouse any of those ideas?

Clinton's confinement of the Democrats is reflected in what Al Gore and Bill Bradley have to say about the middle-class predicament, which is very little at all. How can they raise these unpleasant facts without disparaging their very popular leader or sounding skeptical about the good times so many are enjoying? Bradley does deserve credit for attempting to break free of the fiscal bondage that Clinton has devised—the President's very conservative, even reactionary, posture that fiscal surpluses must be devoted to paying down the federal debt, not for new spending of any consequence. Even Bradley's healthcare plan is framed in the language of noblesse oblige—extending a hand to unfortunates—but does not question the underlying economics that strand working people. Bradley is silent on the fundamentals driving the maldistribution and eroding middle-class security. Gore's economic utterances are even more opaque—a neo-Calvinist mush that enshrines fiscal order above all else. He attacks Bradley as a liberal spendthrift. He promises he will raise taxes only if a recession develops and threatens the precious balanced budget. Raising taxes in a recession is upside-down Keynes—the "root canal" economics reminiscent of Hoover and Coolidge. Even Republican economists now recognize that it's wrongheaded economic doctrine as well as heartless. One hopes Gore is insincere or merely confused.

Has the Democratic Party traded places with Republicans on these central issues of economic policy? Not entirely, but as I have written before, Clinton did essentially govern like a moderate Republican. His accomplishments, when the sentimental gestures are set aside, are indistinguishable from George Bush's. Like Bush, Clinton increased the top income tax rate a bit, raised the minimum wage modestly and expanded tax credits for the working poor. He reduced military spending somewhat but, like Bush, failed to restructure the military for post-cold war realities. He got tough on crime, especially drug offenders, and built many more prisons. He championed educational reform. He completed the North American Free Trade Agreement, which was mainly negotiated by the Bush Administration. On these and other matters, one can fairly say that Clinton completed Bush's agenda. It is not obvious that a Democratic successor in the White House would be much different.

Defenders of Clinton will protest that I am ignoring the harsh political context Clinton faced—the brutally hostile right-wing opposition he outmaneuvered. His greatest accomplishment, it is true, was to stymie Newt Gingrich's half-baked "revolution" and to defuse many of the powder-keg issues Republicans have employed for decades (crime is down, the welfare queen got a job). His success at this has left Republicans with fewer hot buttons to push, so this year their moderates are staging a comeback. The Clinton style may work less well for Democrats if the opponent is not flaming Newt but a pleasant guy who talks compassion or worries aloud about the folks who've been left behind.

Clinton's cultural sensibilities, as opposed to his economics, are genuinely liberal (though he would never use that word), and his faithfulness to social issues like abortion and gay rights further inflamed the right wing's hatred of him. Their blind enmity led them into the sorry spectacle of impeachment, which, for Democrats, was powerfully unifying (and also self-blinding in its way). Clinton did advance controversial social positions, though usually in a self-protecting manner that was less than courageous. Lani Guinier was dumped as too radical after the Wall Street Journal published a maliciously erroneous polemic. Dr. Joycelyn Elders got sacked for announcing that teenagers masturbate. Belatedly, the President does agree now that "don't ask, don't tell" is a failed policy for gays in the armed forces, but he blames the military for its lack of cooperation. When Harry Truman abolished racial segregation in the armed forces, he did not ask the generals and admirals, the sergeants and corporals, if they thought it would be OK.

The problem with Clinton's rope-a-dope style of leadership is that it rewards the opponents for their opposition. The deeper they dig in, the more likely he will back off, postpone action to the indefinite future or invent clever diversions that essentially co-opt the other side's position (his "victory" on welfare reform confounded many conservatives too thickheaded to see that they had won). Clinton's big retreats from party ideals were seen as smart tactical moves, and they often were. But they also became the new starting line for the Democratic Party. Like Bradley, I find myself feeling nostalgia for the stubborn clarity of Ronald Reagan—a leader who believed in a few big things, who repeated them endlessly, never backed off and never admitted defeat, though he frequently lost. The Gipper accomplished great forward progress for his way of thinking.

Clinton instead has talked romantically about a far horizon of progress, then backed away from the messy political conflicts that might actually move the country toward it. The most serious omissions of his presidency define his failure, but are not even talked about in this campaign because he never took up the fight for them. He leaves no legacy on a lot of tough issues, except that he ducked.

Clinton, for example, saved himself a lot of grief by not taking on the military-industrial complex. He simply mimicked Bush's post-cold war defense strategy—the silly doctrine of preparing to fight two wars at once, the occasional violence of cruise-missile diplomacy and selected expeditionary adventures in behalf of humanity. By co-opting the hawks, Clinton wound up on their side. He too wants to build the destabilizing and vastly expensive missile-defense system. If the F-22 or other unneeded new weapons systems are canceled, it will be done by defense-minded Republicans fighting over scarce dollars, not by this President. Clinton's answer to the impossible desires of the arms industry is to propose an astounding increase of $110 billion in the Pentagon budget (this exception to fiscal rectitude is embraced by Gore too).

Do Democrats have an alternative vision for maintaining peace in the post-cold war world? If so, we are not likely to hear about it during this campaign, since the GOP has already moved the goal posts, insisting that even more money be devoted to this bizarre military remobilization in the midst of peace. The Clinton team faced a great moment in history without a coherent vision of how the world might look, now that superpower rivalry was behind us. They opted to continue the status quo, drifting into a dangerous role as "good guy" empire.

To be fair, Clinton was not alone. The country at large didn't want to hear any more about defense issues, and establishment circles were also bereft of new ideas, unable to grasp the great possibilities for reviving a different kind of internationalism, one that is closer to American ideals than massive overseas military deployments and occasional interventions. Reviving or inventing genuine international mechanisms for world peace is a challenge left to future Presidents. To appreciate the scale of the neglected opportunities, think of American leadership at the end of World War II, when the United Nations, the Marshall Plan and the Bretton Woods agreement were invented and launched.

Another great failure of omission that will haunt the next President, no matter who wins, is Clinton's retreat from the central challenge of global warming. After the Kyoto Protocol was signed in 1997, Clinton signaled to the opposition—major industrial sectors and their conservative allies in Congress—that he was not prepared to fight them on this ground either. Instead, he promised he would propose nothing on the legislative front until after Congress ratifies the Kyoto agreement— a cute stratagem that let both sides accept a temporary truce. When opponents are strong and determined, Clinton goes limp. But for status quo interests in Washington, any delay is always a victory. The politics of global warming were always bound to be very difficult, and whatever Clinton proposed might well have been rejected. But that's nearly always the case with important environmental battles, as the Natural Resources Defense Council's David Hawkins, a thirty-year veteran of these struggles, reminded me. It took nearly ten years to enact the 1990 Clean Air Act, Hawkins recalled, but it would have taken even longer if the advocates hadn't started pushing the fight during the early Reagan years. By forcing senators to vote up or down on acid rain, even when the legislation seemed doomed, the environmental reformers also compelled senators to feel the heat back home at the next election. Forcing accountability and educating voters is how they eventually built a majority for passage.

The first rule of politics, Hawkins explained, is that you can never win a fight until you start a fight. Reagan and like-minded conservatives evidently understood this rule too. The scale of Clinton's failure will eventually be determined by whether Democrats rediscover, once this President has retired, that fighting for big ideas that seem hopeless can be the smartest politics in the long run.

The big money owns Election 2000 so far. That could change in the coming months, but right now it's reflected in the emptiness of what candidates from both parties have to say about the American condition. The most pernicious influence of big money is not the repeated scandals in which contributors buy politicians, quid pro quo. The far graver damage from relying on major corporations or wealth holders to finance candidates in both parties is how this automatically keeps provocative, new ideas off the table—effectively vetoed even before the public can hear about them.

Money doesn't just talk in politics, it also silences. Another old friend, a skilled and successful campaign consultant, explained it for me some years ago. "It costs so much to get elected and reelected," he said, "that the system inhibits anyone from taking positions that will be too controversial and will make it more difficult to raise money. Do people in a campaign say that directly? No. What they say is: 'What's the responsible position on this issue?' That's a code word for fundraising. Even when it's not consciously used as a code word, that's the effect." My old friend is working this year for Gore. Clinton didn't invent the Democrats' dependency on the moneyed interests alien to his party's core constituencies (back in the eighties, the architect for House Democrats was Representative Tony Coelho of California, who this year is Gore's campaign chairman). Clinton did, however, elaborate money politics in shrewd new ways. Early in his presidency, when Democrats still controlled Congress and could have enacted genuine campaign-finance reform, Clinton took a pass. Then, in 1995–96, he blew out the gaskets: The White House raised a fortune in uncontrolled soft-money gifts, then used it to manipulate the public mood with a torrent of artful attack ads. Though the legality was arguable, nobody went to jail. This year, Republicans are cheerfully emulating Clinton's strategy, piling up millions for payback time. Democrats lamely complain that the GOP is trying to buy the election.

While there are many other contributing factors, money politics helps to explain why presidential elections are no longer very convincing. Choosing a new leader for the nation was once the most absorbing drama of American democracy, but the process is now caught in a spiral of declining legitimacy. Neither major party seems able to speak plainly, convincingly, on fundamental matters that distress Americans, in part because both parties depend upon the same galaxy of contributors to finance their candidates. Real differences endure, of course, but money makes it increasingly risky for any candidate who thinks anew and outside the accepted boundaries (unless the candidate happens to be rich as Croesus and finances himself).

So as more voters turn away from the empty talk, the voting electorate gradually shrinks further (fewer than half of eligible adults voted in 1996). The question of legitimacy is so obvious that major foundations are spending millions on promoting marginal reforms, especially on educating the populace about why politics and elections should matter to them. The real problem, I suspect, is that many citizens already know too much.

Eccentric new figures like Ross Perot and Jesse Ventura do succeed in drawing voters back into the electoral process—including young voters—but their populist message also threatens established power and allied institutions. So both major parties, aided by the big media, do whatever they can to discourage the intruders, either by ignoring their ideas, ridiculing them or making sure outsiders are excluded from prime-time venues where their irregular views might be widely heard. New voices are blocked out, the old ones given preferred status—this describes the closed circle that is slowly devouring electoral democracy.

It works for the major parties, if not for the country. Incumbents have learned how to live comfortably with a shrinking electorate (witness how very few Congressional seats are genuinely contested this year). Most incumbents are sustained not by building authentic relationships with citizens but by maintaining intimacy with the sources of big money. Outsiders with different ideas—whether it's Pat Buchanan, Donald Trump or Ralph Nader—will be present to leaven the public's interest in Election 2000, but conscientious voters will face the same dispiriting choice: Do they vote their anger at the status quo or do they go along with a disappointing major-party nominee to avoid getting something worse? Making people choose between anger and disillusionment probably feeds the downward spiral.

Clinton, one recalls, never achieved a clear majority in his two presidential races. He always governed with the voting support of less than 25 percent of the adult population. Democracy itself is threatened by this decline, but without some sort of earth-shaking calamity, war or economic breakdown that might inspire popular rebellion, it's hard to imagine that established power centers will relax their hold over the political dialogue. In the long run, the party of Jefferson and Jackson seems especially vulnerable in this shrinking democracy, since Republicans are traditionally the party of money and Democrats must keep moving rightward to match the fundraising, farther away from their historic base.

I once believed that if the Democratic Party lost Congress and the White House it might feel compelled to return to its core values, launch a popular mobilization and take on the big-money interests. The party does have an aggressive core of young new members and old liberal stalwarts who would gladly attempt this, but they are a minority within a minority and are confined by the usual problems of raising money and appealing to a mass-market audience that barely pays attention to politics. After watching how Clinton's straddle succeeded, I am no longer so sure what the party would choose to do.

This will sound corny—hopelessly romantic about America—but I am convinced that a general renewal of democracy (and the Democratic Party) will begin with the people, if it begins at all. That is, one political party or the other must decide to devote some portion of its gigantic cash flow to the unglamorous challenge of reconnecting with citizens at large—not through more opinion polls and focus groups but through listening and teaching, by discussing patiently the large and small priorities that matter to people where they live, by organizing forums where people can learn the facts and respectfully argue out the plausible public solutions. The organizing approach—reviving small-d relationships with ordinary people, patiently, from the grassroots upward—sounds anachronistic in this media age. It's slow and much less certain than designing smart TV commercials, fiendishly more difficult than raising money from a comparatively small number of phone calls to fat cats. Perhaps it is unrealistic to expect either major party to risk its entrenched position by actually encouraging popular intrusion into the closed circle that protects incumbents. Possibly only a new third party with strong convictions, whose leaders have nothing to lose, could be bold enough to attempt such an old-fashioned approach—inviting folks back into a politics that is real.

Yet, if you look around the country, you can see this sort of thing happening now among citizens themselves, people of left and right or neither persuasion. They are trying to reknit the torn fabric of their communities, mobilize a genuine consensus for public action or demand a real voice in governing power. This kind of politics goes forward with real successes, largely beneath the radar of the big media and usually without the least bit of help from organized politics. When it accomplishes something tangible, people can see the connections to their own lives, and their organizations grow stronger. This brand of politics, to borrow a popular phrase, is market-tested.

By comparison, Election 2000 already looks like a failed brand of soap, since so many Americans aren't buying any of it. Restoring credible accountability in the representative system, from the ground up, is the long way back to a robust democracy, for sure. But don't dismiss it as impossible. Leaving aside the fools and scoundrels, of whom there are many, the great saving virtue of Americans is that they do not always believe what they are told by the authorities. Sometimes, they still find their way to the truth about things, despite the media's opacity and the blanket of propaganda for the status quo. When they do figure things out for themselves, Americans sometimes still get real ornery about it.

CONTRIBUTORS

Eric Alterman is a columnist for *The Nation*, MSNBC and a senior fellow of the World Policy Institute. He is the author of three books, *Sound and Fury: The Washington Punditocracy and the Collapse of American Politics*; *Who Speaks for America? Why Democracy Matters in Foreign Policy*; and *It Ain't No Sin To Be Glad You're Alive: The Promise of Bruce Springsteen*.

Frank Bardacke is a bilingual educator, community and labor activist based in Watsonville, California. He was one of the Oakland Seven acquitted after a 1967 Stop the Draft demonstration and an organizer for Teamsters for a Democratic Union. He is the author of *Good Liberals and Great Blue Herons: Land, Labor and Politics in the Pajaro Valley* and one of the translators of *Shadows of Tender Fury: The Letters and Communiqués of Subcomandante Marcos and the Zapatista Army of National Liberation*.

Marshall Berman is a Professor of Political Science at City University of New York and the author of *All That Is Solid Melts Into Air* and *Adventures in Marxism*. His articles have appeared in *Dissent*, *New Left Review*, *New York Times* and *Village Voice*.

Carol Brightman is the author of *Writing Dangerously: Mary McCarthy and Her World*, which won a National Book Critics Circle Award for Biography, and the editor of *Between Friends: The Correspondence of Hannah Arendt and Mary McCarthy*. She is the recipient of an American Academy of Arts and Letters Award in Literature. Her latest book is *Sweet Chaos: The Grateful Dead's American Adventure*.

Benjamin Cheever is the author of *The Plagiarist*; and *The Partisan* (Editor's Choice of the New York Times Best Books of 1994); and *Famous After Death*. A former editor at *Reader's Digest*, he has written for the *New York Times* and *The New Yorker*. He edited *The Letters of John Cheever*.

Stephen F. Cohen is Professor of Russian Studies and History at New York University, Professor of Politics Emeritus at Princeton University, and a *Nation* contributing editor. He is the author of *Bukharin and The Russian Revolution*; *Rethinking the Soviet Experience*; and *Sovieticus*, which was based on his "Sovieticus" columns published in *The Nation* in the 1980s, and the forthcoming *Failed Crusade: America and The Tragedy of Post-Communist Russia*.

Alexander Cockburn, *The Nation*'s "Beat the Devil" columnist, wrote for many years for *The Village Voice*. He has contributed to *The New York Review of Books, Harper's, The Atlantic* and *The Wall Street Journal*, and contributes a nationally syndicated column to the *Los Angeles Times* and the "Wild Justice" column for the *New York Press*. He has published two essay collections, *Corruptions of Empire* and *The Golden Age Is In Us*, co-wrote, with Susanna Hecht, *The Fate of the Forest: Developers, Destroyers, and Defenders of the Amazon*, and with Ken Silverstein, *Washington Babylon*. Cockburn also co-edits the newsletter "CounterPunch" with Jeffrey St. Clair with whom he wrote his recent book, *White Out: The CIA, Drugs and the Press*.

Marc Cooper has covered politics and culture for dozens of publications ranging from *Playboy* and *Rolling Stone* to the Sunday magazines of the *Los Angeles Times* and *The Times* of London. His work is collected in *Roll over Che Guevara: Travels of a Radical Reporter*. He is currently host and executive producer of *The Nation*'s syndicated weekly radio show, *Radio Nation*, and a *Nation* contributing editor.

David Corn, Washington editor of *The Nation*, has contributed articles to the *Washington Post*, the *New York Times*, the *Los Angeles Times*, the *Philadelphia Inquirer*, the *Boston Globe, Newsday, Harper's The New Republic, Mother Jones, Washington Monthly, The Village Voice* and many other publications. He also contributes a weekly column on national politics—"Loyal Opposition"—to the

New York Press. He is the author of *Blond Ghost: Ted Shackley and the CIA's Crusades* and a novel, *Deep Background*, a political thriller.

Arthur C. Danto is the Johnsonian Emeritus Professor of Philosophy at Columbia University. Since 1984, he has been art critic for *The Nation*, and in addition to his many books on philosophy, he has published several collections of art criticism, including *Encounters and Reflections: Art in the Historical Present*, which won the National Book Critics Circle Award for Criticism; and *Beyond the Brillo Box: The Visual Arts in Post-Historical Perspective.*

Mike Davis, who has taught urban theory at the Southern California Institute of Architecture, has been a Getty Institute fellow, a MacArthur Fellow and is now a Professor of History at SUNY, Stony Brook. He is the author of *Prisoners of the American Dream*; *City of Quartz*; and *Ecologies of Fear.* He is a *Nation* contributing editor.

E. L. Doctorow is a best-selling novelist and winner of the National Book Award. His novels, many of which have been filmed, include *The Book of Daniel*; *Loon Lake*; *Ragtime*; *Billy Bathgate*; and *The Waterworks.*

Slavenka Drakulić, a *Nation* contributing editor, has covered the Balkans for the magazine since the late nineteen-eighties. She is the author or *Balkan Express*; *Café Europa: Life After Communism*; *How We Survived Communism and Even Laughed*; *Marble Skin: A Novel* and *The Taste of a Man.*

Martin Duberman is Distinguished Professor of History at Lehman College and the Graduate School of the City University of New York, where he was the founder and first director of the Center for Lesbian and Gay Studies, the country's first such research center. He is the author and editor of some twenty books, including *Paul Robeson*; *Stonewall*; and *Left Out: The Politics of Exclusion/Essays/1964–1999.*

Gerald Early is the Director of the African and Afro-American studies program at Washington University in St. Louis. He is the author of *One Nation Under a Groove: Motown and American Culture*, *Tuxedo Junction*, a collection of essays on American culture, and

The Culture of Bruising: Essays on Prizefighting. He is the editor of *"Aint but a Place": An Anthology of African American Writings About St. Louis*; *The Muhammad Ali Reader*; and *Lure and Loathing: Essays on Race, Identity and the Ambivalence of Assimilation*.

Tom Engelhardt is a consulting editor at Metropolitan Books and author of *The End of Victory Culture* and co-editor of *History Wars: The Enola Gay and Other Battles for the American Past*.

Barbara Ehrenreich's articles have appeared in *The New York Times Magazine*, *The Washington Post Magazine*, *Esquire*, *The Atlantic Monthly*, *Harper's*, *The New Republic*, *Social Policy*, *Vogue*, *TV Guide* and *The Wall Street Journal*. Her books include *Blood Rites*; *The Snarling Citizen*; *The Worst Years of Our Lives: Irreverent Notes From a Decade of Greed*; *Fear of Falling: The Inner Life of the Middle Class*; and *The Hearts of Men: American Dreams and the Flight from Commitment*. She is a National Magazine Award winner.

Susan Faludi is a Pulitzer Prize-winning journalist and author of *Backlash: The Undeclared War Against American Women*, which won the 1992 National Book Critics Circle award for nonfiction and remained on *The New York Times* bestseller list for six months. Her latest book is *Stiffed: The Betrayal of the American Man*.

Eric Foner is DeWitt Clinton Professor of History at Columbia University, President of the American Historical Association and a member of *The Nation's* Editorial Board. He is the author of *Reconstruction: America's Unfinished Revolution, 1863–1877*; *Free Soil, Free Labor, Free Men: The Ideology of the Republican Party Before the Civil War*; and *The Story of American Freedom*.

Tom Frank is co-founder and editor-in-chief of *The Baffler*, the author of *The Conquest of Cool* and co-editor of *Commodify Your Dissent: Salvos from the Baffler*.

Carlos Fuentes is a novelist and writer based in Mexico. Among his many works are *The Death of Artemio Cruz*; *The Buried Mirror: Reflections on Spain and the New World*; *The Death of Artemio Cruz*; *Diana: The Goddess Who Hunts Alone*; and *The Old Gringo*.

Eduardo Galeano is a Uruguayan writer, reporter and novelist whose works include the trilogy *Memory of Fire: The Book of Embraces*; *Walking Words*; *Open Veins of Latin America: Five Centuries of the Pillage of a Continent*; *Days and Nights of Love and War*; *We Say No: Chronicles 1963–1991*; and his study/memoir about soccer, *Soccer in Sun and Shadow*.

Allen Ginsberg, with the publication of *Howl* in 1956, put Beat poetry on the map internationally. His other collections include *Kaddish*; *Mind Breaths*; *Cosmopolitan Greetings*; *Death and Fame*; and *Reality Sandwiches*. He died in 1997.

Philip Green is Emeritus Sophia Smith Professor of Government at Smith College. He is the author of several books, including *Deadly Logic: The Theory of Nuclear Deterrence*; *The Pursuit of Inequality*; and *Equality and Democracy*. He is a member of *The Nation's* editorial board.

William Grieder recently joined *The Nation* as its National Affairs correspondent. For seventeen years he was national Affairs Editor at *Rolling Stone* magazine. He was also an assistant managing editor at the *Washington Post* and has served as correspondent for six Frontline documentaries, including "Return to Beirut," which won an Emmy in 1985. He is the author of *One World, Ready or Not*; *Secrets of the Temple*; *Who Will Tell The People*; and *Fortress America: The American Military and the Consequences of Peace*.

Christopher Hitchens, a longtime contributor to *The Nation*, has been a columnist for the magazine since 1982. He is also a columnist for *Vanity Fair*. His books include *Blood, Class and Nostalgia: Anglo-American Ironies*, two collections including many *Nation* essays: *Prepared for the Worst* and *For the Sake of Argument: Essays & Minority Reports*; *The Missionary Position: Mother Teresa in Theory and Practice*, and the *New York Times* bestseller *No One Left to Lie To: The Triangulations of William Jefferson Clinton*.

Eric Hobsbawm is Emeritus Professor of History at Birbeck College, London, and is the author of a series of radical historical overviews of the last two centuries: *Age of Revolution*; *Age of*

Capital; *Age of Empire*; and *Age of Extremes*. His other works include *Nations and Nationalism Since 1780: Program, Myth, Reality*; *Bandits*; and (co-edited with Terence Ranger) *The Invention of Tradition*.

Molly Ivins, a *Nation* contributing editor, is a columnist for the *Fort Worth Star-Telegram*, where she writes about Texas politics and other bizarre happenings. Her column is nationally syndicated in nearly two hundred newspapers. Her books include *Molly Ivins Can't Say That, Can She?*; *You Got to Dance With Them What Brung You: Politics in the Clinton Years*; *Nothing but Good Times Ahead*, and *Shrub: The Short but Happy Life of George W. Bush* (with Lou Dubose).

Mary Kaldor is the Program Director of the Center for Global Governance at the London School of Economics. She has been the co-chair of the Helsinki Citizens' Assembly. Her books include *New and Old Wars: Organized Violence in a Global Era*; *The Baroque Arsenal*; *The Disintegrating West*; and The *Imaginary War: Understanding the East–West Conflict*.

Stuart Klawans, besides writing a regular column for *The Nation*, has contributed to the *Times Literary Supplement* ("American Notes" column), *New York Daily News* ("Museums" column), NPR (commentaries on *Fresh Air*), *The Village Voice, Grand Street, Threepenny Review, Entertainment Weekly*, WBAI (film reviews on "Soundtrack"), the *Chicago Tribune* and *The New York Times*. He is the author of *Film Follies: Cinema Out of Order*, which was recently nominated for the National Book Critic's Circle Award.

Andrew Kopkind joined *The Nation* in 1982, where he was an associate editor and senior political writer until his death in 1994. While reporting for *The New Republic* in the 1960s he introduced SNCC and SDS to a national audience, as well as covering the emerging Black power movement, the counterculture and anti-Vietnam protests. He was also the *New Statesman's* U.S. correspondent during this period. In the 1970s he produced, with John Scagliotti, "The Lavender Hour," the first gay and lesbian variety program on American commercial radio. His essays are collected in *The Thirty Years' War: Dispatches and Diversions of a Radical Journalist 1965–1994*.

Tony Kushner won both the Pulitzer Prize and the Tony Award for his play cycle *Angels in America*. His other plays include *Slavs! Thinking About the Longstanding Problems of Virtue and Happiness*; *A Bright Room Called Day*; *The Illusion*; *Reverse Transcription*; and *Hydriotaphia*.

Ring Lardner, Jr., a novelist and screenwriter, was one of the Hollywood Ten. He is author of the novel *The Ecstasy of Owen Muir*, and his screenwriting credits include *M*A*S*H* and *The Cincinnati Kid*.

Christopher Layne's articles have appeared in *The Los Angeles Times*, *Washington Post* and *The National Interest*. He is a MacArthur Foundation Fellow in Global Security and a visiting scholar at the University of Southern California's Center for International Studies.

John Leonard, a *Nation* contributing editor, is TV critic for *New York* magazine and the media critic for "CBS Sunday Morning." He has been *The Nation*'s literary editor, editor-in-chief of *The New York Times Book* review, a columnist for *Esquire*, and a TV critic for *Life* and *Newsweek*. His books include *Smokes and Mirrors: Violence, Television and Other American Cultures*; and *When the Kissing Had to Stop: Cult Studs, Khmer Newts, Langley Spooks, Video Drones, Author Gods, Serial Killers, Vampire Media, Alien Sperm Suckers, Satanic Therapists and Those of Us Who Hold a Left-Wing Grudge in the Post-Toasties New World Hip-Hop.*

Deborah Meier, the founder of the Central Park East alternative public schools in New York City, is the author of an educational memoir *The Power of Their Ideas: Lessons for America from a Small School in Harlem.* She has been a MacArthur recepient.

Douglas McGrath is a screenwriter and film director. Among his credits are *Bullets over Broadway* (co-written with Woody Allen and nominated for an Academy Award) and *Emma*, adapted from Jane Austen's novel, which he wrote and directed.

Arthur Miller is the award-winning author of *Death of a Salesman*; *A View from the Bridge*; and *The Crucible*.

Michael Moore is a filmmaker and writer. His movie credits include *Roger and Me*; *Canadian Bacon*; and *The Big One*; the bestseller *Downsize This!*; and the TV series *TV Nation* and *The Awful Truth*.

Allan Nairn has covered U.S. foreign policy and operations for *The Nation* since 1980. His articles have appeared in *The New Yorker*; *The Washington Post*; *The New York Times*; *The New Republic*; *Harper's*; *The Nation*; the London *Guardian*; *Reader's Digest*; and *USA Today*, among others. His coverage of the November 1991 East Timor massacre by Indonesian troops (for *The New Yorker, USA Today* and public radio) won an RFK Journalism Award, a Du Pont-Columbia Broadcast Journalism Award and a Corporation for Public Broadcasting Silver Medallion. His *Nation* articles on Haiti earned him the 1994 George Polk Award for magazine reporting and the James Aronson Award for Social Justice Journalism (First Prize).

Victor Navasky, editor of *The Nation* since 1978, became its publisher and editorial director in January 1995. Before coming to *The Nation* he was an editor at *The New York Times Magazine* and the editor of the satirical journal *Monocle*. He is the author of *Kennedy Justice* and *Naming Names*, which won an American Book Award, and is co-author with Christopher Cerf of *The Experts Speak: The Definitive Compendium of Authoritative Misinformation*, and the stage play *Kenneth Starr's Last Tape* (co-written with Richard Lingeman).

Richard Parker was a co-founder of *Mother Jones* and a managing editor of *Ramparts*. He has worked for a wide range of progressive political organizations and is a member of *The Nation's* editorial board. He is a Senior Fellow of the Shorenstein Center on the Press, Politics and Public Policy at the Kennedy School of Government at Harvard University.

John Pilger has won many international awards for his journalism and filmmaking, including an Academy Award. He has twice been named Britain's Journalist of the Year, and his many other honors include a United Nations Association Media Peace Prize. For many years he was a war correspondent for London's *Daily Mirror*, where he covered Vietnam and Cambodia. His books include *Heroes*; *The Secret Country* (about his native Australia); *Distant Voices*; and the recent *Hidden Agendas*.

Katha Pollitt's "Subject to Debate" column began in January 1994 and appears every other week in *The Nation*. Her 1992 essay on the culture wars, "Why We Read: Canon to the Right of Me . . ." won the National Magazine Award for essays and criticism. Her 1982 book *Antarctic Traveler* won the National Book Critics Circle Award. Pollitt has also written essays for *The New Yorker*; *The Atlantic*; *The New Republic*; *Harper's*; *Mirabella*; *Ms.*, *Glamour*; *Mother Jones*; and *The New York Times*. A collection of her writings, *Reasonable Creatures: Essays on Women and Feminism*, was published in 1994.

Adolph Reed Jr. is professor of political science at The New School University. Among his books are *W. E. B. Du Bois and American Political Thought*; *Stirrings in the Jug: Black Politics in the Post-Segregation Era* and the forthcoming *Class Notes*. He has written for the *Village Voice*, *The Progressive*, and other publications.

David Rieff is a contributor to *Harper's*, *The New Republic*, *The New Yorker*, and the *Washington Post*, among many others, and is the author of *Slaughterhouse: Bosnia and the Failure of the West*; *Los Angeles: Capitol of the Third World*; and co-editor of *Crimes of War*.

Salman Rushdie is the author of the novels *Grimus*; *Midnight's Children*; *Shame*; *The Satanic Verses*; *Haroun and the Sea of Stories*; *The Moor's Last Sigh*; and *The Ground Beneath Her Feet*. His non-fiction includes *The Jaguar Smile* (an account of his travels in Nicaragua); a monograph about *The Wizard of Oz*; and the essay collection *Imaginary Homelands*.

Edward W. Said, the University Professor of English and Comparative Literature at Columbia University, is the *The Nation's* classical music critic as well as a regular contributor on the Middle East. His writing regularly appears in the *Guardian* of London, *Le Monde Diplomatique* and the Arab-language daily *al-Hayat*. His writing, translated into fourteen languages, includes ten books, among them, *Orientalism*; *The World, the Text and the Critic*; *Blaming the Victims*; *Culture and Imperialism*; and *Peace and Its Discontents: Essays on Palestine in the Middle East Peace Process*. His latest book is a memoir *Out of Place*.

Kirkpatrick Sale is a *Nation* contributing editor and the author of *Rebels Against the Future: The Luddites and Their War on the Industrial Revolution: Lessons for the Computer Age*; *The Conquest of Paradise*; *Christopher Columbus and the Columbian Legacy* and *SDS: Ten Years Toward a Revolution*.

Robert Scheer is a *Nation* contributing editor. He was managing editor-in-chief of *Ramparts* and an editor of *New Times*, and has contributed to *Playboy* and *Esquire*. From 1976 he has been based at the *Los Angeles Times*, first as a national correspondent, and now as a columnist.

Jonathan Schell's writings have appeared in *Harper's, The Atlantic, The Washington Post*, and *The New Yorker* where he was the principal writer of *The New Yorker's* Notes & Comments section from 1967 to 1987. From 1990 until 1996, Schell wrote a column for New York *Newsday*. His books include *The Village of Ben Suc*; *The Military Half*; *The Time of Illusion*; *The Fate of the Earth*, nominated for a Pulitzer Prize, the National Book Award and the National Critics Award; *The Abolition*; *History in Sherman Park*; *The Real War*; *Observing the Nixon Years* and *The Gift of Time*. He is the Harold Willens Peace Fellow at The National Institute and teaches at Wesleyan University and the New School for Social Research.

Benjamin Schwarz is a Los Angeles-based correspondent for *The Atlantic* and a former executive editor of *World Policy Journal*. His articles have appeared in *The New York Times, The National Interest, Los Angeles Times* and *The Christian Science Monitor*.

Bruce Shapiro, a regular contributor to *The Nation* writes about crime, justice and civil liberties issues. His 1995 article "One Violent Crime" was a National Magazine Award finalist for essays and criticism, and was included in *Best American Essays 1995*.

Robert Sherrill is the Corporations correspondent for *The Nation*. Among his many books are *Military Justice Is to Justice as Military Music Is to Music* and *The Oil Follies of 1970–1980: How the Petroleum Industry Stole the Show (And Much More Besides)*.

Micah Sifry is a senior analyst at Public Campaign, a leading campaign finance reform organization. For thirteen years, he was an editor and writer with *The Nation*. He has written widely on domestic and international politics, covering everything from third parties in the United States (about which he is writing a book) to the Middle East. He is coeditor, with Christopher Cerf, of *The Gulf War Reader* (Times Books, 1991). From 1993–96, he published *The Perot Periodical*, a quarterly newsletter.

Elisabeth Sifton is a senior vice president of Farrar, Straus and Giroux and publisher of Hill and Wang since 1993. She has had a distinguished career in publishing, as an editor-in-chief at Viking Penguin, executive vice-president at Knopf, and publisher of Elizabeth Sifton Books, which won the Carey Thomas Award for Creative Publishing in 1986.

Clancy Sigal is a novelist, journalist and screenwriter based in Los Angeles. His books include *Going Away*; *The Secret Defector*; *Weekend in Dinlock*; and *Zone of the Interior*. His most recent screenwriting credit was *In Love and War*.

Daniel Singer, *The Nation's* Paris-based Europe correspondent, writes on the Western European left as well as the former Communist nations. He has been a contributor to *The Economist, The New Statesman* and *Tribune*. He is the author of *Prelude to Revolution: France in May 1968; The Road to Gdansk; Is Socialism Doomed? The Meaning of Mitterrand*; and the recent *Whose Millenium: Theirs or Ours?*

Ted Solatoroff, a Nation contributing editor, is a distinguished editor and critic whose work includes the recent celebrated memoir *Truth Comes in Blows*.

Paco Ignacio Taibo II is the winner of seven international fiction prizes, including the Mortiz-Planeta Award, for his crime and historical novels and for his mainstream fiction. He is also the author of the biography *Guevara, Also Known as Che*.

E. P. Thompson was one of England's foremost historians and social critics. His books include *The Making of the English Working Class*; *Customs in Common*; *Towards Exterminism*; and *Witness*

Against the Beast. He was *The Nation*'s British correspondent and a leading figure in Europe's anti-nuclear movement.

Michael Tomasky is a political columnist for *New York* magazine and the author of *Left for Dead: The Life, Death, and Possible Resurrection of Progressive Politics in America*. He is writing a book about the Hillary Clinton–Rudolph Guiliani race. He has been a staff writer for the *New York Observer* and *Village Voice*.

Katrina vanden Heuvel has been editor of *The Nation* since January 1995. She joined *The Nation* in 1984 as assistant editor. She writes frequently about Russian politics and society and is the co-author (with Stephen F. Cohen) of *Voices of Glasnost: Interviews with Gorbachev's Reformers*, and the editor of the magazine's anthology, *The Nation: 1865–1990*. Her articles have appeared in *The Washington Post, The New York Times*, the *Los Angeles Times* and *Vanity Fair*, and she is a regular contributor on MSNBC, CNN and CNBC.

Camilo Jose Vergara, a writer and photographer, is author of *The New American Ghetto* and co-author of *Silent Cities: The Evolution of the American Cemetery*. In 1993, his work was the subject of a BBC documentary. His photographs have been widely exhibited here and abroad, and portions of his archives are represented in the collections of Avery Library at Columbia University, at the Getty Center, and at the New Museum of Contemporary Art in New York.

Gore Vidal has written twenty-two novels, five plays, many screenplays, short stories, well over two hundred essays, and a memoir. He is a *Nation* contributing editor.

Cornel West is Alphonse Fletcher, Jr., University Professor at Harvard University. He is the author of many books including *Prophetic Fragments; The Future of the Race* (with Henry Louis Gates, Jr.); and the best-selling *Race Matters*. He won an American Book Award in 1993 for his two-volume work *Beyond Eurocentrism and Multiculturalism*.

Edmund White is a novelist, critic and biographer. His books include an award-winning biography of Jean Genet, a short biography of Marcel Proust, the essay collection *The Burning Library* and the novels *The*

Farewell Symphony, A Boy's Own Story, The Beautiful Room Is Empty, and, as editor, *The Faber Book of Gay Short Fiction.*

Ellen Willis is director of the Cultural Reporting and Criticism concentration at the NYU School of Journalism and Mass Communication. She was a columnist and senior editor for *The Village Voice*, former pop music critic for *The New Yorker*, and has written for a wide variety of publications, including *Rolling Stone, Mirabella, The New York Times Book Review* and *Newsday*. Her essays on culture and politics have been collected in three books: *Beginning to See the Light:Sex, Hope, and Rock and Roll; No More Nice Girls: Countercultural Essays;* and *Don't Think, Smile! Notes on a Decade of Denial.*

Roger Wilkins is a member of the *Nation* editorial board and a professor of history at George Mason University. During the Johnson administration, he served as assistant attorney general. As a journalist, he has written for the *New York Times*, the *Washington Post*, and the *Washington Star*. While on the editorial staff of the *Post*, he earned a Pulitzer Prize in 1972, which he shared with Woodward, Bernstein, and Herblock, for Watergate coverage. He is the author of *A Man's Life* (1982) and editor with former senator Fred R. Harris of *Quiet Riots: Race and Poverty in the United States.*

Amy Wilentz is the author of *The Rainy Season*, about Haiti under the Duvalier regime. Wilentz edited and translated the writings of Haiti's first democratically-elected president, Father Jean-Bertrand Aristide, *In the Parish of the Poor*. Her essays and articles have also appeared in *Grand Street, The New Republic, The New York Times, New Yorker, The Los Angeles Times, Time* and *Traveler.*

Jon Wiener, a professor of history at the University of California, Irvine, covers academia and campus politics, and also writes about LA. Wiener's articles have also appeared in the *New York Times Magazine, Lingua Franca* and *The New Republic*. A collection of his articles for *The Nation* and other magazines was published by Verso in 1994 as *Professors, Politics and Pop*. His book, *Come Together: John Lennon and His Time*, draws on the Lennon FBI files and explores the relationship of the counterculture and the New Left in the sixties and early seventies. His latest book is *Gimme Some Truth: The John Lennon FBI Files.*

Patricia J. Williams, a *Nation* columnist, is a professor of law at Columbia University. A member of the State Bar of California and the Federal Court of Appeals for the 9th Circuit, Williams has served on the advisory council for the Medgar Evers Center for Law and Social Justice of the City University of New York and on the board of governors for the Society of American Law Teachers. In 1993, Harvard University Press published Williams's *The Alchemy of Race and Rights* to widespread critical acclaim. Her most recent book is *The Rooster's Egg* (Harvard, 1995).

The Nation Institute is an independently funded and administered public foundation focused on defending the First Amendment and strengthening independent media. Projects of the Institute include RadioNation, the nationally syndicated weekly news and public affairs program; an Internship Program for aspiring journalists; a Fellowship Program that supports leading journalists and public policy analysts; and Nation Books, which is co-published with the Avalon Publishing Group, Inc. The Institute also administers an active calendar of public events on social and cultural issues, and funds the research costs of investigative journalism projects.

The Nation Institute is supported by tax-deductible contributions from foundations, corporations and individuals. To find out more about the Nation Institute, please go to www.nationinstitute.org or write us at 33 Irving Place, 8th Floor, New York, NY 10003, USA.